History of the
U.S. NAVY

History of the

U.S. NAVY

1775-1941

Robert W. Love, Jr.

Stackpole Books

Published by
STACKPOLE BOOKS
Cameron and Kelker Streets
P.O. Box 1831
Harrisburg, PA 17105

Interior design by Marcia Lee Dobbs

Maps by Chris Jung

Printed in the United States of America

10 9 8 7 6 5 4 3 2 1

Library of Congress Cataloging-in-Publication Data
Love, Robert William, 1944-
    History of the U.S. Navy Robert W. Love, Jr.—1st ed.
      p. cm.
    Includes bibliographical references and index
    Contents: v. 1. 1775-1941
    ISBN 0-8117-1862-X (v. 1)
    1. United States. Navy—History. 2. United States—History, Naval. I.
Title. II. Title: History of the United States Navy.
VA55.L68 1991
359'.00973—dc   2091-27510
                                                           CIP

To
Robert III and
Kirstie

Contents

Acknowledgments

The late Professor W. Stull Holt of the University of Washington and the late Professor Wesley Frank Craven of Princeton University encouraged me to study the history of the U.S. Navy. I owe a great debt to my colleagues in the History Department of the United States Naval Academy. My discussions of American naval history with professors Craig Symonds and Frederick Harrod repeatedly sent me back to the evidence and profoundly influenced this book. Each of them read and made comments on early drafts of several chapters. I also value the advice and ready assistance of Professor Paolo Coletta, an indefatigable researcher, whose contribution to modern American naval history is immeasurable. Professor Jack Sweetman's friendly, learned skepticism is an always welcome antidote to my latest enthusiasms. The late Professor William Belote kindly bequeathed to me his research notes on the naval history of World War II. Professor John H. Huston allowed me to read and cite his edition of General Henry H. Arnold's diary. I must also discharge an important debt to Professor Michael Isenberg and our colleagues who participate in the history department's "Works in Progress" seminar. I have been helped so much by Professor John Major of the University of Hull and Eric Grove of London that I take this opportunity to express my gratitude. Professor Douglas Brinkley of Hofstra University has shared with me his research on James Forrestal and the Navy's role in the early years of the Cold War. Professor James Bradford of Texas A&M University, Dr. Harold Langley of the Smithsonian Institution, and Professor David Rosenberg of Temple University have been generous in discussing their work with me. I have also learned from the papers of the many hundreds of participants in the Naval Academy's Naval History Symposium over the past fourteen years. The errors in this book are mine alone, however, and no one should, or could, mistake anything in this work as representing the official position on any issue of the U.S. Naval Academy or the Department of the Navy.

I also wish to acknowledge the assistance of the staff of Nimitz Library at the Naval Academy, the Operational Archives and the Navy Department Library at the Naval Historical Center, the Marine Corps Historical Center, the Manuscript Division of the Library of Congress, and the National Archives and the Museum and Manuscript Office of the Naval War College. The Historical Division of the Joint Chiefs of Staff Organization was also helpful. The staffs of the Hoover Institution, the Wisconsin Historical Society Library, the Franklin D. Roosevelt Presidential Library, the John F. Kennedy Presidential Library, the Lyndon B. Johnson Presidential Library, and the Public Records Office, Kew Gardens, London, are due my thanks.

Hundreds of Navy men have shared their experiences with me. I particularly want to acknowledge the help of the members of the Class of 1940 of the Naval Academy. I learned what little I know about the history of the Marine Corps and amphibious operations from Lieutenant Colonel Merrill Bartlett, USMC (Ret.). Research papers written for my naval history courses are the source of continuous enlightenment. This book has been especially informed by the work of Lieutenant Commander Dennis Pricolo, USN; Lieutenant Thomas Belke, USN; Lieutenant Samuel Cox, USN; 1st Lieutenant Darrell Montgomery, USMC; Ensign Thomas Robertson, USN; Ensign Robert Beer, USN; and 2nd Lieutenant Brian Hussey, USMC. Robert Christman helped with the illustrations. Jonathan Ying of St. John's College assisted me early on with a large, bulky manuscipt. As editor, critic, and typist, Suzanne Peake of Annapolis has no peer. My literary agent, Philip Spitzer, worked tirelessly on behalf of this project. I am indebted to a persistent, diligent editor, Mary Suggs of Stackpole Books, who smote many errors and corrected innumerable infelicities of style.

I could not have written this book without the patient support, encouragement, and affectionate toleration of my loving wife, Rose Seals Love.

Introduction

The object of this book is to chronicle and explain the high politics of American naval history, the reasons why statesmen, politicians, bureaucrats, and Navy men accepted certain ideas and adopted particular plans, strategies, and shipbuilding policies rather than others. The book is also concerned with the interplay among international politics, American foreign policy, overall military strategy, naval strategy, tactics, and naval operations. Readers seeking an overarching theory of naval or "maritime" power that explains or codifies the events of this history will be irremediably disappointed. I have found none that will bear the burden of the historical evidence. Nor will readers find any convenient compendium of historical lessons or prescriptions. The simplistic "lessons of history" seldom rise above the level of Napoleon's aphorisms.

Any history of the U.S. Navy must somehow come to terms with the tremendous burden of the legacy of Alfred Thayer Mahan, the famous theorist of "seapower." No historian exerted such a pervasive influence on historians' views of American naval policy. Mahan gave intellectual respectability to the exercise of American military power and to the acquisition of an overseas empire. The reader of *History of the U.S. Navy* will soon notice, however, the absence of what all too easily became the accepted prescriptions of his work. As a piece of propaganda, the conceit of "seapower" still appeals to the U.S. Navy's abiding sense of tradition, but Mahan's ideas on how this amorphous concept should be applied to practical policy and strategic choices had surprisingly little influence on the historical development of the U.S. Navy. Thus, from the standpoint of the historian, Mahan is more important as an actor in the late nineteenth-century drama than as a historian or theorist. I view his works as delightful polemics openly intended to demonstrate the value of capital ship fleets to imperial powers. I have not used his concept of "seapower" as a benchmark to evaluate policy or strategy on the grounds that his thesis does not in any satisfactory way help to explain the events that constitute the story of the U.S. Navy. Nor, I should add, did I find the notion of "command of the sea" terribly useful, although Clark Reynolds' gifted exposition of the role of thalassocracies in world history is an elegant intellectual argument that deserves further study.

In place of the "seapower" and "command of the sea" concepts, I have taken a somewhat different approach. This book attempts to show how presidents, bureaucrats, legislators, and Navy men devised and refined American naval policy by testing its utility as a servant of particular foreign policy goals and interests. The U.S. Navy has served many functions. Social liberals are now using the Navy to express and implement cultural change. Political conservatives view the Navy as a bonding agent of nationalism and a representation of national strength. For others, the Navy functions as a useful symbol of national pride. It is a source of prestige, myths, and, yes, history. As a class, naval officers and civil servants working for the Navy Department have made significant contributions to our national life in many fields: technology, pure and applied science, exploration, navigation, medicine, management, and engineering. These multifarious aspects of American naval activity are, however, and always have been, secondary to the Navy's main business, which is to serve as the handmaiden of diplomacy, the clenched fist of foreign policy. As Secretary of the Navy Hilary Herbert put it in June 1893, at the midpoint in this history, "A nation's navy is the right arm of its diplomacy."[1]

From the founding of the Continental Navy to the opening phase of the new world order of the 1990s, most informed American politicians have considered warships to be useful, flexible tools with which to achieve foreign policy objectives. To bring this dynamic into focus, I have attempted to explain changes in the architecture and objectives of American foreign policy and domestic partisan politics before describing the resulting naval activity. The careful reader will discover that, almost invariably, at least at the outset of an era or a crisis, the Navy was found to be inadequate or inappropriate in some important way to the immediate task at hand. This is largely due to three influences. First, most ships and many weapons have a longer shelf life than the foreign policy problems they were built to help solve or the strategic or tactical challenges they were constructed to meet. More often than not, ships and naval weapons designed to deal with one threat were employed to confront a quite different menace. Second, with rare exceptions, the single most important determinant in American naval shipbuilding policy has been politics—presidential, legislative, or electoral—and its regional and partisan components. Third, the way the electorate rotates the holders of political offices in this democracy is paralleled by the Navy's historic practice of rotating its leading officer personnel. The result is that the play of naval policy is performed by a cast whose actors change constantly. Any snapshot of the Navy's history exposes the transient dynamism and untidiness of this process.

The histories of American foreign policy and the American navies are divided into three fairly distinct eras. Changes in foreign policy objectives were reflected in new missions for the Navy and new configurations of its fleet. In the first era, from the Revolutionary War to the end of the nineteenth century, the Continental Navy and the U.S. Navy served as agents of Continentalism and Maritime Access. As a foreign policy objective, Continentalism encompassed the achievement of political independence and the defense of home territory; territorial expansion to secure natural, defensible coastal, river, or mountain frontiers; and the resolution of the domestic quarrel between competing sectional versions of nationalism. The Navy played a vital role in reaching each of these goals. The corollary to Continentalism was Maritime Access, a policy that sprang from the convergence of the mercantile character of the American economy and the determination of many leading American politicians to avoid an excessive dependence on Europe, her politics, and her markets. Maritime Access embodied the concept of "freedom of the seas," the right of non-belligerent shipping to unimpeded freedom of navigation in wartime, the policy of policing the seas against individual or state-sponsored piracy, the conviction that the United States should insist that the nations of Asia, Latin America, and Africa treat Americans as they did Europeans, and the belief that Americans trading, preaching, or simply residing overseas deserved their government's armed protection. An active Navy featuring active overseas station squadrons was essential to the advancement and enforcement of Maritime Access. In this era, foreign policy, partisan politics, naval policy, and strategy interacted in ways so complex and in such intimate proximity as to make meaningless the argument that the policy choices involved were simply between building sails-of-the-line or frigates, between accepting sail or steam as a means of propulsion, or between adopting a strategy of fleet engagements or a strategy of commerce raiding and coastal defense.

At the dawn of the twentieth century, Europe quite belatedly recognized the United States as one of the Great Powers. American statesmen, often without admitting it or even understanding what was afoot, behaved accordingly. The upshot was that, owing to her peculiar geopolitical position, the United States became, somewhat unwillingly, the arbiter of the balance of power in both Europe and Asia. Strengthed by the nation's mature industrial-agricultural economy and her stable politics, American statesmen used the U.S. Navy's newly constructed battle fleets to establish, defend, and expand the American sphere of influence, to construct a network of outlying coaling stations, far-flung naval bases, and temporary overseas alliances, and to rearrange the balance of power when the occasion demanded. The growth of the U.S. Navy's power and size merely paralleled the concurrent increase in American political and economic influence and coincided with the decline of Europe's imperial system, Britain's fast shrinking international authority, and the last chapter in the history of the Royal Navy's global naval power. By 1945, every informed international statesman looked to Washington to shape the postwar world, the American economy fabricated nearly half of the entire world's annual production of metal-bent goods, and the U.S. Navy had crushed her main wartime rivals and now dwarfed the seagoing forces of America's allies.

The main features of naval power had changed dramatically. Not one ship type performed the tactical function in World War II for which it was designed and built. In the daytime, carriers attacked ships and inland targets, while the fast battleships and heavy cruisers provided the carriers with antiaircraft support. At night, the equation was reversed. Destroyers became radar and sonar pickets, heavy escorts for merchantmen, and antisubmarine escorts for battleship-carrier task forces. And the function and character of bombardment munitions broadened exponentially. The appearance of submarines, sea-based and land-based aircraft, various electromechanical devices, radio communications, and specialized amphibious vessels complicated not only the policy problem of how to balance a fleet but also the strategic and tactical problems involved in operating it.

At the end of the war, the beginning of the third historical era, the U.S. Navy found itself almost overnight called on to take up the role of global bailiff. The two world wars had destroyed Europe's monarchical system, the classical balances of power in Europe and Asia, and the imperial regimes that had long dominated the Eurasian periphery and its appendages. Almost every nation had come to view its bilateral relations with the United States as the most significant aspect of its diplomacy, and only the Soviet Union—moved, as was the United States, by a long history of expansionism and a universalist ideology—challenged America's reluctant assumption of global authority. The U.S. Navy was again called on to serve as the sharp sword of American foreign policy. By conscious decision, the United States adopted a foreign policy of containment of Soviet power and ideology and wittingly assumed a new role as a global superpower, the defender of a stable world order, the advocate of the universalist values of democracy and capitalism, and the often disinterested adjudicator of regional disputes. This position, coupled with the advent of nuclear weapons, the collapse of the traditional world order, the establishment of the great rival Cold War alliance systems, and the accumulation of various overseas military obligations by the United States complicated the questions of naval policy and strategy as never before. The appearance of nuclear munitions, naval reactors, jet aircraft, and airborne and sea-based missiles, and the marriage of nuclear reactors and submarines meant that the definition of a capital ship was no longer clear, and that the function of the capital ship was even less obvious. The invention of the transistor and the microchip made possible the development of missiles that could sink ships or protect them, and even destroy entire cities. Were capital ships to be ship-killers or were they to deliver munitions against enemy home territory? Were they to deter wars or fight them? Did the Navy need a large number of single-purpose ships or a smaller number of multimission vessels? How might the U.S. Navy, configured for the most part to deal with its great Soviet rival, also support American foreign policy goals in situations in which the Cold War contest was only marginally relevant? And when the Cold War ended, was the Navy to continue to be the global bailiff and uphold the New World Order? In identifying and answering these difficult questions, the Navy helped Americans rediscover that naval power plays an essential function in protecting and advancing the Republic's interests.

In this book I employ an occasional naval term. My goal in doing so is to give some nautical flavor to the text, not to awe, confuse, or confound the general reader. Also, I have followed most of the guidelines on writing naval history laid down by the master of all American naval historians, Samuel Eliot Morison. For instance, during World War II the Navy assigned numerical designations to almost every formation of ships and other embarked forces. In an attempt at clarity, I have adopted Morison's recommendation that naval historians assign such formations functional or geographical force names. In a deviation from Morison's advice, however, I have adopted the Naval Institute's useful practice of preceding the name of each naval vessel with the article "the."

A complete list of works consulted for this history would take up another book. Sources for important or controversial evidence, quotations, and interpretations are listed in the notes. For further information, readers should consult the bibliographies, general histories, or special studies listed below.

Three bibliographers have made a significant contribution to the study of the history of the U.S. Navy. Paolo E. Coletta, *A Bibliography of American Naval History* (Annapolis: Naval Institute Press, 1981), is a selected bibliography of about 5,000 of the most important books and articles. The most prolific American naval bibliographer is Myron J. Smith, Jr., whose compilations encompass the entire history of the U.S. Navy. They are: *Navies in the American Revolution: A Bibliography* (Metuchen, N.J.: Scarecrow Press, 1973); *The American Navy, 1789–1860: A Bibliography* (Metuchen, N.J.: Scarecrow Press, 1974); *The American Navy, 1865–1918: A Bibliography* (Metuchen, N.J.: Scarecrow Press, 1972); *American Civil War Navies: A Bibliography* (Metuchen, N.J.: Scarecrow Press, 1972); *The American Navy, 1918–1941* (Metuchen, N.J.: Scarecrow Press, 1974); *World War II at Sea: A Bibliography of Sources in English* (Metuchen, N.J.: Scarecrow Press, 1976); *World War II at Sea: A Bibliography of Sources in English, 1974–1989* (Metuchen, N.J.: Scarecrow Press, 1990); and *The United States Navy and Coast Guard, 1946–1983: A Bibliography* (Jefferson, N.C.: McFarland, 1984). Dean C. Allard, et al., *U. S. Naval History Sources in the United States* (Washington: Department of the Navy, 1979–), identifies manuscript, archival, and other special collections deposited in over 250 American archives and libraries.

Kenneth J. Hagan, *This People's Navy* (New York: Free Press, 1990), which was published too late to be of use for this book, is mostly devoted to the eighteenth and nineteenth centuries and the decades before World War II. Hagan portrays the history of American naval policy and strategy as involving a series of relatively simple, unambiguous choices, such as the choice between heavy capital ships and battle fleets for fleet engagements, or *guerre d'escadre*, on the one hand and light cruisers and other small vessels for coastal defense and commerce raiding, or *guerre de course*, on the other. Hagan's bias in favor of small ships and a small U. S. Navy and his New Left interpretation of American foreign policy are evident throughout his account. Paolo Coletta, *American Maritime Heritage in Brief* (3rd. ed.; University Press of America, 1986), is a valuable, succinct outline that assesses its subject within the context of Alfred Thayer Mahan's concept of "command of the sea." Edward L. Beach, *The United States Navy: 200 Years* (New York: Henry Holt, 1986), contains a lively, eccentric account of the U.S. Navy in the eighteenth and nineteenth centuries. Beach stresses the interest of Navy men in technology and tactical problems but has surprisingly little to say about American naval policy or strategy in World War I, World War II, or the Cold War. Howarth's and Beach's works are documented; Hagan's and Coletta's are not.

Multiauthored studies tend to be more eclectic. Kenneth J. Hagan, ed., *In Peace and War* (2nd ed. rev.; Westport, Conn.: Greenwood Press, 1984), contains eighteen essays on American naval policy. The authors give less weight to abstract strategic concepts as the driving force behind naval policy than to the objective realities of international and domestic politics. Standing rigidly in defense of the older "command of the sea" concept are two volumes written for use as textbooks at the Naval Academy: E. B. Potter, Chester W. Nimitz, et al., *Sea Power: A Naval History* (Englewood Cliffs, N.J.: Prentice-Hall, 1960), and its much truncated successor, E. B. Potter et al., *Sea Power* (2nd ed. rev.; Annapolis: Naval Institute Press, 1981). Neither of the *Sea Power* volumes deals in any serious way with the Cold War. Of these multiauthored histories, only the essays in Hagan, ed., *In Peace and War* are documented.

Three older works are also worth consulting. Fletcher Pratt, *The Navy: A History* (Garden City, N.Y.: Garden City Publishing, 1941), is the most lively account to date. Edgar Stanton MacClay, *A History of the United States Navy from 1775 to 1901* (2nd ed. rev., 3 Vols.; New York: D. Appleton, 1904); and John R. Spears, *History of the United States Navy from Its Origin to the Present Day, 1775–1897* (5 Vols.; New York: Scribner, 1897–1899), were published in the immediate aftermath of the Spanish-American War.

Students of American naval policy should first consult
Charles Oscar Paullin, *Paullin's History of Naval Administration,
1775–1911* (Annapolis: Naval Institute Press, 1968), a collection of
articles published in the U.S. Naval Institute *Proceedings* between
1905 and 1914. Harold and Margaret Sprout, *The Rise of American
Naval Power* (Princeton, N.J.: Princeton University Press, 1939),
leaning heavily on Paullin's articles, analyze naval policy using Mahan's "seapower" concept as a benchmark. Hagan's *This People's
Navy* articulates the antithesis of the Sprouts' influential study.
Robert G. Albion, *Makers of Naval Policy, 1798–1947* (Annapolis:
Naval Institute Press, 1980), takes the story up to the eve of the Ko-
rean War. Paolo E. Coletta, ed., *The Secretaries of the Navy* (2 Vols.,
Annapolis: Naval Institute Press, 1980), and Robert W. Love, Jr.,
ed., *The Chiefs of Naval Operations* (Annapolis: Naval Institute Press,
1980), are multiauthored biographical essays of important figures.
All these works are documented. Short accounts of the careers of
American flag officers may be found in Clark G. Reynolds, *Famous
American Admirals* (New York: Van Nostrand Reinhold, 1978), and
William B. Cogar, *Dictionary of Admirals of the U.S. Navy* (3 Vols., An-
napolis: Naval Institute Press, 1989–). As the learned Professor
Michael Palmer recently observed, however, there exists an urgent
need for an up-to-date administrative history of the Navy.

Two superb specialized works are essential for an under-
standing of important aspects of American naval history: Robert
G. Albion and Jennie B. Pope, *Sea Lanes in Wartime: The American
Experience, 1775–1945* (2nd ed., rev., Hamden, Conn.: Archon
Books, 1968), and Randolph W. King and Prescott Palmer, eds.,
Naval Engineering and American Seapower (Baltimore: Nautical and
Aviation Publ., 1989). Ships' histories abound. *Dictionary of Ameri-
can Naval Fighting Ships* (Washington: Dept. of the Navy, 1959–81)
is a basic reference that provides an account of the operations of
each vessel. This invaluable work is currently being updated by the
Naval History Center. Howard Chapelle, *The American Sailing Navy*
(New York: Norton, 1949), and Howard Chapelle, *The Search for
Speed Under Sail, 1700–1855* (New York: Norton, 1967), are classic
studies. William E. McMahon, *Dreadnought Battleships and Battle
Cruisers* (Washington: University Press of America, 1978), not only
provides useful information on each vessel but also points out the
highlights of its operational history. The dean of modern ships'
historians, Norman Friedman, has written a remarkable series of
detailed design histories. These include *Battleship Design and De-*

velopment, 1905–1945 (New York: Mayflower Books, 1978); *U. S. Battleships* (Annapolis: Naval Institute Press, 1985); *U. S. Cruisers* (Annapolis: Naval Institute Press, 1984); *U. S. Destroyers* (Annapolis: Naval Institute Press, 1982); *Carrier Air Power* (New York: Rutledge Press, 1981); *U. S. Aircraft Carriers* (Annapolis: Naval Institute Press, 1983); and *Submarine Design and Development* (Annapolis: Naval Institute Press, 1984).

Two well-written, carefully documented surveys that treat the U.S. Navy within the broader context of American military history are Russell F. Weigley, *The American Way of War* (New York: Macmillan, 1973), and Allan R. Millett and Peter Maslowski, *For the Common Defense: A Military History of the United States of America* (New York: Free Press, 1984). To place American naval history within the greater context of foreign policy and diplomacy, the reader may rely on Thomas A. Bailey, *A Diplomatic History of the American People* (6th ed., New York: Appleton-Century-Crofts, 1958); Richard W. Leopold, *The Growth of American Foreign Policy* (New York: Knopf, 1962); and Armin Rappaport, *A History of American Diplomacy* (New York: Macmillan, 1975). Thomas G. Paterson, J. Garry Clifford, and Kenneth J. Hagan, *American Foreign Policy* (2nd. ed., 2 Vols., Lexington, Mass.: D. C. Heath, 1988), is a more recent summary of the views of the New Left. Ruhl J. Barnett, ed., *The Record of American Diplomacy* (2nd ed., New York: Knopf, 1950), is a useful collection of basic documents and helpful commentaries.

Chapter One

The American Revolution
1775–1778

When Americans first took up arms against Britain in 1775, they drew on a rich maritime heritage rooted in Europe's great age of overseas exploration and discovery. The British mercantilist system, the colonies' need to import finished goods and export staples, and the relatively low cost of timber had led to the development in North America of several thriving maritime industries. On the eve of the Revolutionary War, Boston, New York, Philadelphia, Baltimore, Norfolk, and Charleston were already prosperous ports, and from Boston Bay to the Chesapeake a large shipbuilding industry had recently matured. America's shipyards built sloops and brigs for Britain's Royal Navy, and her mariners knew how to navigate the major trade routes of the Western world. Still, Americans were keenly aware of Britain's awesome naval might, a force that had crushed the Dutch in three Anglo-Dutch wars in the mid-1600s and had ably defended Britain and her overseas empire over the past century in four great imperial wars against France. After the Peace of Paris ended the Seven Years' War in 1763, Britain's fleet was the dominant factor in the Atlantic balance of power.

At the same time, however, the Royal Navy's presence in North American waters served as one source of the colonies' growing irritation with imperial policy. During the Seven Years' War, colonial governments had repeatedly begged the Admiralty for naval protection for their coastal trade and fishing fleets—more

1

protection than the hard-pressed Royal Navy could provide. And when Parliament adopted a postwar policy of using the Royal Navy to enforce its mercantilist trade laws, Americans began to view the British fleet not as a protector but as a menace to their politics. To collect mercantilist duties—many of which had not been paid for years—the Admiralty established a patrol station off Newport in 1763. This infuriated many Rhode Islanders, and in 1764 Governor Stephen Hopkins ordered the fort on Goat Island to fire on the British schooner *St. John*. A mob of colonists burned a Royal Navy tender the following year and another gang destroyed the tax-collecting sloop *Liberty* in 1769. In June 1772, when word reached Providence that the British cutter *Gaspée* had run aground chasing the Rhode Island packet *Hannah*, Abraham Whipple, an experienced privateer, and a band of angry locals set the 8-gun revenue ship ablaze. John Adams likened Rear Admiral John Montagu, commander of the Royal Navy's North American station, to "a beast of prey" for his vigorous enforcement of the mercantilist Townshend Acts.[1]

For their part, many British strategists believed that they could use the Royal Navy to put down the growing rebellion. Montagu reported in 1773 that he could have "prevented" the Boston Tea Party "by firing upon the town." The Admiralty reacted to the burning of the *Gaspée* by dispatching Captain James Wallace in the 24-gun frigate *Rose* to Newport at the end of 1774, and within six months he had entirely shut down Rhode Island's profitable molasses trade. "A conquest by land is unnecessary" to put down the rebels, for they "can be reduced to distress and then obedience by our Marine," claimed Lord Barrington, secretary of state for war. Taking this line, Prime Minister Lord North responded to the Tea Party by having Parliament pass the Port Act, which closed the port of Boston. Vice Admiral Samuel Graves, who relieved Montagu, stationed eight warships off Boston harbor to clamp off trade, and in March 1775 Parliament passed the Restraining Act, which was intended to thoroughly cripple New England's maritime economy.[2]

Closing Boston harbor caused the colonists to organize to defend their liberties. Meeting in Philadelphia during the fall of 1774, the First Continental Congress decided to boycott British goods, petitioned George III for a return to the imperial policies of 1763, and declared several acts of Parliament "unconstitutional." This set in motion a train of events that led to the exchange of

John Adams.

shots at Lexington and Concord the following year, which in turn caused New England's militia to lay siege to the British troops in Boston. The Second Continental Congress reacted by urging the colonies in May 1775 to arm themselves. A Continental Army was established and George Washington named its commanding general. Washington was ordered to Boston, but before he arrived, the Redcoats took the offensive at Bunker Hill and won a costly tactical victory. Even though they lost, this battle convinced the rebels that they might win on the battlefield if they had enough gunpowder and arms. In the meantime, to recover the ships Captain Wallace had captured, the Rhode Island General Assembly had established for the colony a fleet of two sloops. One of them, Commodore Whipple's 10-gun sloop *Katy*, seized a number of vessels, but his small force was no match for the powerful British frigate *Rose*, which held the Newport station.

Washington's need for arms to besiege Boston led directly to the establishment of the Continental Navy. On 11 August 1775 word reached Philadelphia that two unescorted British brigantines carrying guns and powder were at sea en route to Quebec. Congress reacted promptly, naming John Adams, Silas Deane, and John Langdon to a Marine Committee that was to devise some means of intercepting and capturing those vessels. Adams, an experienced maritime lawyer and one of the most influential men in Philadelphia at the time, favored armed resistance, political independence, and measures designed to create an intercolonial "naval power." Under his guidance, the Marine Committee persuaded Congress to allow Washington to commission warships into his command and to acquire two armed vessels from Massachusetts. The committee also asked the governors of Rhode Island and Connecticut to loan the Continental Army some of their state naval vessels to support the siege of Boston.[3]

Before receiving these instructions from Congress, Washington had, on his own, arranged for the armed schooner *Hannah* to put to sea in September in search of British cargo shipping. Sadly, the *Hannah* took only a handful of minor prizes before the crew mutinied. Undaunted, Washington armed several more schooners. Few of them caught any prizes, although the victories were worth the expense and the aggravation. In November and December, the schooner *Lee* took several British ships off New England, including the brig *Nancy*, which provided the Continental Army with hundreds of muskets and several tons of powder and shot. In January 1776, to prevent further losses, the new commander of the North American Squadron, Vice Admiral Molyneux Shuldham, ordered that "no stores or supplies may be sent in the future except in armed vessels." Because of the fog on the Atlantic coast, he added, convoys are "not to be depended on." By adopting an interdiction strategy, the Americans were compelling the enemy to redistribute his offensive naval forces.[4]

Meanwhile, the inability of Rhode Island's navy to deal with the *Rose* led the colony's General Assembly to instruct Stephen Hopkins, its delegate in Philadelphia, to propose on 3 October 1775 that Congress build a seagoing fleet "at Continental expense" to defend the colonies' coastal waters. Several southern delegates opposed this policy. Maryland's Samuel Chase, a widely known wit, labeled it "the maddest idea in the world, to think of building an American fleet. Its latitude is wonderful. We should mortgage the whole continent." England's economy depended on the American trade, he asserted, and Britain would soon realize that she could not afford to wage war against her best customers, the colonists. Other southerners "agree that a fleet would protect and secure the trade of New England but deny that it would help the southern colonies," Adams noted. This view was not unanimous, however, and a handful of tidewater southerners—including Christopher Gadsden of South Carolina and George Gythe of Virginia—supported the navy measure. The "expense would be great" and "the weight of metal, or the quantity of tonnage may be small," but "a naval force would destroy single cutters and cruisers." While an American fleet could not meet the Royal Navy in battle, "it might oblige our enemies to sail in fleets."[5]

Once Congress had authorized Washington to acquire and operate cruisers, it turned to a second report by the Marine Committee that embodied Adams' plan to establish a Continental Navy. In a resolution adopted on 13 October, Congress voted to acquire and fit out two national warships that were to "cruise eastward" into the North Atlantic and capture British transports "laden with arms and powder" then en route to North America. This marked the birth of the American Navy. Then, after word reached Philadelphia that the British had sacked Portland, Maine, the Marine Committee persuaded Congress to convert two additional merchantmen into warships and to assign them to general duties "for the protection and defense of the United Colonies." This greatly enlarged the mission of the new Navy.

A larger, reconstituted, and more broadly representative Marine Committee was assembled and met nightly for six weeks at a nearby tavern to organize the new establishment. Most of the members seemed less concerned with preparing a coherent plan of action than with rewarding their relatives, friends, and political allies with commissions. Stephen Hopkins, the senior delegate, persuaded the committee to name his younger brother, Esek, a brigadier general of the Rhode Island militia, as commander in chief of the Continental Navy. A merchant skipper with thirty years at sea, Hopkins, like Washington, offered to serve without pay. Silas Deane obtained a captaincy for his wife's brother, Dudley Saltonstall, and the remaining captaincies went to equally deserving relations and friends, most of whom had commanded merchantmen at one time or another. Although he had few political connections, John Paul Jones, a Scottish immigrant with sixteen years at sea, apparently received some support from the Philadelphians and was named Hopkins' senior lieutenant. Meanwhile, Adams, who was familiar with British maritime practices, took on the task of drafting the "Rules for the Regulation of the Navy of the United Colonies." His product was precise, well written, and "less stringent" than the Royal Navy's regulations, although Adams probably copied about half of his draft directly from a British text.[6]

On 9 November George III rejected Congress's Olive Branch Petition and denounced the colonists as rebels. Two weeks later, on 25 November, all Continental Navy vessels were authorized to attack any British warship, transport, or tender, as well as any other armed ship found to be operating against the colonies, and naval agents were hired to procure ships and material for the new fleet. The patriots did not have much time to build new ships and, in any event, did not believe that the war would last long, so before beginning construction of new warships they sought gifts of ships and decided to purchase as many swift raiders as possible. One of these was the new, swift merchantman *Black Prince*, bought from one of the Navy's supporters, Robert Morris of Philadelphia. Renamed the *Alfred* in honor of the medieval founder of the English Navy, she was the first ship commissioned into the Continental Navy. She was soon joined

The ill-fated 697-ton Continental Navy frigate *Raleigh*, one of the thirteen frigates authorized by the Continental Congress in December 1775, was launched on 21 May 1776. Her first captain, Thomas Thompson, was suspended from the service after her first cruise. Her second skipper, the gallant John Barry, ran her aground on an island in Penobscot Bay in September 1778. Captured and taken into the British fleet, her unhappy history illustrates the difficulties of the Continental Navy during the Revolutionary War.

Squadron flagship *Alfred* (left) and the Continental Navy sloop *Providence* (right).

by the brigs *Columbus, Andrew Doria,* and *Cabot;* the 10-gun schooners *Wasp* and *Fly;* and the 12-gun sloops *Hornet* and *Providence.* John Barry, an experienced merchant sailor, rerigged these vessels, and the Marine Committee hired Joshua Humphreys, a Philadelphia ship designer, to convert them into warships.

Carried away by a tide of patriotic enthusiasm that peaked at the end of the year, Congress instructed the Marine Committee to superintend naval policy and on 11 December 1775 authorized the construction of thirteen frigates to serve as the backbone of the new fleet. American shipbuilders, familiar with small, swift, maneuverable brigs, sloops, and schooners, had never built sails-of-the-line—but they had not built a frigate for fifty years either. Their tradition of small-ship building had little or nothing to do with Congress' early decision to build frigates rather than sails-of-the-line. The patriots needed warships that would get to sea quickly, disrupt Britain's blockade, harass enemy convoys, and carry envoys abroad. Schooners and sloops were unsuitable for most of these missions and sails-of-the-line would take too long to build.

Thus the frigate program, the largest public works effort undertaken in North America up to that time, was a reflection of various compromises among competing political and strategic needs. Still uncertain as to the exact naval or maritime demands of the rebellion, Congress chose to build frigates rated at 24, 32, and 36 guns because of their versatility and because a single frigate could overwhelm every enemy warship except another heavy frigate or a sail-of-the-line. "You are enabled to defend yourself against most single ships, and capable we hope of outsailing any of the enemies'" sail-of-the-line, Morris told frigate Captain Nicholas Biddle in early 1777. The seaworthy frigate also provided the means to defend ports and bays, interrupt the resupply of the British blockade, carry cash crops to overseas markets and return home with specie, transport diplomats to and from Europe, show the flag in foreign ports, raid enemy commerce, and harass the Royal Navy's sea lines of communications. No other warship type possessed so much versatility in the age of sail.[7]

The difficulty of disrupting the British blockade was illustrated by the Continental Navy's single fleet operation. Lord Dunmore, Virginia's last royal governor, had organized a small Loyalist squadron that was harassing patriot shipping and settlements on the lower Chesapeake. In December the squadron was reinforced by the arrival of the 28-gun British frigate *Liverpool*, and on New Year's Day 1776 Dunmore bombarded and burned Norfolk. In response, the Marine Committee ordered Commodore Hopkins, the Continental Navy's commander in chief, to sail south to "take or destroy all the naval force of our enemies" in the Chesapeake Bay if they were not "greatly superior to your own," and then to "make yourself master of such forces as the enemy may have both in North and South Carolina." Hopkins was then to return to New England and challenge the British blockade ships off the coast of Rhode Island. If these steps were beyond his means, then Hopkins was "to follow such courses as your best judgment shall suggest." He might also add to his fleet by borrowing ships from friendly state governors.

An icy river and slow recruiting prevented Hopkins from getting under way until February 1777, and by then he had decided that Congress's plan was impractical. Not only was the British fleet active up and down the coast, but he now learned that the *Liverpool* had arrived on the Chesapeake. Also, Captain Whipple had alerted him to a report that there was a large store of supplies at

New Providence in the Bahamas. Hopkins assessed his assemblage of newly rigged, converted merchant vessels manned by sickly, inexperienced crews and decided it was inferior to Dunmore's force, so he decided to avoid the bay, ignore the Carolinas, and raid the Bahamas instead. The wisdom of this move was clear when a storm at sea forced Hopkins to detach the *Hornet* and the *Fly* from the squadron. Unfortunately, he had failed to inform Congress of his drastic change of plans.[8]

New Providence was so important and so vulnerable that the Admiralty had ordered Admiral Shuldham to station a ship there, but he refused to do so, wrongly assuming that the garrison was "able to defend those stores without any additional force." Hopkins landed in March, took poorly defended Fort Montague after firing a few shots, and accepted the surrender of the garrison in the small town of Nassau the next day. Most of the gunpowder had been carried away before the Americans arrived, but it still took fourteen days for them to load the stores onto their ships: seventy-one 9-pounders and 14-pounders, fifteen mortars, more than 10,000 rounds of ammunition, and other stores. During the voyage back to Rhode Island, Hopkins seized a British schooner and her tender, but he could not manage his ships in a fighting formation and therefore was unable to exert tactical control when the *Alfred* encountered the 20-gun British brig *Glasgow*. As a result, the Americans were trapped and outgunned in a melee with Captain Tyringham Howe of the *Glasgow*, a veteran who skillfully damaged Hopkins' ships before escaping unharmed. Concerned about the damage to his squadron and fearful that other British warships were in the vicinity, Hopkins refused to give chase and limped back to New London instead.

Unbeknownst to Hopkins, his descent on Nassau had profound and far-reaching consequences for the rebel cause. By extending the patriots' reach into the West Indies, he had unwittingly widened considerably the geographic and economic scope of the rebellion. In British eyes, a small uprising confined at first to New England now menaced imperial trade and military outposts from one end of their North American holdings to the other. To meet this challenge, the Admiralty's Lord Sandwich reinforced the Jamaica and Leeward Islands stations and stripped the Mediterranean Fleet in order to strengthen the Royal Navy in American waters.

While Hopkins was en route to the West Indies, Philadelphia's Robert Morris obtained a Continental Navy commission for

Captain John Barry, who took command of the *Lexington*, a converted brig that the Marine Committee had recently acquired from Maryland's Council of Safety. Like most Continental Navy captains, Barry was a veteran sailor who knew little about naval tactics or organized warfare; however, he had commanded several armed merchantmen and defended them against pirates. After Humphreys fitted out the *Lexington*, she cleared the Delaware Bay at the end of March 1776. In April, Barry closed on the British sloop *Edward* and, he reported, "shattered her in a terrible manner" during a brief gun duel, after which he seized her powder and arms. Barry reported this action to Congress, unaware that he was the first Continental Navy captain to capture a Royal Navy vessel. Eluding the heavy British frigate *Roebuck*, he returned to the Delaware and patrolled the bay during the summer, taking several more valuable prizes.[9]

The success of Barry's cruise stood in sharp contrast to Esek Hopkins' refusal to challenge the Royal Navy below the Potomac, a decision that enraged southerners in the Continental Congress. Hopkins' offer of his prizes to Rhode Island and Connecticut also poured the acid of sectionalism into the brew of petty bickering, recriminations, and courts martial that befell his squadron upon its return. His decision to leave his cannon at New London especially infuriated Congress. Adams, one of Hopkins' supporters, contended that the commodore was "pursued and persecuted by that anti-New England spirit, which haunted Congress in many other proceedings." Desertions depleted Hopkins' crews, and he made the disastrous mistake of shifting his base to his home port of Providence, Rhode Island. Competing against privateers for sailors and supplies, he found it impossible to prepare his ships for another voyage. The Marine Committee urged him to again put to sea to concentrate on "the destruction of the enemy's fleet in North Carolina or Virginia," an order that took no account of the forlorn condition of his ships. Complaining about Hopkins' failure to organize another fleet operation, Robert Morris pointed out that the *Alfred* was idle and the other ships dispersed on various unrelated duties. Hopkins was not blameless, and his abusive behavior angered Congress and led to his censure in August 1776. Bitter and unemployed, he blasted Congress again, finally admitted that the fleet's problems were beyond him, and asked that someone else be named as a replacement. Hopkins was dismissed from the naval service in January 1778 and returned to Rhode Island politics, but no successor was named commander in chief of the Continental Navy.[10]

The seeming failure of Hopkins' operations was compared by the Navy's critics to Washington's success against Boston. After the Battle of Bunker Hill in June 1775, General Gage refused to mount further offensives, in part because both he and the British government still vainly hoped to settle the dispute over parliamentary authority without a war. These efforts all failed, and by January 1776 General Henry Knox brought artillery from recently captured Fort Ticonderoga to Dorchester Heights on the outskirts of Boston, from where he could pound the British position below. Gage was relieved soon after by General William Howe, whose brother, Admiral Richard Howe, was given the Boston naval command. Deeply committed to peace, Admiral Howe was already quarreling with the Admiralty's Lord Sandwich over British strategy. Howe sought to isolate the conflict to a maritime police action off New England's coast. He reduced the blockade from seventy-five to six ships and used his ships merely to compel the Americans to obey the Navigation Acts.

The friction at sea intensified, however, when Congress in March 1776 passed a resolution authorizing the issuance of letters of marque to American privateers, who were encouraged for the first time to mount attacks on all British ships. Privateering would be, John Adams asserted, "a short, easy, and infallible method of humbling the English, preventing the effusion of an ocean of blood, and bringing the war to a conclusion." This daring step also sent a signal to London that the rebels were unlikely to back down. Such evidence of American resolve unnerved the Howe brothers, neither of whom had the stomach to withstand a bloody siege, so on 17 March the British evacuated Boston and sailed north to the Royal Navy's base at Halifax, Nova Scotia, to regroup. George III had made it clear, however, that he would accept nothing less from the Americans than complete submission to imperial authority, and in response on 4 July 1776 the Second Continental Congress reluctantly issued the Declaration of Independence.[11]

Declaring independence forced waverers to make choices, directed American military efforts toward a single political objective, and came just in time to fortify patriot resolve in the face of greater British determination. Even the half-hearted Howe brothers decided to prosecute the war more vigorously. After months of delay, Admiral Howe agreed to execute the Admiralty's orders to clamp a tight blockade on New England, destroy colonial shipping, and totally isolate the patriots from overseas trade. The fact that the Royal Navy had only twenty of its seventy frigates on station in North America made this difficult. Although the blockade badly crimped shipping north of the Delaware Bay, after the British evacuated Boston it was open to American shipping for the rest of the war. In August, General Howe landed a large army on Manhattan Island, forced Washington to retire to White Plains, and garrisoned New York. Howe's men spread out over New Jersey trying, with little success, to enlist loyalist support. New York, however, remained firmly in enemy hands. David Bushnell, a private inventor, came up with a way to force the British fleet out of New York harbor. He manufactured a one-man, muscle-powered submarine that carried an early limpet mine containing gunpowder and a thirty-minute timer. In 1776 he sent his vessel out to blow up the 64-gun sail-of-the-line *Eagle*, then on station off Governor's Island. The submarine's driver could not attach the mine to the ship's copper-sheathed hull, however, so he set it adrift before escaping and it exploded too far away to do any damage. Supported by a powerful fleet, British troops garrisoned New York for the remainder of the war.

The northern prong of the British attack had even less success than Howe's attempt in New Jersey. In May 1775, Vermont irregulars under Ethan Allen and Benedict Arnold had taken Fort Ticonderoga and its large store of British cannon. In early July, Washington directed Arnold to ride north to Maine, take command of a small army there, and advance westward against the enemy fortress at Quebec. Congress, expecting the French Canadians to join the American rebellion, simultaneously sent a separate expedition to invade Canada under General Richard Montgomery, who occupied Montreal after the British withdrew in November. When he learned that Arnold was about to storm Quebec, Montgomery marched to the southwest to join him, and the Americans attacked the city under the cover of a fierce blizzard. The British repulsed the attack, however, Montgomery was killed, and Arnold was wounded. When British ships brought reinforcements down the St. Lawrence River to Quebec, Arnold had to retire to Fort Ticonderoga in May 1776.

Arnold now began to build a small lake squadron to hold northern New York against an invasion by 13,500 Redcoats under General Sir Guy Carleton. For their part, the British tore apart two schooners on the St. Lawrence and rebuilt them on the northern edge of Lake Champlain, where they had already constructed a vessel drawing 180 tons from local materials. This shipbuilding race was costly. It delayed the start of Carleton's offensive until 11 October 1776, when the superior British squadron sailed south, its advance hastened by a strong north wind. Arnold hid his vessels behind Valcour Island just south of present day Plattsburgh and allowed the British to sail past his station before opening fire. Trying to beat back against the wind, the British made little headway during the day. That night Arnold's squadron escaped south to Crown Point, where it was destroyed over the next forty-eight hours by an enemy in hot pursuit. The Battle of Valcour Island was a tactical victory but a strategic defeat for the British, as Arnold's delaying strategy postponed their offensive until the eve of a bitter winter and compelled Carleton to retire to Canada rather than campaign in the snow.

The Continental Congress was heartened by Carleton's withdrawal, as well as by the early progress of the naval war at sea. A month after Congress had declared independence, Lieutenant John Paul Jones put to sea in the sloop *Providence* on his first independent cruise. During August and September 1776, he took sixteen British ships and destroyed two Nova Scotia fishing fleets. Congress promoted him to captain and gave him command of the *Alfred.* He again sailed onto the Grand Banks and captured six more small prizes plus the armed transport *Mellish*, which was loaded with winter uniforms badly needed by Washington's Continental Army.

Heartened by these operations, Congress supplemented the frigate program in November 1776 with an authorization to lay down three 74-gun sails-of-the-line, five more 36-gun frigates, a brig, and a packetboat. Ironically, the earlier thirteen-ship Continental Navy frigate program was far behind schedule, and had proven to be much more costly than Congress had expected. There were not enough shipyards in any one area to build all these ships and each region wanted the government's business, so the contracts for the vessels were scattered around. This garnered political support for the Continental Navy, but at a high price in resulting inefficiency. Another problem was that the colonies had not manufactured cannon until 1775, when furnaces were first constructed for that purpose in Rhode Island. There was an effort to achieve some economies of scale by setting common standards

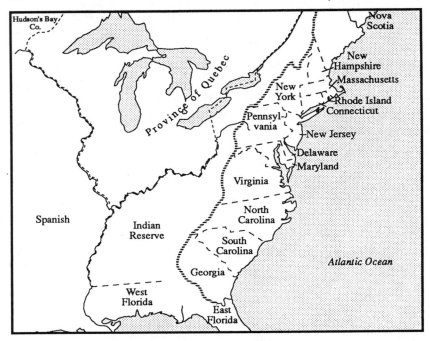

North America during the Revolutionary War

for the ordnance on the basis of designs by David Rittenhouse and by concentrating all naval gun manufacturing at four Pennsylvania ironworks, but this effort failed. Orders for the Continental Army's cannon took precedence over Navy orders, inflation afflicted prices, the demand for guns overwhelmed the capacity of the firms to produce them, and the distribution of the finished guns broke down.

Another problem was that, unlike the Army, the Continental Navy never developed a central commissary system. "Our principal dependence for Navy supplies are upon prizes," the Board of Admiralty confessed as late as September 1780. Moreover, the Army almost always took precedence over the Navy in the distribution of captured arms and supplies. The Americans were inexperienced in producing saltpeter, and relied solely on imported or captured gunpowder during the early years of the war. Importing munitions to the colonies was forbidden by an imperial proclamation in 1774, creating scarcities when the war began that quickly exhausted stockpiles amassed in early 1775 and igniting a fierce competition thereafter among the Army, Navy, and state militias for captured arms. "You will give immediate notice to General Washington of such stores as you may capture which are necessary for the use of the Army," the Marine Committee told John Barry on 29 January 1778, when ordering him out on a routine patrol of the Delaware Bay.[12]

The original shipbuilding schedule specified that the first frigate be completed in March 1776, but none of these ships was ready for another year. Once they were launched, only half of them put to sea. The *Trumbull*, laid down in Saybrook, received her cannon in October 1776, but she drew too much water to cross the bar at the mouth of the Connecticut River and languished there until 1780. A pair of frigates laid down on the Hudson were burned when the British descended on New York, and another pair went up in flames when the British took Philadelphia. A sixth was captured on the Delaware River. The first Continental Navy frigate to get to sea was the *Randolph*, built in Philadelphia. Her cannon were brought on board in November 1776, and she stood out into the Atlantic in February 1777, but after only a few days a gale forced Captain Nicholas Biddle to put in to Charleston for repairs. He took six prizes during his next cruise, but was then bottled up in Charleston harbor when Admiral Howe clamped a blockade on the patriots' southern ports. Although spiced with morale-building heroism, the practical results of these early frigate operations disappointed many of the Navy's supporters.

Like the Americans, the British were handicapped at the start of the war by excessive confidence, but after some early actions they became increasingly realistic in assessing the means needed to blockade America's coast and suppress the constant menace of rebel privateering. The Royal Navy's blockade "would soon make them tired of war," Lord Sandwich predicted in 1777, but he also warned Lord North that "it must not, however, be imagined that any force will be sufficient entirely to execute the purpose of blocking up all the rebels' ports and putting a total stop to their privateering." In this contest for the control of American coastal waters, geography and the indigenous economy favored the patriots. No single port dominated American trade, there were no vital chokepoints through which rebel shipping had to pass, and New England's rugged coastline offered an abundance of harbors and sheltered anchorages.[13]

Sandwich's concern about privateering was well founded. The mission of the American privateer was to pick on weaker enemy merchantmen, while avoiding serious combat at any cost. Whereas a Continental Navy vessel operated under moral and legal injunctions to challenge any enemy warship of equal or lesser strength, the privateer shrank from engaging the Royal Navy, relying instead on speed and stealth to evade enemy patrols and blockade stations. As a type, the privateer was not unique. Schooners, brigs, and larger merchantmen were all drafted into this service, and a large number of American privateers were actually built and armed to conduct these profitable cruises. One distinct American vessel, the letter-of-marque, a converted merchantman armed only for self-defense, was legally entitled to attack enemy vessels and earn prize money, although this activity was entirely incidental to her main function as an armed trader.

Clusters of American privateers began to operate in 1776 off the Gulf of the St. Lawrence, taking small Canadian and British fishing vessels and merchantmen and occasionally raiding poorly defended settlements ashore. These ships operated with relative immunity, owing to the dispersed character of their attacks and their shrewd use of the regional fogs, storms, and high seas to mask their operations and hinder British defensive patrols out of the fleet base at nearby Halifax. American privateers found their most lucrative hunting grounds in the West Indies, however, and it was this area that attracted most of the southern privateers. To safeguard the movement of goods from the British Isles to the West Indies after 1775, the Admiralty established two westward convoy routes, one from Portsmouth, England, the other from Dublin, Ireland. Security for these operations was always poor, the convoys included up to 100 merchantmen and transports and took months to organize, and during the voyage across the Atlantic the loss of stragglers was common. Once the ships reached the Caribbean they dispersed, easy victims for the swarm of American privateers that infested the passages from the Atlantic into the Lesser Antilles.

By 1776, there were 136 American privateers at sea. When British defensive measures reduced this number by half within a year, the Continental Congress reacted by issuing privateering commissions to armed French cruisers operating out of the French sugar islands of Guadeloupe and Martinique. The state governments also issued letters of marque to privateers in increasing numbers, and by the end of the war more than 50,000 American sailors had put to sea on a privateering cruise. Reporting from Halifax in 1777, Admiral Arbuthnot confessed to the Admiralty that the Continental Navy and American privateers had together combined to checkmate the Royal Navy. The British fleets were hard pressed to defend "our trade, which they have really cut up almost without molestation." Although privateering raised havoc with Britain's supply system, it also throttled the development of the Continental Navy. By May 1779, one Bostonian observed that manning privateers was no problem as "men seem as plenty as grasshoppers in the field. . . . Privateering was never more in vogue." Naval officers, rather than appreciating the value of these raiders, despised the privateers for soaking dry the pool of seamen and leaving the Continental Navy's ships with inadequate and inexperienced crews. Many officers felt themselves to be above "those licensed robbers," whom John Paul Jones charged were "actuated by no nobler principle than that of self-interest."[14]

Not only were the British unable to contain the Americans at sea in 1776, but also the more important war on land went badly for them that year and promised to get worse. Fear of monarchs had long kept the British Army small by contrast to the forces of the powers of Europe, and with the onset of the Industrial Revolution the demand for labor in England remained high. This meant that recruiting for both armed services was difficult, so Britain hired foreign mercenaries. The Admiralty not only had to support the established North American command, but also was assigned to transport and supply new Army regiments shipped to the colonies. Within a few years, the War Office had transported about 72,000 soldiers to North America, a body of men that consumed over 120,000 tons of supplies annually. For this purpose, the independent Navy Board employed more than 500 transports, each of which carried from 250 to 400 tons per voyage. The enormity of the shipping effort, however, stretched to the limit the Royal Navy's escort forces and exposed Britain's sea line of communications to frequent American assaults. Nonetheless, if they did not persist in the face of this adversity, explained Lord George Germain, the secretary of state for North America, Britain would "never continue to exist as a great nation after we have lost . . . the American colonies." A bold strategist, Germain convinced the cabinet to undertake complex operations in 1777 designed to sever New England from the mid-Atlantic and southern colonies. While holding New York City, General Howe was to support an invasion from Canada under General John Burgoyne, who was to march from the Richelieu River to Lake Champlain, and then southward along the banks of the Hudson.[15]

Germain's plan went awry from the start. Poor command and

control plagued the entire sequence of operations. Instead of concentrating his army in New York, General Howe struck south against Philadelphia. At first, all went well for the British. The British fleet lifted Howe's army to the mouth of the Delaware Bay, then advanced up the bay against Philadelphia. The small Continental Navy could neither disrupt this offensive nor even provide Washington with information about the enemy's movements. As a result, Washington was defeated at the Battle of Brandywine. Marching overland to Philadelphia, the British penetrated the American lines, dooming the city and forcing Congress to flee. Although Washington inflicted a minor reverse on Howe at the Battle of Germantown, Howe knew that if the British fleet could force its way up the Delaware before the snows of winter ended the campaign, the Continental Army could be cornered like a fox treed by baying hounds. However, for a short time, the defenders of Mud Island denied the British fleet access to Philadelphia. Mud Island finally fell in November 1777, but by then it was too cold for Howe to pursue Washington, who settled into winter quarters at Valley Forge.

Meanwhile, the second stage of Germain's strategy was going awry in the north. From a secure base at Montreal, Burgoyne meandered south along the shores of Lake Champlain until he arrived at Fort Ticonderoga. From there, he fought his way south to Saratoga, but his lines of communications had been severed by American militiamen, and General Horatio Gates' army defeated 5,000 Redcoats on 17 October 1777. Coupled with American naval operations that year, the Battle of Saratoga led directly to an alliance between the United States and France in 1778.

Although the Continental Navy could not defend American waters, its operations on the high seas, plus those of American privateers, had already yielded important results. By mid-1777 the British had been forced to organize most of their North America-bound shipping into heavily escorted convoys. Although only four of the Continental frigates got to sea that year, even their failures kept the British busy. The *Hancock* and the *Boston* stood out of Massachusetts Bay in May 1777 to chase the British frigate *Milford*, but she escaped. Although the American squadron took another enemy frigate and a brig, the *Hancock* struck her colors when trapped by a British warship and the *Boston* fled home, where her captain was dismissed for cowardice. The *Randolph* was still blockaded in Charleston, but the frigate *Raleigh* was more fortunate. She could

not put to sea in the spring of 1777 because of delays in manufacturing her cannon, but that summer Captain Thomas Thompson
finally got under way, rendezvoused with the *Alfred*, and crossed
the Atlantic carrying diplomatic correspondence for Benjamin
Franklin, the American envoy in Paris. With orders to secure
French military assistance and persuade the French monarchy to
sign a military alliance with the united colonies, Franklin had
been carried to Europe in December 1776 by Captain Lambert
Wickes' converted brig *Reprisal.*

There was evidence that Europe was warming up to the American cause. On 17 November 1776, the 14-gun brig *Andrew Doria*
was entering the harbor of St. Eustatius in the Dutch West Indies
when she fired a salute to the Dutch flag. Following an ancient cus-
tom, Johannes de Graff, the governor, returned the honor with a
13-gun salute to the red-and-white-striped American flag, Europe's first salute to America's independence. St. Eustatius soon
after became a bustling depot for military stores shipped by neutral Europe to the American patriots.

The *Reprisal* was the first American warship to enter European
waters. Her appearance signaled the opening phase of a strategic
plan to force the British to disperse their fleets and a naval diplomacy designed to excite tensions between London and Paris. Unhappy with the frigates' inability to disrupt the British blockade of
the American ports, Robert Morris, who was gaining influence
over naval affairs in Congress, argued that since "our infant fleet
cannot protect our own Coasts," the "only effectual relief it can afford us is to attack the enemy's defenseless places and thereby
oblige them to station more of their ships in their own countries,
or to keep them employed in following ours." In January 1777, the
Reprisal sailed into the English Channel and took five British
prizes. Reinforced by the *Lexington* and the *Dolphin*, which rendezvoused with the *Reprisal* in France, Wickes drove into the Irish
Sea in May, eluded several British patrols, captured eighteen
prizes, and provoked a major diplomatic crisis between Britain
and France.[16]

The British insisted that neutrality required that France not
allow the Continental Navy's raiders to operate out of French
ports, and London repeatedly protested France's covert assistance
to the Americans. The French monarchists held no brief for the
republican revolution in the New World, but they ached for revenge against Britain for the humiliation of the Seven Years' War

and hoped in the process to revise Europe's balance of power. The French were not yet convinced that the Americans could win the war, so they decided to prove their neutrality by seizing the *Dolphin* and ordering Wickes to leave French waters. "Our late cruise has made a great deal of noise and will probably soon bring war between Britain and France," Wickes reported. Tragically, on the return voyage home his squadron was destroyed. A British cutter captured the *Lexington*, while the *Reprisal* went down in a storm off Newfoundland. The Anglo-French clash so distressed Germain that he wrote that the American raiders had "such encouragement given them by the French that I was apprehensive . . . that we should have been obliged to have declared war." This was Lambert Wickes' "sincere wish."[17]

In the summer of 1777, Franklin and his fellow commissioners in Paris also had purchased the 14-gun cutter *Revenge*, a vessel they intended to use to attack enemy shipping off the British Isles. She was handed over to Captain Gustavas Conyngham, who had previously commanded the lugger *Surprise* and had taken two British ships during a successful cruise earlier in the year. The French were so alarmed by British protests that they detained Conyngham and his crew, returned the prizes, and confiscated the *Surprise*. Franklin did not despair. He instructed Conyngham to sail in the *Revenge* on 17 July on a cruise that took him back to British waters, where he took two prizes within a week and brought panic to London. His "first adventure greatly raised insurance on the northern trade," diplomat Silas Deane reported to Congress on 23 August, and had "become the terror of all of the eastern coast of England and Scotland."[18]

Conyngham remained in or near British waters for two more months, but Royal Navy patrols were constantly at sea with orders to hunt him down, so he sailed for the Bay of Biscay, putting into the Spanish port of Ferrol. During spring and summer 1778 he made several cruises into the Mediterranean and around the Azores, and was so successful that the British put pressure on Spain to suppress his operations. Having taken dozens of prizes and caused a diplomatic uproar, he decided to return home, and on 1 September he set sail for French Martinique. He hunted down enemy merchantmen and privateers in the West Indies before heading home at the start of the new year, arriving in Philadelphia on 21 February 1779, his ship laden with arms for the Continental Army. He had burned or sent into port sixty enemy vessels. Congress decided to sell the *Revenge* at auction, and she was bought by Conyngham and a Philadelphia firm and fitted out as a privateer. Unfortunately, on 27 April, while chasing two British privateers off New York, she was run down by the British sloop-of-war *Gallatea* and Conyngham was forced to strike his colors.

These American commerce raiders produced a toxic diplomatic chemistry between Britain and France in 1777, which boiled over into reciprocal declarations of war when the French learned about the American victory at Saratoga. In December of that year, London dispatched to Paris an agent who offered Franklin a compromise peace. The British would accept "home rule" for the colonies if the Americans recognized Britain's overall sovereignty. When France's foreign minister, Count Vergennes, learned of this, he promptly negotiated treaties of commerce and alliance with the united colonies. Under the terms of the Franco-American Alliance, signed on 6 February 1778, France was committed to fight for American independence and the Americans were obligated to defend France's colonies in the West Indies. Both powers also promised not to conclude a separate peace and agreed that the Alliance would last "from the present time and forever." Because it seemed to nail French policy to the wall of American objectives, this language was eagerly welcomed by the Continental Congress, which rejected another British overture for a compromise peace and ratified the treaties on 6 June 1778. One week later, British and French squadrons fired on one another in the English Channel, and both powers soon thereafter declared war.[19]

Britain's position had suddenly become very dangerous. Historically, when confronted by a threat from France, British statesmen maintained the European balance of power by creating a coalition with a secondary continental power, but this was impossible in 1778 for two reasons. First, Britain at the time had no friends on the Continent. The Austrians were dedicated to their new tie with France, and so was Spain. Britain had antagonized Frederick the Great of Prussia by signing a separate peace at the end of the Seven Years' War without his consent. Moreover, Britain's ambitious maritime policies in that war and thereafter had also alienated the Dutch, the Swedes, and the Russians. Second, America's curious geopolitical situation confronted Britain with a new strategic equation. In the past, the Royal Navy had secured the flank of the British Isles against her European enemies.

During the American Revolution, however, the Continental Navy and rebel privateers degraded and scattered Britain's naval power, enhancing in turn the danger to British control of the Atlantic from the "unbroken" French fleets at Brest and Toulon. With "no other war or object to draw off their attention and resources," Lord Sandwich explained, the French posed an especial danger to the Royal Navy after 1778.[20]

With the fresh promise of French troops and ships, and buoyed by the victory at the Saratoga, American military operations increased in tempo in 1778. After the terrible winter at Valley Forge, Washington took the offensive during the summer at the Battle of Monmouth. Although this encounter was inconclusive, British power in North America had reached its apex. The Admiralty, charged with the defense of the British Isles, could no longer increase the number of escorts for transatlantic convoys to support the armies of General Henry Clinton, who had just relieved Howe as the British commander in chief.

Britain's logistics problems were exacerbated by the Continental Navy's operations. After his two successful cruises in 1776, Congress had promoted John Paul Jones and given him command of the sloop *Ranger*, which sailed from Portsmouth, New Hampshire, for France on 1 November 1777. The Dutch had been commissioned to build a frigate that Jones was to command, but British agents uncovered this plan and London persuaded the Hague not to sell the ship to the Americans. In France Jones quickly assayed the central strategic reality of the war of the American Revolution. With fourteen vessels sporting 332 guns, the Continental Navy was no match for Britain's North American command, which comprised eighty-nine warships armed with 2,576 guns. On the other hand, the North American fleet was half of the Royal Navy's inventory of 188 warships and had about one-third of its total throwweight. "A single blow" by "ten or twelve sails-of-the-line with frigates would give a good account of the fleet under Lord Howe," John Paul Jones concluded, but he realized that to accomplish this the Americans needed a "continental marine power" as an ally. Meanwhile, the best strategy for the Continental Navy was to bring the war home to the British. Franklin agreed and instructed Jones, who kept command of the *Ranger*, to mount operations "distressing the enemies of the United States by sea, or otherwise" in Europe.[21]

These orders continued the campaign initiated by Wickes

and Conyngham, but for a different purpose. In early 1778, Jones decided to descend upon the British coast to bring the war home to the English and compel the Admiralty to withdraw more ships from the North American commands. With the Franco-American Alliance ready for ratification, Jones sailed around the Bay of Biscay during the winter to prey on British merchantmen and arranged on 14 February for "the American flag for the first time [to be] recognized in the fullest and completest manner by the flag of France, . . . an acknowledgement of American independence." After refitting at the French port of Brest, two months later Jones sailed around Ireland, then south through the North Channel along the western coast of Scotland. There, disguised as a merchantman, he took several small prizes before coming upon the sloop *Drake* off Carrickfergus, Ireland. Jones closed on the enemy and sought to surprise her at night, but a high wind prevented this and during the chase the *Ranger* nearly ran aground. He gave up for the moment and stood out to sea. He was preparing to execute a more important plan: to attack the large port of Whitehaven and "put an end, by one good fire in England, of shipping, to all burnings in America." With a small shore party, Jones spiked the guns of Whitehaven's fort in the broad daylight of 22 April and set fire to a collier in the harbor, but he was chased off by townsmen who forced the Americans to row back to their ship. The alarm was sounded along England's coast that Jones had landed with "a design to burn the town." Although Jones had inflicted little damage on Whitehaven, it was the first time since the Anglo-Dutch wars of the seventeenth century that an enemy had successfully attacked a British port. The raid provided ammunition to British politicians who opposed the American war and immeasurably undermined Parliament's confidence in Lord North's government.[22]

A native of this part of Scotland, Jones mistakenly believed the local magnate, the Earl of Selkirk, to be an important British political figure, and he planned to abduct the peer and ransom him for American prisoners of war. The night following the Whitehaven raid, the *Ranger* anchored in Kirkcudbright Bay. Jones took a party ashore to snatch the earl from his manor house, but a servant told Jones that the victim was away. He ordered his men to return to the ship, but they refused; they were, Jones reported, "disposed to pillage, burn, and plunder all they could." Accustomed to an occasional mutiny, Jones proposed a compromise. Part of the crew marched up to the house and "politely" demanded the

Selkirk's family silver, then returned to the ship. When Jones returned to France, he bought the silver from his crew and shipped it back to Lady Selkirk with a letter explaining that he had "drawn my sword in the present generous struggle for the rights of men" and not "in pursuit of riches."[23]

The morning after the aborted abduction, Jones sped back over to Carrickfergus and enticed the *Drake* into the North Channel, where he hove to, raised the American flag, and fired his broadsides. Exploiting a throwweight of eighteen 9-pounders, superior to the twenty 6-pounders carried by the *Drake*, Jones stood off to prevent the enemy from boarding and taking advantage of his superior manpower. For the next hour there was little maneuvering as the two ships stood and pounded away at each other. When the British struck their colors, their captain was dead and the *Drake* was in sad shape, "her sails and rigging entirely cut to pieces, her masts and yards all wounded and her hull very much galled." A few weeks later, after a cruise that he believed to be "sufficient to show that not all their boasted navy can protect their own coast," Jones put into Brest with his prizes.[24]

While Jones had been preparing for his descent on Whitehaven earlier in the year, in the French port of L'Orient the *Alfred* and the *Raleigh* were loaded with supplies for the Continental Army. They sailed for America in February 1778. Captain Thomas Thompson planned a southerly voyage, hoping to seize some British merchantmen on the way home. On 9 March, however, two small British warships, the 20-gun *Ariadne* and the 14-gun *Ceres*, sighted the American squadron. The *Alfred* was a slow ship, and when the British gave chase, the *Raleigh* had the lee gage and was unable to beat against the wind in time to close up and defend the smaller vessel, which was soon forced to strike her colors. Thompson was now in a spot. With a British prize crew manning the captured *Alfred*, he faced a trio of enemy broadsides that, while individually inferior to his own battery, were collectively far superior. Moreover, the value of his cargo of military stores had been impressed upon him before he had sailed. With little chance of recovering the *Alfred* or her cargo, he decided to run. When the *Raleigh* returned home, the new congressional Board of Marine had Thompson court-martialed for cowardice and dismissed from the Continental Navy.

In the meantime, the stress of diverse operations had forced the British to lift their blockade of Charleston in 1778. Captain Biddle organized a squadron composed of the frigate *Randolph* and two brigs and two schooners from the South Carolina Navy, and sailed in March to hunt down a pair of British sloops and a frigate that were cruising along the coast. They continued south until 7 March when, east of the Barbados, the Americans were spotted at sunrise by the 64-gun sail-of-the-line *Yarmouth*. Biddle signaled the South Carolinians to flee, then turned about, hoisted his colors, and fired on the enemy. Holding the windward gage, the *Yarmouth* stood off, pounding the *Randolph* while the other American ships escaped. Finally, one British broadside hit a powder keg on the *Randolph*'s deck and she exploded into thousands of pieces. "An American ensign," the English captain reported, "was blown upon the *Yarmouth*'s forecastle not singed. The temerity of Captain Biddle in thus engaging a ship so much superior to his own deserved a better fate." Of the crew of 315, only 4 survivors were recovered, found floating on a piece of timber four days after the battle. Within ninety days, five warships of the Continental Navy had been lost—with little to show but glory.[25]

John Barry was nearly as unlucky during his command of the ill-fated frigate *Raleigh*, a ship that he took over from Thomas Thompson in 1778. On 25 September, Barry was escorting a small coastal convoy out of Boston when they were sighted by a pair of powerful British frigates. Barry ordered the American merchantmen back to port and cleared his decks for action. Then the *Raleigh* began to run. While the wind was up, the great speed of the American frigate saved her, but the next day a fog closed in, the wind died down, and the enemy squadron cornered Barry near the mouth of Penobscot Bay. After the *Raleigh* lost two masts during a brief gunfight with the *Unicorn*, the Englishman was joined by his partner, the 50-gun frigate *Experiment*. Unwilling to sacrifice his crew against these formidable odds, Barry ran his ship aground and with his men escaped on foot into the wilderness. The *Raleigh* was refloated by the British, who put her into service flying the Union Jack.

The loss of the *Raleigh* was only the next to the last in a string of disasters that befell the Continental Navy in 1778. When the frigate *Chesapeake* tried to evade the British blockade and get to sea, she too was forced to run aground on the shores of the Chesapeake Bay, refloated by the enemy, and taken into the British fleet.

Of the fourteen ships converted in 1775 by the Marine Committee, only the brig *Providence* remained in service at the end of the year; of the thirteen Continental frigates, there were but four left; and of three cutters bought by Franklin and his fellow commissioners in France, only the *Revenge* still flew the American flag. The British had surged eighty-nine vessels with 2,576 guns into North American waters. To contend with these forces, Congress could count only fourteen warships carrying a total of 332 guns. Although Germain estimated that the Royal Navy had lost 18,000 men through desertion and battle losses to the Americans, the British as a matter of policy wisely refused to exchange prisoners captured at sea. The Continental Navy's manpower problem was worse. American seamen preferred wartime duty in privateers, and by the end of 1778 recruiting for the Continental Navy became so difficult that during the last three years of the Revolution most warships put to sea without full complements.

All else being roughly equal, during most engagements in the age of sail, the level of manning decided tactical victory at sea. American patriotism in the first year of war diminished as the fighting dragged on, and no solution to the recruiting bottleneck was in sight. This, combined with the loss of ships, discouraged Congress. Disenchanted with the Continental Navy and always lingering near the precipice of bankruptcy, Congress in late 1778 allowed work to continue at a slow pace on the *America* at Portsmouth but canceled the other two sails-of-the-line that had been authorized during the winter of 1777 and suspended entirely the rest of the 1776 building program. The Navy's exertions were more valuable than Congress realized, however. Under pressure only from the Americans before 1778, the British had been able to concentrate their military efforts in North America, but this was insufficient to crush the rebels, and this peak in the tempo of British operations in America passed once France entered the conflict.

Chapter Two

To Yorktown and Independence
1779–1781

Shortly after war broke out between Britain and France, the French decided to invade England and, at the same time, to contest the Royal Navy's control of American waters. Although the French inflicted a tactical defeat on Britain's Channel Fleet off Ushant on 23 July 1778, they failed to press home their advantage and retired to Brest after the battle, thoroughly impressed once more with the difficulty of crossing the English Channel. Missing Ushant was a disappointment for John Paul Jones, whose orders to accompany the French fleet as an observer did not arrive in Brest before it had sortied. After his second cruise in the *Ranger*, Jones was promised a better ship and, following a great deal of discussion, was given command of an old East India merchantman, which he converted into a frigate and renamed the *Bonhomme Richard* in honor of his friend, Benjamin Franklin, creator of "Poor Richard."

The French and Spanish fleets were expected to rendezvous in the Bay of Biscay and then move against England, so Jones decided "to make a diversion in the north," first by attacking shipping at Leith, Edinburgh's port, and then by intercepting a convoy of British cargo ships laden with naval stores from the Baltic. To round out his squadron, the French assigned to Jones' command two small frigates, the *Alliance* and the *Pallas*, the corvette *Vengeance*, and the cutter *Cerf*. This formation stood out of L'Orient on 14 August and sailed clockwise around the British Isles,

John Paul Jones in the *Bonhomme Richard* engaging the British *Serapis* off Flamborough Head, 23 September 1779.

Commodore John Paul Jones.

taking seventeen prizes before reaching Scotland's eastern coast. Jones wanted to sail into the Firth of Forth and extract a "contribution" from the port of Leith, but a "sudden storm rose and obliged me to run before the wind out of the Gulf of Edinburgh." His next scheme was to raid British coal stations around Newcastle-on-Tyne, but the French captains rejected this idea, so he decided instead to renew the search for the Baltic convoy.[1]

On 23 September, off Flamborough Head, Jones sighted the Baltic convoy and its escorts, the frigate *Serapis* and the sloop *Countess of Scarborough*. Jones reckoned that his firepower was superior, and as the two squadrons approached each other, he signaled his other ships to join battle. However, the French captain of the *Alliance*, Pierre Landais, ignored Jones' signals, and Captain Cottineau of the *Pallas*, observing Jones' effort to close with the *Serapis*, assumed that the British prisoners on board the *Bonhomme Richard* had taken over the American frigate. The British convoy began its escape, covered by Captain Pearson in the *Serapis*. At 1900, the opposing frigates were within hailing distance. Out of the black night both broadsides spit fire, but during the first or second round two of the six 18-pounders on the *Bonhomme Richard*'s lower gun deck burst, killing several sailors and blowing up the deck above. The rest of the gunners on the lower deck abandoned their stations just as the enemy drew within short pistol range. Fire from the *Serapis* silenced the secondary American battery of fourteen 12-pound guns and, after another thirty minutes, Jones was left with only three 9-pounders for a quarterdeck broadside. He knew that his only chance now was to board the enemy, so when the *Serapis* pulled ahead in order to rake the bow of the *Bonhomme Richard*, Jones rammed her bowsprit over the English stern.

During a momentary lull in the battle, Pearson hailed Jones, asking if he had struck the American colors. "I have not yet begun to fight," Jones screamed back. The *Serapis* turned about to gain a raking position, but Pearson had misjudged the distance between the two ships and fouled his rigging in the *Bonhomme Richard*'s sails, allowing Jones to lash his vessel to the enemy, bow to stern. For the next hour, locked in a deadly embrace, they fired at each other at point-blank range. At first the English held the advantage, but at 2200 an American on a yardarm hurled a grenade through the main hatch onto the *Serapis*' gun deck and it exploded on top of a pile of 12-pound ammunition. Watching the explosion from the quarterdeck of the *Bonhomme Richard*, Lieutenant Richard Dale thought that "more than twenty of the enemy were blown to pieces, and many stood with only the collars of their shirts upon their bodies."[2]

Within moments, the *Alliance* charged onto the scene and fired three devastating broadsides—directly into the *Bonhomme Richard*. Realizing his foolish mistake, Landais retired for a second time. Holed several times over and taking on water, the *Bonhomme Richard* now caught on fire; in the hold below were several hundred British prisoners. When someone released them by mistake, they clambered up the hatches topside only to be driven back down below by the *Serapis*' gunfire. Jones then told the prisoners that the *Bonhomme Richard* would sink unless they fought the fires and manned the pumps. Lieutenant Dale organized damage-control parties to keep the ship afloat; this freed American seamen, who were organized into new gun crews. Jones directed his few cannon against the enemy's mainmast, and at 2230 Pearson, his ship aflame and his decks littered with bodies, struck his colors. Surveying both ships, Jones wrote that "a person must have been an eyewitness to form a just idea of the tremendous scene of carnage, wreck and ruin that everywhere appeared." Jones was unable to save the *Bonhomme Richard*, and she sank next day, but he did manage to reorganize his squadron and escape a British patrol of twelve ships dispatched to intercept the American formation before it made the Dutch port of Texel.[3]

American naval operations and France's entry into the war in 1778 had already forced the Admiralty to redeploy a large number of ships. Long before the Battle of Ushant, the Channel Fleet had been considerably reduced to provide units for the new West Indies Fleet under Vice Admiral John Byron. This fleet had been established to reinforce Admiral Howe in North America. Although the Admiralty had enough sails-of-the-line to deal with the French alone, it now began to fear the prospect of a Franco-Spanish coalition at sea. Out of the 274 warships in commission, more than half had already been deployed to the Newfoundland, Halifax, Jamaica, or Leeward Islands stations. By 1778, four-fifths of all British frigates had been deployed to the western Atlantic or the Caribbean to deal with the Continental Navy and American privateers. This left both the Channel Fleet and the Mediterranean Fleet short of the frigates that they urgently needed to maintain distant stations, blockade enemy ports, escort friendly convoys, and conduct strategic reconnaissance. "There are not ships enough . . . to form a squadron fit to meet the [French] Toulon Fleet," complained Lord Sandwich, "unless we were to sacrifice every other intended service to this object."[4]

Fearing that the French might send a fleet to North America to support Washington's Continental Army, Lord North instructed General Clinton, the British army commander, to consolidate his strength at New York by evacuating Philadelphia. On 28 June, Admiral Howe stood out of the Delaware Bay, only a week before a French fleet of a dozen sails-of-the-line under Vice Admiral Comte d'Estaing arrived from Toulon. Byron's West Indies Fleet, scattered by a storm, was now suspended in mid-Atlantic, and could not reinforce Howe, whose four sails-of-the-line made New York on 29 June and prepared to defend the harbor. On 11 July, d'Estaing's vastly superior force anchored off Sandy Hook while, to the south, Washington prepared to march against New York. It appeared that the British were doomed.

This optimistic view assumed a degree of boldness that the French Navy did not possess. To implement a daring strategy, France had sent to North America her most conservative commander. Plagued by delays, d'Estaing gave up on the New York operation and instead sailed north to attack Newport, a British stronghold since 1776, but his indecision also doomed this move. The British position at Newport was considered hopeless at first, for when d'Estaing entered Narragansett Bay the Americans put the city under siege. Then, on 9 August, Admiral Howe, now reinforced by four sails-of-the-line, was sighted at the mouth of the bay challenging the French to a sea fight. D'Estaing, reckoning on an easy victory, accepted the taunt and stood out to sea. However, once both fleets reached open water, Howe began to run and d'Estaing chased him until both formations were scattered by a hurricane that blew up from the West Indies. Howe limped back to New York and d'Estaing returned to Newport, but by then Byron's reinforcements were closing on the American coast. D'Estaing decided to abandon the siege of Newport and withdraw to the safety of the Caribbean.

By this time, Lord George Germain had already flung a counterstroke to the north, directing Clinton on 2 September 1778 to occupy Maine's Penobscot Peninsula. After careful preparations, Captain Henry Mowett and 700 troops landed at the small port of Castine on 17 June 1779 and secured the area, a bold move that not only established British control of the Penobscot Bay but also threatened New Hampshire's northern flank. Alarmed by this menace, the Massachusetts legislature organized an expedition to retake Castine. In July, the largest American amphibious force assembled during the war set out from Boston with Captain Dudley Saltonstall in command. Built around the *Warren*, the last of the original 32-gun frigates, Saltonstall's squadron included a brig from the New Hampshire State Navy, three Massachusetts Navy brigantines, thirteen privateers, and twenty transports carrying 3,000 volunteers under General Solomon Lovell.

On 25 July, Saltonstall landed troops near the mouth of the Penobscot and opened fire on the British fort that commanded the passage. The bombardment did little damage, so Saltonstall withdrew and issued a call for reinforcements. However, security for the Penobscot operation had been poor from the start and the British had already learned about Saltonstall's plan. While he dithered, the enemy dispatched two brigs and the 18-gun sloop *Nautilus* to cover the bay. These ships were soon joined by Admiral George Collier, who appeared on the scene on 13 August with one sail-of-the-line, three frigates, two sloops, and another brig. When the Americans learned what they faced, Saltonstall was unable to prevent a panic. The privateers ran their vessels aground, as did Saltonstall, who was forced to burn all three naval ships to prevent them from falling into enemy hands. At least 474 Americans were lost during the operation, although most of them made it to the safety of nearby settlements. When he returned to Boston, Saltonstall was roundly condemned for the disaster, found guilty of "want of proper spirit and energy" by a court-martial, and dismissed from the Continental Navy.[5]

Ironically, even minor reverses such as the Penobscot fiasco contributed to the growing impression in London that Britain's naval power was now overstretched, an assessment reinforced by France's 1779 offensive. After withdrawing to the French base at Martinique in the Caribbean following the collapse of the siege of Newport, d'Estaing was reinforced by ships from France under Admiral de Grasse and ordered to challenge Byron's newly formed West Indies Fleet for control of the Lesser Antilles. The French had overrun British Dominica in late 1778, and d'Estaing seized St. Vincent in mid-June of the following year. As a first step toward encircling St. Lucia, Britain's main base in the area, he easily occupied Grenada on 4 July 1779. Two days later, Byron appeared off St. George's with twenty-one sails-of-the-line hoping to dislodge the French, but that afternoon he was driven off after a bloody battle with d'Estaing's superior force of twenty-four ships. Strategically conservative, d'Estaing now forfeited an ideal opportunity to exploit his victory off Grenada by sweeping the Royal Navy out of St. Lucia and descending on Jamaica, Britain's major stronghold in the Caribbean. Nonetheless, the loss of Grenada thoroughly alarmed the British and diverted their attention from North America. "The West Indies will become the principal theater of the war," Germain declared in exasperation.[6]

Spain's entry into the war in 1779 only magnified the problem that Britain's overextended navy faced. Soon after France had declared war, Foreign Minister Vergennes sought out allies in Europe, overcoming monarchical Spain's reluctance to support a republican revolution in the New World with the enticement of French help in recovering Gibraltar. The allies hoped to invade England with a combined fleet, and in August an enormous concentration of sixty-seven French and Spanish sails-of-the-line sortied from Brest and established command of the waters off Plymouth. Britain's Channel Fleet, not half the size of the allied force, was ineffectually commanded and unready to oppose the enemy's movements, but the British were saved by French ineptitude. A dither over where to land tortured Paris that summer and, by the time the decision was made to land in Cornwall in September, foul water and spoiled provisions forced the allied ships to retire to Brest. The Channel Fleet was reinforced soon after, and the British instituted a blockade of French ports intended not only to prevent another invasion but also to shut down the American raiders. British blockade practices were so aggressive, however, that it enraged neutral shippers and London was showered with diplomatic protests over Britain's maritime policy. In 1780, the Dutch declared war over this issue and Russia formed the League of Armed Neutrality with Sweden, Prussia, Austria, Portugal, and Denmark.

Thus, on the eve of the decisive year of the war, British maritime policy had antagonized every major power in Europe. This thrust Britain into a state of strategic isolation. "We have no one friend or ally to assist us," Sandwich complained. New members of Parliament joined earlier critics of Lord North's war policy, and opposition to the American conflict escalated in the House of Commons when maritime insurance rates increased, prices rose, and trade fell off owing to shippers' fear of American cruisers. Despite these difficulties, the Admiralty's achievement over four years of war was considerable. By 1780, for example, the Royal Navy still deployed fifty-nine sails-of-the-line or frigates in North American waters and a reinforced West Indies Fleet in the Caribbean that prevented the French from renewing their offensive.[7]

The Continental Navy was also in distress after several years of war. When Washington proposed a joint Franco-American Fleet expedition against Canada and Newfoundland in early 1779, Samuel Adams, the new chairman of the Marine Committee, told him that "unfortunately the situation of our frigates is such as to afford no reason to expect that they can possibly be collected in season to execute the plan." Concerned by the failure of the frigate policy, in October 1779 Congress reformed the entire system of naval administration, abolishing the Marine Committee and establishing a Board of Admiralty comprising two delegates and three outside commissioners. However, several men appointed as commissioners refused to serve, the board was discredited by the inattention and ineptitude of its members, and most of its work was done by John Brown, its able but overtaxed secretary.

A larger problem was that Congress was deeply in debt and unable to provide the Continental Navy with operating funds. It was "impossible at present to furnish your demands for money," Brown told the Navy's agents in February 1780, inasmuch as "the Treasury can scarcely supply the demands of the Army." As of that year, the Continental Navy was reduced from one hundred ships to five, and privateering—the only American maritime operations that the British could not suppress—constituted the bulk of American naval activity. Operations in European waters were nearly shut down. After his encounter with the *Serapis*, John Paul Jones returned to France, where he found Louis XVI so impressed with his exploits that he lent Jones the 20-gun schooner *Ariel*. After bad weather curtailed two cruises in the fall of 1780, Jones sailed again in December. On the 7th, he closed on a British warship that, after a brief firefight, struck her colors just as night fell but escaped in the confusion. Jones then continued back to America, reaching Philadelphia on 20 February 1781. There, he received a vote of thanks from the Continental Congress, a medal, and command of the recently completed sail-of-the-line *America*.[8]

Other Continental Navy operations fared less well. A few months before Jones returned to Philadelphia, Captain James

Young had taken the *Saratoga* down the Delaware River to raid British transport ships in the Atlantic. He seized three prizes off the Delaware Capes in October 1780, then fled when he was sighted and chased by the British sail-of-the-line *Intrepid*. Young's cruise ended in tragedy when the British recaptured the prizes and the *Saratoga* beat into a gale the next day, never to be seen again. More tragedy was to come. The *Trumbull*, commanded by Captain James Nicholson, was finally fitted out for a cruise and floated over the bar of the Connecticut River. Nicholson slipped past the British blockade and headed south. Due east of New Jersey's Cape May, the *Trumbull* overhauled the 36-gun British privateer *Watt* and engaged her in a gun duel at such close range that the yardarms of the two vessels became locked and gunwads from the *Watt's* broadsides started two fires on board the *Trumbull*. As blood from the grim slaughter washed both ships, the *Trumbull's* mainmast crashed to her deck and the *Watt* escaped into the dark night.

Nicholson returned home and repaired his ship, but local privateers had so emptied the pool of sailors that the *Trumbull* was short 200 men when she next put to sea to escort a small convoy down the coast in August 1781. Off the Delaware Capes she was challenged by the British frigate *Iris*, formerly the *Hancock*, and the American ships were scattered by a dreadful gale that cost the *Trumbull* her foretop mast and main topgallant mast. When the British warships *Victor* and *General Monck* joined the *Iris* and began to fire broadsides at Nicholson, most of his men fled for safety below. Fewer than fifty sailors were left to fight against overwhelming odds, but Nicholson continued firing until twelve of them had been killed or wounded. "Seeing no prospect of escaping in this unneutral contest," he reported, "I struck," thus adding the *Trumbull* to the long list of British prizes.[9]

In spite of these dispiriting losses, the continued rumble of American naval operations wore against the British, whose entire strategy in North America had begun to unravel. From Morristown, Washington's Continental Army watched General Clinton's Redcoats in New York during the winter of 1779, but Clinton could control an area only if his troops occupied the territory, and his forces did not include enough infantry to secure a region long against residents who were either openly hostile to British rule or sullenly uncooperative. London could not provide more men because the Admiralty had no more escorts to defend the convoys necessary to support a larger expeditionary force, and every small test of the British system of maritime defenses added to the on-going strain. That tension did not subside with the general decline in American naval activity—it was more than made up by the new threat to the British from the French Navy and the fleets of the League of Armed Neutrality. On the brighter side for London, Loyalist sentiment seemed high in the Carolinas, and this prompt-ed Clinton to adopt a new southern strategy. He lifted 7,000 sol-diers to Charleston in December 1779. When the British fleet ap-peared off South Carolina, Captain Abraham Whipple's small squadron was just entering Charleston harbor following a cruise around Bermuda. Whipple removed the guns from his ships to re-inforce the shore batteries and repulse the expected enemy as-sault. Charleston was under siege for four months before surren-dering in May 1780, and Clinton thereafter attempted to extend royal authority throughout South Carolina.

The North American puzzle annoyed Paris as much as Lon-don, and Franklin convinced Vergennes to dispatch 5,000 French troops to America under Count Rochambeau, who arrived in New-port, Rhode Island, in July 1780. He and Washington met in Hart-ford in September, agreed on the need for combined operations with a French fleet, and settled on a plan to lay siege to New York the following year. Rochambeau was considerably less eager than Washington to assault the main enemy stronghold, but French pol-icy was now to get the Americans to distract British attention from the West Indies and the Continent. In the spring of 1781, Paris de-ployed another fleet under Admiral François Comte de Grasse from Brest to Martinique. From this base he mounted desultory raids against the British sugar islands of St. Lucia and Tobago. The British naval commanders in the Caribbean were either inept or venal and mounted surprisingly slight opposition. Admiral George Rodney, a brilliant tactician, had raided the Dutch port of St. Eustatius before the locals knew that the Netherlands was at war with Britain. Rodney loaded a fortune in loot on board his ships, then sailed for England to pay off his personal debts with his share of the prize money. Behind he left in command Rear Admiral Samuel Hood, a less talented figure, who failed utterly to arrest de Grasse's operations during the spring of 1781.

Meanwhile, Clinton's southern strategy was about to collapse. After he took Charleston and established a British position in South Carolina, Clinton sailed back to New York, leaving behind a Redcoat army under General Charles Cornwallis, an able field commander. Reacting quickly, Washington sent General Gates south to organize an American army in the Carolinas to check Cornwallis, but Gates lost the Battle of Camden and allowed the British to penetrate into North Carolina. Washington then replaced Gates with one of his best tacticians, General Nathaniel Greene. In short order Greene defeated Cornwallis at the battles of King's Mountain and Cowpens, then killed or maimed one third of the Redcoats on the battlefield before he withdrew from Guilford Courthouse. Beset by these ghastly losses and constantly harassed by Greene, Cornwallis retired to Wilmington, a move that enabled Greene to impale several Loyalist bands in the Carolinas. Cornwallis, unable to challenge the Americans, was anxious to move north, so he marched from Wilmington across the Virginia border, conducted a few raids, then camped at Yorktown on the Chesapeake Bay and called for the Royal Navy to extract his army. All the rival commanders appreciated Cornwallis' situation, which Clinton accurately described as "attended with great risk, unless we are sure of a permanent superiority at sea."[10]

In retrospect, Cornwallis' failure in the South merely confirmed the defeat of a British military effort to reconquer the American colonies that was already doomed. By 1781 King George III had lost faith in Lord North's pro-war cabinet, and almost every other British political leader wanted to end the conflict. With Europe allied in one way or another against British maritime hegemony and the French annually hatching a scheme to invade England, the prospects for victory in America during a protracted war grew dimmer still. Against this formidable adversity, the Royal Navy's ability to control Europe's periphery and the Atlantic counted for little.

These political signposts leading toward an American victory began to concern Vergennes, who now feared that an independent America would face such weak enemies on her landward flanks that she would soon become the "mistress of the whole immense continent." Indeed, he secretly warned the British that the Americans planned at independence to "immediately set about forming a great marine and, as they have every possible advantage for shipbuilding, it would not be long before they had such fleets as would be an over-match for the whole naval power of Europe. When they pleased," they would "conquer both your islands and ours" and "in the end not leave a foot of that Hemisphere in the possession of any European power." Vergennes sent French agents to Philadel-

phia to coerce Congress into sending to Paris negotiators friendly
to France, with instructions "to undertake nothing in the negotiations for peace or truce without" French "knowledge and concur-
rence." Overly eager to please the French, Congress agreed to
these terms, a blunder of appeasement that led to the dispatch of
John Jay, who sailed for France in November 1779 on board Captain Seth Harding's recently commissioned 36-gun frigate *Confederacy*. After a harrowing voyage during which the vessel was saved
only by Harding's skillful seamanship, she reached France and Jay
set out to join Franklin in Paris. After several more transatlantic voyages carrying diplomats eastward and guarding convoys carrying
military stores on the return trips, the *Confederacy* was homeward
bound from the West Indies in June 1781 when she was run down
by two British frigates and Harding was forced to strike his colors.
She was renamed and taken into the Royal Navy.[11]

As the war neared a climax, another American diplomat,
Henry Laurens, was sent to join Franklin and Jay in Paris. Laurens
left Boston in February 1781 on board the *Alliance*, the new command of the redoubtable Captain Barry, whose heroic exploits after he grounded the *Raleigh* on an island off the coast of Maine
had earned him another ship. With his passenger safely delivered
to France, Barry joined a French privateer, the *Marquis de Lafayette*,
when she sailed for America on 31 March 1781. After a brief engagement with an enemy vessel, the French ship turned back, but
Barry continued to cross the Atlantic. On 28 May, the British brigs
Atalanta and *Trespassay* bore down on the *Alliance*, aided by a light
breeze that allowed Barry no steerageway. The brigs kept to the
bow and stern of the American warship and began to rake her
deck with grapeshot, which tore away her rigging and wounded
Barry in the shoulder. For nearly an hour he could not turn his
ship about fast enough to fire his broadsides, and he was limited
to the use of the few bow- and stern-mounted guns. Suddenly,
British gunfire blew away the American flag. The British captains
ceased firing and asked Barry if he wanted to surrender. At just
that moment, a strong breeze came up and Barry turned about,
charging between the two enemy brigs with both broadsides blast-
ing away for the first time and creating havoc on the enemy decks.
Within a few minutes, the English struck, American prize crews
took over their ships, and Barry returned to Boston in triumph.

In spite of the marvelous pluck of patriot captains like Barry,
the Continental Navy lost twenty-four ships armed with 470 guns

to enemy gunfire, bad weather, or misadventure during the Revolutionary War. Surveying "the long list of vessels belonging to the United States taken and destroyed, and recollecting the whole history of the rise and progress of our navy, it is very difficult to avoid tears," complained John Adams in July 1780. The Americans built good, seaworthy ships, but the Continental Navy was poorly administered by Congress. The lack of armaments, supplies, and experienced, disciplined crews was constant, and as a result most of the fleet spent the war blockaded in port. The Continental Navy was unable to lift or even dent the British blockade, provide direct support to the Continental Army, or prevent the enemy from landing on the Atlantic seaboard. The American fleet seldom attempted to defend ports or inlets, and when it did, it usually failed. Although the Continental Navy provided escorts for a large number of merchantmen, the warships usually broke off after getting to sea, seldom defended a merchantman for the entire length of its voyage, and frequently abandoned the mission when the Royal Navy appeared on the scene. Continental Navy raiding of commercial ships took about 200 enemy prizes, but at the cost of several thousand American sailors imprisoned by the British—an ineffective campaign when compared with the privateers' record.

Adams' tears notwithstanding, the Continental Navy's losses were not in vain. Aided by coastal geography and the tempo of American privateering, the Continental fleet contributed to the undermining of the entire British naval blockade. Four of five American merchantmen that left port during the Revolutionary War safely reached their destinations, and despite enormous losses to British patrols, war risk insurance for American merchantmen was always available in American ports, a reflection of the leakiness of the Royal Navy's blockade. The Continental Navy also gave Congress its vital diplomatic link with Europe, and its ships were often assigned by Congress to transport tobacco to the West Indies, where this cash crop was sold for gold or silver desperately needed to sustain Washington's operations against the Redcoats. Continental Navy victories boosted American morale and established a tradition of bravery and daring in the face of overwhelming odds. Americans could surely want for no finer heroes than John Paul Jones and John Barry. The Royal Navy lost 102 ships carrying 2,622 guns to enemy action, and of this total only 16 ships were taken by American privateers, while no British privateer took an American warship.[12]

Although American naval operations and privateering sapped the strength of Britain's economy and military logistics, George Washington, the master of the politics of battle, had long recognized the need to soundly defeat the British Army in the field, so as to allow opposition to the war in London to congeal. He believed that he might win his decisive victory by laying siege to the 13,000-man British garrison in New York, but he needed the assistance of France's West Indies Fleet, now under the command of Admiral de Grasse. Rochambeau had different plans, however, and he warned de Grasse that Cornwallis at Yorktown was more vulnerable than Clinton's New York bastion. The admiral agreed to this strategy and wrote to Washington that he would sail from Cap Français on 13 August 1781 with twenty-five sails-of-the-line, but would neither go north of the Chesapeake Bay nor remain off the American coast past October. Washington reluctantly agreed to go after Cornwallis, although on 15 August he warned Admiral de Barras, who commanded a supporting French fleet, that he would have to "form the junction, as soon as possible, with de Grasse in Chesapeake Bay" to prevent the British fleet from rescuing Cornwallis. Leaving half his troops behind to hold Clinton down in New York, Washington began to move south with the remainder of the Continental Army and General Rochambeau's Frenchmen. Both armies reached Philadelphia on 5 September, where Washington awaited news of the movements of the French fleets.[13]

De Grasse had already arrived at the mouth of the Chesapeake at the end of August. He first landed 3,500 troops to stop Cornwallis from retreating to the south, stationed frigates at the mouth of the bay, and made ready to defend his position. Admiral Hood, who was chasing him up from the West Indies, believed that de Grasse was sailing to Newport to meet Rochambeau, so Hood's West Indies Fleet sped to New York, where Admiral Graves and General Clinton were at the time planning an attack on Rhode Island. Upon Hood's arrival, however, they realized what was afoot, and Graves took command of a fleet of nineteen British sails-of-the-line that appeared at the mouth of the Chesapeake on the morning of 5 September. Meanwhile, Washington was preparing to ferry his army down the Chesapeake to join Major General Lafayette's troops, who were marching overland. A body of 15,000 allied soldiers were about to corner Cornwallis' 7,500 men at Yorktown.

When de Grasse, commanding twenty-four sails-of-the-line, sighted Graves' fleet at 0930 on 5 September, he advanced around Cape Henry and sought the leeward gage, following standard French tactical doctrine. Graves accordingly took the wind, but just at the moment when an order to break the British line and conduct a general chase would have massed his fleet on the isolated French van, Graves told his captains to adhere to the line ahead. At 1615 each van opened up with broadsides, and a two-hour gun duel ensued. Inasmuch as both sides made an equal number of tactical mistakes, the French fleet's numerical edge produced slightly more damage, but it was a victory won by superior command and control and a conservative battle doctrine, not by firepower or innovation. After Graves withdrew, de Grasse watched him for five days, on one occasion drawing the British away from the mouth of the bay to allow Admiral de Barras with eight French sails-of-the-line and a large siege train to slip into the Chesapeake. Nine days later, Admiral Hood with twenty-two British sails-of-the-line arrived off the Virginia Capes, but he was too late to influence events and soon withdrew to New York. De Grasse's victory at the Battle of the Virginia Capes left Cornwallis isolated and at the mercy of the converging Franco-American armies. Washington laid siege to Yorktown, American artillery hammered the British troops when they tried to escape, and Cornwallis finally surrendered on 17 October 1781.

Washington was prepared to besiege New York the following year, unaware that Yorktown had not only sealed Clinton's fate but also closed the book on Britain's entire war effort. In short order, Lord North resigned, Parliament cut off all funds for the war, and a new Whig ministry took office and opened talks with Franklin in Paris. Opposed by almost every power in Europe, the British had little latitude during these negotiations. They were anxious to husband their resources, regroup their forces, and recapture the initiative from the French in the West Indies. On the other hand, Franklin was under orders from Congress not to agree to terms without the consent of the French, whom Franklin and his colleagues, Adams and Jay, rightly distrusted. Violating the 1778 Alliance, which prohibited a separate peace, Franklin went ahead and negotiated an agreement in which Britain recognized American independence and acknowledged her sovereignty from the border of Canada to Spanish Florida in the south and eastward to the Mississippi River. Franklin then presented Vergennes with a *fait accompli*, which the French had to accept. Jubilant, Congress ratified the Treaty of Paris in 1783.

Chapter Three

The Federalist Era
1783–1796

The Articles of Confederation establishing the first government of the United States were drafted one year after the Declaration of Independence but not ratified until 1781, when the Revolutionary War was near an end. Americans did not know whether
they wanted a league or a federated state, so they erected a national government consisting of a single branch, a unicameral
Confederation Congress, in which each state had one vote and the
power to veto any amendment to the organic Articles. Congress
was empowered to requisition, or request, funds from the states,
manage foreign policy, "allow" the creation of military forces and
the prosecution of wars for the "common defense," and mediate
interstate disputes. It was not clear at the time, however, that such
a weak central government would be incapable of providing for
national security.[1]

Long before Yorktown, Congress had virtually ignored the
Continental Navy. The Board of Admiralty, which succeeded the
Marine Committee in 1779, was itself discredited and was abolished by Congress in 1781. Thereafter nearly absolute control of
naval affairs was turned over to Robert Morris, the superintendent
of finance, who reluctantly accepted the responsibility. Morris, a
nationalist, agreed with Adams about the need to maintain a small
fleet and shore establishment after peace was negotiated with the
British. For a short time he pursued an expansionist naval policy,

The 2,200-ton frigate *Constitution*, one of the six heavy frigates authorized by Congress in 1794 to deal with the Barbary corsairs, was launched on 21 October 1797. She saw distinguished service during the Quasi War, the Barbary Wars, and the War of 1812 and thereafter served as the flagship for several station squadrons and as a training ship for Naval Academy midshipmen during the Civil War. Restored many times since, she is the oldest ship still on the Navy's List.

persuading Congress to complete the sail-of-the-line *America*, appointing John Paul Jones as her captain, and resuming construction of the frigate *Bourbon*. He also intended to finish, refit, and deploy the frigates *Alliance*, *Trumbull*, and *Deane*. The *Deane* made four cruises to the West Indies between late 1781 and early 1783, as did several other smaller ships, which took several prizes. Morris expected the French West Indies Fleet to handle British warships in American waters, however, and when word reached Philadelphia that the peace talks had begun in Paris in 1782, he ordered an end to commerce raiding in the Caribbean so as not to upset the negotiations. Moreover, he was largely responsible for turning the Continental Navy into an armed packet service that transported specie, diplomats, dispatches, and cargo between the United Colonies and Europe.

Soon after word of the Treaty of Paris reached Philadelphia, Morris asked Congress to approve a national tax, called an impost, consisting of a 5 percent duty on imports. The tax was intended to provide the Confederation with a constant, reliable source of income, retire the wartime debt, and pay for national defense. In September 1782, Morris announced that he would give the *America* to France as an act of friendship in return for the loss of the 74-gun French sail-of-the-line *Magnifique*, which had just run aground in the ship channel inside Boston Light unless Congress approved his impost plan; shortly thereafter he upped the ante by threatening to sell off all the Navy's remaining vessels as well. After Rhode Island and Georgia refused to vote for the impost, Morris felt that he had no choice but to carry out his threat. Inasmuch as the Confederation was "at the mercy of a single state," as Virginia's James Madison put it, policy was paralyzed. Congress would "in pursuance of such a neutral plan suffer the whole military establishment to be dissolved." Madison worried that "the remaining ships of war too must be sold, and no preparatory steps taken for future emergencies on that side." Personally responsible for some Confederation notes, Morris truly had no other choice. Captain Barry, the last officer on active duty in the Continental Navy, remained with the *Alliance* until she was finally sold off in the summer of 1785. "We can do nothing, . . . neither raise a revenue nor build a fleet," muttered a bitter John Adams. "With the power in our hands of doing as we please, we shall do nothing; with the means of making ourselves respected by the wise, we shall become the scorn of fools."[2]

The Articles poorly equipped Congress to deal with other important issues, including foreign affairs. Chief among the immediate problems was the inability to compel Britain to honor several secondary provisions of the Treaty of Paris. The British, who wanted to create an Indian buffer state to check American westward expansion, refused to abandon their trading posts along the southern shores of the Great Lakes. Neither would they send a diplomatic envoy to Philadelphia, nor open their ports in the West Indies to American trade.

Once the beneficiary of the mercantilist Acts of Trade and Navigation, the United States now became their victim. Parliament prohibited the Royal Navy and British shippers from buying American ships, masts, or naval stores and imposed prohibitively high duties on other American goods entering English ports. "Nothing but retaliation, reciprocal prohibitions, and imposts, and putting ourselves in a posture of defense will have any effect," Adams told John Jay. A strong naval policy would enable the Americans to "astonish the world with a navy in a very few years, not more than eight or ten, equal perhaps to the third maritime power in Europe. This would be amply sufficient for our defence." In accord with mercantilist practice, France and Spain also moved against American shipping, and the resulting imbalance of trade drained specie from the American economy. "The Revolution has robbed us of our trade with the West Indies, the only one which yielded us a favorable balance, without reopening any other channels to compensate for it," Madison complained. Although the French and Spanish intended to exclude Americans from their empires, poor harvests in Europe during the decade forced them to relax their mercantilist laws so much that by 1788 imported American grain was keeping the French peasantry from starvation.[3]

In search of foreign exchange, American merchants sought markets beyond those governed by Europe's mercantilist powers. In 1784, a group of New York shippers sent the merchantman *Empress of China* to Canton. The profits from this voyage were immense, and the China trade thereafter drew an increasing number of American vessels into dangerous but rewarding ventures to the Far East, the Philippines, and the East Indies. That same year, the merchantman *United States* sailed from Philadelphia to Bombay, inaugurating a long and profitable trade with India, and within a short time the fur trader *Columbia* put to sea on her maiden voyage to the Pacific Northwest, establishing an American presence near the mouth of the Columbia River and a fragile claim to the great Oregon Territory.

American mariners also rerouted their commerce away from the British Isles and into the Mediterranean, but there they were attacked by the commerce raiders from the Barbary states of Algiers, Tripoli, Tunisia, and Morocco. A Moroccan cruiser seized the Boston schooner *Betsy* on 27 October 1783 and held her and her crew hostage at Tangier. Alarmed, Congress authorized a commission composed of the American diplomats in Europe, Franklin, Adams, and Thomas Jefferson, to negotiate a treaty with each of the Barbary powers. Before they could act, however, Spain concluded a peace with Algiers that allowed Algerian cruisers to operate beyond Gibraltar. The American merchantman *Maria* was taken off Cádiz on 13 October 1785 by the Algerines, who seized

her cargo and enslaved her crew; more depredations soon followed. A few days later, John Paul Jones, the American naval agent
in Paris, informed Congress that Algiers had issued a formal declaration of war.

Although the Committee of the States, which handled affairs
while Congress was in recess, was specifically authorized "to build
and equip a navy," it could not do so without the assent of nine of
thirteen state representatives, who had to "agree upon the number of vessels of war to be built or purchased." Unfortunately, the
Articles deprived the Confederation of the power to regulate either international or interstate commerce, and in any event
Congress was unable to establish a navy to defend American trade
because of a burdensome debt, another legacy of the successful
but expensive revolution. Without the power to tax, Congress
could neither build nor buy warships nor maintain a shore establishment. New England shipping interests refused to allow
Congress to ignore the Barbary pirates, however, and in 1786 Jay,
the foreign secretary, presented a report encouraging the states in
the pursuit of "such Measures as may conduce to render them a
maritime Power."[4]

Jefferson, the American minister in France, strongly urged
Congress to declare war and lay down a fleet strong enough to
overcome the Barbary navies. Such a war could not be for "a better cause nor against a weaker foe," he claimed somewhat optimistically. Moreover, naval operations against Barbary would "procure us respect in Europe," which would be necessary to improve
American economic relations with the mercantilist powers of the
Continent. Adams, the American minister in London, surprisingly disagreed. Knowing that Congress was unlikely to authorize the
construction of a fleet, he argued for a diplomatic solution: the
United States should follow Europe's lead, pay tribute, and acquire maritime immunity. Despite Jefferson's insistence that the
United States "ought to begin a naval power if we are to carry on
our own commerce," Congress clearly lacked the resources to pay
for a fleet and had no means to levy taxes to raise more revenue.
"The great question," Jay asserted, "is whether we shall wage war
or pay tribute. I, for my part, prefer . . . war." But when Congress
refused to act on his report, Jay instructed Adams to negotiate a
treaty with Morocco in 1786. Although this accord did not require
the payment of tribute, the rest of the Barbary states demanded
exorbitant sums merely to initiate talks with the Americans, and a

tribute treaty was not negotiated with Algiers for another nine years. As a result of the Confederation's inability to deal with Barbary, recorded Rufus King, a Massachusetts nationalist, "Even our merchants charter foreign vessels which are protected from the Barbary cruisers to carry our produce to market." And four years later Jefferson reported from France that American trade with the Mediterranean had "not been resumed at all since the peace."[5]

During the Moroccan crisis, Jefferson argued strongly that the Confederation should establish a navy and prosecute a war against the Barbary powers. Indeed, he even proposed to his political ally James Monroe that a maritime alliance or "convention might be formed" between the United States and the naval powers of Europe "establishing a perpetual cruise on the coast of Algiers which would bring them to reason." Jefferson also saw a fleet as a potential solution to a problem at home. By 1786, several state maritime revenue patrols were conducting a nasty trade war against the coastal commerce of their neighbors. "There never will be money in the treasury," he warned, "till the Confederacy shows its teeth"—in the form of a naval fleet to control interstate commerce.[6]

The problems of foreign and interstate commerce, and the related issues of an unstable currency, unfunded debts, and a weak national government, were among the topics raised in 1786 by Alexander Hamilton at the Annapolis Convention, where representatives of five states issued a call for a meeting of delegates from every state the following May to revise the Articles of Confederation. That meeting, held in Philadelphia, was the Constitutional Convention. Rather than revise the Articles, the leading statesmen of the nation abandoned them and forged a new federal government in which powers were divided unevenly by a system of checks and balances among the legislative, judicial, and executive branches. Most of the debates in Philadelphia hinged on the relative authority of the branches; there was widespread agreement that the national government should "lay and collect taxes," regulate international and interstate commerce, and "provide for the common defense." George Washington presided over the convention, which tailored the new office of the presidency to his talents and, probably, his requirements. Not only was the president to be head of state, he was also vested with the authority to enforce federal laws, conduct foreign policy, and serve as commander in chief of the Army and the Navy. To balance this

power, the national Congress was given the responsibility to declare war, approve treaties, confirm most important executive ap-
pointments, appropriate funds, and, specifically, "provide and
maintain a navy." James Madison, who recorded the convention's
proceedings, claimed that "the palpable necessity of . . . a navy
has protected that part of the Constitution against a spirit of cen-
ture, which has spared few parts."[7]

The new Constitution was then put to a vote in each of the
states. The need for improved national security was a large element of the ratification debate. The Federalists argued the need
for greater security; the anti-Federalists warned of the danger of
standing armies. However, the prospect of creating a national executive to handle foreign policy and of building a navy to enforce
it overcame some objections to the Constitution's more controversial provisions. In April 1788, John Jay wrote "An Address to the
People of New York," voicing his contempt for the old Confederation and urging his neighbors to vote for the new government.
"Other nations [are] taking the advantage of its imbecility," he asserted, while "we permit all nations to fill our country with their
merchandise, yet their best markets are shut against us." Not only
did the "Algerines exclude us from the Mediterranean," but "we
are neither able to purchase, nor to command the free use of
those seas." In the *Federalist Papers*, a series of seminal essays written by Hamilton, Jay, and Madison to persuade Americans to vote
in favor of the Constitution, Madison maintained that America
was "remote from Europe, and ought not to engage in her politics
and wars," but instead should "carry on the commerce of the contending nations." With a small navy to defend this trade, he asserted, "none of them would be willing to add us to the number
of their enemies." Hamilton, who had a more hardheaded, less
idealistic view of the potential of American power, concluded that
the new government "would put it in our power, at a period not
very distant, to create a navy which, if it could not vie with those
of the great maritime powers," would force Europe to pay "a price
. . . not only upon our friendship, but upon our neutrality."[8]

The anti-Federalists, led by Patrick Henry of Virginia, were
less concerned with trade defense than with the security of home
territory. Henry countered Hamilton's thesis by arguing that the
cost of a fleet would be an unnecessary burden; the "condition of
European affairs" was so unstable that "it would be unsafe for
them to send fleets or armies against us." The anti-Federalists

touched a raw nerve when they sounded alarms about standing armies, but in the South even the issue of local defense could be turned to the support of the Constitution. For instance, David Ramsay maintained that "our local weakness particularly proves it to be for the advantage of South Carolina to strengthen the federal government" because "the Congress are authorized to provide and maintain a navy—our coast in its whole extent needs the protection." The most powerful argument for the Constitution was that it would create a strong central government able to deal confidently with issues of foreign policy and national security. The need to establish a navy was only part of a more broadly based demand for enhanced security that led to the ratification of the new Constitution in 1788.[9]

Late that year, in the first national election, George Washington was handed the presidency without opposition. Inaugurated in March 1789 with the first Senate and House, he faced the tremendous problem of forming an executive branch and establishing precedents not only within that branch but also between the presidency and the legislature. In practice, British traditions and Washington's own ideas on to how to organize a government were alloyed. Instead of a cabinet form of government, Washington exploited some of the latent powers of the chief executive's office. The secretaries of the executive departments established by Congress would convene as a cabinet to consider policy, Washington decided, but federal acts would be undertaken in the name of the chief executive. General Henry Knox, the first secretary of war, was empowered to deal with naval affairs, but he faced an Indian war on the frontier in 1789 and for the most part ignored naval questions for two full years. On 21 January 1790 Knox sent to Congress a report on the militia asserting that the "numerous seaports and the protection of . . . commerce require a naval arrangement"—and then arguing that the merchant marine and fishing fleets would provide the ships and sailors to fulfill this need. But Barbary's harassment of American shipping continued, and in 1791 Secretary of State Jefferson proposed that a fleet be built to punish the pirates and defend overseas American trade. Knox prepared a report for Congress on the question, but Americans at the time were already highly suspicious of the military power of the president. One opponent of a navy, Senator William Maclay, claimed that "war is often entered into to answer domestic, not foreign purposes," and charged that the foreign crises were expensive excuses "to have a fleet and army." Although the Senate agreed to build a fleet "as soon as the state of public finances will admit," the issue was not burning, and other matters soon extinguished the few embers of navalist enthusiasm.[10]

Washington enjoyed only three years to organize his government before the first of the wars of the French Revolution forced the United States to define its national security policy within the context of Europe's changing balance of power. Americans favored the republican revolution in France, which began in 1789, but most Federalists, led by Hamilton, distrusted the drift toward radicalism, anarchy, and aggression that emerged in France in 1792. France's declaration of war against Britain in February 1793 posed a major problem for Washington since the Franco-American Alliance of 1778 required the United States to defend the French West Indies in wartime, yet the young republic had no navy to carry out this obligation. Moreover, American statesmen were divided over whether to uphold this commitment. Jefferson favored the French and argued that the Alliance remained in force, but even he agreed that American belligerency at this time would be unwise. Hamilton was willing to abrogate the Alliance and support the British, but he also hoped that the United States could remain technically neutral. From a strategic standpoint, support of the French was impossible—the Americans had no fleet. On the other hand, the French Navy ensured for the moment a tenuous balance of power across the Atlantic that, in turn, might protect America from Britain's revenge. Washington compromised in April 1793 by issuing the Neutrality Proclamation, in which he announced an "impartial" foreign policy. He continued to recognize France's revolutionary government and prepared to receive its new envoy, Citizen Edmond C. Genet, who reached Charleston soon after the Neutrality Proclamation was published.[11]

The French were furious with American neutrality and Washington's seemingly casual indifference to the 1778 Alliance. On his way from Charleston to New York, Genet commissioned four American privateers to operate under the French tricolor against British shipping on the Atlantic coast and appointed Americans as agents of French naval prize courts, measures allowed under the terms of the Alliance. He also aided Americans plotting to invade the colonies of Florida and Louisiana, then under control of Spain, Britain's ally. Since he had no navy to block Genet's activities, Washington had to ask Pennsylvania's governor to use his state militia to prevent Genet from outfitting a British prize as a privateer in Philadelphia, and to fortify Mud Island in the Upper Bay to prevent the newly commissioned French privateers from entering Philadelphia harbor. Genet, blithely ignoring Jefferson's advice, issued more commissions, managed English prizes seized by French privateers just beyond coastal waters, and repeatedly offended the president. The country was in an uproar. In August, Washington asked the French government to recall Genet, and in 1794 Congress passed the first Neutrality Act, which stipulated, among other things, that belligerent warships could not be armed, fitted out, or repaired in American ports.

The French, although indignant about the Neutrality Proclamation, decided that the United States was so weak it would serve France's interests better as a neutral than as a belligerent. If American grain and other exports could be safely shipped to France, then French farmers could leave their fields to join armies that would spread radical revolution throughout central and southern Europe. This commerce grew rapidly after 1793. Because Britain and the United States had no commercial treaty defining their maritime relations, however, American merchantmen were easy prey for British warships on station to enforce Britain's naval blockade of France. During 1794, the Royal Navy seized several hundred American vessels while establishing its dominance in the Channel, the Atlantic, the Caribbean, and the Mediterranean. And in several hundred major and minor battles over the next two decades, the Royal Navy maintained maritime control of Europe's periphery, constantly threatening French power on the fringes of the Continent and imperiling nonbelligerent commerce.

The search by Europe's belligerents for allies during the first year of the wars of the French Revolution set in motion events that led directly to the establishment of the United States Navy. Britain's oldest ally was Portugal, to whom she had been tied by a treaty respecting the trade in Madeira wine since 1492. In October 1793, Portugal honored her alliance with England and turned on France. Before declaring war, the Portuguese Fleet had blockaded the maritime forces of the Barbary powers within the Mediterranean; after joining the First Coalition organized by Britain against France, Lisbon signed a twelve-month truce with the Barbary states that ended this blockade and allowed Barbary's raiders to operate beyond Gibraltar. Within weeks corsairs under the direction of the Dey of Algiers seized the American brig *Minerva* and imprisoned her crew. In return for freeing these hostages, the dey demanded that the United States sign a tribute treaty.

In January 1794, the House of Representatives named a select committee to study relations with Algiers. Stacked with Federalists, who wrote its report, the committee recommended that a naval force be sent into the Mediterranean to defend American trade against the dey's corsairs and to force him to release his American prisoners. Acknowledging that this would engender a "very heavy debt," Federalists such as Samuel Smith of Maryland maintained that "it must be the very worst kind of economy" to tolerate these depredations instead of paying for a fleet. Rather than convert merchantmen into warships, the committee proposed to lay down four 44-gun frigates and two 24-gun frigates. Building the ships would take longer and cost more than buying them, but it would also require the government to create a shore establishment to support the new fleet. The Federalists' purpose was to establish a permanent navy. Hamilton, who had said nothing about creating a navy during Washington's first term, now added his considerable support to the plan.[12]

In February, the Federalists introduced in Congress a bill authorizing the construction and outfitting of six frigates and the establishment of a corps of naval officers. The bill embodied Federalist naval policy and aroused the stiff opposition of the anti-Federalists. Representative Abraham Clark of New Jersey, for instance, warned of the "monstrous expense" and the expansion of executive power through patronage and procurement that would follow. Jefferson's ally, James Madison, who led the Democratic Republican majority in the House, proposed to lease ships from Portugal, and worried aloud that American naval operations in the Mediterranean would entangle the United States in the French wars. Attempting to appease their opponents, the Federalists attached to the bill a clause that would suspend construction of the frigates should the Algerines agree to a "peace." Hoping to avoid friction with France, Madison interpreted this suspension provision to mean that the frigates might be used for no other purpose without the consent of Congress. The vote in the House was less partisan than sectional, however; representatives from coastal districts voted with the majority in favor of the bill and those from rural, western areas almost uniformly opposed it.

On 27 March, President Washington signed the 1794 Naval Act, which authorized Secretary of War Knox "to provide, by purchase or otherwise, equip and employ four ships to carry forty-four guns each, and two ships to carry thirty-six guns each." By this measure the U.S. Navy was established. Congress specified that the frigates be constructed of live oak and red cedar. Few American ships of the period lasted for more than a few years, but vessels whose frames were built from live oak lasted five times longer than the smaller European warships, which used mostly white oak. In effect, the Federalists wanted to build permanence into the fleet. Probably influenced by Joshua Humphreys, a leading Philadelphia ship designer whose concepts seem to have governed the construction of all the vessels, Congress told Secretary Knox that the frigates must be designed "to render them equal, if not superior, to any frigates belonging to any of the European powers." William Penrose, another Philadelphian, wanted to follow British practice and build small, extremely agile frigates, but Knox accepted Humpreys' argument that the French designs were better and his claim that the American ships would "excell if we are to travel after them." Humphreys had never been to sea, never even seen a capital ship, but he knew that the French had transformed some of their 74-gun sails-of-the-line into swift, heavy frigates by cutting them down to a single gun deck. His frigate design called for a ship of over 1,000 tons armed with thirty guns on a single gun deck and a few smaller pieces on the weatherdeck.[13]

To generate political support for building the fleet, Knox "distribute[d] the advantages" to shipyards in Norfolk, Baltimore, New York, Boston, and Portsmouth, New Hampshire. The Carolinas and Georgia supplied timber, and carpenters were recruited from Rhode Island, Connecticut, Massachusetts, and Delaware. New Jersey and Pennsylvania ironworks were assigned to produce the cannonballs and iron ballast, the gun contracts were let to Maryland and Connecticut foundries, and the sails were to be sewn by a maker in Boston.

Delays, confusion, and cost overruns plagued the Navy's first shipbuilding program. Knox fell ill and Alexander Hamilton had to manage the War Department as well as the Treasury. The best timber for the frigates was to be found on Georgia's coastal islands, but an epidemic there brought logging to a standstill for several months. The ships would not be ready for years, but Congressman William Smith of Maryland pointed out to the Navy's Democratic Republican opponents that "what ever gentlemen may think . . . it was probable that we should at some time become a naval power; and even with the most distant prospect of that, it would show economy to prepare for it."[14]

Many Americans suspected that the British were encouraging the Algerines to attack neutral shipping, an economic strategy that the Admiralty itself adopted in 1794 when the Royal Navy seized more than 250 American merchantmen in the Caribbean. Even Hamilton, the pro-British secretary of the Treasury, bitterly condemned this action, and during the spring of that year it appeared that war between Britain and the United States might break out. But the British fleet's victory over the French in the Battle of the Glorious First of June changed matters considerably. Following that action, the Royal Navy so dominated the Atlantic that London was willing to appease the neutral powers by reversing its earlier position and conveying a hint that Britain wanted to negotiate a maritime truce with the United States.

Washington jumped at the bait and agreed to Hamilton's scheme to send Chief Justice Jay to London to settle the outstanding maritime differences and other important issues. The United States was Britain's best customer and the British were in need of no more enemies. Jay persuaded Prime Minister Pitt to agree to evacuate several British posts on the Canadian frontier, end the depredations in the Caribbean, and cede to American ships the right to trade with the British West Indies. They also established joint commissions to deal with the Maine boundary dispute, Revolutionary War debts, and compensation for the recent maritime seizures. In spite of this considerable achievement, Jay's Treaty ignited a nationwide political controversy. Republicans lambasted the treaty, citing its failure to define neutral rights, end the Royal Navy's practice of impressing sailors off American merchantmen, or secure some immediate compensation for the depredations in the West Indies. It was only by the thinnest of margins that the large Federalist majority in the Senate approved the treaty.

The treaty negotiation produced several important results. Most powers, including Spain, France, and the Barbary states, assumed, incorrectly, that Jay's Treaty contained a secret Anglo-American maritime alliance. Word of Jay's mission led directly to an agreement in September 1795 between American agents and Dey Hassan Bashaw of Algiers, in which he promised to release his prisoners and desist from attacking American trade in return for a payment of $650,000, one 36-gun frigate, and an annual tribute of $21,600. Similar agreements were reached with Tripoli in 1796 and with Tunis the following year.

Jay's Treaty washed other shores. To exploit Spain's anxiety, Washington sent diplomat Thomas Pinckney to Madrid. Fearing an Anglo-American combination, the Spanish agreed to allow Americans unrestricted access to the Mississippi River and use of the port of New Orleans. Pinckney's Treaty was favorably received by the Senate. On the other hand, Jay's Treaty, and France's resentment of Washington's Neutrality Proclamation, poisoned the well of Franco-American relations, and American trade with France dissolved after 1796. Convinced that the alliance they believed to be secreted in Jay's Treaty was aimed at France, the French concluded that the Americans not only had failed to honor their treaty obligations but, disregarding the sentimental attachment to France, were about to change sides.

Citing the Navy Act's stipulation that the construction of the six frigates cease if and when Algiers agreed to peace, Jefferson's supporters now insisted that all work on the ships be stopped, but Washington instructed the Senate's Federalists to introduce a bill to put the vessels into commission. In his last annual message on 7 December 1796, he told Congress that he favored "the gradual creation of a Navy. . . . To any active external commerce the protection of a naval force is indispensable. This is manifest with regard to wars in which a State is itself a party." Alluding to the European war, he added that "to secure respect for a neutral flag requires a naval force organized and ready to vindicate it from insult or aggression." Aroused by Jay's Treaty and opposed to intervention in Europe, Jefferson's partisans resisted this line, viewing it as an outrageous violation of the bargain struck with Washington two years earlier. The Senate passed the authorization bill, but to get it through the House the Federalists had to agree to a compromise arranged by Congressman Josiah Parker, which reduced the number of ships from the original six to three: the frigates *Constitution, United States,* and *Constellation.*[15]

Jay's Treaty and Washington's maritime policy also influenced domestic American politics. After Washington took office for a second term in 1793, Jefferson resigned, returned to Virginia, and formed a faction of Republicans that opposed the Federalist policies espoused by Washington, Hamilton, and Vice President John Adams. In 1796 Washington announced that he was retiring. The Federalist candidate, Adams, defeated Jefferson by

only three votes in the Electoral College. Adams' election was almost overshadowed by Washington's great farewell address to the
nation, written only three years before his death. "Europe has a set
of primary interests which to us have none or a very remote relation . . . the causes of which are essentially foreign to our concerns," he declared. American foreign policy should "steer clear
of permanent alliances" and, "taking care always to keep ourselves
by suitable establishment on a respectable defensive posture, we
may simply trust to temporary alliances for extraordinary emergencies." Washington's wisdom was soon tested.[16]

Chapter Four

The Quasi War
1798–1801

When he took office in 1797, President John Adams inherited Washington's cabinet, a bitter feud with fellow Federalist Alexander Hamilton, and widespread discontent with Jay's Treaty. The country was sharply divided over foreign policy. Secretary of State Timothy Pickering, Hamilton's ally, favored close ties with Britain, but the Republican opposition in Congress, orchestrated by Jefferson, contrived and advanced pro-French policies. The "best anchor of our hope is [a French] invasion of England," Jefferson wrote, then "all will be safe with us." Adams was inclined to remain neutral, profit from Europe's distress, and balance Jay's Treaty by negotiating a similar maritime agreement with Paris. Because of the increasing French menace to American shipping, most Americans agreed with Adams' assertion that the national government could not allow relations with France to fester. French privateers operating from Guadeloupe in the West Indies had begun to prey on American trade in 1795, even before Jay's Treaty was ratified, and two years later the French command authorized its privateers to attack American shipping in European and North American waters. Pickering reported to Congress the "monstrous abuse" of France's maritime law to justify the seizure of over 600 American vessels and in 1797 condemned the French as "pirates."

Diplomat Charles C. Pinckney traveled to Paris that year to try to resolve the dispute, but the Directory, France's ruling junta, refused to receive him and ordered him to leave the country.

Commodore Thomas Truxtun's flagship, the *Constellation*, fighting the French frigate *L'Insurgente* in February 1799, in the most acclaimed action of the Quasi War.

Benjamin F. Stoddert, Maryland merchant and Federalist politician, was secretary of the Navy, 1798–1801.

Thomas Truxtun, commodore of the West Indies Station, 1798–1800.

Adams then asked John Marshall of Virginia and Elbridge Gerry of Massachusetts to sail to Europe, form a commission with Pinckney, and try again to negotiate a treaty with the French foreign minister, Marquis Talleyrand. It was the last chance to save the peace. After the trio reached Paris, however, they were approached successively by three of Talleyrand's agents, who demanded bribes to get the talks started. If the Americans did not pay, Pierre Bellamy told Gerry, then "arrangements could be made forthwith to ravage the coasts of the United States by frigates from Santo Domingo." Marshall and Pinckney were indignant. They broke contact and sailed home. In their reports to Adams, the American diplomats referred to the greedy French agents as "X, Y, and Z."[1]

When news that negotiations were ended reached America, the Republicans accused Adams of undermining the talks. Fearing the consequences, he ignored demands from Congress to release the diplomatic correspondence and continued to hope for a peaceful settlement with Paris. The political pressure became intolerable, however, and in April 1798 Adams gave in and sent the documents to the Senate. The response was electric. Overnight, public indignation at French behavior coalesced into a firestorm for war. "The man who, after this mass of evidence, shall be the apologist of France . . . lies between being deemed a fool, a madman, or a traitor," screamed Hamilton. There was a new determination to pay "millions for defense, but not one cent for tribute." Respected statesmen lost their balance, but Adams kept his, deciding to make the most of a bad situation. Adams was a skillful leader whose foul temper and animal cunning made him dangerous to the foes of the young republic, and in his astute handling of the Quasi War with France he proved to be one of the greatest wartime presidents in American history.[2]

Adams' first decision was to reject Secretary of State Timothy Pickering's plan to ask Congress to declare war. He did "not wish" to "declare war," he confided, but thoroughly intended to "wage it." Despite the absence of a formal declaration of war, Congress still had the power to establish the size of the Army and the Navy and appropriate monies for military or naval operations. Thus, even in a limited naval war, the vital constitutional system of checks and balances on executive and legislative action remained intact.[3]

Adams had already moved to increase the size of the new American fleet. On 10 May 1797, the inspiring figure of old Captain John Barry ordered the lines to the new frigate *United States* to be cut and she slid off the ways in Philadelphia. Four months later her sister ship, the *Constellation,* was launched in Baltimore, and a month after that the *Constitution* was launched in Boston. That spring, Adams asked Congress to appropriate funds to complete the three frigates on which work had been suspended under the 1796 compromise. Federalists proposed to increase the number to nine, but the Republicans, led by Pennsylvania's Albert Gallatin, opposed this measure. The Republicans wanted to appease the French; the Federalists hoped to force the pace of the talks. After the XYZ Affair exploded, however, Congress acted quickly. At about this time, Secretary of War James McHenry, widely thought to be an incompetent drunkard, admitted that the Army's coastal fortifications and frontier patrols were overtaxing his poorly managed department and asked that naval affairs be turned over to another agency. On 16 April 1798, Senator William Bingham of Connecticut persuaded the Senate to create a Navy Department, but Republican opposition in the House again stiffened and the bill passed by the slim margin of forty-seven to forty-one. The measure divested the War Department of naval affairs, created a new cabinet office of the Secretary of the Navy, broadly outlined his duties, and authorized him to hire a small staff of clerks. The act was signed by President Adams on 30 April 1798.

Adams nominated former Senator George Cabot of Massachusetts to be secretary of the Navy, and Congress confirmed the appointment before Cabot's letter rejecting the post reached Philadelphia. Adams next asked Georgetown merchant Benjamin Stoddert to take the job, but a friend of Stoddert's warned Secretary of State Pickering that he "cannot believe he will accept" inasmuch as Stoddert "appeared to be a man of good sense." A veteran of the Revolution, Stoddert had served in the Confederation Congress and purchased the land for the new federal city during Washington's presidency. He was a good manager, made sound judgments of men, and confounded his admirer's prediction by accepting Adams' offer. Adams, the commander in chief, established several precedents in his dealings with Stoddert. The president outlined grand strategy, but the secretary directed specific operations. Both men knew the political importance of procurement and promotions, so Adams allowed Stoddert to issue contracts through local Navy agents and to recommend personnel assignments but occasionally overruled him on political grounds.

Stoddert wanted officers "with the true kind of zeal and spirit, which will enable us to make up for the want of great force by great activity," but occasionally the demands of Federalist politics outweighed this high standard.

While Stoddert moved into the Navy's new offices in Philadelphia, Federalists in Congress enacted legislation allowing American warships to "seize, take, and bring to port" armed French ships "hovering" off the Atlantic seaboard. But one French privateer had already entered Charleston harbor and captured an American merchantman, so port defense was Stoddert's first strategic priority, and for this he needed cheap, quickly constructed vessels. The Americans had occasionally employed gunboats during the Revolution, and the War Department, concerned about Indians and pirates on the Ohio River, had laid down two 50-foot gunboats, the *President Adams* and *Senator Ross*, at Pittsburgh in 1797. These vessels entered the fleet when the Navy was established, and Congress authorized the construction of ten more gunboats in May 1798 "for the defense . . . of the harbours of the United States." Two were built at Savannah, two at Charleston, two at Wilmington, one at Beaufort, one at Philadelphia, and two at Newport. Because of Georgia's "exposed" position, Stoddert moved two more to Savannah that fall, but once he was certain that the harbors were guarded, he chose to rely on heavier ships for coastal defense. And, after the fleet went on the offensive in the West Indies that winter, he told Pinckney that he had "little expectation that it is possible to employ these vessels usefully in the present situation."[4]

The Navy's earliest operations were aimed at sweeping French "picaroon" raiders from American waters. In the last week of May, Captain Richard Dale in the sloop *Ganges* stood out of the Delaware Bay and began a patrol that led him from Cape Henry north to New York. Both the frigates *United States* and *Constitution*, and the 20-gun sloop *Delaware*, were also at sea by the end of the month, but the frigate *Constellation*, undergoing sea trials at Baltimore, still needed additional work. While cruising off New Jersey on 7 July, Captain Stephen Decatur in the *Delaware* came upon an American coastal trader that had been plundered by the 12-gun French schooner *Croyable*. He caught up with the enemy privateer that night, forced her to surrender, and then escorted the first American prize of the war into Philadelphia. There she was commissioned into the Navy as the *Retaliation*. Within two months,

American patrol operations had cleared the coastal waters of the picaroons, forcing the French to shift their commerce raiding back to the Caribbean.

The same day that Decatur took the *Croyable*, Congress abrogated the Franco-American Alliance of 1778. Less than a week later, Congress also agreed to Adams' request to acquire a dozen more warships by gifts or lease, establish a Marine Corps, and commission the uncompleted frigates *President, Congress*, and *Chesapeake*. During the next twenty-four months the fleet expanded to more than fifty vessels, most of them converted merchantmen purchased by the Navy or donated by the states, manned by more than 6,000 officers and men. In December 1798, Stoddert asked Congress to appropriate an additional $1 million to build a dozen 74-gun sails-of-the-line and a large number of smaller ships and to establish a chain of Navy yards to build the ships and maintain the fleet. "Had we possessed this force a few years ago . . . we should not have lost by depredations on our trade, four times the sum necessary to have created and maintained it during the whole time the war has existed in Europe."[5]

The debate in Congress over naval policy was reignited by Stoddert's capital ship plan. Early American losses to France, though serious, did not crimp Adams' naval strategy. Stoddert intended not only to win the Quasi War but also to deter Europe's naval powers from trifling again with American neutrality. "Twelve ships of seventy-four guns, as many frigates, and twenty or thirty smaller vessels, would probably be found . . . a force sufficient to insure our future peace with . . . Europe," he told Congressman Josiah Parker, chairman of an ad hoc House Naval Affairs Committee. It would also "make the most powerful nations desire our friendship" once the war was over. Parker had engineered the 1796 frigate compromise, but the French crisis changed his mind about the wisdom of establishing a larger, permanent navy. On 29 December 1798, he argued in favor of the capital ship bill during the House debate, on the grounds that a large fleet was needed to keep the United States out of Europe's wars.[6]

Gallatin, the Navy's most determined opponent, moved to delete the sail-of-the-line authorization, pointing out that the ships were said to cost $2.4 million, whereas Congress was being asked for less than half that amount. Stoddert had claimed that stationing two squadrons in the West Indies was the cause of reduced maritime insurance rates, but Gallatin contended that rates everywhere were being reduced because of the lessening tempo of France's naval activity. In the main, Jeffersonians like Gallatin wanted to defend maritime commerce but opposed Stoddert's request because "a navy would cost far more than it would ever benefit the country." Fleets, they felt, "were used more as engines of power, than as a protection of commerce." Adams and Stoddert made a powerful case, but support for the war with France was at its peak, and in March, with the Naval Act of 1799, Congress authorized the construction of six sails-of-the-line and a number of other measures Stoddert proposed. The problems of building the new American fleet were already beginning to accumulate, however. Simply acquiring in one yard enough timber to lay down a sail-of-the-line proved to be a prodigious undertaking; once the timber was purchased, the lack of adequate storage or transportation added another bottleneck. Congressional generosity was on the wane in 1799, and Stoddert was able to establish only one public Navy yard, in the city of Washington in the new District of Columbia.[7]

While drafting his shipbuilding program, Stoddert also directed American naval operations against France. The basis of American strategy during the Quasi War was an informal maritime alliance with Britain, whose fleet dominated the North Atlantic and whose squadrons in the Caribbean and West Indies cooperated with American naval operations against French bases and privateers. During the summer of 1798, Captain Thomas Truxtun, a veteran Revolutionary War privateer, sailed in the *Constellation* to the Spanish port of Havana, Cuba, where he took charge of an American squadron including the sloop *Baltimore*, commanded by Captain Isaac Phillips. Truxtun received orders to escort a large convoy of merchantmen to the Georgia coast. This mission concluded, Truxtun returned to Norfolk, but the *Baltimore* headed south, escorting another convoy carrying gold back to Havana.

As agents of a neutral power waging an undeclared war against one member of the Franco-Spanish Alliance, Navy captains had to navigate around a thicket of complex issues affecting their operations. For one thing, Britain and Spain were at war, but the United States was neutral in that conflict under the terms of the 1793 Neutrality Proclamation and Jay's and Pinckney's treaties. For another, the Royal Navy's impressment of American sailors, a growing source of friction, continued in spite of the informal wartime alliance. Another ticklish issue concerned Britain's trade regula-

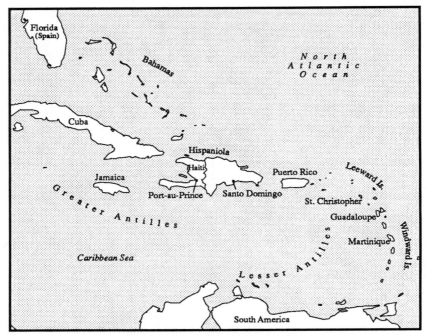

Florida
(Spain)

Bahamas

North
Atlantic
Ocean

Cuba

Hispaniola

Haiti

Jamaica

Port-au-Prince   Santo Domingo

Puerto Rico

Leeward Is.

St. Christopher

Guadaloupe

Greater Antilles

Martinique

Windward Is.

Caribbean Sea

Lesser Antilles

South America

Quasi War in the Caribbean, 1787–1801

tions, which aimed at controlling neutral shipping. Adams argued that the British definition of contraband was imprecise, overly broad, and arrogantly enforced, but Federalist maritime policy did not hold that "free ships make free goods," a position espoused by Jefferson's Republicans, who hoped that it would impair Britain's naval blockade of France. Since the gold carried by the merchantmen escorted by the *Baltimore* was contraband bound for Spanish Cuba, Truxtun instructed Isaac Phillips to defend the convoy against the French but not to fire at British warships holding blockade stations off Havana. On 16 November 1798, three British sails-of-the-line stopped the American convoy and seized several vessels. Confused by his orders, Phillips refused to fight his ship when a British party from the flagship *Carnatic* boarded the *Baltimore*, ordered him to muster his crew, and impressed fifty-five American sailors, fifty of whom were returned later that day. Stoddert and Adams were furious. Phillips, charged with "passive submission" under "circumstances so degrading," was dismissed from the Navy. Adams knew that his protest to London would do no good.[8]

Europe's tensions decided American strategy in the Caribbean, the major theater of operations during the Quasi War. During its global maritime offensive in 1794, the Royal Navy had seized the French West Indian islands of St. Lucia, Martinique, and Guadeloupe. Only Haiti remained in French hands, but it was a tenuous hold. In 1791 a bloody slave revolt had begun in Haiti under Toussaint L'Ouverture, an ex-slave. The radical Jacobin government in Paris dispatched a new governor to Haiti, Victor Hughes, a bloodstained figure of France's recent Reign of Terror. Establishing Port au Prince as his base, Hughes counterattacked, reconquered Guadeloupe, and soon after massacred 1,200 rebels. The British tried in vain to blockade Guadeloupe, but Hughes held out, repulsed several assaults, and in the meantime deployed hundreds of French corsairs to prey on British and American ships in the Caribbean. The French West Indies were cut off from Europe by the Royal Navy, however, and only a few French frigates were sent across the Atlantic to support Hughes' Guadeloupe-based operations.

Stoddert, after considering this history, decided that the fleet's most important mission would be to escort endangered American ships in the West Indies; its secondary mission would be to hunt down French raiders. In October 1798 he extended the fleet's area of operations by ordering Captain Alexander Murray to deploy his small squadron, composed of the brig *Norfolk* and the converted merchantman *Montezuma*, to a base at Basseterre on St. Kitts in the Virgin Islands. Meanwhile, William Bainbridge, one of dozens of experienced young mariners who received commissions as Navy lieutenants during the first summer of the war, was ordered by Stoddert to supervise the refitting of the *Retaliation*. He made a brief shakedown cruise off New Jersey before rendezvousing with Murray's squadron off the Virgin Islands on 8 November.

When American warships in the Caribbean were not escorting convoys, they patrolled for French privateers, but none of Murray's ships carried more than twenty guns and they had to be careful to avoid enemy frigates. On 20 November, after being assured by a British sloop that no French warships were in the area, Murray came upon two foreign frigates. He assumed them to be British but decided to take no chances; he ordered Bainbridge to close and confirm their nationality. Bainbridge sailed toward the pair even after they had failed to answer either British or American signals, and when he was within point-blank range, the frigates *L'In-surgente* and *Volunataire* broke out the French tricolor and sent a boarding party to take over the *Retaliation* without a shot. Murray, who escaped after a chase, was furious with Bainbridge, the first American captain to surrender a U.S. Navy warship to the enemy.

The loss of the *Retaliation* coincided with Truxtun's arrival in Philadelphia, where he conferred with Captains Decatur, Thomas Tingey, and Richard Dale. Together they proposed a new naval strategy to Stoddert. Agreeing to their plan, Stoddert now divided the fleet of twenty-one ships into four squadrons. The first, commanded by Captain John Barry, consisted of the frigates *United States* and *Constitution*, four smaller vessels each mounting twenty-four to eighteen guns, and four revenue cutters. Based in Prince Rupert Bay on the British island of Dominica, Barry was to cruise north to St. Kitts and as far south as Dutch Curaçao. Based at Basseterre, Captain Truxtun's Leeward Island Squadron, comprising his frigate *Constellation* and two brigs, was to escort merchantmen and patrol for raiders between St. Kitts and Spanish Puerto Rico. The Windward Island station, covering the passage between Hispaniola and Cuba, was assigned to Captain Thomas Tingey, whose squadron included the *Ganges*, the brig *Pinckney*, and a revenue cutter. The smallest squadron was the Cuban force, which included only the *Delaware* and two cutters under the command of Captain Stephen Decatur, who was directed by Stoddert to patrol the northern coast of the island. When delays in recruiting and provisioning prevented several ships from sailing, Stoddert decided to provide logistical support for the fleet by shuttling store ships between Atlantic ports and the various Caribbean and West Indies stations.

Having persuaded Stoddert to accept his strategy, Truxtun stood out to sea and headed for his station in the Leeward Islands, where he rendezvoused with Murray in the *Norfolk* and learned of the loss of the *Retaliation*. Truxtun arranged for the *Norfolk* and the *Richmond* to put to sea on 4 February 1799 to escort an outbound convoy from St. Christopher, and the *Constitution* also sailed that day. Appearing off Guadeloupe, Truxtun was headed for Nevis, a Dutch island, when at noon five days later he caught sight of a frigate about fifteen miles away. Shortly, the frigate fired a gun to the windward, the sign of an enemy. It was *L'Insurgente*, the fastest frigate in the French fleet. Truxtun gave chase, and the opposing ship turned to escape, but both captains drove their ships into a squall. High winds snapped *L'Insurgente*'s main topmast, and when the battle began she was unable to maneuver. Truxtun held the commanding windward gage. Achieving a "position for every shot to do execution," the Americans pounded away at will. Although the 38-gun *Constellation* appeared to be at a slight disadvantage when compared to the 40-gun *L'Insurgente*, Truxtun's broadside had a greater throwweight. At 1600, after only seventy-five minutes, the French tricolor was struck. Truxtun ordered Lieutenant John Rodgers and Ensign David D. Porter and a prize crew to take over the captured vessel and reported to Stoddert that "a very fine frigate [was] being added to our infant Navy."[9]

Although Stoddert was elated with the *Constellation*'s victory, he was unhappy with the lack of results from the Dominica force and complained to Alexander Hamilton that Captain John Barry was too "old and infirm" to direct a squadron. "Barry is no doubt brave, and well qualified to fight a single ship," he told Adams, but he kept his units too close together and seemed unable to hunt down any French warships. Stoddert was even less pleased with Captain Samuel Nicholson of the frigate *Constitution* and sent him ashore to supervise the construction of one of the new sails-of-the-line. Stoddert promised Adams that Nicholson would stay at the yard "as long as I remain in office."[10]

During the summer hurricane season, Stoddert decided to recall the four squadrons in sequence, but Truxtun's anxiety to collect his prize money disrupted this plan, and both he and Barry made the American coast in May. While most of the ships discharged their crews and the captains tried to recruit new men and refit their ships, Stoddert wanted to deploy another squadron to raid enemy shipping along the French coast. The plan was well conceived, but thwarted by problems ashore, and in July Stoddert hastily directed Captain Murray in the recently repaired *L'Insurgente* to cross the Atlantic and hunt down French ships in European waters. Stoddert's orders to Murray were written without much thought and specified only that he return to Cayenne by 20 September 1799. Unfortunately, not only did Murray's presence in French waters not cause much excitement, but he also failed to take any prizes and, indeed, was even late arriving at Cayenne and resuming his West Indies patrols.

Disappointed, Stoddert was still bent on attacking the French at the extremities of their maritime empire. The 32-gun frigate *Essex*—built at a cost of $50,000 by public subscriptions at Salem, Massachusetts, whose merchants wanted to reopen their profitable trade with the West Indies—was ready late in the year. On 6 January 1800 she left New York under the command of Captain Edward Preble, who was already known as one of the Navy's best leaders and harshest disciplinarians, a captain whose men often felt the pain of the lash. Although he acknowledged the captain's great ability as a combat leader, Preble's sailing master resigned rather than serve under this "cross, peevish and ill-tempered, surly and proud" martinet. Whipping around Cape Horn, Preble entered the Indian Ocean, recaptured several American merchantmen, cruised for a while in the East Indies, and escorted a merchant convoy back to America.[11]

By July 1799, Stoddert was able to redeploy the squadrons back to their stations in the Caribbean. Ships on the Windward Island and Leeward Island stations operated mostly in deep water, but the Santo Domingo force had a new enemy to deal with in the shallow waters off Hispaniola's rugged coast. Haiti's slave army had split up, one faction led by the black general, L'Ouverture, the other by a mulatto, Benoit Rigaud. On 13 June, L'Ouverture signed an alliance with Britain under the terms of which Britain gave his army aid, L'Ouverture agreed to attack the bases from which French privateers operated, and the Royal Navy was committed to support the rebels at sea. Adams, who approached the Haitian problem carefully, now decided to back the rebels, and embargoed American trade with Haiti to injure Rigaud's army and his French allies.

When Adams got word of the Anglo-Haitian alliance, however, he lifted the embargo and instructed Captain Silas Talbot, the new commander of the Santo Domingo Squadron, to support Toussaint's operations by interdicting arms shipments to Rigaud and by attacking French privateers in Haitian waters. Talbot had few craft that could operate in the shoal waters off the Haitian coast, so Secretary Stoddert assigned to his squadron the 12-gun schooner *Experiment,* which had recently been launched in Baltimore. On New Year's Day, 1800, Captain William Marley in the *Experiment* was escorting a convoy of four merchantmen through the Bight of Leogane on the western, windward edge of the island. Becalmed for several hours in midchannel, they were attacked at noon by ten picaroon barges. The *Experiment*'s guns repulsed the first assault, but after an hour's rest the picaroons rowed out again and concentrated their fire on the schooner. Marley and his crew fought back bravely and saved half the convoy after two more bloody firefights.

Meanwhile, Captain Truxtun was late sailing for his Leeward Island station because of a feud with Talbot and Barry over their relative ranking on the Navy's list. Truxtun was apoplectic when Adams placed Talbot first in order of seniority and agreed to sail only after Stoddert promised that he would never have to serve under Talbot, whom Truxtun roundly despised. Before he set sail, Truxtun altered the *Constellation*'s batteries by exchanging his heavy old 24-pounders on the quarterdeck for lighter 18-pounders and, to adjust for this loss of throwweight in the broadside, by mounting new 24-pound carronades in place of the light 12-pounders on the spar deck. This weakened his frigate's ability to damage an enemy at long ranges, but gave her more firepower at close range and improved the overall sailing characteristics of the ship.

Truxtun reached St. Kitt's with the new year and, on 13 January 1799, arrived on a station "before the road of the enemy at Guadeloupe, where I was informed a very large and heavy frigate, of upwards of 50 guns, was then laying." On 1 February, Captain Citizen Pitot in *La Vengeance* was on the first leg of a voyage from Guadeloupe to France when he spotted the *Constellation* and started to run. The chase lasted until nightfall, when Truxtun closed to within hailing distance and told his gunners "to load and fire and fast as possible, . . . take good aim, and fire directing into the hull of the enemy." During the ensuing gun duel, which lasted over four hours, Truxtun's tactic left Pitot's deck splashed with blood and littered with bodies, but the *Constellation*'s rigging was nearly destroyed. At 0100, just as Truxtun prepared to send a boarding party onto *La Vengeance,* the American's mainmast snapped off at the deck and crashed over the side of the ship. With the sea wreathed in darkness, Truxtun assumed that the enemy had gone down, and the next morning he made for Port Royal, Jamaica, arriving there a week later. Two days earlier, however, *La Vengeance* limped into Dutch Curaçao and Pitot reported that he had just barely escaped a battering from an American sail-of-the-line. With a jury rig, Truxtun had to sail back to Hampton Roads, where he again received a hero's welcome.[12]

. From the first round of hostilities, Adams had stuck like glue to his initial aim of forcing France to sign a trade treaty that respected America's neutral rights. One way of increasing pressure on France was to nurture the Anglo-American rapprochement fashioned in 1796 in the wake of Jay's Treaty by Lord Grenville, the foreign minister, and Federalist Rufus King, the American minister in London. This increasingly close English-speaking relationship, which was enormously useful to American strategy and diplomacy in the Quasi War, survived until Jefferson adopted a pro-French line in 1803. Adams opposed Hamilton's plan to transfigure the rapprochement into an alliance, however, and stood against Hamilton's proposal to declare war against France and her allies. At length Hamilton's Federalists persuaded Congress to bring Washington out of retirement to command a newly formed 10,000-man army, and Hamilton, the senior major general, cooked up a plan to use the army to invade Spanish Louisiana and Florida and assist a handful of unstable Latin American revolutionaries against Spain. The administration should "complete and prepare the land force," Hamilton told McHenry, not only to provide security against invasion, but also because the United States "ought certainly to look to the possession of the Floridas and Louisiana—and we ought to squint at South America." Adams, who had little use for these dangerous and visionary schemes, let Washington retire in peace to Mount Vernon and prevented Hamilton's army from marching southward and widening the war.[13]

At the same time, against the advice of most of his Federalist cabinet, Adams arranged for renewed talks with Paris. When he learned from his son, John Quincy Adams, a young diplomat in Berlin, that Talleyrand was ready to receive American negotiators, the president, supported by Washington, persuaded the obdurate Federalists in the Senate to confirm his nominees to another peace commission "with full powers to discuss and settle by a treaty all controversies" with France. They reached Paris in April 1800, five months after Napoleon had seized power in a coup d'état. He was convinced that Britain was France's main enemy and feared that the Quasi War would escalate, throw the United States into Britain's lap, menace the French West Indies, and threaten the colonies of France's newest ally, Spain. He told Talleyrand to ignore the 1778 Alliance and promise to respect American maritime neutrality; in return, the Americans assumed French liabilities for attacks on American shipping during the war. When the Senate approved the Treaty of Mortefontaine in February 1801, the Quasi War, the United States' first war, came to an end. Just one month earlier, however, Secretary Stoddert had warned Congress that only after America possessed a fleet of sails-of-the-line and "the means of increasing . . . their naval strength" could Americans have "confidence . . . that we may then avoid those wars in which we have no interest, and without submitting to be plundered."[14]

Chapter Five

The Barbary Wars
1801–1806

President John Adams ran for reelection in 1800, but many Federalists supported Alexander Hamilton instead. During Adams' presidency, Virginia's James Madison had built a national political network that evolved into the Democratic Republican coalition, but at election time the party's allegiance was split between Thomas Jefferson and Aaron Burr of New York, both of whom sought the presidency in 1800. Despite his astute direction of the Quasi War, Adams was an unpopular chief executive whose war policies pleased only his most fervent admirers. Foreign policy and its domestic implications played an important role in the election. Whereas Hamilton had wanted to invade and annex Spain's Louisiana Territory, Jefferson believed that the Federalists intended to use the Quasi War against France and French liberalism to suppress liberals in America with the Alien and Sedition Acts of 1798 and Hamilton's national army.

Adams' close association with the Navy made naval policy an issue in the election. "We may regret the necessity of a navy, . . . but we must have a navy, and we must have a military force, or we are not an independent nation," claimed a Federalist newspaper in New York. "We are sacrificing everything to navigation and a navy," countered Jefferson. "What a glorious exchange would it be could we persuade our navigating fellow citizens to embark their capital in the internal commerce of our country, exclude foreigners from that, and let them take carrying trade in exchange:

abolish the diplomatic establishments and never suffer an armed vessel of a nation to enter our ports." Adams came in third at the polls. Neither Jefferson nor Aaron Burr, the Democratic Republican candidates, won a majority in the Electoral College, so the election was sent to the House of Representatives, where Jefferson won by a slim margin.[1]

Although Jefferson proved to be a truly great president, the quality of his cabinet was mixed. Madison, his lieutenant, became secretary of state, and Gallatin, his disciple, was selected to be Treasury secretary. A dispiriting search was conducted to find someone to run the Navy Department. After six men refused the job, Jefferson wondered if "I shall have to advertise for a Secretary of the Navy." At long last Robert Smith of Baltimore was persuaded to take the post. The handful of officers who remained in the Navy apparently liked Smith, but his tenure was marred by a scandal that erupted when Gallatin discovered that Smith had secretly paid $200,000 to his brother's business. In addition, Smith was overburdened by an immense amount of departmental paperwork, and was never able to exert much influence over the president, the cabinet, or the members of Congress. Moreover, by the time Smith finally joined the administration, Gallatin had already won over the president to a policy of strict economy. "If the sums . . . expended to build and maintain the frigates were applied to paying a part of our national debt," Gallatin asserted, "the payment would make us more respectable in the eyes of foreign nations than all the frigates we can build." Gallatin was an immigrant from landlocked Switzerland, and his views on naval policy were shaped by his agrarian perspective and his faith in the importance of national credit. The country could "not support a navy such as could claim respect, . . . such as being an object of terror to foreign nations," he argued. The Navy's consistent foe, Gallatin was more than a match for Robert Smith.[2]

In his inaugural address, Jefferson listed his major goals: peace, economy in government, and states' rights. He sought "peace, commerce, and honest friendship with all nations, entangling alliances with none." In short, the United States lacked any interest in Europe's balance of power. Whereas George Washington in his farewell address had merely urged his successors not to sign another long-term military alliance with any of the Great Powers, Jefferson wanted to avoid involvement with Europe's problems altogether. On the other hand, he was not insensitive to the need to protect American merchant shipping overseas, although he was concerned that the adoption of such a policy might inadvertently lead to a renewed quarrel with France or hostilities with Great Britain. "Peace," he announced, "is our passion." Nonetheless, even the Democratic Republicans admitted that "a navy, well organized, must constitute the natural and efficient defense of this country against all foreign hostility."[3]

Jefferson's intention to cut the cost of the Navy was evident to President Adams long before he left office. Indeed, Gallatin thought it wise as an "economical measure" to "burn" the fleet "at the end of a war, and to build a new one when again at war." The Federalists tried to tie the incoming president's hands by having Congress pass the Peace Establishment Act of 1801. Stoddert, the author of this measure, inexplicably decided to sell off the Navy's smaller ships, perhaps in the hope of keeping as many frigates as possible and continuing the work on the sails-of-the-line, in spite of the looming crisis with Barbary. Once Jefferson moved into the White House, however, he set about with alacrity to end all work on the sails-of-the-line, curtailed improvements to the Navy yards, slashed the shore establishment's payroll, and sold or scrapped seven of the major ships of the fleet, keeping only six in service and another seven laid up in ordinary.[4]

Jefferson also reduced the Army to 5,000 men and in 1802 set a ceiling of 3,000 officers and men for the Navy. Under the Peace Establishment Act, the rank of master commandant had been abolished and the Navy Department retained only the most talented captains from the Quasi War. Secretaries Stoddert and Smith made orderly reviews of their officers, and most of their selections made sense, but the crunching reduction in the officer corps inhibited the development of a professional naval service for several decades. At sea, officers were well paid, but there was little shore duty and officers not detailed to a ship were effectively furloughed with half pay, a status that allowed, even encouraged, other employment. Moreover, neither Jefferson nor anyone else gave consideration to the development of a stable, professional enlisted force; they assumed that the skills of sailors in the pool of merchant seamen were closely related to those required to serve in the Navy. Furthermore, enlisted men signed on a ship for either short service or a specific voyage, and they could easily be paid off, thus eliminating any need to provide for them when the fleet was inactive.

There was some irony in the timing of Jefferson's economies, since he was at the moment taking a tough line on the protection of maritime commerce. Jefferson's position on trade defense, at least as applied to nations other than the great naval powers of Europe, now differed little from that laid down by John Adams. The instant issue concerned the renewed attacks against American shipping in the Mediterranean by the Barbary states of Morocco, Algiers, Tunis, and Tripoli. In July 1800, the brig *Catherine* out of New York was seized by a Tripolitan corsair, and the bashaw proclaimed that if the amount of his tribute was not increased, then he would declare war on the United States. After news of these outrages reached the Atlantic seaboard, the public uproar was heard in Washington, and on 6 February 1802 Congress finally passed a resolution urging the president to deploy the fleet "as he saw fit to protect American commerce and seamen and to commission privateers." Some interpreted this measure as a virtual declaration of war against the Barbary states.[5]

The need to retaliate against the North Africans was underscored by an incident with Algiers. In September 1800, Captain William Bainbridge in the sloop *George Washington* delivered the annual American tribute to the dey. Unexpectedly, the Algerian ruler insisted that Bainbridge transport his own annual tribute to his Turkish overlord in Constantinople and fly the Algerian flag instead of the Stars and Stripes at the main truck of his ship during this voyage. Bainbridge later told Stoddert that the dey's attitude toward the United States "is exactly this: you pay me tribute, by that you become my slaves, and then I have a right to order as I please." Bainbridge's orders were to cement peaceful relations with Algiers, not to start a war, and he could find no excuse to avoid the mission. Within a few days, he stood out to sea and shaped a course for the Dardanelles, carrying as a passenger an Algerian diplomat and the dey's tribute, a selection of zoo animals. "Had we 10 or 12 frigates and sloops in these seas," Bainbridge anguished, "we should not experience these mortifying degradations that must be cutting to every American." Back home, news of Bainbridge's most recent humiliation fed the fire of demands by Congress that the president take stiff action against Algiers and Tripoli.[6]

To solve the problem of the Barbary corsairs, Jefferson adopted a proposal that Adams had already outlined: deploy a naval force to the Mediterranean to compel them to honor their agreements with the United States. In 1801, Secretary of the Navy Smith

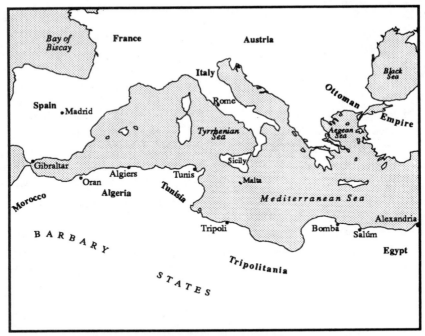

Barbary Wars, 1801–1806

directed Commodore Richard Dale to take command of a squadron composed of the frigates *Essex, Philadelphia,* and *President,* and the schooner *Enterprise.* Once established in the Mediterranean, Dale was to protect American shipping and, if necessary, employ force to compel Barbary's rulers to honor the existing tribute treaties. Jefferson warned Dale not to provoke either Britain or France by demanding that they adhere to the American interpretation of the rights of neutral shipping, however. "Our Nation has suffered as much by the abuse of Neutral rights," he admitted, but "we do not think we ought to go to war, in favor of either" European naval power.[7]

On 1 July 1801, Commodore Dale reached Gibraltar, where the neutral status of the United States allowed him to negotiate an agreement to use the British base for his squadron. Within a few days, he had thwarted a pair of Tripolitan corsairs trying to pass into the Mediterranean to attack American shipping. Dale's ships then progressed along the Barbary coast, visiting Algiers and Tunis and establishing a blockade of Tripoli harbor at the end of the month. After eighteen days Dale was forced to curtail this operation and withdraw to the British base at Malta to get fresh water. Meanwhile, Lieutenant Andrew Sterrett in the *Enterprise* was attacked off Malta by the polacca *Tripoli*. American gunfire so badly mauled this raider that she had to strike her colors, but Sterrett, who lacked the authority to take a prize, had no choice but to release her. When Dale returned to Tripoli, he found the bashaw so impressed with these displays of American naval force that he was ready to negotiate, but the commodore had no brief to secure a new treaty, so he broke off the talks and settled instead for an exchange of prisoners. Neither John Adams nor Thomas Jefferson had intended to establish a permanent American station in the Mediterranean, and Dale's orders specifically directed him to return home after a brief cruise, so he left the *Philadelphia* in the Mediterranean to maintain some pressure on Tunis and Tripoli and sailed back to Norfolk in January 1802.

While Dale was at sea, Congress took up the question of American foreign policy in the Mediterranean, and on 22 January 1802, over minimal opposition, passed a resolution that encouraged the president "further and more effectually to protect the commerce of the United States against the Barbary Powers." Gallatin was opposed to any additional operations. It was "a mere matter of calculation whether the purchase of peace is not cheaper than the expense of war," he declared. He was convinced that a naval campaign against the Barbary corsairs would "not even give us the free use of the Mediterranean trade."[8]

Jefferson, pressured by Congress, overruled Gallatin, decided to send another force into the Mediterranean, and asked Congress to supply funds to support a stronger squadron comprising five frigates and several lesser types. When Commodore Truxtun was asked to take this new command, he refused on the grounds that no captain had been assigned to his flagship. Though there was little doubt that he was the best man for the job, Truxtun's conceit and his active Federalists politics galled Smith. The secretary settled the matter by interpreting Truxtun's rejection as a resignation of his Navy commission and giving the billet to Commodore Richard Morris.

Jefferson instructed Morris to employ his squadron to "effectuate without delay an honorable accommodation with Tripoli, Morocco, and any other of the Barbary Powers with whom we may happen to be at war." Secretary Smith added that he was "to make the handsomest and most military display of force . . . to excite an impression that in the event of negotiations failing you intend a close and vigorous blockade" of Tripoli. Morris sailed in the frigate *Chesapeake* for the Mediterranean in the spring, but the ships assigned to his squadron were dispersed and several months passed before all arrived on station. When they did arrive, many of the vessels were badly in need of repairs, and Morris finally had to send home his flagship and the frigate *Constellation*, a move that weakened his force and undercut his diplomacy. His primary mission was to cow the bashaw of Tripoli, but Morris repeatedly sent his ships off on other duty, tolerated a level of discipline that was altogether too lax, and unnecessarily diverted his attention to Tunis and Algiers. He had accomplished almost nothing when he was recalled by Secretary Smith in the fall of 1803. Challenged over his direction of the squadron, Morris was censured by a court-martial and dismissed from the naval service.[9]

Despite an ongoing crisis with France over the Louisiana Territory, Jefferson was now more determined than ever to achieve his goals in the Mediterranean. Both Dale and Morris had complained about the lack of shallow-draft vessels for work in the shoal waters off the Barbary coast, so Jefferson relaxed his economy drive long enough to secure from Congress in 1803 an appropriation to build the 16-gun brigs *Argus* and *Siren* and the 16-gun schooners *Nautilus* and *Vixen*. He also directed Secretary Smith to deploy a third squadron into the Mediterranean to relieve the ships left behind by Morris. To replace Morris, Robert Smith selected Commodore Edward Preble, a seasoned, sharp-tongued captain who was also one of ablest officers of his day. Although Smith deployed only the frigates *Philadelphia* and *Constitution* to the Mediterranean in 1803, he also assigned to Preble's squadron the schooner *Enterprise* and the four new 16-gun vessels.

Preble sent Captain William Bainbridge in the *Philadelphia* into the Atlantic ahead of the rest of the ships. Bainbridge reached Gibraltar in August and soon discovered that Morocco had deployed her cruisers into the Atlantic to capture American merchantmen. Acting quickly, Bainbridge put to sea, taking one Moroccan corsair before Preble arrived on station in September. At Gibraltar, Preble rendezvoused with Commodore John Rodgers, who was sailing home with the rest of the ships of Richard Morris' squadron. Both Rodgers and Preble wanted to act against the sultan of Morocco, but each commodore also insisted on his right to the overall command. After a nasty quarrel, Rodgers agreed to serve under Preble, and the squadron made for Tangier on the

Moroccan coast. The sultan was so impressed by the swiftness of the American response that he disavowed his earlier declaration of war, released his American prisoners, and reaffirmed his obligations under the Tribute Treaty of 1786. Shortly thereafter, Rodgers sailed for home, leaving Preble to deal with Tripoli.

Meanwhile, the American strategic problem in the Mediterranean had been immeasurably complicated by the loss of the *Philadelphia*. Before Preble reached Gibraltar, Bainbridge had made for Tripoli in company with the schooner *Vixen*. He arrived in late October, only to learn that a Tripolitan corsair was at sea. He detached the schooner and ordered her to patrol the Straits of Sicily. Blown off its blockade station by a violent storm, the *Philadelphia* was sailing back toward the North African coast on the morning of 31 October when another Tripolitan vessel was sighted trying to slip into the harbor. At 1100, Bainbridge began to run her down, but the enemy hugged the coast, and to gain searoom, Bainbridge had to give up the chase and turn about. Suddenly, the *Philadelphia* ran onto a reef covered by about twelve feet of water. At first, Bainbridge believed that he had only hit a sandbar, so he laid on full sail to drive the vessel over the obstacle, but this maneuver failed. The frantic crew now threw most of the guns and water overboard, cut away part of the stern, and even chopped down the foremast, but the ship was stuck. When Tripolitan gunboats began to pepper his ship, Bainbridge struck his colors. The American crew was imprisoned by the bashaw, and Bainbridge and his officers were placed under house arrest.

It was a bleak Thursday morning, 24 November, when Preble learned of the "distressing" loss of the *Philadelphia*. Not only was it humiliating, but he was afraid that it might encourage Tunis or Algiers to renew their attacks on American shipping. Soon he began to receive a barrage of letters from Bainbridge, explaining why he had surrendered his ship and offering suggestions about a rescue operation. Within hours after the *Philadelphia*'s colors had been struck, the tide rose and the Tripolitans floated the frigate free. She was moved into Tripoli harbor under the fort, a symbol of American military impotence.

Preble ached for revenge. On 1 February 1804, Lieutenant Stephen Decatur was ordered to take command of the brig *Siren* and the ketch *Intrepid* and sail for Tripoli harbor on a mission of great danger. Decatur stood off the coast for ten days, then used the cover of darkness to steal into the harbor in the ketch, and at

2330 led a party of sixty men who silently boarded the *Philadelphia* and, after a brief scuffle, killed the Tripolitan crew. Decatur then set fire to the ship and stood on the deck until the flames began to pour from the hatches. "We set fire to her and in less than 15 minutes from the time we first boarded her the flames were bursting out of her ports," reported Midshipman Ralph Izard. "It is astonishing that not one of our men was the least hurt." Enemy gunners started to shoot as Decatur and his crew scampered on board the *Intrepid*. "Before I got out of the harbour," he wrote, the *Philadelphia*'s "cables had burnt off, and she drifted in under the castle where she was consumed."[10]

The news of the burning of the *Philadelphia* reached America shortly after word of her seizure was publicized. Bainbridge's folly was ignored, Decatur and Preble became national heroes, and the public treated the destruction of the ship as a victory. A tonic to public opinion, Decatur's heroism had done nothing to cure the ill of the Barbary corsairs. Navy Secretary Smith exploited the congressional anger at Tripoli to secure another appropriation in March 1804 to construct the sloops *Wasp* and *Hornet*, and to allow Preble to rent or borrow gunboats for his squadron from the friendly kingdom of Sicily.

Still unable to subdue the bashaw, Preble counted three major operational problems that were frustrating his mission. First, as a base for the American squadron, Gibraltar was too far from Tripoli, so Preble shifted his headquarters to the harbor of Syracuse. Second, only the frigate *Constitution* was armed with a broadside of sufficient throwweight to damage the bashaw's forts, thus limiting the usefulness of the rest of the squadron in any frontal assault against the enemy bastion. Third, Preble lacked any small vessels that could run into Tripoli harbor to engage the enemy's gunboat flotilla. Commodores Dale and Morris had already pointed out the need for smaller vessels to Navy Secretary Smith, and Jefferson had asked Congress for authority to construct several gunboats. He expected them "to confine the Tripolitan cruisers within their borders and supersede the necessity of convoy of our commerce in that quarter." Smith sent nine new gunboats to the Mediterranean in late 1804. One was lost at sea, but the rest arrived at Syracuse within forty-eight hours of one another, although they were too late to join Preble's force. In the meantime, he had bribed the king of Sicily into lending him nine gunboats and two bomb boats, each carrying a single 24-pound mortar.[11]

Lieutenant Stephen Decatur, Jr., and his volunteers captured and burned the frigate *Philadelphia* in Tripoli harbor on 16 February 1804.

Commodore Stephen Decatur, Jr.

Edward Preble, commodore of the Mediterranean Squadron, 1803–4.

In January 1804, Preble opened talks with the bashaw. Preble punctuated these fruitless negotiations by moving his fleet from Syracuse to Tripoli to bombard the ancient city, but without a landing force he had no means to assault the fortress. The prospects for a negotiated settlement improved when a French agent was sent to Tripoli to mediate the dispute. Preble offered the bashaw $50,000 in ransom for Bainbridge and the rest of the crew of the *Philadelphia* and asked in return that the Tripolitans promise not to attack American merchantmen in the future. However, the temperament that made Preble such a superb combat leader was unsuited to his new role as diplomat. He ignored the French envoy, neglected to try to understand the bashaw's domestic predicament, and consequently failed to settle the matter during the summer. Exasperated, Preble decided to fight, although he "expected we may suffer much."[12]

The Mediterranean Squadron stood off Tripoli harbor on 3 August 1804, and Preble gave the command to launch his first attack. The American gunboats sailed into the harbor and, after a bloody fight, took three Tripolitan gunboats, which Preble entered into American service and added to his own force. Sadly, the second attack on 7 August was a minor disaster, marked by the explosion of one of the American craft. At this point news from America threw Preble into a fit of depression. After the burning of the *Philadelphia*, Jefferson had promised Congress to send an even larger squadron into the Mediterranean to exact revenge against Tripoli, and Preble knew that the new formation would be commanded by a senior captain to whom he would be subordinate. Anxious to settle the matter before he was superseded, Preble increased his ransom offer to $120,000, but the bashaw rejected the proposal. Preble, now desperate, decided to attack Tripoli once more. He loaded the ketch *Intrepid* with explosives and, on the evening of 3 September, ordered the crew of thirteen volunteers to anchor the vessel among the bashaw's gunboats, light the fuses, and escape over the side before she exploded. The plan was cursed by haste. The *Intrepid* blew up before she reached the anchorage, leaving none of the Americans alive to explain exactly what had gone wrong.

Less than a week later, Commodore Samuel Barron arrived in the Mediterranean to relieve Preble, and with him came William Eaton, an American diplomat. Eaton was the author of a plan to unseat the bashaw by providing military support to his brother, Hamet Karamanli, a rival claimant to the throne. Both Dale and Preble had rejected Eaton's scheme on previous occasions, but after the futile attacks of August Commodore Barron was ready to try anything. He ordered Lieutenant Isaac Hull, captain of the *Argus*, to locate Hamet "and to convey him and his suite to Derna or such other place on the coast as may be determined the most proper for cooperating with the naval force under my command against the common enemy." After Hull had sailed, bad weather forced Barron to lift the blockade of Tripoli and liver disease sent the commodore into a sickbed ashore at Malta.[13]

On 26 November 1804, the *Argus* made Alexandria but Hamet was not there. He was tracked down in Cairo by Eaton and a shore party led by Marine Lieutenant Presley Neville O'Bannon. From them Hamet accepted American gold, with which he bought guns for an army composed of 370 mercenaries and 105 camels. Without telling Hull, Eaton decided to strike 500 miles overland with Hamet in March and assault the bashaw's coastal fortress at Derna. O'Bannon left the party and alerted Hull, who put to sea and closed on Derna on 15 April. There he made contact with Eaton's troops, and at 0200 on 28 April they attacked the city. Barron, still ill in bed, had sent the *Hornet* and the *Nautilus* to support Hull, who concentrated his squadron's fire on the fort. After only ninety minutes the fort fell.

The seizure of Derna, where O'Bannon's Marines first arrived on the shores of Tripoli, heartened Hull, and he asked Barron for more ships and men to hold onto the fort and to mount overland and seaborne assaults on both flanks of the port of Tripoli. Barron was unhappy with the plan, however. For one thing, three of his frigates were worn out, and they needed to return to the United States for repairs before winter came to the Mediterranean. For another, Tobias Lear, the American consul in Malta, was opposed to backing Hamet, whose treachery was notorious. Finally, Barron saw no way that Hull's operation could free Bainbridge and his crew. If Hull succeeded, the hostages would probably be killed before they could be rescued. If Hull failed, then the bashaw would almost surely increase his ransom demand. Therefore, just before he left the Mediterranean to return home, Barron rejected Hull's plan.

Commodore John Rodgers in the *Constitution* relieved Barron on 22 May 1805, and with him came the largest American squadron yet assembled in the Mediterranean. Rodgers also brought a new determination to succeed where Barron and Morris had failed. At the start of Rodgers' progress against Tripoli, the squadron included the frigates *Constitution, John Adams, Essex,* and *Constellation;* the brigs *Argus, Franklin,* and *Siren;* the sloop *Hornet;* the schooners *Nautilus, Vixen,* and *Enterprise;* the bomb vessels *Vengeance* and *Spitfire;* and nine gunboats. This imposing show of force lay off Tripoli on 26 May. Incorrectly concluding that the Americans were giving him one last chance before launching a combined arms attack against his capital in collaboration with Hamet's army, the bashaw was in no mood to quibble. Furthermore, Lear was more than willing to abandon Hamet, whose contempt for the infidel Americans had been barely concealed and who furthermore was by now bankrupt. In the end, Lear agreed to withdraw support from Hamet, and the bashaw accepted a ransom of $60,000 for the release of Bainbridge and his men and promised not to attack American shipping in the future. All this was accomplished despite Rodgers' steely refusal to pay any more tribute.

Commodore Rodgers' attention next turned to the threat to American shipping from Tunis. On 31 July, his ships took up positions across the mouth of Tunis Bay and an ultimatum was dispatched to the bey giving him thirty-six hours to negotiate or be bombarded. Tobias Lear then went ashore to negotiate a treaty, warning the Tunisian that Rodgers preferred fighting to talking. After two weeks, the bey caved in, promised good relations in the future with the United States, and agreed to send a minister to Washington to negotiate a treaty of amity and commerce. His mission complete, Rodgers sailed for America in the summer of 1806.

In 1804, in the midst of the Barbary Wars, Thomas Jefferson had to stand for reelection. When he had entered the White House, he promised to cut the costs of the Navy, which had risen to $3.4 million in 1800 at the height of the Quasi War. Under the blade of Gallatin's stringent economies, this figure fell below $1 million by 1802, but the costs of the campaign against the Barbary powers confounded Jefferson's hopes for greater savings. Although there were no major shipbuilding programs under way, Navy appropriations increased to $1.4 million in 1805. Some of these costs were fixed, but fighting the Barbary pirates was not cheap. Although only six officers and fewer than one hundred sailors were killed in action, naval operations against the North African corsairs cost about $3 million—not counting the loss of the *Philadelphia*—between 1802 and 1806. By an accounting standard, Jefferson might have saved money and lives by paying more tribute. Indeed, Gallatin favored such a policy.

Jefferson, however, understood the foolishness of such a bloodless calculation. The Barbary Wars were popular at home, and Jefferson's principled position in defense of overseas trade burnished his contemporary reputation as a strong president. Nonetheless, after a landslide election in 1804, he wanted to reduce the expense of the faraway maritime embroglio. Soon after Navy Secretary Robert Smith learned that Tripoli had released Bainbridge and his crew, Jefferson decided to suspend most Mediterranean operations, and Smith was directed to order Rodgers to return home with his squadron in 1806. Although the Navy was withdrawing from the Mediterranean, the first Barbary War ended on a note of near-complete triumph.

Chapter Six

Jefferson, Madison, and the Great Powers
1801–1811

Jefferson stood firmly in defense of overseas trade during the first Barbary War, but he was more interested in westward territorial expansion. Over 50,000 Americans lived in the Ohio and Tennessee valleys in 1803, and that region was a hotbox of Democratic Republican politics. The West's prosperity depended on the American right to navigate the Mississippi and deposit cargo in New Orleans, rights obtained from Spain in 1796 in Pinckney's Treaty. However, in October 1802, the Spanish governor closed the port of New Orleans to American trade, an act that menaced not only westward expansion but also the entire American economy.

Behind Spain's move was Napoleon Bonaparte, who planned to reestablish France's North American empire along an axis leading from the granary of Louisiana to the slave-sugar islands of the French West Indies. After Spain changed sides in Europe's war and allied with France, Madrid realized that her Louisiana Territory was quite vulnerable to a British invasion. Moreover, Louisiana's principal value to Spain was its use as an uninhabited buffer between the United States and the Spanish viceroyalty of Mexico. Napoleon offered to solve Spain's problem—and not incidentally put his own plan into effect—by transferring Tuscany to Spain in return for Louisiana, an arrangement embodied in the secret Treaty of San Ildefonso in 1800. Soon after, in the Peace of Amiens of October 1801, the European war was suspended, giving

Napoleon an ideal opportunity to implement his North American plan.

Hints of France's new policy reached Jefferson soon after he took office, and he instantly recognized that it posed an appreciable strategic peril to the United States. New Orleans was "on the globe [the] one single spot, the possessor of which is our natural and habitual enemy," he wrote. Napoleon assembled a powerful French invasion force in Holland in 1802 and ordered it to prepare to strike across the Atlantic the following spring, establish a French presence in New Orleans, and accept the transfer of Louisiana from Spain. Jefferson understood that he had to move fast. The U.S. Army was quite small and the most of the fleet was already in the Mediterranean, so he had little means at hand to prevent the French from occupying New Orleans. Congress reacted to the threat by voting to increase the Army, and Hamilton urged Jefferson to reconsider his longstanding opposition to a military alliance with Britain. Gouverneur Morris, a New York Federalist, asked Congress to abandon Gallatin's economies and lay down a battle fleet that would "be respected by all of Europe." He argued that "the expense, compared with the benefit, is moderate, nay trifling."[1]

Jefferson was struggling to contain the crisis and cool this war fever, but he admitted that Hamilton was partly right. If Napoleon "takes possession of New Orleans," he confessed resignedly, "we must marry ourselves to the British fleet and nation." To prevent France from occupying New Orleans, he obtained from Congress the authority to send James Monroe to Paris to join Robert Livingston, the permanent minister to France. Monroe carried with him secret instructions from Jefferson to buy Louisiana for $10 million, or, should Napoleon turn down the offer, to sail to London to negotiate a military alliance with Britain. Before Monroe reached Paris, however, events in Europe and Haiti laid waste to Napoleon's plan.[2]

In late 1801, Napoleon had sent a large French army to Haiti to suppress Toussaint L'Ouverture's anti-French rebels and reimpose French rule over the whole island of Hispaniola. Jefferson had encouraged this policy at the time because he wanted to reintroduce French power into the Western Hemisphere to counterbalance Britain's preponderant influence. Haiti's ex-slaves and the fevers of their land decimated the French troops, however, and by November 1802 Napoleon had given up on his costly campaign to pacify the island. In addition he learned that the British Admiralty was planning to deploy its own invasion force to the Gulf of Mexico to prevent the transfer of Louisiana, and that Britain's diplomats were organizing another anti-French coalition on the Continent. This meant that Britain was intent on violating the Peace of Amiens and renewing the European war. Unwilling to invest more in his North American scheme, Napoleon announced that he would "cede the whole colony" of Louisiana "without reservation" to the United States. Although Jefferson's West Indies policy had backfired, his diplomats were well positioned to exploit Napoleon's about-face on Louisiana. On 2 May 1803, Livingston and Monroe signed the treaty of cession, and Jefferson soon overcame half-hearted Federalist opposition in Congress to an appropriation of $14.2 million for the immense new territory.[3]

Before Congress approved the Louisiana Purchase, Jefferson had devised a plan to deploy a squadron of shallow-draft gunboats to New Orleans, from where they could push up the Mississippi River and begin to extend American authority into the heart of the territory. He also outlined other measures to explore and settle the region, but defending Louisiana was his initial concern. Navy Secretary Smith had already recognized the need to establish a naval station in New Orleans, and at his request on 28 February 1803 Congress authorized the construction of ten 50-foot, 2-gun schooner-rigged gunboats. The Navy intended to lay down these vessels on the Ohio River and use them to secure the northern anchor of the Louisiana Purchase. When the gunboats were needed in the Mediterranean to reinforce Preble's squadron in 1804, Smith abandoned this plan, but the naval defense of Louisiana continued to worry the president. Clearly influenced by his study of recent European naval history, and perhaps by European galley designs, Jefferson renewed his request for a gunboat building program one year later, and on 2 March 1805 Congress authorized the construction of twenty-five more gunboats "for the better protection of the harbors, coasts, and commerce of the United States."[4]

Jefferson's initial purpose in building the gunboat fleet was to establish American forces in New Orleans and extend the United States into the Louisiana Territory. Of the first twenty-five vessels authorized, only sixteen were actually completed; most of them were deployed to New Orleans, while a few were sent north to naval stations on the rivers of the Ohio Valley. The need for the gunboats was soon evident. Captain John Shaw arrived in New Orleans in January 1806 with instructions to establish a naval station there and to construct a local defense force. Only one month later he received word of a conspiracy against the government led by former Vice President Aaron Burr and General James Wilkinson, the commanding general of the New Orleans garrison, who planned to create an independent western republic along the Mississippi Delta. Shaw took his flotilla upriver, appearing off Natchez with a few gunboats and bomb ketches in an attempt to threaten and overawe Burr's separatist supporters. Scared by the lack of popular support for the rebellion, Wilkinson soon betrayed Burr and arrested their collaborators in the Louisiana Territory. The conspiracy collapsed a few weeks later when Burr was indicted for treason in Virginia. Thereafter, the New Orleans Flotilla was engaged in suppressing Jean Lafitte's pirate gangs, which operated from Barataria Island, and in interdicting the slave trade from the West Indies to Louisiana, which Congress had outlawed in 1806.

Soon after crushing Burr's conspiracy, Jefferson faced the vexing problem of defending American neutral rights against Britain's naval mastery at sea. When the Peace of Amiens collapsed in late 1802 and Britain and France renewed their war, Jefferson promptly issued another declaration of American neutrality. He wanted to remain aloof from Europe's struggle for global power. However, he also threw over the long-standing Anglo-American rapprochement that had begun with Jay's Treaty and replaced Federalist Rufus King in London with Monroe, a pro-French Republican. Monroe was a clumsy diplomat. He not only antagonized Britain's leaders but also failed utterly to convince them not to adopt stiff measures to curtail neutral maritime rights. While the Anglo-American rapprochement was crumbling, the war in Europe was reaching a climax that resulted in a strategic stalemate. In 1805 Napoleon dropped his earlier plans to invade England and instead struck across Europe with his Grand Army. He crushed the Austrians and Russians at Ulm, destroyed the Prussians at Jena the following year, and in 1807 thrashed the Russians at Friedland, leaving France the master of western and central Europe. Meanwhile, the British had concentrated on eliminating the Franco-Spanish naval threat to their Channel flank. Off Cape Trafalgar on 20 October 1805, Admiral Horatio Nelson exploited superior British seamanship and gunnery to sink or capture over half of Admiral Villeneuve's combined fleet. Trafalgar left Britain with nearly absolute maritime ascendancy on Europe's periphery, and the Admiralty in London was eager to exploit this advantage against uncommitted neutrals.

The United States profited greatly from the French wars. Military manpower needs in Britain and Europe had reduced available farm labor, harvests declined, and the demand for imported American grains rose steadily during the Napoleonic wars. Cotton cloth was needed by all the belligerents, and the world's major source of raw cotton was the American South. In addition, shipping rates escalated for the carrying trade around Europe and drew American merchant mariners into a profitable enterprise hauling goods from the West Indies to Europe and between Europe's Atlantic and Mediterranean ports. Inasmuch as these ships were always in danger of being seized by one or another of the belligerents, few Americans quarreled with the abstract concept that trade defense was an essential cornerstone of the Republic's foreign policy. There was another factor that Jefferson had to consider, however. After Trafalgar and Austerlitz, the British cabinet settled on a strategy of employing the Royal Navy to wage a vigorous campaign of economic warfare against France. To avoid previous British trade regulations, French or Spanish goods had been loaded onto American ships in the West Indies. During the voyage to Europe, they would stop off at a neutral port, then sail on to their true destination. In the *Essex* decision of 1805, the British Admiralty outlawed this subterfuge and declared that neutral ships making "broken voyages" might be taken as prizes by blockading vessels of the Royal Navy.

Soon after the victory off Trafalgar and the *Essex* decision, the Admiralty increased the size of its patrol force off the American coast. On 26 April 1806, the British frigate *Leander*, stationed in New York harbor to check on shipping bound for French ports, attempted to stop and search the outbound American merchantman *Richard*; when she refused to submit, the *Leander*'s skipper ordered that a shot be fired across her bow. The shot was poorly aimed, and it killed an American sailor, John Pierce. "A country whose coasts were so much exposed," growled outraged Federalist Barent Gardenier, "and whose cities were so rich, so valuable, and therefore so tempting, should never be unprepared." An anti-British riot erupted in New York, and Jefferson was forced to issue a warrant for the arrest of the *Leander*'s captain for murder and to order all British warships out of New York harbor. Americans were humiliated by the continuous presence of British naval vessels in or near their territorial waters and by Jefferson's unwillingness or inability to do anything about it. "Because there is one leviathan in the ocean, shall every shark satiate his maw on our fatness with impunity?" Federalists asked. Jefferson did not completely disagree with this reasoning and privately admitted that "we should have a squadron properly composed to prevent the blockading of our ports." In fact, the *Leander* affair was so distressing that he confided to a political ally that "the building of some ships of the line . . . is not to be lost sight of."[5]

Jefferson reasoned, however, that the adoption of a capital ship policy was fraught with peril, since Britain's post-Trafalgar naval strategy was to allow no major maritime power to remain neutral. When neutral Denmark refused to give up her fleet to the Royal Navy in 1807, the British Army invaded Zealand and laid siege to Copenhagen while the Royal Navy took over the Danish fleet. The Copenhagen experience was etched in the minds of American statesmen, who feared that if the United States built capital ships, sooner or later the British would attack them. American sails-of-the-line would "be taken and added to the already overwhelming force of our enemy," and would "contribute nothing to our defence." Jefferson had never had much use for a fleet composed of frigates, which he judged to be useful for trade defense but strategically "indifferent" in a contest with Britain. With powerful British fleets of sails-of-the-line at Halifax and in the West Indies, even a large number of American frigates simply could not establish control over their own coastal waters. Jefferson was determined to strengthen the defenses of American harbors and improve his exposed flank in the Gulf of Mexico, however, and to do this he asked Congress in 1805 to build twenty-five more gunboats.[6]

Jefferson attempted to play down the *Leander* affair because at the moment Monroe and Pinckney were in London trying—unsuccessfully, it turned out—to persuade the British to curtail impressment. Because the treaty they negotiated made no mention of impressment, Jefferson refused to send it to the Senate. In 1806, London abandoned the last vestiges of the Anglo-American rapprochement and its earlier policy on neutral rights embodied in Jay's Treaty: by an Order in Council, the Royal Navy was instructed to close all ports in Europe from the mouth of the Elbe River to Brest by tight blockade. Another Order in Council, issued in

Jefferson's gunboats of the type that fought in the War of 1812.

January 1807, prohibited coastal trade between ports under French control. And in November, a third proclamation extended a total maritime blockade to any port in Europe from which the Union Jack was excluded and commanded all neutral ships to stop in Britain before they made for the Continent.

Napoleon, wrongly believing that France could prosper without overseas trade, retaliated with his Continental System. First, in the Berlin Decree of November 1806, he announced a blockade zone around the British Isles and ordered the French Fleet to seize any ship bound to or from Britain or any port within her empire. Then the Milan Decree of December 1807 declared that any neutral vessel honoring Britain's Orders in Council was a "good prize" for French warships or privateers. Although the French Navy could not enforce Napoleon's paper blockade of Britain—whereas the Royal Navy effectively shut down France's overseas trade—Napoleon's Continental System, by outlawing British trade with Europe, was a potent weapon aimed at Britain's manufacturing economy. The result of all this was that neutral shippers who obeyed the British Orders in Council were violating the Continental System, and vice versa. Since the British fleet controlled both the Atlantic and the Mediterranean, in practice neutral merchantmen who traded with Europe were in great danger unless they conformed to the Admiralty's dictates.

Britain's decision to deal stiffly with a wave of desertions from her fleets compounded Jefferson's problems. The British had taken sailors thought to be deserters from the Royal Navy off neutral merchantmen since 1793 and refused to respond to Washington's repeated complaints. Britain's desperate manpower situation added to the gravity of the problem. More American sailors were impressed into the Royal Navy between 1803 and 1806 than in the entire period from 1793 to 1801, and in 1806 the Admiralty announced that its fleet was being instructed to stop American warships and take off deserters, a practice to which the British had theretofore seldom resorted. It was about this time that Navy Secretary Smith decided to send the frigate *Chesapeake* on a brief cruise into the Mediterranean so that the frigate *Constitution* might return home for repairs. Commodore James Barron rode from Hampton Roads to Washington in February 1807 to inspect the *Chesapeake*, but after two months he returned to Norfolk, leaving the ship in the charge of Master Commandant Charles Gordon, who brought the frigate down the Chesapeake in June. Meanwhile Lieutenant Arthur Sinclair recruited a crew, and among the men who signed on were three deserters from the British ship *Melampus*, then attached to Vice Admiral G. C. Berkeley's North American fleet. Berkeley formally protested to the State Department, demanding that the deserters be returned to his custody, but Captain Stephen Decatur, commandant of the Norfolk Navy Yard, reported that the trio were really Americans who had been unjustly impressed into the British fleet before making their escape. Berkeley was livid when he learned that they would not be returned, and he was determined not to return the three to his command.

Signing on British deserters was a well-known practice of the U.S. Navy. Several British officers had complained that U.S. Navy recruiters induced English sailors to desert to American ships during the Barbary Wars, and a French diplomat once charged that half of the hostages from the *Philadelphia* imprisoned by Tripoli were British deserters. The two countries' approaches to the issue of citizenship compounded the problem. Once an Englishman pledged allegiance to the United States, American law held him to be a naturalized citizen. The British, however, regarded him still as a lifelong subject of King George and denounced the American practice as nothing more than a formula to help British deserters avoid capture and condign punishment. Impressment became a serious problem after the French wars broke out in 1793, but Washington tried to solve it with Jay's Treaty. When the British frigate *Carnatic* impressed five American sailors off the American warship *Baltimore* off Cuba in 1798, Adams was preoccupied with the Quasi War. He dismissed Captain Isaac Philips from the Navy for allowing his ship to be boarded but refused to allow the incident to damage the Anglo-American rapprochement. Jefferson had limply protested Britain's impressment policy soon after he entered the White House, but he did no more about it until 1807.

On a beautiful Sunday afternoon in June 1807, Commodore Barron was piped on board the *Chesapeake* and she sailed out of the Chesapeake Bay en route to Gibraltar. Off Lynn Haven Bay, the watch sighted two British warships riding at anchor. Soon the British frigate *Leopard* stood out to sea and, keeping the weather gage, began to run down on the American ship. A surprisingly nonchalant Barron did nothing to prepare his ship for a sea fight, even when it was reported to him that the tompions were being removed from the *Leopard*'s guns. Only after a British officer came on board the *Chesapeake* did Barron become worried. At this point he ordered his crew to general quarters, but the decks were littered with gear and the sailors could do little at this late moment to ready the ship for battle. The *Leopard* aimed several shots across the *Chesapeake*'s bow, drew alongside, and fired her broadsides. Barron struck his colors. A British party came on board and took off not only the three known deserters but also another sailor whom they suspected of desertion, but the *Leopard*'s captain refused to accept Barron's surrender and allowed the American ship to limp back to Hampton Roads in disgrace.

A wave of public indignation spread along the Atlantic seaboard with the news of the *Chesapeake-Leopard* affair, which became a symbol of the nation's humiliation. A court-martial presided over by Commodore John Rodgers found Barron guilty of "neglecting on the probability of an engagement to clear his Ship for action," and he was suspended from the Navy for five years. Not since the Revolution had Jefferson "seen the country in such a state of exasperation." He believed that London would disavow Admiral Berkeley's action. He also feared that if he asked Congress to declare war, then the Royal Navy, fresh from Trafalgar, would bottle up the Mediterranean Squadron, mop up America's overseas trade, and slap a blockade on the Atlantic seaboard.

When a British warship shot at an American cutter carrying Vice President George P. Clinton just a few days later, Jefferson kept his calm. Congress was not scheduled to meet until October, and he refused to call a special session that summer. He first sent an official protest over the *Chesapeake* affair in particular and British maritime policy in general to London. The Admiralty relieved Berkeley, but promoted him at the same time, which only made matters worse. Next, Jefferson recalled the Mediterranean Squadron to home waters. To pressure the British to respect America's neutral rights and end impressment, he finally decided to wage economic warfare against Britain, and France as well. To do this, he had the Democratic Republicans in Congress hastily pass a Non-Importation Act excluding Britain's goods from America's ports.[7]

Jefferson also convinced Congress to pass an authorization bill, introduced in February 1807, to construct 188 more gunboats for harbor defense. About half of these vessels were laid down in New York, Philadelphia, and Baltimore, but the rest were built in the southern ports of Norfolk, Charleston, and Beaufort. Protecting ports, coastal settlements, and inlets was one of Jefferson's major military concerns, and he believed that the gunboat policy met the political goals of efficiency and republicanism and would produce efficient local defense forces. Deployed in harbors and operated in conjunction with shore batteries, the gunboats were to "oppose an enemy at his entrance and cooperate with the batteries for his expulsion." Manned by "the seamen and militia of the port," the gunboats tacked American naval policy away from the seagoing naval aristocracy that Jefferson so distrusted and toward a force dependent not upon the skills of an elite but rather on the meritorious patriotism of the citizenry.[8]

Despite his anger with the Royal Navy over the *Chesapeake-Leopard* affair, Jefferson did not seek war, hoping instead to pressure London into agreeing to accept the American interpretation of neutral maritime rights. "Measures short of war will prevail," Madison assured Pinckney, "with an extension of preparations and arrangements for the event of war." Jefferson sent Monroe to London in April 1807, but the British refused to negotiate on impressment or to modify their blockade regulations, and Napoleon rejected the idea that he abandon his Continental System. To strengthen his hand, Jefferson convinced Congress to pass the

Embargo Act, which prohibited any maritime trade with Europe. The president ordered the few ships left in the fleet to enforce this self-imposed blockade by seizing any American vessel carrying goods bound for Europe. "During the summer [of 1808] all the gunboats . . . should be distributed through as many ports and bays as may be necessary to assist the embargo," Jefferson told Secretary Smith. In all this there was a political paradox. New England opposed the Embargo Act despite the fact that her shipping was the primary target of the maritime policies of the European belligerents. Consequently, enforcement of the act was uneven, prosecutions difficult, and convictions few. In the end the Embargo Act devastated New England's economy and solidified the Federalist grip on the region's politics.[9]

The Federalists failed to seize the moment during the elections of 1808, however, and Republican James Madison won his first term in the White House. Dour and scholarly, he had been a brilliant political operative during the Federalist era, but as president he was plagued by divisions within his own party and an inability to unite men behind hard policies. Even before Madison took office, Jefferson had realized that his Embargo Act was hurting the American economy more than it was influencing Britain or France, and under noisy pressure from the maritime states he allowed Congress to repeal it in March 1809.

Madison, like Jefferson, sought a diplomatic solution to the crisis with Europe and soon after he took office agreed to negotiations with David Erskine, the British minister in Washington, who convinced him that London would repeal the Orders in Council if the United States resumed trading with Britain. Madison hastily lifted all restraints on American trade only to learn to his chagrin that Erskine did not possess the authority to make the deal he had negotiated. The British government repudiated the arrangement, and the Erskine fiasco redounded to the discredit of Madison's administration. Next, Madison proposed to renew the undeclared commerce war against one or more of the European powers unless the harassment of American shipping ended, and he asked Congress for the power to "cause to be issued . . . letters of marque and reprisal against the nation therefore continuing in force its unlawful edicts against the commerce of the U.S." Although a bill containing this authority passed the House in 1809, the stiff provision was excised after Congress settled on a compromise measure to adopt a policy of selective nonintercourse.[10]

In 1810, Georgia Congressman Nathanial Macon introduced two bills intended to lever Britain into conceding on the neutral rights issues. Madison signed Macon's Bill No. 2, which reopened trade with both France and Britain but stipulated that nonimportation would be imposed again on one warring power if the other promised not "to violate the neutral commerce of the United States." Macon had unwittingly led Madison into a trap. In 1811, Napoleon told Madison that France would respect American rights if Washington embargoed trade with Britain unless she revoked the Orders in Council. Madison naively accepted the offer and asked Congress to enact it into law. The British, who had never intended the dispute over neutral rights to lead to war, hastily suspended the Orders on 16 June 1812, but this more moderate policy came altogether too late.[11]

Madison's naval policy did not reflect the rising tide for war. Navy Secretary Paul Hamilton, who replaced Smith in 1809, was a drunken North Carolina planter who did not have the confidence of Congress or other members of Madison's cabinet. As a result of this lack of leadership and the Jeffersonians' general anti-Navy bias, the fleet deteriorated during Madison's first term just as tensions between London and Washington drew taut. Within months of the *Chesapeake-Leopard* affair, there were only two American frigates and four smaller vessels ready for sea duty; this number remained fairly stable for the next five years. The only augmentation of the fleet was the addition of nearly 200 gunboats, which cost roughly $1 million to construct and created an appetite for funds for maintenance and repairs that discouraged most earlier supporters of the gunboat policy.

When Madison took office in 1809, Congress passed an act restricting warships to cruises in American waters, and the following year Democratic Republicans from the western states demanded that appropriations for the Navy Department be reduced once again. Even Paul Hamilton understood the folly of these policies. He pointed out to Congress in 1809 that the gunboats were useful, but only for passive, static harbor defense, and proposed instead to lay down new squadrons of "fast sailing frigates" whose peacetime maintenance "would be much less costly" than the great sums already spent on the gunboats. Hamilton did not fully explain his plan, and it was not seriously considered by Congress, despite the increasing tension over maritime issues between Washington and London.[12]

Macon's Bill No. 2 did nothing to lessen the Royal Navy's presence in American waters. In 1811, the Admiralty dispatched the frigate *Guerrière* to the North American Squadron with orders to patrol off New York, stop and search American merchantmen for cargoes bound for France, and inspect the crews for British deserters. On station in early May, she intercepted and searched the American brig *Spitfire* and took off a passenger, John Deguyo, a native of New York. Again there was a public outcry. Critics heaped scorn on Madison's timid maritime policy, although he had already instructed Secretary Hamilton to deploy Captain John Rodgers in the frigate *President* to hunt down the *Guerrière* and prevent her from harassing any more American merchantmen. At dawn on 12 May 1811, the *President* left Annapolis and cleared the Virginia Capes a few days later in search of the British frigate. At noon on 16 May, Rodgers sighted the 22-gun British warship *Little Belt* and, believing her to be the *Guerrière*, pursued her into the night around Cape Hatteras. After several broadsides were exchanged in the darkness, it was apparent that the Englishman was a far inferior opponent. Rodgers stood off, and the next morning offered to help with the wounded aboard the *Little Belt.*

The British were incensed over the *Little Belt* incident, but Americans viewed it as just retaliation for the humiliations their ships had suffered at the hands of the Royal Navy. Even the most hotheaded American and British commanders understood the need for restraint, however. Like Rodgers, Captain Stephen Decatur in the frigate *United States* was under orders to patrol off New York to protect American shipping. Near the harbor, he closed on two British warships but, unfortunately, while they were exchanging hails an American gunner mistakenly pulled his lanyard and discharged his cannon. Decatur, who did not want to start a war with an error, hastily apologized, and nothing came of the episode.

The skids to war were greased by other issues. After General William Henry Harrison crushed Chief Tecumseh's rebellion at Tippecanoe, Indiana, in 1811, he recovered British arms on the battlefield, confirming American suspicions that British officials in Canada intended to support the creation of an Indian buffer state in the Ohio Valley. Enraged westerners demanded that Congress declare war against Britain, invade Canada, and purge the threat of this coalition to the frontier. Southerners also saw an opportunity for territorial expansion. Napoleon's 1806 occupation of Spain had led to the creation of a Bourbon government-in-exile, which allied itself to Britain, and without a strong regime to protect it, Spanish Florida was now a tempting target for expansionists in the Carolinas and Georgia.

In spite of these diverse strains between Washington and London, Madison did little to prepare for war. Having lost his attempt to get Congress to lay down new warships in 1809, Secretary of the Navy Hamilton did not raise the issue of naval expansion again until November 1811, when he asked Congress to authorize a new coastal defense fleet of a dozen sails-of-the-line and twenty frigates. The House Naval Affairs Committee cut this program to ten frigates and enjoined the Navy to limit its operations to the "defense of your ports and harbors, and the protection of your coasting trade." Partly this reduction reflected the confused state of prewar politics. The Federalists, whose main strength was in New England, usually favored a strong Navy, but New Englanders opposed war with Britain and many Federalists used their vote against Hamilton's program to register their opposition to the western "warhawks." Western and southern Republicans were clamoring for war while opposing naval expansion. House Speaker Henry Clay of Kentucky, the leading warhawk, favored building a fleet that could win "command of our own seas" but felt it was "madness" to build against a British standard. At most, he wanted a fleet of twelve sails-of-the-line and fifteen frigates, but voted against the 1812 building plan because Congress had just passed a costly Army bill. On a close vote, Congress in January struck the ten frigates from the 1812 Naval Act, but compromised by authorizing repairs to the old frigates and appropriating funds to purchase timber to be stockpiled for future Navy construction.[13]

Hanging over the debate about peace or war was the public's deep sense of humiliation over British policy. Americans realized the gravity of war with Britain, but saw no alternative. "Because we cannot maintain our rights against the strong," asked Federalist Josiah Quincy of Massachusetts, "shall we be insulted and invite plunder from the weak?" Even Jefferson, who had ignored the issue of national honor in 1807, argued five years later that "war or abject submission are the only alternatives left to us." Before learning that Britain was suspending the Orders in Council, Madison asked Congress to declare war. "British cruisers have been . . . violating the American flag on the great highway of nations . . . and violating the rights and peace of our coast," he declared. Denouncing further appeasement, he admitted that his policy of "moderation and conciliation have had no other effect than to encourage [British] perseverance and to enlarge pretensions." After voting not to build new ships, the warhawks of the South and West decided to fight, and on 4 June 1812 a sharply divided Congress enacted a resolution declaring war on Great Britain.[14]

Chapter Seven

The War of 1812

1812–1813

On 18 June 1812, when President Madison reluctantly signed the declaration of war against Britain, neither the Army nor the Navy was prepared for the contest. In April, Speaker of the House Henry Clay had forced Madison to call up the militia, but the regular Army totaled only 6,700 troops. Congress voted to increase the Army by 35,000 regulars and 50,000 volunteers. The War Department was poorly equipped to manage the Army, and Madison lacked the initiative and daring needed to direct a major war, although he easily won a second term in the White House in November. Moreover, when hostilities opened, the nation was badly divided, with New England bitterly opposing the war.

The first days of the War of 1812 found Navy Secretary Paul Hamilton trying in vain to mobilize the fleet with the aid of Chief Clerk Louis Goldsborough and only nine assistants. At the time, the Navy included seven frigates, two corvettes, two brigs, and four schooners, and 5,025 officers and men. The sole Navy yard, Norfolk, lacked a drydock and other facilities to refit warships. To make matters worse, the British burned the city soon after the war began. The Royal Navy, on the other hand, operated large dockyards in North America—at Nova Scotia, Bermuda, and Jamaica in the West Indies—making Britain's shore establishment far superior to America's. Overall, the Royal Navy was stronger: in 1812 Britain deployed over 1,000 ships totaling 860,990 tons manned by more than 150,000 officers and men. William Jones, Hamilton's successor at the Navy Department, observed that "the whole funds of government would not defend every point of our extensive coast." On the positive side, most of Britain's ships were busy blockading Europe or watching the North Sea, the Channel, the Irish Sea, or the Mediterranean, and when the War of 1812 broke out, the Admiralty had few reserves to send to North American waters.

Part of prewar thinking about going to war with Britain was the idea of annexing Canada. Jefferson, considering strategy in the midst of the *Chesapeake-Leopard* affair in 1807, dictated to his secretary his notion that "the first blow will . . . be directed against Canada." Madison adopted this as his basic strategy, but Federalist antiwar sentiment doomed it from the start. Madison wanted an army to march north from the Hudson River via Lake Champlain and the Richelieu River and attack Montreal, but when New England's governors refused to allow their state militias to cross into Canada, he decided to seek victory in the northwest. In July, General William Hull crossed from Detroit into Canada, but his troops could not be supplied because a Royal Navy flotilla controlled Lake Erie. To the south at Fort Malden, Britain's main base, General Isaac Brock commanded a regiment of British regulars and a war party of Chief Tecumseh's Indians; when they moved against Hull, he fell back and instructed the Fort Dearborn garrison to evacuate its position. With two fronts in seeming collapse, Hull panicked and on 16 August 1812 surrendered Detroit to the British without firing a shot. Madison now sent for General William Henry Harrison, who rode north, reorganized American troops in the Northwest Territory, and stabilized the front by December.[1]

The second prong of the American offensive had already gotten under way in October, when General Stephen Van Rensselaer took Queenston, Canada, but the state militias again refused to cross the border to reinforce his line. General Brock's Redcoats then arrived on the scene, recovered Queenston, and drove Van Rensselaer back across the frontier. A third American force lunged into Canada in November 1812, led by General Henry Dearborn. He marched north to Rouse's Point in an attempt to take Montreal, but when his militiamen also refused to cross the border Dearborn had to withdraw and make camp for the winter. The failure of the northern offensive left Madison's Canadian strategy in disarray, and in early 1813 the British prepared for a major counteroffensive against the Northwest Territory and New England.

Things went better for a short time on the Atlantic front. Soon after Congress declared war, Madison adopted a maritime strategy of commerce raiding that among other things called for an energetic privateering campaign. As in the Revolutionary War, privateering was quite successful. During the War of 1812 more than 500 commissions were issued to privateers, who seized roughly 1,300 British prizes. Madison expected the Navy not only to attack enemy commerce but also to defend American ports and coastal shipping and prevent the British from landing troops along the eastern seaboard. How all this was to be done with such a small fleet vexed Secretary Hamilton. Commodore John Rodgers, the Navy's senior officer, proposed to take a large squadron to sea immediately, to raid commerce in the West Indies and so unhinge Britain's naval strategy. On the other hand, Captain Stephen Decatur argued that large squadron operations would risk the entire fleet if a superior British force caught the Americans at sea. Decatur's motives were not altogether military—he disliked serving under Rodgers and he wanted an independent command. Prodded by Madison, Hamilton sided with Rodgers, who assembled his squadron in New York one month before Congress declared war. Concerning the "disposition" of his squadron, Hamilton declared, Rodgers should "consult your own best judgement." He could operate "all in squadron or otherwise as in your opinion may be most expedient."[2]

On the day Congress declared war, a rider left Washington headed for New York. Seventy-two hours later, he handed Hamilton's orders to Commodore Rodgers, who within hours put to sea with a squadron consisting of the frigates *President, United States,* and *Congress,* the sloop *Hornet,* and the brig *Argus.* His objective was to attack a fleet of 100 British merchantmen known to be sailing from Jamaica to Canada. As the Americans headed south, however, Rodgers in the *President* sighted the British frigate *Belvidera,* decided to take her on, and so left the American formation and began to run her down. The two vessels engaged at 1620 on 23 June, when Rodgers personally fired the first shot of the War of 1812. After a gun duel lasting four hours, both ships were damaged, and the British frigate fled. Rodgers, whose handling of the battle was uneven, then rejoined the squadron, and the Americans resumed their vain pursuit of the Jamaican fleet across the North

Atlantic. A few orange peels were found in the water on 1 July, but Rodgers had long since lost his prey. Dejected, he stood off the English Channel on 13 July, sailed south around the Madeiras, and then shaped a course for home.

Ironically, Rodgers' frustrating cruise unwittingly served an important strategic purpose. Hard upon the declaration of war, a messenger from Boston had sailed to European waters to warn American merchantmen of the impending hostilities. From his command at Halifax, Vice Admiral Herbert Sawyer intended to deploy one British warship off each Atlantic port to seize American ships when they returned home to seek refuge. Before this British operation began, however, the *Belvidera* made Halifax, Sawyer was warned that Rodgers' squadron was at sea, and he deployed his entire fleet off the port of New York to engage the Americans upon their return. Wrongly positioned, the Halifax Fleet missed Rodgers' squadron, which put into Boston on 26 August with only seven small prizes.

Disappointment over Rodgers' cruise, and the threatening deployment of the Halifax Fleet, convinced Secretary Hamilton to accept Decatur's argument and to adopt a strategy of challenging British operations and commerce raiding with single units or squadrons of only two or three ships. For the remainder of the war, no large American squadron sailed into the Atlantic. To implement this new strategy, Hamilton divided the fleet into three cruising elements. Under Rodgers he established a Northern Cruising Squadron comprising the frigates *President* and *Congress*; under Decatur were the frigate *United States* and the brig *Argus*, making up the Azores Squadron; and a South Atlantic Squadron was put under Commodore Bainbridge, with the frigates *Constitution* and *Essex* and the sloop *Hornet*.

Decatur was the next to put to sea. After refitting the *United States*, he sailed eastward from Boston in October and cruised between the Azores and Canary Islands. When dawn rose on the morning of 25 October, a lookout spotted the British frigate *Macedonian*. There was more than a bit of irony in this encounter. Decatur had met the British captain, John Carden, during the first Barbary War, and they had talked about the relative fighting qualities of their ships. Carden insisted on the superiority of his gun crews, who could handle the agile 18-pounders better than the Americans could work the heavier 24-pounders carried by the *United States*. Moreover, the American frigate was much less maneuverable than the *Macedonian*. When they closed to do battle, Carden had the windward gage, but at first he mistook the *United States* for the smaller *Essex*, and he failed to bear down on his opponent. This error permitted Decatur to stand off and batter the *Macedonian* into submission. When he boarded her he found "fragments of dead scattered in every direction, the decks slippery with blood, one continuous agonizing yell of the unhappy wounded." This "scene . . . deprived me very much of the pleasure of victory."[3]

In June Hamilton had attached Captain David Porter in the *Essex* to Rodgers' squadron, but Porter was not ready to sail when Rodgers departed. Twelve days later, Porter left New York to search for a British frigate carrying gold from South America. He missed this prey but took several other small prizes. On 11 July he chanced upon a convoy of British storeships and troop transports bound for Quebec, escorted by the warship *Minerva*. He ran in his guns, concealed his men, hauled down his colors, and at 0300 fell in with the convoy, disguised as a merchantman. In the darkness he cut out and captured one of the brigs with 200 soldiers on board. He cleared his decks for action at daybreak, but the *Minerva*'s skipper wisely declined to engage. The British convoy continued on to Quebec, while Porter turned to the south. Porter next came upon the enemy sloop *Alert*, tricked her captain into attacking the *Essex* by pretending to run away, then reduced the luckless British vessel to a wreck in eight minutes. Porter was already having trouble handling the large number of prisoners on board his ship, however, so he disarmed the *Alert*, put the prisoners on board, and allowed her to sail for Quebec under parole. He briefly chased one more British warship and then sailed for home. He reached the Delaware Bay in September after capturing nine prizes and 500 prisoners and freeing five American merchantmen and privateers.

The *Essex* was not the only ship that was unready to sail with Rodgers' squadron, for Captain Isaac Hull was still fitting out the 44-gun frigate *Constitution* in Annapolis when war was declared. To avoid being bottled up in the Chesapeake Bay by a British blockade, Hull sailed in mid-July for New York, but the *Constitution* was nearly taken off the coast of New Jersey by a British squadron, and he decided to shape a course for Boston. After replenishing there, Hull took advantage of a westerly breeze and stood out to sea on 2 August heading for the Gulf of St. Lawrence. There he captured

The frigate *Constitution* in action during the War of 1812.

Commodore William Bainbridge.

several British prizes before he got word from an American privateer that a British frigate was operating in the area. Hull decided not to return to American waters but instead to remain at sea, intending either to hunt down this lone enemy vessel or to further disrupt British trade in the area. He justified this dangerous course of action by explaining to Secretary Hamilton that "the force of the enemy is so superior on our coast that it is impossible to cruise with any hope of escaping them, . . . where by cruising off the [Canadian] coast we may do them great injury."[4]

The *Constitution* was heading south about 700 miles east of Boston when, on 19 August 1812, she was sighted by Captain James R. Dacres in the 38-gun British frigate *Guerrière*, then bound for Halifax for repairs. For three hours Hull bore down on the enemy until Dacres decided to fight rather than flee. The American's broadside was superior to her opponent's and the English ship was seriously undermanned, but Dacres counted on his veteran gun crews to win the battle. By retiring with the wind, he repeatedly crossed the track of the *Constitution*, firing a different broadside at every chance. Hull with superior throwweight, also played to his strengths. He maneuvered to avoid raking fire from the *Guerrière* and bore down on the inferior ship, whose aim was less sure than the American's. After a remorseless gun duel, Hull closed and shot away the enemy's foremast and mainmast. Soon, he later reported, she was "entirely disabled." Dacres struck his colors that evening. The British crew, less fifteen dead, were removed, and the *Guerrière*, "a perfect wreck," according to Isaac Hull, was burned the next day.[5]

When Hull returned to Boston, he turned over command of the *Constitution* to Commodore Bainbridge, who had been ordered to hunt down British shipping in the South Atlantic and around the Cape. In company with the *Hornet*, he stood out of Boston on 26 October 1812, expecting Porter in the *Essex* to rendezvous with his squadron at Rio de Janeiro. Leaving the *Hornet* off San Salvador in mid-December, Bainbridge was heading south on 29 December when he sighted the 38-gun British frigate *Java*, en route to the British station in the Indian Ocean. As the ships closed, Bainbridge enjoyed a slight advantage: a larger crew plus superior broadside throwweight. During the preliminary maneuvers, however, Captain Henry Lambert demonstrated that his was the more agile vessel. Crisscrossing each other's track during a battle that lasted over two hours, both ships fought a fearsome gun duel, which ended only after Bainbridge had been twice wounded and Lambert lay dead on his quarterdeck. The better-trained American gun crews took advantage of their superior broadsides and reduced the *Java* to a burning wreck before she finally struck her colors. On the other hand, Lambert's broadsides had inflicted tremendous damage on the *Constitution*, and Bainbridge decided to abandon his cruise and return to Boston for repairs. However, Captain James Lawrence in the sloop *Hornet* remained on station in the South Atlantic into the new year. After evading a British 74-gun sail-of-the-line, he captured one Royal Navy brig carrying gold and defeated the 18-gun enemy brig *Peacock* during a bitter, short engagement off the mouth of the Demarara River on 24 February 1813.

Despite the success of the American squadrons during the first six months of the war, Hamilton was severely criticized by Congress for his inept administration of the Navy Department; at the end of 1812, he was forced out of office. To replace him, Madison turned to former Congressman William Jones, a Democratic Republican from Pennsylvania, who had strongly supported the declaration of war. In early 1813, Secretary Jones took a firm grip on naval policy and strategy. Congress was so elated by the frigate victories that on 2 January, one day after Jones took office, it authorized the construction of four 74-gun sails-of-the-line and another six 44-gun frigates. However, Jones had to remind his senior captains one month later that "our great inferiority in naval strength does not permit us to meet them" in a squadron action "without hazarding the precious gem of our national glory." Although he initially favored the development of a battle fleet, Jones soon recognized that the United States simply lacked the shipbuilding resources to accomplish this in wartime. Nonetheless, to please Congress, he started work on the sails-of-the-line *Washington, Independence,* and *Franklin,* and the three frigates *Java, Columbia,* and *Guerrière.*[6]

Jones dispersed slowly the money for these costly vessels, however. Instead he adopted a vigorous strategy of commerce raiding supported by a naval policy of laying down a large number of swift, smaller vessels that could be built quickly. At his urging, on 3 March 1813 Congress authorized the construction of six sloops of the *Wasp* class. The operational success of the *Wasp,* which slipped past the blockade and cruised in British waters in 1814, inspired Jones to ask Congress later that year for authorization to build another twenty vessels of this type, each armed with about sixteen guns, but few of these ships got to sea during the war.

Jones turned next to the problem of defending the nation's harbors. When the War of 1812 began, Jefferson's gunboat program was complete, with active and reserve flotillas assigned to most major ports, but the fighting characteristics of the gunboats were uneven and repairing them was expensive. Most were 50 feet long, 18 feet wide, and displaced 90 tons; each was armed with one 32-pound long gun and was manned by a crew of one officer and twenty to fifty men. Because the gunboat drew only three feet, close to the shoreline a gunboat flotilla enjoyed a tremendous advantage over enemy frigates, schooners, or sloops. However, they needed a flat calm in which to operate, they were difficult to fight in even a normal chop, and with just a light wind the recoil of the gun rocked the vessel dangerously. Although Jones complained that the gunboats were "scattered about in every creek and corner as receptacles of idleness and objects of waste and extravagance without utility," they performed more effectively than he or many Navy men expected. The gunboat flotillas effectively escorted convoys of coasters through dangerous waters and kept British privateers and other small enemy craft from putting landing parties ashore at will. They also consistently prevented single British vessels from raiding or indiscriminately bombarding American coastal towns. Although the gunboat flotillas were poorly managed and proved to be unattractive duty for naval officers during the war, their mere presence threatened every British vessel smaller than a sail-of-the-line. Over the course of the War of 1812, they were responsible for seizing a large number of important enemy prizes in shallow waters.[7]

During the latter part of 1812, Lieutenant Oliver Hazard Perry's gunboat flotilla patrolled off Newport, Rhode Island, a pattern of operations that was duplicated by the New York-based flotilla, which successfully checked several small British raids in Long Island Sound. Massed formations of American gunboats were often fought audaciously. On 9 October 1813, for instance, twenty-six American gunboats attacked the British frigate *Acasta* and the sloop *Atalanta* at sea in a brisk action that ended only when a storm compelled both sides to retire. One month later, on 13 November, the sail-of-the-line *Plantagenet*, on blockade station off New York, sent some escorting schooners on a chase after the American merchantman *Sparrow*, and they succeeded in running her aground. A

British landing party rowed ashore to take the prize, but local American gunboats arrived on the scene, recovered the *Sparrow*, drove off a number of British gun barges, and even captured one of the enemy schooners. Six months later, on 19 May 1814, the 74-gun sail-of-the-line *Valiant* was bearing down on the American brig *Regent* near Sandy Hook when Commodore Jacob Lewis put his experienced flotilla of eleven gunboats between the brig and her pursuer and began to chase the British ship, allowing the *Regent* to reach port safely. Owing to the presence of these gunboats, throughout the War of 1812 no British warship ever approached an American harbor or shoreline with impunity.

On the other hand, Jones realized that not even the ubiquitous gunboats could defend the nation's entire coastline. Moreover, he was disenchanted with the cost of maintaining the gunboats and so decided to consolidate these dispersed forces into a

U.S. Naval Institute

Commodore Isaac Hull. On 19 August 1812, Hull's frigate, the *Constitution*, defeated the *Guerrière* in one of the most notable single-ship engagements of the War of 1812.

smaller number of flotillas. On 15 March 1813, he ordered all the gunboats north of Boston to be laid up, the crews paid off, and the officers assigned to other duty. To strengthen the consolidated gunboat flotillas in the South, Jones turned to Congress and obtained funds to build over seventy gun barges, stable 70-foot-long platforms armed with two large guns "for the defense of ports and harbors." Thirty-two gun barges were completed in Baltimore, Washington, Norfolk, Charleston, and New Orleans by early 1814, and another thirty-eight were under construction. With "one or more floating batteries," Jones intended the gun barge flotillas to "attack, repel, or destroy" British ships that threatened their stations. Jones tried to establish at least one squadron in each major port, comprising one frigate or sloop supported by a gunboat and gun barge flotilla. Nevertheless, Jones' major concern was the Great Lakes theater, where the collapse of Madison's Canadian strategy a year earlier created an opportunity for the British to launch a counteroffensive. Risking the wrath of the coastal cities, Jones established powerful fighting squadrons on Lake Ontario, Lake Erie, and Lake Champlain, and sent his best younger officers north to take command of these stations.[8]

Jones was fully aware that the war was not going well. Although the Navy won five of nine single-ship engagements in 1812, American losses took about one-fifth of the seagoing fleet. British pride was stung by these defeats, but the power and majesty of the Royal Navy had been barely scratched. In Europe the tide of war turned in Britain's favor when the Russians forced Napoleon to retreat from Moscow in 1812. Wellington evicted the French from Spain the following year and then crossed into France. France's fleet was almost totally blockaded in port, and the Royal Navy now had a ready surplus of warships to send to North American waters.

Lord Liverpool's cabinet first adopted a strategy of trying to mop up the American frigates and privateers and to clear the Atlantic of American trade, then turned to blockading the eastern seaboard. By the end of 1812, several powerful British squadrons were deployed in the West Indies to end American privateering and commerce raiding there, and Vice Admiral Warren, a more militant leader, was assigned to Halifax to relieve Admiral Sawyer. "The naval force of the enemy should be quickly and completely disposed of," the Admiralty firmly instructed Warren. In January 1813, he stretched the Royal Navy's blockade of the American coastline from New York to the Carolinas, established a blockade station off New Orleans, and later extended his area of operations

to include Long Island Sound. And with more ships assigned to
North American waters came new directions from the Admiralty
to avoid single-ship engagements with the U.S. Navy's dangerous
frigates.[9]

American naval captains, unable to challenge the British
blockade, chafed at their inability to get to sea. The *Constellation*,
for example, was bottled up in Norfolk for the entire war. However, more than once the bitch goddess of honor tempted an
American captain to his doom. Captain James Lawrence, who had
commanded the sloop *Hornet* off Brazil, was greeted in Boston as
a hero and received command of the 38-gun frigate *Chesapeake*.
Secretary Jones ordered him to raid British shipping off Canada's
coast, but he had difficulty recruiting a crew in Boston owing to
competition from privateers, and most of the men who signed on
were inexperienced landsmen. Off Boston stood the 38-gun
British frigate *Shannon*, whose veteran commanding officer, Captain Philip Broke, contemptuously dismissed the other British
frigate in his squadron and taunted Lawrence by marching back
and forth at the mouth of the harbor—a violation of the Admiralty's secret order to avoid single-ship duels with the deadly American frigates.

Lawrence, young and headstrong, took the bait and hoisted
anchor on 1 June to sail out and accept Broke's challenge. He had
no idea of what ship or which captain he was about to fight; although had he been aware of Broke's formidable reputation, it
probably would have made little difference to him. Both ships
cleared Boston Light with the *Shannon* in the lead, and for the
next five hours Lawrence chased the Englishman eastward across
the bay until both men were satisfied that they had enough sea
room to maneuver. Then, at 1700, they closed to within fifty yards
of one another, reduced sail, and opened fire. The *Shannon*'s
fierce broadsides, manned by well-trained veterans, overpowered
and badly damaged the *Chesapeake* and she soon lost steering control. Four helmsmen were killed in succession. Unmanageable,
the *Chesapeake* exposed her port quarter to the *Shannon*'s raking
fire. Someone in the *Shannon*'s topworks tossed a grenade into the
Chesapeake's ammunition locker, and the resulting explosion
wreathed her in smoke. Lawrence, mortally wounded by musket
fire, was taken below shouting, "Fight her 'till she sinks, and don't
give up the ship." At the time, Broke was leading a boarding party
onto the *Chesapeake*'s quarterdeck. "In two minutes time the ene-

my were driven sword in hand from every post" and the American struck her colors, he reported soon after. The *Chesapeake*'s loss was the cause of Secretary Jones' decision to abandon single-ship engagements. "It is not even good policy to meet any equal," he warned Commodore Rodgers, "unless under special circumstances where a great object is to be gained without sacrifice. His commerce is our true game, for there he is indeed vulnerable."[10]

This strategy was behind the decision to send Bainbridge in the *Constitution* into the South Atlantic, where he met up with the *Java*. Captain David Porter in the *Essex* was supposed to rendezvous with Bainbridge, but he was late getting under way, and when he arrived off Brazil, he learned that the *Constitution* had been damaged and reasoned that Bainbridge had returned home for repairs. His orders gave him two choices. He might cruise off St. Helena and attack British ships coming up from the Cape of Good Hope, or he might round Cape Horn, enter the Pacific, and attack Britain's trade there. As consumed by the search for glory and wealth as any of his contemporaries, Porter decided on the latter course. Thus, after a "boisterous" passage through the Straits of Magellan, the *Essex* earned the honor of being the first American warship to enter the Pacific Ocean.

After provisioning at Valparaíso, Chile, where he made friends with the local dictator, who was rebelling against Spain, Porter sailed for the Galápagos Islands off the coast of Ecuador, the center of the British whaling industry in the Pacific. Between April and October 1813, the *Essex*, whose 32-gun broadside allowed Porter to rampage at will along South America's coast, took ten well-armed prizes. "A single frigate lording over the Pacific," Washington Irving wrote, "in saucy defiance of their thousand ships, revelling in the spoils of boundless wealth, and almost banishing the British flag from those regions where it had so long waved proudly predominant." Although Irving's elegant exaggeration was matched by Porter's conceit in naming one of his prizes the *Essex Jr.*, his operations did destroy the British whaling industry in the Pacific. The impact on Britain's economy was profound—whale oil was the primary lubricant in machinery as well as the major fuel used for lamplights. One member of Parliament complained that London "burnt dark for a year." Porter's success resulted from his own audacity and from the Admiralty's failure to station any ships in the Pacific during the Napoleonic Wars.

To "put our ship in condition for our return home" and to

provide "relaxation and amusement" for his men, Porter shaped course for the Marquesas Islands, the easternmost archipelago in Polynesia. He anchored off Nuku Hiva, a tropical paradise populated by 40,000 Polynesians. Within days, Porter noted in his journal, it was "helter-skelter and promiscuous intercourse, every girl the wife of every man." Porter dabbled in local politics, got caught up in tribal warfare, and, just before he left, gathered together the natives and his crew and announced that he was annexing the islands to the United States. "Our chief shall be their chief," he declared to the bewildered assemblage. This frolic came to an end in December 1813 when Porter got word that the Admiralty had deployed the frigate *Phoebe* and the sloops *Raccoon* and *Cherub* to the Pacific with orders to hunt down the raider *Essex*. Instead of sailing west to the Indian Ocean or trying to slither back into the South Atlantic, however, Porter decided to do "something more splendid," so he sailed back to Valparaíso to track down the superior British squadron.

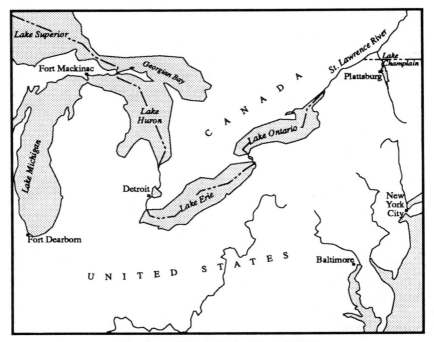

Northern Theater in the War of 1812

Less than a week after the *Essex* reached Valparaíso, two of the British ships arrived, the *Cherub* and the *Phoebe*, commanded by Captain Thomas Hillyer, who had been Porter's friend during Jefferson's war against the Barbary pirates. The two captains met and agreed to fight beyond Chile's territorial waters, but Hillyer turned down Porter's suggestion that the two opposing frigates engage without any interference from the extra British sloop. A British supply ship appeared and replenished Hillyer's ships, and knowing that the *Raccoon* would soon rejoin the British Squadron from her cruise off the Oregon coast, Porter somewhat belatedly concluded that he had best plan an escape. Porter had increased his broadside by stuffing his main battery with short-range carronades, and his ship carried only six long-range 32-pounders. Hillyer, with ample time to look over the American warship, arranged his tactics accordingly. On 28 March 1814, a gusty wind arose. Porter laid on full sail and tried to speed out of the harbor to evade Hillyer's squadron, but in open water the *Essex* was hit by a nasty gale and lost her main-topmast, making her nearly impossible to maneuver. The *Phoebe* and the *Cherub* ran down on the *Essex*, stood off well beyond carronade range, and blasted away without fear of being hit by the returning American gunfire. Porter withstood the slaughter for over two hours, but when he counted more than half his crew among the dead and wounded, he surrendered. Once again, honor had been satisfied but another American ship had been lost to the enemy's already superior fleet.[11]

With the frigates and American trade solidly blockaded, Secretary William Jones turned to alternative naval strategies. The British blockade squadrons prevented the frigates from operating in the North Atlantic, but the enemy cordon was too loose to obstruct the escape of small American schooners and sloops, which slipped out of port to prey on British transatlantic commerce and, only on a rare occasion, to challenge a minor enemy combatant. Jones was also an enthusiast for a renewed offensive against Canada on the Great Lakes, as was Harrison, who commanded the Army south of Lake Erie. The British were based on Fort Malden, under Captain Robert H. Barclay, and he was building up his small fleet with the aim of controlling the lake. As part of Commodore Chauncey's command, Master Commandant Oliver Hazard Perry was directed by Jones to assemble a Lake Erie Squadron to challenge the British. During 1813, both sides engaged in a furious building race that neared a climax in the fall. Barclay's fleet included two ships, two brigs, one schooner, and one sloop; Perry commanded two ships, one brig, five schooners, and one sloop. Although the two fleets were nearly equal in numbers, the American broadside, mostly in carronades, was 896 pounds, about twice the weight carried by the British, who relied mostly on long guns.

The Battle of Lake Erie evolved from Perry's choice of the Bass Islands as an anchorage. From this position, his ships blockaded Fort Malden and severed Barclay's communications to the east. When Barclay ran short of stores, he decided not to withdraw overland but instead to challenge Perry for control of the lake, but his intelligence was poor and he was not told that Perry had superior batteries. Perry, on the other hand, took great pains to scout the British force, and he prepared to exploit his superior throwweight during the upcoming engagement by ordering his captains to close on their opposite numbers and open fire quickly. On the morning of 10 September 1813, Perry sighted Barclay's ships. When the British closed to within a half mile, their guns opened up, half of them concentrating their fires on the *Lawrence*, Perry's flagship. Inexplicably, Master Commandant Jesse Elliott failed to bring up the *Niagara* to support the *Lawrence*, and she was nearly destroyed three hours after the battle began. Dressed as a common sailor to deceive enemy marksmen, Perry escaped in a gig and was rowed over to the *Niagara* in the middle of the action. Taking command of the *Niagara*, which had not been damaged, Perry brought her around and crossed Barclay's "tee," bringing his broadsides to bear on the British flagship *Detroit*. Fifteen minutes later, the entire British Squadron surrendered. "We have met the enemy and they are ours," Perry told Harrison.[12]

Perry's victory cut the supply line across Lake Erie to Fort Malden and compelled British General Henry Proctor and Tecumseh's Indians to retreat eastward along the banks of the Thames River. On 20 September, Perry's ships transported Harrison's army across the lake in hot pursuit. At the Battle of the Thames on 5 October, Harrison destroyed Proctor's army, killed Tecumseh, crushed Britain's power in the northwest, and forced the fleeing enemy troops to withdraw into Canada. However, Harrison was unable to press forward because another British fleet controlled Lake Ontario, and Commodore Chauncey, a hesitant and indecisive leader, was unwilling to bring the enemy to battle. This created a new strategic stalemate in the northwest, and the focus of the war once again turned back to the decisive eastern theater.

Chapter Eight
Defending the Nation
1814–1815

France's fortunes on Europe's battlefields crumbled in 1813 after Napoleon was driven from Russia, and Britain's prospects in North America accordingly improved. American war aims slipped further from sight. The Royal Navy's control of the Atlantic seaboard reduced American trade to about one-tenth of its volume in the last year of peace, Madison's northwest offensive had been smartly repulsed, and Canada was still in British hands. On the other side of the ledger, the American strategy of using the Navy and privateers to attack Britain's commerce in the West Indies was beginning to tell. During the War of 1812, roughly 500 privateers put to sea and captured nearly 1,300 prizes. The British fleet bottled up most of America's frigates in 1813, but the U.S. Navy's smaller swift warships evaded the blockade patrols throughout the war and damaged British shipping in the West Indies and Canadian waters. The British were less concerned with these losses, however, than with the loss of the American market brought on by the war.[1]

In 1813, knowing that the United States was sharply divided over the war, the Admiralty decided to supplement the blockade of the Atlantic seaboard with punitive raids along the coast south of New England, the seedbed of antiwar sentiment. The British struck back at the privateers by attacking their bases. Inasmuch as most privateers operated out of Baltimore, Admiral John Warren, who commanded the North American station, established a blockade force at the mouth of the Chesapeake Bay in February. He sent Rear Admiral Sir George Cockburn in the 74-gun *Broadwater* with three other sails-of-the-line onto the upper bay in April, and Cockburn captured some American ships, destroyed supplies, sent raiding parties up the major rivers, and shot up the Baltimore-Philadelphia highway. Norfolk, where the *Constellation* was blockaded, was burned during one of these raids. Commodore Joshua Barney's small Chesapeake Gunboat Flotilla was powerless to obstruct Cockburn's operations, and Cockburn finally retired from the upper bay in September. Perhaps by then he realized that he had forfeited an opportunity to land troops and inflict a much more telling blow. Warren's orders to Cockburn to raid American commerce on the Chesapeake Bay rather than land troops and occupy Baltimore or Washington, then both poorly defended, was the most wrong-headed strategic decision of the war.[2]

Cockburn's 1813 raids were a prelude to a major offensive Britain launched the following year. In Canada, General George Prevost assembled a large army and prepared to strike south along the Richelieu River, cross Lake Champlain, and march down the Hudson Valley to New York. A supporting advance under General Drummond was to seize Fort Niagara. In New England opposition to the conflict was so bitter that Massachusetts, Connecticut, Maine, and New Hampshire refused to let their militias cross into Canada, Boston bankers boycotted federal bond issues, and New England farmers sold their produce to the British Army. If Prevost could cut off New England from the rest of the country, Lord Liverpool believed, then his diplomats could divide the United States at the peace table. To destroy harbors, harass Madison's weak government, and prevent Madison from reinforcing the Great Lakes theaters, the British planned to use their fleet to conduct raids along the Atlantic seaboard. This comprehensive strategy, asserted Lord Castlereagh, the foreign minister, was aimed at nurturing secession in New England, enlarging Canada, and forcing Madison to agree to peace terms he had previously rejected.[3]

The Americans were also preparing their own strategy. General Dearborn mounted a weak offensive along the Niagara River front, but when he was pushed back he was relieved by Secretary of War John Armstrong, who took direct command of operations in the field. This was no improvement. Armstrong ended up losing the entire line from Fort George to Buffalo, New York. In March 1814, however, the Americans counterattacked along two lines of advance: Brigadier General Winfield Scott defeated the British at Chippewa and General Jacob Brown fought a new British commander and his fresh reinforcements to a standstill at Lundy's Lane. Although the Americans were pressed again to withdraw from Fort Erie in September, winter was approaching and with it the end of this indecisive frontier contest and Madison's plan to conquer Canada.

"It is impossible to attach too much importance to our naval operations on the Lakes," Navy Secretary Jones told Commodore Chauncey. "The success of the ensuing campaign will depend absolutely on our superiority on all the Lakes—and every effort and resource must be directed to that object." During 1813 and 1814, Jones transferred supplies, guns, and his best officers to those commands, resisting demands that he improve coastal defenses and diverting material from the seagoing fleet to Chauncey's squadron on Lake Ontario and Lieutenant Thomas Macdonough's squadron on Lake Champlain. Chauncey, still inert, wasted his resources and failed to seize several opportunities to strike at the British. Macdonough, who had fewer assets, quickly built up his squadron, developed a superior tactical organization, and prepared to obstruct General Prevost's offensive.[4]

The British put their plan into motion in the spring of 1814. Their fleet struck with great violence along the Atlantic coast in a series of punitive, diversionary raids. Vice Admiral Cochrane, who commanded a fleet of twenty warships and thirty transports carrying General Robert Ross and his landing force of 4,000 British regulars, was bent on humiliating Madison's government and undermining morale by sacking Washington. To retaliate against Baltimore for privateering operations, he intended to reduce that city as well. Jones learned of Britain's plans to raid Washington and Baltimore in May 1814, but he was "not equally impressed with the apprehension of immediate danger" since the British ships on "the Chesapeake . . . were satisfactorily engaged in conflagrating farm houses, and depredating upon slaves and tobacco, on the shores of the Patuxent [River]." Commodore Barney had prepared for eight months to defend the capital with his small Chesapeake Flotilla—one sloop, a cutter, two gunboats, and nine heavy gun barges.

At 0800 on 1 June Barney's vessels stood at the mouth of the Patuxent when his lookouts reported two British schooners on the horizon. During a lethal action the next day, the Chesapeake

The New Orleans Flotilla gunboats attack British ships in the early phase of the Battle of Lake Borgne, 1814.

Commodore Oliver Hazard Perry, victor in the Battle of Lake Erie, 1814.

Commodore Thomas Macdonough, commander of the Lake Champlain Flotilla, 1812–14, and victor of the Battle of Lake Champlain.

Flotilla's gunboats and gun barges suffered heavy casualties but drove off the enemy, who made sail and tried to lure Barney's vessels within range of the guns of Cockburn's 74-gun sail-of-the-line. Too wise to fall into this simple trap, Barney withdrew, the British in pursuit, and established a line across shallow St. Leonard's Creek where the enemy could not follow. The British then brought up their heavy guns and blockaded the Chesapeake Flotilla while their raiding parties burned and pillaged up and down the Patuxent. Two American infantry regiments and 100 Marines reinforced Barney's command, and on 25 June he launched an abortive counterattack against a superior force led by two British frigates, inflicting serious damage before escaping from the creek and running upriver to Nottingham. After a few skirmishes with the main body of the advancing British force, Barney fell back on Washington, leaving Lieutenant Solomon Frazier to destroy the American gun barges before they could be captured. On 22 August the barges were blown up, one by one, within Cockburn's sight near Point Pleasant, fifteen miles from Washington.[5]

When Barney and his 500 sailors reached Bladensburg on foot, General William H. Winder ordered them to hold the last of three defensive lines he had erected to defend the road to Washington. Neither Madison nor Secretary of War Armstrong had bothered much with the capital's defenses, believing the city to be invulnerable, and so no prepared works were ready to obstruct the invaders. Winder now failed to slow up Ross' Redcoats as he might have by destroying bridges or ambushing them as they marched through Maryland's thick forests. When the enemy charged the American works at Bladensburg, Winder's first two lines collapsed, but gallant Barney mounted a frantic counterattack, urging his sailors on with the rousing battle cry, "Board 'em! Board 'em!" To Barney's distress, Ross outflanked the Americans, some of whom escaped, and thereby opened the road to Washington. The British entered the capital hours later, burning the White House, the Capitol, and the Navy Yard.[6]

Admiral Cochrane next turned on Baltimore, which was guarded by Fort McHenry, one of the few coastal forts dating back to the 1794 Fortification Act that the Jeffersonians had completed. Cochrane landed Ross' troops between the Back and the Patapsco rivers, but Ross was killed when he met stiff American resistance at North Point. His replacement, Colonel Arthur Brooke, was finally stopped on the outskirts of Baltimore by earthworks and entrenchments stoutly defended by Major General Samuel Smith's Maryland Militia. Not long after, on 13 September, Cochrane's fleet arrived off Baltimore and, in a futile demonstration of British firepower, bombarded Fort McHenry all day and all night. Francis Scott Key eulogized the heroes who defended Fort McHenry in the anthem "Star Spangled Banner." Unable to reduce the stout fort, Cochrane ordered the British troops to board their transports, and his fleet retired back down the Chesapeake. Within one month Cochrane's ships had returned to the West Indies for the winter, and he began to prepare for a more serious stroke against the southern flank of the United States.

The British had concentrated their ships on the Chesapeake during the summer of 1814, but they did not neglect secondary operations. A British expeditionary force slashed up the Connecticut River in April, burning several American vessels and terrifying the local militia. Another small British landing party occupied the port of Wareham on Cape Cod, and the Royal Navy's blockade prevented any American warships from putting to sea to defend the region. Finally, in August, Nova Scotia's governor launched a major local offensive up the slithery neck of Penobscot Bay. He took Castine, a small but strategic port, and, overcoming minimal resistance, advanced forty miles north to Bangor, Maine. A few days later, Captain Charles Morris in the frigate *Adams*, returning from a successful cruise against British shipping on the Grand Banks, closed the Maine coast. Intending to evade the Halifax Fleet's patrols, Morris entered Penobscot Bay, but after running his ship aground on the Isle au Haut he had to head upriver for repairs. On 3 September, he realized that the British controlled the bay and were blocking his line of retreat, so he burned the *Adams* to prevent her from falling into enemy hands.

The Royal Navy could put landing parties ashore along the Atlantic seaboard because the Americans possessed no capital ships to challenge the powerful British covering fleets and because the British blockade immobilized America's frigates. Evading the enemy's patrols became a preoccupation of the American commodores, and none was more frustrated with the blockade than Stephen Decatur, whose frigate *President* had been stuck in New York harbor for several months. On the night of 14 January 1815 he decided to escape. Unhappily, one of the beacon ships guiding his vessel though the channel drifted off station and he grounded the frigate and then strained her hull when he made her free.

Soon after, a British patrol, led by the *Endymion,* sighted the *President* and overhauled the weakened American vessel after a brief stern chase.

Decatur now faced a choice between fighting his ship or surrendering to a superior enemy. He assembled his crew, warned them that escape was impossible, and outlined a bold plan to board the enemy and capture her. Since her hull was distorted, however, the *President* could not close on the hostile ship, and the *Endymion* proved to be altogether too elusive. Decatur changed tactics and decided to batter his opponent with his broadsides. This was so successful that when the *President* swung around and momentarily presented the *Endymion* with her stern, the Englishman could not rake Decatur's deck. At this moment, however, the British frigates *Tenedos* and *Pomone* closed to within range of Decatur's ship. The *President* had suffered only slight battle damage, and 80 percent of her crew were uninjured, but Decatur now saw no choice but to strike his colors. Because he had surrendered his ship, Decatur was later tried by a court-martial. While many embarrassing questions might have been asked about his uneven conduct of this battle, his great reputation as a warrior saved his naval career.[7]

The British were also active on America's southern flank in 1814. The Admiralty and the War Office in London arranged to transport General Pakenham and several veteran regiments from Europe to Jamaica, where they rendezvoused with the Royal Navy's West Indies Fleet and sailed into the Gulf of Mexico. Lord Liverpool's strategy was "to obtain command of the embouchure of the Mississippi, so as to deprive the back settlements of America of their communications to the sea." On 8 December, part of Vice Admiral Cochrane's fleet and transports dropped anchor off Ship Island, nearly seventy miles from New Orleans. Since General Andrew Jackson, the new Army commander in the South, had garrisoned forts St. Philip and Bourbon on the Mississippi below New Orleans, Cochrane ruled out pressing upriver. He decided instead to cross Lake Borgne, march around the Bayou de Pecheurs, and attack the city on its landward flank. Lake Borgne was too shallow for his ships, however, so Cochrane transferred his troops to small boats and relied on his gunboats and gun barges to force a passage across the lake.[8]

The New Orleans gunboats had not been inactive up to this time. In 1813, Commodore Daniel Paterson's vessels supported

General Wilkinson's seizure of Mobile, transporting the assault troops to the front, providing gunfire support for the Army's maneuvers, and maintaining communications with New Orleans. Thus, when Cochrane appeared on Lake Borgne nearly two years later, he faced several veterans. Unfortunately, their forces were unequal to the demands of their precarious strategic situation. On 10 December 1814, Lieutenant Thomas Catesby ap Jones, who commanded a flotilla of five gunboats and three smaller craft, saw Cochrane's gun barges and gunboats enter Lake Borgne from the gulf and advance on his station. For the moment, however, Jones' small formation blocked any British troop movement. In the face of overwhelming odds, he decided to withdraw slowly, pick positions where he could fight briefly and withdraw again, and so delay the entire British movement.[9]

Over the next four days the Americans retired slowly, but on the 14th Jones could no longer make headway against the wind and tides and was forced to turn and fight with no line of retreat. He formed his vessels into a tight line abreast with springs on his cables and awaited the approach of Captain Nicholas Lear, whose command included one sloop, forty-two powerful carronade launches, and a bomb craft. After rowing for thirty-six hours against the current, the British crews relaxed briefly while they ate breakfast, then formed up and bore down on Jones' line, opening up the battle with a withering salvo. The Americans inflicted some damage on the leading British vessels, but within a few minutes Jones was badly wounded, and soon after, all his gunboats had surrendered.

The bitterly fought gunboat Battle of Lake Borgne, which cost more lives than many frigate engagements, illustrated some of the virtues as well as the faults of Jefferson's gunboat policy. On several points Jefferson had been right. The gunboat was cheap to build, easy to man, and perfectly suited the defense of harbors and ports, enclosed waterways, and shallow reaches. In fact, Jefferson had not built too many gunboats—he had not built enough, considering the length of America's coastline, the large number of ports and harbors, and the gunboats' limited strategic mobility. The frigate victories in 1812 brought glory to American commodores and lifted national morale, but once Britain turned her attention and resources to the American war, the blockade of America's ports was established at a relatively small cost. The Royal Navy did pay a high price to attack America's coasting trade or harbors, however, thanks to the Navy's oft-maligned gunboats and gun barges.

After Jones' defeat, a few small American craft remained on Lake Borgne to harass the movement of the boats ferrying the British troops to the bayou. Because Cochrane had few shallow-draft vessels, this movement took several more days, and it was not until 23 December that General Pakenham's troops were all ashore at their camp along the bayou. Commodore Paterson in New Orleans still had the schooners *Carolina* and *Louisiana* under his command. He sent Lieutenant John D. Henley in the 2-gun *Carolina* up the waterway to harass the British bivouac in the darkness, and this diverted Pakenham's attention from an unexpected attack on his rear by Jackson's army. Pakenham brought up his heavy guns after this brief reverse, while Paterson took the *Louisiana* up the bayou to support Henley's diversionary fire. After British gunfire blew up the *Carolina* on the 27th, Paterson pulled the *Louisiana* out of the fray in time to get her back to the city, where her guns were offloaded and added to Jackson's artillery. Neither Jones' gunboat action nor Paterson's harassing operations were in any way decisive, but taken together they gave Jackson a bit more time to prepare his defensive works. Pakenham, a wretched tactician, now ordered his troops to make a frontal assault on Jackson's lines, and the British ranks were torn apart by the well-entrenched defenders. After three more frontal assaults failed at the cost of over 2,000 British casualties, Pakenham admitted defeat and retired on the afternoon of 8 January 1815, thus ending the battle and leaving New Orleans in American hands.

In the fall of 1814, while the British were preparing to attack New Orleans, Madison was under great pressure to negotiate an end to the war. In August, he named a peace commission consisting of diplomat Quincy Adams, Speaker of the House Henry Clay, and Albert Gallatin, and they sailed to Europe to meet Britain's envoys at Ghent in Flanders. London demanded that an Indian nation under British military protection be established in the Northwest Territory, that America cede parts of Maine and northern New York to Canada, and that the Americans agree to British control of the Great Lakes. The British refused to discuss impressment or neutral rights.

While the commission was drafting its response to Britain's demands, Commodore Thomas Macdonough prepared to meet Captain George Downie on Lake Champlain. The odds were against the Americans for many reasons, one being that Napoleon's defeat had allowed the British to ship a large army of veterans from France to Canada. "My mind is made up for the worst and my consolation is that whatever disasters we may sustain, the vindictive desperation of the enemy will unite and purify the country and I trust enable us to sustain the conflict and preserve our institutions undefiled," Navy Secretary Jones told Madison. Because the U.S. Navy now controlled both Lake Ontario and Lake Erie, the British commander, General George Prevost, decided to shift the weight of his attack to the east and cut New England off from the rest of the country by moving from his base at Montreal to New York via Lake Champlain, the Richelieu River, and the Hudson River. He was mindful of the Duke of Wellington's advice that "naval superiority on the Lakes is the *sine qua non* of success in war on the frontier of Canada." There had been little action on Lake Champlain before Prevost's offensive got under way, although back in June 1813 two American sloops were captured, giving the Royal Navy's small flotilla uncontested control over the region for the moment.[10]

Obsessed with the lack of money and in despair over the defeat of France, America's informal ally, Jones adopted a "purely defensive" strategy on the Great Lakes in 1814. He was concerned about a renewed British offensive in the Northwest Territory, but did "not anticipate anything to disturb our complete control on Lake Champlain." Jones nonetheless arranged for shipbuilding materials to be sent north and instructed Macdonough to exercise a vigorous command of the American naval forces in the area. Two remarkable shipbuilders, Adam and Noah Brown, had already converted a steamer hull into the 19-gun *Ticonderoga*, and in June Macdonough proposed that they be paid to construct another vessel to strengthen his squadron. Jones wanted "not to add to the naval means on Lake Champlain as suggested by Commodore Macdonough," but Madison wisely disagreed and allowed Macdonough to complete the 24-gun brig *Eagle*. A few weeks later Jones "regret[ted] commencing the new ship," but Madison was firm on "the critical importance of preventing the enemy from gaining a naval supremacy" on Lake Champlain. This was his best strategic decision of the war. Years later Madison recorded that after he made the decision, Jones obediently advanced "the experiment for reinforcing our little squadron." Macdonough also restored the *Saratoga* and several gunboats. While he was readying his squadron,

Macdonough learned that the British were about to launch a spoiling attack. He quickly brought his guns ashore and on 14 May drove off a formation of British galleys and a single bomb sloop.[11]

Hurried construction meant that the American squadron was soon ready to fight. Macdonough anchored his ships off Plattsburgh, his landward flank defended by 3,000 scratch troops from the New York and Vermont militia and volunteer invalids from the local hospitals. After crossing the border in mid-August, Prevost's 12,000-man army had repelled a party of American skirmishers and continued to march to the south. Then, on 3 September, Captain Downie took command of the Royal Navy's Lake Champlain squadron, which consisted of his flagship, the *Confiance*, three sloops, and twelve gunboats. The opposing forces' firepower was roughly equal: the British had ninety-two guns with a throwweight of 1,900 pounds; the Americans, eighty-six guns with a slightly greater throwweight.

Macdonough deployed his vessels in a line from the shoals of Cumberland Head in the north to Crab Island to the south, a short distance across the critical chokepoint at a bend in the lake off Plattsburgh. Forty yards west of his line, Macdonough stationed his gunboats. It was just after 0800 on 11 September 1814 when Downie's formation reached Cumberland Head and he could assess for the first time the tactical problem he faced. If he formed his line outside the bay, his guns would be out of range of the enemy. On the other hand, if his vessels entered the bay before lining up, they would be exposed to American raking fire. To avoid either of these dangers, Downie divided his squadron into three sections. He ordered his gunboats to engage the southern anchor of Macdonough's line, sent two sloops around Cumberland Head to outflank the northernmost American vessel, and brought his flagship and one sloop down on the center, where the *Saratoga* and the *Ticonderoga* awaited the British assault. The climactic battle of the War of 1812 was about to begin.

When the British gunboats closed and opened up, Macdonough held his fire until most of the enemy vessels were within range of his long guns. He then sighted a 24-pounder on the *Confiance* and touched the fuse. The shot passed the length of the deck of the British flagship and destroyed the wheel. At this signal, all the American batteries opened fire. To the north, the *Eagle* engaged two British sloops. They attempted to outflank her, but both ran into shoal water and one lost her main boom and half of her crew to the *Eagle*'s broadside. Drifting south, the second British sloop came alongside the *Saratoga*; Macdonough fired one bow gun and she struck her colors. Meanwhile, the British sloop *Linnet*, having forced the *Eagle* to retire to the west, turned along the American line and ran south, firing at the *Saratoga*, which was now caught between Downie's flagship and the *Linnet*'s furious broadside. Macdonough's starboard battery was destroyed within moments.

Macdonough was ready for something akin to this contingency. He tripped the bow anchor, dropped a stern anchor, and waited for a northerly breeze to bring the *Saratoga* about. At this moment, however, the wind died down, the ship remained motionless, and the *Confiance* and *Linnet* increased their deadly raking fires. Macdonough had also planned for this turn of events. Two kedges had been dropped over each side of the bow before the battle began and lines were strung to the quarters. When Macdonough and his men began to haul on one kedge line, the ship came around, and the *Saratoga*'s fresh broadside soon hammered the *Confiance* into submission. Macdonough then turned his attention on the *Linnet*, which quit the fray after only fifteen minutes. With Downie dead and the three largest ships in the hands of American prize crews, the rest of the British squadron hastened to escape. That same morning, the British Army had launched a landward attack on the American defenders of Plattsburgh, but the first British assault was repelled. When General Prevost learned about Downie's defeat in the Battle of Lake Champlain, he abandoned the invasion of New York and began to retreat back to Canada.[12]

Blown across his deck twice by splinters, knocked out for a few moments by a large timber, and hurled across the deck by the decapitated head of a gun captain, Macdonough emerged from the battle amazingly unscathed. He had saved the republic. Never again would a European power seriously plan to invade the continental United States. Reflecting on the Battle of Lake Champlain, Secretary Jones, who was not given to hyperbole, observed that "to view it in the abstract, it is not surpassed by any naval victory of record; to appreciate its results, it is perhaps, one of the most important events in the history of our country." In Commodore Macdonough's honor Congress struck a gold medal, and the state of New York awarded him a grant of 1,000 acres on Cumberland Head so that he might look out on the scene of the most important naval battle in American history.[13]

The news of Macdonough's victory struck London like a thunderbolt. At one stroke, Britain's grand strategy in North America was in disarray. The cabinet asked Wellington to replace Prevost, but he refused. There were not enough troops to overwhelm the Americans, he said, and Britain faced a renewed crisis in Europe. Indeed, Britain's position in Europe was on the verge of eroding. After entering Paris and exiling Napoleon to Elba, the allies met at the Congress of Vienna in 1814 to shape Europe's new balance of power, but national interests clashed and the victors were on the brink of splitting apart when the Anglo-American peace talks got under way at Ghent. The American diplomats realized that the British were in a vise and that they cared less about faraway North American issues than the European settlement. The American negotiators exploited Macdonough's victory skillfully, and the British finally agreed to an end to the War of 1812 in the Treaty of Ghent. This peace appeared to leave all the major prewar issues unsettled. Both London and Washington accepted "the status quo antebellum"—the formal diplomatic and military situation as it existed before the war.[14]

Although the warhawks of 1812 failed to annex Canada, end impressment, or force Britain to accept America's definition of neutral maritime rights, they nonetheless achieved other important national objectives. Clay's basic strategic assessment was correct. So long as the French wars occupied Britain's attention, she could not divert enough resources to defeat the United States. Macdonough's victory on Lake Champlain put an end to Britain's plans to dismember the United States and create a buffer Indian client state to fence in westward expansion. After a painful reappraisal of the North American balance of power, the British tried to appease the hotheaded Americans. Certain after Waterloo that the Napoleonic Wars were at an end, Castlereagh even assured Quincy Adams, the new minister in London, that "the Admiralty was now occupied in prescribing regulations" on impressment to "prevent all cause of [future] complaint." The real loser in the War of 1812 was Spain. Jackson's victory at New Orleans tore open the western flank of Spanish Florida, territory that Spain could hold no longer on her own. Fought over the most fundamental American foreign policy objectives of continentalism and maritime access, victory in the War of 1812 meant that these goals were partly reached, though in ways not precisely documented in the diplomatic terms of the peace.[15]

Chapter Nine

Maritime Access and the Monroe Doctrine
1816–1828

Barely a week after the Senate approved the Treaty of Ghent, President Madison asked Congress to declare war on Algiers. On the eve of the War of 1812, an Algerine cruiser had seized the Salem merchantman *Edwin*, and Tunis and Tripoli had allowed the Royal Navy to enter their harbors to reclaim wartime British prizes from American privateers. Both acts were violations of the tribute treaties. Madison, furious over these incidents, was unable to retaliate while the country was at war with Britain. With the signing of the peace, however, the Navy had plenty of ships, the country was determined to end Barbary's piracy, and on 3 March Congress declared war.

To prosecute the last of the Barbary Wars, Navy Secretary Benjamin Crowninshield ordered Commodores Bainbridge and Decatur to assemble two separate squadrons, but for reasons that are unclear he gave Decatur more support than Bainbridge in preparing for the expedition. As a result, Decatur cleared New York harbor on 20 May 1815 with the fast frigate *Guerrière*, the frigates *Macedonian* and *Constellation*, three sloops, and a pair of schooners. Arriving off Spain's southeast coast, he came upon Algiers' largest frigate and an escort, both of which he captured. He entered Algiers harbor in June and brandished his guns at the dey's forts, and negotiations soon were underway. Peace, Decatur quipped, was best dictated "at the mouth of a cannon." Diplomat William Shaler warned the dey that Americans would no longer pay him tribute and convinced him to release his American prisoners, promise to stop harassing American shipping, and pay an indemnity for violating the old treaty. Decatur almost upset the deal by offering to return the two captured frigates, but with the end of the French wars even Algiers' nuisance value was nil. One year later an Anglo-Dutch Fleet charged into the harbor and destroyed the fortifications.

Standing out of Algiers in June 1815, Decatur made for Tripoli, where he humbled the bashaw into agreeing to terminate his own tribute treaty. A menacing appearance at Tunis brought the same result. Decatur left the Mediterranean for home just as Bainbridge's squadron reached Gibraltar. "I have been deprived of the opportunity of either fighting or negotiating," he grumbled sourly. Madison's plan was to do more than just conduct a punitive operation, however, and Bainbridge's appearance signaled the establishment of the first of the Navy's postwar station squadrons. This was affirmed in 1816 when Crowninshield approved a long-term lease of facilities from the British for an American naval base at Port Mahon on Minorca.[1]

Because the Treaty of Ghent directly addressed none of the causes of the War of 1812, many Americans believed that it had brought merely a temporary armistice. The British were also concerned, fearing that the United States would renew the war and invade Canada for the third time in forty years. The U.S. Navy nearly shut down operations on the Great Lakes in February 1815, but British Foreign Minister Castlereagh pointed out that the Americans now "had so much advantage" in that theater that the Royal Navy needed to build up its own forces. "The Americans by their proximity would be able to prepare . . . for attacks much sooner than . . . the British could be prepared for defense," he told Quincy Adams, the new American minister in London. Madison reacted by having the Army construct a string of forts from Fort Wayne at Detroit to Fort Montgomery at Rouse's Point on Lake Champlain. If the war was renewed, his strategy "would be to take the lakes themselves." Within two years, however, both sides recognized that this costly arms race was not improving their security and that the causes of the War of 1812 were melting away. This assessment led to the 1817 Rush-Bagot Agreement, under which each nation agreed to deploy on Lake Ontario no more than one lightly armed 100-ton vessel, a similar vessel on Lake Champlain, and one each on the two upper Great Lakes. This naval arms limitation agreement brought to an end the postwar arms race on Canada's border.[2]

This easing of tensions also produced the Anglo-American Convention of 1818, which addressed several territorial issues. The negotiators drew the boundary west along the 49th parallel from the Lake of the Woods to the Rocky Mountains, but both powers claimed the entire Oregon Territory. America's stake in the territory was based partly on a trading post established at the mouth of the Columbia River some years earlier by John Jacob Astor. At Astor's urging, in October 1817 President Monroe instructed Captain James Biddle to sail the sloop *Ontario* into the Pacific, visit Astoria, and peacefully demonstrate the American claim to the disputed territory "by some symbolical or appropriate mode adapted to the occasion." Unable to settle the rival claims, the negotiators of the 1818 Convention agreed on a joint occupation of the Oregon Territory for ten years, an arrangement that was renewed two times over the next several decades.[3]

Americans were keenly aware that the nation had been ill prepared to fight the War of 1812; they had watched the British blockade American ports, burn the capital, and invade New York, Michigan, Illinois, and New Orleans. Now the National Republicans, led by House Speaker Henry Clay and South Carolina's John C. Calhoun, demanded strong measures to improve national defense. These included building a system of coastal and inland forts, expanding the fleet, and reorganizing the Army and Navy. In 1814 Navy Secretary Jones had complained of the absence of any professional staff to help him direct wartime naval operations and manage the shore establishment, and he convinced Congress to create a Navy Board of Commissioners to advise and assist the civilian secretary. Jones left office in December of that year, and Madison asked the senior officer on active duty, Commodore John Rodgers, to become the next secretary of the Navy. Rodgers declined, and the president turned to Benjamin Crowninshield, a seafaring merchant from Massachusetts. Madison then named Rodgers to chair the new Board of Commissioners.

In the legislation creating the Board of Commissioners, Congress used inexact language to describe its duties, and this spawned a host of troubles. Crowninshield told Rodgers to nominate two other commodores to fill out the board, but Congress had spelled out neither the commissioners' authority nor their relationship to the Navy secretary, and a quarrel erupted between the two men about the board's function. Rodgers reasoned that Congress intended the commissioners to direct operations, supervise naval personnel, and report to the president; Crowninshield wanted them to manage the shore establishment and report to the secretary. Crowninshield relied in part on the precedent established in the 1790s by Stoddert, a strong secretary, who exercised unchecked command authority over his department. Rodgers wanted to adopt the British practice of charging a Board of Admiralty with the authority to supervise naval policy and operations. Individual authority, and a clear chain of command, was to be replaced by corporate civilian-military responsibility.[4]

They appealed to Madison, who had helped to write the Constitution, to decide the issue. He ruled that civilian control of a military department meant that executive authority must be vested in a political appointee, someone subject to confirmation by the Senate and removal by the president. An important if abstract point was involved. In theory, and often in practice, the secretary established policy, which uniformed naval officers implemented. In theory, a naval officer might be removed from the service only for violating Navy regulations or the Articles of War, whereas the secretary served at the pleasure of the president. Although the secretary was an appointed, unelected official, he nonetheless represented the elected authority of the president and was charged with giving form and detail to the president's political decisions. Naval officers were in principle unable to make political decisions, for they owed their loyalty to the government, not to the administration, which might change with every election. Madison, siding with Crowninshield, held that the Constitution required direct political, civilian control of the Navy Department.[5]

Articulating the correct principle, Madison now applied it wrongly. Nothing in his decision prevented him from giving the board a writ to conduct operations or manage the fleet under the secretary's direction as Rodgers was urging, but Crowninshield objected strongly to this chain of command and the president gave in. The result was that the commissioners were endowed with authority over the "civil" affairs of the department. In spite of this convoluted arrangement, the commissioners, often criticized as too conservative under Rodgers' leadership, performed valuable work for the Navy. Rodgers' major accomplishment was the construction of the first American drydocks in Philadelphia and New York, work that began in 1827 and was completed six years later.

In 1822 Rodgers persuaded Congress to create a special billet for an ordnance officer, a job first held by Master Commandant Stephen Cassin. With Cassin's guidance, the commissioners standardized testing for new guns, fixed quantities of powder, shot, and wads, and established quality controls for ordnance manufacture. However, Rodgers failed to get Congress to reduce and reform the Navy yards or to consolidate all naval gun manufacturing at a single national gun factory.[6]

After the great naval victories in the War of 1812, the Navy rode the crest of a wave of popular enthusiasm when the peace was ratified. The danger of renewed hostilities with Britain and Decatur's successful operations against Barbary led many to argue in favor of a strong peacetime fleet. "The surest pledge that we can have of peace," wrote Secretary of State John Quincy Adams, "will be to be prepared for war." America's "only effectual defence is a naval force." Crowninshield had little trouble in April 1816 persuading Congress to approve an eight-year program to build nine 74-gun sails-of-the-line, a dozen 44-gun frigates, and three steam batteries "for the defense of the ports and harbours." One *North Carolina*-class sail-of-the-line, two frigates, and two sloops were to be laid down each year at an annual cost of $1 million. The Crowninshield program constituted the first long-term, peacetime American naval shipbuilding policy. However, many of the dangers of 1816 soon evaporated and others were dispersed by diplomacy or naval force, and so by 1819 the nation possessed a relatively large fleet, a program of naval expansion, and "many naval officers on duty and so little for them to do," noted Navy Secretary Smith Thompson.[7]

The Era of Good Feelings, which began when Virginian James Monroe entered the White House in 1817, was marked by an absence of party politics, remarkable economic growth, and a new departure in American foreign policy. Monroe named Quincy Adams as his secretary of state and kept Crowninshield at the Navy Department. Although he did not have to fight a major war, Monroe faced serious problems in international politics. The first problem concerned Spanish East Florida, where an alliance of the Creeks and the Seminoles threatened America's outposts in the Southeast. The First Seminole War broke out in 1816 when the Indians raided West Florida, but the following year General Jackson, supported by the Navy's New Orleans Flotilla, thrashed the Creeks and pushed the Seminoles back into East Florida. Jackson's incursions were bitterly protested by the Spanish, although they could do nothing to stop Jackson or to deflect Quincy Adams' demands that Spain either suppress the Seminoles or sell East Florida to the United States.

At the same time, South American rebels and a pirate gang under Jean Lafitte occupied Amelia Island in the Gulf of Mexico and proclaimed the establishment of a renegade republic of Florida. This menaced not only Gulf shipping, but also Quincy Adams' plan to annex this Spanish possession. At a special cabinet meeting on 30 October 1817, Monroe ordered the Navy to dismantle the pirate base. On 23 December, a squadron under Captain John Henley in the *John Adams* closed on Amelia Island and put ashore a landing party that overran the pirates after three days of fighting. Spain now faced the fact that she could neither deter the Americans nor defend East Florida, so she sold that territory to the United States for $5 million in the Adams-Onis Treaty of 1819. When Lieutenant Matthew C. Perry in the *Shark* stood into Key West on 26 February 1822, he had the honor of taking possession of East Florida. Spain's position in the New World had not completely collapsed, however, and Madrid rejected Quincy Adams' offer to buy its colony of Texas.

Spain was especially distressed in 1819 by revolutions in Latin America, a complex series of wars that erupted in Buenos Aires in 1810 and spread quickly throughout the Spanish empire, led in the north by Venezuela's Simón Bolívar and in the south by Argentina's José San Martín. The success of these revolutions created a dilemma for Monroe. He sympathized with the rebels but was concerned that the new, weak republics were often convulsed by civil wars and territorial clashes. Moreover, he was aware that Austria's Metternich, Europe's most skillful statesman, was arranging for a "great expedition" backed by the French fleet to help Spain recover her empire in the New World.

The revolutions and the demise of Spanish naval power also occasioned an outbreak of privateering in the Gulf and Caribbean. In 1819, Monroe ordered Commodore Oliver Hazard Perry to take command of a squadron composed of the frigate *Constellation*, the sloop *John Adams*, and the schooner *Nonesuch*, obtain an accounting of privateering licenses issued by Venezuela, and then sail to Buenos Aires to suppress piracy against American shipping in the Río de la Plata. Perry's ships arrived at the mouth of the Orinoco on 15 July, crossed the bar, and sailed 300 miles upriver to Angostura. There he persuaded officials of the Bolívar government to order their privateers not to harass American shipping. Just a few days after the Senate approved his nomination as the American envoy to Buenos Aires, however, Perry died of yellow fever. Monroe, uneasy about offending Europe, delayed naming a replacement, and the new envoy did not reach Buenos Aires until October 1820, by which time the entire region was engulfed in war and Britain was swiftly becoming the dominant outside influence.[8]

None of the rebel republics at first possessed navies, but they needed ships to deny mobility to Spain's armies in Cuba and Peru and to challenge the small Spanish Fleet at sea. To harass Spain's trade, the rebels often hired former British and American officers and supplied them with ships and naval or privateering commissions. Blank commissions, which were illegal, were commonplace in this trade, and many of the privateers were no more than pirates. They cared little about maritime law and often preyed on neutral shipping. This problem was acute in the Caribbean, an area so important to American trade that it ranked second only to Britain in dollar volume in 1816. From 1775 to 1815, Spain had allowed American trade with her Caribbean colonies to flourish, in part to prevent European incursions there and in part because Madrid was incapable of enforcing her mercantile laws. With the onset of the Latin American revolutions, Spain began to view this commerce as illegal—it violated her sovereignty, slit her blockades, and aided her enemies. She declared a blockade of South America's Atlantic and Gulf coasts, but her means of enforcing it were only a handful of frigates based on Cuba. The United States was neutral in this conflict. Monroe was edgy about Europe's attitude, but he wanted to help out the rebels and at first allowed them to fit out privateers in New Orleans or one of the other expanding Gulf ports.

This policy did not please everyone. Commodore Charles Morris, who commanded the Gulf station, was charged with protecting American shipping, but federal officials in New Orleans frustrated his efforts by refusing to enforce the Neutrality Acts. Americans owned and operated many of these privateers, and when Quincy Adams tried to suppress their activities by having them arrested, sympathetic New Orleans juries refused to bring in convictions. American opinion supported South America's rebels and cared little about offending Spain. On both sides privateering soon degenerated into piracy. One observer documented over

3,000 incidents from 1815 to 1822, and Quincy Adams claimed that the Spanish and rebel "paper blockades" were merely an excuse for "a war of extermination against neutral commerce." Monroe was forced to act. In 1819 Congress passed an act "to Protect Commerce," instructing the Navy to station "a suitable naval force" in the Caribbean and authorizing it to seize any ship suspected of piracy. At the same time, Quincy Adams informed Spain that the United States did not recognize her paper blockade and would prevent rebel or Spanish warships or privateers from harassing American trade.[9]

Monroe's newly energetic policy against privateering led Congress in May 1820 to authorize the construction of five 12-gun *Alligator*-class schooners for Caribbean operations, and in the fall of the following year Navy Secretary Samuel Southard established the West Indies Squadron, consisting of the sloop *Hornet*, two schooners, two brigs, and three old gunboats under the command of Lieutenant Lawrence Kearny. Soon after his arrival in the Caribbean, however, Kearny discovered that he did not have enough shallow-draft vessels to operate inshore where the pirates hid out. On 16 October, while cruising off Cape Antonio, the 12-gun brig *Enterprise* came upon four pirate vessels plundering three American merchantmen, but in the shallow water the warship could not maneuver. Kearny sent five small boats to chase down the pirates, and several of the gangs were caught, but the rest got away. Despite these operations, several New England insurance companies complained that piracy had not declined and begged the administration "to see some vigorous measures adopted to check the progress of this growing evil."[10]

In response, Southard gave Captain James Biddle command of the West Indies Squadron in 1822. It now also included the frigates *Macedonian* and *Congress*, a corvette, a sloop, and a schooner—a formidable collection of firepower. Biddle was told to defend trade and American interests in a vast area north of the equator from the tip of West Africa to the Gulf of Mexico. This great increase in firepower did little to curb the pirates because the West Indies Squadron still lacked any fighting craft that did not draw a great deal of water. Moreover, rancid diplomatic relations between the United States and Spain caused by Monroe's support for the rebels undercut Biddle's attempt to cooperate with Spanish officials in Cuba and Puerto Rico, where the pirates were based. In effect, those officials refused to allow the squadron to operate in

Spanish territorial waters. And pirates were not the only danger to the West Indies Squadron. In the fall of 1822, over 100 officers and men were felled by a peculiarly deadly form of yellow fever. The commissioner was so alarmed that Commodore Rodgers carried two naval surgeons in the schooner *Shark* to Pensacola to investigate in October. Angry over his predicament, Biddle resigned his command.

The knotty problem of Caribbean piracy was inextricably linked to the broader issue of American foreign policy in the Western Hemisphere. In 1820, Tsar Alexander II issued a ukase, or proclamation, claiming that the southern boundary of Russian Alaska extended down the Oregon coast to California and urged the Russians to colonize the Pacific Northwest. Russia also backed Metternich's plan for the Holy Alliance to provide military support to the Spanish in Latin America. Britain opposed Russia's claims to Oregon, however, and hoped to dominate South America's trade, so in 1823 Foreign Minister George Canning warned Metternich that Britain would use the Royal Navy to prevent the Holy Alliance from intervening in Latin America. Just before he made this dramatic move, however, Canning decided to enlist additional support, and he proposed to Monroe that Britain and the United States issue a joint declaration against Metternich's scheme.

British and American aims in Latin America were in many ways parallel, but Quincy Adams believed that the United States need not appear as "cockboat in the wake of the British man-of-war" and should adopt an independent line. Monroe's cabinet was aware that Britain opposed European intervention, but when they debated the issue, they did not know that Canning had threatened to use force to uphold his policy. In March 1823, Monroe had defied Spain's protests by recognizing the Latin American republics, but his great Annual Message of December contained an even stiffer position. "As a principle in which the rights and interests of the United States are involved, that the American continents . . . are henceforth not to be considered as subjects for future colonization by any European powers." In return, America would not interfere in Europe's balance of power. "In the wars of the European powers in matters relating to themselves we have never taken any part, nor does it comport with our policy to do so." That same day Monroe secretly instructed his envoy in London to tell Canning that the United States would "unite with the

British Government in measures to prevent the interference of the Allied powers in the affairs of South America, and particularly in sending troops there." This threat proved to be unnecessary. The Monroe Doctrine was issued after Canning's threat reached Vienna and forced the Holy Alliance to abandon its plan to aid Spain. A clear statement of the need to defend twin goals of continentalism and maritime access, the Monroe Doctrine became the rock upon which American policy in Latin America rested for over a century.[11]

The conflict between the Monroe Doctrine and Monroe's antipiracy policy caused a host of problems for Commodore David Porter, who relieved Biddle in command of the West Indies Squadron off Puerto Rico in February 1823. He increased the number of smaller vessels in his command, fitting out eight 50-ton schooners and five small barges, purchasing a store ship, and obtaining a converted Hudson River ferry, the *Sea Gull*, the first steamer to conduct naval operations. Added to the three schooners and three sloops already on station, Porter now counted sixteen vessels with 133 guns and over 1,150 men under his command. He knew that he needed the cooperation of Spain's officials, so he sent two small schooners to deliver a conciliatory letter to Puerto Rico's governor at San Juan. When one of these ships entered the harbor she drew fire from the forts, killing her commanding officer. Porter was angry, but his orders told him not to upset the Spanish, and he needed their cooperation to eradicate the pirates. An apology from Puerto Rico's governor was gracefully accepted.

During the spring and summer of 1823, Porter's squadron scoured the coasts of Hispaniola and Cuba, and by October most of the pirates there had been either killed, captured, or run ashore. Porter's "zeal and enterprise," claimed Monroe, meant that "the piracies . . . in the neighborhood of . . . Cuba have been repressed." But the West Indies Squadron was again stricken by yellow fever and, for the second time in his life, Porter was felled by the dread disease. Violating orders, he returned to Washington, and within a short time quarreled not only with Southard but also with Quincy Adams and Monroe. By the time he recovered, the cabinet considered Porter a foolhardy, foul-tempered pest.

Upon his return to the West Indies in November 1824, Porter was thrust into a stew of confused diplomacy. Navy men in the Caribbean had known for many years that piracy was, in Perry's words, "openly permitted by the Spanish Authorities." In October, pirates from the small Puerto Rican port of Fajardo had emptied an American warehouse in St. Thomas in the Danish West Indies. Lieutenant Charles T. Platt in the *Beagle* sailed to Fajardo to investigate, but when he and another officer went ashore dressed in civilian clothes to talk to local officials, they were thrown into jail and not released until the loot could be spirited away. Porter, indignant over this affront, sailed into Fajardo the next day with almost his entire squadron and, under a flag of truce, sent a letter ashore demanding an explanation. When he saw the Spanish preparing to defend their village, he assembled a 200-man landing party, went ashore, captured the battery, spiked its guns, and marched into town. The captain of the port appeared and profusely apologized. Porter departed that afternoon, and that evening he wrote a report to Southard explaining his actions.[12]

For Monroe and Adams, the timing of the Fajardo incident could not have been worse. Monroe was aware that the West Indies Squadron "would attract the attention, not of Spain alone but . . . [also] of the powers of Europe," and Porter's orders had been written with the "desire rather to err on the side of moderation" rather "than to risk a variance with any of the nations concerned." Southard ordered Porter to return to Washington and charged him with "disobedience of orders" and "insubordinate conduct." He had a good case, and a court-martial found Porter guilty, but merely suspended him from duty for six months—with full pay and rations. Instead of rejoicing, Porter denounced the court and the Monroe administration, rejected the verdict, resigned his commission, and soon took command of the newly formed Mexican Navy. He was replaced on the West Indies station by Captain Lewis Warrington, a less mercurial figure who defeated the pirates using his predecessor's tactics and British cooperation. Warrington simply handed over any pirates he caught to the Royal Navy for a quick hanging. Southard's decision to establish a Navy yard at Pensacola to support the West Indies Squadron strengthened his hand. Soon the secretary reported to Congress that "piracy, as a system, has been repressed" off "Cuba and now requires only to be watched, by a proper force, to be prevented from afflicting commerce . . . in that quarter." With these stout measures, the end of Latin America's revolutions, and better relations with Spain, by 1829 the menace of Caribbean piracy was reduced to a mere annoyance.[13]

In an election decided by the House, John Quincy Adams defeated Andrew Jackson and entered the White House in March 1825. His presidency was frustrated because Jackson's supporters undermined his domestic program and rejected his foreign policy. He was dedicated to the Monroe Doctrine, and when rumors spread that Britain and the Holy Alliance were about to go to war, he declared that he would not intervene in Europe. The United

Commodore David Porter, commander of the West Indies Squadron, 1823–24.

U.S. Navy Department

States would use its Navy only to defend the "rights of their national independence." He kept several members of Monroe's cabinet, including Navy Secretary Southard, although Southard had difficulty dealing with a Congress that was increasingly hostile to naval expansion.[14]

The Navy's 1816 Crowninshield program envisioned the construction of a battle fleet of 74-gun sails-of-the-line, but the end of the Barbary Wars and better relations with Britain reduced the tempo of American naval operations. There were four sails-of-the-line in commission in 1820, but only the *Columbus* was on active service, and when she returned from the Mediterranean Squadron that year, she was laid up in ordinary for a quarter-century. The rest of the fleet ready for service consisted of three frigates, the new sloops, and a handful of lesser vessels. In 1820, Congress, disenchanted with the high costs of peacetime naval expansion, amended the 1816 program by halving the $1 million annual appropriation and by pushing back, to 1827, the date by which the entire plan was to be finished. The sail-of-the-line *Pennsylvania* was laid down in 1822, but work progressed so slowly that she was not completed for fifteen years.

Quincy Adams intended the United States to "become in regular process of time and by no petty advances a great naval power," and Southard set out to refurbish the fleet. He ordered work begun in 1825 on two new frigates under the Crowninshield program, and the following year Congress passed a private relief act allowing the Navy to purchase the *Hudson*, a frigate built by an American shipyard on order from the bankrupt Greek government. Pointing out that only four sloops were in service, Southard asked Congress in 1825 for several more. Congressman Lemuel Sawyer and other Jackson Democrats were generally "satisfied with the present number of ships" and charged that Southard's plan was intended "for the gratification of national vanity," but Congress supported the Navy's request anyway. Ten 700-ton *Boston*-class sloops were built over the next three years. Using funds earmarked for repairing vessels already in commission, Southard also rebuilt the sloops *John Adams* and *Peacock*. Both Southard's expansion plan and the Crowninshield program were brought to a halt in 1827, when a heated decade over naval policy ended in a defeat for the administration. The 1816 and 1820 acts, now expired, were replaced by a measure authorizing $500,000 each year over the next six years to acquire oak framing timber, but Congress refused to construct any more vessels. Some residual shipbuilding authority still remained, however. The fleet had grown in the decade since the War of 1812 from thirty-five ships to fifty-two, and an average of sixteen vessels were deployed to one of the four overseas station squadrons yearly, but the triumph of Jackson's Democrats in Congress in 1827 meant that postwar naval expansion was at an end.[15]

On the other hand, America's overseas trade was greatly increasing, perhaps nowhere more than in the Pacific, and Quincy Adams was eager for American shippers to improve their position there. "The American continents, henceforth, will no longer be subject to colonization," he wrote in 1823, but "the Pacific Ocean, in every part of it, will remain open to the navigation of all nations." Again, his troubles with Congress obstructed his strategy. He persuaded Congress to authorize a South Seas exploring expedition in 1825, but no funds were appropriated for the project.

When Quincy Adams could take executive action, however, he was more successful, and in December of that year an opportunity arose to extend America's reach into the Pacific. When Commodore Isaac Hull of the Pacific Squadron learned that the crew of the Nantucket whaler *Globe* had mutinied, he dispatched Lieutenant John "Mad Jack" Percival in the schooner *Dolphin* to hunt down the renegades, who were reported to be in the Marshall Islands. Pursuing this unsuccessful mission—only two mutineers were captured—Percival put into Honolulu on 9 January 1826, the first American warship to visit the Hawaiian Islands. He was followed by another visitor, Master Commandant Thomas Catesby ap Jones in the *Peacock*, who had been ordered by Southard to sail from Chile to Tahiti to explore the Society Islands on behalf of New England merchants. Jones concluded a simple treaty with the Tahitians concerning the treatment of American ships and sailors, and another, more important agreement with Hawaii's King Kamehameha covering trade and routine maritime issues. Southard wanted Jones to visit Astoria and reinforce the American claim to the jointly administered Oregon Territory, but the *Peacock* was unable to cross the bar at the mouth of the Columbia and Jones had to abort this part of his mission.[16]

The importance of the Pacific frontier was underlined by Southard in late 1827 when he advised Congress that "the establishment of a regular passage . . . through the Isthmus of Panama" was needed to improve communications with the newly established

Pacific Squadron. "At least four vessels of respectable size ought to be constantly in the Pacific," he asserted, "but the distance from the United States renders this impossible, unless six vessels in commission be devoted to that object." Although the Senate ignored Jones' treaty, his diplomacy laid the foundation for the subsequent American bond with Hawaii. Southard was so enthused by Jones' venture that he instructed Master Commandant William B. Finch in the sloop *Vincennes* to return to Honolulu in 1829 and reaffirm the American relationship with the native monarchy. Finch then sailed into the South Pacific, returning to America by way of the Indian Ocean and the Cape of Good Hope, the captain of the first Navy warship to circumnavigate the globe.[17]

The Pacific Squadron was established not to develop America's interest in the mid-Pacific, however, but to defend American shipping off South America during the rebellion against Spain. Before the Napoleonic Wars, American merchantmen stopped over in Chilean ports on their way to the Pacific Northwest or the Orient, and in 1815 New England's whaling fleet returned to the southeast Pacific. Over twenty-five ships "had turned Cape Horn to take fish in the Pacific," Monroe reported in June 1816. That month, however, he had to deal with the seizure of an American whaler by royalist officials in Lima. Monroe briefly considered sending a frigate into the Pacific to protect shipping, but in a fit of economy rejected the idea.[18]

Soon almost no American ships were safe between Chile, the rebel stronghold, and Callao, Peru's main port. Admiral Cochrane, a British soldier-of-fortune hired to command the Chilean Navy, was determined to ruin the brisk American carrying trade with the loyalists, and the loyalists intended to shut down neutral shipping to the rebels. Monroe walked a tightrope. He refused to become involved in Latin America's wars against Spain, but he intended to defend maritime access in South American waters. After news of the rivals' war against American trade reached Washington, Monroe sent Captain Biddle in the sloop *Ontario* into the Pacific in October 1817 with orders "to secure respect to our commerce in every port and from every flag" in the southeastern Pacific. Biddle stood off Valparaíso on 25 January 1818. Spain had issued a blockade order covering the length of Chile's coast, but deployed only two ships and a brig to enforce it, a formation that foolishly attempted to prevent Biddle from entering the harbor. He learned that neither side was willing to respect neutral rights, and so found himself racing up and down the coast, using bluster and threats, to get American ships released.[19]

Biddle was relieved in early 1819 by Captain John Downes in the 38-gun frigate *Macedonian*. Tensions increased in August when Downes learned that the Spanish had seized several American ships and Cochrane announced that he intended to blockade every Peruvian port. Downes had to race to Acapulco and demand that the royalists release the merchantman *Cossack* and her imprisoned crew. After repeated protests, the Spanish backed down and the ship was freed. "Nothing but the presence of the *Macedonian*," he reported from Valparaíso, "has saved the American property in this port. Between the Spaniard and the Chilean squadron a small part of any of our vessels would have escaped destruction."[20]

Within days Cochrane's rebel fleet, composed of one frigate and a few sloops, appeared off Callao and established its blockade. On the night of 5 November he led a party that boarded the Spanish frigate *Esmeralda*, slaughtered the crew, and took over the ship. The loyalist shore batteries opened fire on the ships in the harbor, hitting the captured vessel, a British frigate, several merchantmen, and the *Macedonian*. Several Americans were killed when a rumor that Downes was assisting Cochrane ignited riots in Callao and Lima, and four days later Spanish gunboats fired at the American schooner *Rampart*, forcing her master to abandon the vessel. Downes, stranded ashore during the riots, was furious about this incident, but he refused to return fire for fear it would involve the United States in the war. Instead, he demanded that the viceroy pay compensation. After some hard bargaining, the Spaniard backed down and returned the *Rampart* to her owners. With this issue partly settled, Downes organized a convoy of American ships and escorted them out of Callao on 24 November en route to safer ports. Prior to 1819, Spanish operations posed the greater danger to American shipping, but Cochrane soon became the scourge of all neutral trade on the Pacific coast. Following the *Rampart* affair, Downes learned that the rebels were blockading the American merchantmen *Zephyr* and *Panther* in the port of Payta, so he sailed south to rescue them. Thoroughly frustrated, he was eager to leave the Pacific when the *Independence* appeared on the scene to relieve the *Macedonian* in June 1821.[21]

The constant menace to American trade in the southeast Pacific led Monroe in January 1824 to establish a permanent Pacific

Squadron. Commodore Hull took a powerful force—the frigate *United States*, the sloops *Peacock*, and the *Dolphin*—around Cape Horn and established a base at Callao. He put into Valparaíso, 1,700 miles away, on 27 March, and learned that a British squadron of one sail-of-the-line, two frigates, and two sloops had entered Callao. The presence of these two forces considerably reduced the danger to neutral shipping at the same time that the military situation ashore stabilized. Cochrane's blockade had worn down the Spanish, and in December the rebels routed the royalists at Ayacucho and took Lima. Less than two years later the last Spanish redoubt fell, and in 1827 Madrid tacitly accepted the independence of the Latin American republics.

The Monroe Doctrine also conflicted with American sympathies in the Greek war for independence, which erupted in 1821. The Turks attempted to suppress the revolt with terror, thus arousing western support for the Hellenic cause. When Egypt provided Turkey with aid, the Greeks turned to the Great Powers, but they feared to intervene unilaterally, break up Turkey, and disturb the balance of power. After an 1822 massacre at Scio, Monroe in his 1823 Annual Message expressed "a strong hope" that the Greeks "would succeed in their contest." The following year, however, the Greek Navy was crushed off Budrum. Its ships scattered into the Aegean Sea and turned to privateering to support the rebellion. Southard told Congress in December 1823 that augmenting Commodore Thomas Catesby ap Jones' Mediterranean Squadron "will not be necessary," but he changed his strategy a few months later when he learned that the Greek pirates had begun to attack the American carrying trade to the Near East.[22]

In May 1824 Southard named Commodore Rodgers to take command of a powerful squadron built around the sail-of-the-line *North Carolina* and the frigate *Constitution*. He was to enter the Mediterranean, make contact with the Turks, and try to negotiate a treaty giving American trade most-favored-nation status—a major element of maritime access—and allowing a consul to reside in Constantinople. The *North Carolina* stood out of Hampton Roads on 27 March 1825, and the squadron rendezvoused at Gibraltar one month later. Rodgers sent his ships into the Aegean, where they escorted American merchantmen to Turkey, visited Greek ports, and tried to seek out the Capudan Pasha, a Turkish leader with whom Rodgers hoped to negotiate a trade treaty. Rodgers' operations considerably reduced attacks on American shipping. After anchoring in Port Mahon for the winter, he returned to the eastern Mediterranean in 1826, located the Turkish fleet, and pressed in vain the case for a trade treaty. This naval diplomacy may have failed because of a rumor circulating in Europe that Monroe intended to support the Greek rebels in return for a naval base in the Aegean.

Once Rodgers retired from the Aegean later that year, however, the tempo of Greek operations increased and did not recede until Lieutenant Lawrence Kearny in the *Warren* reached the area in the summer of 1827. He escorted convoys through the islands and in September initiated an active patrolling schedule. Later that month, he captured an armed Greek brig making for the port of Carabusa and burned another pirate brig a few weeks later. In October, Kearny came upon the abandoned American brig *Cherub,* which had been plundered by pirates near the island of Syra, rescued her, and ran down another pirate gang who had attacked the freighter *Rob Roy* and escaped with her cargo. Determined to root out the pirates of Myconi, the *Warren* swept the surrounding waters with small boats, and Kearny put ashore a landing party to collect evidence. Then, on 15 November, the *Warren* appeared off Myconi and Kearny delivered an ultimatum to the island's leaders, threatening to bombard the port unless they surrendered the loot from the *Cherub.* Twenty-four hours elapsed with no reply. Kearny fired two warning shots into the town and directed that a third shot land in the market square. The Greeks quickly capitulated, and the loot from the American ship was returned. Kearny realized that the source of the problem was the rebellion, however, and reported that "piracy has . . . the present seat of the Greek government, for its fountain head."[23]

The problem was changed dramatically in July 1827 by the negotiation of the Treaty of London. Recognizing that the Greeks might never win independence alone, and unable to withstand public pressure to intervene, Britain, France, and Russia agreed to establish a combined multinational fleet to prevent the Turks from overrunning Greece. This force appeared in the eastern Mediterranean within months, and on 20 October at the Battle of Navarino annihilated the Turkish fleet. This victory erased Turkish naval power in the Aegean and allowed the Greeks to reassert their authority in the region. In the near term, however, the allied victory at Navarino only complicated the American problem. Because the Greek privateers were no longer needed to repel the

Turks, their attention quickly returned to victimizing neutral merchantmen. Without a larger squadron to patrol the area, Lieutenant Kearny warned Southard, American trade was in greater
danger than ever.

Southard and Rodgers quickly turned to Congress with a request for more "indispensable" sloops to reinforce the Mediterranean Squadron, claiming that "nothing but the presence of a
force which they dread can intimidate or control" the Greek pirates. Southard was disenchanted with patrols and hoped merely
to increase the number of ships on station to a level that would
produce a system of convoys to protect the reduced level of American traffic. Although the Greek war had heated up, he told
Congress, "the presence and activity of our vessels . . . have protected our . . . growing commerce from serious interruption." Indeed, he had even come around reluctantly to support a proposal for joint Anglo-American cooperation in convoying operations.
While this strategy and the Navy's request for more sloops were being challenged in the Senate by the Jacksonian Democrats, other
forces were at work. Ironically, the engagement off Navarino had
been triggered by a misunderstanding. The primary mission of
the allied force had been to establish maritime order in the
Aegean Sea in the hope that this would indirectly support the
Greek cause.[24]

When the destruction of the Turkish Navy resulted in an increase in Greek piracy, the commander of the French fleet informed the Greek patriots that he would destroy any armed Greek
vessel that ventured ten miles beyond the mainland. From the flagship *Constitution*, Commodore Daniel Paterson, the new commander of the Mediterranean Squadron, alerted Washington that
"should the allies carry this measure vigorously and rigorously into
effect," it would "soon suppress piracy." When their threats were
ignored, the Great Powers decided to act, no longer concerned
about hampering the ability of the Greeks to withstand the Turks.
In January 1828, the allied fleet descended on the main pirate
base at Carabusa, destroyed it and most of the pirate flotilla, and
then remorselessly dispatched a series of punitive expeditions
against the remaining Greek forces in the northern waters of the
archipelago. Shortly before he left office, Navy Secretary Southard
confirmed the results to Congress, announcing in 1829 that the
threat to American commerce from the Greek pirates had nearly
been eliminated.

Whereas American involvement in the Mediterranean re-

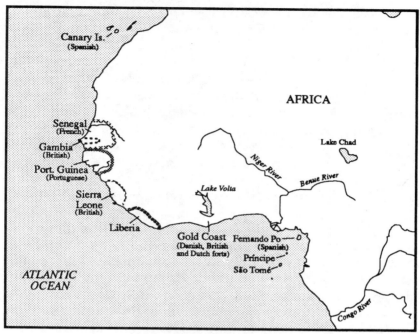

West Africa, 1816-1828

flected a single-minded dedication to maritime access, naval operations in African waters arose as a product of the movement to suppress the Atlantic slave trade. Two related pieces of legislation formed the foundation of American policy on this issue. In 1800, Congress had prohibited American ships or crews from engaging in the Atlantic slave trade to Brazil and Cuba; seven years later the importation of African slaves into the United States was outlawed, a trend against the slave trade foreseen by the Constitutional Convention in 1787. The first act assigned the Navy the responsibility for enforcing this policy. Then in April 1818 this authority was strengthened when Congress approved President Monroe's request to permit American warships to seize slavers flying the Stars and Stripes in the Caribbean and off West Africa. A year later Congress, trying to deter the traffic, defined slave trading as piracy, a crime punishable by hanging; this further reinforced the Navy's role.

On 3 March 1819, Congress enacted another measure, the Slave Trade Act, which authorized Monroe to recognize a private agency to handle the resettlement of Africans recaptured from slavers taken along the West African coast. The effect of this law was to provide a subsidy for the American Colonization Society, a private group whose immediate goal was to end the slave trade by establishing an African colony of former captives, and whose long-term objective was to transport all American blacks back to their native Africa as a solution to the domestic problem of slavery. Navy Secretary Smith Thompson supported this policy, but Secretary of State Quincy Adams worried that the establishment of a West African settlement of ex-slaves would "plunge us deep enough into the plan to bind the honor of the nation to further appropriations" to defend the new colony. Adams was overruled on this point by Monroe, who assigned responsibility for the project to the Navy in January 1820, thus initiating a long and intimate relationship between the Colonization Society and the department. Meanwhile, Thompson had dispatched Lieutenant Edward Trenchard in the sloop *Cyane* to West Africa with orders to suppress the use of the American flag by slavers in those waters. Arriving off the African coast in March, Trenchard soon arrested four slavers flying the Stars and Stripes and released their captives ashore.[25]

In 1821, Lieutenant Robert Stockton, one of the founders of the Colonization Society, persuaded Thompson to give him command of the schooner *Alligator*, and to order him to establish on the African coast the ex-slave colony to be known as Liberia. Guided by the advice of agents at Freetown, the capital of the British colony of Sierra Leone, Stockton selected a site near Cape Mesurado and landed there on 12 December for a palaver with the local chief, King Peter. These negotiations did not get off to a good start. King Peter was angry at the British for disrupting the slave trade from which his tribe had long profited at the expense of its enemies, annoyed by the patrol operations of the *Cyane*, and offended by Stockton's brusque demands for a cession of part of the tribe's domain. When the chief started to threaten the American landing party, Stockton drew his pistol, cocked it, and pointed the barrel at the chief's head. Just as King Peter threw up his arms, the sun shone through the clouds and he announced that "divine" intervention was compelling him to accept Stockton's offer![26]

Following Liberia's establishment, Stockton returned home. He was followed off the African coast by Lieutenant Matthew C. Perry in the sloop *Shark*, which arrived on station in September 1822. By that time the occasional American patrols had been sufficient to force the slave traders to stop flying the Stars and Stripes, and Perry reported to Washington that while he was off the coast he "could not even hear of an American slaving vessel." "To continue our exertions to repress the slave trade," Secretary Southard told Congress in 1823, he intended "that the commander of the West India squadron . . . detach one or more of the vessels belonging to his command to cruise along the African coast, occasionally touching at Cape Mesurado and ministering to the wants of the people there." Dispatching a schooner or sloop to visit the colony and patrol West African waters soon became an accepted aspect of American naval operations; at least one warship was assigned to this duty every year for the next twenty years. In spite of these somewhat irregular deployments, the American naval agent in Liberia advised the Navy Department in 1832 that the "slave trade on this section of the coast has nearly ceased," with only two slavers flying French colors still "engaged in the illicit traffic." The suppression of part of the Atlantic slave trade by the West African patrol, however, coincided with the collapse of the broad and ambitious effort of the Colonization Society to transport all American slaves back to Africa.[27]

Chapter Ten

Maritime Access in the Age of Jackson
1829–1840

General Andrew Jackson of Tennessee won the 1828 presidential election partly because of his personal popularity as a hero of the War of 1812 and partly because of the paralysis of Quincy Adams' National Republican administration. Jackson's Democrats skillfully tarred Quincy Adams with the charge of "aristocracy," southerners liked Jackson's promise to honor states' rights, and several former Federalist leaders sought a stronger chief executive. Although Jackson's tenure was dominated by domestic issues, his expansion of the powers of the presidency and his faith in vigorous government shaped his forward foreign policy and his behavior as commander in chief. He was convinced that the "bulwark of our defense is the national militia, which in the present state of our intelligence and population must render us invincible." He disliked professional armies and asserted that as long as the nation was worth defending, "a patriotic militia will cover it with an impenetrable aegis."[1]

In the absence of any real threat to American home territory from Europe, Jackson pursued a vigorous policy of continentalism, or westward territorial expansion, and shortly after he came to office this provoked a series of wars with the Indian nations. Whereas Quincy Adams had been ambivalent about westward expansion, in 1829 Jackson adopted a policy of removing the Indians to lands west of the Mississippi. His agents imposed more than ninety punitive treaties on the Indians, and hostilities erupted in

1831 with the Sacs and Fox tribes in the Black Hawk War. Although removal of the Cherokees from Georgia proceeded peacefully, Florida's Seminoles put up a stout resistance in the Second Seminole War, beginning in December 1835. Supported by a small Navy detachment that constantly moved troops up and down the rivers and waterways crisscrossing Florida's swamps, the Army spent the next seven years under eight different commanders chasing down fewer than 1,200 braves, who skillfully defended an Indian population that had already shrunk to less than 5,000. After burning the Indians' crops and razing their villages, the Americans reduced the Seminoles to about 250 souls by the spring of 1842, and Washington at long last declared a bitter victory.[2]

The frontier outlook behind this fearsome policy was shared by the new secretary of the Navy, John Branch of North Carolina, a former senator who owed his appointment to his support of Jackson's effort to create a new national Democratic Party. Like most of the early Jacksonians, Branch held an agrarian perspective, but he was nonetheless a well-educated, articulate official whose long dominance of North Carolina's public life testified to his political ability. It suited Jackson's partisan purposes to extol the virtues of the militia, but as president he also frequently confessed to the need for the Navy as "the best standing security of this country against foreign aggression." Jackson held that the "ocean rolling between us and most of the governments with whom we are likely to have collision" meant that the United States had "nothing to apprehend from attempts at conquest." Nevertheless, he shared with his predecessors a view that the determined defense of maritime access was a necessary feature of American grand strategy.[3]

Accepting this calculus meant that Branch could at the same time be mostly indifferent to the size of the U.S. Navy as compared to the naval forces of the Great Powers. When he took office he declared that the Navy needed to build no more sails-of-the-line or frigates, although he did ask Congress to underwrite an ongoing program to stockpile materials for mobilization shipbuilding in the event of a crisis. Jackson's naval policy was to "discontinue, for the present, the building of ships of war, unless for some object or immediate emergency." Moreover, Branch sternly objected to using funds appropriated for repairs to rebuild old ships from the keel up, a "deception" he charged Quincy Adams had employed to reconstruct the *John Adams*. This came partly from Branch's Jeffersonian concern for economy but also from the fact that many of the ships that had been authorized and laid down under the 1816 Crowninshield program were still incomplete. For example, the sail-of-the-line *Vermont* was laid down in 1818 but not launched until 1848; the frigate *Santee*, laid down in 1821, was not launched until 1855 and not commissioned for another three years; and the sail-of-the-line *Virginia*, laid down in 1822 in the Boston Navy Yard, remained on the stocks there for the next sixty-two years.[4]

Other factors shaped Jackson's early naval policy, including the end of the Latin American wars of independence; the decline of piracy in the Caribbean after 1825; and an increasing, profitable American trade with South America, the Pacific, and the Far East. With five frigates, ten sloops, and four schooners in the fleet, Branch had to support several overseas station squadrons, each composed of one large ship and several lesser vessels. However, he soon found that he did not have enough of these inferior warships, and to sustain the increasing tempo of cruising he persuaded Congress in 1830 to allow him to lay down the schooners *Experiment, Boxer,* and *Enterprise.* Like nearly all of the Navy's smaller vessels, these schooners were expected to support a frigate during a squadron action in wartime, but mostly to cruise singly in peacetime on distant station, "defending our property on the ocean from pirates or open enemies."[5]

Although Branch was comfortable with the general political philosophy of most inland Democrats, he was surprisingly eager to expand the boundaries of maritime access. Since 1784 Americans had traded with the Ottoman Empire, and while the Turks were usually courteous and often expressed an interest in a commercial treaty with Washington, they had always somehow avoided formal negotiations. In 1829, the Great Powers forced Constantinople to grant independence to Greece, and Jackson assumed in 1830 that the Sublime Porte would want to widen its contacts with the West. To negotiate a treaty, Secretary of State Martin Van Buren named Charles Rhind, a New York merchant, and Captain James Biddle, who was about to take command of the Mediterranean Squadron. When they made the port of Smyrna, Rhind left Biddle behind and rode alone to Constantinople, where through the fog of international intrigue he saw a desperate need by the Turks for new friends.

Rhind's Treaty contained the familiar provisions of American trade arrangements of the time—a most-favored-nation clause and a definition of the extraterritorial legal rights of Americans in Turkey—but in one respect it was unique. Rhind wanted to restore the pre-Revolutionary War export of American-built warships, and in return for a Turkish pledge to allow the Americans to trade in the Black Sea, he promised to help the Turks acquire warships built in the United States to replace those lost at Navarino in 1829. Biddle, confounded by this novelty, fussed with his fellow commissioners, and, before the Senate approved Rhind's Treaty, the offending clause was excised. Before it was amended, the Rhind Treaty had trespassed across the boundary of maritime access by violating the Monroe Doctrine's promise that the United States would not become involved in the European balance of power.[6]

Beyond Europe the Jacksonians' enforcement of maritime access was more muscular, as evidenced by Secretary Branch's request to Congress in 1831 for funds to "provide a sufficient force to visit occasionally the Indian and Chinese seas," a force that eventually became known as the East India Squadron. Concern for the safety and expansion of American trade in the western Pacific was also expressed in Jackson's decision to deploy a punitive expedition to Quallah Batoo, Sumatra, in 1831. Since 1783, Yankee mariners had shipped opium from India to Sumatra, where they traded it for pepper before returning home to Salem. This commerce grew so rapidly that, by the end of the Napoleonic Wars, Salem had a virtual stranglehold on the Western pepper trade. The trade became violent, however, and Sumatra's Malays, desperate for opiates, earned a justifiable reputation for ferocity. On 9 February 1831, the rajahs of Quallah Batoo, a small village, boarded the American merchantman *Friendship*, killed three sailors, took over the ship, grabbed several hostages, and stripped the vessel of her fittings, cargo, and specie. Po Quallah, the pirate leader, boasted that he would "cut off every American vessel that falls in my power." Master Charles Endicott escaped, however, and with the help of three other American ships recovered the *Friendship*, but he was unable to punish the murderers or recover his goods. "Within the space of twelve months," he warned the rajahs, "a big ship from the United States would most assuredly visit Quallah Batoo and punish the aggressors."[7]

Word of the plunder of the *Friendship* reached Washington at the height of a cabinet split between Jackson and Vice President John C. Calhoun, a crisis that threatened the breakup of the new Democratic Party coalition. Jackson dismissed Calhoun's supporters, including Navy Secretary Branch, and replaced them with his own partisans. The new secretary of the Navy was Levi Woodbury of New Hampshire, a quintessential Jacksonian, of whom a fellow politician complained that he "keeps snug and plays out of all the corners of his eyes." Woodbury's first order of business was to deal with Quallah Batoo. The *Friendship* was owned by Congressman Nathanial Silsbee of Massachusetts, a formidable figure who insisted in letters to Jackson and Woodbury that they exact some retribution from the Sumatrans for plundering his vessel.[8]

The frigate *Potomac*, completed in 1821 in the Washington Navy Yard but never before commissioned, had been fitted out recently to replace the *Guerrière* on station off the west coast of South America with the Pacific Squadron. Already Secretary Woodbury had given her captain, John Downes, the additional duty of transporting Martin Van Buren, a participant in Jackson's cabinet shuffle, to his new post as minister to the British court. Downes' orders were again amended on 9 August 1831. After dropping off Van Buren in London, the *Potomac* was to round the Cape of Good Hope and shape a course for Sumatra, and there "demand of the rajah . . . restitution of the property plundered . . . and the immediate punishment of those concerned in the murder of the" crew "of the ship *Friendship*." When his ship reached Cape Town, Downes learned about a number of other atrocities committed by the Malays of Quallah Batoo, and when he made the coast of China, more chilling tales came his way. By February 1832, the *Potomac* was closing the north coast of Sumatra, but no other ships were in the vicinity to provide Downes with additional intelligence.[9]

Woodbury's orders to Downes were quite specific in one respect. After presenting "a demand" for "prompt redress," he was "authorized . . . to vindicate our wrongs," capture the "offenders . . ., retake such part of the stolen property as can be found," and "destroy the boats . . ., forts, and dwellings near the scene of aggression." Woodbury also impressed Downes with the need to inflict "ample punishment" on the natives. Stopping off at Cape Town, China, and Java, Downes had learned that there was little real government on Sumatra and that the tribesmen were fierce fighters. Not taking any chances, he decided to assault their forts and take five local rajahs hostage as an "important preliminary step towards opening a successful parley."[10]

At 1430 on 5 February, the *Potomac*, disguised as a large Dutch merchantman, anchored off Quallah Batoo, and a boat was lowered to carry a party ashore to reconnoiter. The sailors turned back, however, when they drew fire from the forest and the hostile intent of the natives became evident. "No demand for satisfaction was made previous to my attack," Downes later explained, "because I was . . . satisfied that no such demand would be answered except only by refusal." When night fell, one launch, four cutters, and a lifeboat lifted a landing party of about 250 sailors and Marines onto a beach one mile from the village. Dividing into five groups, they descended on the rajahs' forts, assisted by gunfire from the *Potomac*, and engaged overwhelming numbers of Malays, who defended their positions with muskets, swords, javelins, and small cannon. By 2000, the forts were in flames and, except for two casualties, Downes' men returned safely to their frigate. The *Potomac* stayed off Quallah Batoo for another twelve days while the rajahs assured Downes that they would no longer molest American merchantmen. When he was satisfied, Downes hoisted anchor and made for the Sandwich Islands.[11]

When the *Potomac* closed on the South American coast at the start of summer to join the Pacific Squadron, Downes learned that news of his attack on Quallah Batoo had ignited a firestorm of Whig criticism against the Jackson administration. The Whigs charged that Jackson had acted highhandedly in dispatching Downes' mission, that hundreds of men and scores of women and children had been massacred, and that Downes' foray had failed to secure an indemnity. The Whigs were in an awkward position, however; they prefaced their accusations with vocal support for an active policy of trade defense and tried not to impugn the honor of Downes or his men. In a nutshell, the Whigs condemned Jackson's abuse of executive authority, a continuing partisan theme that encompassed his handling of domestic policy and foreign relations. "If the president can direct expeditions against the Malays," the pro-Whig *National Intelligencer* declared on 10 July 1832, "we do not see why he may not have the power to do the same in reference to any other power or people." Jackson, they charged, was usurping Congress' power to declare war. Jackson's partisans sprang to his defense, while the Whigs tried to get him to give Congress all of the correspondence dealing with the Quallah Batoo affair. In spite of Woodbury's public support for the raid, he privately wrote to Downes that Jackson "regrets that you were not able before attacking . . . to obtain fuller information" and complained that Downes had not issued "a previous demand . . . for restitution and indemnity" before attacking the forts.[12]

When Woodbury's insulting letter, obviously intended for Congressional consumption, reached Downes at Valparaíso, he was furious. He hired Jeremiah Reynolds, a talented publicist, as his personal secretary, and during the voyage home Reynolds interviewed the entire crew and composed a detailed account of the episode. By the time that the *Potomac* stood into Hampton Roads, however, the Whigs had dropped the issue. They realized they could not attack Jackson without slandering the popular Downes. Woodbury's reading of Reynolds' account of the attack on Quallah Batoo led Jackson to uphold Downes' actions in his next annual message to Congress at the end of the year, and Woodbury reported in December 1832 "that the result of that visit has been to silence all exultation and menaces of further violence from those sea robbers." Nonetheless, Downes' single punitive operation had failed to suppress the Sumatran pirates. Barely two years later, on 27 May 1834, the Sumatrans tried to board the *Derby of Salem*, then loading pepper off Trabangunchute, and only resolute action by the crew prevented the bark from being overwhelmed. "It is high time that the American government had a sloop of war on this coast from March to August to protect our commerce," Captain Jonathan P. Felt indignantly reported to his employers after the episode.

After additional depredations, Commander George Read in the *Columbia* was dispatched to deal with the Sumatrans again in 1838. Mindful of Downes' problems, Read negotiated at length with the pirate rajahs to secure restitution for lost American property and the arrest of several of the natives. But when this diplomacy failed, Read resignedly burned down another village, a punitive step that reduced the danger to American shipping in the area for several years.[13]

The goal of expanding American trade in the Pacific also led Navy Secretary Woodbury in 1832 to promote the diplomatic mission of Edmund Roberts, a New Hampshire merchant captain who was given the Navy title of captain's clerk and sent out in the sloop *Peacock* to establish formal commercial relations with several Asian and Indian Ocean trading partners. Because he refused to perform the degrading kowtow before the court of Cochin China, Roberts was unable to conduct any negotiations there. He was more successful in Siam, where he arranged a trade treaty, and in

Muscat, whose sultan ruled most of East Africa as well as the spice-rich island of Zanzibar. Although many American merchants traded with China by the time Roberts reached the Far East, the Manchu court in Peking was so hostile in its few dealings with foreigners that the country was not on his agenda.[14]

After Roberts returned to the United States and the Senate approved his two treaties, he decided to sail back to the Far East to exchange the ratification and to try for the first time to penetrate the isolated Japanese market. Unfortunately, Roberts died of cholera en route to Japan, curtailing for the moment American diplomatic interest in relations with that island empire. The Roberts mission, concern for Hawaii, and continuing problems with the pepper trade to Sumatra caused Jackson in 1835 to establish an East India Squadron, comprising the *Peacock* and the schooner *Enterprise*, under the command of Commodore Edward P. Kennedy. With an area of operations stretching from the China coast to Hawaii, the East India Squadron was responsible for "protecting as well as extending [American] commerce" in the western Pacific, defending the growing number of missionaries who sailed into the Pacific to convert heathen peoples, and preventing any foreign naval power from annexing the strategic Hawaiian Islands.[15]

Andrew Jackson's uncommon willingness to resort to force to defend American interests adorned his foreign policy and was demonstrated in the Falkland Islands crisis of 1831. When Buenos Aires had declared her independence from Spain on 25 May 1810, she continued her mother country's claim to the offshore islands, a claim disputed by the British. The British had evacuated their small garrison from the unpopulated archipelago on the eve of the American Revolution. However, after 1810 Argentina was racked by the revolution, repeated coups among the patriots, civil wars, and frontier conflicts, and for years the government of Buenos Aires was unable to exercise much authority in the islands, which by that time were mostly used by New England's commercial sealing and whaling fleets. It was a "distressing spectacle," John Forbes, the minister to Buenos Aires, told Secretary of State Martin Van Buren, to watch the Argentines "falling through the evening twilight of despondency into the darkness of an almost hopeless anarchy."[16]

Into this vortex stepped Louis Vernet, a wealthy Franco-German adventurer who established a settlement in the Falkland

Sound and was named Argentine military governor in 1829. A roguish schemer, Vernet planned to grab control of the fishing and sealing trade in the South Atlantic by asserting his authority as governor to prohibit American ships from killing seals or cattle on the islands. A decree to this effect so profoundly imperiled American rights that when a copy reached Washington, Jackson immediately announced his opposition to "any measures" that "impose any restraints whatever upon the enterprise of our citizens engaged in the fisheries in question." Buenos Aires had "no good title to these Islands . . . from any fact connected with their history." This laid down a line of policy regarding the Falklands that Washington followed for the next 150 years.[17]

Even before he learned about Jackson's stance, Vernet had trouble enforcing his decree; the reigning junta in Buenos Aires was preoccupied with threats of a renewed civil war and so was unable to provide him with a patrol vessel. Therefore, Vernet armed his own schooner and hired several former British naval officers. In August 1831, they seized three schooners from Stonington, Connecticut, looted the ships, imprisoned the crews, and extorted ransom for their release. When Vernet returned to Buenos Aires with his loot and hostages, the American consul lodged a protest, but the Argentine government announced that it was "indifferent" to the incident, refusing to repudiate, acknowledge, or condemn Vernet. Meanwhile, Master Commandant Silas Duncan in the corvette *Lexington* had been ordered to duty with the Brazil Squadron that was charged with the usual mission of protecting American citizens and commerce. A hero of the battle of Lake Champlain, Duncan was resourceful and intelligent, and when he reached Buenos Aires on 29 November he decided to force the Argentines to accept responsibility for Vernet. On 6 December, Duncan warned the Argentine foreign minister that the *Lexington* would sail for the Falklands in three days and "put an immediate stop" to further depredations against American ships unless Buenos Aires disowned Vernet and charged him with piracy. Duncan fully recognized the dangers in this course of action. If Buenos Aires sustained Vernet's position, explained George Slacum, the American consul in Buenos Aires, then "our commerce round the Cape would be exposed to robbery and destruction." On the other hand, both Duncan and Slacum understood that moving against Vernet's gang might indirectly encourage the British to reassert their claim, and they recognized that there were "powerful reasons why England should not be permitted to colonise" the archipelago.[18]

The Argentines did not know how to reply to Duncan's ultimatum. Disowning Vernet would weaken their claim to the Falklands, but exercising sovereignty was beyond the means at hand. In any case, there were no ships available to prevent Duncan from carrying out his threat. At noon on 9 December, the *Lexington* left the dock in front of Government House and made for the mouth of the Río de la Plata; five hours later, the Argentines proclaimed that the entire matter was a "private" issue. Duncan closed on Port Louis on 28 December, but a storm prevented him from entering the harbor for three days. He arrested Vernet's lieutenants, destroyed the fort, and recovered some of the loot from the Stonington sealers. Vernet's colony was like a prison camp, and most of the settlers were begging to go back to the mainland. Their pleas fit neatly into a plan of action that Duncan concocted during his stay in the Falklands.[19]

Sailing on 21 January, he reached Montevideo two weeks later and announced his intentions: if the Argentines tried Vernet's men for piracy, then he would return them to Buenos Aires; should Buenos Aires refuse to do this, then Duncan would take the prisoners to the United States to stand trial there. He then sailed for Rio to rendezvous with the new commander of the Brazil Squadron, Commodore George Rodgers, who had just come from the United States without any specific instructions on the South Atlantic crisis, although Jackson had restated the American position in his most recent annual message to Congress. Within days after Rodgers' departure, word of the Vernet affair reached Washington from the crew of the sealer *Breakwater*, and Secretary of State Livingston dispatched John Baylies to Buenos Aires. A special envoy, Baylies was told to protest the seizures, defend Duncan's operation, and persuade the Argentines to promise that they would stop molesting American ships. Duncan's prisoners, of course, provided some leverage for this approach.[20]

Rodgers reached Rio in early April, but his handling of the affair undermined American interests in the South Atlantic. To appease Buenos Aires, he ordered Duncan to release Vernet's gang, thus discarding the only trumps Baylies had to play. Baylies "threatened" General Rosas in Buenos Aires with the use of "naval force" to get "reparations" and "justice," but his mission achieved little and ended in what President Jackson termed the "suspen-

Commodore John Rodgers, commander of the Mediterranean Squadron, 1804–6; commander of the Atlantic Squadron, 1812; and chairman, Board of Commissioners, 1815–36.

sion" of relations for the next decade. The Vernet affair renewed British interest in the Falklands, although Rear Admiral Sir Thomas Baker of the South Atlantic Squadron warned London on 25 February 1832 that it would be "prudent to delay" to avoid any involvement in the "angry discussions" between the United States and Argentina. Baker's report sparked the interest of the Admiralty as to "whether . . . the treaties with Spain" gave Britain "possession of the Falkland Islands." The British waited for American interest to cool, and then the foreign minister, Lord Palmerston, instructed the Admiralty to dispatch "one of His Majesty's ships" to "the Falklands for the purpose of exercising the rights of sovereignty." On 2 January 1833, the small British warship *Clio* anchored in Berkeley Sound and forced an Argentine Navy schooner to withdraw. The captain raised the Union Jack over

Britain's newest crown colony. London ignored all subsequent Argentine protests about this action, but the British did avoid harassing any American ships for many years.[21]

The Falkland Islands crisis was a product of the turmoil in Latin America that followed the collapse of the Spanish Empire, a process from which Americans tried to profit by aggressively pursuing the twin objectives of maritime access and continentalism. The Monroe Doctrine, which had the effect of discouraging the Great Powers from allying with Spain's successors in the New World, provided an important strategic tool in advancing the cause of westward expansion and North American hegemony. During Jackson's presidency, the issue of Texas annexation began to focus the attention of American statesmen on the debility of Mexican power and the exposed western flank of the United States. Two years after Spain had refused to sell Texas to the United States during the negotiations over the 1819 Adams-Onis Treaty, the Spanish viceroy in Mexico City granted a huge tract of land to Moses Austin of Missouri on the understanding that Austin would attract 300 American families to settle in the undeveloped province. This agreement was reaffirmed by the Mexicans after they successfully rebelled against Spanish rule and achieved independence in 1822, and within eight years 30,000 Americans had migrated to Texas.

In August 1829, Jackson revived Henry Clay's earlier attempt to buy Texas from Mexico, but his diplomacy failed owing as much to the ineptitude of Jackson's envoy as to Mexican opposition. Four years later, General Santa Anna, Mexico's dictator, denounced his constitution, established a strong central government in Mexico City, and abrogated several agreements with the Texans. The members of Stephen Austin's Committee of Safety, alarmed by these threats to their liberty, roused their fellow Texans and on 4 October 1835 proclaimed Texas' independence and declared war against Mexico. While General Sam Houston was raising an army to defend Texas, Santa Anna and more than 5,000 Mexican troops crossed the Rio Grande. However, their northward march was delayed by the heroic stand of a mere 200 Americans who held the strategic Alamo fortress in San Antonio. After Santa Anna slaughtered the defenders of the Alamo to a man on 6 March 1836, he laid siege to Goliad, and when that garrison foolishly threw down its arms and surrendered, the Mexicans shot all their American prisoners of war in a bloody act of revenge against the rebels.

Jackson realized that Americans were deeply shocked by the massacres at the Alamo and Goliad and heartened by Houston's resistance. Nevertheless he feared that open support of the slave-holding Texas rebels would split the Democratic Party along regional lines and deny his vice president, Martin Van Buren, victory in the November 1836 election. When the rebellion erupted, therefore, Jackson invoked the 1818 Neutrality Act and Navy Secretary Mahlon Dickerson instructed Commodore Alexander Dallas of the West Indies Squadron to defend American neutrality, protect trade with Mexico, and "sustain the honor and interest of the United States" in the Gulf. To accomplish this mission, Dickerson told Congress, he had deployed "an unusually large force . . . in the Gulf of Mexico, and in the West Indies" where American "commerce be more exposed than in any other quarter."[22]

Because the movement of Santa Anna's army depended completely on supplies shipped from New Orleans to Texas, Dickerson's seemingly cautious decision unwittingly undermined the Texans' cause. To interdict supplies bound for the Mexican Army, the Texans established their own navy, purchasing four small schooners and sending them on cruising patrols off the mouth of the Rio Grande. Two American merchant brigs carrying supplies to the Mexican Army depot at Matamoros were captured on 3 April by the former slaver *Invincible.* In response, Commodore Dallas dispatched Master Commandant William V. Taylor in the *Warren* to the mouth of the Mississippi, where he found the *Invincible* and took her without resistance. When he learned that Taylor had escorted the *Invincible* back to New Orleans for trial on charges of piracy, William G. Bryan, the Texas agent there, complained that "Dallas is no friend to Texas."[23]

Behind much of this activity were several New Orleans insurance firms that were profiting from the Mexican trade and indifferent to the plight of Texas. Public opinion in New Orleans and elsewhere in the United States unquestionably favored the Texans' cause, however, and Jackson's neutrality policy was sharply criticized by his opponents. Indeed, the trial of the *Invincible* in New Orleans was marked by the unseemly haste of Texas' partisans to get the ship released and her crew freed. Dickerson got in step with public opinion on 18 May by modifying his orders and crisply reminding Commodore Dallas that "the Mexican as well as Texas" ships in the Gulf were "interrupting our lawful trade and should be captured." One week later Jackson sent word to Dallas to shift as many vessels as possible to the Florida coast to support naval operations in the Second Seminole War. By this time, the tide of the war in Texas had already turned. Laying siege to the Alamo and Goliad so delayed the Mexican Army's progress that Houston had time to organize his own formidable army, and on 31 April the Texans routed the Mexicans at the Battle of San Jacinto and captured Santa Anna. To save his own life, Santa Anna signed two treaties on 14 May 1836 that recognized the independence of Texas.[24]

Jackson was now under fire for his neutrality policy. When Congress demanded that he recognize Texas, Jackson replied that "we should stand aloof . . . until Mexico itself or one of the great foreign powers shall recognize the independence of the new government." A dogged foe of southern interests, Van Buren as president kept Secretary of State John Forsyth at the State Department; both men understood the volatility of the Texas issue and were determined to ignore it entirely. A new government in Mexico City repudiated Santa Anna's treaties, but the Mexican Navy's renewed blockade of Texas' ports in 1837 failed entirely. Van Buren followed Jackson's neutrality policy nonetheless, and Forsyth endorsed Commodore Dallas' strategy of escorting American ships between New Orleans and Matamoros, Tampico, and Veracruz, a policy that Texas bitterly protested. Mexico's maritime operations, never energetic, ended in April 1838, when the French Navy blockaded Veracruz and Tampico so as to force the Mexicans to pay reparations to Frenchmen injured during Mexico's ruinous revolutions. Termed the Pastry War, this farcical conflict doused for the moment Mexico's hopes of recovering Texas.[25]

Jackson was less cautious in dealing with the volatile French Claims Crisis. The claims in question emanated from French seizures of American merchantmen before the Quasi War and had been such a sore point in Franco-American relations that Monroe in his great 1823 annual message demanded "a just indemnity for losses sustained in the later wars . . . under unjustifiable seizures." A revolution in France seven years later brought to power a pro-American monarch, Louis Philippe d'Orléans, and on 4 July 1831 he signed the Franco-American Claims Treaty in which France promised to pay its debt to the United States in six annual installments. The payments got entangled in an unrelated dispute between the king and Parliament, however, and the Chamber of Deputies refused to appropriate the first installment in 1834. Charging that the French "won't pay unless they're made to," an infuriated Jackson asked Congress for the authority to confiscate

French ships in American ports and sell them off to pay the debt. The French minister, deeply affronted, asked for his passport, and the stunned Chamber of Deputies in Paris voted not to make any payments until Jackson retracted his threats and issued an apology, an ultimatum Jackson dismissed with blistering profanity. The crisis worsened considerably. France severed diplomatic relations, and Jackson responded in December 1835 that "the honor of my country shall never be stained by an apology from me for the statement of truth and the performance of duty." "No apology" was the catchword of the day as well as the basis of American policy. Former President Quincy Adams, who hated Jackson but supported him on this issue, worried privately that "if the two countries be saved from war, it seems as if it could only be by a special interposition of Providence."[26]

Jackson had been convinced in 1834 that the existing fleet was "sufficient to guard our commerce" against any non-European opponents, but when the French Claims Crisis erupted, the French government put its navy on alert and sent a powerful squadron across the Atlantic to defend France's West Indian sugar islands. The result was an abrupt change in Jackson's naval policy. One year earlier Navy Secretary Dickerson had used his authority under the Crowninshield program to lay down the small steamer *Fulton II*, which was completed in early 1837. "It can hardly be doubted that the power of steam is soon to produce as great a revolution in the defense of rivers, bays, coasts, and harbors as it has already done in the commerce . . . in Europe as well as America," Dickerson told Congress. In addition, the sail-of-the-line *Pennsylvania* was launched in 1836, and the sails-of-the-line *Ohio*, *Columbus*, and *Delaware* were hurriedly repaired. Also in 1834 Congress agreed to build one frigate and one sloop and to purchase two storeships. When it was clear that the experiment with steam plants would be successful, Jackson instructed Dickerson to ask Congress in 1835 to authorize the construction of the first of four steam sloops, presumably for harbor or coastal defense operations in shallow waters. The Navy secretary conveyed this request to Congress with the prediction that the introduction of steam into fleets "will greatly diminish the frequency as well as the horrors of such [naval] war . . . as it will hold out much greater advantages to the defending than to the attacking party."[27]

The French Claims Crisis also caused the secretary to ask Commodore Rodgers' Board of Commissioners to prepare a broad survey of the Navy's needs. "Our naval force in commission is not adequate to the protection of our rapidly increasing commerce" in the face of the French threat, he observed. Often neglected by historians, the Rodgers Report, as the board's survey became known, was a milestone in the development of American naval policy; it laid down several lines of action that subsequent Navy officials would pursue. After a perfunctory recommendation to reorganize the Board of Commissioners by assigning each of its members executive responsibilities, Rodgers suggested the creation of a "home squadron" to defend the East Coast and "serious and early attention" to the "preparation of a considerable number of steam vessels" for the fleet. The commissioners wanted Congress to authorize a two-stage building program, which would produce a fleet of thirty-five frigates, twenty-five sloops, twenty-five steamers, and twenty-five smaller vessels. The only link in the report between strategy and policy was the proposal to establish the Home Squadron, and Rodgers apparently settled on force levels merely by estimating the Navy's ability to recruit sailors under wartime conditions. Nonetheless, the Rodgers Report was remarkable, showing not only the seriousness of the French Claims Crisis but also demonstrating that many senior Navy men backed a long-term policy of naval expansion and the development of a fleet of steamers.[28]

By the spring of 1836, when Rodgers issued his report, the Franco-American crisis had evaporated. The Senate rejected a request by Jackson to improve coastal fortifications on the grounds that $5 million, the sum of the claims involved, was too small an amount to justify a war with France. Meanwhile the British, concerned about the stability of the regime in Paris, persuaded the French that Jackson was unlikely to back down in the face of French naval pretensions. The Chamber of Deputies reversed itself, reinterpreted Jackson's statements, and meekly voted to pay the bill for the old American claims. Although Jackson had risked war with France over a trivial issue, the result of the affair was heightened respect for the United States from the Great Powers and a demonstration of Britain's interest in keeping peace in the Atlantic even at the expense of Europe.

Jackson's stiff position during the French Claims Crisis enhanced his reputation as a strong president. His personal popularity plus the new Democratic Party machine sufficed to elect Van Buren to the White House in 1836. Shortly after Van Buren

took office, however, the aftershock of Jackson's disastrous economic policies plunged the country into the Panic of 1837, a depression of the business cycle that lasted throughout the remaining years of the Democratic administration. Van Buren's lack of
interest in foreign affairs and naval policy was in large measure
attributable to the consuming demands of domestic politics during the Panic.

For the first two years of his presidency, Van Buren kept Mahon Dickerson at the Navy Department, but in 1838 Dickerson's
health declined and the chief executive turned to James K. Paulding, a well-known literary figure who had served as a naval agent
and who was a confidant of the late Commodore John Rodgers.
No reactionary, Dickerson took advantage of the Navy's mobilization during the French crisis to begin increasing the number of
men in the fleet, a figure that rose dramatically from 6,250 in 1837
to 11,250 five years later. Under his stewardship, the officer corps
also increased in size. There were only thirty-seven captains in
1835, but by 1842 that figure had risen to sixty-eight. One reason
for this expansion was the commissioning of a number of vessels
authorized under the 1816 Crowninshield program on which
work had begun long ago but which were brought into the fleet
during the war scare with France.

The French crisis had just died down when a dispute erupted
with Britain concerning the Canadian border with Maine. This
was followed immediately by a series of cross-border raids from
New York into Canada in retaliation for the burning of the American merchant ship *Caroline* by Canadian hotheads on 29 December 1837. In addition, the collapse of American credit in the financial markets of England had a ripple effect that created a
depression in Britain, and this badly strained relations between
London and Washington. Matters were worsened by the arrest of
Alexander McLeod, a Canadian who was accused in a New York
court of murdering an American during a border raid in 1837.
Palmerston, the aggressive British foreign minister, demanded
that Washington arrange for McLeod's release and threatened
hostilities when Van Buren tried in vain to explain that as president he had no authority over New York's state judiciary.

These incidents created a series of war scares that pock-
marked the Van Buren presidency and compelled Congress to reexamine the relative strength of the American fleet and the forces
assigned to coastal defense. In 1839, Congress established the

Corps of Steam Engineers and authorized the Navy secretary to appoint an engineer in chief, a billet that had been filled over the past four years under a "private contract." Taking quick advantage of the spoils system, the Whigs in 1841 gave the job to a lawyer who was the son of former Navy Secretary Smith Thompson. "His engineering was purely nominal," one wit complained, "and confined to a very prompt and efficient drawing of his salary." The act also established billets for several assistants and specified that each steamer was to be manned by at least eight engineers.[29]

The Navy's new Corps of Engineers was needed because the Van Buren administration was reluctantly presiding over the birth of the American steam fleet with the launching of the steamer *Fulton II* in 1837. Robert Fulton, an inventor and political gadfly, had originally adapted the steam engine to the paddlewheel in 1807, and that year his steamboat *Clermont* first appeared on the Hudson River. During the War of 1812, Navy Secretary Jones had contracted with Fulton to build the *Demologos*, a fast blockade runner and the first steam warship ever constructed. After the war, however, the *Demologos* was employed merely as a receiving ship since the development of steam vessels for the American fleet seemed totally unnecessary. Steam engines were expensive, dirty, and notoriously fragile. Breakdowns were common. Steamers began to burn coal rather than wood, so steam-driven warships were more or less tied to fixed routes between coaling stations. In addition, their cruising radius was quite short. These characteristics made steam vessels inappropriate for a navy that was almost wholly dedicated to dispersion to overseas stations for long-distance cruising missions. The *Fulton II*, on the other hand, had been authorized by Congress for port and harbor defense during the war scare over the French Claims Crisis.

Neither Secretary Paulding nor Commodore Isaac Chauncey, the new chairman of the Board of Commissioners, expressed much enthusiasm for the construction of a fleet of steamers along the lines proposed in 1836 by Rodgers, but in March 1839 Congress authorized construction of the paddlewheel steam frigates *Mississippi* and *Missouri* and one other experimental steam warship. If Congress was alarmed about a war with Britain, Chauncey's analysis of the most probable American naval strategy might have been disturbing. He envisioned that the new steam frigates would be employed as "floating batteries" for wartime harbor and port defense, while the larger ships were "scattered" into small squadrons with the objective of "destroying the enemy's commerce, carrying the war into the enemy's sea, and contending for the mastery of the ocean." Neither Chauncey nor Paulding had an opportunity to test this plan during Van Buren's presidency, since the ugly crisis with Britain lapped over into the next administration.[30]

Chapter Eleven

Defending Maritime Access
1841–1845

In 1840, the Democrats renominated President Martin Van Buren, but he had been discredited by the Panic of 1837 and the Whig candidate, General William Henry Harrison, won the election easily. Harrison died soon after he was inaugurated, leaving no presidential legacy other than the appointment of a Whig cabinet led by Daniel Webster, the secretary of state, and Navy Secretary George Badger of North Carolina. Badger found the Navy under attack not only by Congress but also by a clique of younger officers led by Lieutenant Matthew Fontaine Maury, the author of a series of articles in the *Southern Literary Messenger* published under the pseudonym "Harry Bluff." Detailing the "evils of the deranged system" of management, Maury claimed that "never before . . . has the spirit of discontent, among all grades in the navy, walked forth in the broad light of day, with half such restive but determined steps." Maury's charges were echoed by two prominent captains, Robert F. Stockton and Matthew Calbraith Perry, who asserted that the Board of Commissioners had been excessively conservative under Commodore John Rodgers and had collapsed into disarray at his death in 1837. Maury's critique notwithstanding, successive administrations had already asked Congress to revise the board's charter; in 1833, for instance, Levi Woodbury had suggested a "different arrangement of the Navy Board . . . to apportion its ordinary business among the several members." Congress, however, failed to act on any of these proposals.[1]

Badger, apparently agreeing with Maury's analysis, announced in May 1841 that a "thorough reorganization" was long overdue. Before he had time to do anything, however, he resigned from Tyler's cabinet along with the rest of the Whigs, with the exception of Webster. Tyler replaced them with his own allies, including Abel Upshur, a brilliant Virginia jurist, who became the next secretary of the Navy. Upshur concurred with Badger's diagnosis of the department's woes, and adopted a plan proposed by Congress in 1838 to divide "the duties now performed by the Board of Navy Commissioners" and assign these functions "to separate bureaux." In an act passed in September 1842, Congress replaced the Board of Commissioners with five bureaus. The Bureau of Yards and Docks was to be headed by a captain, as was Ordnance and Hydrography; a naval constructor was to run the Bureau of Construction, Equipment and Repair; a naval surgeon would be in charge of Medicine and Surgery; but either an officer or a civilian might manage Provisions and Stores. The new law specified that each bureau chief was to be nominated by the president, be confirmed by the Senate, and be responsible to the secretary of the Navy. The old board was the exclusive preserve of line officers, but with the establishment of the bureau system, staff officers, technicians, scientists, and civilian specialists began to create new and more secure organizational niches. For example, the increasing importance of the Corps of Engineers was acknowledged in 1845 with the enhancement of the billet of engineer in chief, whose incumbent was charged with representing the views of the Navy's engineers to the bureau chiefs, line officers, the civilian secretariat, allies in Congress, industry, and the infant American engineering profession.[2]

Congressional interest in the Navy in 1842 was stimulated by continuing tension with Britain over the *Caroline* incident, the Maine boundary question, American anger at British support of Texas' continuing independence, and London's claim to the entire Oregon Territory north of the mouth of the Columbia River. Transatlantic relations had in fact grown so bitter that in May 1841 President Tyler warned Congress that additional appropriations were needed to assure that the country was "in a state of entire security from foreign assault." Although Harrison and Tyler had promised during their 1840 campaign to seek a détente with the British, and had even put out preliminary feelers in London, the quarrel heated up again in November 1841 over the *Creole* affair and the transatlantic slave trade to Cuba and Brazil.[3]

The United States had outlawed the importation of slaves in 1808, one year after Britain did. Thereafter, the British adopted a diplomacy designed to persuade or coerce all other maritime powers to negotiate antislave trade treaties, which permitted the Royal Navy to stop and search any suspected slaver sailing under a European flag. Alone among the Western powers, the United States consistently rejected these overtures for two important reasons. First, Britain's violations of American neutral rights before the War of 1812 remained a sore point between Washington and London. Second, the Admiralty refused to give up the right to impress deserters, although the Royal Navy had abandoned this practice at the end of the Napoleonic Wars. The United States was committed to eradicating the slave trade, but defending her maritime rights against what appeared to be yet another British effort to police the seas served a far more direct and immediate American national interest. Thus, while American warships on station in the West Indies or off the West African coast were ordered to suppress American participation in the slave trade, they were also warned not to interfere with foreign-flag shipping.

Following these strict orders occasionally led to some extraordinary situations. On 10 November 1821, Lieutenant Matthew C. Perry in the *Shark* was patrolling the waters off the ex-slave settlement of Liberia when he overtook the West Indies–bound French slave schooner *Caroline*, loaded with a cargo of 133 Africans. After inspecting her papers, Perry had no choice but to allow her to proceed. "The officers, not feeling the same responsibility as our commander, blamed him for what they considered his timidity and want of feeling," wrote Midshipman William F. Lynch. "We offered to become his security against any pecuniary loss" if he seized the ship and freed the slaves, but "our security was not deemed sufficient, and the slaver [was] released." The number of European flags that slavers could safely fly declined rapidly from 1816 to 1835, and five years later most of them flew the Stars and Stripes, a choice that gave them a high degree of immunity since there was seldom more than one American warship on station off the African coast during the 1830s.[4]

The *Creole* affair threw into sharp relief the vexing issues of slave trade diplomacy and American naval strategy. In 1833, Parliament had abolished slavery in Britain's West Indian colonies, and thereafter London not only tried to suppress the slave trade but also supported abolition beyond its empire, both to advance the humanitarian cause and to level the terms of trade. In November 1841, the American coaster *Creole* departed Virginia on a legal voyage with a cargo of slaves bound for sale in New Orleans. Once at sea, the slaves revolted, took over the ship, and sailed for the Bahamas. British officials there promptly hung the ringleaders of the mutiny but refused on humanitarian grounds to return the remainder of the slaves to American custody. This flagrant violation of American maritime rights further inflamed anti-British passions in the United States and renewed fears that war would break out with Great Britain that year.

It was against this background of transatlantic tension that Badger examined American naval strategy in 1841 and found that the dispersion of the fleet and the emphasis on trade defense was being achieved at too high a price. Of the seventy-six vessels in commission, only thirty-five were fit for duty on distant station. Six of these ships cruised the Pacific, two patrolled the East Indies, five were deployed to the Mediterranean, and another five operated in the South Atlantic. With four ships in transit and another four under repair, only nine remained to defend the Atlantic and Gulf coasts if war were suddenly to erupt. On 31 May, Badger warned that the result of "a war with Great Britain" would not only involve a "great interruption" in American overseas trade, but also "a naval force comparatively small might, on our very shores, have seized our merchant ships and insulted our flag." There was "no suitable means of resistance or immediate retaliation" against this threat. To correct this strategic imbalance, Badger advanced the view that it was "necessary that a powerful squadron be kept afloat at home at all times." Congress agreed, and on 1 August established the Home Squadron by dismantling the West Indies Squadron and enlarging the area of operations of the Brazil station. Secretary Upshur immeasurably strengthened this new command in 1842 when he assigned to it the recently commissioned paddlewheel frigates *Missouri* and *Mississippi*.[5]

The last gasp of the Board of Commissioners under Badger in 1841 may have been to help to prepare the annual report, which went up to Congress in December, soon after Upshur took office. This seminal statement of American naval policy lit off a vigorous debate in Congress, owing largely to the recent war scare, a timeliness that rescued naval affairs from its usual place on the back burner of the public agenda. Upshur justified his request for a 50 percent increase in naval appropriations by claiming that the Navy

The 3,220-ton paddlewheel steamer *Mississippi* was laid down in 1839 and completed in early 1842.

Abel Upshur, Virginia jurist and politician, was secretary of the Navy, 1842–44.

was faced with the problem of executing two distinct and almost contradictory missions: coastal defense and overseas commerce protection. Historically, the country had relied on the geographical advantage of shallow coastal waters as a shield against invasion, a topography that constricted enemy attacks to specific points along the coast that could be fortified and defended with light naval forces. Europe's possession of shallow-draft steamers negated this advantage, and so Upshur wanted to strengthen coastal defenses in two ways. Recalling Jefferson's gunboats, he asked Congress to lay down a large number of small iron-hulled steamers to protect harbors, bays, and other estuaries, a program that would create "a cheap and almost an imperishable naval force" and subsidize the growth of the domestic iron industry. There was some irony in Upshur's support for this scheme inasmuch as he contended that static harbor and coastal defenses would be inadequate to repel an invasion of the Atlantic seaboard and, he argued, the American fleet would thereafter have to confront "the enemy upon the ocean."[6]

To meet an invader at sea, Upshur proposed to have ready a fleet of steam frigates that would form the nucleus of the new Home Squadron. He was imprecise on exactly how many ships he wanted for this command, but inferred a rough division of the fleet into equal forces, one dedicated to commerce protection and the other to coastal defense. Upshur realized that organized naval "resistance" against an invader would probably be necessary "at the precise time when we are least prepared to make it successfully," and so he proposed as a long-term goal to bring into commission an American fleet that was "half the naval force of the strongest maritime power in the world."[7]

Although some Americans feared a British invasion, it took a suspension of belief to conclude that one could be mounted quickly or enjoy more than transitory military success. Senator Thomas Hart Benton of Missouri, a rigid Jacksonian, attacked Upshur's building program on the grounds that no invading enemy could sustain operations inshore against an aroused American militia. "If hundreds of thousands were not enough to cut them up, millions would come—arms, munitions, provisions arriving at the same time." The militia system was "cheap" and "omnipotent" and mitigated against Upshur's "impracticable" and "senseless" concept "of building and keeping eternal fleets to meet the invader and fight him at sea." Upshur's strategic proposal was at one end of a spectrum of thought whose opposite end was bounded by Benton's assertions; in the center was a consensus on the need for a naval strategy of peacetime trade defense based on dispersed deployments of station squadrons comprising ships that could, in an emergency, concentrate to supplement coastal defense fortifications and undertake cruises against enemy commerce.[8]

If Upshur's attempt to use a foreign naval standard to measure the American fleet was unusual, then his devotion to the enforcement of maritime access reassured lawmakers less alarmed than he was about the dangers of international politics. The secretary asserted that the coasting trade was tied to overseas commerce and that the enterprise of both bound together farmers, planters, mechanics, and manufacturers; the defense of maritime commerce was, therefore, "our principal interest." To this policy was linked continentalism, a goal fostered by the westward movement, which had resulted in a growing number of American settlements in Mexican California as well as outposts at the mouth of the Columbia River in the jointly administered Oregon Territory. Protection of these enclaves not only fostered continental expansion but also had begun to necessitate a more active defense of the American commercial frontier in the Pacific. To this end, Upshur wanted Congress to establish a naval base along the West Coast, or in the Hawaiian Islands, and to double "the number of vessels now employed" in the Pacific.[9]

The Democratic opposition in Congress to Upshur's policy was led by Senator Benton, who maintained that the American "coast and cities could be defended without great fleets at sea." Also ranged against increasing appropriations for shipbuilding were Senator Levi Woodbury of New Hampshire, a former secretary of the Navy, and former President Quincy Adams, who now served in the House. Benton was motivated by sectionalism and principle, but Woodbury's stance was purely partisan. Quincy Adams held that Upshur's goals were too ambiguous and his plan too extravagant. This opposition laid the groundwork for a protracted debate in Congress that degenerated into a nasty sectional dispute over how to apportion the spoils of any new shipbuilding program. Opponents of the measure used the dispute as a distraction to pare down the appropriations and paralyze any further action on the entire program. Noting the successful operation of the Navy's small iron steamer *Michigan* on the Great Lakes, in 1842 Congress authorized the Navy to contract with shipbuilder Robert L. Stevens to construct at his Hoboken, New Jersey, shipyard a 420-foot-long, 6,000-ton "war steamer, shot and shell proof, to be built principally of iron," carrying eight large guns.[10]

The construction of the first American ironclad warship, known as the Stevens Battery, was doomed, however, by a race between two technologies. Metallurgical advances producing stronger guns that fired shells with greater velocity also permitted the manufacture of thicker, more resistant iron armor plates. Designer Robert Livingston first intended to install 4- to 6-inch-thick armor in the Stevens Battery, but he soon learned that European rifled guns fired shells that might penetrate 6-inch plate. These problems were never wholly overcome. The Stevens Battery never went to sea, although work on her continued until 1854, when—after great expense to the Navy and the Stevens family—the project was suspended. Congress fumed about the cost of this fiasco. France commissioned the seagoing ironclad *Gloire* in 1859, and Britain completed the ironclad *Warrior* a year later, but both were only protected by 4-inch armor and were therefore thought to be vulnerable to rifled gunfire. A New Jersey senator tried to persuade Congress to complete the Stevens Battery during the first year of the Civil War, but most on the Hill agreed with Senator Daniel Clark. "I would rather have one *Monitor* than have this monster."[11]

The Stevens Battery was originally proposed during the transatlantic crisis with Britain in 1841 for which much of the blame could be laid at the feet of Lord Palmerston, Britain's pugnacious foreign minister. That year the British electorate threw Palmerston and his fellow Whigs out of office, however, and Sir Robert Peel, a moderate Tory, became the new prime minister. Burdened by domestic issues, Peel was committed to a peaceful settlement of several disputes with the United States, and he instructed Britain's minister in Washington, Lord Ashburton, to agree to Secretary of State Webster's plan that the two nations try to settle the outstanding issues and thereby reduce bilateral friction. During June and July 1842, Webster and Ashburton made equal concessions on the issues of the Maine boundary, the line between the Connecticut and St. Lawrence rivers, and a slice of disputed territory that separated Lake Superior and the Lake of the Woods. On the maritime questions, Ashburton acknowledged Britain's "regret" over the *Creole* affair and Webster promised not to mention the argument over the *Caroline*, although both men agreed that further incidents had to be prevented.

Webster and Ashburton also sought to deal with the gnarled question of the Atlantic slave trade, an issue that had vexed Anglo-American relations for more than two decades. Both men despised the trade, but Webster knew that Congress was poised to reject any treaty with Britain that allowed the Royal Navy to stop American flag vessels on the high seas. He proposed instead that the Navy maintain a force of a minimum of eighty guns off West Africa to supplement the more impressive British naval effort by arresting slavers flying the Stars and Stripes. Ashburton agreed to this and a provision was inserted into the treaty specifying that the British and American naval squadrons off Africa would operate "in concert and cooperation." By arguing that this joint cruising convention did not "place the police of the seas in the hands of a single power," Webster outflanked considerable opposition at home to the antislave trade articles and convinced the Senate to approve the treaty.[12]

Soon after the Webster-Ashburton Treaty was ratified, Navy Secretary Upshur established the four-ship African Squadron and assigned command of it to Captain Matthew Calbraith Perry. In June 1843 the *Saratoga* cleared Sandy Hook en route to the coast of West Africa. Upshur was an intelligent, vigorous defender of southern slave society, but he detested the Atlantic slave trade and even coached Perry on the tactics and guises used by slavers to elude British patrols. In fear of the deadly yellow fever and malaria that threatened all Western ships in the waters of West Africa, Perry selected Porto Praira in the Cape Verde Islands as his base and prohibited his men from going ashore between the Cape Verdes and Angola, even though this meant that his ships had to shuttle back and forth along the coast and that only two vessels at most might be on station at any time.[13]

Upshur also ordered Perry to defend the flourishing legal American commerce with West Africa against pirates who lurked along the coast, encourage the Africans to trade with American merchants, and prevent neighboring tribes from harassing the colonies of former American slaves in Liberia and Cape Palmas, a settlement founded by the Maryland Colonization Society. Off the Liberian capital, Perry fired a broadside and sent landing parties ashore to deter an attack on the Liberian settlers. He then shaped a course for the Ivory Coast just leeward of Cape Palmas, where he intended to deal with the vexing affair of the *Mary Carver*. This merchant schooner had been seized by tribesmen from the village of Little Berribee, who had murdered the crew and taken several women passengers ashore, where they were raped and tortured. This brutal incident had aroused American public opinion, and even before he landed, Perry had decided to demand that the local rulers of four villages execute the murderers and pay an indemnity of $12,000. If they refused, then Perry had plans "to chastise them." Inasmuch as the indemnity was beyond the means of the tribes, Perry's intentions were clear to his subordinates. The palaver ashore with the kings of Little Berribee took place in a tent pitched so that the commodore would not have to risk entering any of the villages, an acute danger since one of the rulers, Ben Krako, a chief of fearsome size and strength, was the prime suspect in the *Mary Carver* atrocity.[14]

When Perry quizzed the natives, he trapped Krako in a tangle of lies and stepped up to the African to arrest him. At that very moment someone fired into the crowd and a fight erupted. Krako's interpreter bolted for the woods, only to be cut down by an American musket. Krako tried to escape too, but a handful of Marines jumped him and, after a furious struggle, clubbed and stabbed him senseless. Carried on board the *Macedonian,* where Surgeon Duberry tried to save his life, Krako succumbed a day later. After Perry was finished with Little Berribee, the *Macedonian* weighed anchor. Behind them, recorded Purser Bridges in his journal, the Americans left "an open space of blackness and smoking ruins, where half an hour before, the sun had shone upon a town." News of the Berribee operation spread along the coast quickly, and even induced the warlike Kru tribesmen to stop attacking Liberia and bothering Cape Palmas. Because Krako had been a feared tyrant and a constant menace to the other tribes in the area, Perry became a local hero. After this incident, the Americans had little trouble signing trade treaties with the surrounding villages. "Since your settlement of the Berriby piracies," Commander Joel Abbot of the *Decatur* told the commodore, "there is no national flag that is so highly respected by the Natives as the American."[15]

Those commodores who followed Perry in command of the African Squadron over the next twenty years discovered that suppressing the slave trade was more difficult than protecting American commerce or defending Liberia. Slave vessels were the fastest under sail, flew the flags of many nations, and carried several sets of forged papers. Collaboration with the British was the key to controlling slave trade, but the Royal Navy's arrogant handling of several incidents was enough to discourage American naval officers and made them less than enthusiastic about their mission. Perry and his successors were also handicapped by the stricture that they were not to stop vessels flying other flags nor to allow British warships to stop or search slavers flying the Stars and Stripes.

One of the African Squadron's additional duties was to explore new markets for American goods and report back to Washington about the geography of the African coast. Collecting data that would assist in the development of overseas commerce was part of the synergy of American naval policy in the nineteenth century, although explorers and their patrons were often stimulated by an interest in more purely scientific researches. The apex of this movement to learn more about the world came in June 1842, when Lieutenant Charles Wilkes returned to New York at the conclusion of a four-year voyage with the Exploring Expedition. In the spirit of Captain Cook's great voyages of the previous century, the Navy Department during the age of Jackson sponsored a number of "scientific" ventures, but this one had gotten off to an especially difficult start. After nearly a decade of discussion, Congress had appropriated funds for a Pacific expedition in 1837, but Secretary of the Navy Paulding was unable to find a serving captain to command the squadron so he turned to Wilkes, a brutal, brilliant, and cantankerous lieutenant.

Wilkes stood off Hampton Roads in August 1838 with the 500-ton sloops *Vincennes* and *Peacock* and four schooners. He split up his squadron at Tierra del Fuego five months later to explore the South Atlantic, then they rendezvoused at Callao, Peru, in June 1839. Across the South Pacific they sailed and surveyed, reaching Sydney, Australia, in November; from there, the *Vincennes* continued westward, enabling Wilkes to discover the continental land mass of Antarctica. After charting Tonga, the expedition sailed to Fiji, where Wilkes avenged the murder of a pair of his officers by killing fifty-seven natives. The squadron stopped off in Hawaii before scouting the coast of the Oregon Territory. There the *Peacock* went down trying to cross the bar at the mouth of the Columbia River on 18 July 1841. Wilkes then circumnavigated the globe, striking from Singapore in February 1842 around the Cape of Good Hope and into the Atlantic, and returning to the United States in the summer.

No cheering crowds or official reception greeted the Exploring Expedition; instead, a court-martial found Wilkes guilty of illegally flogging his Marines. The results of the voyage were nonetheless considerable. Published in twenty-two volumes and a dozen atlases over the next decade, Wilkes' findings significantly improved navigation in the Pacific, fostering greater American trade with the Far East and political interest at home in the mysteries of Asia and the Pacific. Wilkes had surveyed 800 miles of the Pacific Coast's inland waterways from the Puget Sound to the San Francisco Bay and the Sacramento River, reporting on the fertility of the land, the extent of the protected anchorages, the weakness of Britain's hold on the Pacific Northwest, and the fragility of Mexico's writ in California. Wilkes also underlined the importance of the Hawaiian Islands to the control of the northeastern Pacific, an issue already highlighted by Upshur's proposal to establish a naval base in the archipelago and by an announcement by Secretary of State Webster in 1842 that the United States did not intend to annex Hawaii but would oppose with force a similar attempt by any of the Great Powers. This extension of the Monroe Doctrine beyond the Pacific frontier illustrated the increasingly close connection between North American continentalism and the defense of maritime access along the Pacific Rim.[16]

The establishment of the East India Squadron on the eve of the First Opium War between Britain and China illustrated the growing importance of maritime access in the western Pacific. Recurrent problems with the Sumatrans of Quallah Batoo and pirates along the China coast caused President Van Buren in 1838 to dispatch Commander George Read and a squadron to revisit Quallah Batoo, and then to sail on to Macao, one of only two ports in China then open to Western merchants. Turkish and Indian opium had first entered China during the Napoleonic Wars; it was one of the few foreign goods in sufficient demand to allow Westerners to penetrate China's rich market. Trading and traders commanded little respect from China's Confucian society, however, and this attitude was reflected in China's dealings with Western merchants. The Manchu court in Peking purposefully kept trade with the West small by restricting European and American merchants to the port of Canton, by requiring them to deal exclusively with the Co-hong, a trading guild controlled by imperial officials, and by permitting the Co-hong to set artificially high prices for Western goods and to compel Western merchants to use regulated warehouses.

The East India Company thrived under this restrictive system, but when it lost its monopoly over Britain's Asian trade, other merchants, including some Americans, entered the market and wittingly violated an assortment of Chinese regulations. The Manchu court, unable to halt two centuries of Russian expansion, regarded all Europeans with constant suspicion and haughtiness. Chinese officials feared that the aggressive opium merchants would drain their nation of its silver reserves and destroy its people's health. To suppress the opium trade, Commissioner Lin Tse-Tsu was sent to Canton, and in March 1839 he demanded that the Western merchants surrender their opium stocks to his men. When they refused, he cordoned off their warehouses and effectively imprisoned them in their own quarters. Commodore Read with the frigate *Columbia* and the sloop *John Adams* stood into Macao one month later, only the fourth American naval commander to visit China. After assessing the standoff, Read felt inclined to drive up the Bogue and relieve the merchants in Canton, an operation he believed "would have been more of an amusement than a trouble for us," but he was deterred by the presence of thousands of Chinese milling about the warehouses.[17]

The British had by now arranged to turn over $10 million worth of opium to Lin, and he agreed in return to allow the Western merchants to escape to Portuguese Macao. The Americans on Macao begged Congress for an "agent to be sent out to China to negotiate . . . a commercial treaty, with a naval force for the protection of persons resident there and property." The British responded to Lin's policy by surging ships onto the Royal Navy's China station, blockading Canton, and employing a small steamer to tow larger warships from Macao up the river to Canton, where they menaced the city and supported British Army punitive operations along the riverbanks. The British troops quickly and ruthlessly sliced through the pathetic Chinese shore defenses during a subsequent advance on Nanking.[18]

Although American merchants in China told Commodore Read that they were not trading in opium, in fact they controlled about 10 percent of the market. They asked Washington in May 1839 to assign to China a diplomat and a permanent naval squadron, to ensure that Americans shared in the rewards from the peace between China and Britain at the end of the First Opium War. This request was followed in April 1840 by a petition to Congress by Boston and Salem merchants asking that the administration send another squadron to Chinese waters to prevent Britain from monopolizing the China trade. In this instance, the interests of Boston merchants coincided with those of northern evangelical Protestant churches, which sponsored a growing number of missionaries who sailed to the Far East to convert the Chinese to Christianity. Commodore Read had left China in 1839 while the British were preparing to mount their initial offensive in the First Opium War, and when he arrived home, Navy Secretary Paulding selected Commodore John Downes to organize a new squadron and return to the Far East. President Van Buren clearly hoped that this measure would increase trade with China and so correct a traditional imbalance of payments.

Downes turned down the billet, citing his age, and Paulding turned to a younger man, Commodore Lawrence Kearny. This able and dynamic officer left Hampton Roads in late 1841 and made the port of Macao on 22 March 1842. Kearny's orders required him not only to protect American interests and citizens in Canton, but also to respect China's peculiar customs and political culture and prevent Americans from smuggling opium into China. Although the First Opium War was at an end, several American merchants had lost goods or were imprisoned by the Chinese during the fighting, and Kearny decided as a first step to obtain compensation for these wrongs. While dealing with the Chinese on this issue, he took advantage of their prostration by hinting that he might bombard Canton unless the Manchu court's diplomats agreed to grant the United States concessions equal to those conferred on Britain. The result was an exchange of letters in which the Chinese promised Kearny to open four additional "treaty ports" to Americans, conclude a commercial agreement providing for most-favored-nation status for the United States, and regularize customs and criminal laws under which resident aliens fell.

Secretary of State Webster raced to consolidate this accomplishment by asking Commodore Foxhall A. Parker, the new commander of the East India Squadron, to transport Minister Caleb Cushing to Canton in 1844. A skillful diplomat, Cushing nonetheless had tremendous difficulty making contact with the faraway Manchu court after he reached China. To support Cushing's demands, Parker sailed the *Brandywine* up the Bogue and anchored off Canton. Cushing then threatened to travel to the forbidden imperial capital unless the Chinese began serious negotiations. These measures seemed to work. The Chinese relented and dispatched an accredited envoy to Wanghia near Macao for talks. While Parker and Cushing were negotiating with the Chinese, however, a riot broke out in Canton against the American merchants, one of whom shot a demonstrator to protect his warehouse. When this news reached Lieutenant E. G. Tilton in the *St. Louis*, then anchored off the Bogue, he sailed up to the port of Whampoa and proceeded to Canton with a landing party of sailors and Marines who restored order there and prevented a mob attack on American businesses. "We must act with decision and energy in order to make a lasting impression on the vile but unfortunate creatures whom it appears the mandarins are either unwilling or unable to control," the new American consul in Canton told Commodore Parker.

Whereas the British insisted on protecting their nationals by stationing ships in the treaty ports, Cushing knew that the East India Squadron could not support this expense, so he took the opposite position. The Treaty of Wanghia required that "the local authorities . . . shall defend them [American nationals] from all insult or injury on the part of the Chinese," but time would demonstrate that this was something the Manchu court was often unwilling or unable to do. The ratifications were returned to China the following year by the next commander of the East India Squadron, Commodore James Biddle, who sent ships to visit the new treaty ports and established a permanent consulate in Canton. Although the disturbances there had subsided, he nonetheless on one occasion was forced to deploy the *Vincennes* to Whampoa and send a landing party ashore to protect Americans during an antiforeign uprising there. As Biddle confessed, however, it would be difficult "to protect my countrymen without giving just cause of offense to the Chinese or wounding unnecessarily their national pride."[19]

As Kearny had recognized, moreover, the defense of American commercial interests on the Asian mainland rested mostly on Britain's willingness to employ force to maintain its own treaty rights. Washington should deploy to the China coast one "of our large class ships . . . to impress the Chinese with a sense of respect for the United States," he had cautioned before sailing home. The East India Squadron now had three constituencies: merchants, missionaries, and diplomats. American envoys and commissioners moved from place to place in their frustrating dealings with the agents of the wily, truculent Manchu court, which still refused to allow foreign diplomats to reside in Peking. The ships of the squadron also provided a measure of force—significant in a regional context—and a setting of fitting pomp and dignity that the commodores and diplomats thought necessary to deal with the Chinese. Other than transporting diplomats up and down the China coast, often serving as offshore legations, sending landing parties ashore to defend threatened merchants, and occasionally chasing down pirates, however, the small, overworked East India Squadron could do little to improve American trade or protect the small but growing number of Christian missionaries in China.[20]

The First Opium War not only thrust the East India Squadron into the maelstrom of Far Eastern politics but also highlighted the utility of steam-driven ships for riverine operations and exposed some of the problems associated with the new technology. The steam frigates *Mississippi* and *Missouri* were commissioned in 1842, but a controversy about their sea trials set the stage for a debate over the tactical merits of the competing propulsion systems, sail and steam. Few questioned the effectiveness of steamers for inshore operations or harbor defense, but the high cost and great weight of coal—and the unreliability and fragility of the early steam machinery—seemed to preclude the economical use of these ships for protracted peacetime cruising on distant stations. Breakdowns were common, experienced engineers were scarce, and spare parts were not readily available overseas. Moreover, the *Mississippi*, armed with ten medium guns, had exposed wooden paddlewheels that were vulnerable to an opponent's gunfire. She barely made nine knots and required constant replenishment of her coal bunkers, a tiresome, dirty chore for all hands. Coal was unavailable in most of the ports visited by the station squadrons, and when it was, the British often controlled its supply. Navy officials were uneasy about becoming overly dependent on Britain's network of coal depots. Although the *Mississippi* saw good service, the *Missouri* was plagued with trouble. Attached to Parker's squadron, which transported Cushing to China in 1843, she was anchored en route in the shadow of the fortress of Gibraltar when a fire ignited in her storeroom, the flames spread into adjoining spaces, and the ship blew up and sank.

The loss of the *Missouri* dampened only for a moment the enthusiasm of younger Navy officers for steam propulsion. When Commodore Perry took command of the newly established

African Squadron in 1842, Captain Robert F. Stockton became the leading proponent of steamships in Washington. Energetic and temperamental, he brought to America an eccentric Swedish engineer, John Ericsson, who was hired to work in the Philadelphia Navy Yard in 1842 designing and building the experimental frigate *Princeton*. Stockton, who bore some of the costs of the project out of his own considerable fortune, intended to construct a warship to "perform any service" with the Home Squadron or on distant station, and he crammed all the latest technology into the concept for his ship. Not only was the *Princeton*'s hull constructed of iron, but the main drive was connected to Ericsson's revolutionary screw propeller. The installation of the screw propeller allowed Stockton and Ericsson to place the main drive and the steam engines below the waterline where they would be immune to enemy gunfire. In addition to a pair of Paixhans guns, one at the bow and another at the stern, the *Princeton* carried a dozen pivot guns along the center line, and two of the biggest cannon yet built, named the Oregon and the Peacemaker, both 12-inch breechloaders. Ericsson, who built the Orator—called the Oregon by Stockton—used three iron bands to secure the breech of his gun against the force of the explosion in the barrel. Stockton, who built the Peacemaker, employed thicker metal and reinforced his barrel with wrought iron. Ericsson thoroughly tested his gun, but Stockton was less careful and apparently was satisfied with what many thought were inadequate tests of the Peacemaker.[21]

Proud of his ship, Stockton named her in honor of his birthplace, and on the morning of 28 February 1844 a large party of national officials came on board the *Princeton* for a historic cruise down the Potomac River. The Peacemaker was fired successfully several times during the afternoon, suitably impressing the guests. On the return leg, by request the gun was fired one last time. The barrel exploded, killing Abel Upshur, now secretary of state, and Representative Thomas Gilmer, who had just been nominated to the secretaryship of the Navy, and several others. Stockton, who was standing on the safe side of the gun and thus escaped injury, was subsequently exonerated by a Navy court of inquiry, but he blamed Ericsson for the disaster, and this undeserved slander prevented Ericsson from getting any Navy business for the next decade. On the larger canvas of national policy, too, this tragedy produced profound and long-ranging results.

Chapter Twelve

The Mexican War
1846–1848

America's annexation of Texas in 1845 led to the Mexican War. The Republic of Texas was established soon after Houston's 1836 victory at San Jacinto, but Mexico immediately vowed to recover Texas and threatened war if Texas were admitted to the Union. American diplomats responded that an attempt to reoccupy Texas would involve Mexico in a war with the United States, but they were more concerned that Mexico's political chaos and indebtedness would invite European intervention, a violation of the Monroe Doctrine. France's naval blockade of Mexico's Gulf coast during the 1838 Pastry War alarmed Washington, as did the continuing presence of powerful British naval squadrons in the West Indies and Pacific Ocean. Rumors occasionally reached Washington that Mexico intended to cede her Pacific ports to one of the Great Powers in return for the cancellation of her obligations.

On the night of 6 September 1842, Commodore Thomas Catesby ap Jones' Pacific Squadron lay at anchor in the Peruvian port of Callao when the frigate *Dolphin*, the flagship of the Royal Navy's Pacific Squadron, stood into the harbor, remained for a few hours, raised sail, and put to sea. Meanwhile, Jones learned of a rumor that California had been ceded to Britain and that Mexico and the United States were at war. Acting with the unanimous agreement of his officers, he sent one ship to Panama with a dispatch, stationed a second vessel at Callao, and took the frigate *Congress* and the sloop *Cyane* north to Monterey, the capital of Upper California. Jones could not find the *Dolphin*, but there were so many rumors that war had broken out that he occupied the port on 19 October.[1]

Secretary of State Webster shied away from the issue of Texas. President Tyler wanted to resolve the matter but did not want war with Mexico as the price. When Jones learned on 20 October that his earlier intelligence was wrong, he withdrew from Monterey, leaving to Webster the job of placating the irate Mexicans by agreeing to send Commodore John Sloat to replace Jones. At the same time, Tyler soothed American expansionists by refusing to censure the commodore for acting precipitously. The incident acted to expose the vacuum of power on the Pacific coast. Soon after, Webster left the administration. He was followed as secretary of state by Abel Upshur, who put more starch into the administration's foreign policy, ignored Mexico's threats, and in the summer of 1843 opened annexation talks with Texas.

After Upshur died in the 1844 *Princeton* tragedy, Tyler selected the South's greatest spokesman, John C. Calhoun, to be his third secretary of state. Calhoun was worried about British intervention in Texas, and he viewed annexation as the vehicle that would propel him into the White House. Britain sought "naval ascendancy and political preponderance" in the Gulf and Caribbean in order to monopolize the production of "the great tropical staples," Calhoun reckoned, so he quickly negotiated an annexation treaty with Texas and sent it to the Senate. Alarmed, the Mexicans replied with a blustering threat of war if the treaty were ratified. This led John Y. Mason, the new Navy secretary, to alert Commodore David Conner of the Home Squadron that ratification "must lead to actual hostilities." The treaty went down in the Senate, however, under the combined opposition of Senator Henry Clay and former President Martin Van Buren, both of whom used the event to improve their chances of succeeding Tyler.[2]

Calhoun's Texas scheme was seen as a plot to increase the power of the southern slave states in the Senate, and this made his candidacy unacceptable to northern Democrats at the 1844 convention. The convention deadlocked between Calhoun and Van Buren. George Bancroft, the leading Democrat of Massachusetts, was pledged to support Van Buren, but he decided that Van Buren's cause was lost and switched Massachusetts' votes to dark-horse candidate James K. Polk of Tennessee, the Speaker of the

House, who won the nomination. The Whigs turned for a third time to Senator Clay, but during the campaign Polk lured the South with a strong stance on Texas while dredging up the American claim to the entire Oregon Territory, an issue that split the Whigs. Neither westward expansion nor eastern public opinion influenced American policy on Oregon nearly as much as the maritime objective of annexing ports on the San Diego Bay, the San Francisco Bay, and the Strait of Juan de Fuca—the final frontier of continental security and the gateway to the Pacific and the Orient. Polk capped his campaign, and won the election, by promising to force Britain to accept a Pacific Northwest boundary of "Fifty-Four Forty or Fight!"

With only a few months left in office, Secretary of State Calhoun moved with haste, persuading Congress to annex Texas by means of a joint resolution that required only a simple majority in each house rather than the approval of two-thirds of the Senate. His resolution was passed in February 1845. Anxious to get Texas to accept this arrangement, Tyler now instructed Captain Robert Stockton to take command of a small flying squadron built around the steamer *Princeton*, sail to Galveston, convey the news to the Texas legislature, and lobby against British and French diplomats who were working furiously to obstruct annexation. Two months later, Stockton returned to Washington and reported to his friend Polk, the newly elected president, that the Texans had enacted their own annexation measure.

To his cabinet Polk named James Buchanan of Pennsylvania as secretary of state and George Bancroft as secretary of the Navy. A fair number of naval officers predicted trouble ahead with Mexico, but there was nobody within the Department of the Navy to prepare war plans other than the secretary, and Bancroft supposed that Polk would find a way out of the crisis through diplomacy. This conviction, Bancroft's gentle character, and the Navy's bureaucratic inertia discouraged calls for preparedness that year. In the wake of a discouraging report by the bureau chiefs about the relative size of the fleet, Bancroft admitted that the "navy is poorly equipped with sea going steamers," but insisted that "no additional appropriations are required" to fill this void. Despite ongoing crises with Britain and Mexico, he dismissed a proposal by his bureau chiefs to lay down over sixty steam warships. He did, on the other hand, ask Congress for permission to lay down three steam frigates, five sloops, and a pair of gunboats, although he

Commodore Robert Stockton, humanitarian and U.S. senator from New Jersey, was captain of the screw-frigate *Princeton* in 1844 and commodore of the Pacific Squadron, 1846–47.

continued to maintain that Europe posed no threat to American territory. The Texas crisis notwithstanding, Congress ignored Bancroft's requests, a hesitant approach justified in part by the notion that the Navy could purchase and convert merchant steamers into coastal patrol ships should the seaboard be imperiled.[3]

Bancroft's first year in office stressed an energetic stewardship of continuing resources. He visited every Navy yard except Memphis and Pensacola, urged more economical management of the Navy, and then turned to major personnel reforms. His most important contribution as secretary was his role in the establishment of the Naval Academy, a project that had been advanced by almost every secretary since Crowninshield in 1816. Most of the many schemes to organize a naval college had run aground on the rocks of congressional opposition to the expense, but the Jacksonians especially looked with disfavor on the establishment of skilled elites with entrenched interests and specialized technical authority. To complicate matters, opinion in the fleet was by no means uniform. Many officers believed that the traditional system

U.S. Navy Department

George Bancroft, historian and politician, was secretary of the Navy, 1845–46.

of educating midshipmen at sea had been thoroughly proven, while a largely younger group argued that a more formalized setting with a standardized, structured curriculum was badly needed. By the time the Polk administration took office, the sensational tragedy of the *Somers* mutiny—in which Captain Alexander S. Mackenzie had hung three men, including the black-sheep son of the secretary of war, for mutiny after a court martial of dubious propriety—was proving the catalyst to action.[4]

Bancroft decided to establish a naval college—without first asking Congress—by acquiring Fort Severn from the War Department, and then by moving Professor William Chauvenet's small Naval School from the Philadelphia Navy Yard to the Annapolis site. This brought to a successful end a long campaign by Commodore Perry and others to establish a permanent training school for midshipmen. Commander Franklin Buchanan chaired a board that drafted a curriculum, established the rank of naval cadet, and arranged a course of study consisting of two years of education at Annapolis, three years' training at sea, and a final twelve months on board a training ship. Because existing law allowed the Navy to educate only boys who held warrants as midshipmen, Bancroft ordered all midshipmen not at sea to report for classes, which began on 10 October 1845 under the direction of Buchanan, the first superintendent. Bancroft's concern with economy paid dividends. When Bancroft turned to Congress for funds to repair Fort Severn in 1846, he could cite the Naval School's successful establishment within existing appropriations, and this cut away most of the traditional opposition to a permanent national naval academy.

The Naval Academy was established at a time of a renewed sense of national crisis. American policy over Oregon and Texas was the consummation of the continentalist strategy envisioned by the early nationalists. In short, the struggle with Mexico ended the era of territorial expansion and inaugurated a new era of consolidation of American hemispheric authority. Elected as an expansionist, Polk's vision went beyond continentalism. He clearly saw the nexus between that objective and a more aggressive search for maritime access, particularly in the Pacific.

In 1650, after eradicating Christian missionaries, Japan's shogun, or military ruler, had closed the four islands of his nation to foreign intercourse, migration, and commerce, a foreign policy of negation that persisted well into the nineteenth century. Japan's isolation caused hardships for shipwrecked Western seamen, and several American sailors languished in Japanese prisons in the nineteenth century. In addition, American merchants wanted the use of Japan's ports to expand their trade with East Asia and the South Seas. When the Senate approved the Treaty of Wanghia in 1845, Bancroft instructed Commodore James Biddle, the new commander of the East India Squadron, to exchange ratifications with China at Canton and then to try to negotiate a similar treaty with Japan. The East India Squadron stood into Edo—or Tokyo—Bay in the summer of 1846. Bowing to restrictive orders, Biddle could not threaten the Japanese, but he went beyond his instructions by allowing them to board his flagship and scuffle with his men. He gave up and sailed home shortly thereafter to report on his failure. If nothing else, Biddle's mission to Japan had exposed the means *not* to use in dealing with the shogun. Then, as the East India Squadron sailed eastward across the calm Pacific, James Biddle received new orders from President Polk, alerting the old commodore to prepare for a new war with Mexico.[5]

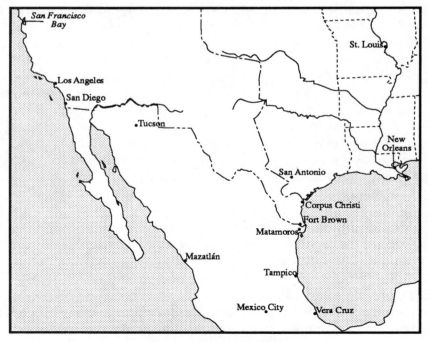

Mexican War, 1846–1848

Mexico City broke diplomatic relations on 31 March 1845 when Texas accepted annexation. Polk did not want war, but he did not intend to back down. In June, he dispatched General Zachary Taylor and a small army to Texas and, on the same day, directed Commodore John Sloat to concentrate his Pacific Squadron off the Mexican coast where it could menace the port of Mazatlán. If hostilities broke out, Bancroft told Sloat, the Pacific Squadron was to concentrate, sail north quickly, seize California, and blockade Mexico's Pacific coast ports. There was activity in the Gulf of Mexico as well. In September, John Slidell was named Polk's envoy to Mexico, and the president instructed him to try to negotiate a settlement in Mexico City. At the same time, Polk worked to calm the British, who were opposed to American annexation of Texas and who seemed ready to go to the brink over the Oregon question. Bancroft moved a few ships that were returning from the Mediterranean Squadron into the Gulf to join Commodore Conner's Home Squadron, which was directed to position ships off Vera Cruz to apply pressure to Mexico City during Slidell's negotiations. The threat of war on two fronts hung uneasily over Washington during the humid summer and fall of 1845.

Polk then developed another stratagem. His friend Captain Stockton had been given command of the frigate *Congress* in the fall, and Bancroft instructed him to transport the new American commissioner to the Hawaiian Islands. Before Stockton sailed, however, Polk gave him a second set of sealed orders, which he opened only after his ship cleared the Virginia Capes. After delivering the commissioner, Stockton was to sail for the Pacific coast, position the *Congress* so that he might strike suddenly north against British Oregon or south against Mexican California, and await news from Washington. With this forward deployment, Polk had stationed Stockton where his powerful frigate would be useful regardless of the outcome of American diplomacy.

At the same time, General Taylor's army in Texas was put on alert, but the Mexicans backed down for the moment in late October 1845, and the crisis momentarily abated. In the long run, however, only a strong Mexican regime could accept the loss of Texas without a war, but in 1845 Mexico City's central government was weak and preoccupied with a rebellion in Tampico, an uprising in Yucatán, and a plot against its authority in the province of Baja California. When the Mexicans appeared to be ready to talk in late 1845, Conner withdrew his ships from Vera Cruz to ease the tension, but a coup in Mexico City soon brought into power a new dictator, who refused to concede anything to the Americans. Early in 1846, Polk instructed Taylor to occupy a stretch of contested Texas territory bounded by the Nueces and Rio Grande rivers. To support Taylor, Commodore Conner arranged for a naval escort to defend the movement of a convoy of Army transports, which sailed from New Orleans and put Taylor's troops ashore near the port of Corpus Christi. Taylor headed south to establish a camp on the Rio Grande opposite Matamoros. Conner now believed that the Mexicans were too weak to fight, but Taylor was convinced that war was inevitable. He prematurely proclaimed a blockade of the mouth of the Rio Grande in early April, which a handful of station ships enforced by closing the river to Mexican shipping. The rest of the Home Squadron was still riding at anchor at Pensacola, however, because Conner, a methodical strategist, refused to move prematurely and rejected out of hand Captain John L. Saunders' plan that "the whole squadron immediately make a dash upon all the [Mexican] ports except Vera Cruz and gain possession of them." Conner was unwilling, he declared, to conduct "predatory warfare," a stance thoroughly at variance with Polk's forward policy.[6]

Trouble appeared suddenly on another flank, prompted in part by Polk's campaign to dislodge Britain from the Oregon Territory. Prime Minister Sir Robert Peel announced in 1845 that Britain would not only defend her claim to British Columbia between the 49th and 54th parallels, but would also fight to hold onto the territory between the 49th parallel and the Willamette Valley to the south. For years the British had rejected a longstanding American proposal simply to extend the border along the 49th parallel westward to the Pacific Ocean. After lengthy discussions in London in late 1845, Minister Louis McLane warned Polk that the British were preparing for naval operations in the Pacific. The U.S. Navy's Pacific Squadron off Mazatlán included three 44-gun frigates and four 20-gun sloops, but Commodore Sloat understood that there was in the vicinity an even more powerful British fleet under Rear Admiral George F. Seymour, whose ships were also off the Mexican coast awaiting the outcome of the negotiations. Polk needed to avert war with Britain if he was to deal successfully with Mexico, but he could not appear to back down on the Oregon issue, so he decided on a hard line as a counter to Peel's bold threat. "The only way to treat John Bull was to look him straight in the eye," he confided to a friend. Sloat was secretly alerted by Bancroft to be ready to join forces with Biddle's East India Squadron off the Oregon coast when the Mexican crisis ended. Tethered by a thin string, Sloat awaited war, but he was in poor health and word soon reached Washington that he was tending to dither. Thus, Sloat lost Bancroft's confidence, and Bancroft considered having Stockton, now in the Pacific with the frigate *Congress*, take command of the Pacific Squadron in 1846, although he too decided to wait upon events.[7]

The crisis heated up over the winter. On 3 February 1846, Polk received from McLane a second and more ominous warning concerning the Royal Navy's preparations for war, and he chose to raise the stakes and force a settlement. He successfully appealed to Congress to pass a joint resolution that unilaterally ended the Anglo-American occupation of the Oregon Territory, thus jolting London into deciding on peace or war. Despite Peel's strong line, Britain's interest in the question was on the slide. The flood of American pioneers into the Willamette Valley had caused the British Hudson's Bay Company to move its headquarters from Fort Vancouver on the Columbia River up to the Strait of Juan de Fuca. The Foreign Office, no longer concerned with the territory south of Puget Sound, now focused on holding on to the San Juan Islands. Moreover, Britain at the time was recuperating from a recession and badly in need of the American trade, and a major political crisis had cleaved the Tories in half. The opposition Whigs were also divided, however. One Whig leader, Palmerston, opposed any compromise, but his rival, Lord John Russell, allowed Peel's cabinet to remain in office until the question was resolved. This paved the way for Lord Aberdeen, the Tory foreign minister, to fashion an agreement with McLane that embodied the historic American position on the boundary issue. Somewhat earlier Polk had casually referred to the "comparatively worthless territory north of 49 degrees," but he could not now publicly back down from "Fifty-four Forty," so he sent the Oregon Treaty to the Senate without any recommendation, correctly expecting it to be approved. It extended Canada's border westward along the 49th parallel and conferred on the United States two-thirds of the disputed region, including the protected anchorages of Puget Sound.[8]

Freed from the menace of war with Britain, Polk had already shifted his attention to Texas and California. By the spring of 1846, neither Mexico nor the United States believed that avoiding war was possible, and both sides therefore were building up their

forces. "We have a great naval force at Mazatlán," Bancroft told
Minister McLane. "Were Mexico to venture on war, every port
from San Francisco to Acapulco lies open to our ships. In the Gulf
of Mexico we have a still larger force." As late as April, Bancroft,
alone among Polk's advisers, still thought that diplomacy might
resolve the crisis. At a 9 May cabinet meeting he urged Polk to let
Mexico strike the first blow, suggesting that this would unite all
Americans behind the administration's war policy. Polk rejected
this line on the grounds that the country was too "excited and impatient" to tolerate further appeasement. That night the news
reached Washington that Mexico had declared war two weeks earlier and that Mexican dragoons had crossed the Rio Grande and
attacked the American camp. Taylor had counterattacked on the
8th, driving the enemy from Palo Alto, and three days later, back
in Washington, Congress declared war. After thrashing the enemy
at Matamoros on the 24th, Taylor launched a stunning drive that
took his army deep into northern Mexico, stalling only after he
seized Monterrey on 24 September.[9]

The United States at last began to prepare for the campaign
against Mexico. The War Department called up the militia, and
several new regiments joined the Army that summer. And, on 13
May, soon after declaring war, Congress authorized the Navy to acquire six steamers, four bomb brigs, three steam-schooner gunboats, and three storeships. Although these vessels were to be used
to prosecute the Gulf campaign, the most immediate threat to
American interests in May 1846 was on the Pacific coast, where
Commodore Sloat had concentrated his Pacific Squadron off the
Mexican port of Mazatlán. From the squadron surgeon, who had
visited Guadalajara, Sloat heard the news of the fighting in Texas
and Taylor's victory at Palo Alto. He had held orders to govern his
conduct once war broke out. He was to "at once possess . . . the
port of San Francisco, and blockade or occupy such ports as . . .
[his available] force might permit." Sloat was unaware that the
Oregon question was about to be resolved, however, and he was
concerned by the presence along the Oregon coast of the 88-gun
sail-of-the-line *Collingwood*, the new flagship of the Britain's Pacific Squadron and by far the most powerful warship in the area. Uncertain what to do, he dallied at Mazatlán, sending the *Cyane* north
carrying a letter to Thomas O. Larkin, the American consul in
Monterey, announcing Sloat's intention to "visit" California within a few weeks. He did not put to sea until 7 June and failed to ap-

pear off Monterey until 2 July. Even then, he hesitated to take decisive action, although it was by now clear that the United States and Mexico were at war.[10]

Five days later, Sloat learned about the Bear Flag Revolt. In early 1845, Brevet Captain John C. Frémont had led a party of sixty Army topographers and engineers over the Sierras and into northern California, but the Mexicans were alarmed when he harassed some of their settlements, and Frémont's party was forced to withdraw to southern Oregon. Meanwhile, Polk had dispatched Marine Lieutenant Archibald H. Gillespie to California with secret orders instructing Frémont to establish a command post near Sutter's Fort in central California. Gillespie also carried Polk's private instructions to Larkin, who was to assist any rebellion of Americans that Frémont could stir up against Mexican rule.

In May 1846, American settlers in northern California declared their independence, formed the Bear Flag Republic, and on 15 June overran the small Mexican garrison defending the provincial capital of Sonoma. To support this movement, Larkin had asked Sloat to send the sloop *Plymouth* to Monterey, where she lay at anchor when war broke out, but Sloat's continuing indecision deprived his subordinates of his guidance. Commander John B. Montgomery had anchored the sloop *Portsmouth* in San Francisco Bay, and Gillespie repeatedly asked him to support Frémont, but Montgomery refused to do so without orders from Sloat. He wrote in his diary that he was frustrated by his inability to "facilitate the ultimate designs of our government, which my present neutral position necessarily forbids." Prompted in part by Montgomery's complaints to Larkin, Commodore Sloat decided to act. On the morning of 7 July he sent a party ashore to demand the surrender of the Mexican garrison at Monterey and to post a declaration that "henceforth California will be a possession of the United States." Two days later, Montgomery landed and peacefully took possession of the small settlement of Yerba Buena on San Francisco Bay. Sloat then sent a company of thirty-five dragoons north to San Jose, where they met up with Frémont's small Bear Flag Army, but the commodore was horrified to learn that Frémont possessed neither official orders nor a formal declaration of war.[11]

Alarmed by the confusion, Sloat began to wonder how the Pacific Squadron might gracefully withdraw from California, a personal agony that was relieved by the arrival in Monterey Bay of

Commodore Robert F. Stockton in the *Congress* on 15 July. Stockton quickly went ashore to confer with Sloat. Sloat, suffering from poor health and a narrow view of the swirl of events, quickly offered to relinquish his command. On 23 July, Stockton took command of operations ashore, and six days later he relieved Sloat as commodore of the squadron. He quickly denounced the uneasy truce Sloat had arranged with General José Castro, the commander of the Mexican forces in California. Stockton was already concerned by the news that the British sail-of-the-line *Collingwood* had been seen in California waters. He interpreted this as an omen of unexpected trouble: Either the British intended to support Mexico's army in California or they were there to goad the Mexicans into mounting a counteroffensive on their own. Stockton had few men under his command, so neither prospect was encouraging. He decided that he had to establish a grip on California quickly and then occupy Baja California before Mexican reinforcements arrived on the scene or the British had a chance to intervene.

Having already extended American authority over northern California, Stockton decided to move on Castro's battalion of Mexicans at Los Angeles. Frémont's troops boarded the *Cyane*, which transported them to San Diego where they were to cut off Castro's line of retreat. Meanwhile, Stockton in the *Congress* stood into San Pedro Bay and put ashore a large landing party that occupied that small port and prepared to march on nearby Los Angeles. When Castro realized that Frémont and Stockton were about to converge, he told his men to scatter and fled to Sonora. This allowed Stockton to enter the city on 13 August. "We have chased the Mexican Army more than 300 miles along the coast . . . [and] ended the war," he trumpeted.

The next day a small band of Marines and Bear Flag troops overran San Luis Obispo and captured the former Mexican territorial governor and his staff. Leaving Lieutenant Gillespie and forty-eight men to hold Los Angeles, Stockton returned to San Francisco, announced that he intended to blockade Mexico's Pacific ports, land at Acapulco to protect American shipping from Mexican privateers, and march overland to Mexico City. Frémont was ordered to expand the Bear Flag Army to 400 men and extend his writ over all of California. These grandiose plans were upset by Captain José Flores, who assembled a battalion of Mexican irregulars that drove Gillespie's drunken, undisciplined rabble out of Los Angeles in September. Stockton reacted by sending Captain

William Mervine in the *Savannah* to San Pedro to join Gillespie and try to recover Los Angeles, but Flores soundly trounced Mervine's landing party on 8 October. Stockton arrived two weeks later, decided that he was outnumbered, and shifted his base to San Diego. He was unaware of the whereabouts or intentions of Frémont's Bear Flag Army.[12]

In the meantime Polk had ordered Brigadier Stephen Kearny to lead a cavalry battalion into the southwestern desert to take the Mexican fort at Santa Fe. After investing that outpost, Kearny and 100 dragoons rode west, crossed into California, and on 6 December lost a skirmish at San Pascual with a small force of Mexican irregulars. One of Stockton's patrols met Kearny and escorted him to San Diego six days later, and there they found Stockton preparing to march north and recover Los Angeles. Stockton wanted Frémont's Bear Flag troops to strike south from Santa Barbara and menace Flores' rear, but Frémont was quite slow and Stockton refused to wait in San Diego until their offensive was coordinated. Rejecting Flores' last-minute plea for a truce, he set out on 29 December. Flores wanted to prevent the converging American forces from uniting, so on 8 January he tried to block Stockton from crossing the San Gabriel River about twelve miles from Los Angeles. Thanks to Stockton's considerable skill as a tactician, however, the Americans routed the Mexicans and Flores fled to the west. He tried again to disrupt Stockton's march toward the Los Angeles River the next day but was again crushed, and Stockton took the surrender of the city on 10 January 1847.

Only a few days after Stockton completed the conquest of California, he was relieved of his command by Commodore W. Branford Shubrick, who arrived in the *Independence*. Shubrick soon learned from Kearny that he and Stockton had quarreled not only about the overall military command during the march to Los Angeles but also about Stockton's unwise decision to appoint Frémont, a mercurial figure, as the provisional governor of the territory. Armed with orders from Washington that named Kearny to this post, Shubrick and Kearny both turned on Frémont, who was eventually arrested and court-martialed for resisting Kearny's authority.

With California secure, Shubrick stamped his own mark on the war by seizing Baja California and strengthening the blockade of Mexico's Pacific coast. Stockton had taken the first move in this direction in August 1846 when he instructed Lieutenant Samuel

Du Pont in the *Cyane* to harass Mexican trade in the Gulf of California. On 2 September, the *Cyane* appeared off the port of San Blas, where Du Pont sent a landing party ashore to spike the guns of the small fort. He stood off the port of Guaymas on 6 October and sent ashore another landing party, which captured a Mexican brig during a brisk action with the defending battery. Du Pont then established a close blockade of the major port of Mazatlán, an operation so effective that the city soon began to run short of supplies. Nearly three dozen vessels tried to run the American blockade, but Du Pont seized twenty-three of them.

Once he had cleaned up matters in California, Shubrick strengthened the blockade. In late October 1847, Captain Elie A. F. La Valette in the *Portsmouth* appeared off Guaymas, sent a landing party ashore, and with the support of two heavy guns forced the surrender of the port the next morning. Meanwhile, on 30 September, Commander Thomas Selfridge in the *Dale* closed on the port of Mulije, which had recently been recaptured by the Mexican Army from a rebellious band of Indians. Under Lieutenant Thomas T. Craven, a landing party of Americans went ashore, drove a Mexican force nearly twice its number inland, and captured a sloop and a schooner. Then on 10 November Shubrick took station off Mazatlán with a force composed of the *Independence, Congress, Cyane,* and *Erie.* He sent La Valette into the town to demand its capitulation, but the colonel of the Mexican garrison there angrily rejected the offer, tore up the printed instrument of surrender, and dared the Americans to attack. Within a few hours, 600 American sailors and Marines in three lines of boats rowed ashore, regrouped on the beach, and marched into the town plaza where they raised the American flag before the retreating Mexican colonel could fire a shot. Commodore Shubrick imposed an occupation government over Mazatlán under Captain La Valette, who encouraged the residents to believe that the United States intended to annex the region in the peace treaty, a line Shubrick also took in his dealings with the hapless leaders of Baja California. Thus, not only did American naval operations strangle Mexican trade on the Pacific coast, but they also added to the political pressure on Mexico City during the last year of the war.

Meanwhile, on the Gulf front, Commodore Conner and General Taylor had exchanged views about joint operations against Mexico as early as May 1846. Even before the conflict had begun, Conner and the Home Squadron had established so preponderant a presence off Mexican waters that no enemy naval vessel ever went to sea after the war was declared. So, after escorting troops for Taylor's army to Corpus Christi, there seemed to be little for the Home Squadron to do. Although the Mexican Congress on 25 June authorized the issuance of letters of marque and reprisal to privateers, this effort failed completely. And when the Mexican agents tried to hire privateers in Europe, several admiralties gruffly warned them to discontinue the practice. Thus, Conner's major responsibility early in the war was to clamp a close blockade on Mexico's ports, shut down her maritime trade, and prevent shipments of munitions from Europe from reaching the Mexican Army.

Based on his survey of the Mexican coast in 1845, Conner had decided to establish an advance base on Anton Lizardo, an off-shore island about a dozen miles south of Vera Cruz. There he anchored a storeship, using the base as a rendezvous for the colliers that supported his steamers. Conner intended to employ the larger steamers to carry dispatches and supplies between Anton Lizardo and his bases at New Orleans and Pensacola. In addition, he believed that the steamers would be useful for hunting down any Mexican merchant ships, commerce raiders, or privateers that attempted to operate in the gulf. The American sloops, which could stay at sea during bad weather, were assigned to blockade stations, but the slow sails-of-the-line were almost useless for blockade operations. To augment his force, Conner asked Bancroft to provide the Home Squadron with a large number of shallow-draft vessels that could operate close to the coastline and up some of the major rivers.

On 14 May 1846 Conner issued a blockade order covering Vera Cruz, Alvarado, Tampico, and Matamoros, but before the American blockade stations could be established the Mexican naval steamers *Guadalupe* and *Montezuma* escaped from Alvarado to Havana. They had been built by the British before being commissioned into the Mexican Navy, but on the eve of the war with the United States the Mexicans turned them back to British registry for fear that they would be taken by the Americans. The Army's blockade of Matamoros had shut down Mexican movements on the Rio Grande, so Conner was able to shift most of his forces to the south. The *Falmouth* captured the Mexican merchant schooner *Criolla* on 24 May, and the *Somers* took another merchant schooner, the *Amada*, that same day. In the meantime, Conner assigned the sidewheel steamer *Mississippi* to cover Vera Cruz, where the major blockading force would be stationed, and he also sent the sloop *St. Mary's* to establish a blockade station off Tampico.

Shortly after declaring "defensive" war against the United States, the Mexican government found itself under assault from foreign and domestic enemies. Polk attempted to sow confusion and discord in the enemy camp and exploited the resulting internal divisions without remorse. In May, Conner dispatched Commander Duncan Ingraham in the *Somers* to Yucatán to "conciliate" the rebel governor at Compeche and to induce him and his rebel regime to stay out of the war. Polk also sent Commodore Alexander Slidell Mackenzie on another secret mission to Havana to meet with ex-president Santa Anna, who had gone into exile there the year before. In return for a substantial bribe, Santa Anna promised Mackenzie that he would return to Mexico City and work for a negotiated settlement of the war. With Mackenzie's help, Santa Anna landed at Vera Cruz on 16 July and made his way to Mexico City where he was still a popular figure. Santa Anna betrayed Polk, however. He opposed any compromise, disrupted secret talks with Washington, and won back the presidency in December. Although Santa Anna was marginally more competent than Mexico's other generals, none of them was a fair match for Zachary Taylor or Winfield Scott. For his part, Bancroft had begun to worry that Mexico was threatened by "disintegration, which may render it necessary in the pursuit of peace, to deal with her province by province, state by state."[13]

While Polk disrupted Mexican politics, Conner clamped a tight blockade on Mexico's Gulf coast ports. When he received reinforcements for his Home Squadron in July, he extended his operations to the ports of Tecoluto, Tuxpan, and Soto la Marina. Poor logistics hampered the blockade from the start; there were few storeships, and fresh water, coal, and fresh fruit had to be shipped from New Orleans to the Anton Lizardo base. Conner was aware of these problems, but he was never able to infuse Secretary Bancroft with any great sense of urgency about them. For this Conner was not entirely to blame. Bancroft was proving to be an indolent war leader. The Bureau of Provisions and Clothing under Gideon Welles served the fleet admirably, but Conner constantly criticized the other material bureaus, although he himself was partly at fault for not keeping the department fully abreast of his needs.[14]

Getting supplies of fresh water was another dilemma for Conner, and this directly led to a series of assaults on the Mexican base at Alvarado. After some American landing parties trying to get water ashore skirmished with Mexican forces around Vera Cruz, Conner decided to seize Alvarado. A wide, shallow bar at the mouth of the Alvarado River had prevented him from establishing a close blockade there, and the commodore worried that this tactical problem would worsen during the fall. The Mexican fleet of three brigs, three schooners, and three gunboats was dispersed in the channel and upriver, but Conner discounted these light forces and his reconnaissance disclosed that the enemy shore batteries were also weak. For the Americans, the major problem was that only their schooner gunboats could cross the bar.

Conner had to call off the first attack on Alvarado on 28 July after the frigate *Cumberland* ran aground on a reef and all attention turned to saving the ship and her crew. After she was refloated, a passing storm further delayed the operation, and it was not until the afternoon of 6 August that Conner struck for the second time. He positioned his larger ships off Fort Santa Teresa at the mouth of the river and, at dusk, they bombarded the Mexican batteries. However, he had not reckoned on an unusually strong current, so powerful that it prevented even the steamers *Mississippi* and *Princeton* from keeping station or inflicting any damage on the enemy positions. After a brief gunboat action, another storm threatened the entire squadron, and Conner gave up and withdrew to Anton Lizardo.

The failure of the first two assaults on Alvarado brought Conner under attack by the American press, and Secretary Bancroft raised questions about Conner's ability to command American naval operations off Mexico. He selected Commodore Matthew C. Perry as Conner's relief, but then changed his mind, giving Perry command of the steamer *Mississippi* instead and sending him back into the Gulf as the commodore's deputy. In the meantime, Bancroft himself had fallen under a cloud. Polk sent him to England in September 1846, and named as his successor John Y. Mason, a seasoned politician who had headed the Navy during the waning days of the Tyler administration. This shuffle of figures did Polk little good. Although a weak manager, Bancroft was a deft politician, commanding respect within the cabinet and on Capitol Hill. Mason, a better administrator, had almost no political following and exerted little influence on Polk's war policy. He was shrewd enough to exploit the patriotic fever of the moment, however, and on 3 March 1847 Congress authorized the construction of the sidewheel steam sloops *Saranac* and *Powhatan* and the steam frigates *San Jacinto* and *Susquehanna*, although none of these vessels entered the fleet during the war.[15]

During Bancroft's last days in office he had managed to unsettle Commodore Conner about his future, and Conner was further discomfited by a letter from Commodore Charles Morris warning that Polk was "anxious" that the Home Squadron "do something which will answer" the Navy's critics and "make newspaper noise." This refreshed Conner's determination to take Alvarado, and he devised a plan for a third attack. The Home Squadron appeared off the mouth of the river on 15 October; the *Mississippi* bombarded Fort Santa Teresa, while the *Vixen* led a column of smaller vessels in front of the Mexican guns. None of this did much good. After midday, Conner sent the *Vixen* at the head of a line of gunboats that charged across the bar, but the small steamer *McLane* ran aground while trying to lead the second division into the channel. "What is to be done now?" Conner asked Commander Joshua Sands of the *Vixen*. With great bravado, Sands proposed to "go ahead and fight like hell!" With no gunboats, this was patently impossible. Conner, disconsolate, was forced to retire once more. The *Vixen* withdrew, the *McLane* was refloated, and the Home Squadron headed back to Anton Lizardo.

As an alternative to attacking Alvarado once again, Perry now proposed an assault on Tabasco, a town about seventy miles up the Tabasco River from the port of Frontera. Frontera was poorly defended, but Perry faced the familiar problem of getting his gunboats over a shallow bar. The Tabasco's current, however, unlike the Alvarado's, was relatively weak. Led by the *Vixen*, several schooner gunboats crossed the bar on 23 October, but the *McLane* again went aground. Nonetheless, Perry pressed forward, captured several Mexican steamers, and took Frontera. After the American gunboats started upriver the next day, the Mexicans abandoned the only fort that had been defended, and on 25 October Perry anchored off Tabasco, fired a few shots over the rooftops, and the city surrendered. The Mexican garrison had merely retired from the town, however, and now counterattacked. Perry could not hold his position without destroying the port. "From motives of humanity," he was "determined . . . not to fire again," and so the American formation withdrew downriver to Frontera and the Gulf. Other than humiliating the Mexicans and exposing their weakness, by now all too evident, the Tabasco operation was of little military consequence. On the other hand, Perry's success improved his position in Washington and the victory boosted the Home Squadron's morale.[16]

Meanwhile, General Taylor was pressing the Mexican Army in northern Mexico, and he asked Conner to support his operations by taking the port of Tampico, five miles up the Pánuco River. Conner was opposed to another attack until he learned that Santa Anna had withdrawn his forces from Tampico, and that the port, the second largest on the Mexican Gulf coast, was virtually undefended. With two small steamers, four schooners, and a landing party of 300 sailors and Marines, Conner took Tampico on 14 November and seized several Mexican schooners and gunboats, which he put under his own command.

One of Polk's reasons for wanting control of Tampico was to support the Army's inland advance from Vera Cruz to Mexico City. With the breakdown of peace talks in September 1846 and Santa Anna's ascendancy, Polk had dropped the idea of a compromise. He now wanted to crush Mexico and end forever any threat to America's southern flank. He knew that Stockton had secured San Francisco and guessed that Mexico's resistance on the Pacific coast would soon crumble. On the surface, the military objectives of the war had already been achieved. Nonetheless, Polk wanted Mexico to formally recognize her losses—just the assurance that Santa Anna was now unwilling to proffer.

Polk had expected Zachary Taylor to strike into central Mexico from Monterey, but the roads in the region were poor, and Taylor's army was tired, so he arranged an undeclared truce with the enemy along a 200-mile-long front. This led General Winfield Scott, the Army's commanding general, to propose that the Home Squadron land a second army on the Gulf coast and that it advance overland to Mexico City. It was a fine plan and Scott was a superb general, but both he and Zachary Taylor were Whigs, and Polk correctly thought that they both had political ambitions. Polk asked the Senate to give Senator Thomas Hart Benton, a Missouri Democrat, a commission as a lieutenant general, but when the Senate refused, Polk gave the job to Scott. Troops were detached from Taylor's army in November 1846 and transferred to Scott's command. When Santa Anna learned of this he moved north and attacked Taylor, only to be thoroughly routed at Buena Vista in February 1847.

While Scott was on his way to the theater, Conner planned the Vera Cruz landing. On 4 March, forty transports carrying the vanguard of the invasion army reached Anton Lizardo, and two days later Conner and Scott boarded the *Petrita* and reconnoitered several landing sites near Vera Cruz. Scott wanted to take the port and quickly move inland to avoid prolonged billeting in the miasmic tidewater, but the formidable fortress at San Juan de Ulloa guarding the harbor's entrance obstructed a seaward assault. Scott therefore decided to land three miles south of the city, and Conner's staff accordingly prepared their invasion plan. On the 9th, the troops were shifted from the Army transports to the warships off Anton Lizardo, then the squadron steamed north to an anchorage off the landing site. While the *Spitfire* conducted a diversionary bombardment of San Juan de Ulloa, Conner positioned his heavy ships where they might provide gunfire support for the landing and put the troops ashore in sixty-five specially built, shallow-draft surfboats. The Mexicans decided not to contest the beachhead, so Scott's army marched safely ashore to the music of the squadron's band. That evening 10,000 men were ashore, and the next day Scott laid siege to Vera Cruz. On 22 March, his field artillery shelled the city, supported by Commander Josiah Tattnall's bombardment flotilla of two small steamers and four schooners, which were in action until Vera Cruz surrendered on the 27th.

Despite this victory, a few days later Conner was relieved of his command by Commodore Perry, who had participated in the initial operations in the Gulf of Mexico and then returned to Washington in early 1847. Perry's reports on Conner's conduct of the campaign undermined Polk's confidence in his principal naval commander and played a role in Conner's relief. A more energetic figure, Perry was anxious for the Home Squadron to take a larger part in the war. Once Vera Cruz had surrendered, General Scott decided to move against nearby Alvarado, expecting to capture cattle, horses, and mules there for his overland march. After Conner's unsuccessful attack one year earlier, however, the Mexicans had strengthened Alvarado's seaward defenses with guns from their fleet, most of which was blockaded upriver. On the other hand, Scott's position in Vera Cruz now exposed Alvarado to a landward attack. Perry planned the operation with the help of Brigadier General John A. Quitman, whose troops started out on the road to the Madelin River on the afternoon of 30 March. Perry was to shift the squadron from Anton Lizardo to Alvarado and bombard the city, diverting the defenders' attention away from the main landward blow.

One of the most bizarre episodes of the Mexican War was thus set in motion. While Quitman's army was on the march, Lieutenant Charles G. Hunter in the converted steamer *Scourge* sailed from his station off Vera Cruz south to support the joint operation against Alvarado. That evening, the *Scourge* arrived off the bar at the mouth of the Alvarado River. After firing a few rounds at nearby Fort La Vigia, Hunter withdrew for the night. At dawn, he again closed on the fort but, to his surprise, when the *Scourge* opened fire, the Mexicans ran up a white flag and surrendered. When Hunter went ashore, he was told that the small Alvarado garrison had left the city in the darkness of the previous evening. Bringing his ship across the bar, he ran up the Stars and Stripes over Alvarado and chased a handful of errant Mexican vessels upstream.

The next morning the *Scourge* appeared off the small village of Tlacotalpan, and Hunter sent an officer ashore to accept its surrender on April Fool's Day. That same morning, Perry with the Home Squadron stood into Alvarado and landed a party of Marines. They were joined that afternoon by Quitman's column, which had just entered the city. Although the Americans now held Alvarado, both Perry and Quitman were furious at Hunter because his premature demonstration had scared off the Mexican troops and they had taken with them the horses and mules that were the object of the operation. Perry had Hunter hauled before a court-martial, which found him guilty of "treating with contempt the authority of his superior." Hunter was dismissed from the squadron and publicly reprimanded.[17]

Polk wrote in his diary on 10 April that he had just received the "joyous news" that Scott and Conner had landed and taken Vera Cruz, a military victory that the president immediately tried to exploit. That same day he instructed Nicholas Trist, the State Department's chief clerk, to sail for Mexico, where he was to join Scott's army and be ready to negotiate a peace treaty with the Mexicans. Polk directed Trist to demand, as a minimum, that the Mexicans cede California and New Mexico to the United States and agree on the Rio Grande as the southern boundary of Texas.

Secretary of State Buchanan informed the Mexicans of Trist's mission in the hope that they would negotiate an end to the war before they suffered additional defeats in the field and lost more territory.[18]

Once Scott had left Vera Cruz on 9 April, Perry decided to shut down as many ports as possible along Mexico's Gulf coast. On 18 April Perry took Tuxpan with a landing party of 1,500 men—the same day Scott decisively defeated Santa Anna at Cerro Gordo. Two months later, Perry took four steamers up the Tabasco River and landed more than 1,100 men, who occupied Tabasco City that same day. He repulsed Mexican counterattacks on 24 June, but continued enemy pressure convinced him to evacuate the area a month later. Mexican resistance in front of Mexico City was stiffening, so Polk ordered Perry on 4 August not to bother taking any more ports. Encountering brisk enemy defenses during the summer campaign, Scott's army faced superior numbers in every battle, but impressive American leadership, tactics, engineering, and artillery invariably overcame the inept Mexican Army. On 8 September, Scott launched his final offensive against the capital at Chapultepec Park, a 200-foot hill guarding the twin approaches to the city. After a week of combat, a Marine detachment overran the defenders and the capital surrendered.

The Treaty of Guadalupe Hidalgo ending the Mexican War was the product of a confusing interplay of events that followed Trist's arrival in Mexico in the summer of 1847. Polk distrusted Scott, a political rival, and when he learned that Scott and Trist were working in concert, he also lost confidence in Trist. Told in October that the Mexicans had rejected his basic demands, Polk recalled Trist to Washington, now intending to add Baja California to the list of territories that Mexico would have to cede as the price of peace. Trist upset Polk's plan, however, by ignoring the recall order and ably negotiating a treaty on the basis of Polk's original instructions. The Mexicans accepted the Rio Grande boundary, ceded California, Arizona, New Mexico, Colorado, and parts of Utah and Wyoming to the United States, and received a payment of $15 million. Trist allowed them to keep Baja California. Polk was quite justifiably angry with Trist, but he was stuck with Trist's treaty and reluctantly sent it up to the Senate. The opposition on Capitol Hill was divided between some expansionist Democrats, who wanted "all Mexico," and the northern Whigs, who opposed extending slavery, but by a comfortable majority the Senate approved the treaty on 25 May 1848.

This did not entirely settle Mexico's fate. She was still rent asunder by the Yucatán Rebellion of 1838, which had been supported by the Americans after 1846. Although Perry had backed Yucatán's efforts to win independence from Mexico, with the ratification of the Trist Treaty American interests in the area had been served and the rebels were left to fend for themselves. To prevent the collapse of their insurrection, in early 1848 Yucatán's leaders considered asking Great Britain to annex the entire peninsula. Polk got wind of this move and announced in April that he would use force to oppose the annexation of the Yucatán on the grounds that such a step would violate the Monroe Doctrine. The Yucatán rebels were therefore left to their fate when Commodore Perry boarded the *Cumberland* and departed for New York on 15 June. He put into Norfolk to find that Polk's war policy had alienated most northern Whigs and a small number of northern Democrats, and that the president, who had accomplished everything he set out to do when he entered the White House, was not running for reelection. Polk, who died within a year, was perhaps the most thoroughly ruthless and completely successful commander in chief in American history.

Chapter Thirteen

Defending Manifest Destiny
1848–1852

The acquisition of the Pacific coast during the Mexican War fulfilled the basic foreign policy goal of continentalism; at the same time, it created vexing political and strategic issues for Polk's successors. A fragile consensus was achieved on a national maritime strategy, but this was soon overshadowed by the politics of sectional confrontation. Many Whigs had opposed the war, but they smelled victory in 1848 when Polk retired and nominated General Zachary Taylor as their presidential candidate. The Democrats turned to Senator Lewis Cass of Michigan, a champion of sectional compromise, but he lost to Taylor when antislavery radicals divided the Democratic Party in New York, giving the Whigs their second chance at the executive branch.

The most influential men in Taylor's cabinet were the new secretary of state, John M. Clayton, and former Congressman William B. Preston of Virginia, who gave up his House seat to take over the Navy Department. He had little interest in naval affairs, however. He wanted to use naval policy to prevent the disintegration of the Whig Party and to engineer Taylor's reelection in 1852, a goal endangered by the split within both parties over the issue of slavery in the Mexican Cession. When California and New Mexico applied for admission to the Union in 1849, New England abolitionists seized the chance to raise the whole question of slavery, but they were frustrated by Whig moderates like Navy Secretary Preston and Senator Henry Clay of Kentucky, who fashioned the Compromise of 1850.

How to govern the new territories became such a dominant political issue that it invested every other national question, including foreign policy. In 1848, naval chaplain Walter Colton, the author of seven books describing his adventures in the fleet, reported in the Philadelphia *Independent North American* that a prospector had found gold at Sutter's Fort in northern California. During 1849 alone, tens of thousands of Americans took one or another of the various overland trails to California, or embarked on long voyages to the Isthmus of Panama or around Cape Horn to reach the gold fields of the Sacramento Valley. Indians threatened the overland trails, however, and the voyage around Cape Horn was long, arduous, and expensive. In short order, attention turned to laying down and defending a rail line across the waist of Central America, and to constructing a waterway to link the Atlantic and Pacific oceans. These projects plunged American statesmen and naval leaders back into the volatile politics of the Caribbean, and once again threatened to pit the United States against Britain's maritime might.

The presence of a powerful British squadron off the Pacific coast of Latin America during the Mexican War had frightened the government of New Grenada, which was worried that the Royal Navy might seize its province of Panama. After Stockton conquered California in 1846, President Polk negotiated a treaty with Bogotá that gave the United States an exclusive right to build a railroad or a canal across the Isthmus of Panama. In return, Polk committed the United States to defend the "neutrality" of the route and to ensure that "free transit of traffic might not be interrupted." Work started on the Panamanian Railway soon after the California Gold Rush began, and the line was completed in 1855. The president's extraordinary military commitment to New Grenada upset Congress, however, and the Polk-Mallarino Treaty was not approved by the Senate until June 1848, at the close of the war with Mexico.[1]

London reacted with alarm to this threat to its longstanding dominance of the Caribbean—Britain controlled the strategic area that stretched from Jamaica to British Honduras—and the Admiralty's attention turned toward Nicaragua, the most likely site of any transoceanic canal. The British possessed a dormant claim to the Mosquito Coast of Honduras and Nicaragua, and they now decided to exercise it. In 1848 the Royal Navy seized the vital port of Greytown, a smugglers' haven situated at the mouth of the

San Juan River, and in October of the following year, a British warship entered the Gulf of Fonseca on the Pacific coast and took possession of the strategic Tiger Island. The Taylor administration was
furious at these apparent violations of the Monroe Doctrine, and
many Americans construed them to be part of a British plot to undermine the United States' preferred position under the Polk-
Mallarino Treaty. "Now as we are gaining greatness in the Pacific,"
George Bancroft warned Secretary of State James Buchanan in
March 1849, Britain "has seized the key passage to the Pacific." All
five of the Central American republics, fearing additional British
encroachment, beseeched Washington for protection, and the nation braced for another transatlantic crisis. "Great prudence" was

The rugged, ubiquitous 792-ton sloop-of-war *Cyane* was launched in 1837 and
served the U.S. Navy until 1871.

demanded "on both sides," Secretary of State John Clayton
warned, otherwise a "collision" between the United States and
Britain would be "inevitable."[2]

However, the Central American question was a secondary issue for Lord Palmerston, the British foreign minister, and he was
diverted from attending to it by a series of shattering revolutions
that rocked Europe in 1848. Nonetheless, while disavowing the
seizure of Tiger Island, Palmerston grimly insisted on keeping
Greytown, although the Foreign Office knew that most of the English-speaking residents were nothing more than pirates. The
Americans were upset with Britain's strategic expansion in Central
America, but the excitement over the Nicaraguan crisis soon van-
ished, allowing Secretary Clayton to begin to negotiate a compromise on this question and others with Henry Lytton Bulwer, the
new British envoy to Washington. Their talks resulted in a treaty
that obligated Britain and the United States to cooperate with
each other in building any isthmian canal, and bound both parties neither to demand exclusive control over a canal nor to claim
a unilateral right to fortify it. The Senate swiftly approved the Clayton-Bulwer Treaty of 1850, but its terms were bitterly attacked by
nationalist Democrats like Senator Stephen Douglas of Illinois,
who claimed that the Whigs were guilty of "truckling to Great
Britain" in a matter vital to American security.[3]

The administration was shaken to its core soon after, when
President Taylor fell ill during a strenuous Fourth of July celebra-
tion and died five days later. He was succeeded by Vice President
Millard Fillmore, who shuffled the cabinet, naming Senator
Daniel Webster secretary of state and North Carolina's governor,
William A. Graham, secretary of the Navy. The raging sectional
controversy had by now undermined the Whig Party's traditionally expansionist naval policy. Graham was inclined to allow Navy appropriations to increase at the modest pace they had followed
since the Mexican War, but he ignored complaints that most of
these additional funds were earmarked for woefully corrupt shipyards and for subsidies to steamship firms that built vessels that
were supposed to be "convertible" to warships in a national emergency. On the one hand, Graham denounced the increasing habit
of his fellow Whigs to compare the American fleet with the naval
forces of the Great Powers, asking in 1851 only for authorization
to build one sailing warship and one steam vessel "to test and keep
pace with the improvements of the age." On the other hand, his

appeals to national prestige—without any comprehensive strategic justification—fell on deaf ears on Capitol Hill. Maryland's John P. Kennedy, who succeeded Graham at the Navy Department in the last year of the Fillmore administration, also found Congress resistant to an expansionist naval policy. Proposing to "maintain that position of relative strength which had been our policy heretofore to assume," Kennedy asked Congress to lay down three screw frigates and another trio of screw sloops, but his request was met with stony silence, and the Navy received approval only to razee, or cut away the upper decks, of the sails-of-the-line *Franklin* and *Constellation* to increase their usefulness to the station squadrons.[4]

Indeed, Fillmore's administration was enlivened only by the start of Perry's great voyage to Japan, a project principally sponsored by Secretary of State Daniel Webster. Shortly after Taylor took office in 1849, Commodore John H. Aulick of the East India Squadron reported to Webster that an American merchantman had rescued several Japanese sailors in the Pacific and brought them to San Francisco. Aulick saw the chance to repatriate them as a vehicle for putting relations between the United States and Japan "upon a more easy footing" and "a favorable opportunity for opening commercial relations." The concept of opening up Japan to American trade was not new; it had been pressed since 1839 by Aaron H. Palmer, an agent for several steam engine manufacturers. He collected a library on Far Eastern affairs, and some of his ideas found their way into Secretary of State James Buchanan's 1847 report to Congress on Asia. Two years earlier, Polk had dispatched Commodore Biddle on a mission to Japan, but Biddle was specifically forbidden to employ force to accomplish his objectives and was told not to insist that the Japanese sign any agreement. Hamstrung by these restrictive orders, he was humiliated by local Japanese officials and his mission was judged a failure. Palmer, undaunted by this setback, next persuaded Maine's Senator Hannibal Hamlin to get Congress to pass a resolution asking the State Department to employ the East India Squadron to rescue stranded American sailors thought to be languishing in Japanese jails and to try again to open commercial relations not only with Japan but also with Korea, Cochin China, Siam, and Burma. Palmer apparently hoped that establishing American coaling stations in the Far East would lead to an increased demand for his steam machinery.[5]

In 1851, Fillmore approved Webster's plan to dispatch another naval mission to Japan armed with specific orders to deliver a letter from the president to the emperor in the capital of Edo, later named Tokyo. Commodore Aulick of the East India Squadron was selected to carry out this assignment. In June of that year he sailed for the Far East, carrying Fillmore's letter and the authority to negotiate a treaty, but with no instructions about using force if the Japanese rejected his advances. Webster had also asked Aulick to transport a diplomat to Brazil. During the voyage south they quarreled, the Brazilian accused Aulick of extortion, and in November 1851, after Aulick arrived in the Far East, word reached him that he had lost his command and was being recalled to Washington to explain his behavior.

Navy Secretary Graham selected Commodore Matthew C. Perry, an accomplished naval diplomat, as Aulick's relief. Admitting his "deeply fostered aim" to "push forward," Perry at first complained to Graham that this was "a retrograde movement" for his career, but once assured that his new command would be "enlarged" to confer "distinction" on him, Perry began to prepare singlemindedly for his mission to Japan. During 1852, he selected his captains and his staff, studied Japanese history, politics, culture, and geography, and persuaded Webster to allow him to write his own orders, instructions that purposefully awarded the commodore "large discretionary powers." If the Japanese refused to agree to a "relaxation of their system of exclusion" after a friendly approach, then Perry was to "change his tone" and see that they were "severely chastised." On 24 November 1852, in Annapolis, Perry bid farewell to Fillmore, who handed him another letter addressed to Japan's emperor. It asked that shipwrecked American sailors be "treated with kindness," that "our steamships and other vessels . . . be allowed to stop in Japan and supply themselves with coast, provisions, and water," and that Japan suspend or "change its ancient laws as to allow a free trade" with the United States.[6]

Shaping a course around the Cape of Good Hope, Perry sailed across the Indian Ocean and arrived in Hong Kong in April 1853, only to find China in the midst of a civil war between the imperial army and Taiping rebels. Perry, wholly concerned with his mission to Japan, intended to sidestep the Chinese problem for the moment. To watch over the interests of American merchants and missionaries in China, he deployed the sloop *Plymouth* to Shanghai, but took the rest of the squadron with him to visit the

Ryukyu Islands in May. He anchored in the port of Naha, surveyed the surrounding waters, set up a temporary base for his mission, and established two supply ports for American steamers. On 2 July, the sidewheel steam frigates *Susquehanna* and *Mississippi* and the sloops *Saratoga* and *Plymouth* stood out to sea and set sail for Japan. Eight days later, the East India Squadron anchored off Uraga in the Bay of Edo. After a few hours, the American ships were surrounded by Japanese guardboats and junks, but Perry was determined not to repeat Biddle's mistakes so he refused to allow the Japanese to attach lines to the American ships or to permit Japanese sailors to come on board. In short order, a minor official told Perry that Fillmore's letter would be received at the port of Nagasaki, where the Japanese allowed the Dutch to maintain a small trading post. Perry refused. He was aware that the Japanese placed great value on the superficial dignity and status of "face," and he did not want to lower himself to the level of the Dutch merchants, whom he knew the Japanese treated with contempt. Instead, he demanded to be met by high officials of the government and threatened to sail up the river to Edo, where the figurehead emperor resided in the imperial palace.[7]

Perry instructed his men to survey Edo Bay and conduct an occasional gunnery practice to make clear his intentions. Frightened by the black smoke of the American steamers and terrorized by the great roar of the cannons, the Japanese relented. New envoys from Edo arrived, and a special building was erected ashore for the talks. On 14 July, Perry, his officers, and 250 heavily armed Marines came ashore with great pomp and ceremony, marching to music provided by the squadron's band. This procession was watched warily by thousands of Japanese. The imperial envoy agreed to deliver Fillmore's letter to the emperor, and Perry explained that he intended to return with four warships the following spring for a reply. Perry weighed anchor within days and sailed back to the Ryukyus, where he found the Americans there almost under siege. He threatened to march on the Japanese regent's palace unless the Okinawans stopped molesting the Americans and agreed to establish a coaling station. With this accomplished, he shaped a course for Hong Kong. Soon after he arrived there, the East India Squadron was increased to ten ships.

Herbert Marshall, the minister to China, pestered the commodore to disperse his units along the Chinese coast to protect Americans caught in the middle of the Taiping War. Meanwhile, in September 1853, four Russian warships appeared off Nagasaki, and the commodore told Japanese officials that he had come to negotiate a trade treaty between Russia and Japan. The Japanese rebuffed this overture and the Russians left. When their squadron reached China, however, the Russian commodore arranged for a meeting with Perry, during which he suggested that they join forces, return to Japan, and compel the Japanese to sign a joint trading agreement. Perry, alarmed that the Russians intended to spoil his carefully laid plans, brushed aside the proposal. When he learned that the French also were sending a squadron to Edo Bay, the wily commodore decided that he had to move swiftly. Just as he was about to sail in January 1854, however, Perry received a letter from Secretary of the Navy James Dobbin instructing him to detach the *Susquehanna* for duty at Macao under the control of Robert M. McLane, the new American envoy to China. Effectively ignoring Dobbin's orders, Perry replied that he could not spare the *Susquehanna* without jeopardizing the mission to Japan.

A few days later, the East India Squadron was at sea en route to Japan. Perry stopped over at Naha for two weeks, warned the regent that he would seize the Ryukyus for the United States if Japan refused to negotiate, then sailed for Edo Bay. Perry's first visit and the appearance of the Russian Squadron in Japanese waters had touched off a boisterous debate among Japan's leaders, most of whom were well informed about the humiliating treatment accorded to China by the Western powers in the wake of the First Opium War. Against Japanese traditionalists stood a new generation of military barons who intended to acquire European weapons to prevent their country from being dominated by the Westerners and to preserve the existing political and social order. They forced the ruling shogun to refer the question to his regional warlords and to the emperor, who for centuries had been merely a figurehead. They decided to accept the American plan. Perry was unaware of this, of course, and when the East India Squadron arrived at the Uraga anchorage on 15 February 1854, the seven warships carried provisions for eight months. The commodore was prepared for a long stay.[8]

Perry was therefore surprised when he learned that five imperial commissioners were waiting to talk with him. They jockeyed over where the squadron would drop anchor and finally agreed to a compromise site off Yokohama, where the Japanese erected another special compound ashore for the upcoming negotiations.

Perry and his entourage landed amidst suitable ceremony. Six weeks after he returned he had his agreement. The Treaty of Kanagawa, signed on 31 March 1854, provided that Japan would open up the ports of Shimoda and Hakodate to trade and the purchase of supplies by American ships. One port was designated as a haven for shipwrecked mariners, and the Japanese agreed to receive an American diplomat and allow him to reside in Shimoda. During a great feast on board Perry's flagship at the end of the talks, the head of the Japanese delegation "threw his arms about the Commodore's neck" and with "a tipsy embrace" announced "with maudlin affection" that "'Nippon and America, all the same heart.'"

Perry returned home a hero, and the volumes he published about his great mission to Japan excited interest in America's position in the Pacific and the Far East. In 1855, Washington named Townsend Harris, an experienced Far Eastern merchant, as the first American envoy to Japan, and he negotiated a second treaty that opened up four more ports to American trade and established extraterritoriality, harbor dues, and tariff schedules. Although Perry did not strictly "open" Japan to intercourse with the West, he did create an opportunity for a faction of Japanese rulers, alert to the turmoil on the mainland, to alter their country's long-standing isolationist policy. Perry's successful mission was a milestone in the development of the United States as a major transpacific power.[9]

Chapter Fourteen

The Empire of Trade
1852–1860

By the time Commodore Perry set sail for Japan in 1852, the Whigs had been defeated at the polls by Democrat Franklin Pierce, a vibrant champion of "Young America" who promised to conduct a more vigorous defense of American interests abroad. But Pierce was unable to control his own Democrats on domestic issues, and soon after he entered the White House his popularity evaporated. To defuse the tensions of sectional and partisan strife he often turned to foreign affairs, although this maneuver seldom succeeded. One of the keys to Pierce's election had been the support of the leader of the North Carolina Democrats, State Representative James C. Dobbin, who was rewarded with the secretaryship of the Navy. An advocate of offshore continentalism and maritime access, Dobbin took seriously Pierce's charge to reverse the languishing "condition and strength and efficiency" of the Navy, clearly a reference to the poor condition of many of the older ships and the lack of larger war steamers. During the 1840s steam had joined, not supplanted, sail in the fleet, but as late as 1853 the Navy included only seven seagoing steamers, and four of them were under construction.[1]

In his first annual report Dobbin attempted to correlate the Navy's building program to specific foreign policy goals. The acquisition of the Pacific coast gave the United States an "elevated rank," perhaps placing her "among the great powers." The great oceans protected America's home territory, but without a fleet they were merely "a shield without a sword." In the wake of the settlement with Britain over Oregon and the defeat of Mexico, Dobbin argued that coastal defense against Europe's naval powers was only one of the Navy's missions, and that defending overseas trade and upholding maritime access were also important objectives. Virginia Congressman Thomas S. Babcock, who chaired the House Naval Affairs Committee agreed. Europe's Great Powers were "our competition," he declared, "and with them are to be our contests."[2]

The fleet included about seventy vessels in 1853, but only half of them were ready for service, hardly enough to support five widespread, overseas station squadrons and also react to recurrent war scares with their inevitable calls on the Navy to provide a visible defense of the coast. Moreover, of the ships in service, none of the steamers carried more than ten guns. To remedy this, Secretary Dobbin proposed to lay down six large screw-driven steam frigates and to install a steam engine in the razeed frigate *Franklin*. Over opposition from Congressman Thomas Hart Benton, an old Jacksonian, Congress enacted the proposal. The passions aroused over the *Black Warrior* affair—the seizure by Spanish authorities of the American steamer—influenced the vote, as did the ongoing Greytown crisis and the outbreak of Europe's Crimean War.

The 1854 Navy Act authorized the construction of the screw-frigates *Colorado, Merrimack, Minnesota,* and *Wabash,* and the large screw-sloop *Niagara,* each armed with a battery of Lieutenant John Dahlgren's new rifled shell-firing guns. Despite the modernity of their ordnance, these ships were designed to meet the needs of the station squadrons. They had wooden hulls, no armor, and small auxiliary steam engines that made only about nine knots. The first news about the Crimean War demonstrated the vulnerability of wooden hulls to explosive shells, but neither Dobbin nor Congress expressed any interest in laying down armored ships, a strong hint that neither the Pierce administration nor Congress was much concerned about the prospect of a war with one of the European powers. Congress also did not lose sight of the gargantuan costs of the Stevens Battery, an ongoing project employing more than 500 workmen at the time.

Dobbin then asked Congress for seven more steam sloops in 1854, but his plan was ignored, although he repeated it for two years. In 1856, at the suggestion of the Senate Naval Affairs Committee, he reiterated his request for large shallow-draft sloops for the defense of southern ports and islets, and, in March 1857, during the final days of the Pierce administration, Congress authorized the construction of the screw-sloops *Brooklyn, Hartford, Lancaster, Pensacola,* and *Richmond.* Expanding on the foundation established during the Mexican War, Dobbin's shipbuilding program propelled the growth of steamers in the fleet; counting all types, from 1853 to 1860 the number increased from six to thirty-eight, while the number of vessels without auxiliary steam declined from fifty-nine to forty-four.

Dobbin intended his naval shipbuilding to support Pierce's energetic foreign policy. In his 1853 inaugural, Pierce declared that his "administration will not be controlled by any timid foreboding of evil from expansion. Indeed, . . . our position on the globe renders the acquisition of certain territories not within our jurisdiction eminently important for our protection." Thus "with a view to obvious national interest and security," he appointed a fellow expansionist, William L. Marcy, as his secretary of state. Their immediate focus was on Cuba, one of two remnants of Spain's empire in the New World. Before the Mexican War, Washington had adopted a consistent policy on Cuba, which rested on the Monroe Doctrine and the presumption that the United States would eventually supplant Spain as the governing power. During the Mexican War, Polk had sent an envoy to Madrid to purchase Cuba, but the Spanish indignantly rejected this offer. Spain's domestic chaos weakened her overall position, however, and this was reflected in the eruption of several rebellions in Spanish-held territories, including one led by General Narciso Lopez, a Venezuelan renegade who escaped to the United States after staging an unsuccessful uprising in 1849. Secretary of State Webster did not oppose Cuban annexation, although the island's plantation slavery made this a volatile issue, but he was determined not to suborn American filibustering.[3]

As a result, the Home Squadron was instructed to prevent American filibusters from sailing from New Orleans to Cuba, but Lopez nonetheless succeeded in May 1850 in landing 500 armed men on the island. Unable to generate any local support there, he withdrew, his ship standing into Key West just ahead of a pursuing Spanish cruiser. Webster had Lopez prosecuted for violating the Neutrality Acts, but a sympathetic New Orleans jury refused to convict the hero. This encouraged Lopez to organize another expedition, which slipped out of New Orleans and sailed to Cuba where a landing was made in August 1851. This time, however, the Spanish Army was lying in wait. Lopez and fifty followers were caught and executed, and the governor general in Havana threatened to slaughter the rest of the filibusters, many of whom were sons of the most prominent families of Louisiana.

To force the Spanish to release the hostages, Webster persuaded Fillmore to instruct the Home Squadron to concentrate just off Cuban waters in a show of force. At the same time, he privately apologized to the Spanish and suggested that it was not in their interests to further inflame American public opinion. The British, not wanting to encourage annexation, told Spain bluntly to release its American prisoners. Madrid relented, the imprisoned filibusters were freed, and Congress passed a resolution of apology and compensated Spain for damage to its New Orleans consulate during a riot. When Britain and France tried to persuade Fillmore to sign a tripartite guarantee of Spanish rule over Cuba, however, he gruffly rejected the proposal.

Pierce was the legatee of this diplomacy when Cuban annexation resurfaced in February 1854. This time the question arose because of the unthinking, illegal seizure by Spanish authorities in Havana of the American steamer *Black Warrior*, an old coaster that for years had plied the seas from Mobile to Cuba to New York. This silly act of Spanish arrogance was met with an uproar from all factions in the United States. The *New York Herald* even suggested that Pierce should "simply fit out, in a week at farthest, three or four war steamers, and dispatch them to Cuba with peremptory orders to obtain satisfaction." Speaking for friends in the administration, Congressman Babcock warned that the *Black Warrior* affair was offering American expansionists an opportunity to defy Britain and oust Spain from Cuba. Unless Madrid apologized and instructed her agents in Cuba not to bother American shipping in the future, the United States should "take redress into our own hands." Unwilling to press matters that far, Pierce instead allowed the Spanish to appease the vessel's owners. Meanwhile, Secretary of State Marcy instructed the American ministers to Spain, France, and Britain to meet in Ostend, Belgium, and discuss what was to be done about the future of Cuba.[4]

In October 1854, James Buchanan from London, John Y. Mason from Paris, and Pierre Soule from Madrid met at Ostend to discuss the issue. After the trio conferred, they sent a secret report to Marcy—later described as the Ostend Manifesto—in which they resurrected Polk's plan to buy Cuba from Spain, but added the provocative suggestion that should Spain reject the offer "we shall be justified in wresting it from Spain if we possess the power." Pierce sympathized with the Ostend Manifesto, but by now the whole issue of Cuba had become entangled with the sectional crisis over the Kansas-Nebraska Act. Then in November the Democrats lost control of Congress, partly because of attacks by northern Whigs against the president's Cuban policy. The administration's loss of congressional support doomed the Ostend Manifesto, and Pierce steered away from the issue for the remainder of his presidency.[5]

The collapse of Cuban annexation did not sound the deathknell of Pierce's activist policy in the Caribbean, however, for it was designed to achieve a second objective: reducing British influence in the region. To further this goal, Pierce had outlined an acquisitive naval-base policy, but he lacked the will to adopt a truly militant stand, and Congress was unwilling to support his policy. In addition, the Great Powers were active in their determination to check American designs. In 1853, for instance, British and French agents defeated Pierce's half-hearted attempt to negotiate a lease on a naval base on Samaná Bay in the Dominican Republic.

Elsewhere, Pierce's policy was equally unsuccessful. He had little use for the restrictions of the Clayton-Bulwer Treaty respecting a isthmian canal, and he believed that the first step toward undermining the status quo in Central America was the acquisition of an American naval base in the Colombian province of Panama. After several false starts, an opportunity to press the matter arose in April 1855, when Panamanians in Colón rioted, damaged the American railway's property, and killed fifteen Americans. The American commissioner in Panama now warned Pierce that Colombia was incapable of governing Panama, and proposed that a Navy squadron be dispatched to occupy and annex the isthmus from coast to coast. As in the Cuban affair, Pierce was unwilling to move so boldly, but in September he did dispatch the *Independence* and *St. Mary's* to Colón. A landing party went ashore and held the railroad station for three days to guarantee the right of transit. Simultaneously an envoy was sent to Bogotá, carrying Pierce's proposal that Colombia cede several islands in the Bay of Panama to the United States for a naval station, and that Colón and Panama City be turned into self-governing cities under the U.S. Navy's protection. The Colombians quickly rejected this humiliating scheme. Nevertheless, the need for a naval base in Central America and the hope that a canal might one day be built did not expire. One of the Pierce administration's last acts was to prepare for an expedition led by Lieutenant Tunis A. M. Craven, which investigated a route for an isthmian canal. Many men were lost on this mission, however, and the tragedy soured Americans on the possibility of developing a waterway across Panama.

The British were mildly annoyed that Pierce was treating American obligations under the Clayton-Bulwer Treaty indifferently, and irritation exploded in rage over the Greytown affair. To profit from the demand for transportation from the Atlantic seaboard to California, entrepreneur Cornelius Vanderbilt's Accessory Transit Company had acquired a monopoly from the Nicaraguan government to carry passengers from Greytown up the San Juan River, across Lake Nicaragua to Lake Managua, and overland to the Pacific coast. To avoid the British authorities in Greytown, an old pirate den, Vanderbilt was given permission by the Managua regime to erect his firm's offices, warehouses, and hotel on the island of Punta Arenas, at the mouth of the San Juan. Punta Arenas was one of a number of Honduran Bay islands then the object of a bitter territorial dispute between the British and the government of Nicaragua. British interest in the area was underscored in 1852 when London announced that the islands had been annexed to the new crown colony of British Honduras. The following year, when the British brusquely ordered Accessory Transit to abandon Punta Arenas, Commander George Hollins in the sloop *Cyane* landed a company of Marines who occupied Greytown while Commander James T. Gerry in the sloop *Albany* convinced Greytown's officials to withdraw their demand.

Sparks flew again in May 1854 when the American master of one of Vanderbilt's steamers shot a native boatman and touched off a riot in Greytown. American consul Solon Borlund held the mob off at gunpoint to defend the master, but was himself injured by British officials when they arrested him for threatening to shoot the rioters. After being released, Borlund fled to Washington where his demands for some support were warmly received. President Pierce instructed Hollins to take the *Cyane* back to Greytown and extract an apology and an indemnity for the damages to American property. Although he was to do this without "a resort to violence," it was made clear that "these people" had to be "taught that the United States will not tolerate these outrages." The *Cyane* arrived off Punta Arenas on 11 July. The next day Hollins issued an ultimatum: He would bombard the town unless the British paid the indemnity. His demand was met with silence, however, so he sent a steamer to evacuate the town, and at 0900 on the morning of 13 July, the *Cyane* opened fire on the city. The destruction slowly continued until midday, and that afternoon Hollins put a landing party ashore to complete the burning of every structure still standing.[6]

Pierce strongly supported Hollins' attack on Greytown, and when news of the destruction of the city reached London, the First Lord of the Admiralty worried that Britain was "fast drifting into a war with the United States." Although Britain's position in Central America was important, Lord Palmerston's ministry was hamstrung in reacting by the outbreak earlier that year of the Crimean War, which pitted Britain and France against Russia's drive for southward expansionism against Turkey. The war was already stretching Britain's naval resources to the limit. In addition, the Greytown episode erupted amidst the flowering of a warm détente between Washington and London, and the important Canadian Reciprocity Treaty had just been signed on 6 June 1854. Thus, the British Foreign Office protested the Greytown operation to James Buchanan, the American minister in London, but at the same time the governor of British Honduras was told to avoid any more disputes with either the Americans or Nicaragua's volatile regime.[7]

The impulse to extend continentalism through extraterritorial annexation was also evident in Pierce's policy in the Pacific, where the acquisition of Hawaii became the litmus test of his program. The islands had for several decades been a major port of call for American ships plying the Pacific, and by 1840 Honolulu was established as the base for the American whaling industry in those waters. Protestant missionaries had reached the islands twenty years earlier, clothing some of the natives, deforming their easygoing culture with heavy doses of Puritanism, and clashing occasionally with Navy captains and merchant masters who defended their crews' right to some pleasure ashore.

American maritime use of Hawaii increased in importance during the Age of Jackson, and concerns heightened that either Britain or France might try to annex the islands. Rumors of various British annexation plots reached Washington during the transatlantic war scare of 1841, and Secretary of State Webster drafted a special message, which Tyler sent to Congress the following December, announcing that the United States would forcibly oppose "any attempt by another power . . . to take possession of the islands, colonize them, and subvert the native [pro-American] government." When an eager Royal Navy captain tried unsuccessfully to take over Hawaii in 1843, Secretary of State Upshur asked London to repudiate his actions. At the same time, the Senate was told that Tyler "might feel justified . . . in interfering by force to prevent its falling into the hands of one of the great powers of Europe." The Tyler Doctrine effectively extended the protections of the Monroe Doctrine into the eastern Pacific.[8]

After the acquisition of California and Oregon in 1846, Washington's position on Hawaii hardened. Secretary Webster complained bitterly in 1850 when a French landing party briefly occupied Honolulu. Soon after becoming president three years later, Franklin Pierce decided to prevent another such episode, firm up the evolving American protectorate, and secure the exclusive rights to a coaling station and small naval base at the mouth of the Pearl River near Honolulu. He sent Commissioner David George to the islands in 1854 to negotiate a treaty of annexation with the native monarchy, but this agreement contained an unfortunate provision promising eventual statehood for Hawaii, and for this reason the Senate rejected it. Americans were willing to support maritime access, and often were eager to expand the boundaries of continentalism, but they were unwilling to entertain overseas military obligations.

The debate over the Hawaiian treaty exposed America's strategic dilemma in the Pacific, where only the small East India and Pacific squadrons were responsible for an immense area of operations. To remedy this, Secretary Dobbin proposed in 1856 to split the Pacific Squadron into northern and southern commands, which would permit an increase in the tempo of cruising operations in the South America-Hawaii-Puget Sound strategic triangle. Although Congress ignored this proposal, Dobbin was able to enlarge the vital Mare Island Navy Yard on San Francisco Bay to serve as a repair base for ships of the Pacific and East India squadrons. With the increasing American maritime activity in the Pacific and the Far East, a trend that was accelerating before Pierce took office in 1853, having to return ships to the East Coast for repairs was clearly inefficient.

American policy toward China was tied to the expansion of trade in the Pacific. In the wake of the 1844 Treaty of Wanghia, the United States demanded compliance with its treaty rights but wanted to keep a low profile, avoid disputes with the faraway Manchu court in Peking, and allow Britain and France to take the lead in exploiting China's political and military weakness. American statesmen realized that the East India Squadron could not uphold American policy unilaterally but resisted acting in concert with the powers of Europe. This approach was tested by the Taiping Rebellion, which pitted antiforeign Chinese rebels against the Manchu dynasty and all Westerners living or trading in China's treaty ports. The rebels aimed to break up Britain's trade, but Americans were also attacked, and U.S. Navy commanders were on occasion called on to support British operations in order to defend common interests. When Commander John Kelly reached Shanghai in the sloop *Plymouth* in 1854, he found that the imperial army was threatening Westerners in the city. He offered to help, and a multinational force of 400 men, including American sailors and Marines from the *Plymouth*, was formed under British command. In the short but hard-fought Battle of Muddy Flat, this small army thrashed a much larger body of imperial troops. Still, the trouble continued, and on 11 November Lieutenant George Preble in the chartered shallow-draft steamer *Queen* joined a combined Anglo-American operation against the port of Taiho during which 100 Chinese pirates were killed, 50 junks destroyed, and 3 villages burned.[9]

The Taiping Rebellion overlapped the Second Opium War, which evolved from the *Arrow* incident. On 8 October 1856, Chinese imperial troops in Canton boarded the British merchantman lorcha *Arrow*, seized a dozen Chinese sailors, and forced the master to lower the Union Jack. A goodly portion of the difficulties between Westerners and Asians before, during, and after the Taiping Rebellion involved touchy questions of face, race, honor, and status, and the *Arrow* incident was no exception. The humiliation of the *Arrow*—precipitated by an unusually shortsighted local Chinese commissioner—enraged the local British commanders. The Chinese ignored their complaints, so the Royal Navy's warships cleared the river of imperial junks and Royal Marines stormed and reduced several nearby Chinese forts. Called upon to protect the American settlement in Canton by the American consul, Commander Andrew H. Foote in the *Portsmouth* soon arrived on the scene and sent a landing party of Marines and sailors ashore to defend the merchants' warehouses. The situation grew so serious that Foote was joined by the new commander of the East India Squadron, Commodore James Armstrong, who arrived in his flagship, the 1,500-ton screw-frigate *San Jacinto*.[10]

Armstrong approved of Foote's actions, but he felt that the presence of his ships in the Bogue off Canton had led the Chinese to believe that America and Britain were working together against the Peking government and that this was what endangered the Americans in Canton. He wrongly assumed that the local Chinese officials made a distinction between the Western powers and would somehow reward the Americans for their neutrality. Things would improve, he reasoned, once he withdrew. Then, on 15 November, while preparing to retire, the *San Jacinto* was brought under fire by five Chinese forts along the river, and Armstrong, now infuriated, decided to retaliate. The *San Jacinto* drew too much water to operate inshore and the *Levant* was grounded, but the *Portsmouth*'s guns easily silenced the forts within ninety minutes. A party of sailors and Marines landed, took one fort by storm, and frightened the Chinese into evacuating the other four bastions and leaving behind 168 guns. More than 500 Chinese were killed, at a cost of only 7 American dead. "Our Navy though small is still able to punish any insult . . . to our Flag come from whom it may," observed Seaman William H. Powell. Foote's conduct of these operations was so skillful that it earned the enthusiastic praise of the nearby British commander. Soon after, the Chinese commissioner rendered a belated apology and the affair was ended. The American envoy to China, Peter Parker, then waging a losing campaign to get Washington to adopt a more vigorous policy, reported that Armstrong's operations had been "conducted to secure" an "important prestige in the mind of this haughty government." Navy Secretary Dobbin was willing to go one step further. In his 1856 annual report he asked for appropriations to build "one or two steams of light draught, to be used in Chinese rivers . . . for the protection of the immense property belonging to [American] citizens." However, Congress ignored this early appeal to establish a Yangtze patrol and resisted deeper involvement in Asian politics.[11]

Anglo-American naval cooperation on the China station was matched by the collaboration of the respective squadrons off the West African coast. However, where British and American goals differed, there was little cooperation, and that was especially true in Latin America. Britain's imperial policy repeatedly clashed with America's dedication to maritime access in Latin America, and friction was stimulated by Washington's willingness to adopt a more muscular stance there than in Asia. This was evident during the second Falkland Islands crisis in 1854. Although the British had ejected the Argentines and formally occupied the Falklands in 1833, New England ships continued to hunt seals in the rookeries for another two decades, ignoring the complaints and decrees of a succession of British authorities. Then, in December 1853, matters took a nasty turn. The Mystic whaler *Hudson*, commanded by Master Henry Clift, and her tender, the schooner *Washington*, were anchored off New Island when six vengeful seamen deserted, hiked to Port William, and swore to Governor George Rennie that Clift and the captain of the schooner, Master William Eldridge, had violated a recent decree against seal hunting. Rennie sent Lieutenant Henry Boys in the brig *Express* to New Island to arrest the two Americans. Word of their capture soon reached Commodore W. D. Salter with the Brazil Squadron in Rio, and he immediately ordered Commander William Lynch in the brig *Germantown* to sail to the Falklands and investigate the dispute. Lynch was to avoid "as far as possible all cause of collision," but he was at the same time to "keep a watchful eye on the interests of our citizens" and secure the release of the Americans.[12]

Lynch stood into Port William on 2 March 1854, aware that Rennie had already asked for support from the Royal Navy's powerful South Atlantic Squadron in La Plata river. Enraged by the arrests, Lynch sent a messenger ashore carrying a threat to arrest Rennie as a pirate. He also trained the *Germantown*'s guns on the hapless *Express* and threatened to blow her out of the water unless the Americans were freed. After the Americans were released, Lynch and Rennie exchanged a few nasty letters, then the *Germantown* stood off the Falkland Islands. "The massacre of the animals" by the Americans "had almost destroyed the rookeries," Rennie sadly reported soon after.

The issue of sovereignty over the Falklands continued to divide Britain and Argentina for many years, while the death of the sealing trade brought to an end American interest in the South Atlantic islands. In a fitting climax to the triangular diplomacy of the Falklands dispute, the Admiralty "disavowed the conduct of the . . . *Express*," agreed to pay damages to the American sealers, but

Matthew C. Perry was commodore of the Home Squadron, 1847–48, and commodore of the East India Squadron during the voyage to Japan, 1853–54.

questioned whether Lynch's "language" and "demeanor are consistent with the usages of civilized nations." Lynch's bravado earned him a hero's laurels at home, one of the few bright spots in the otherwise grim record of failure of Pierce's overly ambitious foreign policy.[13]

The Democrats dumped Pierce in 1856 and turned to former Secretary of State James Buchanan, a prosouthern expansionist, who handily defeated John C. Frémont, the candidate of the newly organized Republican Party. Soon after Buchanan entered the White House, however, the Panic of 1857 engulfed the economy,

Commodore Perry and his party meet with Japanese under a tent at Kanagawa, Japan, in 1854. The Japanese were intrigued by the miniature railroad that Perry transported with him to Japan and with other evidence of advanced Western industrial technology.

2,900-ton screw-sloop *Hartford* was commissioned in 1859. She served as Farragut's flagship ᴧg the attack on Mobile Bay, as the postwar flagship of the Asiatic and North Atlantic squadrons, ᴀs a training and cruise ship for Naval Academy midshipmen until 1912.

and domestic politics began to fracture under the weight of sectional rancor. Caught in the jaws of this political cataclysm, Buchanan proved himself a disciple of Polk's expansionism, with a clear intent to reduce Britain's influence in Central America, annex Cuba, and actively defend maritime access. He maintained an office in the State Department and tried desperately to conduct a vigorous diplomacy, undertake an expansionist naval policy, and develop a nationalist approach to foreign policy that would divert attention from the sectional wrangle. Buchanan's Cuban policy was thwarted by northern suspicions of southern designs, however, and Congress rejected once again an administration plan to purchase Cuba from Spain. The resulting paralysis stymied Buchanan's Cuba policy, although the importance of the old Caribbean trade to the national economy was already beginning to decline owing to the use by American shippers of the new regional canal and railroad systems.

The Democrats' renewed effort to annex Cuba collapsed after the congressional elections of 1858, during which Buchanan's ability to avert more sectional strife was further undermined by the electoral vigor of the new Republican Party. Because the Republicans and Whigs were both committed to observing the spirit as well as the letter of the Clayton-Bulwer Treaty, the new Congress refused to allow the president to make additional commitments to defend American rights to an isthmian canal in Central America, rebuffed Buchanan's attempts to link American interests in the region to the independence of those republics, and rejected the McLane-Ocampo Treaty of 1860, in which the Mexicans had agreed to sell to the Americans a transit route across their country.

The force behind many of these projects was Navy Secretary Isaac Toucey, an elderly Connecticut Democrat, whose experience in Polk's administration and prosouthern bias fitted him for Buchanan's cabinet. This sectional outlook was reflected in Buchanan's handling of foreign relations and Toucey's naval shipbuilding policy, arenas in which Buchanan sought somehow to conciliate southern interests. In his first annual report, Toucey laid down the line that comparing the fleet to the naval forces of the Great Powers was an inappropriate standard for American naval policy. The administration did not want to compete with the European powers "in the magnitude of their naval preparations," he told Congress in December 1857. If this illustrated the Democrat's commitment to Jeffersonian frugality—a tone set by Toucey's concern with an "overgrown naval establishment" and his promise not to foster the development of "a great navy in time of peace"—it also mirrored Upshur's concern for peacetime preparedness, a "true policy" under which the administration was dedicated to building a fleet "unsurpassed in . . . completeness" so that "no event shall take us altogether by surprise."[14]

The old Jeffersonian interest in protecting ports evidenced itself in Toucey's plan to build a number of small steamers combining "great speed and heavy guns" that would be "formidable in coast defense," especially in exposed southern waters. Led by Florida Senator Stephen Mallory of the Naval Affairs Committee, Congress authorized the Navy in March 1857 to lay down five shallow-draft steam sloops, the design for which was chosen by a board composed for the first time of line officers, naval constructors, and the chief engineer. "We are compelled to build . . . vessels as other nations do," Mallory declared, invoking the seldom-used European standard as a benchmark for American naval policy. Steam warship building was accelerated by a war scare in early 1858. The commander of the Royal Navy's West Indies station decided to try to clamp down on the use of the American flag by vessels engaged in the Atlantic slave trade between West Africa and Cuba. After the Royal Navy stopped and searched a number of renegade slavers flying the American flag in the Caribbean, and British cruisers had fired at a few American vessels that refused to submit to inspection, Secretary of State Lewis Cass dispatched a series of stiff, angry protests to London. At the height of this furor in June 1858, Senator Mallory asked Congress to amend the annual naval appropriation bill and authorize the Navy to construct ten more shallow-draft sloops with "full steam power" and screw propellers.[15]

Northerners were unsympathetic with Buchanan's apparent opposition to Britain's antislave trade policy, however; and this issue, like so many others, became entangled in the web of domestic political sectionalism that forced Mallory to reduce his proposal to seven vessels. While Mallory was compromising, London was conciliating. The crisis caught Britain off guard. Exhausted by the Crimean War, she was unprepared to deal with the rambunctious Americans and yet eager to maintain good relations with her best market. After Buchanan demanded that the Royal Navy not stop any American vessel regardless of the purpose of her voyage or her cargo, London backed down and announced on 8 June

1858 that the Admiralty no longer claimed the right in peacetime to search foreign vessels without treaty consent. Later in the year Toucey again tried to stoke the fires of fleet expansion by alluding to the summertime war scare when he asked Congress to lay down another ten steam sloops of "light draught, great speed, and heavy guns" to defend the "inland seas." By this time there was little passion left on Capitol Hill over the affair and concern over the Panic of 1857 was peaking. As a result, Toucey's request went unanswered.[16]

The legatee of Pierce's Caribbean policy, Buchanan also faced the nagging problem of American filibustering, an activity that enraged the North and held the South in thrall. William Walker, the greatest filibusterer of the era, was a soldier of fortune whose first foray had been an abortive raid on Baja California in 1853. At the head of a band of American adventurers and Central American revolutionaries, Walker landed two years later in Nicaragua, where his support of the Constitutionalist Army soon led to his election as president. In May 1856, Pierce recognized Walker's regime. He had become a legend in the United States and was mistakenly thought to be the advance agent of American annexation. The British viewed diplomatic recognition as an overt violation of the Clayton-Bulwer agreement on the strategic balance in the Caribbean. Although Secretary of State Marcy distrusted Walker, he refused to move against him. In short order, however, Walker alienated Vanderbilt by revoking Accessory Transit's steamship monopoly and angered Nicaragua's neighbors by mounting raids across their borders. Vanderbilt organized and subsidized a Central American alliance that overthrew Walker's government, and Walker escaped from Nicaragua early in 1857 only at the intervention of Commander Charles H. Davis.

Undaunted by this setback, Walker returned home and assembled a new expedition of 200 men, who later that year slipped past an antifilibustering patrol established in the Gulf by Commander Frederick Chatard in the *Saratoga*, and landed at Punta Arenas. Vanderbilt and the Central American governments now formally asked Washington to intervene, and as a result, Commander Hiram Paulding in the *Wabash* sped to Greytown, arriving there on 6 December 1857. With a party of 300 sailors and Marines, Paulding went ashore and arrested the filibusters. Walker was unceremoniously returned to the United States within a few days. The Nicaraguans thanked Paulding for his quick action, but Walker's southern supporters complained that Paulding had violated the 1818 Neutrality Act by arresting the filibusterers on foreign soil. Not knowing which way to turn, Buchanan censured Chatard for letting Walker evade his patrol, agreed that Paulding had made a "grave error" by arresting Walker's gang, but in the same breath defended Paulding as a "gallant officer" who believed at the time that he was "promoting the interest of his country." Walker, a deranged rogue, was unwilling to give up. He slipped through another Navy patrol in 1860 and landed in Honduras, but he was captured and put before a firing squad. Supporters in the United States mourned his passing as a symbol of the collapse of southern aspirations for Caribbean expansion.[17]

Unable to bring Congress to heel behind his expansionist Caribbean policy, Buchanan refused to risk more censure from the Hill by associating his aims in the Far East too closely with those of the Great Powers. Yet the occasional need for the East India Squadron to collaborate with the European squadrons on the China station became evident at the outset of the Second Opium War. Pressured by the Taiping rebels to resist Western influence, the Manchu court had looked away when the Taipings massacred a large number of foreign nationals, including a French priest, and ignored British demands that Peking use imperial troops to defend Western treaty privileges. Britain and France declared war, and an allied force took Canton in January 1858. Two months later Flag Officer Josiah Tattnall in the *Minnesota* reached Canton with a passenger, William Reed, the first fully accredited minister to China since Cushing, who carried instructions to negotiate another treaty with Peking at the end of the war.

When the Manchu court ignored the loss of Canton, the Western diplomats met in Shanghai and decided that their forces would advance up the Peiho River to increase the pressure on Peking. On 26 April the *Minnesota* and the *Mississippi* rendezvoused with fifteen British and French warships at the mouth of the Peiho. The Chinese still refused to negotiate, so the allied fleet crossed the bar, reduced the nearby Taku forts, and steamed upriver to the undefended port of Tientsin where they anchored at the mouth of the Imperial Canal, which led to Peking. His capital now threatened, the emperor agreed to open negotiations. Reed was escorted ashore for the talks at the village of Taku by Commander Samuel Du Pont, who later described the Chinese officials in a letter to his wife. "The poor creatures knew an evil hour was fast approaching and they had the mark of panic in their faces." The negotiations ended on 18 June 1858 with the signing of the Treaty of Tientsin, which opened up eleven Chinese ports to American trade, allowed the American minister to reside in Peking, and extended extraterritorial legal protections to American nationals in China. The Chinese soon signed similar agreements with the British and French. Because of the Navy's lack of ships, Reed insisted that the Treaty of Tientsin once again provide that the Manchu court would defend American nationals from its own citizens. Should this fail, the treaty contained a most-favored-nation provision that would allow the East India Squadron to adopt the British fleet's aggressive practice of navigating China's inland rivers. The Americans had once more expanded their toehold in China by following in Europe's wake. This was foreign policy on the cheap, but it succeeded.[18]

A year later, after helping to revise the Treaty of Kanagawa with Japan, Commodore Tattnall in the *Powhatan* stood out of Hong Kong on 17 June 1859 in company with the *Minnesota* and *Germantown* and shaped a course for the mouth of the Peiho River. His mission was to deliver a passenger, John E. Ward, the new American minister, who was carrying the ratified Treaty of Tientsin to Peking. Four days later the formation appeared off the Taku bar, where a large Anglo-French fleet had gathered. Tattnall now learned that the Chinese had rebuilt the Taku forts, that they were insisting that the Western diplomats land on the Gulf of Chihli to the north, and that the Western admirals had declared their intention to fight their way upriver. Shifting his broad pennant to the light, shallow-draft *Toey-wan*, Tattnall entered the river on 24 June, but the small paddler ran aground near the forts and had to withdraw the following morning before the battle began. In the fight that ensued, clever Chinese tactics and good gunnery resulted in the loss of the British admiral's flagship gunboat and damage to another of his vessels. On the grounds that "blood is thicker than water," Tattnall agreed to allow the *Toey-wan* to be used to tow British launches into position so that the Royal Marines might land and advance on the forts, a clear violation of the recently signed Treaty of Tientsin. This landing was also poorly planned and directed, and the Chinese bravely held their forts in fighting so bitter that when the British and French retired they counted 450 dead and wounded. They withdrew to Shanghai, and Tattnall followed. Deciding to accede to Peking's demand, his ships sailed north later that summer to Pehtang, where Chinese officials met Minister Ward and transported him to Peking for the exchange of ratifications. Once again, the Americans had taken advantage of Europe's willingness to use force to exploit China's weakness and end her isolation. As for Tattnall's assistance to the British during the battle for the Taku forts, Secretary Isaac Toucey was unwilling to be overly critical of his overseas commanders and told the commodore that his decision "met with the approbation of the Navy Department."[19]

Buchanan's firm line on maritime access in the Far East was matched by his rugged stance on a nagging dispute with Paraguay, a problem he inherited from the Pierce administration. In 1853, Pierce's secretary of state, Daniel Webster, had approved a scheme devised by Edward Hopkins, a former naval officer. Hopkins urged negotiating treaties with Argentina, Paraguay, and Uruguay that would permit unrestricted international navigation on La Plata River and its tributary system. Hopkins, a quarrelsome adventurer, had for years tried to get a monopoly for his steamship company from Carlos Antonio López, Paraguay's mercurial dictator. His chance appeared in 1852 when General Rosas was ousted as dictator of Buenos Aires and Argentina opened up the Paraná and Uruguay rivers to international trade. John Pendleton, the Ameri-

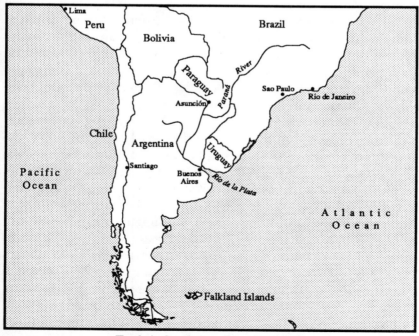

Trade in South America, 1852–1860

can minister in Buenos Aires, made his way up the Paraguay River to Asunción and convinced López to sign a navigation agreement with the United States. The Senate approved this agreement, known as the Pendleton-López Treaty, in 1854. To underscore the importance of this diplomacy and investigate the potential for American trade in the region, Navy Secretary John P. Kennedy instructed Lieutenant Thomas J. Page in the 350-ton paddlewheel steamer *Water Witch* to steam into the South Atlantic, report to the commander of the Brazil Squadron, and survey the La Plata, Paraguay, and Paraná rivers in order "to extend the bounds of science" and determine the "probable extent" of American "commercial intercourse" there. Navy oceanographer Lieutenant Matthew Fontaine Maury, one of the enthusiasts behind this mission, told Page to try to find out if the La Plata and Amazon systems were connected by some undiscovered river network.[20]

Page, no diplomat in uniform, was wholly unprepared for the nasty thicket of intrigue into which he stepped when the *Water Witch*, the first American warship to enter Paraguayan waters, reached Asunción on 1 October 1853. At first things went well. He persuaded López to allow the *Water Witch* to steam up the Paraguay River to Bahia Negra, but López refused to allow him to go farther. López did not want to establish the precedent of free international navigation on Paraguay's rivers on the Brazilian border; he feared that this would encourage the Brazilians to operate in that remote region and that if they did so they would one day dominate Paraguay. On the other hand, Asunción's control of the upper Paraguay River prevented the Brazilians from exploring the Mato Grosso, the rich interior of their own country.[21]

Seventeen days later, while Page was preparing for his journey, Edward Hopkins, the newly appointed American consul, appeared in the capital. Hopkins and López had done business since 1845, but their once friendly relations had recently turned sour. In November, Page in the *Water Witch* proceeded up the Paraguay River to Bahia Negra, near the point at which the borders of Paraguay, Brazil, and Bolivia meet. Inasmuch as he already had permission to navigate Brazil's inland waterways, Page foolishly ignored López's injunction to go no farther than Bahia Negra and continued on to Corumbá, Brazil. As a result, when Page returned to Asunción in December, López accused him of violating Paraguay's laws. López now suspended talks with Brazil over a river navigation treaty and ordered the Brazilian negotiator to pick up his passport. After this break with Brazil, López felt sufficiently secure to allow Page to resume his explorations.

Eight months later, in August 1854, the climate suddenly darkened. Hopkins burst into the presidential palace, bullwhip in hand, and demanded that López print an apology in Ascunción's official newspaper for a fracas between a soldier and Hopkins' younger brother. López was unnerved. He expressed his regrets for the incident but refused to print the humiliating apology. On 2 September, he ordered Hopkins to leave the country. That same day, Hopkins, who now feared for his life, sent a message to Page asking for help, and Page returned to the capital in the *Water Witch*. Page soon became involved in a petty feud with the foreign minister, who was reluctant to allow Hopkins to leave the country before he paid his debts to the government. Tired of haggling, Page took the *Water Witch* "up to a position [near the city dock], with her guns doubled-shotted, bearing in the direction of the Presidential palace." His intent was to threaten López so that he would not try to prevent Hopkins from departing. In retaliation, four days after the *Water Witch* stood out of Asunción, López declared an end to foreign navigation on Paraguay's rivers. Page, who wrongly considered López to be bound by the unratified Pendleton-López commercial treaty, warned Washington that the Paraguayan dictator was "unscrupulous" and not to be trusted.[22]

Soon after, Page received the instrument of ratification of the treaty from Washington and the State Department's instructions to deliver it to Asunción. He decided not to test López's decree, thus infuriating the Brazilians, and remained with the *Water Witch* while Lieutenant Murdagh took the commercial steamer *Buenos Aires* up to Asunción. López refused to accept the treaty. This infuriated Page, and four months later he directed Lieutenant William N. Jeffers to take the *Water Witch* up the Paraná River through Argentina to the Paraguayan frontier. On 1 February 1855, Jeffers approached Itapiru, a Paraguayan fort containing six large cannon situated on a small hill, which controlled all movements near the confluence of the Paraná and Paraguay rivers. When Jeffers steamed into the shipping channel on the Paraguayan side of the Paraná, the commander of the fort ordered him to turn back. Jeffers continued upriver. When the *Water Witch* was beneath the fort, the Paraguayan commander ordered his gun crew to fire a warning shot over the bow of the ship. Unfortunately, their aim was bad, and the shot struck the helm and killed the American pilot.

Both sides now opened fire. The fort fired twelve shots and hit the *Water Witch* ten times. Jeffers' poorly trained gunners got off only one three-howitzer broadside before abandoning their battle stations and seeking cover below. The vessel's hull was riddled with holes and the portside paddlewheel was badly damaged. With the pilot dead, the vessel ran aground, then broke free and drifted downstream. Jeffers limped back to Corrientes, Argentina. There he reported to Page, who was furious about the Paraguayan attack. Page tried to persuade Commander William D. Salter of the Brazil Squadron to retaliate against Paraguay by sending the brig *Germantown* up the Paraná River. "The fort at Itapiru ought to have been knocked down," Page contended. "We should . . . be even with the Paraguayan government." Salter refused to retaliate, however, until he received instructions from Washington. Page took some satisfaction from Brazil's decision to send a powerful naval squadron up to the Paraguayan border, which forced López to concede Brazil's right to navigate Paraguayan waters up to the Mato Grosso. When Navy Secretary Dobbin learned of the *Water Witch* incident, he approved of Page's actions, but for the moment he also applauded Salter's restraint. Page published several volumes about his explorations after his return to the United States and wrote of the need to cultivate political and commercial ties with La Plata basin before "alliances are made elsewhere" that would exclude American trade from the great interior rivers of the region.[23]

Beset by domestic political strife, Pierce was unwilling to retaliate against Paraguay for the *Water Witch* affair in 1855, but Buchanan took a far more muscular line two years later. He asked Congress for authority to coerce Paraguay into submission "in the event of a refusal" by Asunción to an American demand for an apology and damages. Armed with a congressional resolution, Navy Secretary Toucey very publicly organized the largest peacetime American punitive expedition ever assembled in the age of sail—a squadron comprising eleven steamers and eight sailing ships carrying 200 guns, and a landing force of 2,200 sailors and 300 Marines. On 9 October 1858, Toucey instructed Commodore W. Branford Shubrick to take his imposing force into La Plata River, establish a blockade of Paraguay at the junction of the Paraná and Paraguay rivers, and destroy the Paraguayan fort at Humaitá. Then he was to proceed upriver, lay siege to Asunción, and occupy the city. Upon learning about Shubrick's mission, General

Urquiza, Argentina's dictator, sent word to López that he should "expect the worst" and proposed that he accept Argentine mediation of the dispute, the alternative being certain defeat.

Shubrick arrived at the mouth of La Plata in December and began to move up the Paraná to the Paraguay River. Urquiza tried to persuade the Americans to wait until López agreed to a peaceful settlement. "The steamers of the fleet were a lot of broken-down hulks unworthy of the name of ships of war, and a laughingstock to other nations," recalled Lieutenant S. R. Franklin. "It was the best we could do, and as they frightened López into making the terms we demanded, they answered our purpose as well as a better-equipped force." López sent for the American minister in Buenos Aires, and they hastily signed an agreement in which López apologized for the *Water Witch* affair, promised to compensate the Navy and Hopkins, and opened up all of Paraguay's ports and rivers to American navigation. Lieutenant Page returned to South America with two small steamers, and explored and charted several Paraguayan and Uruguayan rivers during 1859. In December 1860, he returned home with a remarkable record of the geography and economy of the region, but publication of the report was curtailed when he resigned his commission to join the Confederate Navy the following spring.[24]

Bad timing also frustrated some of Buchanan's other projects. For instance, under a contract signed in May 1859 between Secretary Toucey and the Chiriquí Improvement Company, the Navy received title to sites for bases or coaling stations at both the Chiriquí Lagoon and the harbor at Golfito Duke on the Pacific Ocean, as well as exclusive access to some of the firm's coal reserves. Congress appropriated funds later in the year for a naval expedition to the area under Captain Frederick Engle, who was assigned to survey the sites, verify the Chiriquí Company's titles, and check on the quality of the coal. Engle returned to Washington after inspecting the area, elated at the prospects of finally establishing an American naval base in Central America. His announcement that his mission had been a grand success came in January 1861, just days before the entire matter was buried under the burden of the Civil War.

Chapter Fifteen

The Civil War at Sea
1861–1865

The election in November 1860 of Republican Abraham Lincoln, who was committed to ending slavery in the territories and to high protective tariffs, ignited the secessionist movement in the Deep South. South Carolina passed an ordinance of secession on 20 December 1860, and a few months thereafter, state militias throughout the South took over most of the federal arsenals. They also seized control of many of the coastal forts, including Forts Sumter and Moultrie in Charleston Harbor, Fort Pulaski off Georgia, Forts Gaines and Morgan in Mobile Bay, Fort Caswell near Wilmington, North Carolina, and Forts St. Philip and Jackson below New Orleans.

Unwilling to contest these moves and so precipitate a war that Lincoln would have to wage, President Buchanan moved to assert federal authority by putting into effect a scheme suggested by Lieutenant General Winfield Scott, the Army's commanding general, to reinforce Fort Sumter. Troops boarded the chartered steamer *Star of the West*, and she secretly departed New York for the run south soon after New Year's Day 1861. Nine days later, she entered Charleston harbor, but about two miles from Fort Sumter a Confederate battery on nearby Morris Island opened fire on her. Within a short time the *Star of the West*, flying a large American flag, was also brought under fire by Fort Moultrie, and was forced to retire from the harbor. Later that day she steamed back to New York.

Having failed to reinforce Fort Sumter, Buchanan turned his

attention to Fort Pickens on Florida's Santa Rosa Island, a stronghold that controlled the entrance to Pensacola Bay and access to the Pensacola Navy Yard, still in federal hands. Navy Secretary Isaac Toucey directed the frigates *Macedon* and *Sabine* to rendezvous with the sloops *Brooklyn* and *St. Louis* off Pensacola Bay, and ordered the squadron to reinforce the small Fort Pickens garrison and prevent the Florida militia from landing on the island. Toucey soon modified this order, however, after Florida's Senator Stephen Mallory arranged an armistice under which the militia promised not to assault Fort Pickens if Washington did not attempt to reinforce the garrison. This truce lasted until 4 February, when Florida joined Alabama, Georgia, Louisiana, Mississippi, South Carolina, and Texas to form the Confederate States of America. Unwilling to use force to confront secession, Buchanan left these problems to his successor.

During the winter of 1860, Lincoln had preached union in the North and held out the hand of conciliation to Virginia, North Carolina, and the border states, a posture he maintained even after he entered the White House in March 1861. "The Union of these states is perpetual," he claimed in his inaugural address. "No state, upon its own mere notion, can lawfully get out of the Union." Most new presidents dismissed civilian workers of the other party from the Navy yards to create jobs for their own partisans, but Lincoln, playing for time, ordered the new secretary of the Navy, Gideon Welles, not to remove any Democrats from the Norfolk Navy Yard while Virginia's leaders were meeting at Richmond to consider secession. This policy of appeasement was reflected elsewhere in the disarray that Welles found when he became secretary of the Navy. Seventy of the 300 officers on active duty had already resigned to join the new Confederate Navy, and most of the department's civilian clerks were political appointees, pro-South Democrats left over from the Buchanan administration. Welles had to create an Office of Detail to verify the loyalty of the remaining officers, investigate new applicants, weed out those who harbored Confederate sympathies, assign new officers to billets, and handle routine transfers.[1]

By the first week of April, only Fort Sumter and Fort Pickens remained in Union hands, symbols of the impending clash. To conciliate the South, Secretary of State William Seward urged Lincoln to withdraw federal troops from Fort Sumter, but to leave the garrison at Fort Pickens in place since the Florida keys controlled the entrance to the Gulf of Mexico. He also suggested that the president seize a pretext to challenge Britain, France, Spain, or all three, and then "convene Congress and declare war against them," thus unifying the country through the vehicle of a foreign conflict. Lincoln rejected this bizarre plan and turned instead to the immediate problem of Fort Sumter, an isolated outpost in the middle of Charleston harbor that was within range of shore batteries commanded by Confederate General Pierre G. T. Beauregard. General Scott warned Lincoln that Fort Sumter could not be held, a view Welles shared. The "impression has gone abroad that Sumter is to be evacuated and the shock caused by that announcement has done its work," Welles told the president. Lincoln disregarded this advice and instead agreed to a plan to reinforce Fort Sumter devised by Gustavas Vasa Fox, a former Navy officer and unofficial presidential adviser. This plan involved assembling a relief expedition consisting of an escort force that included the steamer *Powhatan* and a flotilla of small, fast steam gunboats, and a troop transport carrying a handful of landing boats. The steamer would defend the formation during the passage to Charleston, and the gunboats would cover the movement of the federal troops into the harbor. "If their vessels determine to oppose our entrance," he explained, then "the armed ships must approach the bar and destroy them or drive them on shore."[2]

Seward believed that a confrontation at Fort Sumter would bring on a war, which he still wanted to sidestep. Without telling Welles, he prevailed on Lincoln to detach the *Powhatan* from the Fort Sumter expedition and to deploy her instead in support of Fort Pickens. Bypassing the Navy Department, Seward then forwarded Lincoln's secret instructions to this effect directly to the ship. Lieutenant David Dixon Porter in the *Powhatan* stood out of New York on 6 April and steamed south to rendezvous with the fast transport *Atlantic*, which carried Army Captain Montgomery C. Meigs' Fort Pickens reinforcement battalion. They reached the Florida keys on the morning of 17 April. Meigs reinforced Fort Taylor at Key West and Fort Jefferson on Dry Tortugas, and landed soldiers and Marines at Fort Pickens the following day. Porter, who anchored the *Powhatan* at the mouth of Pensacola Bay, wanted to force an entry into the bay, but the plan was canceled at the last minute because Fort Pickens was barely defensible. Porter's expedition left the Union in command of the bay, however, and so closed off the most important Navy yard south of Norfolk. In the meantime, Captain Andrew Foote, the commandant of the

New York Navy Yard, alerted Welles to the Fort Pickens expedition. In a fury Welles confronted Lincoln and Seward, and forced Lincoln to agree to issue his orders to the Navy through Welles in the future.

Jefferson Davis of Mississippi, the Confederacy's new president, learned about Fox's Fort Sumter plan two weeks before the transport *Baltic* carrying 200 Union soldiers stood out of New York on 8 April. He had ordered Beauregard to demand the surrender of Major Robert Anderson, who commanded the fort's garrison, but that same day Davis was handed a letter from Lincoln stating that "an attempt will be made to supply Fort Sumter with provisions only." Anderson told Beauregard twice that he would not surrender, but that "if you do not batter us to pieces we will be starved out in a few days." The Confederate cabinet ordered Beauregard to wait for Anderson to evacuate the fort peacefully, and he planned to withdraw at noon on 15 April. The appearance of Fox's

Gideon Welles, founder of the Republican Party in Connecticut, was secretary of the Navy, 1861–69.

Gustavas Fox, assistant secretary of the Navy, 1861–66.

U.S. Navy Department

U.S. Navy Department

formation off Charleston at 0300 on 12 April changed their minds. Only Georgia's Robert Toombs, the secretary of state, opposed Davis' decision to prevent Fox from reaching the fort. "It is unnecessary; it puts us in the wrong; it is fatal," he said. After Anderson once again refused to surrender, the Fort Johnson battery on the mainland fired a signal shell over Fort Sumter at 0430, and other Confederate guns began firing thirty minutes later. Fox was frantic. Of the ships needed to run the blockade, only the *Pawnee* had reached the rendezvous point ten miles off Charleston by 0600, and her captain stubbornly refused to support the transports until the *Powhatan* arrived. Fox rowed into the harbor and "saw, with horror, black volumes of smoke issuing from Sumter." Although Anderson returned fire at 0700, Fort Sumter soon appeared to be a shambles.[3]

Fox arranged a truce with Beauregard that allowed Anderson's men, less one casualty, to board the *Baltic* for the voyage back to New York. "You and I both anticipated that the cause of the country would be advanced by making the attempt to provision Fort Sumter, even if it should fail; and it is no small consolation now to feel that our anticipation is justified by the result," Lincoln told Fox. Before Beauregard fired on Fort Sumter a large number of northerners, perhaps a majority, did not believe that antislavery politics was an adequate reason to fight a civil war. After Fort Sumter, the proponents of the Union grew far stronger, and a body of northern opinion was already weighing what an independent Confederacy would mean to the geopolitics of North America. To the Union, an independent, militarily strong Confederacy posed an immense strategic and economic challenge; preventing another nation from controlling the "great inland lake" of the Caribbean and the mouth of the Mississippi was a powerful motive for waging war. The guard "posts [of] the Caribbean, are in themselves alone of sufficient importance to create and justify a war, even a long and bloody war," announced the *New York Daily Tribune* on 11 January 1861.[4]

The bombardment of Fort Sumter forced the undecided in the North and South to make choices. Virginia's Richmond Convention had voted in March to remain in the Union, but Lincoln used the incident in Charleston harbor to justify a call for 75,000 volunteers for militia duty. This in turn moved Virginia to reverse course and join the Confederacy, along with North Carolina, Arkansas, and Tennessee. Maryland intended to quit the Union, but Lincoln prudently flooded the state with federal troops who ruthlessly suppressed secessionists there. This movement was supported by the Union Navy's new Potomac Squadron, which attempted to establish federal control up and down the river. Complete success was elusive, but the presence of the Potomac Squadron at this critical time permitted Lincoln to transport federal troops to Washington, a Union island now surrounded by a lake of Confederate hostility. Public opinion over secession was so evenly divided in the other border states of Delaware, Missouri, and Kentucky that they remained in the Union almost by default. Still, Lincoln was uncertain about the constitutionality of many of the military measures taken in April. Thus, although he called Congress into special session, he quite deliberately postponed the first emergency meeting for three full months.

The Union entered the Civil War with enormous political advantages, not all of which were entirely apparent in 1861. Most important, the North had an established national government, a permanent Army and Navy, good international credit, and a small but functioning national bureaucracy. The North also had superior political leadership. Although Lincoln was a poor administrator and a meddlesome commander in chief, he nonetheless saw beyond the military dimensions of the Civil War. He husbanded his military authority by shifting, often unfairly, the blame for defeats to his generals and admirals, and successfully unified the North under the umbrella of the war aim of maintaining the Union, which was elevated to the status of a virtue while rebellion was treated as sin. Moreover, Lincoln exploited the willingness of Congress and the state governments in the North to subordinate institutional, factional, and regional quarrels to the larger goal of military victory over the South.

The North also enjoyed a superior economic base for waging war. There were about 20 million whites in the Union states, only 6 million in the Confederacy. In addition, the North had a far more industrialized economy; there were 110,000 manufacturing plants and shops in the Union, only 18,000 in the Confederacy. The northern states produced nearly 600,000 tons of pig iron in 1860; southern output that year barely exceeded 35,000 tons. Four modern, large iron foundries were situated in the North; the South could rely only on the Tredegar Iron Works in Richmond. To transport its armies to the battlefield, the North possessed several major railroad arteries served by 22,000 miles of track; the South had to rely on four main lines with barely 9,000 miles of track. There was a large plant capacity to build barges and steamships in the North, almost none in the South. In New York, moreover, a large number of plants and shops building steam engines and machinery were already flourishing, an essential element in constructing new railroads, hauling machines, steamships, and naval vessels. Because of these advantages, northerners, including Lincoln, badly underestimated the potential of more intense Confederate patriotism and significantly better generalship. The North in 1861 was also heedless of the need to harness national resources in support of a rational, coherent, strategic war plan.

Confederate defenses seemed poorly arranged during the summer of 1861, so Union enthusiasts called for an offensive "on to Richmond." This was the battle cry when General Irvin McDowell's Union Army set off for the Confederate capital, only to be checked on 21 July at Manassas Junction, Virginia, in the first Battle of Bull Run. The carnage there stunned the generals, the troops, and the politicians on both sides. Although the Union Army left the battlefield first—encouraging many southerners to conclude rashly that the war was over—both governments soon grasped the need to mobilize their societies, organize major forces to conduct protracted campaigns, and erect and defend extensive supply networks.

Lincoln's cabinet reflected his uneasy national position and an early dependence on established Republican leaders, one of whom was Navy Secretary Welles, an ex-Democrat who had founded Connecticut's Republican Party. After Welles tangled with Seward over the Fort Sumter operation, Lincoln decided to muffle Seward's most vocal critic and at the same time energize the Navy Department. With Welles' approval, Gustavas Fox was named the new assistant secretary of the Navy. With sixteen years of commissioned service, Fox understood the complexity of operational problems far better than did Welles, but he lacked the secretary's political acumen and wizened ruthlessness. "Coolness and placidity" were Welles' greatest assets, thought Lieutenant Porter, who disliked but respected the secretary. Welles and Fox made a daunting combination. A powerful executive and one of Lincoln's best cabinet officers, Welles reorganized the Navy during the early stages of the war. In July 1862, Congress approved his plan to assign the shipbuilding functions of the Bureau of Equipment and Recruiting to the new Bureau of Construction and Repair and to create a new Bureau of Steam Engineering. The work of the former Bureau of Ordnance and Hydrography was divided between two new bureaus: Ordnance and Navigation. Within a few years, Welles had shifted the Office of Detail to the Bureau of Navigation, which created, for the first time, an effective Navy personnel office.[5]

Meanwhile, the Union's military fortunes had begun to decline. General Scott, clearly too old and tired to wage hard war, had prudently warned Lincoln against seeking a fight at Bull Run. After this first major Confederate victory, Scott urged Lincoln to direct the fleet to blockade the Confederacy while the Army laid siege to her borders, a proposal critics derisively called the Anaconda strategy. Scott argued that the blockade would deprive the South of foreign trade, while a landward siege would force Davis to defend the full length of his frontiers, thus exposing thinly held areas to costly federal raids. When weakened, the South could be punctured by Union thrusts down the Mississippi River, east from New Orleans into Alabama, and south from Washington to Richmond and into the Carolinas. Scott believed that this strategy would cost the Union Army few casualties and impose such unremitting economic and military pressure on the South that the seceding states would eventually rejoin the Union. Lincoln rejected some of the features of the Anaconda plan since its implementation would demand more political patience than he believed the North would possess after a few years of war. Lincoln apparently thought that he had only four years to prove that he could reunite the nation by military means. As an alternative to the Anaconda plan, however, the president mindlessly adopted a strategy of advancing everywhere. His first step was to concentrate Union troops into two major armies: The western army was to take the offensive against Confederate positions along the Mississippi, while the larger Army of the Potomac was to advance on Richmond. Lincoln did, however, accept one key feature of the Anaconda strategy—economic warfare. By the summer of 1861 he had already taken measures to blockade the South and prevent the Confederacy from establishing economic or diplomatic ties with Europe.

Organizing and maintaining the blockade was the Union Navy's major contribution to the war. When Welles learned that the Confederates planned to razee the *Merrimack*'s hull and turn her into a slow casemated ram, he named an ad hoc board, headed by Commodore Silas Stringham, to consider Union shipbuilding pol-

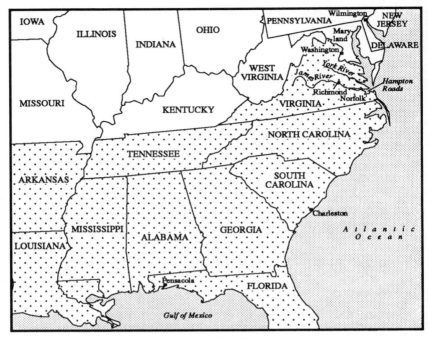

American Civil War

icy in light of this new menace. The pressure on Welles to do something was mounting daily. "If there are not now on hand steam vessels . . . to complete the blockade," Massachusetts Governor John
Andrew told him on 16 July, then "it is a matter of more importance
to use the sailing vessels for that purpose immediately than to wait
for steam gunboats to be completed for it." The Stringham board
examined the old Stevens Battery, but in May 1861 recommended
against rebuilding this relic. Two months later Congress convened.
Within weeks it had acted on Welles' request for an appropriation
for "one or more iron-clad steamers or floating batteries" whose design was to be selected by Commodore Joseph Smith's newly constituted Ironclad Board. This board examined several plans, took
bids, and eventually accepted one proposal to build the *New Ironsides,* a 3,500-ton wooden-hulled steam frigate distinguished by an
armor belt amidships, and another controversial plan to lay down
the 738-ton *Galena*-class armor-plated gunboats.[6]
        Cornelius S. Bushnell, a successful shipbuilder, discussed his
bid with John Ericsson, the eccentric ship designer whose shame-
ful treatment by the Navy after the 1844 *Princeton* disaster had un-

derstandably left him embittered. He wanted "to construct a vessel for the destruction of the rebel fleet at Norfolk and for scouring the Southern rivers and inlets of all craft protected by rebel batteries." Bushnell saw the genius in Ericsson's design and arranged for him to see the Ironclad Board, whose members were so impressed that they informally advised Welles to go ahead with the project. Welles agreed, and Ericsson promised to build the raftlike 172-foot *Monitor* within three months.[7]

Creating the blockade fleet transfigured the Navy. Before the Civil War, the fleet seldom relied on steam for cruising, but after 1861 no vessel was constructed without a steam plant. Soon after the first shots were fired at Fort Sumter, Welles ordered the construction of several 1,240-ton *Ossipee*-class screw-sloops that could operate in deep water against Confederate blockade runners and raiders, and contracted for twenty-three *Unadilla*-class steam gunboats. The Corps of Engineers mushroomed, fed by the needs of this new construction, and Captain Benjamin Isherwood, chief of the Bureau of Steam Engineering after 1862, became one of the Navy's leading figures. Under his influence, Welles decided to rely almost exclusively on the thirty-six coastal monitors for heavy operations in shallow waters and assigned them his highest priority.

One other reason Welles attached such urgency to the *Monitor* building program in 1861 was the threat of British intervention following a series of Union humiliations. British military preparations during the *Trent* affair sparked concern within the Navy about defending northern shipping and the Union coastline against an assault by the Royal Navy. Although he had earlier opposed the monitor program, and any investment in ironclads, Captain John Lenthall, the influential chief of the Bureau of Construction and Repair, proposed in November 1861 to lay down a fleet of twenty ironclad steam frigates to fend off British or French naval intervention. Such vessels, Ericsson asserted, might even "beard the British lion in his den." Lenthall wanted to lay down several double-turreted *Miantonomah*-class oceangoing monitors and insisted that the United States had the opportunity to "start equal with the first powers in the world in a new race for supremacy of the Ocean." However, Welles had no interest in joining an international naval arms race in ironclads in the middle of the Civil War—in spite of the crisis over the *Trent* affair. He settled instead on building only the seagoing ironclads *New Ironsides* and *Dunderberg*, an ill-fated vessel. On the other hand he did agree to the construction of thirty-seven double-ended ironclads, designed to ob-

viate the need to turn around when operating in the narrow channels of Confederate shipping channels or rivers. By 1865, the
Union Navy had built and launched 179 new warships, all driven
by steam plants.[8]

To obtain ships from the merchant marine, Welles issued a
commission to his brother-in-law, George D. Morgan, as Navy
agent and gave him wide powers to buy vessels for the Union fleet
in New York. By the end of 1861, Morgan had purchased ninety
vessels—and accumulated $70,000 in fees for himself. John M.
Forbes, a Boston patriot who headed up the purchasing effort in
New England, worked for free. From their efforts, by the end of
the war the Navy had acquired by purchase or transfer from other executive departments 479 vessels of various types. Welles' vig-
or in expanding the Union Navy boded ill for the South, but all
the monitors and most of the lesser ironclads would not begin to
enter the fleet until 1862.

The threat of the ex-*Merrimack* came about as a result of a vigorous naval policy adopted by the Confederacy. From scratch President Davis had to organize a central government in Richmond,
expand and exploit the South's small industrial economy, and establish a new national army and navy. He also had to confront the
contradiction between the Confederate principle of states' rights
and the need for a strong central government to orchestrate the
war effort and coordinate domestic and international policy. It was
not surprising that Davis, an Army veteran, seldom turned his considerable talents to the tangled issues of naval policy or strategy,
although therein lay the means of survival for a coastal power in
the modern age. He named former Florida Senator Mallory his
Navy secretary, and Mallory laid down three major goals for the
Confederate fleet: to defend the South's harbors, forts, and inlets;
disrupt Union naval operations in Southern waters; and attack
northern oceangoing commerce. Mallory expressed little concern about lifting the Union blockade, believing that it was not of
sufficient military importance to justify diverting Confederate assets from more pressing tasks. A man of great talent and energy,
he understood that the South suffered from shortages of materiel,
manpower, skilled shipbuilding labor, shipyards, and industrial
managers. In addition, the Confederate Army was accorded priority for many resources.

Confederate shipbuilding policy was founded on the notion
that the South could not afford to build a fleet of wooden frigates

since they "would fall easy prey to" the Union Navy's numerous steam frigates. Mallory intended to overcome this "inequality of numbers" by "invulnerability," and work was soon begun at the Norfolk Navy Yard on an ironclad that "could traverse the entire coast of the United States, prevent all blockades, and encounter, with a fair prospect of success," the Union's blockade squadron. In some respects, a predecessor of the vaunted Laird ram, the *Virginia* was intended as an interim measure to defend Confederate ports and prevent the Union Navy from exercising unfettered control over southern waters. Launched five years earlier but burned to the waterline and scuttled before Norfolk fell, the frigate *Merrimack* was raised, repaired, and fitted with a 170-foot armored casemate citadel fabricated by the Tredegar Works, the sole factory in the South with a mill large enough to roll used rails into two-inch-thick iron plate. Her draft was too deep to allow her to maneuver in shoal water, and she made only four knots at top speed, but the vessel was a potent warship with an ugly broadside. As an extra touch, a ram was added to her bow before she was recommissioned and renamed the *Virginia*. Commander John Mercer Brooke, who was in charge of raising and converting the vessel, reported that she would be "a good boat for harbor defense."[9]

Mallory also decided to purchase ships and guns abroad, and assigned James D. Bulloch to sail to Europe to direct this effort. He arrived in England in May 1861, and by midsummer had signed contracts with various British firms to build and arm several warships. For the cruiser program, Bulloch decided on wooden hulls, sails, and supplementary steam engines. These vessels were cheap, only $200,000 each, but they were only about 200 feet long and had limited firepower. The design of the Confederate cruiser allowed her captain to disguise his ship as a merchantman yet, with a top speed of fourteen knots, pounce on Union flag vessels. For the ram program, Bulloch arranged for Laird's of Liverpool to construct several vessels with steam engines, iron armor, and shallow draft for quick maneuvering in harbors, bays, and inlets, in shoal water, and up rivers. He planned to accept delivery of the cruisers and rams in England and man them there with Confederate officers and foreign crews, who would then sail to Spain or the Azores to fit out for commerce raiding or the voyage home.

Bulloch's activities led to a host of troubles between Britain and the United States. Union foreign policy was aimed at preventing the Great Powers from recognizing the Confederacy, providing legal backing for the blockade, and cutting off the flow of arms from Europe to the South. Lincoln and Seward got off to a rocky start in early 1861, but once the president realized that Seward was his most effective cabinet officer, the men became close friends. Lord Lyons, the British minister in Washington and Seward's most formidable opponent, recognized that Seward's considerable talents would make him "the fiercest of the lot" of Lincoln's cabinet. Seward's first problem after the fall of Fort Sumter was to deal with the related problems of the blockade and the legal status of the Confederate States. In 1856, in the wake of the Crimean War, the powers of Europe had negotiated the Declaration of Paris, which was intended to govern the future conduct of maritime war. "Blockades, in order to be binding, must be effective: that is to say, maintained by a force sufficient really to prevent access to the coast of the enemy," the agreement read. This clear definition of an effective blockade was intended to put an end to the confusion over "paper" blockades that could not be enforced.[10]

The Declaration of Paris also stipulated that a blockading fleet might seize contraband or enemy goods carried by enemy ships at any time, and immunized noncontraband enemy goods carried by neutral ships and neutral goods carried by enemy ships. In addition, the powers forswore the right to commission privateers, theretofore an important element in American maritime strategy. When invited to sign the treaty, the Pierce administration staunchly refused to give up the right to employ privateers in wartime unless the British agreed to revise the agreement to immunize all noncontraband goods, a compromise that London stiffly rejected. In 1856 the Americans sought to weaken the effectiveness of naval blockades; for their part the British tried to strengthen the legal underpinnings of this strategy upon which the Royal Navy had traditionally relied. When the Civil War erupted and Lincoln issued blockade orders, however, Seward hastily offered to ratify the Declaration of Paris, but this new diplomacy ran aground on the rock of Britain's opposition.

Lincoln's proclamation of a blockade of the ports of the seven seceding Confederate states on 19 April 1861 compelled the British and French to hastily assess their respective positions on the American conflict. Lord Palmerston, Britain's prime minister, and Lord John Russell, the foreign minister, not only sympathized with southern nationalism but also hoped to weaken the United States strategically by dividing the Union and thereby revising

North America's balance of power. Such a result would, they assumed, strengthen Canada's relative position and lessen the influence of the United States in the Caribbean and the Gulf of Mexico. Suspicious of Palmerston's longstanding anti-American bias, Seward tried to block the establishment of ties between Richmond and London by directing Charles Francis Adams, the American minister in England, to warn Russell that if London recognized the Confederate regime, then "diplomatic relations between . . . Great Britain and" the United States "will be suspended." Unwilling to take this risk, Palmerston decided instead to issue a neutrality proclamation, recognizing the South as a belligerent and thus permitting Richmond "to solicit loans, contract for arms, . . . send commissioned cruisers to sea, exercise all rights of search and seizure," and send diplomats abroad. Bulloch's activities were protected by this ruling. Seward was unhappy with this outcome, a result of Lincoln's hasty decision to announce the blockade rather than to declare certain domestic ports to be closed. Although Lincoln consistently refused to admit that the Confederacy was an independent nation, after the British announcement he had little choice but to instruct Welles to order the Union Navy to adhere to the Declaration of Paris.[11]

The French, who followed suit with their own neutrality proclamation, showed more interest in southern independence than the British, but they had much less diplomatic leeway. Napoleon III had spent huge sums to rebuild the French Navy, but in 1861 it was still greatly inferior to Britain's fleet. France was entangled in her Mexican imbroglio and in maintaining her position on the Continent during a decade of turmoil in Central Europe and had little choice but to follow Britain's lead in American affairs. Seward depicted the continuing danger to the Union when he cautioned Adams to be alert to European maneuvers: "If they determine to recognize [the Confederacy], they may at the same time prepare to enter into [an] alliance."[12]

Diplomatic recognition and military assistance from Britain and France were the bearing beams of Confederate diplomacy inasmuch as Europe's support offered Richmond a quick, obvious means to victory. Most southern statesmen had been planters before the war, however, and after secession they continued to view the British and French as customers rather than latent allies. This wrong-headed approach led Jefferson Davis in 1862 to conclude that he could demonstrate the South's importance to Europe by imposing an embargo on cotton exports, a nonintercourse measure intended to cripple Britain's textile economy and force London to come to the aid of the Confederacy to restore trade. Davis was not overly concerned with the Union blockade, therefore, and even looked forward to the frictions it might generate between Washington and London. "The blockade answers our purposes exactly," the *Charleston Mercury* declared. "It will force Great Britain and France to choose between the friendship and commerce of the Confederate States" and the Union. But British warehouses were overstocked with cotton when the Civil War began, and within two years Brazil, India, and Egypt were increasing their cotton shipments to Liverpool. As foreign or maritime policy, the Confederate cotton embargo not only failed to influence Europe, but also perversely reinforced the Union Navy's blockade before it was fully established.[13]

In the wake of Britain's neutrality proclamation, Davis escalated his campaign to win full diplomatic recognition and more military assistance by naming James Y. Mason his minister to Britain and John Slidell to France. It was public knowledge that they intended to run past the Union blockade standing off Charleston and travel to England on board the Confederate cruiser *Nashville*. To bottle up the *Nashville* in Charleston, Welles surged Union ships onto that blockade station, and on 16 October ordered Commander John B. Marchand in the sidewheel steamer *James Adger* to cross the Atlantic and position his vessel in the English Channel in case the rebel cruiser escaped. Mason and Slidell then changed their plans and chartered the coastal packet *Theodora*, which easily slipped past the Union patrols off Charleston under the cover of a rain squall on 12 October 1861. Off Cárdenas, Cuba, the coaster ran out of coal, and she was escorted into Havana harbor by a friendly Spanish gunboat.

Captain Charles Wilkes in the *San Jacinto* was en route home from West Africa at the end of the month when he put into Cienfuegos, Cuba, for coal. It was there he learned that Mason and Slidell were in Havana, and that they had booked passage to St. Thomas on board the British intercoastal packet *Trent*. Wilkes studied several maritime law books before deciding to capture Mason and Slidell, overruling his executive officer, Lieutenant D. M. Fairfax, who told him that seizing them might lead to war with Britain. Holding the Confederate envoys to be traitors, Wilkes concluded that, because the captain of the *Trent* was aware of their mission, he had wittingly decided to bring "contraband" on board his ship, thus making her a legal prize. No other action he might take "would so effectively non-plus [the] diabolical schemes" of the rebels as a move "to take the steamer as a prize." On 8 November, the *San Jacinto* took station in a narrow strip of the Old Bermuda Channel, about 230 miles east of Havana. When the *Trent* appeared, Wilkes fired one shot across her bow and sent a party of Marines aboard. After an unseemly scuffle with the diplomats' families, they brought Mason and Slidell back to the *San Jacinto*.[14]

The *Trent* affair outraged British public opinion, and before Palmerston and Russell could decide what to do, the cabinet was awash in indignation. The Admiralty alerted its North American Station to prepare for war, and Queen Victoria signed a proclamation on 4 December 1862 forbidding the export of gunpowder, caps, lead, or saltpeter. The transport *Melbourne* was loaded with 30,000 Enfield rifles and other military stores, and 8,000 troops were embarked for the voyage to Canada where they were to supplement the regular garrison and make ready for an American invasion. The reaction in the United States was predictable. Welles congratulated Wilkes for his "intelligence, ability, decision, and firmness," and the *New York Times* praised him for capturing the two "distinguished malignants." Overnight, Wilkes became one of the first Union heroes of the Civil War.[15]

Seward, who disliked Welles, was alarmed from the start, and quickly "scouted the idea of letting the prisoners go." After his first blush of enthusiasm, Welles decided that Wilkes had acted rashly and without regard for the diplomatic consequences. There was a general agreement both in Britain and America that the Union's legal case might have stood on firmer ground had Wilkes simply seized the *Trent* and hauled her into a prize court for carrying belligerent dispatches. The government had "white elephants on our hands," warned Lincoln, and Seward soon after instructed Adams in London to quietly disavow Wilkes' actions. Welles now came full circle, calling Wilkes "impulsive" and "erratic."[16]

Fearful that Palmerston's policy might lead to war with the United States, Prince Albert, Victoria's consort, prevailed upon him to soften Britain's official demand that Washington release its Confederate hostages. In turn, Seward replied with a lengthy defense of the Union position on neutral rights and the blockade, a tome published while Mason and Slidell were secretly hustled on board a British steamer that awaited them in Boston harbor. Within a few months, Seward and Russell had made amends, and had negotiated the 1862 Seward-Lyons Anti-Slave Trade Treaty in which the United States gave the Royal Navy permission for the first time to stop and search suspected slavers flying the Stars and Stripes off West Africa and in Cuban waters. While Anglophobia still ruled public opinion in the North, the *Trent* affair forced the British to examine the prospects of war with the United States under the most provocative circumstances, and to decide that the defense of Canada against a Union invasion was at least for the moment beyond the reach of British military assets. This view was reaffirmed after the clash in early 1862 in Hampton Roads. The *Monitor*'s appearance was noted with alarm in London, and Russell warned the cabinet to "think of our position if . . . the Yankees [begin] turning on us by means of iron ships [and] renew the triumphs they achieved in 1812–13!" According to the London *Times*, "There is not now a ship in the English navy, apart from . . . two [armored vessels], that it would not be madness to trust to an engagement with the little *Monitor*." So long as Canada was at risk, Britain was unlikely to side with the Confederacy.[17]

The collapse of the Peninsula Campaign that summer and Lee's invasion of Maryland in the fall raised the South's prospects for European diplomatic recognition. Palmerston proposed to his cabinet on 14 September that Britain and France issue a joint offer to Washington and Richmond of "mediation on the basis of separation and recognition accompanied by a declaration of neutrality." Russell liked this formula. Should Lincoln reject it, he was "ready to recognise the Southern States as an independent State." This would bolster the Confederacy's credit in Europe, increase the Union Navy's problems in enforcing the blockade, and remove many of the obstacles then preventing the South from acquiring more military and naval assistance from abroad. A discussion on this step by the British cabinet was scheduled for late October. The Union victory at Antietam put a brake on Palmerston's plan to recognize the Confederacy, however, and while neither he nor Russell stopped thinking about mediation after Antietam, they were thereafter more inclined to Lord Granville's view that such an offer would be "premature" until the military picture in North America was clarified. Palmerston was constantly reminded that Canada could not be defended, and the Admiralty reiterated its opposition to any British action that might lead to war with the United States until the spring of 1863, when "our naval force could more easily operate upon the American coast."[18]

Seward understood after Fort Sumter that of all the Great Powers, Britain's opinions and policies counted the most, and he adjusted his maritime diplomacy throughout the war accordingly. Britain was starved for cotton by 1862 and Palmerston was blaming Washington for this plight. The British were angry with the North over this and other maritime issues, but they were also upset by the Confederate announcement in 1861 that Richmond planned to resume the Atlantic slave trade at the end of the war. Moreover, paralysis gripped British foreign policy in the face of conflict over how to respond to the provocation of the Union blockade. Minister Lyons wanted to use the ineffectiveness of the blockade as a club against Seward, while in London the Admiralty was happy to keep track of the expanded rights of blockading forces articulated periodically by the State Department. The masters of the Royal Navy expected that these American positions might someday be put to good advantage in the cause of British interests. Thus, Jefferson Davis' oft-stated, bitter complaint that London was unwilling to hew to a strict line of policy on the blockade was essentially correct.

As for the French, Confederate Minister John Slidell reported from Paris that Napoleon III preferred to recognize the Richmond government but that he depended so completely on British good will that "he will make any sacrifices of his own opinions and policy to retain it." In effect, French maritime policy was shackled to the stalemate in Whitehall. Seward craftily exploited this state of affairs, adopting a different diplomatic tone with the French.

Because he did not fear the French, his approach to them was abrupt, often blunt, on occasion threatening. This model was not useful in dealing with Britain, however. The danger there to the Union cause was real and omnipresent during the first two years of the war. When he warned the British not to move against the Union, Seward did so with great care, at least until the turn of the tide of the war meant that caution no longer was so necessary.[19]

The July 1863 Union victories at Vicksburg and Gettysburg completed the revision of the terms of transatlantic maritime diplomacy, a process that began after Antietam. London was on the verge of intervening in September 1862, but nine months later this had all changed, with Palmerston's cabinet now determined to remain aloof from the American scene in the expectation that the Confederacy would eventually fall. Seward exploited this attitude by pressing the British to stop selling warships being built in English and Scottish yards to the Confederate Navy. These transactions had been the source of Union complaints since 1861, but by the time Seward's campaign began to have an impact on the Foreign Office, the Confederate commerce raiders had already taken a fearful toll of Union merchant shipping.

Chapter Sixteen
The Raiders
1861–1865

In early 1861 Confederate Navy Secretary Mallory launched a campaign to raid Union shipping by issuing commissions to a handful of southern privateers. "Jefferson Davis might as well have thrown a lighted match into a powder magazine, as menace the commerce of the North with privateers," the *New York Times* snorted angrily. "The effect of his proclamation upon our community has been only to deepen and make tenfold more intense the hatred and indignation of the public." Davis had high hopes for his privateering strategy. He expected a swarm of Confederate raiders to seize Union shipping in European waters and bring their prizes into Britain's ports for condemnation and sale. This plan was undermined by London's June 1861 neutrality proclamation, which effectively prohibited either belligerent's armed vessels from entering British waters. Another menace to southern commerce raiding was Lincoln's threat to try Confederate privateer crews for piracy. When the crew of the captured privateer *Savannah* was actually hauled into federal court in New York, Davis forced an end to the proceedings by threatening reprisals against an equal number of Yankee prisoners of war. This small victory notwithstanding, Confederate privateers took only forty prizes in 1861, and the following year the entire rebel privateering campaign collapsed because of the inaccessibility of neutral ports and the difficulty of bringing prizes into blockaded southern ports.[1]

Commerce raiding by Confederate Navy cruisers built in Britain proved to be immensely more successful than the South's abortive privateering effort. The most effective raider was the 1,050-ton screw-sloop *Alabama*, constructed by Laird's of Liverpool. Launched as the *Henrico*, she stood out of Liverpool on 29 July 1862 and sailed for the Portuguese Azores, where she was fitted out and commissioned into the Confederate fleet as the *Alabama* by the inspiring, resourceful Captain Raphael Semmes. For the next two months Semmes in the swift *Alabama* raided Union commerce in the North Atlantic, taking twenty ships before he charged onto the Newfoundland Banks to attack the northern grain trade there. Next he sailed south to Brazilian waters, where he ravaged Union ships returning from the Pacific. Semmes then made for Cape Town and on to the East Indies, where the *Alabama* took seven prizes before retracing her route around Africa and back to Europe. After spending nearly two years on a commerce raiding voyage that took him over 75,000 miles, Semmes had burned or paroled more than sixty Union prizes worth $6 million. When he put in at the French port of Cherbourg on 11 June 1864, the *Alabama* was badly in need of an overhaul.

Although Navy Secretary Welles refused to withdraw many ships from the Union blockading squadrons to hunt down the Confederate raiders, he was not insensitive to the wound that they inflicted on northern morale. A few Union ships had been kept on station overseas and in the Caribbean to deter the raiders, but only in 1863 was he ready to send them out to keep his promise to Congress to conduct an "active pursuit" of the "rebel-pirates." One of these Union hunters was the 1,550-ton screw-sloop *Kearsarge*, commanded by Captain John A. Winslow. In pursuit of the *Alabama*, the *Kearsarge* made the waters off Cherbourg only a few days after Semmes arrived in June 1864. Winslow dropped anchor off the harbor, waiting for the Confederate raider to stand out to sea. When he learned of Winslow's arrival, however, Semmes abandoned his plan to repair his sloop, reasoned that he was cornered, and decided to fight rather than risk being interned by the French.

After taking on coal, Semmes gallantly steamed out of Cherbourg to accept the *Kearsarge*'s challenge, opening fire on the Union ship once both Americans were clear of French territorial waters. With chain cable stacked in tiers to protect her vital spaces, the *Kearsarge* had an immense defensive advantage over the unarmored *Alabama,* and Winslow did not even begin to fire until he was within 1,000 yards of his opponent. Steaming on opposite courses, the ships circled each other, each captain trying to cross the other's bow and rake his enemy's deck. Because her powder and shells had deteriorated in storage, the *Alabama*'s broadside was ineffective. "After the lapse of about one hour and ten minutes," Semmes reported, "our ship was . . . in a sinking condition, the enemy's shell having exploded in our side, and between decks, opening large apertures through which water rushed with great rapidity." Semmes struck his colors, threw his sword into the sea, and abandoned ship. While Winslow rescued the rebel crew and the *Alabama* sank, a nearby yacht picked up Semmes and his officers and helped them to escape to England.[2]

Another successful southern commerce raider was the 191-foot-long screw-sloop *Florida,* built for the Confederate Navy by William C. Mission and Sons of Liverpool in 1861. On 22 March 1862, the *Florida* sailed from England for the West Indies, where she was fitted out as a raider by Lieutenant John N. Maffitt. Although Maffitt and most of his crew had contracted yellow fever, the *Florida* ran the Union blockade off Mobile Bay, anchored under the protection of the guns of Fort Morgan, and provisioned for her first cruise. On 19 January 1863, Maffitt escaped back into the Gulf and sailed down to South America, capturing more than a dozen prizes and eluding a small Union squadron assigned to run her down. Maffitt stood into Brest harbor in August, and the *Florida* was laid up there for five months undergoing repairs. Maffitt, by now near death from the fever, was relieved by Lieutenant Morris. He returned to the West Indies, then hunted down Union ships around the Canaries before heading for the neutral port of Bahia, Brazil, in the fall of 1864. Morris and half his crew were ashore on the night of 7 October when Commander Napoleon Collins in the *Washusett* came alongside the *Florida* and took over the Confederate ship. Ignoring protests about this flagrant violation of Brazil's neutrality, Collins towed his prize back to the United States. Shortly thereafter, she went down in a collision off Newport News with a Union troop ferry. Collins was court-martialed for violating Brazilian neutrality, but he had by that time become a national hero in the North and was later promoted for his audacity. During her career as a raider, the *Florida* had taken thirty-eight Union ships worth over $2 million.[3]

The Union countered the Confederate commerce raiders by sending out small hunting squadrons to track them down, destroy them at sea, or blockade them in neutral ports, and by putting diplomatic pressure on Britain and France to end the sale of warships to the Confederate Navy and shut down European ports and yards to southern cruisers. Charles F. Adams, the indefatigable Union minister in London, relentlessly complained to Lord John Russell that the sale of these commerce raiders to the South not only offended Washington but also violated Britain's own neutrality laws. Palmerston's cabinet felt uncomfortable with these private transactions, and its discontent was increased in March 1863 when Congress authorized the president to commission Union privateers. It was ironic that this measure, the Union Privateering Act of 1863, was enacted for reasons having little to do with international diplomacy. It had been pushed through Congress by New York speculators, who hoped to share in the huge sums of prize money then being collected by the Union Navy's blockading squadrons. To keep this monopoly for his officers and men, Welles persuaded Lincoln not to issue any commissions to northern privateers. This was not understood in London, however, and with few Confederate-flag merchantmen at sea, the British saw the Privateering Act as merely another attempt to threaten reprisals against them if the Palmerston government decided to support the South.[4]

This new Union menace only added to the prime minister's earlier worry about establishing a precedent in international law by allowing sales of warships that might be used to undermine Britain's traditional blockade strategy. These factors, magnified by Adams' nagging, resulted in a decision by the British authorities in April 1863 to impound the 120-ton wooden screw-sloop *Alexandra* at the Toxteth dock in Liverpool to prevent her imminent transfer to the Confederate Navy. On the surface this seemed a decisive move, but in truth it was rather tentative, an illustration of indecision rather than firm resolve. During the summer of 1863, Palmerston and Russell finally agreed not to intervene in the Civil War, but it was not until early fall that the cabinet reluctantly took the legal steps necessary to curtail the transfer of more warships from British yards to the Confederates. With the Union by then ascendant on the battlefield, Seward had already begun to take a rougher line with London, and the entire issue reached its climax over the Laird Rams.

The Laird Rams were a pair of vessels fitted with iron "piercers," or rams. Armed with powerful 9-inch rifled guns, these ships had been purchased by Confederate Navy agent Bulloch at the request of Secretary Mallory, who intended to deploy them for harbor defense and in raids on northern ports. In addition to these two vessels, the firm of Thompson Brothers was also building another *Alabama*-class screw schooner and an armored frigate at its yard on the Clyde River. In early September 1863, Minister Adams heard a rumor that the *Alexandra* was about to escape, and emphasized to the British the need to act quickly. "It would be superfluous in me to point out to your lordship," he warned Russell, "that this is war." Although the rumor proved to be false, this and similar threats turned the tide. Russell issued an order on 3 September that effectively impounded the Laird Rams, and the ships were later purchased for the Royal Navy. Early in the war, the British had adopted other practices that reflected its policy of benevolent neutrality toward the Confederacy. For instance, they permitted Confederate captains to recruit crews in British ports, and Confederate cruisers were allowed to remain in British waters longer than the twenty-four hours permitted under recognized international law. In addition, these vessels were allowed to return to neutral British ports before three months had elapsed, another violation of international maritime law. At the same time that he ordered the Laird Rams be impounded, Russell directed the Admiralty to end these practices.[5]

With the Laird Rams project about to collapse in the summer of 1863, Bulloch understood that his mission to England would soon draw to a close, so he hastily made secret arrangements for some of the impounded vessels to put to sea. He had limited success, but he was able to acquire the *Sea King*, a steamer built on the Clyde, which was commissioned beyond British waters as the raider *Shenandoah*. During her career, the *Shenandoah* burned or sank about $1 million worth of prizes, ravaging the Union whaling fleet in the Bering Strait for four months after Lee surrendered at Appomattox. Ironically, it was during the Civil War that whale oil lost much of its value as a strategic commodity. Petroleum was discovered in Pennsylvania in 1859, and over the next five years it replaced whale oil as an all-purpose lubricant, and kerosene replaced whale oil as lamp fuel. The northern whaling trade never fully revived. After making arrangements for the transfer of the *Shenandoah* in early 1863, Bulloch shifted his base to

Stephen R. Mallory, U.S. senator from Florida, was Confederate secretary of the Navy, 1861–65.

France, and in July arranged for the L. Arman shipyard at Bordeaux to build two rams and four *Alabama*-class screw-schooners for the Confederate Navy. In addition, he contracted to purchase guns for the rams from the English firm of Armstrong. When Secretary Seward learned about this project, he fired off the first of a barrage of menacing protests to Napoleon III. By this time the emperor was eager to improve relations with Washington in order to reduce Union opposition to France's occupation of Mexico, and so he directed his agents to compel Arman to sell the vessels elsewhere.

The powerful, seagoing ram *Stonewall* was purchased by Denmark, but when she did not arrive in time to help the Danes defend Schleswig and Holstein in their war against Prussia and Austria in late 1863, they canceled the sale. Arman secretly transferred the ship back to the Confederates, and Mallory sent Captain T. J. Page to Copenhagen to take command of the *Stonewall* in December 1864. Within a month he had sailed to Quiberon Bay, where he took on supplies and readied his ship for the voyage across the Atlantic. When Page put to sea, however, he ran into a terrific storm that forced him to seek refuge at Ferrol, Spain. Meanwhile, Welles had dispatched Captain Thomas T. Craven with a Union squadron composed of the wooden frigates *Niagara* and *Sacramento* to hunt down the French-built ram, and he reached Coruna, nine miles up the coast from Ferrol, only a few days after Page put into that port. When he learned of the nearby Union force, Page decided to fight. On 25 March 1865 the *Stonewall* cleared the harbor and Page issued a challenge to the Union ships to do battle, an offer Craven declined to accept. "If we had gone out," he later insisted, "the *Niagara* would most undoubtedly have been easily and promptly destroyed." Although this assessment was probably correct, it led to Craven's conviction by a postwar court-martial for failing to act aggressively and allowed Page to escape across the Atlantic to Havana, where his ship was seized at the end of the war.

The *Stonewall* episode underscored many of the problems that afflicted Confederate maritime diplomacy. The French and British decisions to shut down Confederate warship contracting provoked bitter, eloquent complaints from Jefferson Davis to the effect that neither power was willing to act on its principles, but these outbursts fell on deaf ears in Paris and London and failed to reverse Europe's decision in 1863 to end its support of the cause of southern nationalism.[6]

On the other hand, the commerce raiding operations cost the Confederacy relatively little, and the benefit was disproportionate to the effort involved. Although the Union's coastal trade was largely immune to the Confederate raiders, by the end of the war these warships had sunk about 5 percent of the Union merchant fleet and had disrupted about one out of every 200 Union voyages in the overseas trade. Still, throughout the war the lack of open ports was a major impediment to a successful commerce raiding campaign. Because the Confederate raiders could not deposit prizes in neutral British or French ports, they burned most of them at sea, although many ships carrying a large number of passengers were allowed to proceed under bond or parole. Over 200 northern merchantmen were burned, sunk, or sent into the Confederate ports of New Orleans, Charleston, or Wilmington for condemnation. While these losses put a slight crimp in northern shipping, Union trade with Britain and Europe felt little effect. When losses to the Confederate raiders resulted in greatly increased insurance rates for Union merchant shipping, traders merely sought a neutral flag, usually British, under whose protection they could sail with immunity. By the end of the war, nearly 75 percent of the North's trade with Europe was carried in foreign bottoms.

Indeed, over the course of the war, about half the Union merchant fleet adopted foreign flags of convenience, which the Confederate raiders were forbidden to attack. The Confederate depredations merely accelerated a downward trend in the size of the American merchant fleet already under way, however. For at least a decade before the Civil War, the American merchant marine—which relied mostly on older wooden clipper ships and paddle-wheel steamers—had lost cargoes to the growing British merchant fleet of iron-built sail and steam vessels. This meant that while the Confederate raiders wounded the American merchant marine, raised southern morale, inconvenienced the North, and strained Washington's relations with Europe, they had virtually no impact on the outcome of the Civil War.[7]

Chapter Seventeen
The Peninsula Campaign
1862

The uneven early performance of Union arms on the battle-field did not match the consistent success of Lincoln's maritime diplomacy. Soon after the Union lost the first Battle of Bull Run, Lincoln turned to Major General George B. McClellan, who succeeded Winfield Scott in late 1861 as the commanding general of the Union Army. An able strategist, McClellan was almost alone among Union generals in his dislike of frontal offensives against entrenched lines and in his adoption of detailed plans of maneuver embodying joint operations. The meticulous preparations that his campaigns required conflicted with Lincoln's impatient demand in early 1862 that the Union armies take the offensive against the main southern army under General Joseph Johnston, who stood at the time between Washington and Richmond. Unwilling to wait, Lincoln assumed personal direction of the Union Army on 10 March, left McClellan in charge of only the Army of the Potomac, and peremptorily ordered him to move south. Instead of advancing overland, however, McClellan chose to exploit Union naval control of the Potomac River and the Chesapeake Bay by mounting a huge amphibious operation to outflank the Confederates and advance on Richmond. This set the stage for the great Peninsula Campaign.

McClellan could consider this ambitious operation because in April 1861 Welles had established the Potomac Flotilla and instructed it to hold the Union banks of the river from the capital to the mouth of the Chesapeake Bay. During the war, Union steamers patrolled these waters continuously, protecting the passage of troop transports and cargo shipping to and from Washington and harassing the opposing Confederate batteries along the Virginia banks. In planning his flanking movement, McClellan was misled by poor intelligence into believing that Johnston would hold his army at Manassas, and so he decided at first to embark the Army of the Potomac in 400 transports, steam down onto the Chesapeake Bay, and land at Urbana, less than fifty miles from Richmond. Confederate attention to these movements was to be diverted by an amphibious landing aimed at taking Raleigh, North Carolina. McClellan assembled a division of New England fishermen under the command of Major General Ambrose Burnside and trained these troops in small boat operations and forced landings. McClellan intended Flag Officer Louis Goldsborough's North Atlantic Blockade Squadron to take Fort Macon and occupy the nearby Beaufort harbor area so that Burnside's men could land, advance from Roanoke Island inland, and menace Raleigh. This would force the Confederates to divide their army so as to deal with the southern threat.

Burnside took Roanoke Island easily, but Goldsborough needed sixteen gunboats, two days, and his entire stock of high-explosive ammunition to reduce the 9-gun battery in Fort Barlow at Pork Point. The result was that Goldsborough's gunboats could not support Burnside's movement against Raleigh. The ensuing delay gave the Confederates time to erect formidable lines in front of Raleigh, and Burnside had to abandon his proposed overland movement. Moreover, McClellan now learned that Johnston was falling back south of the Rappahannock River, so he boldly changed his plan. He now proposed to outflank the Confederates by shipping the Army of the Potomac even farther south to the Union base at Fortress Monroe. From there, he would work his way up the peninsula bounded by the York and the James rivers, shifting his balance from one river to another and thereby avoiding the sieges and pitched battles he so disdained. Whenever his opponent built up defensive lines, McClellan intended to exploit the Union Navy's mobility to attack the Confederate rear. These great movements would envelope any Confederate forces that opposed his progress on the peninsula and crush the shallow defenses to the east of Richmond.

In early March, McClellan explained his strategy to Flag Officer Goldsborough. Goldsborough was to establish control over the lower Chesapeake Bay, secure an anchorage in Hampton Roads that covered the mouth of the James River, and defend the passage from that anchorage to the Union base at nearby Fortress Monroe. To do this, Goldsborough concentrated a powerful force at Hampton Roads, including the screw-frigates *Minnesota* and *Roanoke*, the sailing frigates *St. Lawrence* and *Congress*, and the sloop *Cumberland*. Laying off the mouth of the Elizabeth River, this formation was assigned to blockade a rebel gunboat squadron on the James River and to prevent the breakout onto the Chesapeake Bay of the menacing Confederate ironclad *Virginia*, which, Mallory had assured Jefferson Davis in February, would soon be able "to keep our waters free from the enemy."[1]

To relieve the trapped James River Flotilla, Confederate Captain Franklin Buchanan in the recently completed *Virginia* got under way from the Norfolk Navy Yard on the morning of 8 March and steamed down the Elizabeth to Hampton Roads. Goldsborough, well aware of the presence of the *Virginia* at Norfolk, had inexplicably neither prepared his squadron for combat nor devised any battle plan to exploit his opponent's weaknesses and avoid her strengths. After an opening exchange of broadsides, during which shot from the *Congress* bounced harmlessly off the *Virginia*'s armor, Buchanan rammed and sank the *Cumberland*. Escorted by the armed tugs *Raleigh* and *Beaufort*, the *Virginia* next went after the *Congress*, forcing her to run ashore, where she erupted into flames and was destroyed by Confederate gunfire. During this exchange, however, Buchanan was wounded. Lieutenant Roger Catesby ap Jones relieved him and headed for the *Minnesota*, but thirty minutes elapsed before the *Virginia* turned around, and Jones could navigate no closer than 2,000 yards to the grounded Union screw-frigate. At the end of the day, the *Virginia* chugged back to the Confederate anchorage at Sewell's Point, her armor intact and her crew almost unharmed.

When Assistant Secretary of the Navy Gustavas Fox had learned about McClellan's plan, he recognized the need to deal quickly with the threat to the Peninsula Campaign posed by the Confederate ironclad. Ericsson had almost completed work on the *Monitor*, but she had not yet undergone her routine sea trials when, on 6 March, Fox directed her captain, Lieutenant John L. Worden, to steam south to Hampton Roads to reinforce Goldsborough's

The Union Navy *Monitor* engaging the Confederate ironclad *Virginia* (ex-*Merrimack*) in Ha
Roads, Virginia, 9 March 1862.

Rear Admiral Franklin Buchanan was the first Superintendent of the U.S. Naval Academy, 1846; commander
of the Confederate Chesapeake Bay Flotilla, 1862, and
of the Confederate Mobile Bay Flotilla, 1864.

squadron. When Worden stood out of New York, workmen were still on board and "no part of the vessel was finished." After a terrifying southward voyage during which the *Monitor* was repeatedly swamped and nearly sank twice, Worden entered the Chesapeake Bay in the late afternoon of the 8th, heard gunfire from Hampton Roads, and later that evening dropped anchor alongside the *Minnesota*. A thick fog settled over both Union vessels.

When Roger Catesby ap Jones brought the *Virginia* out the next morning, Worden got up steam and closed to defend the Union formation. "I got under way as soon as possible and stood directly for her," Worden recalled, "in order to meet and engage her as far away from the *Minnesota* as possible." For two hours, the pair of remarkable warships dueled. Although the more agile *Monitor* was able to prevent the *Virginia* from firing on the helpless *Minnesota*, Worden's guns could not penetrate the southern ship's armor. At the same time, Jones was unable to inflict any damage on the *Monitor*. Jones grounded the *Virginia* while trying to break off from the *Monitor*, but just as Worden closed to within fifty feet to hammer his opponent into submission, the Confederate gunners shifted their fire from the turret to the pilot house of the Union vessel. "When being within ten yards of the enemy a shell from her stuck the pilot house near the lookout hole, though which I was looking, and exploded, . . . filling my face and eyes with powder and utterly blinding and in a large degree stunning me," Worden wrote. With the captain temporarily blinded, Lieutenant Samuel D. Greene took command and retired to the east. Once the *Virginia* freed herself, Jones withdrew up the Elizabeth River to the Norfolk yard for a variety of minor repairs. The *Monitor*'s pilot house was badly damaged and Greene had to turn the vessel from starboard to port just to aim at the enemy, with the result that he fired only a few rounds at safe range and decided not to chase his opponent under the guns of the Confederate forts. "The very serious danger of grounding in the narrower portions of the channel and near some of the enemy's batteries, which it would have been difficult to extricate her, possibly involving her loss," led Worden to agree with Greene's decision. "Her loss would have left the vital interests in all the waters of the Chesapeake at the mercy of future attacks from the [ex-] *Merrimack*." However, Assistant Secretary Fox, who was watching the battle with crowd of spectators on the northern shore, was furious, and he ordered that Greene be relieved of his command.[2]

Although the Battle of Hampton Roads appeared to end in a stalemate, Goldsborough soon realized that this was because the disparities in the ordnance of the opposing vessels gave the *Monitor* an advantage. Whereas the *Monitor* fired solid wrought iron and brass shot designed to penetrate the *Virginia*'s armor, the Confederate ironclad, expecting to confront only the wooden Union frigates, carried only explosive shells. Goldsborough was concerned that if the Confederates armed the *Virginia* with solid brass-tipped bolts, sortied again, and closed and fired once more at point-blank range, then the *Monitor* might be defeated. He was unaware that weak engines and ineffective steering rendered the *Virginia* almost unseaworthy and nearly impossible to maneuver. To prevent a body blow to Union political morale, Lincoln instructed Goldsborough not to expose the *Monitor* to "unnecessary" risks, and Welles warned him repeatedly not to bring the vessel within range of the Confederate shore batteries. As it was, the Union Navy now controlled Hampton Roads and the great Peninsula Campaign could begin.[3]

Soon after the news of the battle reached Washington, Mc-Clellan's army of 120,000 men boarded transports that carried them down the Potomac to Fortress Monroe, leaving behind 50,000 troops to defend Washington and 24,000 men under General Nathanial P. Banks to fend off a thrust up the Shenandoah Valley by a secondary Confederate army under General Thomas "Stonewall" Jackson. Before departing, McClellan had alerted Secretary of War Edwin M. Stanton that he intended to move from Hampton Roads up the banks of the York River toward Richmond, and "that the Navy should at once throw its whole available force, its most powerful vessels, against Yorktown." From that anchor the Confederates had entrenched a line across the peninsula, a step ordered by Jefferson Davis over the objections of General Johnston, who was naturally worried that McClellan would use the Union fleet to outflank the position.

Fox, who agreed with McClellan's strategy, had apparently promised him that the North Atlantic Squadron would support the Army's movements, but that was before he learned that Goldsborough distrusted McClellan and was stubbornly refusing to cooperate with him. Rather than trying to outflank Yorktown, Goldsborough insisted that the Union forces first take Norfolk, end the menace of Norfolk's batteries to Union shipping, recover the Navy yard, and destroy the *Virginia*. Goldsborough's obsession with taking Norfolk upset McClellan's plans and delayed his movements, although maneuver rather than speed was at the core of McClellan's strategy. Goldsborough was especially worried when he learned from Union spies that Mallory had assigned Captain Josiah Tattnall to command the *Virginia*, and that Tattnall, a skillful, aggressive fighter, was preparing to reenter Hampton Roads. Goldsborough reinforced his squadron with a jerry-rigged ram to use against the *Virginia*, planned to sink hulks in the Elizabeth River to blockade the rebel ironclad, and readied his forces for a joint movement against the city. This foolishly ignored McClellan's correct estimate of the situation. Owing to the layout of the surrounding Confederate railroads, if the Union troops seized Yorktown and opened up the James River, then Norfolk would fall. The capture of Norfolk alone, however, would have no influence whatsoever on Yorktown's defenses.[4]

McClellan reached Fortress Monroe on 2 April, followed within three days by transports carrying most of the Army of the Potomac. He was expecting General McDowell's corps—which included Major General Ambrose Burnside's division, the only division in either army trained and equipped for amphibious operations—to arrive shortly. When word reached Lincoln that Jackson had driven up the Shenandoah Valley, however, he ordered McDowell to a central position at Fredericksburg so that he might either support McClellan or block a Confederate drive on Washington. McClellan was crushed but refused to concede defeat. He had by now reached a compromise with Goldsborough, agreeing to a simultaneous attack on the Yorktown line by the Army and a Union squadron consisting of the newly arrived armored gunboat *Galena* and a flotilla of lesser gunboats. Both McClellan and Goldsborough were again victimized by poor intelligence, however, leading them to overestimate not only the strength of the Confederate lines but also the firepower of the forts along the York River. After one week of timid reconnaissance, Goldsborough told McClellan that none of his vessels was strong enough to pass beyond those positions. This left McClellan no choice but to lay siege to Yorktown.

Goldsborough's exaggerated assessment of the Confederate Army compelled McClellan to postpone his offensive for a month, a delay that seemed to favor Johnston, whose force was growing daily. His army had already reached Richmond, and, under the direction of General Robert E. Lee, southern troops were erecting formidable new defensive works to the east of the city. While the Confederates prepared to defend Richmond, Goldsborough and a detached Union Army moved on Norfolk, overrunning the Confederate batteries on Mulberry and Jamestown Islands before laying siege to the city. Goldsborough was reluctant to send his vessels against the shore batteries until Union troops landed and the enemy was engaged on his landward flank, but these tactics so prolonged the entire operation that the Confederates had time to remove their heaviest guns from Norfolk and transport them to Richmond. And, before Norfolk fell on 11 May, Tattnall burned the *Virginia* after removing her battery and loading it onto the Confederate tugs *Beaufort* and *Raleigh*. They carried the guns up to Fort Darling on Drewry's Bluff, a 100-foot-high earthwork on the right bank of the James River eight miles below Richmond. While many considered this to be an impregnable position, Mallory was warned by Confederate Brigadier General R. E. Colston that "earthen forts are insufficient defenses against fleets." To strengthen Drewry's Bluff, Mallory ordered that a barricade be thrown across the river. Obstructions and torpedo mines devised by Captain Matthew F. Maury were planted in the riverbed, and several old hulks filled with stone were sunk directly beneath Fort Darling's guns. Finally, Mallory directed the gunboats *Patrick Henry* and *Jamestown* to plug the narrow remaining gap in the barricade.[5]

Goldsborough, overly cautious, was still concerned about the *Virginia*, even after the Confederates suddenly evacuated the Yorktown line on 4 May and the batteries at Mulberry and Jamestown Islands defending Norfolk simultaneously fell into Union hands. McClellan was impatient with Goldsborough, and that same day he privately urged Captain John Rodgers of the *Galena* to take some Union gunboats up the James past Drewry's Bluff to the outskirts of Richmond. Rodgers was eager to advance, but Goldsborough opposed this operation for over a week. The impasse was broken when Lincoln, on a visit to Fortress Monroe, learned from Rodgers that "there was a great opening for a naval movement up the James River," and the next night Rodgers wrote to his wife that Goldsborough had sent for him earlier in the day and said "that he had received orders from the president to send me up the river." Goldsborough instructed Rodgers not only to suppress fire from the Confederate batteries along the banks of the river, but also to send Marine landing parties ashore to completely destroy each rebel fort before steaming up to the next one. Slowly progressing up the James, Rodgers' flotilla did not reach City Point until 13 May, and by this time he fully realized that most of the Confederate defenses were incomplete. Indeed, between City Point and the outskirts of Richmond, Drewry's Bluff was the only well-defended enemy strongpoint.[6]

At 0735 on the morning of 15 May, Rodgers sighted Fort Darling and the obstructions in the river that would mark the limit of his advance. He stationed his wooden vessels about 1,300 yards from the fort but anchored the *Galena* within 600 yards of the enemy guns, and ten minutes later the Union ships opened fire. From the start of the battle, the barricade prevented Rodgers' vessels from being able to maneuver, and as a result the Confederate gunners improved their aim as the day wore on. The *Galena* was battered by thirteen shot and shell, but Rodgers refused to retire, although his solid shot was ineffective against the earthworks and his supply of explosive shells was low. The "experiment with the *Galena*," he later reported, "demonstrated that she is not shotproof." Lieutenant William Jeffers in the *Monitor* steamed up to support the flagship, but he could not elevate her 11-inch guns sufficiently to bring them to bear on the fort and had no choice but to withdraw. "Tell Captain Jeffers that is not the way to Richmond!" shouted a Confederate officer. At 1100, Captain J. R. Tucker in the Confederate gunboat *Patrick Henry* finally found the range, and a well-aimed shot passed through the *Galena*'s bow gun port and set her on fire. Quick action by the brave crew saved the ship, but the successful Confederate defenses had left all Rodgers' vessels either crippled or in ineffective positions, so he turned back, leaving the Confederates in possession of the James above Drewry's Bluff. It was "impossible to reduce such works [at Fort Darling], except with the aid of a land force," Jeffers now concluded. There were six subsequent Union attempts to force Drewry's Bluff, but each one was repulsed. "Without the Army," Goldsborough told Welles, "the Navy can make no headway towards Richmond."[7]

McClellan rejected an advance up the James. He was already considering an overland movement across the peninsula to Harrison's Landing, a site on a flat plain that he and Rodgers carefully selected to ensure that the Union gunboats could defend all its flanking approaches. At the same time, he exploited Union command of the York River to deploy one detached, specially trained division upstream in transports escorted by gunboats to seize West Point. This deft stroke compelled Johnston to evacuate the center of the peninsula and withdraw behind the earthworks east of Richmond. Without coming to grips with the main body of the Confederate Army, McClellan had overcome divided counsels, Goldsborough's reluctant support, and Lincoln's interference, and had forced the enemy to absorb enormous casualties at a slight cost to his own troops. Expecting at any time to link up with McDowell's corps from Fredericksburg, McClellan next crossed the Chickahominy to Seven Pines and established powerful forces on both the northern and southern banks of the river. Gripped by fear at McClellan's presence within sight of Richmond, Jefferson Davis overruled Johnston's objections to a counteroffensive and ordered him to mount a frontal assault on the Union Army on 31 May. Not only did the rebels fail to dislodge McClellan at Seven Pines, but also the Union troops again suffered far fewer casualties than they inflicted. One of the Confederate wounded was Johnston, who was replaced by General Lee. Alarmed, Mallory recorded that "we are looking for a battle before the city in a few days."[8]

Even before the Battle of Seven Pines, McClellan learned that Lincoln, personally directing the armies in the field since February, had instructed McDowell to join Banks and Major General John C. Frémont to check another thrust by Stonewall Jackson up the Shenandoah Valley toward Harper's Ferry northwest of Washington. Although Lincoln concentrated an overwhelmingly superior force against Jackson, he did not name a local tactical commander to coordinate the operation, and while the Union generals were quarreling with one another, Jackson's troops escaped from the trap. This fiasco moved Lincoln to surrender command of the armies around Washington to Major General John B. Pope and to name Major General Henry Halleck as his chief military adviser. By now Lee had energized the Army of Northern Virginia, and he went on the tactical offensive against McClellan during the Seven Days' Battles. These Confederate assaults only hurried McClellan's arrival in late June at Malvern Hill on the James River, a position that he had intended to occupy days before Lee took command. While Mallory was pleased that the Seven Days' Battles "have resulted in the triumphant success of our arms," he was greatly concerned that Lee's casualties were so "heavy" that he might not be able to keep fighting.[9]

Even Lincoln was so impressed by McClellan's skillful moves that he confessed after the Seven Days' Battles that McClellan had "effected everything in such exact accordance with his plan, contingently announced to us before the battle began." After repulsing a savage attack by Lee on Malvern Hill on 1 July, McClellan retired to his formidable camp at Harrison's Landing to await the arrival of the reinforcements that he believed Lincoln to have earlier promised. Lee took up a defensive position on the perimeter of Harrison's Landing, but he was shaken by the events of the past week. "The great obstacle to operations here is the presence of the enemy's gunboats," he told Davis, which not only "protect our approaches to him," but also "prevent us from reaping any of the fruits of victory and expose our men to great destruction" in another offensive. Worried about the inherent weakness of his position once McClellan was reinforced, Lee was considering a withdrawal to Richmond so that his battered army might be reequipped and refreshed.[10]

During June 1862, Gideon Welles became disenchanted with Rear Admiral Goldsborough, but instead of relieving him, the secretary established a new and independent force, the Union Navy's James River Flotilla under Rear Admiral Charles Wilkes. Wilkes was rightly thought to be more aggressive, but he had only fifteen gunboats under his command, in addition to the ironclad *Galena* and the *Monitor*, and many of them badly needed repairs and reequipping. Reminding Wilkes of his reasons for establishing the new command, Welles specifically instructed him to cooperate closely with McClellan. Wilkes' restless energy soon resounded throughout the flotilla, but he quickly discovered that he had far too few shallow-draft gunboats to support McClellan's proposed advance up the James. Moreover, Confederate guerrillas on the riverbanks were constantly harassing Union transports. To suppress their ambushes Wilkes ordered a number of armored scout canoes from the Navy Department so that his own sharpshooters might be better protected and therefore more mobile. On the other hand, detaching units to escort transports and to suppress Confederate bushwhackers reduced the overall strength of the force Wilkes had to support McClellan's upriver movement. This led to Welles' decision to reinforce Wilkes by ordering Captain David D. Porter to steam from New Orleans to the Chesapeake with the mortar gunboat flotilla of the Mississippi River Squadron. Porter's vessels could not reach Hampton Roads until August; nonetheless, considering the "favorable" strategic position that McClellan had created at Harrison's Landing, Secretary of War Stanton concluded that it "looks more like taking Richmond than any time before."[11]

Then, in a bizarre turn of events, Lincoln decided that invading eastern Tennessee was more important than seizing Richmond. He had promised McClellan 50,000 troops to reinforce the Army of the Potomac at Harrison's Landing, but his new strategic emphasis on the western theater made this impossible. He was impatient for a victory and angry with McClellan for his apparent reluctance to confront Lee. On 26 July 1862, General Halleck in effect ordered McClellan to assemble his transports, embark his army, retire from the James River, and return to Washington. Although Welles was soon complaining that Halleck "plans nothing, suggests nothing, and is good for nothing," for the moment Halleck had Lincoln's ear. When he learned about Halleck's devastating decision, Admiral Wilkes was astounded, and he appealed to Welles to urge Lincoln to rescind Halleck's order. Once reinforced by Porter's mortar gunboats, the James River Flotilla might force Drewry's Bluff and reach a position to the north from where the *Monitor* could shell Richmond. Welles questioned this claim not only because of the failure of Rodgers' earlier attack, but also because he had learned that the Confederate ironclad *Richmond* had reinforced Drewry's Bluff. He was also aware that personal relations between Lincoln and McClellan were poor, and that Lincoln was firmly against further operations on the York Peninsula. Consequently, he refused to challenge Halleck's decision and instructed Wilkes to cover McClellan's withdrawal.[12]

The Army of the Potomac boarded Union transports at Yorktown for the trip back to Washington. McClellan had believed that he could use the mobility that the Union fleet gave his army to compel the enemy to waste himself in attacks on Union trenches. Not only did he establish the only amphibious division in the war, he also used the fleet to move regular troops about, reconnoiter enemy positions, and provide his army with mobile artillery. Lincoln wanted a thoroughly aggressive general who would take the offensive and defeat the enemy without too much concern for subtlety, and he belatedly realized that McClellan would never do this. Other than the destruction of the *Virginia*, the Union's only long-term benefit from the entire campaign was the occupation of Norfolk, but this was important inasmuch as it decisively staunched the Confederate's ironclad program. The last Union naval vessel departed Fortress Monroe on 28 August 1862. With Lincoln's decision to end McClellan's great Peninsula Campaign, the North was bereft of any grand strategy to force the South to rejoin the Union.

Before all of McClellan's army arrived in Washington, Jefferson Davis agreed to General Lee's plan to invade Maryland, crush Pope, menace Washington, and put an end to the war. Lee defeated Pope at the Second Battle of Bull Run on 29 August, crossed the Potomac at Leesburg, and, one week later, concentrated his army at Frederick, Maryland. By now, however, McClellan's troops had landed in Washington and he took the field to hunt down Lee's invaders. At Antietam Creek, during the bloodiest single day of the Civil War, McClellan abandoned his usual tactics and attacked Lee's lines, but he failed to inflict a decisive defeat on the Confederates. After losing at Antietam, Lee retired across the Potomac back into Virginia. McClellan pursued, but so slowly that Lincoln replaced him with General Ambrose Burnside, who moved south across the Rappahannock River on 13 December and fell into the maw of Lee's army at Fredericksburg. Only a few weeks after Admiral Du Pont failed to take Charleston, Burnside's successor, General "Fighting Joe" Hooker, suffered another disastrous setback in May 1863 at Chancellorsville. The Confederate victories at Chancellorsville and Charleston induced Lee to invade Pennsylvania, acquire much needed food and supplies, and strike a telling blow at the Union. The Army of the Potomac repulsed this daring stroke at Gettysburg on 4 July 1863. Gettysburg was a defensive Union victory, however, and afterward neither Lincoln nor his generals had any strategic plan to defeat the South.

Chapter Eighteen

The War for the Mississippi River
1861–1863

Lincoln, an experienced Illinois politician, knew that support for the war in the Midwest was weaker than elsewhere in the North. Scott pointed out in the Anaconda plan that the Confederacy was especially vulnerable along its western flank, where the Union's superior railroad system could shift troops around the theater faster and supply its armies with more munitions than the enemy's primitive transportation system. Exploiting this advantage hinged on winning control of the Tennessee and Mississippi rivers, a costly and dangerous venture that diverted manpower and material away from the vital Washington-Richmond axis. Lincoln probably questioned whether the Midwest campaign would be militarily conclusive, but its political importance to the infant Republican Party was beyond dispute.

Navy Secretary Welles showed little interest in this aspect of Scott's Anaconda strategy in early 1861. Lincoln had assigned the western theater to the Army; the Navy was at the time burdened by the problems of establishing the great blockade squadrons in the Atlantic and the Gulf of Mexico. Therefore, when boat designer James B. Eads of St. Louis, Missouri, submitted plans to Washington to build a squadron of river gunboats and made suggestions about their use, Captain John Lenthall, the chief of the Navy's Bureau of Construction and Repair, responded with little enthusiasm. For one thing, the shallow water of the Midwestern rivers seemed to rule out the use of a screw propeller, but the only effective alternative, side-mounted paddlewheels, could be disabled by a single shot. Lenthall turned the project over to Naval Constructor Samuel Pook, who came up with the ingenious idea of protecting the paddlewheel by locating it between high twin armored sterns. Pook also suggested cramming all the machinery below the deck and protecting the vessel by bolting 2.5-inch-thick iron plates to the hull above the waterline. Welles then turned the project over to the War Department, where it was referred to General McClellan, who had established a river force for the Army's Department of the Ohio in the summer with the assistance of his Navy liaison officer, Commander John Rodgers. As the first vessels for the Army's Western Flotilla, McClellan had already ordered the conversion of the three wooden sidewheelers *Tyler, Lexington,* and *Conestoga.* Armored with thick oak bulwarks, they were thereafter generally known as timberclads.

McClellan was succeeded by Major General John C. Frémont in the West, who signed a contract with Eads in August 1861 to build seven 175-foot-long ironclads for the Western Flotilla. Welles was indifferent to the Western theater, however, and Commander Rodgers' responsibility for the flotilla was at first largely administrative. A veteran of the fleet, he was humiliated by being outranked by every newly commissioned colonel in the area, and could do nothing to prevent his gunboats from being repeatedly commandeered by these nominally superior officers for a variety of minor operations. Rodgers so antagonized Frémont by his complaints over this issue that the general asked Lincoln to appoint a new flotilla commander. Rodgers' replacement was another experienced naval commander, Captain Andrew H. Foote. His arrival in the West coincided with the launching of the first Union ironclad at Carondelet, Missouri, on 12 October 1861, and with the delivery of a pair of converted river snag boats. Sensitive to the Army's problems, Foote attacked the root of Rodgers' old dilemma by securing from Frémont an order stating that Foote was to be "in charge of and commanding this [naval] expedition." Armed with this writ, he convinced Welles to promote him to the temporary rank of flag officer. Although these measures strengthened Foote's position with respect to the Army, he could not surmount delays in outfitting his commissioned vessels or in acquiring weapons and equipment for the squadron of twenty-eight mortar boats that Frémont had also purchased.[1]

A southern thrust into Kentucky first brought the Western Flotilla into action. To anchor the outer defensive perimeter of the Confederate stronghold of Vicksburg, Mississippi, Jefferson Davis sent troops to occupy Columbus, Kentucky, in September 1861. The political cost of this move was high. Opinion in Kentucky about the war was sharply divided, and the state had declared herself neutral, a deadlock that had left her in the Union by default. This stalemate was broken when the Confederates occupied Columbus, and Kentucky's resentful legislature voted against secession. To challenge the southern position at Columbus, Frémont assembled a small force under Brigadier General Ulysses S. Grant, who was to garrison Paducah, thereby blocking any northward movement by the Confederate forces. Assigned to Grant's command, Flag Officer Foote had established a naval base at Cairo, Illinois, and over the winter of 1861 he and Grant prepared a plan to attack the nearby rebel stronghold at Fort Henry. This was too risky for the new theater commander, General Henry Halleck, but Foote circumvented his opposition by asking Gideon Welles to take up the matter with the War Department. The Navy secretary approved of this plan and persuaded Secretary of War Stanton to direct Halleck to support Grant's operation.

The Union plan was to employ the Western Flotilla to conduct a diversionary attack on low lying Fort Henry, while Grant's army struck the main blow in a landward assault. Despite a heroic effort, Foote, faced with a shortage of trained crews, could assign only four ironclads and three gunboats to this operation. Against Fort Henry, Foote adopted frontal assault tactics, overruling the opposition of his boat captains. On 6 February 1862, he sent his gunboats to a position within 300 yards of Fort Henry, where they were to commence a rapid fire. Since the timberclads were kept far to the rear, their long-range bombardment was less effective but still distracting. "The scene in and around the fort exhibited a spectacle of fierce grandeur, . . . the deafening roar of the artillery, the black sides of five or six gun-boats, belching fire at every port-hole," observed one participant. This pounding continued for two hours while Grant's troops prepared to storm the fort from the landward approach, but the Navy's gunfire was so intense that the defenders quit before Grant had a chance to attack. By this time, however, most of the Confederate troops had already retired to Fort Donelson, a stronger position twelve miles to the southeast on the high ground of the west bank of the Cumberland River.[2]

Grant, exploiting Fort Henry's fall, relentlessly advanced on Major General John B. Floyd's Confederate troops in Fort Donelson. To prevent reinforcements from reaching Fort Donelson, Foote's gunboats struck from Fort Henry south along the Tennessee River to Muscle Shoals, Alabama, destroying an important bridge along the railroad from Columbus to Bowling Green. Grant hoped to attack Fort Donelson rapidly, but Foote wanted to wait until his crews were rested, his vessels repaired, and a mortar boat flotilla brought up. This time, General Halleck overruled Foote, instructing him to bring his gunboats up the Cumberland River to support Grant's army. The operation began on the morning of 13 February 1862, when the *Carondelet* closed on Fort Donelson and opened fire. Once again the rebels' attention was diverted from Grant's movement, and Grant was able to close off the Charlotte Road, the Confederate's last line of retreat. Foote drove the Western Flotilla to within 400 yards of the Confederate batteries at Fort Donelson the next day, but the rebel gunners high on the bluffs now had the advantage and delivered a murderous fire down on the weak topsides of the Union gunboats. First, the *Carondelet* was damaged, then the *Louisville*. The flagship *St. Louis* was hit fifty-nine times, lost steering, and had to retire. Seriously injured, Foote decided to withdraw the gunboats. Captain John Rodgers, still in the theater, issued a stinging criticism of Foote's tactics. "Ironclads were to fight wooden ships and stone forts at distances which leave the ironclads impregnable to the artillery opposing them," he declared. Nonetheless, when the Confederates tried to escape from Fort Donelson they were bloodied by the Union Army and on 16 February accepted Grant's demand for an "unconditional surrender."[3]

The collapse of Fort Donelson opened up the Cumberland River to a movement southward by the Western Flotilla. Foote now headed downriver, destroying the Tennessee Iron Works above Dover and occupying Fort Clarksville on 19 February. He then divided his force, taking most of the Western Flotilla on an armed reconnaissance along the Mississippi as far south as Columbus, which was evacuated by the rebels before Foote occupied it on 4 March. Although he had earned the respect of Welles and Fox, Foote's relations with the Army soured after the capture of Fort

Donelson, and he was drained of energy by his wounds. To replace Foote, Welles named Captain Henry C. Davis, assuring Lincoln that the new commander's "affable manner would enable him to get on well with the Army" while his "scientific caution would discourage unnecessary risks of the flotilla." Davis' primary concern was defending his vessels, not only to prevent a repetition of the losses incurred at Fort Donelson, but also to block the Confederates from advancing on the Union rear.[4]

Before being relieved, Foote had instructed Captain Henry Gwinn to take the 450-ton timberclads *Tyler* and *Lexington* south down the Tennessee River to Eastport, Mississippi. From there, Gwinn steamed farther south until he came upon a body of Confederate troops who were fortifying Pittsburg Landing, Tennessee, a position just to the northeast of the important enemy railroad junction at Corinth. With covering fire from the Union gunboats, Gwinn led a landing party ashore and stormed the Confederate battery, but he was repulsed. Grant was by now advancing overland toward Corinth, and within a few days his army arrived at Pittsburg Landing. Halleck instructed Grant not to lay siege to Corinth until he was joined by a converging Union army under Major General Don Carlos Buell. Buell had seized Nashville on 25 February, and his troops were soon marching southwest to reinforce Grant at Pittsburg Landing.

The loss of Fort Henry, Fort Donelson, Columbus, and Nashville undermined the Confederates' cordon defense of Tennessee. Jefferson Davis reacted by concentrating a large army southeast of Corinth under General Albert S. Johnston. On the morning of 6 April, Johnston attacked Grant's left flank near Shiloh Church and nearly took Pittsburg Landing before darkness fell. That evening, Captain Gwinn moved the *Lexington* and *Tyler* down the Tennessee River to cover Grant's flank and provide counterbattery fire against the advancing Confederate artillery. While Grant rallied his troops and relied on the Union guns to repulse a succession of Confederate charges, Johnston exhausted the southern reserves in a series of desperate frontal assaults against the Union lines. Johnston was killed during one of these charges. That same night the advance elements of Buell's army reached the east bank of the Tennessee, where they were loaded onto Union boats and taken across the river to reinforce Grant's men at Pittsburg Landing. At dawn on 7 April, Grant counterattacked, inflicted dreadful casualties on the Confederate army, and forced it to retreat to Corinth.

Gunboats and mortar boats bombarding Island No. 10 on the Mississippi River during the Civil War.

Admiral David Dixon Porter was commander of the Mortar Flotilla of the East Gulf Squadron, 1862; of the Mississippi Squadron, 1863–64; and of the North Atlantic Blockading Squadron, 1864–65.

Grant's victory at Shiloh gave the Union possession of western Tennessee, and Halleck appeared on the scene soon after to coordinate the entire offensive. Moving slowly, he occupied Corinth on 29 May, then divided his forces, sending Buell eastward into eastern Tennessee while instructing Grant to hold the Union position in the Mississippi Valley. By this time the Union Navy's assault on Memphis had already begun. The last Confederate stronghold on the Mississippi to the north of Memphis was Fort Pillow, a position commanding the eastern bank of the river approach to the city. In April, the Western Flotilla mortar boats were positioned in front of the fort, and they began to lob explosives over the bluffs and into Confederate works. In spite of Captain Davis' reputed concern for the security of his forces, he was unprepared when the Confederate River Defense Fleet's ram boats attacked the Western Flotilla in a lightning attack at Plum Point Bend on 10 May 1862. During this battle, the Union ironclads *Mound City* and *Cincinnati* were sunk, and the rebels damaged several other vessels and inflicted heavy casualties before they withdrew. Although both ironclads were later raised and brought back into service, the reversal at Plum Point led Assistant Secretary Gustavas Fox to complain that another Union defeat of this magnitude would cause "Halleck . . . to fall back and we should lose St. Louis, Cairo, and everything."[5]

This interpretation of the setback at Plum Point, echoed by a number of highly critical newspaper accounts of the battle, angered Davis. And he was furious about the appearance on the river of Brigadier General Charles Ellet's nine-boat Ram Fleet, a new, independent, Army riverine command recently created by Secretary of War Stanton. Ellet wanted to attack the Confederate River Defense Fleet south of Fort Pillow, but his rams were unarmed, and he abandoned his plan when Davis refused to support the operation. Annoyed by this timidity, Ellet then dispatched a ram south to scout the enemy position, and it returned with the news that Fort Pillow had been evacuated. This intelligence finally moved Davis to begin the Union fleet's southward movement. Meanwhile, Captain J. E. Montgomery was preparing for action with his eight converted steamboat rams of the Confederate River Defense Fleet. At 0500 on the morning of 10 June 1862, he left Memphis and steamed downriver in a double line to Hopefield Bend, the Union anchorage. His appearance there completely surprised Davis. The Union vessels were tied up to the riverbank, their steam engines shut down. The Confederate *General Bragg* and two other rams struck the unarmored stern of the guard boat *Cincinnati* and damaged her, but Ellet's Ram Fleet was by now ready for action and their maneuvers shattered the rebel attack. At the end of the Battle of Hopefield Bend, four Confederate rams were sunk and three more were captured. By this point, however, General Halleck's seizure of Corinth had already exposed Memphis to a landward attack, and the Confederates evacuated the city before it surrendered to Captain Davis. With seven of eight vessels of the River Defense Fleet lost, and Memphis in Union hands, the Union forces had laid open the Mississippi River to a movement south to the Confederate stronghold at Vicksburg.[6]

After both Memphis and New Orleans fell to the Union Navy, Lincoln had to choose between Admiral David G. Farragut's proposal to attack Mobile Bay and General Grant's plan to advance on Vicksburg. Strongly influenced by Jefferson Davis' publicly proclaimed determination to hold on to Vicksburg, Lincoln postponed the Mobile Bay operation and instructed Navy Secretary Welles to order Farragut to support Grant's campaign. After tak-

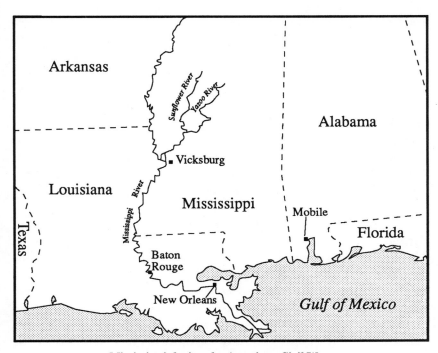

Mississippi during the American Civil War

ing New Orleans, Farragut had steamed up the Mississippi, accepting the surrender of Natchez on 12 May. Ten days later, he reached a position just south of Vicksburg. The Confederate batteries there easily repulsed a brief attack by the Union forces, and Farragut concluded that the forts were positioned so high on the bluff that they were immune to his gunfire.

Meanwhile, Davis had led the Western Flotilla from Memphis down the Mississippi past the Vicksburg forts to a rendezvous south of the city with advance elements of the Gulf Squadron. Discouraged by the strong defenses of Vicksburg, Farragut then retired back to New Orleans only to receive explicit orders from Welles to embark Brigadier General Thomas Williams' division and steam back upriver to assault Vicksburg. Welles took this move despite Halleck's reluctance to send troops westward from Corinth to support the naval operation. On 28 June, Farragut led the Gulf Squadron through a three-mile-long gauntlet of fire under the Vicksburg batteries, and rendezvoused with Davis' Western Flotilla off the mouth of the Yazoo River three days later. And, on 1 July, four Western Flotilla mortar boats joined a dozen Gulf Squadron mortar boats under Commander David Dixon Porter, and this force began to lob explosives against the Confederate forts. The vulnerable Union transports were by now stranded on the Mississippi south of the city, unable to pass safely under the Vicksburg batteries. To move them north for a joint attack on the rebel forts, Union Army engineers dug a canal across a wedge of land separating the two federal forces, beyond the reach of the enemy's cannon. Before much work could be done, however, Welles decided to withdraw Porter's mortar force from the Mississippi and transfer it to Virginia to support General McClellan's Peninsula Campaign, a move that considerably weakened the Gulf Squadron. "No doubt but what Vicksburg will soon fall," Farragut told Welles on 6 July, "but it must be by [Union] troops coming down on the rear."[7]

Davis had devised a plan to steam north up the Yazoo on an armed reconnaissance, and for this operation he had assembled a formation consisting of the ironclad *Carondelet*, the gunboat *Tyler*, and the ram *Queen of the West*. On 15 July, this force was surprised by the Confederate ironclad *Arkansas*, which was steaming south to support the defenders of Vicksburg. During the ensuing action the *Arkansas* ran the *Carondelet* aground and then chased the other two vessels through the middle of the Union fleet. At the end of the day, the Union Navy was humiliated and the *Arkansas* was anchored safely under the guns of the Vicksburg forts. A gallant tactical victory, the *Arkansas*' sortie proved to be a strategic mistake, for it relieved the Western Flotilla of any waterborne threat to its flank from the Yazoo River. Farragut's position was nevertheless now in peril because of the falling level of the Mississippi River, and so he withdrew once again back to New Orleans, while Davis steamed upriver to a new Union base at Helena, Arkansas.

When Farragut retired to New Orleans, the Confederates mounted a counteroffensive. Supported by the *Arkansas*, Confederate troops attacked the Union garrison at Baton Rouge, Louisiana, but this operation was broken up by the ironclad steamer *Essex* and two Union gunboats, which helped to repulse the rebel advance on the outskirts of the city. Crippled by engine problems during the first phase of this operation, the *Arkansas* gamely joined the battle on the second day, but she was unable to maneuver and was blown to pieces by a magazine explosion caused by shells from the *Essex*. The Confederates then reinforced Port Hudson, a few miles north of Baton Rouge and 150 miles south of Vicksburg. Meanwhile, to the east, a successful Confederate thrust toward Louisville had undermined Grant's operations west of Corinth, thus easing for the moment the converging pressure on Vicksburg.

Unhappy with the stalemate before Vicksburg, Gideon Welles had decided to force Secretary of War Stanton to agree to resolve the divided commands on the Mississippi. He did this by persuading Congress in September 1862 to pass an act placing the Western Flotilla under the Navy's jurisdiction. Stanton, however, refused to transfer Ellet's Ram Fleet to this new naval command. Welles was disenchanted with Captain Davis' well-known timidity and, after the Union defeat at Plum Point Bend and the failure of the first attack on Vicksburg, he recalled Davis to Washington and installed him as the chief of the new Bureau of Navigation. As Davis' relief, Assistant Secretary Fox sponsored Commander David D. Porter and rounded up the support of Seward and other cabinet members. Porter was a most unlikely candidate—he was distrusted by Welles, disliked by many of his fellow officers, and dismissed by Stanton as a "gas bag who makes a great fuss and claims credit that belongs to others." Welles needed a blooded, aggressive leader in the west who would be cowed by neither the Confederates nor the Union Army, however, so he picked Porter

to command the Mississippi Flotilla and promoted him to the newly established rank of rear admiral.[8]

Shortly thereafter, Lincoln named Grant to command the entire Army of Tennessee, and the general established his new supply base at Holly Springs in December 1862. Grant divided his
troops into two armies. The first, under Major General William T.
Sherman, was loaded on board transports at Memphis. Supported by Admiral Porter's gunboats, Sherman was to mount an assault on Vicksburg from banks of the Yazoo River north of the city.
At the same time, Grant intended to strike south along the Mississippi Central Railroad from Holly Springs to Grenada and draw
the Confederate Army away from Vicksburg. This strategy failed,
largely because Grant completely depended on the single railroad
line from Grand Junction to Grenada. Southern cavalry tore up
the track, raided Holly Springs, and left Grant's army to live off
the land. For this and other reasons, before the end of December
1862 Grant was forced to break contact and retreat north to Grand
Junction.

Porter was already making ready to move onto the Yazoo, and
Sherman readied for the assault against the rebel forts on Chickasaw Bluffs, which guarded Vicksburg's northern flank. In planning this operation, Porter assured Sherman that he could land
the troops behind the powerful Confederate batteries. However,
when he sent an armed reconnaissance up the Yazoo on 12 December, the new ironclad *Cairo* struck a mine and sank, and the
rest of the vessels could make little headway against the
formidable booms and obstacles in the river and the well-posi-
tioned rebel guns. Sherman was nonetheless determined to advance, although Porter warned him that the gunboats could neither close on the forts nor elevate their guns enough to hit
anything on the high ridge. On 29 December, Sherman's troops
waded through the swamps below the forts, but the rebel artillery
on the heights was too strong and by nightfall the Union assault
had been thoroughly repulsed. A few days later, Sherman and
Porter decided to pull back to the mouth of the Yazoo River.

The Union was now without any overall strategic plan to take
Vicksburg, and none was ever really developed during the next six
months of the campaign. Instead, Grant and Porter constantly improvised, reacting to enemy movements and exploiting Union
manpower, material, and naval superiority to overwhelm their opponents with brute force. In January 1863, Grant reorganized his

army, establishing a base north of Vicksburg at Milliken's Bend. All his operations against Vicksburg that winter failed, however, and he had to wait until the spring when the rains ended and the river began to fall. In the meantime, Welles instructed Admiral Farragut in New Orleans to support a northward movement by General Banks, whose army was to overrun Port Hudson, advance upriver, and assume a position below Vicksburg to divert Confederate attention from Grant's spring offensive.

To cut off Port Hudson, and Vicksburg, from supplies coming from the Red River, on 3 February Admiral Porter sent the ram *Queen of the West* and the gunboat *Indianola* south past the Vicksburg batteries with orders to establish a blockade force at the mouth of the Red River. Although the *Queen of the West* destroyed several Confederate vessels, she ran aground on the riverbank directly beneath a strong enemy fort and quickly fell into southern hands. She was repaired and assigned to a small rebel squadron that ran down, overwhelmed, and destroyed the *Indianola* on 24 February. Meanwhile, the plan to overrun Port Hudson was abandoned within a few weeks largely because of poor communications between Grant and Banks and because Banks refused to cooperate with Farragut when the admiral began to move against Port Hudson. Farragut in the *Hartford* led elements of the Gulf Squadron beneath the Confederate batteries at Port Hudson on 14 March, but the withering enemy gunfire destroyed the *Mississippi*, badly damaged several other ships, and turned back every Union vessel except the flagship and a single escorting gunboat. However, the presence of this small but powerful Union naval force on the Mississippi north of the city cut off Port Hudson from reinforcements and supplies from the Red River, and isolated Vicksburg as well.

In early April 1863, Grant marched south along the western bank of the Mississippi River to a new base at Hard Times, followed by Porter's gunboats and transports. Most of these vessels successfully made the passage under the Confederate batteries. As a diversion to this movement, Grant had dispatched raiding cavalry into the Mississippi countryside. Next, he ordered General Sherman to cross the Mississippi River north of Vicksburg and enter the Yazoo, a grand feint designed to cover the principal Union movement across the Mississippi south of the city. On 30 April, Grant's army embarked in the transports and, covered by Porter's gunboats, steamed south to a new base at Bruinsburg on the east bank of the Mississippi. Relying on his men to savage the land for food and fodder, Grant cut free from his base at Bruinsburg and marched overland to dislodge General Joseph Johnston from the city of Jackson. Then Grant turned to the west, defeated the Vicksburg garrison under General John C. Pemberton at Champion's Hill, and advanced on the city. Pemberton's attempt to retreat to the city was cut off when Sherman overwhelmed the weakened Confederate batteries at Chickasaw Bluffs and thus closed the circle. Under siege by converging armies supported by the Union transports on the Mississippi, Pemberton surrendered Vicksburg on 4 July 1863. Grant's victory at Champion's Hill encouraged Banks to move on Port Hudson, and on 27 May he laid siege to the city, whose defenders were so demoralized by the loss of Vicksburg that they surrendered on 8 July. Admiral Farragut announced that the fall of the city would lead to "establishing once more the commerce of the States bordering on this river."[9]

The political consequences of the Vicksburg campaign overshadowed its military importance. Contrary to some claims, Vicksburg was not a major link between the eastern and western Confederate states, mostly because the transportation systems east and west of the city were quite primitive. Shipments of European arms continued to slip through the Union blockade of the Confederacy's Atlantic and Gulf ports, and arms and supplies from Mexico reached the South's armies long after Farragut took New Orleans in 1862. Nor did Grant's seizure of Vicksburg stop Davis from shifting troops across the Mississippi River, although he had long since bowed to southern regionalism by refusing to transfer men routinely from one military department to another. After the fall of Vicksburg, the Mississippi Flotilla was assigned to patrol the river and its tributaries, but as late as August 1863 there were only five vessels on station from the mouth of the Red River to Natchez, seven between Natchez and Vicksburg, and eleven from Vicksburg to the mouth of the White River. With forty-five vessels to patrol the rivers from Donaldsonville, Louisiana, to Cairo, Illinois, Porter held fewer than fifty stations along the entire length of the Mississippi. He reported that the waterway was vulnerable not only to guerrilla raids but also to the movement of Confederate troops and supplies. Indeed, southern leaders seldom complained about problems moving cattle, arms, food, or men across the river. And, while Pemberton's army had surrendered at Vicksburg, the fall of the city released other divisions in the region that were badly needed in the east, where the contest would be decided.[10]

Following the seizure of Vicksburg, Union leaders could not decide what to do next. Generals Grant and Banks met and agreed to support Admiral Farragut's persistent call for a joint assault on Mobile, but Lincoln's military adviser, General Halleck, rejected this plan and instead instructed Banks to lead an expedition up the Red River to dislodge the Confederates from Shreveport, Louisiana. Establishing Union—and Republican—control over the politics of Texas, Arkansas, and Louisiana appealed to Lincoln. Seward hoped that establishing a Union army in Texas might put pressure on the French Army, which had occupied Mexico since 1861. In addition, the arrival in the Mississippi Flotilla of a large number of shallow-draft light gunboats, ordered in 1862 by Captain Davis, made possible operations along the tributaries of the Mississippi. Once Halleck persuaded Porter to back the Red River campaign, Banks reluctantly fell into line.

The grand progression up the Red River turned into a fiasco for which General Banks was unfairly blamed. In April 1864, Rear Admiral Porter, now a vigorous champion of the expedition, led his gunboats over the rapids at Alexandria in support of a parallel landward movement by a large Union army that was only partially under Banks' command. The whole advance was extremely slow because some Union troops were detached to organize local elections and because Porter spent too much time confiscating cotton shipments. Then, to the consternation of both commanders, General Sherman, now commanding in the West, recalled one Union division from Louisiana without consulting Banks, thus weakening his force considerably. When the Confederates counterattacked at Sabine Cross Roads on 8 April, Banks retreated back to Alexandria. This turn of events left Porter's gunboats stranded as the unpredictable river level began to fall at the end of spring—a danger Banks had warned Halleck and Porter about before the operation got under way. With Porter's assistance, the Union forces checked the Confederate pursuit at Pleasant Hill, but the gunboats soon lost their landward support when the Army withdrew. Porter was expecting the Red River to rise in the spring, but the previous winter had been especially dry and the water level was now dangerously low. An Army engineer suggested constructing small dams to lift the river level around the Alexandra rapids, and as a result all but one of the gunboats escaped capture or destruction on 14 May. Both Porter and Halleck blamed Banks for the disaster, and this wrongful assessment was endorsed by Grant, who persuaded Lincoln to relieve Banks of his command.

In spite of the Red River fiasco, the loss of Vicksburg and the opening of the Mississippi River had already dealt a dreadful political blow to the Confederacy. Wartime politics rather than military strategy had made Vicksburg an important symbol of Confederate independence, and Jefferson Davis committed his prestige and a large southern army to defend the city. When it fell, Confederate morale in the West was shattered and Confederate prospects for Europe's support evaporated. The South also lost control of the economic lifeline of the Ohio Valley. Leading Copperhead Democrats there had from the time of Fort Sumter opposed the Civil War, in part because they feared the permanent loss of the Mississippi trade and the use of the port of New Orleans. Although the Mississippi Flotilla's patrols could not prevent the Confederates from crossing the river after 1863 following the surrender at Vicksburg, Union commerce from the Midwest began to flow once again down to New Orleans. This stimulated the economies of Ohio, Indiana, Illinois, and Missouri and erased that region's concern about losing forever this vital economic artery. After the summer of 1863 Lincoln's Republicans were politically ascendant in state elections in the Midwest and the Old Northwest. This not only improved Lincoln's prospects for reelection in 1864 but also undermined the Democrats' chances of forcing Washington to open talks on a compromise peace with the South.

Chapter Nineteen

The Union Blockade
1861–1865

Controversy adorned every measure Lincoln took in the West, but few northerners disputed the usefulness of the Union Navy's blockade, a strategy that took shape only days after Fort Sumter. Indeed, the blockade was the one aspect of General Winfield Scott's Anaconda plan that was not widely criticized, and Navy Secretary Welles believed that it would be the Navy's key contribution to the northern war effort. Within a few weeks, he had begun to withdraw most of the three dozen ships deployed to the overseas station squadrons. He also directed Captain Samuel F. Du Pont to organize a Blockade Board, which was to draft a strategic plan for the campaign. "Closing of all insurgent ports" and "cutting [coastal] intercommunications with the rebels" were the major strategic objectives, Welles wrote. The 3,500-mile Confederate coastline included 180 harbors and navigable inlets, but there were few large ports and an overall lack of rail and modern road transport. So, for strategic purposes, Du Pont divided the enemy coast into four large zones, one for each major Confederate port, and proposed having one Union Navy command responsible for each area of operations. Welles agreed. The North Atlantic Blockade Squadron was assigned the area from the Chesapeake Bay to Wilmington, North Carolina; the South Atlantic Blockade Squadron was to patrol from Wilmington to the Florida keys; and the Eastern and Western Gulf Blockade Squadrons were responsible for the southern and western ports of the Confederacy. To defend federal shipping to and from the Pacific coast against Confederate privateers and cruisers, Welles kept four ships on duty in the West Indies with Flag Officer Garrett J. Prendergast's Home Squadron, until he had to abolish this command in August.[1]

It was soon clear that Lincoln had issued the blockade proclamation too hastily and had given too little thought to the great number of vessels the Union Navy would need to enforce it. After establishing the great blockading squadrons in 1861, Welles worked tirelessly to tighten the blockade, and most of the new monitors, ironclads, and lighter vessels that entered the Union fleet during the war were assigned to duty on the Atlantic or Gulf blockade stations. Blockade work was tiring, costly, boring, and occasionally dangerous, but prize money earned by those Union crews who seized Confederate blockade runners meant that it could also be profitable—especially for the North Atlantic Blockade Squadron, which took most of the prizes. For at least three years, however, the blockade was not strategically effective because of the complex logistics involved. By 1862, each of the four blockade squadrons required an average of 3,000 tons of coal every week just to support the Union steamers. Until New Orleans fell to Admiral Farragut, blockading vessels had to come to one of the two major Union coaling depots to refill their coal bunkers: Port Royal or Pensacola. The depots' stocks were often low, and steamers spent a great deal of time waiting for coal and transiting between the depot and their blockade stations. On the other hand, the presence of the Union Navy's blockading forces, in particular the North Atlantic Blockade Squadron off Virginia and North Carolina, made it necessary for the Confederates to tend to their coastal defenses and reduced the manpower available to their armies in the field.

Maintaining the blockade fleet was another major problem. During the first two years of the war, most of the blockading vessels were too old or unseaworthy to keep up with the rugged tempo of operations, and until 1864 recent conversions made up most of the flotilla assigned to interdict blockade runners bound for the important Confederate port of Wilmington. The seakeeping quality of most of these vessels was degraded immeasurably by the wartime installation of heavy gun batteries for which the hulls had not been designed. Engine breakdowns were so common that at any given time at least a third of the steam-driven blockading vessels were disabled. So daunting was this problem that Flag Officer

Samuel P. Lee, who relieved Goldsborough in command of the North Atlantic Blockade Squadron after the Peninsula Campaign collapsed in 1862, instructed Captain Ludlow Case of the Wilmington Blockade Force "not to keep more than one of the little vessels moving about at a time, even at night."[2]

Welles was frustrated by the ineffectiveness of the early blockade operations, and this made him prey to a number of ill-considered schemes aimed at achieving quick results. In late 1861, he approved a project to supplement the Charleston Blockade Force by sinking a number of stone-laden whalers in the main ship channels leading into the harbor. This idea failed because Charleston harbor's powerful currents quickly created new channels for the Confederate blockade runners to transit. Moreover, the deployment of the Stone Fleet was close to being an open admission to Europe that the regular Union naval blockade was ineffective and, therefore, illegal. Britain's foreign minister, Lord John Russell, claimed that sinking the Stone Fleet violated conventional blockade practices, endangered safe navigation, and represented a Union "plot against the commerce of nations." Strongly worded British protests notwithstanding, the Union Navy sank a total of 78 stone-laden vessels in various southern harbors and channels during the Civil War as part of its costly campaign to create obstacles to Confederate shipping.[3]

To reinforce the blockading squadrons, at the end of 1862 Welles reestablished the Home Squadron, named Rear Admiral Wilkes to this new command, and slowly strengthened it over the following two years. Wilkes' first move was to establish patrol stations about fifty miles off Wilmington and Charleston to intercept Confederate blockade runners heading to or from British Bermuda or the West Indies. Eventually, Wilkes also established blockade stations off Cuba, Bermuda, and the Bahamas to catch blockade runners en route to Confederate ports from those havens before they could escape to the open seas. Although the Home Squadron did not capture a large number of blockade runners, Wilkes' operations clearly contributed to the difficulties that the swift and agile southern blockade-running fleet encountered.

Du Pont's 1861 Blockade Board had not only recommended how to organize the fleet, but had also proposed that the Navy seize key positions off the Confederate coast that might be used as advance bases. "The President [has] been told up and down by [Assistant Secretary] Fox . . . that the blockading squadron cannot

Rear Admiral Samuel F. Du Pont, commander of the South Atlantic Blockading Squadron, 1861–63.

Admiral David Glasgow Farragut, Navy's first admiral, was command East Gulf Blockading Squadron, 186

keep at sea in the winter without depots for coal, etc.," Du Pont explained. The first of these positions was Hatteras Inlet off the North Carolina coast. It seemed an ideal location for a Union advance base because it was situated near the major Confederate ports of Wilmington and Beaufort. Over 100 Confederate blockade runners had passed through the channel in July and early August alone. On 26 August, in the first amphibious operation of the Civil War, Flag Officer Silas H. Stringham's North Atlantic Blockade Squadron closed on Forts Clark and Hatteras, defending the inlet, reduced them after a brief exchange, and supported the landing of 900 Union troops under Major General Benjamin F. Butler, who took the surrender of the enemy garrison. For a variety of reasons, however, Hatteras Inlet was not developed as an anchorage for the blockade squadron.[4]

Gustavas Fox had already convinced Flag Officer Du Pont, who had just been named to command the South Atlantic Blockade Squadron, that he should descend on Port Royal, a deepwater sound situated between Savannah and Charleston, two large, busy Confederate ports. Port Royal would be isolated once the Union Navy was established at the mouths of the Broad and Beaufort rivers, Fox pointed out, because it could not be reinforced from the landward flank owing to the presence of a large, impassable swamp. However, Port Royal was well defended by two strong Confederate forts, Beauregard and Walker, which protected the entrance to the sound. To conduct just this kind of operation, Welles had already ordered the construction of nearly two dozen 500-ton steam-driven gunboats, each carrying five to seven guns, and they were built and launched within ninety days. Du Pont assembled a force of eleven larger warships and a gunboat flotilla, and this formation put to sea and rendezvoused in Hampton Roads with transports carrying Brigadier General Thomas Sherman's 13,000 Union soldiers. A dreadful storm delayed their departure until 28 October. When the expedition finally stood out into the Atlantic, Du Pont's covering force ran into a hurricane off the Carolina coast that caused the loss of the sidewheeler *Governor* and three cargo ships and damage to several other vessels. When Du Pont and Sherman arrived at the bar off Port Royal on 4 November, however, they agreed to a change of plans, with the result that the naval batteries were assigned the job of reducing the forts.

At 0800 on 7 November Du Pont in the 46-gun flagship *Wabash* led two columns of fourteen vessels each up the channel between Forts Walker and Beauregard. A small Confederate defense force, composed of a converted river steamer and two gunboats, appeared on the scene, fired a few shots, and discreetly retired. Du Pont had intended to lead his columns back and forth beneath the weak north flank of Fort Walker, but the confusing battle overcame his captains, the Union formation broke up, and thereafter most of the ships operated independently. Although the Confederate batteries returned a brisk fire, the throwweight of the Union guns was at least five or six times greater. At 0100 Fort Walker was evacuated, and the rebels abandoned Fort Beauregard ninety minutes later. The Union transports then entered the sound and Sherman's troops marched ashore to take possession of both forts. Overnight, Du Pont became one of the first Union heroes of the Civil War. In a rare moment of hyperbole, Welles asserted that the seizure of Port Royal had "taken the vitals out of the rebellion."[5]

After the fall of Port Royal, Lincoln urged Welles to direct Admiral Du Pont and the South Atlantic Blockade Squadron to move against Charleston, the Confederate's key blockade-running port. Lincoln's and Welles' overly optimistic view of the Charleston operation increased after the epic clash between the *Monitor* and the *Virginia*, but both men had vastly overrated the *Monitor*'s offensive firepower. In his zeal Welles had let a large number of contracts to build more monitors, and Fox now pressed Du Pont to employ a formation of monitors in a frontal challenge to Fort Sumter. Although he believed Fox to be "intelligent and brave," Du Pont concluded that Fox was obsessed with the monitors just as the administration was obsessed with the Charleston operation.[6]

Du Pont was certain that a frontal attack on Charleston would not succeed. He badly wanted to take the city. This symbolic seedbed of secession was also the major gap in his blockade operations. Of fourteen established Union stations in the South Atlantic, thirteen were reasonably successful, but swift Confederate blockade runners had confounded Du Pont's best efforts to shut down their nighttime runs in and out of Charleston. In March 1863, Du Pont sent Lieutenant John Worden in the *Monitor* to attack Fort McAllister, a seven-gun stronghold that guarded the Ogeechee River south of Savannah. Worden made repeated assaults, but was unable to inflict any damage. Convinced that the effectiveness of the *Monitor* had been exaggerated, Du Pont warned Welles that she was lacking in "destructiveness as against forts." Fox persisted, nonetheless. Given to homey, biblical allusions, he replied to Du Pont that the "fall of Charleston is the fall of Satan's kingdom." Fox also had another motive: "My duties are twofold," he told Du Pont. "First to beat our southern friends; second to beat the Army." Du Pont responded in a letter to Welles that cautioned that "troops are necessary." While the monitors had "impenetrability," they had "no corresponding quality of aggression." Under enormous pressure from Lincoln and Welles, Du Pont finally agreed, against his better judgment, to send a gunboat and seven monitors against Fort Sumter.[7]

Attacking at 0230 on 7 April 1863, Du Pont's columns exchanged a furious gunfire with the Confederate batteries. The Union flotilla fired 139 shots and was hit 411 times by southern projectiles. Fifty Union sailors were dead, over twice that number were wounded, and five of the monitors were too badly damaged to continue the action. After being punished for two hours, Du Pont had to retire. The double-turreted monitor *Keokuk* sank the next day. With the unanimous agreement of his captains, Du Pont reported that a renewed attack would be futile. "These monitors are miserable failures where forts are concerned," he told General Hunter. Du Pont's opponents agreed. "Their monitors are great humbugs," Confederate General Beauregard asserted confidently, "more terrible in imagination than in reality." Preceded by the disaster at Fredericksburg, the Union defeat at Charleston raised Confederate morale and served as another embarrassing reminder of Lincoln's uneven performance as commander in chief.[8]

When Lincoln learned that Du Pont was about to retire from the squadron's anchorage one week after the attack against Charleston, he personally ordered the admiral to hold his position. The president appeared at the Navy Department the next day and seemed to a reporter to be "the very picture of a man whose wits had left him." Welles and Fox blamed Du Pont. He was "prejudiced against the monitor class" and "would attribute the failure to them, but it is evident he has no taste for rough, close fighting," they agreed. This unfair assessment found its way into Welles' account of the battle, which he released to the press. Du Pont responded by demanding that the Navy also publish the correspondence containing his early reservations about the operation. Soon after learning that he might be "sacrificed," Du Pont received a letter from Welles informing him that he was being relieved on account of his "opposition to a renewed attack on Charleston." Du Pont's professional courage, which emerged a bit late, insulated his successor, Rear Admiral John A. Dahlgren, from Washington's continuous pressure to keep on attacking Fort Sumter.[9]

Until 1864, enforcing the blockade was difficult, as the failure of Du Pont's attack on Charleston underlined. During the first three years of the war, a fleet of swift Confederate blockade runners steaming from the West Indies to the Atlantic and Gulf ports carried a cornucopia of arms and military equipment, consumer goods, and luxuries from Europe to the South. They were hindered but not deterred by the Union blockade. Indeed, 80 percent of the blockade runners carrying arms from Europe reached their Confederate destination. Until Richmond was under siege in 1865, no major Confederate Army units ever suffered from a serious shortage of artillery, ammunition, or small arms, although the southerners had to contend with a confusing variety of mixed-caliber batteries and never enjoyed the reserve munitions with which the Union troops were endowed. There were severe shortages in the South during the Civil War, but these resulted more from the reluctance of the Richmond regime to regulate trade than from the Union blockade.

The Union blockade squadrons achieved somewhat greater success in staunching the export of southern commodities, although from 1861 to 1864 more than 90 percent of the cotton shipped from the Confederacy to Europe passed through the blockade. Nonetheless, owing both to the Confederate embargo measure and to Farragut's seizure of New Orleans, the volume of the cotton trade fell precipitously in 1862. Loss of this essential source of foreign exchange, which was desperately needed to purchase arms and equipment in Europe and ship them to the South, was crucial. With the collapse of the prewar cotton trade came a parallel decline in Confederate credit in Europe, crippling the South's ability to recover after the reversal at Gettysburg in 1863.[10]

Neither Jefferson Davis nor Navy Secretary Mallory worried greatly about the blockade, although both were aware of the Union Navy's huge investment in this strategy. Davis' attitude was explicable by his disinterest in the Confederate Navy and the immense trust he placed in Mallory, his most skillful cabinet official. The upshot of Davis' attitude was that the Confederate Army and Navy rarely planned or conducted joint operations, unlike the Union forces, which worked together, if not always harmoniously, throughout the war. Davis seldom complained to Mallory about the blockade, and when he did it was to express anger at European diplomatic practices rather than annoyance over the absence of any effective counterblockade strategy. This attitude seemed to be justified by the early success of the blockade-running operations.

After the Union fleet seized a few vessels that had sailed directly to southern ports from the British Isles, the blockade runners quickly abandoned this route. Thereafter, contraband was shipped to the Bahamas, where it was transferred to one of a growing fleet of fast blockade runners for the last leg of the voyage to Wilmington, Charleston, Mobile, or New Orleans. "The blockade of the port [of Charleston] was so imperfect that vessels entered and departed with so little risk that the export of cotton and import of supplies did no suffer any material interruption," Admiral

Dahlgren reported in July 1863. The Confederates also shipped contraband from Europe to the neutral Mexican port of Matamoros, and from there transported it across the Rio Grande to Brownsville, Texas. By 1864, however, the blockade began to influence Confederate military operations. Davis, dedicated to states' rights, had rejected a plan to empower a Confederate Navy officer to control all blockade running until that year, and when he finally took this step, it was far too late to make any difference to the outcome of the war. As a result, the South did not efficiently apportion its blockade-running tonnage between civilian and military demands, middlemen and speculators dictated the mix of European imports, and an excessive fraction of this tonnage consisted of unnecessary but profitable luxury goods. Nonetheless, the Confederate logistics system was more responsible than the Union Navy's blockade for the southern supply problems. In early 1865 Lee's men were starving—while southern warehouses held more that 50 million rations of meat and bread.

Assuming that the blockade was destined to fail, Mallory worried little about using the Confederate Navy to attack the Union blockading squadrons. He was constantly fearful, however, that the opposing naval forces would land troops and establish lodgments on the Confederate coast, and so he put his energies into defending harbors and repulsing Union attacks on inlets, ports, and coastal forts. To do this he persuaded the Richmond Congress early in 1861 to authorize an ambitious plan to lay down fifty armored vessels in southern shipyards. During the war, twenty-two of these vessels were completed. Only five large, seagoing ironclads were to be used against the Union blockade; the rest of the Confederate fleet was dedicated to harbor or river patrols. Of the seagoing Confederate ironclads, only the *Arkansas* and the *Virginia* ever put to sea, but neither of these vessels could operate in rough water. Mallory hoped that the Confederacy's foreign-built cruisers would force Welles to withdraw ships from the Union blockade, although these ships were designed not to disrupt the blockade but to raid enemy commerce.

In the end, as a measure to cut off trade between the South and Europe, the Union blockade failed—at least until the final year of the war. Of 2,054 wartime attempts to run the Wilmington blockade, for instance, 1,735 succeeded. It appears that 2,960 vessels pierced the blockade in the Gulf, and about two-thirds of this number reached their destinations after Farragut took New Orleans and tightened the blockade in 1862. On the other hand, many of these vessels were engaged in interstate coastal trade, which the blockading stations sharply curtailed. Sailing vessels accounted for most of the Confederate losses. Of 1,149 blockade runners captured by the Union fleet, only 210 were steamers. Of 355 blockade-running vessels damaged or run aground, only 85 were steamers. Steam plants were essential to the establishment of the Union blockade, and necessary for the rapid movement of large bodies of Union troops to points on the Confederate coast, but the appearance of steamers in the Civil War apparently favored the South in the final accounting. The most effective element of the blockade proved to be the seizure of southern ports, for no port was ever truly closed until it was captured. To the extent that blockade duty wore out ships needed for landing operations, the blockade strategy delayed rather than advanced the day of Union victory. At a political level, however, the blockade proved to be an essential cornerstone in the Union effort to prevent Europe from intervening in the Civil War. It was a continuing reminder of Union control over the Confederacy's territorial waters, and this by itself mitigated Richmond's claims of independent sovereignty.[11]

The course of military operations in North America during the last year of the conflict simply confirmed the wisdom of the Great Powers' decision to accede to Union diplomacy. In April 1864, Lincoln named General Grant to the command of all Union armies. When Grant rode east to lead the northern offensive against Richmond, General William T. Sherman was left behind in command of the western theater. Grant and Sherman had already agreed that Sherman would launch his own offensive aimed at striking deep into Georgia, taking Atlanta, and destroying the large Confederate army defending the city. Admiral Farragut, who had always wanted to shut down blockade running into Mobile Bay, now raised anew the argument that a Union attack from the Gulf would tie down Confederate reserves in Alabama and prevent Davis from using those troops to reinforce the southern army in Georgia. Welles agreed with this strategy, and at long last Farragut was allowed to mount his attack on Mobile Bay.

The Confederates had erected a formidable defense for Mobile Bay. Three forts guarded the only channel deep enough for Union ships to navigate. To the east, Fort Morgan, a masonry structure with a casemated battery of forty-five guns, rested on the edge of a fingerlike peninsula that stuck out into the channel. To the northwest lay Fort Powell, which protected the shoal waters of the passage. And in the middle of the channel was Fort Gaines on Dolphin Island. Over half of the deep channel was defended by three lines of moored torpedoes, or mines, and a buoy marked the western boundary of the minefield about 150 yards from the edge of the peninsula. President Davis had assigned a Confederate squadron under Rear Admiral Franklin Buchanan to defend Mobile Bay. It included the newly constructed *Tennessee*, a slow and not very maneuverable casemated ironclad that carried two 7-inch pivot rifles fore and aft and two 6.4-inch rifles on each broadside, and the light steam gunboats *Selma, Gaines,* and *Morgan.*

To assault Mobile Bay, Farragut was assigned a division of Union troops under Major General Gordon Granger, and a formidable invasion force of wooden ships, transports, and the monitors *Manhattan, Tecumseh, Chickasaw,* and *Winnebago.* Farragut was alert to the presence of the Confederate minefield, but he guessed that most of the torpedoes were harmless because of their crude works and their long immersion in the channel. His major tactical problems were the gunfire from the forts and the threat from the southern squadron. During their approach, the Union monitors were to advance in a single line slightly ahead and to the right of the ships. When the formation entered the channel, the monitors were to engage the forts while the wooden ships were running the channel, then the monitors were to protect the ships against a counterattack by the *Tennessee*, the best armed of all of the Confederate ironclads. The day before the attack, Granger landed troops on Dauphin Island, one step in a larger movement to outflank Fort Gaines.

At 0700 on 5 August 1864, Farragut was ready. He had lashed his wooden ships together in pairs, and had tied himself high in the rigging of the *Hartford* so that he could see the entire battle. Carried by the morning flood tide, the Union columns approached Fort Morgan, the *Tecumseh* slightly ahead of the *Brooklyn.* They drew the first Confederate fire. At this moment, Buchanan in the *Tennessee* emerged and began to bear down on the Union flotilla, attempting to cross the "tee" of Farragut's column. Captain Tunis A. M. Craven in the *Tecumseh* tried to ram the Confederate ironclad. Instead he struck a mine that exploded, sinking his monitor. Craven stood back and allowed his pilot to be the last man to escape through the turret tower's tiny opening, then went down with his vessel.

The rest of the Union monitors steamed safely into Mobile Bay, but the loss of the *Tecumseh* frightened the captain of the wooden ship *Brooklyn*, and he started to reverse course to get out of the channel. Captain James D. Alden's hesitation caused the Union ships to congregate below Fort Morgan, and the Confederate gunners inflicted heavy casualties. When Farragut saw what was happening, he yelled down to Percival Dayton, the flagship's captain, "Damn the torpedoes!" or words to that effect. The *Hartford* passed by the *Brooklyn* and charged onto the bay, and the first column of Union ships followed the flagship. From the *Brooklyn's* quarterdeck it was now apparent that Farragut had safely transited the minefield, so Captain Alden slowly turned the *Brooklyn* around and led her column into the bay as well. There Farragut's monitors engaged the Confederate squadron. The wooden, side-wheel steamer *Metacomet* ran down the *Selma*, which surrendered, while Farragut's ships battered away at the *Gaines*, which was beached by her crew. The *Morgan* sought shelter under the guns of Fort Morgan, as had the *Tennessee*, but Buchanan again valiantly sortied out against the *Hartford*, creating a great melee. To protect the flagship, the *Monongahela* and the *Lackawanna* each rammed the *Tennessee*, but Buchanan kept up steam. Finally his vessel ploughed into the bow of the *Hartford*, whose guns could inflict no damage on the Confederate ironclad.[12]

The battle was almost over, however. The primers used by the *Tennessee's* gun crews had gone bad, and Buchanan could get off only one last shot against the *Hartford* before the *Lackawanna* tried to ram him again. This maneuver was flawed, and the *Lackawanna* mistakenly punched into the *Hartford*, but within moments the *Chickasaw* closed on the *Tennessee* and the Union gunfire closed the shutters on the Confederate's gun ports. One round wounded Buchanan. The *Manhattan*, armed with a 15-inch gun, then moved in, her fire puncturing the *Tennessee's* armor. By 1000, the Confederate flagship was dead in the water, surrounded by Farragut's squadron, and unable to return fire. After fighting an extraordinary battle against overwhelming odds, Buchanan had no choice but to surrender. In control of Mobile Bay, Admiral Farragut began to move on the outposts, and on the evening of 5 August, the defenders evacuated Fort Powell and blew it up. The next day, Fort Gaines surrendered. Farragut and Granger then laid siege to Fort Morgan, which held out until the end of the month.

While Farragut was moving against Mobile Bay, General Sherman was advancing toward the outskirts of Atlanta. The city fell on 2 September 1864, thus erasing Sherman's concern that Confederate troops from Mobile would reinforce the army he faced in Georgia. Although Granger laid siege to Mobile over the winter, the city remained in Confederate hands while the Union Navy ruled the bay.

Farragut's victory on Mobile Bay and Sherman's capture of Atlanta had a powerful effect on Civil War politics. After the failure of the Peninsula Campaign, discontent with the Lincoln administration had ripened during 1862. In addition, the way Lincoln conducted the war undermined the authority of state governments in the North, increased federal debts and taxes, and generally inflated the economy. To oust Lincoln in 1864, the Democrats nominated General McClellan, who favored a compromise with the South. Republicans and a handful of War Democrats united under the banner of the Unionist Party and supported Lincoln's reelection. The race appeared to be close until that August. Then the victories at Atlanta and Mobile Bay sealed the ultimate fate of the Confederacy, and the argument that the Union needed to negotiate a compromise to settle the war lost its force. McClellan was handily defeated in November and Lincoln won a second term in the White House.

Grant had come east by this time to take command of the land campaign against Lee. He understood that to defeat Lee he had to overcome the immense advantage conferred on the Confederates by their interior lines of communication. McClellan had tried to accomplish this by exploiting superior Union mobility and logistics, but he could not contend with both Lee's brilliant counterthrusts and Lincoln's meddling. Two years later, Grant, now the Union Army's commanding general, could expect the Union fleet to harry the Confederacy's eastern flank while Sherman's army impaled the enemy on its western flank. Whenever Grant made contact with Lee, moreover, the Army of the Potomac would enjoy crushing local superiority and plentiful reserves. In April 1864, Grant began to descend on the Lee's Army of the Rapidan. To support Grant's lines of communications, Rear Admiral Lee's North Atlantic Blockade Squadron was to cover the movement of troops and supplies to a number of bases along the Virginia tidewater. In addition, Grant asked Admiral Lee to support a thrust up the James River by General

Butler's Army of the James, which was then positioned at Fortress Monroe.

With covering fire from five Union ironclads and ten gunboats, part of Butler's troops occupied City Point on the James on 5 May, and part overran Bermuda Hundred the same day. "We have landed here, entrenched ourselves, destroyed many miles of railroad, and got a position [from] which . . . we can hold against the whole of Lee's army," Butler told the War Department. Jefferson Davis had already ordered General Beauregard to come north from Charleston to reinforce Richmond, however, and on the 16th he counterattacked at Drewry's Bluff, forcing Butler to draw back along the York River to a defensive position at Bermuda Hundred. "This predicament of Butler," Porter wrote some years later, "gave rise to the celebrated letter of General Grant, in which he speaks of Butler's being as completely 'hors du combat' as if he were enclosed in a bottle with the cork in." At the same time, the main Union force, the Army of the Potomac, slashed into the Wilderness on 5 May, and inflicted and absorbed terrible losses at Spotsylvania Courthouse three days later. Then Grant shifted to Lee's right flank, crossing the Pamunkey River with such determination that Lee barely had time to slip between the Union vanguard and the open road to Richmond.[13]

By 3 June, these movements found Grant at Old Cold Harbor and Lee at New Cold Harbor, confronting each other just a few miles northeast of the Confederate capital. Grant could not dislodge Lee's lines, however, so he again struck southward, crossing the Potomac River and reaching City Point on the night of 15 June. To defend his new headquarters against a counterattack by a nearby flotilla of Confederate mine vessels and fire rafts, Grant asked Admiral Lee to establish a barrier astride the river. Five days later Commander Thomas T. Craven's men sank four hulks filled with stone in the main channel at French's Reach and stretched a cable-and-boom obstruction across the river. "The enemy probably was well pleased at the Federals obstructing the channel," Porter commented, because "he knew that his position could not be assaulted by a naval force." The Union's offensive against Petersburg ground to a halt after three days. Grant confessed that taking Richmond would be more difficult than he imagined. He decided nonetheless to remain on the York Peninsula where he could constantly pressure Lee and where the Union fleet provided reliable protection for the flanks of his army.[14]

The turn of the tide in Virginia was matched by a renewed

Union determination to strengthen the blockade. Du Pont's failure to take Charleston in 1863 did not discourage his relief, Admiral Dahlgren, who was bent on taking the Confederate bastion. Upon assuming command of the South Atlantic Blockade Squadron in July, he abandoned the plans for another naval assault, deciding instead to use the fleet to support a series of amphibious landings by Brigadier General Quincy A. Gillmore's Union Army division. In preparation for a move against Morris Island, Gillmore's men occupied nearby Folly Island. Then, on 10 July, four Union ironclads shelled Fort Wagner while Army troops crossed Lighthouse Inlet, but when they landed and tried to advance to the fort, they were pinned down on the beach by Confederate gunfire. On 17 August, after two prolonged bombardments, Fort Wagner was reduced to rubble by naval gunfire and shore-based artillery, and Gillmore began to advance. Dahlgren was preparing to assault the fort on 6 September, but the Confederates evacuated it overnight and abandoned Morris Island entirely the following day.

Dahlgren believed Fort Sumter to be totally exposed by the

Library of Congress

Rear Admiral John A. Dahlgren, an ordnance expert who commanded the South Atlantic Blockading Squadron, from mid-1863 to 1865, standing in front of a 30-pound Dahlgren rifle on board the 1,500-ton screw sloop *Pawnee* in Charleston Harbor in 1864.

fall of Fort Wagner. On the night of 1 September, his ironclads shelled Sumter for five hours, but the defending garrison was intact and refused his demand that they surrender. "All we have to do is to go in and take possession," he declared. He prepared to conduct a small amphibious assault of the fort, but it was dosed by misadventure. Relations between Dahlgren and Gillmore had gone sour; they no longer spoke to each other, and each man was planning on his own to conduct essentially the same landing. Matters worsened when Gillmore learned of Dahlgren's plan and insisted, quite unreasonably, that the Navy allow the Army to command the entire operation. Dahlgren's reply was sharp and surly. As a first step, Dahlgren ordered Commander Edmund R. Colhoun in the single-turreted monitor *Weehawken* to take station in the narrow channel separating Sumter from Morris Island to cover the landing. The *Weehawken* ran aground in shoal water on 7 September and she was seriously damaged by gunfire from three enemy batteries before being freed by steam tugs. The *New Ironsides*, which covered the rescue, took fifty hits from Fort Moultrie's guns and was also forced to withdraw.

Dahlgren's security was so poor, moreover, that Charleston's defenders soon knew his battle plan. The Confederate gunboat *Chicora* sortied, Fort Sumter's garrison was armed with rifles and grenades, and the guns of Forts Moultrie and Johnson were aimed at the spot near Sumter's southern face where the Union men were to land. Late on the night of 7 September, small boats carrying nearly 500 Marines and sailors were towed to within about 400 yards of Fort Sumter, and the men began to row toward the island. When the first landing party stepped ashore, they were stunned by grenades thrown from the fort and pinned down by gunfire from the *Chicora* and the forts. The assault force ashore surrendered, and the rest of the boats escaped. Dahlgren again decided to blast Fort Sumter into submission, and after a bombardment lasting forty-one days between late October and early December, he observed that "the only original feature left [of Sumter] is the northeast face; the rest is a pile of rubbish." Still the fort would not surrender. Dahlgren and Gillmore were by now caught up in a quarrel so violent that Lincoln had to order them "to courteously confer" about future operations to overcome the seemingly invincible Confederate stronghold in Charleston harbor.[15]

Although Mallory was not overly concerned about the blockade, he did not intend the Confederate Navy to remain passive while the Union fleet stood off southern ports; he repeatedly employed his handful of ironclads to disrupt enemy operations. In early 1863, a pair of small Confederate ironclads modeled after the *Virginia* attacked the Charleston Blockade Force, but they were driven back into the harbor by the superior Union ironclads. Then, in May, word reached Washington that the Confederates had completed the ironclad ram *Atlanta* in Savannah and planned to send her out against the Savannah Blockade Force. Du Pont instructed Captain Rodgers in the single-turreted monitor *Weehawken* to steam from Charleston to the Warsaw, Georgia, blockade station and check this move. Rodgers arrived off Savannah on 10 June 1863. Seven days later the *Atlanta* appeared, as expected, in the early morning hours, and began to enter the sound. Within a few moments, however, the *Atlanta* ran aground and could not free herself, a perfect target for the superior Union guns. The *Weehawken* weighed anchor and, in company with the *Nahant*, advanced on the helpless Confederate ironclad at 0515. Rodgers fired just five shots, putting two rebel gun crews out of action, blowing the roof off the ram's pilothouse, and piercing her casemate. After fifteen minutes, the *Atlanta* struck the Stars and Bars.

Mallory was working in the meantime to complete more ironclad rams to disrupt the Union blockade. One of these vessels, the *Albemarle*, was finished in mid-1864, and Mallory deployed her to the North Carolina sounds. When Lieutenant William B. Cushing learned that Admiral Lee could not spare any ironclads from the North Atlantic Blockade Squadron to send out against her, he volunteered to attack the *Albemarle* in a commando-style operation. He fixed a spar torpedo to the bow of a small launch and on the night of 27 October 1864, in the darkness, came alongside the ironclad. Cushing placed his torpedo under the *Albemarle*'s hull just before the Confederate lookouts saw his boat and opened fire. Within seconds the device exploded, ripping a great hole in the bottom of the *Albemarle*, which caused her to sink. Although most of his men were captured and two died when the Union launch went under, Cushing and one sailor escaped by swimming to safety. Many southerners remarked at the unsurpassed daring of Cushing's remarkable exploit.

Other Confederate efforts to make the blockade more costly for the Union fleet achieved somewhat greater success. Built in Charleston as a private venture, the 50-foot *David* was armed with one torpedo, a 70-pound explosive charge bolted to the end of a bow spar. On the night of 5 October 1863, Lieutenant William T. Glassell in the *David* sortied from Charleston Harbor and drew alongside the ironclad steamer *New Ironsides* without being detected. When the Confederate torpedo exploded under the steamer's starboard quarter, it caused some damage, but Glassell panicked, abandoned his boat when she went dead in the water, and was captured by Union sailors. His assistant engineer was able to relight her boilers, however, and the *David* escaped back to Charleston. The escapade was so famous that the *David*'s name became the generic term for an entire class of Confederate small bow spar torpedo boats, but subsequent attacks by these vessels never disrupted any Union operations.

The success of the *David*-type torpedo boat moved Mallory to support another project organized by a civilian, Horace L. Hunley. He built a 26-foot-long bicycle-powered submersible that he fitted with a bow-mounted spar torpedo. Although one trial in Mobile Bay ended when the vessel ran aground and killed her nine-man crew, Mallory directed that the *Hunley* be transported by rail to Charleston to help disrupt the blockade. After three more underwater disasters in that harbor, however, it became clear that she could not maneuver effectively while submerged. When she made her maiden sortie in February 1864, therefore, the *Hunley* remained on the surface and closed slowly on the new Union screw-sloop *Housatonic*. The Union lookouts sighted the *Hunley* only after it was too late, and she rammed the *Housatonic*. Both vessels sank within minutes. The Confederates were buoyed by this triumph, but their other experiments with submersibles were quite costly and less rewarding.

While the Confederate fleet could do nothing to lift the blockade, which became increasingly effective during 1864, neither could the Union fleet entirely shut down blockade running into Charleston. And, by the end of the year, it was evident that only a landward approach to Charleston would compel the city to surrender.

Wilmington, the other remaining Confederate coastal bastion, also served as a magnet for Union naval activity. Good railroad lines connected Wilmington to Richmond and to the interior of the Confederacy, and, after the Union blockade began to thicken in 1862, Wilmington was the foremost Confederate blockade-running center. Situated at the fall line of the Cape Fear River, the city was defended against seaward approaches by the powerful batteries of Fort Fisher at the mouth of the river. Welles had wanted to take Fort Fisher for years, but Admiral Lee's North Atlantic Blockade Squadron did not have enough vessels to mount this operation until the autumn of 1864. As always, there was the question of command. For two years Lee had been the object of considerable envy and criticism owing to the large sums of prize money he collected. Welles defended him until 1864, when he had had enough and decided to find a relief. Inasmuch as Farragut was ill, Welles turned to Rear Admiral Porter, who was lobbying in Washington for the billet. "Porter . . . received from the Navy Department all the facilities which [Admiral] Lee had applied for in vain," Captain Benjamin F. Sands observed bitterly. Porter increased the patrols' tempo and set out decoys to lure blockade runners into a hedge of traps. He, too, seized a large number of prizes, but discovered that as long as Wilmington was open the blockade was incomplete.[16]

Porter faced two problems in planning the Fort Fisher operation. There were no Union Navy bases nearby, and the Army's local commander, General Butler, was irremediably uncooperative. Although Welles pointed out to Lincoln that "the public expect this attack" and "to procrastinate much longer will be to peril its success," Butler was in no hurry to provide the necessary troops. In November 1864, he leisurely brought up his division from the Bermuda Hundred, a movement whose slow pace was the object of Porter's biting criticism. Instead of assaulting the position, Butler concocted a scheme to blow up the fort using a large floating mine. Porter liked the idea. He selected the old, rotting steamer *Louisiana* and had it loaded with 215 pounds of black powder and a detonator. After fighting storms during the middle of December, Porter's squadron appeared off the Cape Fear River. On the night of 23 December, a tug towed the *Louisiana* to within 300 yards of Fort Fisher and dropped anchor. The timer was set, the crew escaped in rowboats, and everyone waited for the explosion. Nothing happened. Twenty minutes later, Fort Fisher's guns fired on the ship and produced five separate, spectacular explosions. This created a brilliant fireworks display, but the Confederate fort was undamaged.[17]

Ignoring this setback, Porter's vessels closed on Fort Fisher at dawn the next morning, and within an hour his guns had momentarily silenced the Confederate batteries. Butler's transports carrying 6,500 men were supposed to arrive shortly thereafter, but he did not appear until the next day. He then decided to land about five miles south of Fort Fisher, and during the day 100 Union boats put about 2,200 Union soldiers ashore. Porter's squadron then closed in and resumed its bombardment. Butler later claimed that the Navy's gun crews were ineffective, that only three of the seventy-five Confederate guns were dismounted, and that at the end of the day over 800 rebels were still manning the fort. Announcing that Grant had ordered him to conduct an assault, not a siege, he ordered his men to retire and board their transports, and the division sailed back to Hampton Roads. "Here was our fleet of six hundred guns commanding a peninsula two miles wide only, and able to cover for many miles any number of troops we might land," Porter complained, but "from beginning to end the military [Army] part of the expedition has been a failure." The North Atlantic Squadron withdrew to Beaufort, and from there Porter wired a blistering indictment of Butler to his old friend, General Grant, charging that Butler was incompetent and hinting that Butler, a former Congressman, owed his rank and command to Republican Party "politics."[18]

When his own position was less secure in the early years of the war, Lincoln needed "political" generals like Butler and Banks, once important Republican figures; but in late 1864 the president had just been reelected and could now allow them to be discarded. Grant agreed with Porter's charges. He also badly wanted Porter to capture Fort Fisher so that blockade-run supplies from Wilmington could not reach Lee. "Hold on wherever you are for a few days and I will endeavor to send the troops back again and without the former commander," he replied. Grant replaced Butler with Major General Alfred H. Terry, a far more competent military leader. In the meantime, however, Porter was alarmed to discover that Butler's criticism of the Navy's gunfire was essentially correct. The next time, he told his gunners, they were to direct their fire at the enemy parapets rather than at the Confederate flags.[19]

With Terry in command of the troops, Porter and a formation of sixty-two Union vessels appeared off Fort Fisher on the evening of 12 January 1865. Porter sent a squadron composed of the *New Ironsides* and other ironclads to within 700 yards of the beach the next morning and, once in position, they opened fire. At 0800, the troops landed, dug a trenchline across the peninsula, and isolated the fort from the mainland. Terry brought his artillery over the beach the following day and began formal siege operations, but Fort Fisher was skillfully defended by Colonel William Lamb's 1,500 men, who fought fiercely throughout the first day of the battle. To assure Union success in this second attack, Porter had organized a special landing party of 2,000 sailors and Marines who had practiced landing and assault tactics before the operation. On 15 January, he put these men ashore to support Terry, but when they stormed the fort they were repulsed. This diverted Lamb's attention from Terry's advance, however, and Porter renewed his shelling of the enemy position. The defenders' guns fell silent in the early afternoon. At 1500, the steam whistles in the Union fleet all blew at once, a signal for Terry's troops to assault the parapets. Seven hours later, after a seesaw battle during which the Confederates were chased from the fort and hemmed in at the end of Federal Point, Lamb surrendered. Wilmington was cut off from the sea, and the blockade of the Confederacy's Atlantic coastline was virtually complete.[20]

As a part of the effort to close the blockade, these final exertions were probably unnecessary. As early as September 1864, financier Gazaway Lamar reported to Confederate Treasury Secretary George Trenholm that "the fleet blockading Wilmington is so numerous that the port may be considered closed." "Charleston is not much safer," and Mobile was "shut up." Lamar confessed that "unless we can get safer harbors"—which the presence of the Union Navy made impossible—"blockade running must be abandoned." The Confederacy had decided in 1861 to bring its blockade running into only a handful of established ports, so each time the Union Navy closed a southern port the result was the loss of an unnecessarily high fraction of Confederate overseas trade. And, after the fall of Fort Fisher, of the major Confederate strongpoints along the coast only Charleston still remained in southern hands. In spite of repeated exertions, Dahlgren's South Atlantic Blockade Squadron had neither prevented blockade runners from using Charleston nor taken Fort Sumter. "So many [Union blockading] steamers were repairing as to make even the blockade inefficient," he confessed in December 1864, and several ships entered and departed Charleston the following month. When Sherman marched north from Savannah into the Carolinas in January 1865, however, Admiral Dahlgren renewed the pressure on the Charleston garrison with the help of ships released from the Wilmington Blockade Force. Caught between these converging forces, the city surrendered on 18 February.[21]

Although the North's triumph now seemed inevitable, the South still held Richmond, fielded two large armies, and possessed the resources to conduct protracted guerrilla operations aimed at disrupting any Union occupation. To end the carnage, Lincoln met with Confederate Vice President Alexander H. Stephens on 31 January 1865 on board the Union steamer *River Queen* in Hampton Roads; however, these talks ran aground when the Confederates rejected Lincoln's demand that the Union be reconstituted. Three days earlier, Grant and Porter had met at City Point and planned the final descent on Richmond, an offensive made much easier by the Union Navy's control of the Chesapeake Bay, Hampton Roads, and the lower York and James rivers. Grant decided that General Thomas Schofield's corps would board transports at Annapolis and sail south to Fort Fisher, where they were to support a movement by the Navy's Wilmington Blockade Force up the Cape Fear River against Wilmington. On 19 February, Porter led a squadron consisting of the monitor *Montauk* and fifteen gunboats in an attack on Fort Anderson, about halfway between Fort Fisher and Wilmington. Weakly defended, it was abandoned after a withering naval bombardment lasting several hours. This exposed Fort Strong on Big Island, which Porter took six days later. Porter now began to clear the Cape Fear River to provide an advance base for Sherman, whose army was about to cross into North Carolina and march inland parallel to the coast.

Schofield's corps was now detached, but Grant still had about 90,000 troops divided between the Army of the Potomac, which he used to lay siege to Richmond, and the Army of the James, which was almost surrounding nearby Petersburg. Porter, who assumed tactical command of the James River Squadron in March 1865, had established Union control of the James River up to City Point and repulsed several attempts by Admiral Raphael Semmes' defending Confederate Navy vessels to disrupt Union shipping. Semmes tenaciously held Drewry's Bluff, however, and Porter could not move beyond that position. General Lee was aware by this time that he was hopelessly outnumbered, especially after Union cavalry raided the Shenandoah Valley, and he knew that Grant intended to launch his spring offensive within weeks. Lee, ever resourceful, concocted a last-ditch plan: a local attack that would seize the enemy arsenal at City Point, relieve the siege of

Richmond, and allow half the Confederate Army to hold Richmond while the rest escaped to the south to join Johnston in the Carolinas and overwhelm Sherman.

"We are upon the eve of events fraught with the fate of the Confederacy," Mallory warned Naval Agent Bulloch in France. On 25 March, Lee threw nearly half his best troops against the Union right opposite Petersburg. At one point during this offensive, the attackers briefly overran Fort Stedman, and elsewhere they advanced toward City Point, which was only about ten miles from the Confederate lines. To guard that position, Porter had sent several gunboats up the Appomattox River with instructions to hold the critical pontoon bridge there "at all times" so as to obstruct the enemy move. However, Lee's last offensive had already been blunted when the Union Army recovered Fort Stedman. On 29 March, Grant's final blow struck at both ends of the Confederate line, and two days later the entire right flank of the Confederate position was exposed. Mallory reluctantly ordered Admiral Semmes to destroy his three ironclads and the gunboats that had defended the James River on 2 April, and to have his crews join Lee's army, which was evacuating Richmond. "The naval operations of the Confederacy east of Mississippi would cease," he confessed at last. To prevent Lee from escaping, Grant flung his divisions in pursuit and dispatched Sheridan's cavalry to a position astride the only line of retreat available to the Army of Northern Virginia. When he realized that he was trapped, Lee surrendered to Grant on 9 April 1865 at Appomattox Court House, and a week later Johnston surrendered to Sherman in North Carolina. The War Between the States was over.[22]

Chapter Twenty
The Return to the Station Squadrons
1865–1880

Andrew Johnson, a War Democrat who became president after Lincoln's assassination in April 1865, soon fell afoul of the Radical Republicans over Reconstruction. Questions of how to treat the defeated Confederate states and return to peacetime electoral alignments divided northern Republicans and soon wedded the northern Democrats to the solidly Democratic South. There were no serious overseas threats, and this allowed politicians, in their partisan struggles, to wield the Navy itself as a weapon.

Navy Secretary Welles and Secretary of State Seward both remained in Johnson's cabinet and steadfastly supported him throughout his 1868 impeachment by the House and trial in the Senate. Owing to Johnson's preoccupation with domestic politics, Seward took the lead in postwar foreign affairs, protected from the Radicals to some extent by his close wartime association with Lincoln. A visionary, Seward laid the foundations for an American sphere of influence in the Caribbean and an empire of trade and annexation in the Pacific. The long-term influence of his vision and diplomacy on American foreign policy and naval strategy was profound.

French military rule in Mexico was Seward's most pressing postwar problem. Spanish, British, and French naval forces had seized Vera Cruz in 1861 to compel the Mexicans to pay long-overdue debts. When the Spanish and British withdrew, the French remained behind. Napoleon III, emperor of France, concocted a scheme to create a Roman Catholic empire in the New World and cajoled Austrian Archduke Ferdinand Maximilian into accepting the throne of Mexico, backed by 40,000 French Army regulars. A Mexican rump led by former President Benito Juárez retreated into the countryside, organized an army, and mounted a ferocious guerrilla campaign against the French after 1863. Juárez appealed for American assistance, but Seward explained that, for the moment, the Union could do nothing to thwart this blatant violation of the Monroe Doctrine. Congress was anxious for Seward to act, however, and the House passed a resolution condemning "the deplorable events" in Mexico and warning Napoleon III that the United States would not remain "indifferent spectators" to French adventurism in North America. Seward responded sharply that the eve of Grant's climactic invasion of Virginia was "not the most suitable time we could choose for offering idle menaces to the Emperor of France."[1]

The issue of Maximilian's regime came to the fore shortly after Appomattox. Andrew Johnson, who had just become president, long had advocated a "day of reckoning" with France. He felt that "an expedition into Mexico" would be "a sort of recreation" and wanted "the French concern" to be "quickly wiped out." To pressure Maximilian, Grant dispatched General Philip Sheridan with 50,000 men to the Texas border, and Seward sent General J. M. Schofield to France to tell Napoleon III to "get out of Mexico." Welles strengthened the Gulf Squadron and prepared to coordinate operations with Sheridan, but at the same time he pointed out to Johnson that the country was exhausted from the Civil War and confidentially warned that it was questionable whether the Gulf Squadron could deal with a major deployment of the French fleet to the region. The overall balance of power clearly favored the Americans, however. On 12 February 1866, Seward abruptly demanded that Napoleon III tell Washington "when French military operations may be expected to cease in Mexico." At the time, Bismarck's successful drive to unify Germany under Prussian leadership was weakening France's position in Europe. Caught up in this whirlwind, Napoleon III had little time for his interests in Mexico. In April, he promised Seward that the French Army would quit Mexico within a year, leaving Maximilian to the mercy of Juárez and his insurrectionists.[2]

Seward's iron-fisted support for the Monroe Doctrine in Mexico was complemented by renewed interest in the United States in building an isthmian canal to connect the Atlantic and Pacific oceans. Attention to this project increased in 1869 when an Anglo-French consortium completed the Suez Canal, which for the first time linked the Mediterranean with the Indian Ocean. After the Civil War, Secretary Seward negotiated one canal treaty with Nicaragua and another with Colombia, the latter agreement allowing the United States to build a canal through the Colombian province of Panama. Others favored a Mexican route. Captain Robert Shufeldt, an energetic officer with an entrepreneurial bent, began to lobby for an expedition to Tehuantepec. In 1870 he was given command of the seagoing ironclad monitor *Miantonomah* and directed to survey the area and evaluate it as a future canal site. Shufeldt's report cautioned that any canal had to be defensible since it would create "an extension of the Mississippi River to the Pacific Ocean" and transform "the Gulf of Mexico into an American lake." Shufeldt proposed building the canal in southern Mexico, but the best American prospect for the project at the time seemed to be the private Panamanian Isthmus Canal Company. However, this venture failed to raise the enormous capital needed to begin construction and soon declared bankruptcy. The failure of Seward's canal policy did nothing to lessen his interest in extending America's defensive perimeters, increasing the authority of the United States in the Caribbean, and employing the Monroe Doctrine to reduce Europe's influence in the Western Hemisphere.[3]

From these goals came an aggressive campaign to acquire naval bases in the Caribbean, a policy that spanned the doomed presidency of Andrew Johnson and his immediate successor, U. S. Grant. Shortly after the Confederacy surrendered, Seward opened talks with Denmark concerning purchase of the three islands of the Danish West Indies, but the Danes would sell only two. A price of $7.5 million was stipulated in a treaty signed in 1867, but by then relations between Congress and Johnson's administration were acidic, the Senate frowned on the venture, and nature conspired to upset the arrangement. While Congress was debating the treaty, the sloop *Monongahela* visited Charlotte Amalie in St. Thomas, the spacious harbor that had first attracted Seward's interest in the islands. On the afternoon of 18 November 1867 an earthquake created a tidal wave that carried the ship over the warehouses of Frederickstad harbor on St. Croix and dropped her onto the main street. The redux of the wave then dragged her back to the coral reef at the edge of the town. Although the *Monongahela* was refloated and later repaired, once the news of this disaster reached Washington the House resolved that "further purchases of territory are inexpedient." Seward toyed with acquiring naval bases in Cuba, Puerto Rico, and Martinique and asked Congress in 1868 to buy the Dominican port of Samaná Bay, which appeared on the market after a coup in Santo Domingo. However, as a result of the antipathy in Congress toward the Johnson administration, the immense national debt left over from the Civil War, and a general hostility to overseas territorial acquisitions, nothing came of this scheme.[4]

Seward's vision, which extended to the Pacific, was not limited to continentalism or its corollary of coastal defense. After Captain William Reynolds in the screw-sloop *Lackawanna* claimed Midway Island on 28 August 1867, Seward persuaded Congress that December to make Midway the first overseas possession of the United States. Also that year Seward negotiated a major treaty with Russia to purchase Alaska for $7 million. Critics complained that Alaskan cows gave frozen milk and dubbed the deal "Seward's Folly." Some proponents viewed the move northward as a means of outflanking British Canada; others, in the mistaken belief that the tsar had supported the Union during the Civil War, saw it as a way of thanking Russia. Democratic opponents failed to prevent approval of the Alaskan treaty by the Republican Senate. With the acquisition of Alaska and Midway, the protectorate over the Hawaiian kingdom, and the opening of the transcontinental railroad, the strategic Alaska-Hawaii-California triangle was formed. Seward negotiated a commercial reciprocity treaty with the Hawaiian regime in 1867, but the Senate ignored this agreement and devoted its attention instead to the impeachment of Andrew Johnson. The secretary of state expressed his regret that American politics could not focus on "the higher but more remote questions of national extension and aggrandisement."[5]

Navy Secretary Welles was also at swords point with Congress after 1865 owing to the rift between Johnson and the Radicals, Welles' loyalty to the president, and the postwar revival of extreme partisan politics. The Radicals were angry with Welles and hostile or indifferent to the Navy's interests, and Congressman Elihu Washburne, one of their leaders, attempted to discredit Welles, reduce his patronage power, and slash naval appropriations. At the end of the war, the fleet consisted of 471 ships armed with 2,455 guns, and the vessels embodied some of the most advanced naval architecture, ordnance, and steam engineering of the day. Welles understood that the coastal monitors, so "formidable in war," were "unsuited for active service in peace." Of the remaining seagoing monitors, the "Department"-class *Miantonomah* and *Monadnock* sailed to Russia. They were reported to have good seakeeping capabilities, but even this was in doubt. Welles laid out a plan to maintain a modest postwar fleet and complete construction of the seagoing monitors, but Congress would not support it. Instead, Congress demanded that most of the fleet be demobilized, refused to improve the Navy yards, and canceled most of the wartime shipbuilding programs. While the monitors rusted, Washburne had Congress reduce the Navy's manpower ceiling below its prewar level, so low that there were not enough sailors to man some of the larger overseas station ships. And, in 1868, Congress instructed Welles to sell off the ironclads, keeping only the seagoing monitors, the *Passaic*-class coastal monitors, and Ericsson's *Dictator*—which became a rotting icon. As a result of wartime damage, obsolescence, and lack of maintenance, one critic claimed that among the various craft being sold "there is no vessel . . . worthy of the attention of a first-class buyer."[6]

The picture was not wholly one of decline and inactivity. Welles reestablished the station squadrons and once again transfigured the fleet into a force capable of upholding maritime access in the Pacific and Latin America. In 1865 he announced that he planned to send "one or more of our naval vessels . . . annually to display the flag . . . in every port where our ships may trade." Overseas, forward deployment proceeded apace, with dispersion replacing concentration as national naval strategy. Two years later, the Mediterranean and African squadrons were combined into a European Squadron, a command that went to Admiral Farragut. At the same time the Brazil Squadron was reestablished and its name changed to the South Atlantic Squadron. The Pacific Squadron was retained, but the East India Squadron became the Asiatic Squadron and its area of operations was extended into the Indian Ocean and westward to the eastern coast of Africa. The wartime blockade squadrons were disestablished and the old Home Squadron was disbanded, its responsibilities divided between the new Gulf Squadron and the new North Atlantic Squadron. Trade defense and presence once more became the fleet's primary missions. Europeans were not oblivious to this decision. When tensions arose in 1868 as a result of stalled negotiations over the *Alabama* claims—reparations claimed by Washington as a result of the damage done to Union shipping by British-built Confederate raiders—the Admiralty attempted to include in its estimates a possible threat to Britain from the United States. Prime Minister Disraeli caustically observed, however, that the "Americans have no navy, and not an ironclad, except for coastal defense." While inexact, Disraeli's remark illustrated the impact of the American decision to disregard a European standard as a benchmark for its naval policy.[7]

The postwar Navy was sharply divided by a feud between the line officers and the engineers. Line officers believed that Welles was firmly in the camp of the staff, and took as one piece of evidence for this his decision to extend the bureau system to the Navy yards, thus depriving the local commandant of much of his daily authority. To recapture control of the Navy, line officers promoted various schemes to reorganize the department in ways that would deprive the secretary of some of his statutory power. Eventually, these assaults coalesced into a generalized campaign against the basic structure of the bureau system, the bastion of staff authority. Rear Admiral Samuel Du Pont fired off the first round in 1864, after Welles had dismissed him from command of the South Atlantic Blockade Squadron. Du Pont asked his business associate, Congressman Henry Winter Davis, to introduce in the House a bill that would establish a Board of Admiralty—dominated by line officers and responsible directly to the president—to dictate naval policy. The Du Pont plan was supplanted in 1865 by Farragut's scheme to establish a board composed of all the admirals, whose task would be to "harmonize and concentrate" the work of the bureaus with fleet operations. Vice Admiral David Dixon Porter echoed the views of most line officers in his support for these measures.[8]

Welles opposed the creation of any new boards with statutory jurisdiction over naval policy, and he dealt roughly with many of his opponents. For instance, he claimed to be unable to locate any important billets for Rear Admirals Louis Goldsborough, John Dahlgren, or John Rodgers after the war. The pervasiveness of steam technology and the demand for engineers and other specialists created an asymmetry, obvious to all, that underscored the line's uneasiness with Welles. By 1867, staff officers, a minority of those who held regular commissions, occupied about half of the shore billets. Few constructors or engineers were unoccupied, but nearly one-quarter of the line was ashore on half pay awaiting orders. "In a great sea fight," complained one line officer, "the honor of the nation is not in the hands of constructors and engineers, but in that of captains and admirals."

Porter, whom Welles found to be "officious, presuming, and meddlesome," was sent to superintend the teenaged cadets of the Naval Academy. Such vindictiveness was "all wrong, wrong from beginning to end," complained one of Porter's partisans in 1867. Porter was so eager to discredit Welles, and advance his own reorganization plan, that he fed stories of Navy extravagance and mismanagement to Congressman Washburne, the leader of the Navy's Radical opponents on the Hill. Welles rightly suspected that Porter had "fostered a factious clique at Annapolis" to undermine his authority and to persuade Congress to side with the views of the officers of the line. His suspicions were well founded. Charging that there was a "war going on between the engineering department and those who belong to the Navy proper," Senator James W. Nye introduced a bill in December 1867 to create a "board of survey" to provide the secretary with "professional advice." Welles struck back with the constitutional argument that such a board was intended to "supercede" the powers of the civilian secretary.[9]

The Radical Republicans suspended their criticism of the Navy when the Senate put President Johnson on trial in 1868, however; and they scarcely wanted to slander the newly elected Grant administration, which entered office in March 1869. Nonetheless, the Senate that year passed the Grimes Bill, which directed the president to name a "wholly advisory" board of officers to investigate naval policy. The forces opposing its enactment were great. The Secretary of the Navy was afraid of encroachments upon his authority, and congressmen on the House Naval Affairs Committee, which usually led its Senate counterpart, did not want functionaries intervening between them and the bureau chiefs. In addition, staff officers were rightly convinced that the scheme was a product of the line officers' attempt to dominate the material bureaus and the shore establishment, and they predicted that line officers would try to monopolize the new board. Against such formidable opponents, the bill failed in the House.

This issue of civilian versus military control of American military policy was being played out on a larger stage with more profound results at the same time that Welles and Porter were dueling for ascendancy in the Navy Department. When the dispute between President Andrew Johnson and the Radical Republicans over Reconstruction policy grew increasingly bitter in 1867, Congress passed the Tenure in Office Act in an effort to prevent Johnson from firing either Secretary of War Edwin Stanton or the Army's commanding general, Ulysses S. Grant. After the president dismissed Stanton, Grant refused to obey further orders from the White House and the House impeached Johnson, who escaped conviction by only one vote after a partisan trial in the Senate. To create a strong Republican Party that would last beyond Reconstruction, the Radicals needed a popular national leader. They found him in Grant, who announced his candidacy for the presidency while he was still serving as commanding general. With carpetbaggers controlling the South, the Democrats were crushed by Grant's landslide in the 1868 elections, and the Radical Republicans under New York Congressman Thaddeus Stevens and Senator Charles Sumner of Massachusetts won a viselike grip over Congress.

For his first secretary of the Navy, President Grant named Adolph E. Borie, a Philadelphia merchant whose only political accomplishment had been to subscribe to a fund to buy a house for the general in that city. Gideon Welles was livid. Borie, he snapped, was a "nonentity." Even Borie admitted that he was "only a figurehead" and told his friends that Grant intended that the Navy Department be "managed by Admiral Porter," who moved from Annapolis to Washington soon after the inauguration. Borie went home to Philadelphia while Porter, as stubborn and intemperate as ever, announced his determination to change American naval policy overnight and settle some old scores as well.[10]

Within a few weeks, Porter had issued forty-five general orders, the most important bearing on the questions of steam and the related dispute between the staff and line officers. The admiral confided to a friend that he intended to make the engineers "the most inferior corps in the Navy" by throwing "them so clear overboard that there won't be enough of them left to tell the tale." Porter first rescinded part of an order issued by Gideon Welles giving staff officers all the privileges of assimilated rank. Next, he copied a long-standing British practice by directing that "all vessels . . . be fitted with full-sail power" and that ships "provided with full-sail power should not use their steam except under the most urgent circumstances." And finally, Porter turned on Commodore Benjamin

Isherwood and replaced him as chief of the Bureau of Steam Engineering with Isherwood's archrival, Captain James W. King. Isherwood was exiled to Mare Island Navy Yard in California.[11]

Isherwood's engineers reacted with alacrity, besieging Grant and Borie with their complaints. They had powerful political allies, including John Roach, a corrupt Chester, Pennsylvania, shipbuilder who was closely associated with Isherwood. Borie, distraught by the snarling feud, caused a small scandal by getting drunk during a June Week ball at the Naval Academy in 1869. Within days he resigned from the cabinet. Grant was persuaded by Senator Alexander G. Cattell of New Jersey to name his business partner, George M. Robeson, as Borie's replacement. In return, Robeson awarded the Cattell brothers several lucrative contracts for supplies and equipment. Over the next seven years the secretary received nearly $300,000 in bribes.[12]

Secretary Robeson wisely avoided the ongoing quarrel between the staff and the line, rescinding Porter's writ and naming him to head a powerless Board of Inspection and Survey. Welles' friends told him that Porter had been relegated to the status of an unwelcome "intruder in the Department" who no longer exercised power. Porter reacted by organizing the line officers into the Naval Association, but within a few years he recognized that this group's exclusiveness was retarding its growth. He then persuaded the members to disband the organization and establish a successor, the Naval Institute, whose membership was not restricted to line officers and whose purpose was to be to spread professional and scientific knowledge throughout the Navy. For six years after its founding in 1873, the Naval Institute expanded gradually, establishing chapters at most naval stations and yards, sponsoring monthly meetings in Annapolis where its members read papers, and publishing some of these presentations on an irregular schedule in the journal *Proceedings*. In 1879, Lieutenant Commander Allen D. Brown convinced Porter and the rest of the Institute's trustees to award an annual gold medal and a cash honorarium for the year's prize essay as an incentive to more writing on naval affairs, and soon Commanders Alfred Thayer Mahan and William T. Sampson arranged for the regular quarterly publication of *Proceedings*. The journal was now to disseminate news and views on naval issues and provide a forum, beyond control of the Navy Department, where questions of naval policy, strategy, and tactics might be debated.[13]

When Porter was evicted from the Navy Department in 1869, he left behind a shipbuilding program in shambles. In one of his first major steps, Robeson in September of that year appointed Rear Admiral Louis Goldsborough to chair a special Board on Steam Machinery to investigate Isherwood's *Wampanoag*. Designed and laid down in 1863 as a fast cruiser whose mission was to hunt down the swiftest enemy commerce raiders, she was completed after the war and in 1868 underwent sea trials during which she made 16.7 knots in rough water and set a world record. She was the apogee of American steam technology, the fruit of the application of all of Isherwood's great talent, and the pride of the Corps of Engineers. A "faultless" vessel was her captain's description, and he drove her to a speed record as the "fastest in the world" that was unsurpassed for nearly two decades.[14]

At the altar of speed, however, Isherwood had sacrificed armor, firepower, and spaces for stores, munitions, and the crew. The steam plant alone weighed almost 1,200 tons, almost one-third of the ship's total displacement of 4,215 tons, and it took up 175 feet of the *Wampanoag*'s 355-foot length. She burned 6.25 tons of coal each hour at top speed, but her small bunkers did not hold much coal so her cruising radius was short. These deficiencies assumed a peculiar importance given the station-cruising mission of the Reconstruction Fleet, and the Goldsborough board's highly critical report ultimately led to her decommissioning. Ironically, during the remaining seven years of Navy Secretary Robeson's tenure, the staff engineers seemed firmly ascendant. At his behest, in 1871 Congress raised the relative rank of staff officers up to the grade of captain, curtailed the authority of executive officers over the staff, and equalized the precedence between the staff and line. The line fought back. In addition to cataloging the faults of the *Wampanoag*, Goldsborough complained about the "lamentable" condition of the Navy, which he asserted was "really a consequence of the present bureau system."[15]

Robeson's decision to overhaul most of the monitors imperiled every other shipbuilding proposal over the next decade. Because of the costs of this effort, few new vessels were laid down between 1865 and 1881 and Congress was willing to authorize the construction of only ten vessels for the fleet. Repairs to the *Tennessee* alone cost $1.8 million over ten years, and during Grant's presidency the Bureau of Construction and Repair spent over $6 million annually, most of it on Robeson's "great repair" policy. A decision in 1873 to replace the monitors' wooden parts with iron parts greatly increased the already high costs of this program. On the other hand, overall manning levels remained fairly constant, with naval personnel in the 1870s hovering around 9,000 officers and men; and because of the monitor overhaul program the Navy yards remained quite active.[16]

Although Robeson was committed to repairing the monitors, he was not totally against new construction, and proposed in 1870 to lay down an experimental seagoing monitor with twin turrets, full-sail rigging, and a pair of 15-inch smoothbores. When the British sailing monitor *Captain* capsized, his plan was cut short. Robeson then turned back to the general principles of the over-haul scheme and started an expensive program to completely re-build several of the seagoing ironclads with iron hulls. Despite this reactionary line, Robeson was willing to countenance an occa-sional experiment, as evidenced by his request to Congress to lay down a pair of small iron-plated torpedo boats. These boats were authorized in March 1871 and commissioned three years later.

The experimental 4,215-ton screw-frigate *Wampanoag* was commissioned in September 1867. She served as the flagship of the North Atlantic Fleet in 1868, but the following year the Goldsborough Board found her unfit for duty and she was laid up in ordinary.

Admiral John Rodgers, commander of ...estern Flotilla, 1861, and of the Asiatic ...dron, 1872.

And, despite his coolness toward Porter, Robeson agreed to ask Congress to authorize the construction of the experimental 173-foot, 800-ton torpedo boat-ram *Alarm*, which was built from plans prepared by the admiral.

Robeson soon became one of the main targets of Grant's many opponents, who correctly accused his administration of being corrupt. In February 1872 editor Charles Dana of the *New York Sun* published a series of articles accusing Robeson of graft and bribery, and minority Democrats and dissident Republicans on the Hill forced the House to conduct an investigation of the charges and moved once again to slash naval appropriations. Congress backed down after Grant was reelected that November, however, and Robeson remained in office throughout Grant's trouble-ridden second term. Robeson's acrimonious relations with the Hill meant that, when the British commissioned the *Devastation*, the world's first true battleship, and the other European naval powers followed suit, Congress was in no mood to adopt a capital ship policy. In spite of Robeson's problems with Congress, he was a crafty politician who manipulated the overhaul program to keep Navy yards busy with Republican workers during local, state, and national elections. His stockpiling policy also kept Navy storehouses and depots full of material purchased from firms that contributed to friendly Republican candidates.

Grant was little interested in naval policy, which Robeson managed, or in foreign affairs, which was mostly left to his cautious secretary of state, former New York Governor Hamilton Fish. Instinctive expansionists, neither Grant nor Fish possessed Seward's strategic vision or his political sagacity, and Grant was easily influenced by speculators and an odd assortment of private advisers. He was intent on acquiring a naval base in the Caribbean, but his maladroit diplomacy led to a series of misadventures in that important region. Although Grant discarded Seward's plan to buy the Danish Virgin Islands, he embraced the former secretary's scheme to annex the Dominican Republic, despite the decisive defeat in Congress in 1869 of two resolutions to lease a site on the Bay of Samaná. Without enthusiasm Fish negotiated a treaty of annexation later that year with Santo Domingo, but this diplomacy won little public support and became a casualty of a bitter feud between Grant and Charles Sumner, the leading Radical Republican in the Senate.

Grant's interest in acquiring naval bases in the Caribbean was stimulated in part by the outbreak of the first Cuban civil war, which had erupted in 1868 when the Spanish captain-general in Havana refused to implement political and economic reforms demanded by a revolutionary government in Madrid. By the early spring of the following year, the eastern half of the island was held by a rebel army led by General Thomas Jordan, an American adventurer whose troops were armed by gunrunners paid by Cuban agents in New Orleans and New York. Determined to put down the Cuban revolution, the Spanish rejected overtures for mediation from General Sickles, the American minister in Madrid, instead proclaiming a naval blockade around Cuba, deploying several cruisers to the Caribbean, and acquiring a flotilla of thirty small Ericsson steam gunboats from an American shipyard.

Americans sympathized with the Cuban rebels. In August 1869 Grant instructed Secretary Fish to recognize the rebels, and Navy Secretary Robeson ordered a detachment of six vessels from the North Atlantic Squadron to Cuban waters, a force that was soon strengthened by the arrival of five more ships. Robeson sent several screw-frigates and sloops into the yards for repairs, and forty-four rotting monitors were readied for operations, but it was nonetheless evident that the fleet lacked enough seagoing vessels to operate against the Spanish Navy. For this and other reasons Fish was not eager to confront Spain, so he persuaded Grant to reverse course and convince Congress to defeat a bill recognizing the rebel Cuban belligerency in 1870. He also rejected Sickles' scheme to resurrect the Ostend Manifesto with its demand that Spain sell Cuba to the United States. On the other hand, Fish strongly protested Spain's declaration that her forces in Cuba would subject rebel gunrunners to the death penalty for piracy, since the State Department knew that most of these men were Americans.[17]

For three years, while the Spanish flotilla tried unsuccessfully to enforce its blockade of Cuba, the U.S. Navy's new Caribbean Squadron was diverted to deal with another crisis in Panama. A few ships remained off Cuba to prevent filibusters from landing, to prevent the Cuban rebels from illegally using the American flag, and to check any attempt by the Spanish to seize American flag vessels in international waters. One of the more active gunrunners was the fast paddlewheel steamer *Virginius*, a former Confederate blockade runner, which had repeatedly evaded Spanish and American patrols and delivered several loads of arms to the rebels in Cuba. Then, in late 1873 her captain, Joseph Fry, brought her into Kingston, Jamaica, for urgent repairs. Carrying another cargo of munitions, Fry was eighteen miles off Cuba on 31 October when the *Virginius* was sighted by the Spanish cruiser *Tornado*. The Spaniard gave chase and Fry made for Jamaica, but the *Virginius* was overhauled after an eight-hour run less than twenty miles off Kingston. She was boarded, taken over, and escorted back to Santiago the next day. After quick, drumhead trials by a Spanish maritime court, Fry and thirty-six of his men were shot on 7 November and another fifty-one sailors were condemned to death—in spite of the loud objections of the American vice consul, who was forced to remain in his office to avoid anti-American rioters in the streets.[18]

Word of the executions reached Jamaica within days. British Commodore A. C. de Horsey dispatched the *Niote*, which arrived in Santiago soon after and threatened to bombard the city if another American prisoner was shot. A few days later, Commander William B. Cushing in the *Wyoming* steamed through the narrow channel into Santiago harbor, his guns run out and his men at action stations. "If you intend to shoot any more of the *Virginius* prisoners," he told a Spanish official, then "you would better first have the women and children removed from Santiago as I shall bombard the town." The reaction in the United States to this latest Spanish outrage was instantaneous. There were anti-Spanish rallies in cities from Boston to New Orleans, several Congressmen called for an invasion of Cuba, and Sickles urged Grant to ask Congress to declare war. Although Fish questioned Robeson's assurances that the Navy was prepared to fight Spain, Grant directed that every ship be assembled off Key West as soon as possible. If the Spanish had killed Fry and his men illegally, the *New York Times* editorialized, then "there will be nothing left . . . but to declare war."[19]

The 1873 Key West concentration was a haphazard affair. Despite tension with Spain over Cuba since 1869, the Navy had made no plans to employ the fleet to pressure Madrid or to defeat the Spanish in the event of war. There were no storehouses at Key West, nor any stores. Nonetheless, on 8 December, Robeson instructed "all the ships of the various squadrons to rendezvous at Key West." Admiral Porter and the fleet remained there for several weeks and conducted slow-paced evolutions. "Moving at a rate of four and a half knots," observed Commodore Foxhall Parker, Porter's chief of staff, "the vessels before us were in no respect worthy of a great nation" nor sufficiently powerful to successfully contest the Caribbean with even the decrepit Spanish fleet. "The authorities in Washington allowed the foreign attachés to come and inspect us, and report our warlike condition," Lieutenant Robley D. Evans recalled. "We were dreadfully mortified over it all."[20]

Grant told Robeson at the height of the crisis that he would ask Congress for extra funds to pay for the fleet concentration; a supplemental appropriation of $4 million was passed later that year, although Robeson argued that the real cost exceeded $5 million. The armored vessels were in such poor shape that Congress earmarked $900,000 for their "reconstruction." Rather than devising a new building plan, however, Robeson applied these windfalls to the "great repair" policy, selecting the seagoing monitor *Puritan* and the four *Miantonomah*-class seagoing monitors for conversion. Because of Robeson's quarrels with Congress, work was suspended again in 1876. When at last the *Puritan* was launched in 1882, she displaced 6,060 tons; still incomplete, she did not enter the fleet for another fourteen years. Congress also reacted to the deteriorating condition of the fleet on the eve of the *Virginius* affair by authorizing the construction of seven small 650-ton steam vessels and the 2,300-ton wooden sail-and-steam frigate *Trenton*. Completed in 1876, the *Trenton* was a floating compromise between the press of new technology and the more traditional needs of the station squadrons. Robeson was unenthusiastic about these projects, however; his heart was devoted to the monitor overhaul program. "Every ship built, rebuilt, or substantially repaired" since the Civil War had been done "by me," he boasted in 1882. In short, during Robeson's tenure the weakened sword of the fleet acted as a brake on a more forward American foreign policy.[21]

Already alarmed by the lack of preparedness, Fish now learned to his consternation that the *Virginius*'s American registry was probably illegal, a discovery that undercut the technical side of his case against Spain. Moreover, the U.S. economy was in the grip of the disastrous Panic of 1873, a calamity that overshadowed every other partisan consideration. Possessing little leverage, Fish nonetheless sent an ultimatum to Spain, demanding an end to the killings, punishment of the bloodthirsty Santiago commander, an apology, and reparations. Fish had overestimated Spanish power and ignored the utter destitution of Spanish politics, and his diplomacy received powerful support from the British, whose ambassador in Madrid warned the Spanish about the dangers of provoking the hotheaded Americans. Spain hastily agreed to all of Fish's terms except the apology, a small matter that was soon forgotten. In defending the settlement on 5 January 1874, Grant admitted that the *Virginius* had illegally flown the American flag, although he held the Spanish reaction to be morally wrong and politically intolerable.

The immediate crisis evaporated, but the Cuban revolution became more violent. Rear Admiral A. C. Case held "united fleet" maneuvers off Key West later that year, and in 1875 another incident forced the nagging issue to the fore. Robeson orchestrated another fleet concentration off Port Royal, South Carolina, and recalled a number of ships from their stations in Europe and South America. Neither Fish nor Grant wanted to go to war with Spain over Cuba, however, and Fish now proposed that Europe put pressure on Madrid to end the fighting. Grant's opponents leaped on this seeming violation of the Monroe Doctrine, but

Fish's diplomacy came to naught. The Great Powers were loathe to get involved in the confusing conflict. Thereafter, Spanish blockade operations were more restrained, and the civil war ended with a truce in 1878. The most important outcome of the *Virginius* affair was that it illustrated the Navy's decay and the difficulty of establishing American hegemony in the Caribbean without a battle fleet that could wrest those waters from one of Europe's smaller navies.

On the other hand, the Navy's primary postwar mission was not to operate against first- or second-rank maritime powers, but to protect and promote commerce by its constant presence on the periphery of Eurasia and in Latin America. Station squadron commanders of the postwar Navy did not generate proposals to reconfigure the fleet; rather, this impulse came mostly from officers who were more influenced by the political and diplomatic temperatures of Washington or the capitals of Europe, or by exposure to new technologies. On distant station, presence and trade defense required dispersion, mobility, and endurance. To exert power on distant station the level of force did not have to be great to be sufficient. And while the 1873 concentration crisis worried some, the Navy's condition perfectly fit the needs of a traditional American foreign policy.[22]

Grant had picked up some of the threads of Seward's Caribbean policy, but his administration was far less interested in developing American maritime trade or increasing the Navy's presence in the Pacific. The vastness of this area of operations explained the size and prestige of the powerful Asiatic Squadron, which Rear Admiral Stephen C. Rowan was named to command in 1867. He supported a more vigorous policy to defend American interests in China, and in 1870 arranged for the steam sloop *Alaska* to make the first passage by an American warship 600 miles up the Yangtze River to Hankow. This trip, and irregular patrols upriver over the next twenty years, were made to reinforce the squadron's right to free navigation on China's inland rivers, a right first articulated in the 1858 Treaty of Tientsin.

However, Rowan's major problem involved relations with the Hermit Kingdom of Korea, a sometime Chinese tributary, which had for centuries followed a policy of absolute exclusion from international intercourse. A handful of French Roman Catholic missionaries had landed in Korea a few years earlier, but the king in Seoul went along with nationalist pressure behind an antiforeign campaign that ended with the execution of nine priests in 1866. Details of this atrocity reached the West from the survivors of the shipwrecked American merchantman *Surprise,* who had been saved by the Koreans and made their way back to the safety of China's treaty ports. Expecting similarly benign treatment, the merchant schooner *General Sherman* made her way up the Taedong River with the help of the tides in September 1866, intending to trade in Pyongyang and defying orders posted along the riverbanks to leave. When the Taedong fell, the ship was stranded. The Koreans sent out fire rafts to burn her and massacred the crew while they were swimming ashore.

To avenge their dead countrymen, a French squadron blockaded the mouth of the Han River leading up to Seoul, but the Korean Army repulsed an attack on Kanghwa Island at the mouth of the river and forced the invaders to withdraw. In 1868, Commander John Febiger sailed to the peninsula in the screw-sloop *Shenandoah,* in an attempt to learn about the fate of the American crew of the *General Sherman,* but he was simply ignored. Korean opinions of the West were also colored by the antics of Ernest Offert, a German soldier of fortune, who planned to steal relics from the imperial tomb and ransom them for an agreement to trade with the Europeans. Although his gang failed to break into the temple, Offert told the court about his plan anyway, thus confirming the Korean view that Westerners were dangerous barbarians indeed.

Although Febiger reported that the American merchantman deserved its fate, Admiral Rowan at first was inclined to try to "open" Korea to American trade. He was dissuaded by George F. Seward, the consul in Shanghai, who doubted that there was any market for American goods on the impoverished peninsula. Rear Admiral John Rodgers, who replaced Rowan two years later, was more determined. At the very least, he told Secretary Robeson, he intended to "secure the right of having an agent in Korea to superintend events." Secretary Fish agreed, and a month later the State Department sent a copy of Perry's Treaty of Kanagawa to Frederick C. Low, the American minister to China, along with instructions to negotiate a similar agreement with the Koreans. Rodgers was to support Low's mission with a "display of force." Unfortunately, Low and Rodgers never really decided whether their purpose was to punish the Koreans for the *General Sherman* affair or appease them in the hope of negotiating a trade treaty.[23]

With Low, and five shipwrecked Koreans whom he intended

to repatriate, Rodgers in the screw-frigate *Colorado* sailed from Nagasaki in May 1871. "If we do not succeed now," he worried, then "some other power . . . will probably be more fortunate." A few days later, the squadron closed on Inchon. There Low parlayed with some minor Korean officials, explained his mission, and outlined Rodgers' plan to send the iron-sidewheel gunboat *Monocacy*, the iron tug *Palos*, and some steam launches up the Han River to survey the approaches to Seoul. On 1 June, these vessels steamed in front of a fort on Kanghwa Island. Without warning, the Korean battery erupted with volleys of quick but poorly directed fire. The Americans responded with a shelling so effective that the Koreans had to flee from the fort, but during the action a strong current threw the *Monocacy* onto a rock in the channel and the steam launches soon ran out of ammunition, so the Americans had to withdraw.

After the survey group returned to its anchorage, Rodgers and Low agreed that American prestige throughout Asia might suffer unless the squadron mounted a punitive operation. Rodgers issued an ultimatum, giving the Koreans ten days to apologize. Meanwhile, the *Monocacy* was repaired and a plan of battle was drafted. Though the Korean king had notes posted ashore denying responsibility for the attack, he nonetheless reaffirmed his policy of isolation and rejected any further talks. At 1130 on 10 June 1971, the *Monocacy* and the *Palos* opened fire on Kanghwa Island while Commander L. A. Kimberly's landing party of 650 sailors and Marines in small boats were towed toward the shore. The gunboats made slow progress against the swift current, however, and the landing party was inadvertently put ashore on a mud flat beneath one of the forts. "It was too late in the day to attempt a further advance into a country wholly unknown," recalled Lieutenant Commander Winfield S. Schley, the landing force adjutant. The next morning the Marines led the way in bitter fighting up to the citadel, supported by the *Monocacy*'s smoothbores. Eleven Americans died before the stronghold fell, but Schley reckoned that the Koreans lost about 350 of 5,000 men defending the forts.

Rodgers held Kanghwa Island overnight, but he began to withdraw on the 12th. Although Schley claimed that "the object of the expedition had been fully accomplished and the insult to the flag had been avenged," Korea's king rejected Low's final note. Rodgers had failed to "open" Korea to American shipping, but his punitive operation possibly prevented similar attacks on American merchants or ships of the scattered Asiatic Squadron elsewhere in the Far East. On the other hand, the incident caused the Koreans, who were well aware of the humiliations inflicted by the West on China and Japan over the past few decades, to resolve to avoid any entanglement with and subordination to Western naval powers. There was, therefore, some irony in the fact that the other "power" that Rodgers believed would inevitably follow the American lead was Japan. In 1876, a joint Japanese force arrived off the Korean Peninsula and compelled the king to sign a trade treaty.[24]

Rodgers' failure to open Korea to American diplomacy and trade symbolized the missed opportunities of the entire Grant administration, which was at the time seriously discredited at home by scandals that racked the country up to the eve of the elections of 1876. Navy Secretary Robeson, one of the Democrats' favorite targets, was subjected to four partisan investigations in the 1870s, which thoroughly undermined public confidence not only in his secretaryship but also in the Navy itself. In January 1876 Congressman Washington Whitthorne, the Democratic chairman of the House Naval Affairs Committee, attempted to impeach Robeson for accepting bribes, and during the presidential election campaign later that year the Democrats charged that the recent fleet concentrations were evidence that Robeson was mismanaging the Navy. These charges, with the Democrats' promises to end the Republicans' corruption and economize, made the condition of the Navy a public issue for the first time in a decade.

The public's cynical attitude toward the Navy was not reversed by the controversial, hotly contested 1876 election, which brought to the White House Rutherford B. Hayes, an Ohio Republican who was untainted by the Grant administration's scandals. His interest in naval affairs was confined to an attempt to lower the dinning level of public uproar about Robeson's corrupt practices. The lame-duck Democrats on the Hill were furious over the "stolen election," and Congressman Whitthorne introduced a bill in March 1877 to reorganize the Navy Department along lines suggested by Porter. Days later, he again arranged for naval appropriations to be slashed to a new postwar low. Later that year Senator John Sherman even suggested that the Navy become a subordinate bureau of the War Department, then being run by his brother, General William T. Sherman. Furthermore, a disastrous downturn in the business cycle struck with the Panic of 1877, and falling federal revenues increased the burden of servicing the seemingly large postwar national debt. The Democratic majority in the House in 1879 advanced a new fiscal policy of retrenchment and allowed postwar Navy appropriations to reach another low-water mark.

This general line of policy was etched deeply in thinking on Capitol Hill. Republican Senator George S. Boutwell, for example, argued that the country was territorially impregnable against any foreign enemy and that naval appropriations were wasted "except as such are necessary for coast defenses" built around floating bat-teries supported by "torpedoes and steam-rams." He believed that mines had reached a technical state of "such perfection . . . that there is not a navy on the face of the earth which could enter a harbor that is protected by these modern inventions." Even the classic argument in favor of a strong Navy—trade defense—no longer seemed terribly important. The United States had been one of the world's great shipping powers before the Panic of 1857, but the size of the American merchant marine had fallen so dra-matically that twenty years later it included only 15 of 300 steamships engaged in the Atlantic and Pacific transoceanic trade. Although publicist Jerrod Kelley was arguing that naval expansion was needed to stimulate the rebirth of the maritime industry, few politicians during Reconstruction accepted this sophistry owing to the dazzling growth of the industrial economy and the increase of the export trade in grains and other agricultural commodities.[25]

Because of the willingness of successive Republican adminis-trations to enforce maritime access overseas, it was also clear that the level of naval defense of trade had far less to do with the health of the shipping industry in an era of laissez faire than did the iron laws of supply and demand. Turning to coastal defense, Boutwell opposed the expense on the grounds that "the pre-eminence" of American economic power was extraordinary and "so valuable is it a market for the products of the world, that we can command our rights by withdrawing our diplomatic representative from any country on the face of the earth." With little opposition from the administration, Boutwell's general stance prevailed. From 1877 to 1881 Congress authorized no new shipbuilding, and neither Hayes nor his Navy secretary, Richard Thompson, seemed overly concerned about changing this policy. Frauds, political jobbery, and indifference had left the Navy in a "deplorable condition," lamented Commander Alfred Thayer Mahan.[26]

Secretary Thompson knew little about naval affairs, but he was an experienced, honest Indiana Republican workhorse who understood that he had to disassociate the Navy from Robeson's corruption and improve the department's management. He assembled a policy board consisting of the bureau chiefs and met with it weekly, but while this greatly improved management it left no important legacy. He reorganized the yards in a vain attempt to root out inefficiency and corruption. When Congress alleged fraud at the Philadelphia Navy Yard on iron contracts for the reconstruction of the 3,265-ton ironclad monitor *Puritan*, Thompson assigned an ad hoc board to investigate the charges. Designed by John Ericsson and laid down in 1864, she was incomplete when the war ended the following year and work on her was suspended. When work resumed on the rotting ship under Robeson's "great repair" policy in 1874, her hull was found to be so badly deteriorated that the contractor, shipbuilder Roach, designed and laid down an entirely new 6,060-ton vessel bearing little resemblance to her predecessor. Because of Robeson's quarrels with Congress, however, work on the seagoing monitor was suspended two years later; she was not launched until 1882 and did not enter the fleet until 1896. This scandal further discredited the Navy. Thompson thoroughly disapproved of Robeson's policy of using appropriations intended for repairs to rebuild ships from the keel up, but because he continued Robeson's aggressive overhaul policy he was forced to resort to this fiscal vehicle by 1880 to complete several of the smaller steamers that Robeson had ordered. Thompson also moved the Navy Department from its temporary Civil War quarters to the new State-War-Navy Building next to the White House on Pennsylvania Avenue. Unfortunately, his new proximity to the president did nothing to enhance his minuscule influence with Hayes.

Thompson reasoned that unless he could clean up the corruption, Congress would not modernize the fleet. He largely succeeded in keeping the Navy free of scandal during his tenure in office, but he was weighed down by the burden of the past, his deference to Congress, and a conviction that any plans to modernize the Navy had to come from the Hill. A Massachusetts Republican, Congressman Benjamin Harris of the House Naval Affairs Committee, took the lead in 1878 by introducing a bill to establish an annual $3 million appropriation for new construction. The measure provided for the sale of older vessels, stipulated that the proceeds be invested in new shipbuilding, and directed the secretary to appoint a board of line officers chaired by Admiral Porter to administer the fund. The Democrats, who controlled the House, voted down Harris' bill, however, and Congressman Whitthorne ordered his Naval Affairs Committee to launch another highly publicized investigation into Robeson's contracts. The result of this furor was to focus public attention once again on the condition of the fleet, and two liberal New York newspapers even called for rebuilding the Navy, but the issue was so charged with partisan politics that nothing was done. The Republicans won control of the House in November 1878 and passed the Harris bill in 1879, but the Senate's Democratic majority, not wanting their opponents to take credit for rebuilding the Navy in the upcoming presidential elections and concerned that it would expand Republican patronage, voted it down.[27]

Hayes' conservative naval policy was mirrored by his consistent disinterest in foreign affairs, a reactionary view Thompson never overtly challenged. Thus, it was only on the grounds of expanding American exports after the Panic of 1877 that Captain Robert Shufeldt was able to convince Thompson to give him command of the *Ticonderoga* and allow him to circumnavigate the globe on a voyage to investigate the status and potential for American trade in Africa, South Asia, and the Far East. Overseas trade required "the constant protection of the flag and gun," declared Shufeldt, who trumpeted the fleet not only as the protector but also the "pioneer of commerce." Bypassing Europe, Shufeldt shaped course for Africa in November 1878 to visit the American protectorate of Liberia, where he tried but ultimately failed to settle an arcane border dispute with British officials in the neighboring colony of Sierra Leone.[28]

The crew was rested on the island of St. Helena during July 1879, then Shufeldt sailed around the Cape of Good Hope and into the Indian Ocean. He visited ports along the eastern coast of Africa before making for the Red Sea and the British naval base at Aden. From this southern anchorage, the Royal Navy controlled the route north to the Red Sea and the new Suez Canal beyond, as well as the approaches to the Persian Gulf. "The ubiquitous gunboat is the real exponent of British Naval Power on all distant seas," he reported. "It is inexpensive to build and economical to commission, yet it flies the flag, carries the gun, and conveys the idea of power on ordinary occasions as effectively as its larger consort." Shufeldt found that Britain's imperial writ held sway west of Singapore, but to the east in Asia lay unexploited opportunities, not only for American commerce and influence but also for Shufeldt's career. In the great Western contest for power in China, Japan, and Korea, Robert Shufeldt saw a level field and fortune beckoning.[29]

Chapter Twenty-one
The Birth of the Steel Navy
1881–1889

President Hayes refused renomination in 1880, so the Republicans picked another "dark horse," Congressman James A. Garfield of Ohio. Garfield defeated General Winfield Scott Hancock, the Democratic candidate, in a landslide. By the time Garfield took office in 1881, manufacturing and, to a lesser extent, agriculture were on the rebound from the Panic of 1877, trade was improving, and tariff receipts were rising. From 1881 to 1890 the federal government enjoyed an annual surplus of $100 million. Republicans favored high tariffs to protect domestic manufacturers, not to raise revenue, and so, for the first time in many years, the cost of rebuilding the Navy did not bother Congress overly much.

Foreign policy considerations played their part in moving the Republicans to adopt a vigorous program of naval expansion. The War of the Pacific between Peru and Chile, which broke out in 1879 and lasted five years, saw both belligerents deploy British-built cruisers more powerful than any in the U.S. Navy. This raised the question of how the United States was to uphold the Monroe Doctrine and defend its trade and other interests if its fleet was outgunned by South America's lesser naval powers.

Garfield paid off his political debts by naming as secretary of state the leader of the Halfbreed faction of the Republican Party, Governor James G. Blaine of Maine. The new president tried to appease the South by appointing William H. Hunt, a Louisiana Unionist, as his secretary of the Navy. Hunt initiated a round of

policy conferences between influential legislators and naval officers, and quickly was persuaded that the fleet was so decrepit that
"unless some action be had in its behalf it must soon dwindle into
insignificance." Part of the problem was that neither Robeson nor
Thompson, his immediate predecessors, was able to forge a consensus within the Navy on a shipbuilding program, and this inertia allowed Congress to avoid the issue. Hunt sought some common ground, finding that naval officers and Congressmen both
generally agreed that the backbone of the new fleet should consist of metal-hulled steam cruisers designed for coastal defense,
peacetime overseas cruising, and wartime commerce raiding.
These meetings created bonds of mutual concern and were one
of the two important legacies of Hunt's brief tenure.[1]

Hunt's second legacy was a proposal to create the Office of
Naval Intelligence, which was finally established in the Bureau of
Navigation in 1882. ONI's function was to send naval attachés
abroad to collect information about foreign fleets, naval policy,
technology, strategy, and tactics. Navy officers had traveled to Europe occasionally over the past fifty years to investigate specific
questions, but the creation of ONI regularized the flow of information and expanded and directed its dissemination. Hunt hardly had time to get a grip on the Navy's problems, however, when
Charles J. Guiteau, a rejected Republican placeseeker, went
berserk and assassinated President Garfield.

Blaine, Garfield's secretary of state, focused on Latin American affairs, attempting to fashion a vigorous long-term policy designed to squeeze British influence from the hemisphere. To consolidate Latin America behind Washington, Blaine persuaded the
president to sign invitations to a hemispheric conference in Washington. However, the plan collapsed in November 1881 when the
new president, Chester A. Arthur, asserted his authority by replacing Blaine, Hunt, and the rest of Garfield's cabinet with his
own appointees. During his brief tenure as secretary of state,
Blaine had also outlined a vague but ambitious policy of commercial expansion in the Pacific and the Far East, where the perils of piracy, storms, and pandemics still raised havoc with American maritime commerce and its guardians, the Asiatic Squadron.
Typhoons and cholera were ever-present visitors on distant station
during the Gilded Age. Of five ships deployed to the Far East in
1877, Rear Admiral Thomas Patterson reported that only one was
suitable for extended cruising. Patterson based his squadron in

the Japanese port of Yokohama and sent ships out in patrols to hunt down and turn back steamers and large junks carrying illegal Chinese "coolie" immigrants to Hawaii and San Francisco, where there was an insatiable demand for unskilled labor to work on the transcontinental railroads.[2]

In April 1880, the Asiatic Squadron was joined by Captain Robert Shufeldt in the *Ticonderoga*, then on the last leg of her historic circumnavigation of the globe. Shufeldt's mission was to investigate the political economy of Africa, the Arabian Peninsula, the Persian Gulf, Southeast Asia, and the Far East. Shufeldt, im-

Rear Admiral Alfred Thayer Mahan, historian and president of the Naval War College, 1886–89 and 1892–93.

U.S. Naval Institute

pressed by the mercantile power of the British and French empires along the maritime belt from Africa to the Malay Peninsula, did not believe that American influence could penetrate the surface of imperial power there. He entertained far greater hopes for American prospects in East Asia. At the very least, he told Washington, none of the Great Powers had cornered these markets for which successive secretaries of state had had such high expectations.

To the orders he had written for himself before his departure, Shufeldt had appended an instruction that his command visit Korea and try to establish trade relations between the Hermit kingdom and the United States. When Shufeldt arrived in the Far East, he concocted a scheme that gave him a powerful ulterior motive to fulfill this mission. First, he would need to win flag rank by being named to the command of the Asiatic Squadron. Second, he intended to offer his services to Peking in the lucrative post of "Admiral in Chief to the Emperor of China and the Son of Heaven." While the Chinese and Russians jostled for control over Korea, Shufeldt used the Japanese to try to open up secret talks with the Korean emperor in Seoul, but this ploy failed. Shufeldt was then ordered to return home, and the *Ticonderoga* sailed for Mare Island Shipyard in San Francisco Bay in late 1881.[3]

Shufeldt returned to Washington soon after Blaine, his good friend, took over the State Department. Shufeldt still wanted to negotiate a trade treaty with the Koreans, command the Asiatic Squadron, and loot the Chinese Navy. Back in Washington in 1881, he found in ONI the aegis for his scheme. Blaine persuaded Hunt to appoint Shufeldt as the first American naval attaché to China, and in the spring of 1882 Shufeldt used friendly Chinese intermediaries to deal with the Koreans while he drafted his own treaty, which included an exchange of diplomats, a tariff agreement, and most-favored-nation status for the United States. The single point of contention was whether the United States would recognize China's suzerainty over Korea. The Chinese demanded that the treaty contain a provision acknowledging this ancient relationship, but the Japanese opposed it. Korean attitudes toward the West had changed markedly since the *General Sherman* affair of 1866 and the 1871 Low-Rodgers mission, as a result of dramatic changes in Northeast Asia's balance of power. Russia's expansionism, Japan's new muscularity, and China's attempt to reassert her hegemony on the peninsula now made the Koreans eager to acquire more outside contacts, although they were anxious not to of-

fend any of their powerful neighbors. In addition to this compli-
cation, there were the usual clouds of suspicion created by the
diplomatic maneuvers of the envoys of the Great Powers. Shufeldt
arranged for a secret meeting to deal directly with the Koreans,
and in early May he boarded the *Swatara*, which stood out of the
Chinese port of Chefoo in a fog so dense it masked her movements
from British, German, and Japanese observers.[4]

Slowed by the bad weather, Shufeldt did not reach the Korean port of Chemulpo until 14 May 1882, when his Chinese escort
was joined by a lone, wary Japanese gunboat. One week later, he
signed the Treaty of Chemulpo, which opened Korea to Western
trade but left unanswered Korea's fate in the looming struggle between Japan and China. Shufeldt's achievement was extraordinary. So was his anguish when he learned that William E. Chandler, whom Arthur had appointed secretary of the Navy in late
1881, had ordered him "summarily relieved" for critical comments
written about Chinese officials in a letter to a friend, who had foolishly let a newspaper reporter read the admiral's correspondence.
Ironically, Chandler had more important work for Shufeldt.

Chester Arthur disliked the vigor but not all the substance of
Blaine's active foreign policy. He also understood the need to increase the size of the fleet. No European power posed a threat to
American home territory, but American trade with Europe, Latin
America, and Asia was an important element of the gross national product and coastal defense still remained as powerful a public
argument for naval expansion as did trade protection. Indeed,
Commodore William G. Temple argued that any new shipbuilding program should consist of monitors, rams, and torpedo craft
to reinforce the Army's coastal fortifications and defend harbors,
bays, and inlets. "There should be so many of them, that in spite
of any possible destruction of them by the enemy, some one
should be sure to get his ram or torpedo under the bottom of each
[enemy] iron clad, and wipe them all out of existence in a single
day or night." The Navy could not ignore that the station
squadrons needed vessels to defend overseas trade and enforce
American foreign policy, although few in the 1880s predicted that
within a decade the United States would require a battle fleet to
establish American naval dominance in the Western Hemisphere.
Viewed as a national institution, the Navy in 1881 was an embar-
rassment. Navy yards were cesspools of unregenerate corruption,
most crews were dominated by foreign nationals, and many offi-

cers were superannuated figures who languished for years without promotions and demonstrated a notable lack of competence. So much old material had been piled up, Secretary Hunt complained that "it encumbers the wharves and grounds of our navy-yards, and presents an unsightly appearance sometimes ghastly and discouraging to those whose labors are to be performed near it." Much like repairing a statue or public building, reconstructing the Navy was viewed by many as part of governmental housekeeping.[5]

Before leaving office, Hunt named an advisory board chaired by Rear Admiral John Rodgers to draft plans for a new shipbuilding program. The Rodgers Board first met on 28 June 1881 to consider three different proposals, and it quickly took up one to build new cruisers. Rodgers was strongly influenced by Chief Engineer Benjamin Isherwood, who prevailed on his colleagues first to fix the speed of each new vessel and then to establish the other characteristics. For the new cruisers, the board agreed on a sustained speed of 15 knots. A predicate of this decision was that the cruiser would be employed in wartime for commerce raiding and would not confront battleships in fleet actions. The cruisers would be steam driven but would still need "full sail power," observed Commander Robley D. Evans, "because we have no coaling stations abroad." Rodgers then turned to the question of iron or steel for the hull. Isherwood and the other engineers and the naval constructor favored iron; all the line officers, excepting Rodgers, voted for steel because it would save weight, strengthen the hull, and reduce the chance for major damage from grounding or collisions.[6]

Rodgers rejected a plan to build a class of heavy 5,000-ton armored cruisers on the grounds that "in time of peace iron-clads were not necessary for carrying on the work of the United States Navy" and because American industry was unable to roll steel for larger caliber guns. "We should not buy our guns abroad, but should make them ourselves," he declared in June 1881. Another plan, this one to lay down a fleet of oceangoing marine rams, was vigorously advanced by Rear Admiral Daniel Ammen, a respected figure, but Rodgers reasoned that the ram was useless as a station ship and might easily be a casualty of long-range gunfire on the open seas. After deliberating for five months, the Rodgers Board finally reached a compromise that reflected the tensions between the operational needs of the station squadrons and the visionary Navy of the technical bureaus. Rodgers' plan asked Congress for appropriations to repair existing wooden-hulled ships and for the construction of two new steel cruisers. Each of these 2,500- to 3,000-ton vessels was to be equipped with "full sail power and full steam power." Rodgers understood that Congress was clearly ready for a new naval shipbuilding plan, although the Democrats, led by Congressman Whitthorne, were effectively holding up passage of the Harris Bill, which provided for a fund for new construction, because they feared that the Republicans would take credit for rebuilding the Navy in the upcoming midterm elections.[7]

The result of this partisan squabble was that naval expansion was momentarily stalled on the Hill when William Chandler became secretary of the Navy in 1882. A seasoned New Hampshire Republican, he gave shape to Arthur's determination to rebuild the Navy and laid down two related lines of policy. He asked Congress to limit expenditures for the repair of older ships, in spite of opposition from the administration's supporters who wanted to be able to dispense shipyard work to their partisans. Although the 1883 Pendleton Act put the Navy's white-collar employees under the protection of the new nonpartisan Civil Service Commission, shipyard workers were not covered by this early Progressive measure. Most Reconstruction and Gilded Age politicians considered the yards to be hiring halls for party loyalists, and repairing older vessels kept the yards busy. Chandler complained in 1884 that this meant that the "ships have been made to drag out a protracted existence for the benefit of the yards." The minority Democrats used delaying tactics to hold up an appropriation for the new ships in Congress in early 1882, but ex-Secretary George Robeson, now a New Jersey Congressman, came to the Navy's rescue. To the Democrats' dismay, he attached to a regular appropriation measure the Harris Bill, which funded the two cruisers and added monies to construct five of his beloved double-turreted monitors, and he persuaded Congress to enact the entire package on 7 August. This act also empowered the Navy's Survey and Inspection Board to prune the fleet and prohibited the Navy from spending more to repair a vessel than 30 percent of the contemporary cost of the same new ship. This move, paradoxically, led both to a reduction in the number of ships in the fleet and to pressure on Congress to build even more new ships. Moving swiftly, Chandler's Survey and Inspection Board condemned forty-four ships, about one-third of the number on the Navy list.[8]

Chandler was by now distrustful of the material bureaus, and he ignored them by naming another advisory board headed by Rear Admiral Shufeldt to design the two new cruisers and super-intend their construction. Shufeldt's writ was indeed even stronger than it first appeared to be. With Chandler's blessing, Shufeldt rewrote the Rodgers Board's plan, proposing instead on 3 March 1883 that four new armored cruisers and a steam dispatch boat be laid down. Although the November 1882 elections had re-turned a Democratic majority to Congress, there was still time in March 1883 for the lame-duck Republican majority to enact the Shufeldt Board report and authorize construction of the White Squadron, consisting of the 4,500-ton protected cruiser *Chicago*, the 3,189-ton protected cruisers *Atlanta* and *Boston*, and the 1,500-ton dispatch boat *Dolphin*. Although these ABCD ships were to be midwives to the use of new steel technology, the bureaus felt that the very existence of the Shufeldt Board was anathema, for its ex-traordinary charter challenged their status as the repositories of technical expertise. Captains T. D. Wilson, William Shock, and Montgomery Sicard, the respective chiefs of the Bureaus of Con-struction, Steam Engineering, and Ordnance, tried to undermine the new building program by preparing plans for the new cruisers at a pace that was, at best, glacial. Not only did they resent the Rodgers Board's supervisory authority, but they also intended to thwart Chandler's policy of building the new ships in privately owned yards.

Chandler was determined to launch one of the cruisers in time for the 1884 presidential election, but his plan went awry. Working from incomplete, deliberately incorrect blueprints pre-pared by the bureaus, shipbuilder John Roach turned in the low bid for one of the four vessels. The source of many of Robeson's woes, Roach had for many years contributed to Chandler's politi-cal campaigns, and his business partner was the powerful New York merchant banker J. P. Morgan. While in office Chandler re-ceived thousands from Roach, and Roach was paid back when Chandler awarded all four contracts to his firm. However, Roach's corruption and lack of technical expertise caused a political scan-dal when the program got mired in cost overruns. When Roach prepared to turn over the *Dolphin* to the Navy in June 1885, she was declared unfit for service. Chandler's ill-advised decision to award all the contracts to Roach backfired on the Republicans, dosed the Democrats' charges of corruption and mismanagement, and played an important role in the election of 1884. Amidst this uproar, little was said about the strategic deployment of the new cruisers in peace or war or about their tactical employment, but enough questions were raised to cause Chandler to initiate a search for some answers. The White Squadron was "fitted for general service," he announced. At the same time, he put reformers and traditionalists alike on notice that American naval policy "is not now, and never has been . . . to maintain a fleet able at any time to cope on equal terms with the foremost European armaments." Not until the 1890s would an administration consciously adopt a European benchmark as a standard for American naval policy.[9]

How to operate the White Squadron was a vexing question, one Chandler thought might be answered when he approved a plan crafted by Commodore Stephen B. Luce to found the Naval War College in Newport, Rhode Island. Its purpose was to derive "fundamental principles" of warfare "of general application on land or sea" and to study and teach "the evolution of strategic principles based on naval engagements of the past." After Luce settled in Newport and signed a lease for an abandoned poorhouse, he selected for his faculty Captain Alfred Thayer Mahan, a malcontent at sea who had already written one book on naval operations during the Civil War; James Russell Soley, a history professor at the Naval Academy; and Tasker H. Bliss, an Army artillery lieutenant. Luce hoped that their studies might overcome "the crass ignorance of naval officers" and the "imbecility of our Navy Department" about strategy and operations. "It must strike anyone who thinks about it as extraordinary that we members of a profession of arms should never have undertaken the study of our real business." Neither these comments nor the general plan to divert, even temporarily, the best naval officers from sea duty to academics ashore won the Naval War College many friends among the bureau chiefs. The school's existence over the next decade was precarious, being assured only by its obscurity and by several powerful patrons.[10]

Chandler also tried to increase public support for the Navy and shrewdly exploited the tremendous interest in the tragic *Jeannette* expedition to publicize the peacetime, nonmilitary value of the fleet. Lieutenant A. W. Greely of the Army Signal Corps and a twenty-five-man exploring party had been transported by the steamer *Jeannette* to Lady Franklin Bay, Grinnell Land, north of

Greenland. They established a base camp in 1881 and made arrangements to pick up food and other supplies the following summer. As a result of stupidity and misfortune, the rations and gear were never delivered, and rumors about the gruesome fate of Greely's explorers started to filter back to the American press. When Democrats on the Hill began blaming the War Department for the fiasco, Chandler volunteered to organize a Navy rescue mission.

U.S. Navy Department

Rear Admiral Stephen B. Luce was founder and president of the Naval War College, 1884–86, and commander of the North Atlantic Squadron, 1886–89.

He persuaded Congress to pass a supplemental appropriation for the Navy to acquire, refit, and commission the large whalers *Thetis* and *Bear* and to put into commission the rugged steamer *Alert*, which the British offered as a gift in a gesture of transatlantic support. Amidst considerable fanfare, Commander

,189-ton, steel-hulled cruiser *Atlanta*, one of the three "ABC" cruisers, served in the Squadron olution in 1889–90.

The *Texas*, the U.S. Navy's first coastwise battleship, c. 1896.

U.S. Navy Department

Winfield Scott Schley's three-ship rescue squadron stood out of New York on 1 May 1884 and sailed for Newfoundland, north to Greenland, across Baffin Bay, and into the ice pack, which was at the time just starting to open. He made Cape Sabine on 22 June and there found Greely and seven of his crew, emaciated but still alive. Schley soon discovered that they had survived only by eating the flesh of their dead comrades. He was alert to the consternation that news of this cannibalism would provoke, so he carefully concealed the existing evidence, kept his men and the survivors quiet, and orchestrated a triumphal arrival in New York, which was presided over by President Arthur. The rescue of the *Jeannette* survivors immeasurably boosted the Navy's prestige. "The American heart was thrilled as it had not been since Richmond fell," editorialized the *United Service Magazine*.[11]

Schley's dramatic accomplishment notwithstanding, once the Democrats took control of Congress in March 1883 they rejected Chandler's requests for more new shipbuilding. The following year Arthur bowed out and the Republicans turned to Blaine as their presidential candidate. The Democrats chose New York Governor Grover Cleveland, who tarred the Republicans with charges of graft and corruption and frequently cited the example of Roach's contracts as evidence of his charges. The Republicans claimed credit for naval expansion, but the corruption charge stuck and Cleveland won at the polls by a close margin, the first Democratic president since the Civil War. In March 1885, the Democratic majority in the House passed a naval authorization bill that resumed construction of the steel navy and authorized building the unprotected cruisers *Newark* and *Charleston* and two other vessels.

To run the Navy Department, Cleveland named William C. Whitney, a New York banker, who declared that the administration was committed to continuing the general building policy laid down by Chandler. The United States "had no vessel . . . which could have kept the sea for one week as against any first-rate power," he claimed in March 1885, charging that this was the result of Robeson's policy of lavishly repairing older hulls, which had cost $75 million since the Civil War. Moreover, "the yards have been nests to hold lazy heelers . . . of the Republican party." Congress approved Whitney's request for a cap of 20 percent of original cost on all overhauls, and this virtually assured that the entire fleet would have to be rebuilt over the next decade.[12]

Intent on discrediting his Republican predecessors, Whitney dedicated himself to John Roach's ruination. He brought in his own accountant to investigate Chandler's shipbuilding fund, launched yet another investigation of Roach's business practices, and convinced the attorney general to invalidate Roach's existing Navy contracts. Whitney refused to accept delivery of the dispatch boat *Dolphin* and, when more defects were discovered in the White Squadron cruisers, ordered the bureaus to take over and complete the construction of these ships. Roach, the nation's largest shipbuilder, was forced to declare bankruptcy. Assuming that the Navy yards were sinkholes of Republican jobbery, Whitney tightened accounting procedures and ordered an inventory of equipment stored in Navy depots. The inventory uncovered $1 million of rotting clothes and enough canvas to rig the entire British fleet. No new contracts were let until 1887, by which time Whitney had decided to use the shipbuilding program to create Democratic allies in the private shipyards.

Whitney's short-term goal was to tar the Republicans, bankrupt Roach, and arrange for the Democrats to take credit for enlarging the Navy, but his policy clearly illustrated that both parties were now firmly committed to naval expansion. Aware that one reason for the delay in completing the White Squadron cruisers was that Roach had to use the Navy's experimental plans, Whitney decided to purchase European designs for his new ships. In December 1885, Congressman Hilary Herbert, an Alabama Democrat who chaired the House Naval Affairs Committee, introduced a bill to build ten new ships and finish the double-turreted monitors. A House-Senate compromise reduced the number of ships to four, but Whitney prevailed in subsequent years. Thus, during Cleveland's first term, thirty ships totaling over 100,000 tons were laid down, including six monitors, one more unprotected light cruiser, six armored cruisers, and the second-class coastal battleships *Texas* and *Maine*. Although these vessels were called battleships, the decision to build them did not represent a determination to erect a battle line, for each ship was expected to fulfill more than one tactical mission. The 7,000-ton *Maine*, for example, carried only four 10-inch guns and did not possess the endurance to fight in an overseas fleet action or to serve as the flagship for a distant station squadron. The battleship *Texas* marked a real milestone in the evolution of the steel Navy, however. A double-bottomed vessel that made 16 knots, she had her guns distributed over two decks and she was the first American warship since the original *Monitor* to be equipped with gun turrets. The 5,800-ton protected cruiser *Olympia* made 21 knots, and her main battery had four 8-inch guns.

The increasing range of naval guns exposed the vulnerability of the nation's coastal defenses, an argument raised by an important 1885 ONI report on naval tactics written by Commander William Bainbridge-Hoff. He pointed out that new naval guns capable of firing 10,000 yards would revise fleet tactics and necessitate overhauling coastal defenses since ships carrying these guns would be immune to existing shore batteries and might be defeated only by "a fleet designed for coastal defense"—heavy cruisers and fast patrol boats bearing automotive torpedoes. Bainbridge-Hoff's findings influenced the joint Army-Navy Endicott Board, which recommended in 1886 that the Army arm its coastal forts with new all-steel, high-velocity long-range guns and that the Navy build heavy gun barges for harbor defense. When asked about this by Congress, however, Navy men defended the second-class battleship as a better means to defend the coast and as a useful instrument for the trade defense on distant stations. The latter was especially important, and Whitney in his 1887 annual report argued that the fleet existed "largely for the purpose of protecting the mercantile marine and assisting its healthy development."[13]

More than partisan politics and strategic uncertainty slowed new shipbuilding. In 1886 the Democrats passed an act stipulating that shipbuilders were to use only materials of "domestic manufacture." Such a policy fell in line with the national consensus favoring protectionism, and bespoke an uneasiness over importing fabricated steel from potential international rivals in Europe. On the other hand, Andrew Carnegie and other steel makers took years to build the plants to manufacture the quality of armor that the Navy Department needed. Nevertheless Congress, determined to have national control over the suppliers of the "new Navy," in 1886 established the Naval Gun Factory at the Washington Navy Yard, a site that had not been used for shipbuilding since 1825 and had been thereafter mostly dedicated to the manufacture of other naval equipment.

Although Cleveland pursued an ambitious policy of naval expansion, foreign policy under Secretary of State Thomas Bayard lacked much cohesion or strategic synthesis. This became evident during the Samoan crisis. Lieutenant Charles Wilkes' Exploring

Expedition had visited the Samoan Islands in 1838, and the usefulness of establishing an American base there became evident
during the Civil War, when the Union fleet encountered difficulties pursuing the Confederate raider *Shenandoah.* After the war Seward announced that he intended to acquire a coaling station in
the islands. The need for some American position in the South Pacific was also underscored by the completion of the transcontinental railroad, which brought increased trade between California and the British colonies of Australia and New Zealand. Of the
fourteen Samoan Islands, Savaii, Upolu, and Tutuila were the
largest, and before the Civil War American merchantmen had discovered an excellent harbor at Pago Pago on Tutuila. A San Francisco firm bought a large tract of land from the natives to construct a coaling station in 1868. American political influence in
the islands increased, and four years later President Grant dispatched Commander R. W. Meade in the *Narragansett* into the
South Pacific with orders to negotiate a treaty with Samoa giving
the United States exclusive rights to a naval station. Meade arrived
at Pago Pago in February 1872, remained there for nearly a
month, surveyed the harbor, and signed a treaty with the local
chief giving the United States "exclusive" rights to establish a
"naval station" in return for American "friendship and protection"
of the Samoans. Meade's treaty was rejected by the Senate, however, owing both to the ambiguous nature of the defense provisions and to a personal quarrel between the president and Senator Charles Sumner, the stubborn chairman of the Foreign
Relations Committee.[14]

Grant refused to give up. In 1874 he sent another envoy to
the islands to acquire a site for a naval base, but the diplomat became entangled in tribal politics and wound up for a time as the
premier of the islands! Two years later, Chief Le Mamea came to
Washington from Samoa to negotiate yet another treaty, giving the
United States the right to erect a coaling station at Pago Pago in
return for a promise to mediate disputes between the rival tribes,
or between the natives and other Western powers. Although this
time the treaty was approved on the technical grounds that it did
not confer a protectorate over the natives, in practice it obligated
the United States to defend the Samoans on Tutuila against European incursions.

The problem of European intervention in Samoa arose after
the Great Powers met at the Congress of Berlin of 1878. There, in

complex negotiations, the British wound up supporting the demands of Hamburg shipping interests that they be granted rights to Apia harbor. The following year, both Britain and Germany coerced the Samoans into signing treaties granting them rights to construct coaling stations in the islands. The resulting turmoil was exacerbated both by local tribal rivalries and by the zealotry of the German, British, and American consuls assigned to defend their respective national interests in the islands. One visitor, English author Robert Louis Stevenson, recorded in 1889 that there was "a new conspiracy every day" against the fragile native regime.[15]

Secretary of State Bayard was so concerned in 1887 that he called a conference in Washington with the British and German ambassadors to discuss the Samoan tangle, but they could find no common ground between the Anglo-German demand for partition of the islands and the American insistence that they be allowed to remain independent. To strengthen their position, the Germans deployed a squadron composed of the two gunboats and a corvette to the islands. Once these ships appeared on the scene, the Germans engineered a coup and installed their own client on the throne. In response, the ousted pro-American king armed his supporters and, in December 1888, they ambushed and killed some German sailors from a nearby gunboat. In retaliation, the pro-German king declared martial law, and the German gunboats shelled the rebels' villages.

American reaction was vigorous. The screw-steamer *Nipsic* had already reached Samoan waters in November, and on 13 January 1889 Rear Admiral Lewis A. Kimberly, commander of the Asiatic Squadron, sailed for the islands in the light frigate *Trenton*. The rebuilt screw-steamer *Vandalia* rendezvoused with the Asiatic Squadron in Apia harbor on 22 February. Cleveland had recently tangled with Berlin over an unrelated tariff issue, so he was already annoyed with the Germans. He signed a measure hastily enacted by Congress authorizing Kimberly to pay $500,000 to purchase 121 acres of land for a coaling station at Pago Pago and an appropriation of $100,000 for the Navy to develop the harbor. A minor war scare gripped the country, with the *New York World* expressing the hope that "the presence of this small fleet will have the effect of cooling the hostile officers of the German gunboats."[16]

Bismarck, the German chancellor, did not take the matter so seriously, however. Concerned exclusively about Europe's balance of power, he was using German colonial and naval policy to gather middle-class electoral support for his Junker regime, not as a vehicle to increase Germany's influence overseas. He invited London and Washington to send delegates to another conference in Berlin to settle the matter, and this offer was accepted by the new Harrison administration on 14 March 1889. Two days later, however, a violent hurricane swept over the Samoan islands. The British warship *Caliope* steamed out of poorly protected Apia harbor and rode out the storm at sea, but the winds and swells sank two of the German gunboats and ran the German corvette aground. At the peak of the storm, the *Trenton* and the *Vandalia* "settled to their gundecks," while the *Nipsic* was saved only by the decision of Commander D. W. Mullan to run her up on the beach. Both the German and American squadrons suffered great loss of life, and, according to Admiral Kimberly, the Americans were now left with "almost no . . . warships worthy of the name in the Pacific Ocean."[17]

This great tragedy put the affair of Samoa into perspective, and the *New York World* was now reminding its readers that "the awful devastation wrought in the harbor of Apia makes our recent quarrel with Germany appear petty and unnatural." The *New York Times* commented, "Serious as that disaster is, it is slight compared to what might have resulted from keeping up the absurd fiction that we have Samoan 'interests' that need looking after." Once the Germans and British adopted this viewpoint, then Secretary of State Blaine's continued rejection of partition left them with no alternative but to agree to a tripartite condominium over the islands and the restoration of the legitimate pro-American monarchy, an arrangement finalized in Berlin on 14 June 1889. Despite this harmonious outcome, three-power rule failed to suppress tribal hatreds and commercial rivalries in Samoa during the next decade. Meanwhile, the Democrats attacked Harrison for undermining Samoan independence and the Republicans moved toward a policy of partition. In the aftermath of the Spanish-American War in 1898, President McKinley negotiated a second treaty with Germany, which gave Berlin sovereignty over the larger Savaii and Upolu islands and allowed the Navy to take over all the lesser islands, including Tutuila. Seward's vision of an American maritime empire in the Pacific was beginning to take shape.[18]

Chapter Twenty-two

Great Power Status and the Battleship Fleet
1889–1897

The Democrats renominated Cleveland by acclamation in 1888, and when James G. Blaine of Maine decided not to run, the Republicans chose Indiana's Benjamin Harrison, a corporate attorney and grandson of President William Henry Harrison. Despite winning a slim majority of the popular vote, Cleveland lost in the Electoral College. The Republicans, who tended to favor naval expansion more than the Democrats, also won control of both houses of Congress. Intelligent but brittle, Harrison selected a talented cabinet, headed by Blaine at the State Department; Benjamin Tracy, a veteran New York politician, became secretary of the Navy. In response to Tracy's request, Congress in 1890 reestablished the assistant secretaryship of the Navy, a post that went to James Russell Soley, a distinguished professor from the Naval War College.

Tracy had no background in naval affairs, but he entered office firm in the conviction that Cleveland's hesitant foreign policy was inappropriate for a great power of the economic and political vigor of the United States. To correct this, Harrison and Tracy launched an aggressive drive to acquire overseas naval bases in the Caribbean and in the Pacific, and it was not long before Tracy clashed with Blaine, whose overriding concern was to achieve hemispheric solidarity. Tracy urged Blaine to purchase the Danish islands of St. Thomas and St. John, but Blaine demurred on the basis that while the islands "are destined to be ours" they

"should be among the last West Indies taken." Tracy then seconded a plan approved by Harrison to acquire a share with the French
of a new coaling station in the Portuguese Azores, but again Blaine
turned down the scheme.[1]

The issue of Caribbean naval bases also divided Blaine and
Tracy. Just before he left office in 1889, Cleveland had obtained
an option to acquire a naval base at Mole Saint Nicholas in Haiti.
The site had been offered by Florvil Hypolite, president of the provisional Haitian government, who needed American support and
arms shipments to defeat a rebel army led by his long-time rival,
François Legitime. The insurgents blockaded the Haitian coast,
but the American government favored Hypolite, and Rear Admiral Stephen B. Luce, who commanded the North Atlantic
Squadron, declared Legitime's blockade illegal and dispatched a
few ships to escort American merchantmen carrying munitions to
the government's army. After securing the option on Mole Saint
Nicholas, however, Cleveland had vacillated, and finally decided
to refuse to exercise American rights to the base. When the Republicans returned to the White House in 1889, Tracy urged Harrison and Blaine to acquire the Mole, and the president supported the Navy secretary's plan to take the initiative to resolve the
matter.

Eager to conclude a deal, Tracy sent the *Yantic* to survey Port
au Prince in December 1889 and instructed the new commander
of the North Atlantic Squadron, Rear Admiral Bancroft Gherardi,
to negotiate directly with Hypolite's government. These talks
stalled, however, when the presence of American warships in the
port stirred up nationalist resentment against the provisional cabinet. President Hypolite was worried about a renewed insurgency
by Legitime's gang. After a full year of twisted dealings, Gherardi's
patience was worn thin. Returning to Haiti in January 1891 in the
cruiser *Philadelphia*, he found Hypolite unwilling to sign the deed
unless his cohorts approved of the arrangement. Gherardi decided that a loud squadron gunnery practice in the harbor during
this debate would speed the deliberations of the Haitian cabinet,
and he asked Washington for permission to take the Mole by force
if Hypolite continued to deceive and delay. Tracy, who had el-
bowed Gherardi into adopting a more forward stance, sanctioned
this muscular attitude and diverted the new White Squadron cruisers to Haitian waters in April, when the crisis came to a climax. At
this juncture, Frederick Douglass, the American minister to Haiti,

The 10,288-ton *Indiana*, the U.S. Navy's first front-line, ocean-going battleship, was authorized in 1890 and completed five years later.

Benjamin F. Tracy, N
lawyer and Republican p
was secretary of the Navy,

convinced Blaine to accept Hypolite's rejection of the transfer, and Harrison and Tracy were compelled for the moment to accept Blaine's position.

If the administration could not acquire a naval base in Haiti, then Tracy wanted Blaine to take advantage of an offer made by the Dominican Republic tyrant Ulises Heureaux. He was offering to lease Samaná Bay to the United States in return for American military support in any "just war" with the neighboring government of Haiti. Blaine rejected these terms on the grounds that they would involve the United States in a series of endless Hispaniolian wars and that they violated the Jeffersonian doctrine against entangling alliances. Again frustrated with nostrums he thought to be outdated, Tracy sent Rear Admiral Gherardi in the *Philadelphia* to inspect Samaná Bay in 1891, but the cruiser's arrival stirred up local nationalism and Heureaux decided that he could not remain in power unless he withdrew his offer. In late 1891, after these bitter struggles, Tracy prevailed on Harrison to demand that Blaine adopt a stiffer line to serve America's expanding maritime needs, but Blaine's calculated lack of enthusiasm had already dealt a lethal blow to the president's naval-base policy. Furthermore, the administration was already busy dealing with the more immediate issues of Chile and Hawaiian annexation.[2]

Secretary Blaine wanted to conciliate Latin American nationalism and direct it against British imperialism to the advantage of the United States. The focus of much of his attention was Chile, a British client for many decades, where a civil war erupted in January 1890 between President J. M. Balmaceda and the Chilean Congress over an issue of domestic finance. The Army supported the president, but the Chilean Navy joined forces with the Congress to form a junta headed by the commander of the sea forces, Captain Jorge Montt. Washington inclined toward Balmaceda, but, above all, wanted to prevent European intervention in the conflict. Tracy sent Rear Admiral William P. McCann with units of the Pacific Squadron to cruise off the Chilean coast, protect American merchant shipping and citizens there, and report to Washington on the course of the war. McCann warned Tracy that Montt's rebels had won the first battle and would probably overthrow Balmaceda were they to acquire more arms from abroad. To this end, Montt had dispatched an agent to New York to meet with W. R. Grace, an influential shipping magnate. With Grace's help, the Chileans chartered the American schooner

Robert and Minnie, which was anchored in San Francisco Bay, and purchased 5,000 rifles and tons of bullets. Meanwhile, a Chilean merchantman, the *Itata*, steamed north from Iquique to San Diego. Then, in an odd turn of events, the plan came unglued when the local marshal discovered that the plotters were intending to smuggle arms out of the United States, a violation of federal antifilibustering laws. He boarded the *Itata* just in time to be taken prisoner when she sailed. The *Itata* rendezvoused with the *Robert and Minnie*, the arms were transferred to the larger vessel, the kidnapped marshal was put ashore, and the *Itata* shaped a course south for Chile.[3]

Harrison, who was then on the Pacific coast, telegraphed Washington with instructions that the Navy was "to recover possession of" the *Itata*. For his part, Tracy was anxious to act, not only because the *Itata* had been legally detained in San Diego but also because her arrival in Chile would work against American foreign policy. He assigned this mission to Commander George Remey, captain of the cruiser *Charleston*, who sped south from Mare Island to Acapulco Bay in search of the *Itata*. Meanwhile, Captain Montt instructed the modern Chilean cruiser *Esmeralda* to steam north at full speed to rendezvous with the *Itata* and escort her back to Chilean waters. The opposing cruisers met off the coast of Mexico. Awaiting the appearance of the *Itata*, the decks of both warships were cleared and the crews prepared for action once she arrived. They waited in vain, however. The *Itata* avoided the area completely, standing into Valparaíso a few days later with the *Charleston* in hot pursuit. Admiral McCann, who had tried to arrange a truce in the civil war before the rebels had defeated Balmaceda, now convinced Captain Montt to disavow the *Itata*'s actions and order her to transfer her munitions to an American ship and return to San Diego in company with the *Charleston*. A wave of emotional anti-Chilean outrage swept over the United States in reaction to the *Itata* affair, but Grace pointed out that the insurgents had already won the civil war, and this argument finally convinced Harrison to permit the *Itata*, minus her cargo, to return to Chile.

The *Itata* affair poisoned the well of good relations between Washington and the new government in Santiago. Then, in early October 1891, Balmaceda's cause collapsed when he took his own life, and Harrison recognized the rebel regime. The cruiser *Baltimore* had replaced the *Charleston* on station off Valparaíso and, although a series of minor incidents marred the summer months, by 25 September 1891 Commander Winfield Scott Schley told Washington that "the presence of a vessel is no longer demanded" because "everything [is] quiet." Tracy insisted nevertheless that she remain at Valparaíso, and when the crew learned that the ship would not be sailing soon, they began to demand some liberty.[4]

On the afternoon of 16 October, Schley relented and allowed some of his sailors to go ashore. Trusting them to avoid trouble, Schley neglected to make provisions for an adequate shore patrol to prevent any untoward incidents. Although the petty officers in town warned their men to be careful, and there were a number of signs suggesting that the local mob was lying in wait for them, the thirsty bluejackets still set out for the nearest bars. In the early evening, a fight broke out in the True Blue Saloon and the ensuing brawl spilled out onto the streets of Valparaíso. There, a mob of Chileans attacked the Americans, while the local constabulary watched approvingly. After two Americans were beaten to death, the police arrested thirty-six sailors, but released them the next day. Schley's cable reporting the riot at the True Blue Saloon hit Washington like an electric shock, and the entire country was soon caught up in a minor war scare. Plans were made for the body of one of the dead sailors, Boatswain's Mate C. W. Riggin, to lie in state in Independence Hall in Philadelphia. Captain Robley "Fighting Bob" Evans, who arrived in Valparaíso harbor shortly thereafter in the *Yorktown*, echoed public opinion when he asserted that Schley's men "went ashore . . . for the purpose of getting drunk . . . which they did on Chilean rum with good United States' money. When in this condition they were more entitled to protection than if they had been sober."[5]

Although Schley damaged his reputation by disingenuously asserting that his men had been sober, Tracy insisted that this point was not at issue. Sober or not, he argued, at least they deserved the protection of the Chilean police. Pressing this tough position, Tracy badgered Harrison into dispatching a stiff protest to Santiago, demanding both an apology and reparations. "We are on the verge of war here," British diplomat Cecil Spring-Rice reported to London, noting that "President and the Navy are bent on it." Secretary of State Blaine once again counseled restraint. Fearing for the future of "hemispheric solidarity," he engineered a series of delays in Washington that gave Montt's newly elected government time to take charge in Santiago.[6]

The Chileans, unaware of the uproar in Washington, gruffly rejected Harrison's first demand for reparations. This led the president to order Tracy to prepare for war and to ask Congress on 27 January 1892 to consider a declaration. Tracy purchased thousands of tons of extra coal from London, New York, and California, and made arrangements to transport it to Montevideo, Uruguay, which he intended to use as a coaling station for the fleet that was to be assembled under Rear Admiral Gherardi. "After the fleets concentrated," he wrote, "they were to proceed to Chile, drive the Chilean men-of-war under the guns of the fort in Valparaíso, then attack the whole coast of Chile." On the other hand, Tracy knew that the long sea line of communications from the Atlantic seaboard to the Pacific coast of Chile, the lack of an isthmian canal, and the danger that the Chileans might find allies among the other Latin American republics or in Europe meant that a protracted war with Chile might not be easily won. Tracy did not want war, believing that loud threats would be enough to force Chile to back down. Leaks to the press about the Navy's preparations reinforced reports reaching Santiago from Britain to the effect that Harrison was not bluffing. Five days after the president sent his blistering war message to Congress, Montt cabled his government's apology to Washington and offered to pay reparations. Although many credited Blaine's patience with averting war, Harrison's demands and Tracy's preparations were the real levers that forced Chile to reverse her position.[7]

Tracy achieved only mixed success, as the engineer of this more muscular naval diplomacy, but the occasional victories were more than overshadowed by the enactment of his legislative program. Some of Tracy's program was clearly influenced by the naval historian Alfred Thayer Mahan. Long ignored and near death, Admiral David Dixon Porter was still on active duty as head of the Board of Inspection and Survey when Tracy became secretary. Tracy asked for Porter's advice, and during the summer of 1889 the old admiral made suggestions that guided Tracy through the labyrinthine ways of naval politics. Porter also introduced Tracy to Captain Mahan. Mahan had taken over the presidency of the Naval War College after Luce went to sea in 1886, but he had been removed abruptly two years later and exiled to a ship in Puget Sound. Rear Admiral Francis Ramsay led the opposition to the War College and Mahan's studies, complaining that the school wasted needed space and offered no practical studies in its curriculum, and arguing that it should be moved to Annapolis as an appendage of the Naval Academy. These views were seconded by Captain Winfield Scott Schley, chief of the Bureau of Equipment. Mahan fought back, bypassing the chain of command and successfully persuading Porter, Luce, and others to prevail upon Secretary Tracy to allow him to return to Newport, a step Tracy took in August 1889. When Porter fell ill, Mahan became one of Tracy's main advisers. Mahan was by now convinced that "the outward aspirations of the United States will only be fulfilled by the Republicans."[8]

During his first term at the Naval War College, Mahan had lectured on his theory of "sea power," which he based on the experiences of the British fleet during the age of sail. Encouraged by Luce, he tried to categorize and codify the elements of maritime power, and in 1890 Little, Brown, and Company published his manuscript under the title *The Influence of Sea Power Upon History*. The "term 'sea power,' . . . was deliberately adopted by me to compel attention . . . and to receive currency," Mahan told his British publisher. "I deliberately discarded the adjective 'maritime,' being too smooth to arrest men's attention or stick in their minds." In arguing that "there are certain teachings in the school of history which remain constant, and being, therefore, of universal application, can be elevated to the rank of general principles," Mahan was adopting a line of reasoning advanced formerly by Luce, who believed that there were a number of "immutable" strategic principles that could guide the conduct of national security policy in peace and war. "How to view the lessons of the past so as to mold them into lessons for the future, under such differing conditions, is the nut I have to crack," he told a friend. While writing at Bar Harbor, Maine, in the summer of 1886, he found his answer.[9]

At home with the newly fashionable school of economic determinism, Mahan grounded his studies on a somewhat simplistic understanding of Adam Smith's *Wealth of Nations*, the bible of modern capitalism. He viewed statecraft and warfare mainly as a means to the end of economic security and prosperity, and assumed wrongly that an active foreign trade was essential to an industrialized nation's economic health. Maritime powers grew or declined in relation to their ability to exploit international trade, which was but one component of the greater synergism of "sea power." While he catalogued other parts of this concept, Mahan was mostly interested in the "military science" of naval policy and strategy and its application to the creation of "sea power." And, like most authors, Mahan wanted to sell books and earn money. Therefore, to make his highly technical manuscript "more popular" with the reading public, he added a preface to his War College lectures enumerating the characteristics of successful sea powers.[10]

Despite his economic orientation, Mahan proved himself to be a predecessor of Halford Mackinder and a later generation of geopolitical determinists when he compared nations whose "geographical position" was "directed upon the sea" with "a people one of whose boundaries is continental." Suggesting that "a country is in this like a fortress," he noted that the "extent of territory," or the size of the country, was a critical factor. Maritime empires also needed long coasts, secure harbors, and adequate rivers, a "physical conformation . . . upon which a healthy sea power depends." The size of the population was also important, since maritime powers needed a labor force "readily available for employment on shipboard and for the creation of naval material." Finally, peoples who exhibited an acquisitive "national character" and were blessed by "intelligent direction by a government fully imbued with the spirit of the people and conscious of its true general bent," would be successful imperial sea powers.[11]

In the first volume of *Influence*, Mahan explained the seventeenth- and eighteenth-century European wars for empire as efforts to acquire "command of the sea" and its seaborne trade. To accomplish this, a successful naval power concentrated its fleet and deployed it to destroy the enemy's navy, blockade his ports, and isolate and overrun his colonies. Rummaging over a century of British naval history, Mahan discovered that victory at sea was almost always won by a fleet of capital ships, maintained in peace and war, and strategically concentrated in combat against an enemy's main fleet. "A principle of ageless application," he wrote nearly twenty years later in an analysis of the Russo-Japanese War, "is the inexpediency, the terrible danger, of dividing the battle fleet, even in times of peace, into fractions individually smaller than those of a possible enemy."[12]

Mahan maintained that naval battles in the age of steam would be fought in much the same way as they had been during the age of sail—that is, according to the same immutable strategic or tactical principles—although somehow routines would change to fit new technology. For instance, the fore-and-aft gunfire arcs and the greater range of rifled guns meant that battleships would forswear the line ahead and adopt a line-abreast formation. Because the ram was slow and the torpedo had little endurance, Mahan believed them to be useless during high-speed, deep-water fleet engagements. The principle of strategic concentration of the battle fleet would always apply, and Mahan therefore argued that developing forces for commerce raiding or coastal defense wasted resources. "It is not the taking of individual ships or convoys . . . that strikes down the power of a nation; it is the possession of that overbearing power on the sea which . . . closes the byways by which commerce moves to and from the enemy's shores." Undergirding the deterrent of a fleet in peace, and enabling squadrons to concentrate in war, a network of overseas bases was essential to strategic success either in the age of sail or the age of steam.[13]

Mahan's theory of seapower informed a politics eager for intellectual justification. His book sold well in England, and its reception there reverberated back across the Atlantic. Within two years, Mahan was hailed as a formidable historian, one of a new and powerful generation of American intellectuals. The nation was searching for a new strategic role to play in the wider world, one that more closely comported with the reality of American economic might and political vitality than the accomplished goal of continentalism and the older, less relevant objective of maritime access. Mahan's greatest influence on American history was that he helped to persuade an entire generation that the United States should behave in the international arena much like the Great Powers of Europe. This was exactly what Mahan intended to do, and he confessed to a friend, Republican Congressman Henry Cabot Lodge of Massachusetts, that he planned "to make the experience of the past influence the opinions and shape the policy of the future."[14]

Mahan was heeded for the simple reason that he brought a vastly simplified history into line to support an easily understood naval policy. Navy Secretary Tracy used Mahan's architecture to defend specific foreign policy objectives and a practical shipbuilding program, first embodied in his 1890 annual report, a seminal document containing a proposal to lay down three *Indiana*-class battleships. Soon after taking office, Tracy had created three boards to examine naval strategy, material, and building policy. The Strategy Board was to consider deployments and missions for each squadron in the event of a war. The Material Board was merely a means by which Tracy could coordinate the work of the bureau chiefs, most of whom opposed the increasing influence of line officers over shipbuilding policy. The most important of the three boards was the Policy Board, chaired by Commodore McCann, who prepared a plan to build nearly 200 warships of all classes based around a force of battleships. Tying technology to strategy, McCann urged Tracy to lay down a battleship with an especially large coal bunker and a cruising radius of about 15,000 miles. The McCann Board's plan was attacked in the press as overly expensive and unnecessary, however.

The result was that Tracy's more modest program received a friendly reception on the Hill. He explained that he was adopting a very long-term goal of slowly building up an Atlantic Fleet of twelve battleships and a separate Pacific Fleet of eight battleships, both of which were to be supplemented eventually by sixty cruisers and twenty monitors. "Armored battleships," he insisted, would "raise blockades" off the American coast and "beat off the enemy's fleet on its approach," and he denigrated any continued reliance on cruisers with the assertion that commerce raiding in wartime would fail to "prevent a fleet of ironclads from shelling our cities." Nonetheless, he made a bow to the past with the concession that cruisers were still "essential adjuncts of an armored fleet."[15]

The strategic problem was outlined in the Naval Institute *Proceedings*' prize essay in 1889: "By building unarmored ships and arming them with heavy guns and torpedoes," the author asserted, the United States had tried to "grasp one horn of the dilemma while avoiding the other." Meanwhile, foreign armor had "grown thicker and thicker," and this trend would surely end "not in the abandonment of armor." A bill authorizing "sea-going, coastline battleships designed to carry the heaviest armor and most powerful ordnance . . . with a coal endurance of about five thousand knots" emerged from the House Naval Affairs Committee early in 1890. It was soon passed by both houses, then controlled by the first clear Republican majorities since Reconstruction. The Battleship Act of 1890 provided for the construction of the three 10,288-ton battleships *Indiana*, *Massachusetts*, and *Oregon*, which carried a mixed-caliber battery of four 13-inch slow-firing, breech-loading rifles in armored turrets at the bow and stern, eight 8-inch guns in four wing turrets, and four 6-inch guns in casemates. Capable of a top speed of 17 knots, the *Indiana* was protected by an armor belt of 18-inch face-hardened nickel steel and a 2.7-inch deck. The low freeboard, moderate speed, and fairly small coal bunkers meant that these *Indiana*-class ships embodied several strategic compromises, but they represented nonetheless a major step along the path toward the creation of a battle fleet.

The *Indianas* represented a step into the future of Great Power naval competition, but the 1890 Naval Act was also burdened by the Navy's commerce raiding tradition. This was illustrated by the authorization for the construction of the fast cruiser *Columbia*, a 7,375-ton ship designed with such massive coal bunkers that she could steam for more than 100 days over 25,000 miles at half speed. With a top speed of 22 knots, she was designed to hunt down enemy steamships and escape from the swiftest capital ship, and she carried two 6-inch guns, eight 4-inch guns, four torpedo tubes, and a single 8-inch gun aft to fend off pursuers during a stern chase. Tracy saw this as only the start, however. "Even when all the ships now authorized are completed," he told Congress the following year, the fleet would "not have a fighting chance against a respectable [attacking] fleet of foreign ironclads" owing to the length of the American coastline, the Navy's lack of offshore bases, and the vulnerability of the ports and harbors. "Nothing short of a force of battle ships, numerous enough to be distributed in the separate fields of attack and able to concentrate on any threatened point within their own field, will prove a complete protection."[16]

The attraction of America's traditional commerce-raiding strategy also explained the decision to commission the torpedo boat *Cushing* in 1890. For about ten years after the Civil War, Navy men believed the spar torpedo boat was a useful means of defending harbors and ports, and in July 1869 Navy Secretary Robeson leased Goat Island at Newport, Rhode Island, from the War Department and established the Navy's torpedo station there. Its mission was to follow European advancements in the field and develop weapons for deployment in the American fleet. Navy experts realized that the use of the spar torpedo almost invariably led to the suicidal destruction of the vessel bearing the weapon, but a solution to this problem was at hand. One year earlier a British factory manager, Robert Whitehead, had invented a self-propelled, automotive torpedo. Rear Admiral Charles Stedman observed a demonstration of the Whitehead automotive torpedo two years later in Europe and reported to Washington that it was likely to change the character of naval warfare. Five years after the White-head system was proved, the Navy purchased a slightly different Lay automotive torpedo, and Newport began to conduct experiments in its use. The spar torpedo system was doomed by the automotive torpedo, and the experimental *Lightning*, commissioned in 1876, was the last American torpedo boat to be armed with a spar.

During the 1880s Newport's engineers devised various ways to tow torpedoes and designed several steam launches to carry them, but this promising work received surprisingly little attention owing to the interest in the construction of the White Squadron. Many Navy officers viewed the problem of harbor defense as something of a misguided anachronism. "This country has been thus far absolutely without a successful automobile torpedo," complained Tracy in 1890, a deficiency he correctly argued "does not seem to have received the attention which its gravity demanded." Helped along by Tracy's prodding, a licensed self-propelled torpedo finally went into production later that year, although questions of how to employ it would still require years of debate and experimentation. Continued problems with torpedo manufacture culminated in the establishment of a Navy torpedo plant at Newport in 1907. This facility was not only to produce a steam torpedo under a British license but also to develop and test new models for the fleet. The work of conducting research was subordinated to production, however. The plant rapidly became a mainstay of the local economy and the manufacturing facility received the vigilant protection of Rhode Island's Congressional delegation.[17]

The impending marriage of the steam launch with the automotive torpedo posed a threat to capital ships and large cruisers that the Navy could not ignore. Large flotillas of small torpedo boats were a major feature of most European fleets by 1887. That year Congress authorized the Navy to purchase the wooden steam yacht *Stiletto* from the Herreshoff Manufacturing Company, and she was armed with an experimental automotive torpedo by the Newport station. The *Stiletto*'s sea trials led directly to the construction of the 105-ton steel-hulled torpedo boat *Cushing*, which had a top speed of 22.5 knots. Her entry into the fleet in 1890 provoked a new debate over the mission of the torpedo boat. Some officers argued that these small craft posed a deadly threat to enemy battleships or armored cruisers. To do this, however, a torpedo boat had to maneuver to within a striking range of about 600 yards from her target, a distance well within the range of accurate naval gunfire, fire her 28-knot torpedoes, and escape before being sunk by the opposing battery. To be successful against a cruiser or battleship, the torpedo boat had to have high speed and quick handling to reduce the time during which she would be under fire from the heavier vessel's rapid firing guns.

This worked perversely against building more endurance or range into the torpedo boat, and her short cruising radius led critics to assert that her most appropriate role was as adjunct to harbor or coastal fortifications. For the next decade, this issue was not resolved. The Navy laid down thirty-five torpedo boats over the next ten years, ranging in size from the 12-ton portable torpedo boat, which was carried on board a battleship, to the large 225-foot *Stringham*. To a naval power of the second rank, such as the United States, the construction of torpedo boats represented an attempt to overcome the supremacy of the British battleship fleet by technological leapfrogging.

The short cruising radius of its new torpedo boats and battleships renewed the Navy's interest in the issue of basing, a matter whose urgency was underlined by a study commissioned by Secretary Tracy in 1892 on comparative "Coaling, Docking, and Repair Facilities." The primary thesis of this report was that commerce raiding was not a sound naval strategy for the major maritime powers. For one thing, the speed of some of the newest coal-burning transatlantic merchantmen met or exceeded that of most American warships. In short, the prey might outrun the hunter. And, while coal-burning cruisers required frequent refueling, there were few overseas coaling stations that were not in foreign hands. This made little difference in peacetime to the station squadrons, but most neutral ports would be closed to American warships in wartime, thereby exposing the Navy's commerce raiders to enemy fleet operations. The importance of a naval basing policy was also highlighted by the sharp contrast between the lack of American overseas coaling stations and the global network of naval bases and coaling stations erected over the past several decades by the Royal Navy.[18]

The need for more coaling stations for the fleet and for American merchantmen had its most immediate effect on American policy in the Pacific. Indeed, the final initiative of the Harrison administration was an attempt to annex Hawaii, which Tracy wanted both for use as a commercial coaling station and as a naval base for the Pacific Squadron. Since President Pierce's attempt to annex the archipelago in 1854 had collapsed, the issue of Hawaii had become entangled with a rivalry between competing sugar producers in Louisiana and the islands. Although most Republicans favored closer American supervision of Hawaii than did the Democrats, Cleveland had extended the practical American protectorate over the islands in 1887 by acquiring an exclusive right to erect a naval station at the Pearl River harbor.

In 1889 when a native uprising against King Kalakaua, the hereditary monarch, moved him to accept an offer of assistance from the American minister in Honolulu, J. L. Stevens, the uneasy political relationship between the United States and Hawaii flared up. Stevens called upon a landing party from the *Adams* and later reported that the "appearance" of Marines and sailors in Honolulu during the crisis "had a favorable effect" in suppressing the armed challenge to the pro-American king. Kalakaua died shortly thereafter, however, and was succeeded by Queen Liliuokalani, who more resolutely opposed increasing American influence in the islands. After her coronation she dismissed her entire cabinet, then headed by Sanford Dole, a powerful pineapple magnate and an advocate of annexation. Since the McKinley Tariff of 1890 had resulted in a reduction in the price of sugar, many American planters in Hawaii favored annexation so that they could benefit from the federal subsidy for domestic sugar producers.[19]

Dole, with Stevens' help, now set in motion his plan to overthrow Liliuokalani. When the coup began on the morning of 27 January 1893, Stevens asked Captain G. C. Witse of the cruiser *Boston*, the flagship of the Pacific Squadron then riding at anchor in Pearl Harbor, to send a landing party ashore to keep order. After the queen was deposed and Dole's clique was in power, Stevens insisted that Witse place the new regime under American protection. Within a few weeks, Rear Admiral John S. Skerett reached Hawaii, assumed personal command of the Pacific Squadron, and surveyed the situation. He reported to Washington that the Dole government held power only because of American military support and could not survive a fair election. From Harrison's perspective this made all the more urgent the passage of legislation annexing Hawaii, but it was ammunition for those who condemned extraterritorial acquisitions on the basis of interest or principle. Stevens negotiated a treaty of annexation with Dole, and Harrison sent it to the Senate just before he left the White House. The Democrats strongly opposed the outgoing administration's annexationist policy, however, and prospects for the treaty were poor.

Harrison ran for a second term in 1892 but was defeated by former president Grover Cleveland, who entered the White House in March 1893. For his Navy secretary, Cleveland selected Alabama Congressman Hilary Herbert, who had served six years as chairman of the House Naval Affairs Committee. Herbert had originally opposed the construction of battleships but was now a convert to the cause of building a battle fleet. He brought in former Congressman William Gibbs McAdoo of New Jersey as assistant secretary and replaced many of the bureau chiefs, but he generally hewed to the naval policy originated by Harrison and Tracy.

Within months Herbert pledged "to increase both the number of battleships and torpedo boats" so that the fleet might be better prepared for "war-like operations," but the Panic of 1893 struck the economy, trade slackened, and federal revenues plunged. Cleveland adopted strong measures to restrain federal spending, and the battleship program fell victim to the ax of economy. Other factors set the stage for this decision. Most of the ships authorized under the Tracy program were not yet in commission, and the Navy had been jolted by several incidents suggesting that its leadership was grossly incompetent or crooked. Shortly after Herbert took office, the *New York Times* charged several admirals and captains with negligence or fraud in various matters, and these scandals were capped in February 1894 by a real tragedy. The old frigate *Kearsarge* struck a well-charted reef off the coast of Nicaragua and went down, an event whose symbolic implications transcended the instant disaster. Muckraking newspaper stories about this incident eroded public confidence in the Navy, and support on the Hill for new battleship construction collapsed.[20]

The political importance of the *Kearsarge* episode was magnified by the "armor scandal," which pitted the Navy Department against steel manufacturers and involved charges of price gouging and oligopoly. Tracy was benignly indifferent to price fixing by the "steel trust," firms dominated by industrialist Andrew Carnegie, and when Harrison was defeated, Tracy found work with Carnegie. Since the White Squadron had been laid down, the relationship between the Navy and the steel trust had developed into an alloy of mutual need and suspicion. Carnegie and his only rival,

Bethlehem Steel, both had invested huge sums to produce armor for naval shipbuilding, and most naval leaders agreed with the position taken by Captain William Sampson, the chief of the Bureau of Ordnance, that the domestic production of armaments was an essential component of national security policy. Through a system of Navy inspectors working in the steel plants, the material bureaus tried to enforce a rigid system of quality control in the face of industry demands for looser regulation. Sampson and other officers trusted this system, but they were always worried that it could be corrupted.[21]

An energetic manager, Herbert sidestepped the lingering, self-conscious feud between the staff and the line, and the handmaiden of this quarrel, reorganization of the Navy Department. But he took one step in early 1894 that led indirectly to the development of a war planning staff. He directed the Naval War College to prepare tactical war plans that the North Atlantic Squadron was to test during evolutions and maneuvers. This launched the War College annual war game of examining strategy, tactics, and new technologies in hypothetical combat simulations. The need to develop tactical and strategic doctrines was underscored by Herbert's most important policy decision: to abandon completely the armored cruiser program and dispense with the traditional naval strategies of wartime commerce raiding and coastal defense. Chandler's cruiser program, Herbert concluded, had provided enough ships to sustain the peacetime overseas station squadrons, but he was convinced that these vessels would be of limited "military value" in a fleet action as compared to the battleships that the Navy would need to challenge a major European power. For political convenience, however, Herbert cloaked the new strategy in the garb of tradition, defending the establishment of the battle fleet as a means to "protect our citizens in foreign lands" and "render efficient aid to our diplomacy."[22]

Democratic majorities in both houses of Congress, federal deficits due to the Panic of 1893, and the malodorous influence of the armor scandal conspired against Herbert's plan to resume battleship building that year. In December 1894, however, he persuaded Cleveland that naval shipbuilding might stimulate the economy and help drag the country out of the depression. Congressional Republicans were eager to support this policy, and Carnegie, J. P. Morgan, and the steel trust were not altogether without influence among the Democrats. Many politicians feared that the industrial shipbuilding complex developed over the past decade would rust or disintegrate unless new Navy projects kept it busy. In addition, an array of new foreign policy problems diverted attention from domestic issues and invited renewed awareness of national naval and military policy. In December 1894, Cleveland approved Herbert's request to Congress for funds to lay down three more battleships. Nevertheless, Congress remained uneasy about the establishment of a battle fleet, and a strong sentiment lingered on the Hill that the construction of a fleet of battleships would somehow entangle the United States in the European balance of power. The result of this political clash was a legislative compromise. The Democratic Congress went along with the administration in March 1895 and authorized the "sea-going, coast-line" battleships *Kearsarge* and *Kentucky*, six gunboats, and three torpedo boats.[23]

In December 1895, Herbert asked for three more *Kearsarge*-class battleships, but by that time the entire shipbuilding program was bogged down by strikes in the steel plants and disruption in the shipyards, precursors of the recurrent labor union troubles of the next century. In addition, naval policy began to take on a more partisan cast as the presidential elections neared. The Republicans, who now controlled the House, favored building four more battleships, but Senate Democrats would agree to lay down only two. The authorization bill was stalled by a few Populists led by South Carolina's Senator "Pitchfork" Ben Tillman. His rustic views on foreign policy and naval affairs were quaint, but his contrived opposition was soon overcome by Secretary Herbert's promise to refurbish the shabby Charleston Navy Yard. During the summer of 1896, Congress reached another compromise, authorizing the three battleships *Alabama, Illinois,* and *Wisconsin,* and another ten torpedo boats.

Although Cleveland supported moderate fleet expansion, he and his secretary of state, Richard Olney, enunciated a firm nonannexation foreign policy. Shortly after he took the oath, the president withdrew the Hawaiian annexation treaty from the Senate and invited former Queen Liliuokalani to visit Washington, where her plea for independence was met with sympathy. However, Cleveland was unwilling to move against the Dole republic, which Republicans in Congress supported and to which Cleveland reluctantly extended diplomatic recognition. With this move came a renewed American commitment to the traditional protectorate over the islands, and Secretary Herbert directed the Pacific Squadron to be prepared to prevent any foreign intervention in Hawaiian affairs.

Cleveland's hesitant foreign policy in the Pacific was mirrored by his inconsistent attitude during the Venezuelan frontier crisis, although the outcome was a positive step in the direction of enhanced American hegemony in the Western Hemisphere. The border in question was an area that divided British Guiana and Venezuela, and the quarrel was simmering even before the British Foreign Office in 1840 employed geographer Robert Schromburgk to elaborate its claim to the territory. To resolve the question, the British repeatedly proposed that Caracas accept the Schromburgk Line, but the Venezuelans consistently rejected this offer. Talks broke down after gold was discovered in the disputed area, and Venezuela severed diplomatic relations with Britain in 1887 to protest London's arrogance and to alert Washington to the need to back their claim. Interest in the issue in the United States was thereafter stimulated by the former American minister to Venezuela, William L. Scuggs, whose lobbying on behalf of Venezuela resulted in the passage by Congress in early 1895 of a resolution supporting arbitration of the question. The British, however, deemed this to be an unacceptable vehicle by which to reach a settlement.

Anti-British sentiment was soon fired up by the seizure of the Corinto, Nicaragua, customs house by a Royal Navy squadron sent there in April to protect British merchants from local hooligans and to collect overdue debts. Cleveland's Hawaiian policy, and his inability to reverse the course of the Panic of 1893, had already undercut his earlier popularity at home. Now he became the object of vicious partisan attacks on the grounds that he was allowing Britain to violate the Monroe Doctrine. "The support of the Monroe Doctrine should be established and at once—peacefully if we can, forcibly if we must," insisted Republican Senator Henry Cabot Lodge. Cleveland reacted by having Secretary of State Olney inform the British on 20 July 1895 that "the United States is practically sovereign on this continent, and its fiat is law" and demand that Britain accept American arbitration of the Venezuelan frontier question. Unhappy with this confrontation, the British prime minister, Lord Salisbury, ignored the degree of American determination behind what Cleveland called Olney's "twenty-inch gun note."[24]

When Salisbury missed Olney's deadline, Cleveland asked Congress to authorize him to appoint a boundary commission and impose its findings by force if Britain ignored or rejected them. The United States would "resist by every means" any British move to violate the Monroe Doctrine, he declared. "War If Necessary," headlined the *New York Sun* in early 1896. Indeed, Rear Admiral Gherardi at the Naval War College, angered by the lack of an operational plan during the Chilean crisis, was hard at work on a plan, later codenamed Red, outlining an American strategy for a war with Britain over the Monroe Doctrine. Gherardi's Red Plan articulated some assumptions widely held by Navy men about the need to develop supporting overseas coaling stations. Neither Cleveland nor Salisbury had really intended to allow the Venezuelan issue to push them this near to the brink, however, and Salisbury ultimately realized that the equation of power in the Caribbean now favored the United States and that his imperial policy of "splendid isolation" from Europe had left Britain without any continental allies. Germany was encouraging a rebellion against British rule among the Dutch Boers of South Africa at the time, and Canada was still utterly indefensible. These considerations led Salisbury to agree to American mediation in March 1896. A multinational commission was created the following year, and in 1899 it awarded a vital sector of Orinoco Basin to Venezuela. When pressed to act, Cleveland had staked out a strong position in support of an advanced concept of the Monroe Doctrine, a posture that enhanced the Great Powers' respect for the United States, although the lessons of this incident were ignored by at least one power of lesser rank, Spain.[25]

From John Adams to William Seward, most visionary American statesmen believed that Spain would someday quit Cuba and that the island would be absorbed by the United States. Despite the crises over the 1854 Ostend Manifesto and the 1873 *Virginius* affair, Spain held on while American resistance to overseas acquisitions became somewhat more rigid. However, the Wilson Sugar Tariff and the Panic of 1893 depressed the price of Cuban sugar from eight cents per pound to two, destroying Cuba's planters and its urban middle class and providing the spark to a rebellion against Spain's corrupt, inefficient military rulers. Guerrillas launched sporadic operations the following year, and on 9 February 1895 the patriots issued a declaration of Cuban independence. Americans quite naturally sympathized with this revolution against European colonialism, and many urged Washington to assist the rebel cause. Cleveland generally opposed interventionism, however, and soon after the war erupted he issued a neutrality proclamation.

The war soon grew bloody. In an attempt to suppress the violent uprising, Spanish General Valeriano Weyler resettled large numbers of Cuban peasants in guarded camps to cut away support for the rebels. Aghast at the savagery this strategy entailed, Congress passed a resolution demanding that the president recognize the patriot junta. He refused to act, however, on the grounds that the president was solely responsible for establishing and carrying out American foreign policy. Cleveland was also inclined to remain aloof from the Cuban civil war, and judged the policy line urged upon him by Congress to be unwise. However, Cleveland warned in December 1896 that if Spain did not grant Cuba some form of autonomy, then "our obligations to the sovereignty of Spain will be superceded by higher obligations, which we can hardly hesitate to recognize and discharge."[26]

Chapter Twenty-three
The Spanish-American War
1898

The Spanish-American War was provoked by the Cuban Revolution, but this bloody conflict in Cuba played only a minor role in the 1896 presidential elections in which Senator William McKinley, an Ohio Republican, crushed William Jennings Bryan, a populist Democrat. McKinley promised to maintain a strong currency, keep high tariffs, annex Hawaii, and "enlarge" the fleet. His cabinet included John Sherman, secretary of state, and former Massachusetts governor John D. Long, secretary of the Navy. Long was a poor choice who warned McKinley early on that he had "no special aptitude for the Navy." A cautious, stable figure, he struggled to restrain the impatient vigor of Assistant Secretary Theodore Roosevelt of New York, an outspoken advocate of a muscular foreign policy and naval expansion. "I make a point not to trouble myself overmuch to acquire a thorough knowledge of the details pertaining to any branch of the service," Long confessed, with the result that he never truly mastered his department. The Republican platform advocated a strong foreign and naval policy, but McKinley wavered for a few months before declaring that he opposed building a large battleship fleet as that might bring on unwanted "foreign complications."[1]

The Cuban war intensified in 1897, but McKinley's first major foreign policy crisis was his request to Congress in mid-1897 to annex Hawaii. Japan bitterly objected to annexation, for strategic and political reasons. High unemployment in Japan caused by the

Panic of 1893 was partially relieved by emigration to Hawaii, and the Japanese worried that the United States would extend its "Oriental exclusion" immigration policy to the islands. Japan also worried that the United States would become a Pacific naval power and rival if she constructed a naval base in the islands. Commodore Perry's treaty in 1854 had lit a fuse of discontent among a faction of Japanese who wanted to overturn the ancient shogun system. Conservatives wanted to maintain isolation, while progressives feared that insularity would expose Japan to the same Western powers that had infringed upon Chinese sovereignty following the Opium Wars.

One of the most reactionary feudal rulers was Lord Mori, whose cannon guarded the Straits of Shimonoseki. He protested Japan's conciliatory policy by firing on Western shipping in 1863, in defiance of several treaties. The Tokagawa shogun in Tokyo was too weak to punish him, and an international reaction followed. Although the screw-sloop *Wyoming* engaged the Japanese batteries briefly in 1864, there were only two American ships in the Far East at the time, and both were busy trying to hunt down Confederate raiders. Washington therefore declined to join a seventeen-ship multinational fleet, which reduced Mori's forts and shot up his small flotilla later that year. Frightened by this display of power, Tokyo signed the one-sided Convention of 1864, which expanded Western rights in Japan and provided that the Japanese pay a $3 million indemnity to the European powers. Japan's anguish over this humiliation led to a civil war, which ended in the defeat of the shogun and the restoration to power of the Emperor Meiji in 1869. During the Meiji Restoration, the grip of the samurai warrior caste was broken, and the Japanese resolved not to ignore the West but instead to absorb the methods of modern industry and technology that had put Asia at Europe's feet. Japan industrialized rapidly, and by 1890 her gross national product far surpassed that of her Asian neighbors. She sturdily resisted foreign encroachments, demanded parity in all dealings, and in 1894 denounced the last of the unequal treaties. Moreover, she reversed her historic policy of isolation and became a trading nation. By 1895 Japan's interests in Korea, a sometime Chinese tributary, represented an important element of her economy.

Korea's future was the first issue to divide modern Japan and the United States. America's interest in Korea stemmed from a clause in the 1881 Shufeldt Treaty that obligated the United States to "exert" its "good offices" should the Great Powers deal "unjustly or oppressively" with Korea. "America is to us our Elder Brother," declared Korea's king, who received the first American minister in Seoul with unconcealed delight. Another envoy, Ensign George Foulk, tried to persuade Washington to back Korean independence, but the Chinese obstructed his efforts, and by 1894 China's domination of Korea was firmly reestablished. Therefore, when a revolt erupted in southern Korea, the king asked the Chinese Army to put it down. Japan quickly moved its own army to Korea, replaced the king with a pro-Japanese regent, and successfully ambushed the Chinese fleet at the Battle of the Yalu River, the first engagement between ironclad fleets.[2]

Following this defeat, China sued for peace to end the Sino-Japanese War. America's minister in Seoul asked Washington to order the Asiatic Squadron to send a warship to Inchon to protect Korea's independence during the peace talks, but Cleveland was a determined noninterventionist and Secretary of State Olney turned down the scheme. In the 1895 Treaty of Shimonoseki, China accepted Japan's domination of Korea and ceded the Liaotung Peninsula, Port Arthur, the Pescadores Islands, and the island of Formosa. The Germans and French were disturbed by these concessions; so were the Russians, who feared that Japan would establish a naval base at Port Arthur. These three Great Powers "invited" Japan to "reconsider" the Treaty of Shimonoseki and in so doing save the "peace of the Far East." Confronted by this formidable array of Europe's military and naval might, the Japanese could do nothing but retreat. They evacuated the Liaotung Peninsula and withdrew from Port Arthur—which the Russians soon occupied—and ached for revenge over the Triple Humiliation.[3]

With this history, Japan was in no mood to be humbled again over the issue of Hawaii in 1897. When the Dole republic moved to prevent Japanese immigrants from entering Honolulu in March of that year, shrill protests blasted from Tokyo to Washington. McKinley reacted by having Secretary Long order Rear Admiral L. A. Beardslee of the Pacific Squadron to transfer the cruiser *Philadelphia* and the old sloop *Marion* to Hawaiian waters, where they were to remain "for the present." The Japanese more than matched this move by sending the powerful battle cruiser *Naniwa* steaming across the Pacific to Honolulu in April to intimidate the Dole regime. McKinley then calmly upped the ante by ordering

Beardslee to concentrate all four of his ships in Hawaiian waters. Following this escalating crisis closely, Captain Mahan warned Assistant Secretary Roosevelt, his close friend, that there was a "very real present danger of war."[4]

At the president's request, Captain Caspar F. Goodrich's Naval War College faculty now prepared the first strategic plan for operations against Japan. Assuming that neither side would have allies, he fixed the Navy's objective as the destruction of Japan's fleet. Goodrich divided his campaign into four phases. The American battleships, cruisers, escorts, and fleet train would first concentrate on the East Coast, then steam around South America to San Francisco Bay. The fleet would then sail to Hawaii, establish an advance base, and then strike into the western Pacific to search out and destroy Japan's fleet, presumably in the vicinity of the Philippine Islands. The plan suggested many problems that the fleet would face fighting in the Pacific. Supporting the movement would be a nightmare. Neither Mare Island nor Bremerton Navy Yard on Puget Sound was large enough to support the fleet on the Pacific coast, let alone prepare it for the great advance into the western Pacific.[5]

Nonetheless, McKinley stood ready to go to the brink with Japan over Hawaii in the early summer of 1897 and pressed on with negotiations with the Honolulu government. When the *Naniwa* arrived at Pearl Harbor, Long instructed Beardslee to prevent the Japanese from intimidating the Dole republic. "If the Japanese openly resort to force," Beardslee was to "land a suitable force, and announce officially provisional assumption of a protectorate pending [the] ratification of [the] treaty of annexation." Tensions increased on 16 June when Secretary Sherman signed a treaty of annexation with Hawaii. McKinley was worried by the intensity of Japan's protests, so he kept the newly constructed battleship *Oregon* on the Pacific coast to signal his resolve on the issue. He also considered reinforcing Admiral Beardslee's squadron by sending the second-class battleship *Maine* to the Pacific, although he decided against this as he did not want to weaken the Atlantic Squadron at a time of tension with Spain over Cuba. As it was, warned Admiral Goodrich, even with reinforcements the Pacific Squadron was inferior to the Japanese fleet with its two new battleships. He told McKinley that if war broke out this disparity might make it "necessary for us to abandon the Sandwich [Hawaiian] Islands temporarily and with our fleet fall back to the support

of San Francisco." To avoid a bitter fight in Congress with antian-
nexation Democrats and improve relations with Japan, McKinley
directed that annexation be postponed until tempers cooled. By
the fall Japan had withdrawn its squadron from the eastern Pacific. Goodrich's study of a Pacific war set in motion a line of thinking that influenced successive generations of naval strategists, and
his counsel may have encouraged McKinley to delay Hawaiian annexation. But the most immediate and important outcome of the
crisis was to provide McKinley with a model of how to use ships'
movements to lever concessions on foreign policy from strong opponents.[6]

Despite the war scare over Hawaii, and increasing tension
with Spain, Navy Secretary Long followed McKinley's broad lead
and resisted Roosevelt's schemes for fleet expansion, which he labeled a "mistake." The geographical "remoteness from foreign
powers," Long told Congress, and the "devotion of our people" to
commerce made war but a mere "last resort" of foreign policy. And
he steadfastly opposed "any policy that involves military entangle-
ments." In December 1897, on the eve of the Spanish-American
War, he slashed the Herbert shipbuilding program, asking
Congress to appropriate funds for only one battleship. Instead of
using naval appropriations to coerce the Spanish, Long told
Congress that he intended to "put ships into reserve in order to
reduce running expenses." That the president did not curb this
enthusiasm for retrenchment was a measure of McKinley's un-
readiness for the moment to adopt a sharper diplomacy on the
Cuban question.[7]

The economy was recovering from the Panic of 1893, and
McKinley had to wrestle with many important domestic issues during his first year in office. He was anxious to feel his way carefully
through the minefield of foreign relations and military policy, and
the pressure he applied against Spain that year was restrained. He
refused to recognize Cuba's rebels, persuaded Spanish Prime
Minister Mateo Sargasta to relieve General Weyler and end
Weyler's brutal *reconcentrado* strategy in Cuba, and had Congress
appropriate $50,000 for Cuban relief. But he also insisted that
Spain grant Cuba autonomy and warned that the United States
could "no longer remain a disinterested spectator." Publisher
William Randolph Hearst of the *New York Journal* fabricated accounts of atrocities by Spaniards against innocent Cubans, but
when reporters actually neared the battlefront they found that

both sides had engaged in terrible savagery. McKinley's quiet pressure plus the tempo of rebel operations were beginning to take their toll. Madrid hinted at eventual autonomy, although the Spanish firmly resisted Cuban independence.[8]

On 10 January 1898 rioters in Havana, led by Spanish Army officers, destroyed several pro-independence newspapers, and Consul Fitzhugh Lee warned that "if Americans and their interests are in danger ships must be sent." The North Atlantic Squadron's winter maneuvers were being held off Newport to avoid antagonizing Madrid, but McKinley now ordered it to steam to Key West to bolster his diplomacy. In response to Lee's cable, he told Navy Secretary Long to send a battleship to Havana to signal American "friendship" for Cuba and interest in order in the Caribbean. While Long was making these arrangements, the diplomatic landscape erupted. On 9 February, the *New York Journal* published a letter written to Madrid by Spain's ambassador in Washington, Dupuy de Lome, which Cuban agents had stolen from the mails. De Lome called McKinley "weak" and urged Spain to continue with its policy of duplicity and delay on the grounds that McKinley was too stupid to see behind Spanish lies. McKinley cared little about this Spanish functionary's barbs, but the de Lome letter deprived all subsequent Spanish bargaining of the crucial cloth of good faith. McKinley now had to discount every Spanish promise, inasmuch as outright acceptance might be thought to demonstrate that he was easily fooled.[9]

While this storm brewed, Captain Charles D. Sigsbee in the battleship *Maine* stood into Havana harbor. Three nights later, on 15 February 1898, an explosion ripped her hull apart and killed 260 sailors. Confused as to the cause of this tragedy, Sigsbee felt that "public opinion should be suspended," and McKinley promised an investigation "to fix the responsibility." The bizarre behavior of Spain's officers in the riot one month earlier led many to believe that they were responsible for the disaster; Roosevelt, an astute judge of international politics, felt that "the *Maine* was sunk by . . . the Spaniards." It seemed unlikely that the rebels were guilty, because discovery of such a plot would have completely alienated their American support. Rather than blaming the rebels, the Spanish claimed that an internal explosion had caused the ship to sink. Captain William Sampson, an ordnance expert, was named to chair the Navy's board of inquiry. In Havana, hard upon the disaster, he examined a considerable body of evidence and concluded that the cause was external. In an effort to dampen the call for war by American jingoes, who were by now rallying public opinion behind the slogan "Remember the *Maine*," McKinley suppressed the finding. A few years later Long wrote that "it will probably be found that . . . the Spanish government . . . was innocent of the design, though it was possible that some of its subordinates or possibly some insurgent Cuban foreseeing the effect, may have been responsible."

Less important than the true cause of the tragedy was its political fallout. The sinking of the *Maine* so strongly riveted American attention on Cuba that McKinley could no longer wait on events. He sent an ultimatum to Madrid on 27 March, demanding that the Spanish stop prosecuting the war, open talks with the rebels, and agree in advance to American mediation if these negotiations failed to bring about independence for Cuba by 1 October. Sargasta conceded some minor points but refused to initiate a ceasefire, rejected American mediation, and stood firm against Cuban independence. His diplomacy having failed, McKinley was left with no choice but to go to war. On April Fool's Day, the text of Sampson's report on the *Maine* was published by the "yellow" press, and the result was a furor on the Hill. "The destruction of the *Maine*, by whatever exterior cause, is a patent and impressive proof of a state of things in Cuba that is intolerable," McKinley told Congress. He had "exhausted" diplomacy and now asked Congress to declare war. A last-minute Spanish move to suspend Cuban hostilities came too late, and Congress declared war within a week. By greatly underestimating McKinley's statesmanship, Spain now faced certain, humbling defeat alone.[10]

Partially restrained by Long's inertia, Assistant Secretary Roosevelt was mostly responsible for the flurry of Navy activity in the early months of 1898. For four years the Naval War College had studied plans for a war with Spain and considered attacks on Cuba, Puerto Rico, the Philippines, the Canary and Balearic islands, and a bombardment of Spain's major ports. The planners also wanted the Asiatic Squadron to attack Spain's small fleet in the Philippines to prevent the enemy from raiding America's Pacific shipping and to pressure Spain's Army in Cuba to surrender. The North Atlantic Squadron would then blockade Cuba and Puerto Rico. The Newport planners expected the United States to acquire naval bases in Cuba and the Philippines when the war was over, but the effect of wartime strategy on postwar diplomacy was not considered.

McKinley was apprised of these concepts, but they guided his conduct of the Spanish-American War in only the most general way. He had agreed in late 1897 to a Navy plan to attack Spain's Philippine Fleet. He had also decided to blockade Cuba once Congress declared war, and he intended as a final step to invade Cuba and occupy Havana. His views were flexible, however, and he adjusted his strategy to exploit unexpected opportunities. Roosevelt, an enthusiast for the Manila strike, personally selected Commodore George Dewey, an extremely able leader, to command the Asiatic Squadron in late 1897, and before Dewey sailed in December the two discussed the Philippine operation. None of those who studied the plan expected it to set in motion events that would lead to the annexation of the Philippine Islands. After he arrived on station, Dewey concentrated four cruisers, two gunboats, and a cutter at Hong Kong, purchased a collier, and awaited an order to sail.

When Congress declared war on 25 April, Dewey's Asiatic Squadron was riding at anchor in Hong Kong harbor. Led by his flagship, the modern 5,870-ton cruiser *Olympia*, the formation included the light cruisers *Raleigh* and *Boston*, the revenue cutter *McCulloch*, the two gunboats *Concord* and *Petrel*, and the 4,400-ton cruiser *Baltimore*, which had arrived from Hawaii only three days earlier. At midnight, Dewey received a message from the Navy Department, approved in advance by McKinley, which directed him to "proceed at once to the Philippine Islands." Setting sail from Mirs Bay two days later, Dewey's ships appeared at dawn on 1 May at the entrance to Manila Bay. The bay was defended by powerful shore batteries and a Spanish squadron composed of one older cruiser and several smaller vessels. Dewey had to lead his squadron through a channel that the Spanish easily might have mined, although the American consul in Manila had reported on 10 March that "the bay and its channels are both free from mines and torpedoes." On the basis of this intelligence and his own considerable experience with mining in deep, tropical waters, Dewey took a serious gamble, dismissing the mine threat as a "specious bluff."[11]

On 1 May, Dewey could not be absolutely certain that this was the case. The Spanish military position in Manila was desperate, not hopeless, but the foolhardiness of Spain's leaders in the Philippines mirrored the strategic ineptitude that led Spain to war with the United States in the first place. To defend Manila Bay, Admiral Patricio Montojo had positioned his ancient ships in the shallow

waters opposite the Cavite arsenal, far away from any possible support from the Lunetta battery's modern 9-inch guns shielding the
city. This decision merely invited Dewey to attack the Spaniard's
strong points in detail. Once the Asiatic Squadron passed safely
into the bay, Dewey sighted the enemy fleet at Cavite and shouted
to the *Olympia's* captain, "Fire when ready, Gridley." Over 100 guns,
half greater than 4 inches, pounded the Spanish into submission
during a one-sided gun duel that cost the lives of only seven Americans. At midnight, when over 400 Spaniards were dead and seven
of their ships badly damaged, desultory sniping from the Lunetta
battery prompted Dewey to send a message ashore threatening to
bombard the city unless the shooting stopped. At sunrise, Manila
Bay, now under American control, was silent. The classic strategy
of bringing an enemy port under the guns of an American fleet had
undermined Spanish power in the Philippines and was about to upset the balance of power in the Pacific.

Manila and Hong Kong were linked by cable, and Dewey asked
the Spanish governor general, who had not surrendered the city,
to allow him to use it to communicate via Hong Kong with Washington. When the Spaniard refused, Dewey cut the cable, and thus
was on his own when he first encountered the labyrinthine politics
of the Philippine insurrection. One part of McKinley's campaign
to shock Madrid into withdrawing from Cuba was Dewey's attack
on the Philippines, chosen merely because they "belong to Spain."
Dewey's orders said nothing, however, about taking the islands, nor
was he told how to deal with a squadron of German warships that
entered Manila Bay a few days later.

Vice Admiral Otto von Diederichs' Asiatic Squadron was ordered on 2 June to steam from Hong Kong to Manila Bay to investigate "the wishes of the natives and foreign influences upon
the political situation." Under the guidance of young Kaiser Wilhelm II since 1890, German foreign policy had grown increasingly acquisitive, and Chancellor Bernhard von Bulow found no difficulty persuading the kaiser, one of Mahan's devotees, that
"control of the sea may depend upon who rules the Philippines."
The Germans wanted some compensation if the United States or
Great Britain annexed the Philippines—in spite of the fact that
there was no historic German interest in the archipelago, few German interests in the region, and no accepted place for Germany
in the existing balance of power in the Pacific. "There is, to the
German mind, something monstrous in the thought that a war

should take place anywhere and they not profit from it," Secretary of State John Hay told Senator Lodge. Diederichs, who was not informed of the kaiser's objectives, entered Manila Bay on 12 June.[12]

Some minor incidents over three weeks between the American and German squadrons convinced Dewey that Diederichs' activities were part of a larger German policy aimed at thwarting American ambitions in the Far East. German ships mysteriously came and went from their anchorage nightly, and when Dewey demanded the right to board them to determine whether they were helping the Spaniards in Manila, Diederichs tied the issue into a knot of legal complexities. While Diederichs did nothing overt to interfere with American operations, Dewey never forgot the German's abusive attitude and disruptive behavior, and his opinion colored the Navy's views of German foreign policy for many years to come. Also, Dewey felt that because of Diederichs' presence in Manila Bay, he did not have enough ships to detach one vessel to the Spanish Caroline Islands to establish an American presence there before the peace talks began. Meanwhile, back in America, Dewey's victory in Manila Bay made him a national hero overnight, propelled him into consideration for the presidency in 1900, and earned him a promotion by Congress in 1899 to the rank of Admiral of the Navy for life.

Some of Dewey's annoyance with the Germans stemmed from the fact that they distracted his attention away from the siege of Manila, whose Spanish commander was still stubbornly refusing to surrender. Dewey sent a message to Navy Secretary Long on 7 May that he could "take the city at any time, but I have not sufficient men to hold" it. To overrun Manila "and thus control the Philippine Islands," he estimated, would require a "well equipped force of 5,000 men." McKinley accepted Dewey's assessment and instructed the War Department to support the movement against Manila. Transports carrying Major General Wesley Merritt's division stood out of San Francisco and shaped a course for the Philippines on 28 May. The loss of Manila Bay, intended to shock the Spanish into surrendering Cuba, had a paradoxical result. Sargasta purged his cabinet, planned to reinforce Luzon and Havana, and refused to negotiate. This led McKinley to reason that the U.S. Army would have to invade Cuba.[13]

During these days, Teddy Roosevelt's presence in the Navy Department hurried preparations for war. He persuaded Long to increase the department's request for shipbuilding during the current session of Congress to take advantage of the war fever. Both houses in May authorized construction of the second battleship *Maine* and also provided funds for the 12,500-ton battleships *Ohio* and *Vermont* of the same class, armed with main batteries of four 12-inch guns, and for twelve torpedo boats and sixteen larger torpedo boat destroyers.

Measures were already in hand to prosecute the war in the Caribbean. In March, Secretary Long had ordered the commander of the North Atlantic Squadron, Rear Admiral Montgomery Sicard to return to Washington, owing to his ill health, and named as his successor Commodore Sampson, author of the recent report on the *Maine* tragedy. Next, Long wired Captain Mahan, who had retired and was vacationing in Italy, directing him to return home and join a Strategy Board composed of himself, Sicard, and Rear Admiral Crowninshield, the decorative chief of the Bureau of Navigation. "Some of the Atlantic coast cities and towns were nervously excited over the possibility of an attack by a separate Spanish man-of-war," Long wrote, and so in April and May "the department was compelled to modify the rule of concentration adopted as the guide of its conduct during the war." Long established a Flying Squadron of cruisers under Captain Winfield Scott Schley at Norfolk and a smaller Northern Patrol Squadron under Commodore John A. Howell, who was to guard American waters above the Delaware Bay. The South Atlantic Squadron was instructed to withdraw from the Brazilian coast to Key West on 26 March, and the small European Squadron received orders to rendezvous at Lisbon and return to American waters.

Two weeks earlier Long had ordered Captain Charles E. Clark, who had just assumed command of the battleship *Oregon* on the Pacific coast, to return to the Atlantic. She stood out of San Francisco Bay on 19 March, ran down to Callao, Peru, fought her way though a violent gale in the Straits of Magellan, and arrived at Rio de Janeiro at the end of April. "It was at Rio that we first received word that war had been declared," Clark wrote. He soon learned that four heavy Spanish cruisers and three fast oceangoing torpedo boats had departed the Cape Verde Islands the day before. "If this Spanish squadron were headed for the West Indies, as I was inclined to believe, the necessity for the *Oregon*'s presence with our fleet was all the more urgent." He raced over the last leg of the historic dash, which ended on 26 May with the arrival of the battleship at Key West.[14]

Long was being asked in the meantime to revise his strategy by Commodore Sampson, who took command of the newly enlarged North Atlantic Squadron in late April and quickly evaluated Spain's plight. "The country has nothing to fear from an attack along our northern coast," he reminded the secretary. Instead of holding Schley's Flying Squadron at Norfolk, Sampson proposed that Schley transfer the battleship *Massachusetts* to the North Atlantic Squadron so that he, Sampson, might descend on Havana, whose defenses he had just recently inspected. "My present plan contemplates an attack [upon Havana] the very moment the dogs of war are let loose," he reported, while complaining that "my force is now too small for that purpose." Sampson wanted to reduce the Spanish forts at the entrance to Havana harbor, then menace the city with a punishing naval bombardment. He was convinced that this would force the Spaniards in Cuba to surrender. This strategy was vetoed by Long, who knew that the Spanish cruisers were at sea and worried about what they would do when they arrived in the Caribbean. "The lack of docking facilities makes it particularly desirable that our vessels should not be crippled before the capture or destruction of Spain's most formidable vessels," he told Sampson. The Army was approaching mobilization in such a casual manner, moreover, that Long was afraid that "there may be no United States troops to occupy any captured stronghold or protect it."[15]

After McKinley announced a blockade of Cuba, Long moved to prevent the Spanish from reinforcing the island. At the same time, he modified his earlier standing orders against attacking forts. While he did "not wish a bombardment of forts protected with heavy cannon" such as Havana, he told Sampson on 26 April that "it is within your discretion to destroy light batteries which may protect vessels you desire to attack, if you can do so without exposure to heavy guns." From various reports by Lieutenant William S. Sims, the naval attaché in Paris, Sampson now learned that Rear Admiral Pascual Cervera's four fast cruisers were heading for the Caribbean. Assuming that Cervera intended to take on coal at San Juan, Puerto Rico, Sampson decided to intercept the Spanish cruisers there and overwhelm them with his heavier battleships. With the battleships *Iowa* and *Indiana*, the armored cruiser *New York*, two monitors, and a torpedo boat, he stood out of Cuban waters on 3 May and steamed for Puerto Rico. The slow monitors had a 6-knot speed, and the passage to San Juan took

U.S. Navy Department

Admiral William Sampson, commander
North Atlantic Squadron, 1898.

Commodore Winfield Schley, commander of
the Flying Squadron, 1898.

nine days. When Sampson's formation was off Cap Haitien, Long
warned him "not [to] risk crippling your vessels against fortifications as to prevent them from soon thereafter successfully fighting
[the] Spanish fleet . . . if they should appear on this side." However, when he arrived off San Juan on 12 May, Sampson bombarded the enemy batteries for several hours. The flagship *New
York* and the *Iowa* each took one hit during this exchange.[16]

Long had in the meantime ordered Schley's Flying Squadron
to sail for Key West, sent three cruisers into the Caribbean to locate and shadow Cervera, and alerted Sampson that his opponent
would either "haul up for Santiago . . . or pass through the Yucatán
Channel and endeavor to operate in the Gulf of Mexico." To prevent Cervera from entering American waters, Long directed
Schley on 19 May "to establish a blockade at Cienfuegos with the
least possible delay." Sampson had returned to Key West by this
time, but Cervera was nowhere to be found. Guessing that Samp-

son would be at San Juan, Cervera had stopped off at Martinique for coal, but the French refused to assist him, so he steamed to Dutch Curaçao, where the officials were more helpful. On the 18th, Sampson learned that Cervera was heading for Cuba, so he returned to Key West at full speed and ordered Schley's Flying Squadron to steam south and blockade the port of Cienfuegos. Unbeknownst to the Americans, Cervera had decided to head from Curaçao for Santiago, but when he arrived there on 19 May he could think of no more to do than to drop anchor and await Sampson's arrival. Upon learning that Cervera might be at Santiago, Sampson decided "to make no change in the present plans" and told Schley to "hold your squadron off Cienfuegos." He reasoned that "if the Spanish ships have put into Santiago they must either come to Havana or Cienfuegos to deliver the munitions of war" they were carrying. Mahan's Strategy Board in Washington apparently disagreed. At 1230 that same day Long intervened with a cable to Sampson that he was to "send word . . . to Schley to proceed off Santiago with his whole command." Sampson conveyed this to Schley, but it took the Flying Squadron over a week just to steam from Cienfuegos to Santiago. Delayed by bad weather and his 6-knot gunboats, he did not appear off Santiago until 26 May. Then, because his ships could not take on coal in the storm, he decided to return to Key West. The weather cleared the following day, however, and on the 28th the Flying Squadron finally established a loose blockade of Cervera's fleet.[17]

Sampson's battleships joined Schley's cruisers off Santiago on 1 June. Assuming command of both forces, Sampson instituted a close blockade, positioning his five heavy ships in an arc five miles around the entrance to the harbor. At night he moved his ships closer in to shell Fort Morro and other Spanish positions. A landing party of 650 sailors and Marines under Captain Bowman McCalla was put ashore on Guantánamo Bay on 10 June, and it overran the port after a week of fighting. With a secure base to support his blockade, Sampson turned his full attention to the problem of Santiago. A four-mile long inlet, surrounded by hills, led into the spacious harbor. The shipping channel at the mouth of the inlet was only 125 yards wide and it was well defended by electric mines and floating log booms, the Fort Morro battery, and Spanish guns in the nearby hills. Sampson could not risk sending his battleships into the channel, so he approved a daring plan devised by Lieutenant Richard Hobson to bring the old 7,000-ton merchant collier *Merrimac* into the channel, scuttle her, and block the passage, thus shutting Cervera's squadron in the harbor. Three hours before sunrise on 3 June, Hobson used the high tide to move the *Merrimac* into the harbor, but before he could reach position, the Spanish guns opened fire, disabling her rudder. She sank in the wrong place, merely narrowing the channel rather than closing it. Unwilling to put his heavy ships at risk, Sampson decided that the Army should land and approach Santiago from its landward flank. "If 10,000 men were here, city and fleet would be ours within 48 hours," he cabled McKinley on 1 June.[18]

McKinley originally had intended for American forces to attack Havana, but Cervera's dash to Santiago had upset this plan, so he suspended the Havana operation until the fall and ordered Brigadier General William R. Shafter, who had assembled an Army corps at Tampa, to prepare to take Santiago. Shafter was ready to ship 5,000 troops to Cuba to support the rebels in early May, but Secretary of War Russell A. Alger failed to warn the Navy that a troop convoy had been assembled and was about to put to sea. "To my utter amazement . . . it [the troop movement] is to be made tomorrow," Long complained on 8 May, "and not one word has been said to me about furnishing a convoy." After Long told McKinley that no Navy escort was available, the Army scrapped its first plan to invade Cuba.[19]

Over the next few weeks, Shafter enlarged his swampy Tampa camp to 25,000 men, the War Department chartered twenty-six more rusty transports to carry them to Cuba, and Long instructed Rear Admiral George Remey at Key West to assemble an escort force to cover the movement of the Army convoy across the Florida Strait. In Tampa, confusion reigned. McKinley was anguished by Shafter's repeated postponements. On 8 June, responding to Sampson's urgent appeal, the president ordered Shafter to leave at once for Cuba with at least 10,000 men. As luck would have it, soon after the transports stood out to sea, a report reached Remey that three Spanish ships had been spotted cruising along the coast, and he told Shafter to return to port while he sent out a small squadron to hunt them down. While Remey investigated, Shafter kept his seasick, sweat-drenched troops on board the transports at quayside waiting for the all-clear. Remey discovered a few days later that the mysterious vessels were in reality American steamers, so on 14 June the Army convoy got under way again on the first leg of the great expedition to Cuba.

So slow were the transports that it took Remey's squadron, composed of the battleship *Indiana* and sixteen lesser escorts, six days to make the passage. The trip was marred by constant friction. The 7-knot convoy, spread out along the horizon, chugged toward Cuba, ablaze at night with running lights despite the apparent danger of Spanish torpedo boats. The escort skippers warned Shafter by megaphone and semaphore to dim his lights and conform to some convoy discipline, but he refused. "A smart Spanish officer could not have failed to inflict a very serious loss" by launching a torpedo attack at night against the convoy, observed one passenger, Captain Alfred Paget, the British naval attaché. On 20 June, the fleet appeared off Daiquiri, eighteen miles east of Santiago, bombarded the port, and landed Shafter's 16,000 troops with little trouble. He moved slowly inland toward Santiago, supported on occasion by offshore bombardments by Sampson's ships. The troops took El Caney and San Juan Hill but suffered heavy casualties, so Shafter suspended his offensive and called on Sampson "to force the entrance [to Santiago] to avoid future losses among my men."[20]

This set the stage for the battle off Santiago. During a lull in Shafter's offensive, Cuba's Spanish governor foolishly ordered Admiral Cervera to escape from Santiago at any cost. On the morning of 3 July Cervera learned that the battleship *Massachusetts* was taking on coal at Guantánamo, and that the heavy cruiser *New York*, Sampson's flagship, was riding at anchor five miles from the main American body, so he seized the chance to sortie. He had no idea of what to do or where to go if he escaped, however. When Sampson saw that the Spanish ships were steaming out of the channel, he signaled Commodore Schley, whom he had left in tactical command in the heavy cruiser *Brooklyn*, and ordered him to engage the enemy with his cruiser and the battleships *Oregon*, *Indiana*, *Iowa*, and *Texas*. The battle began when Cervera unexpectedly dashed directly toward the *Brooklyn*. Schley, fearing a Spanish torpedo attack, turned to starboard, nearly crossing the bow of the *Texas* and forcing her to reduce speed and veer away to avoid a collision. Schley was now thoroughly confused. Instead of turning back toward the enemy, his cruiser steamed around in a complete circle before rejoining the battleships, which were, by then, chasing the Spanish fleet along the Cuban coastline.

The fast *Brooklyn* soon steamed ahead of the battleships and they easily overwhelmed the enemy in a brief but violent action.

Lieutenant Commander Richard Wainwright in the 800-ton converted steam yacht *Gloucester* gallantly challenged two Spanish destroyers, which were also engaged by the *Indiana*'s heavy batteries. One was sunk by a 13-inch shell and the other struck her colors. The *Maria Teresa*, Cervera's flagship, took thirty hits before she was run onto the beach. The cruisers *Oquendo* and *Vizcaya* next were brought to book and forced to run aground. The 14-knot fast cruiser *Colón*, however, led the *Brooklyn* and *Oregon* on a fifty-five-mile chase that ended only after she reduced speed, took several minor hits, and ran aground. At the end of the battle, the entire Spanish squadron had been sunk or captured, one American and 160 Spaniards were dead, and Cervera and his captains were prisoners of war. Although the enemy had been crushed, American gunnery and command and control were very poor. Only 3 out of every 100 American shells fired hit a Spanish ship, and Schley's unsettling behavior during and after the battle created an instant controversy. He first claimed credit for leading the squadron to victory, then hastily apologized to Sampson, who was distressed about the *Brooklyn*'s bizarre movements. This was the origin of the bitter Sampson-Schley feud, which led to a postwar court-martial that investigated Schley's conduct and eventually involved the president. The dispute ended only with Sampson's death soon after.

Cervera's defeat did not solve Shafter's problem, so the general continued demanding that Sampson force the Santiago channel and shell the city. Sampson still refused to risk his ships by sending them into the channel. Relations between the two grew so rancorous that McKinley ordered them to "confer at once for cooperation in taking Santiago." At the same time, however, Secretary Long was cautioning Sampson not to risk the battleships, so Sampson began to shell the city from long range. This did little real damage, although it scared the Spanish a great deal. When Shafter renewed his offensive, Santiago surrendered on 14 July. Bitter at Sampson's refusal to risk his ships in the channel, Shafter kept the commodore from accepting Spain's capitulation. Sampson retaliated by instructing his sailors to seize all the Spanish ships in the harbor after the Army tried to take them over. McKinley was annoyed by their petty bickering; he knew that another Spanish army still occupied Havana and that the war might not yet be over.[21]

McKinley's strategy of stunning Madrid climaxed with the seizure of Puerto Rico. During the Santiago campaign, General Nelson Miles, the Army's commanding general, assembled a second army that was sent by transport to Puerto Rico, escorted by Sampson's North Atlantic Squadron. They landed at Port Guánica and brushed aside feeble opposition. Sampson believed that San Juan, the Spanish stronghold, could be "destroyed from the water and may yield without much resistance" to a "proper show of naval strength," but Miles wanted the glory and asked Washington to instruct the Navy to allow him to assault the position. Mahan, now running the Navy's Strategy Board, called Miles' landings in Puerto Rico "a military stupidity so great that I can account only by a kind of obsession of vanity," an ungenerous but not inaccurate description. Before this quarrel got any hotter, however, the Spanish surrendered.[22]

By the time Miles had landed on Puerto Rico, Washington was abuzz with rumors that McKinley was about to order Commodore John C. Watson's newly assembled Eastern Squadron, a force built around the battleship *Oregon*, to raid Spain's poorly defended Atlantic coast. Watson was eager for action, expressing the "hope we can get between their home ports and some of Camara's squadron." He was referring to Admiral Manuel de la Camara, who had sailed from Cádiz to Suez on 16 June with a fleet of two cruisers, six escorts, and four troop transports. When Sims, the naval attaché in Paris, informed Washington that Camara's ships would enter the Suez Canal in early July, Mahan's Strategy Board predicted that he planned to attack Dewey's Asiatic Squadron in Manila Bay or to intercept the cruiser *Charleston*, then escorting transports carrying General Merritt's 1st Division from California to the Philippines. Long reacted by ordering the cruiser *Boston*, the seagoing monitor *Monterey*, and the gunboat *Monadnock* to reinforce the Asiatic Squadron in July. The Americans could not have known that Sargasta's purpose in deploying Camara's fleet was not to challenge Dewey, but simply to reassert Spain's claim to the Philippines when peace talks were arranged.[23]

When Sargasta learned that Watson's Eastern Squadron was taking on coal, he anxiously recalled Camara's ships. The protected cruiser *Charleston* had appeared in the Marianas, stopped off at Guam on 20 June, fired a challenge, accepted the surrender of the Spanish garrison, and raised the American flag over Agana. Merritt reached Manila Bay on 15 July, established a base at Cavite, and within days laid siege to the city. Three days later Spain asked France to arrange a ceasefire, based on the conditions of an American withdrawal from all Spanish territory and independence for

Cuba. McKinley stiffly rejected this proposal and allowed Madrid to wait in anguish for two weeks for his reply. On 30 July he conveyed his terms to Spain: independence for Cuba, the cession of Puerto Rico and Guam to the United States, and the unconditional surrender of the Manila garrison. If Spain continued to resist, Shafter and Sampson were to advance on Havana in the fall and Watson's Eastern Squadron was to shell Spain's undefended Atlantic ports. This bloody threat left Sargasta with no choice but to capitulate. McKinley had accomplished more than he intended. The 400-year-old empire of Columbus was in utter collapse.

The Spanish-American War began over Cuba but ended in a bitter debate over the fate of the Philippines. On board Dewey's flagship during the Battle of Manila Bay on 1 May 1898 was a member of the Philippine Assembly, a band of anti-Spanish rebel nationalists. Dewey's victory led their dynamic leader, Emilio Aguinaldo, to declare the islands independent of Spain in June without first seeking the commodore's approval. Aguinaldo's patriot army cooperated with Merritt's troops during the siege of Manila, but Merritt refused to recognize the Filipino regime. Dewey, the senior commander in the theater, was confused by the problem and expressed little interest in the ultimate fate of the islands. With 13,000 starving men on his hands, the Spanish Army commander in Manila arranged for a short, "bloodless" exchange of gunfire, followed by the city's surrender. Dewey's guns fired a few broadsides on 13 August, the Spanish responded by raising a white flag, and Merritt's troops began to march into the city. Then Aguinaldo's rebels, who also wanted to occupy Manila, upset the arrangement by charging the Spanish redoubts. Two Americans were killed during the fighting. Dewey, who blamed Merritt and Aguinaldo in equal measure for this fiasco, took this and other incidents as evidence that the Philippine Assembly was too weak and unstable to govern or defend the islands.

Owing to the severed telegraph cable between Manila and Hong Kong, neither Dewey nor the Spanish command in the Philippines knew that, on the day Manila surrendered, Madrid's envoys were signing an armistice in Washington. McKinley sent a delegation to Paris to negotiate a treaty, but, on 26 October, he alone made the major decision of the peace talks—to annex the Philippine Islands. Madrid reckoned that the Democrats would object to annexation and so procrastinated until the congressional elections in November returned Republican majorities to both the House and Senate. On 10 December, after McKinley threatened to renew the war, Spain agreed to the humiliating peace treaty. Anti-imperialists, mostly Democrats, opposed Philippine annexation on the grounds of traditional American anticolonialism and because the Constitution could not follow the flag. Others, including Captain Mahan, favored the acquisition of a naval base in the islands but opposed any commitment to defend the entire archipelago. Navy Secretary Long looked warily on annexation. "If I could have my personal preference," he confided to his diary, "I would . . . be rid of the Philippines and of everything else except our own country." No responsible American wanted to return the Philippines to Spain, Germany and Japan both clearly wanted to annex the islands, and most Republicans recognized that Philippine independence would not last long without an American guarantee. As attractive as granting independence to the Filipinos was, McKinley insisted that any American protectorate over the islands would be worthless unless the entire territory were defended. His reasoning was persuasive, and the Senate approved the peace treaty on 4 February 1899.[24]

The Philippine Insurrection was touched off when the Treaty of Paris dashed Aguinaldo's hope that the United States would grant independence to the Philippines. When General Merritt tried to disperse the Filipino Army around Manila, the rebels refused to move. Aguinaldo had decided to resist the Americans, and at 2330 on 4 February, the Filipinos attacked along the length of the sixteen-mile perimeter surrounding the capital. They were repulsed everywhere but in the north, where Major General Arthur MacArthur's troops had to fall back. To support MacArthur's counterattack, Captain Whiting in the *Charleston* moved close inshore and opened fire on several enemy positions with his 8-inch guns. He was soon joined by the gunboats *Concord* and *Callao* and the monitor *Monadnock*. Within two days, the Filipino offensive was repulsed and the second battle for Manila was over. Major General Ewell S. Otis, who relieved Merritt, realized, however, that the American role in the Philippines had taken a new turn.[25]

Otis decided to move quickly against the southern Visayans, an island group that was also threatened by separatist bands. An expedition stood out of Manila Bay bound for the port of Iloilo 300 miles to the south on the island of Panay. On 11 February, Captain Wilde in the *Boston* landed a party of fifty men under Lieutenant Albert Niblack, who braved opposing gunfire, occupied the town, and prevented the retreating rebels from destroying it. Eleven days later a landing party from the gunboat *Petrel* went ashore on Cebu and secured that island. By 2 March, the Visayans group was in American hands.

By this time MacArthur's troops, supported by the Philippine Squadron, had advanced on Aguinaldo's army, ousted them from the region just north of Manila, and pursued them into northern Luzon during a brutal campaign that ended in early June 1899 with the fall of Malolos, an enemy stronghold. Then, on 10 June, Major General Henry Lawton launched a second drive to overcome a 5,000-man Filipino army that held the shoreline between Manila and Cavite. This assault began when the *Monadnock* opened fire on the stronghold of Parañque, a withering barrage that forced the enemy to abandon his slit trenches and fall back to the Zapote River. Three days later, Lawton boarded the *Helena* and steamed northward to reconnoiter the opponent's new position. When the *Helena* neared the mouth of the Imus River, a hidden 6-inch rifled gun opened fire on the American formation and nearly hit the gunboat *Callao*. A formation of three American gunboats quickly silenced this battery. Lawton's troops attacked the insurgents at noon that day, their advance supported by the *Helena*'s powerful guns. Devastated by this display of American firepower, Aguinaldo retired to the village of Imus, but Lawton's remorseless pursuit soon forced him to order his troops to scatter. Although Cavite was secure, Otis' exhausted division had been decimated by fevers and had lost a large number of volunteers whose terms of enlistment were at an end.

While the Army awaited the arrival of reinforcements, the Philippine Squadron established a blockade of Luzon to prevent foreign arms from reaching the poorly equipped insurgents. On 17 September 1899, Naval Cadet Welborn C. Wood in the 1,400-ton blockade gunboat *Urdaneta* entered the mouth of the Orani River near Manila, but the vessel soon ran aground. While Wood and his men bravely tried to free their ship, Filipinos in a nearby village brought the stranded vessel under a brisk enfilading fire. Wood and several others were killed, and the rest of the Americans were taken prisoner. A week later, Commander W. T. Swinburne brought the *Helena* in company with several gunboats within gun range of the *Urdaneta* and provided covering fire for an American rescue party, which freed the stricken vessel.

After fresh troops arrived in the Philippines, General Otis renewed his offensive in northern Luzon against the vital railroad leading to Lingayen Gulf, the last key line of communications held by Aguinaldo's rebels. Exploiting the mobility provided by the Philippine Squadron, Otis embarked two regiments under Major General Wheaton, who was instructed to outflank the enemy. On 7 November 1899, the *Princeton* and the *Helena* led the Philippine Squadron into Lingayen Gulf, where they bombarded insurgent forts; meanwhile the Army waded ashore and captured the rebel port of San Fabian that evening. Although this stroke outflanked Aguinaldo's main body, Wheaton's lethargy during the next few days allowed the Filipino Army to escape Otis' trap.

Aguinaldo had avoided destruction in northern Luzon for the moment, but his army was nonetheless badly bruised, and he decided in December 1899 to divide his troops into several independent forces and launch a guerilla campaign. Meanwhile, Otis pressed home his advantage by instructing Wheaton to pursue Aguinaldo into the rugged interior of northeast Luzon while a second American force was directed to take the enemy port of Vigan on the eastern coast. On the afternoon of 24 November, the *Oregon* in company with the gunboats *Callao* and *Samar* anchored off Vigan, and the following day Captain Wilde bombarded the Filipino defenses and sent ashore a landing party of sailors and Marines, who overran the city without opposition. Aguinaldo was again trapped between an American stronghold on the coast and an advancing force moving toward him on his landward flank. The Filipino Army dispersed, and within a few weeks the Americans had surrounded the remnants of the insurgent force on the tip of Luzon. On 11 December, Aguinaldo's military deputy surrendered to Captain Bowman McCalla at the port of Aparri. Although Aguinaldo himself was still at large, this surrender marked the end of organized resistance on Luzon.

General Otis turned to the occupation of more of the southern Philippines. The *Nashville* and *Helena* and the gunboat *Merivales* landed troops at several hemp ports in southern Luzon and then helped to occupy the islands of Catanduanes, Samar, and Leyte without meeting much resistance. A treaty of occupation was negotiated with the Muslim sultan of Sulu. In 1900 Aguinaldo took heart from the declarations of Democratic presidential candidate William Jennings Bryan, who denounced the war and promised to grant independence to the Philippines if he were elected. By this time the Americans had adopted a counterinsurgency strategy of attacking the peasantry, which supported the guerrillas in a conflict conducted with unusual ferocity on both sides. "We certainly did a good job on the river," recalled Lieutenant Yates Stirling of his duty in the gunboat *Castine* during a punitive operation on the Gardara River. "After we had finished up, there was little left to speak of. We burned the villages; in fact, every house for two miles from either bank was destroyed by us. We killed their livestock, cattle, pigs, chickens, and their valuable work animals, their carabaos. It seemed ruthless; yet it was after all war, and war is brutal."[26]

When McKinley crushed Bryan at the polls in November 1900, much of the spark was drained from the Filipino rebels. Aguinaldo's capture further demoralized his followers, and most of them surrendered or suffered defeat in detail over the next year, although outbreaks of anti-American violence continued sporadically until 1906. The United States had not only ousted Spain from Cuba, Puerto Rico, and the Philippines, but also demonstrated that it intended to hold on to its new Pacific empire.

Chapter Twenty-four

Naval Policy and the Open Door
1899

Philippine annexation brought the United States into Far Eastern politics, and China's debility advanced that process. The turmoil on the mainland following the 1895 Sino-Japanese War caused the Great Powers to establish permanent spheres of influence in China with the thought that these territories might be annexed to their empires if China was dismembered. The Germans, following their new policy of "world politics," were first, occupying Kiachow Bay in November 1897 and establishing a naval base for their Pacific Squadron at Tsingtao. Russia forced Peking to sign twenty-five-year leases on the Liaotung Peninsula, Port Arthur, and nearby railroads; Japan obtained concessions in Fukien Province; and France won a ninety-nine-year lease on Kwangchowan Bay and the right to build a railroad from French Indochina to Yunnan. Britain, committed to free trade since 1844, was distressed at these moves, but it joined in and forced the Manchu court to allow the Royal Navy to build a naval base at Weihaiwei and to improve Britain's trading concessions in the Yangtze Valley.

Diverted by the war with Spain, the United States opposed these moves in principle but was more concerned with defending American merchants and missionaries against China's frequent, violent antiforeign outbreaks. Commodore Dewey was especially concerned about this danger, and pointed out to Navy Secretary Long in December 1897 that all the European powers were increasing their naval forces in Asian waters. Whereas France and Russia deployed battleships in the Far East and the British had three battleships and three armored cruisers on station off China, the U.S. Navy's Asiatic Squadron totaled only five smaller cruisers and gunboats. Unless America was prepared to defend its China trade, Dewey warned, it might be lost. Matters worsened in 1898 when Kuang-hsu, China's newly crowned emperor, initiated the "One Hundred Days" of political and economic reform only to be betrayed by an erstwhile ally, Shanghai governor Yuan Shih-kai, and soon imprisoned by the treacherous Dowager Empress Tzu Hsi.

American Minister E. H. Conger was so alarmed by the Tzu Hsi coup that he warned Dewey that unless naval protection was available, Americans residing in China would have to flee to the European legations. Dewey responded by dispatching Commander Frank Wilde in the cruiser *Boston* to Tientsin and by stationing small bodies of Marines there and in Peking, but Wilde reported that there was little danger for the moment to the American community in China. Nevertheless, Conger warned Washington that naval forces, the spheres of influence, and the treaty ports were the "chief elements of foreign potency" in China, and strongly urged a more muscular tone to America's Far Eastern diplomacy and the establishment of an Asiatic Squadron base on the China coast.

The Boxer Rebellion forced Washington to reexamine American aims in China and led to the announcement of the Open Door Policy. The Boxers, a violent, superstitious, secret North China society originally opposed to the Manchu dynasty, fell under Tzu Hsi's sway in the early 1890s and became an armed outlet for fanatical anti-Western xenophobia by the end of the decade. The Asiatic Squadron occasionally sent vessels up the Yangtze to visit American settlements during the decade, but when anti-Christian riots broke out in the valley from Chungking to Ichang and beyond in 1891, only a German gunboat was available. Marines and sailors were landed to defend the American community at Kiukiang, but they took no part in suppressing the uprisings. Congress was so alarmed by this turmoil that in 1893 it authorized the construction of three gunboats especially designed "for service in China or elsewhere." Although Tzu Hsi encouraged Boxer gangs to attack Western missionaries in Shanghai and Hopei, the large Boxer rising in 1899 centered in North China.

Wrestling with the related problems of the Boxer outrages, the spheres of influence, and the possible partitioning of China, Secretary of State John Hay stumbled upon an old British policy favoring free trade with China, termed the Open Door, and decided to adopt it to reach American ends. Neither McKinley nor Hay was willing to accept a British offer to issue a joint statement taking this line, but they did want to prevent the partitioning of China and protect American rights within the European spheres of influence. As a result, nonpartition and respect for international trading rights formed the basis for the first Open Door note, which Hay circularized in September 1899. Europe's reaction ranged from Italy's acceptance to Russia's equivocation, but Hay avoided this inconvenience by simply declaring on 23 March 1900 that the Open Door Policy had been accepted with commitments that were "definitive."[1]

The Boxer Rebellion around Peking was by now so serious that the Western ministers there asked their governments to stage a combined naval demonstration in North China waters, but Hay rejected the plan for the moment. He did, on the other hand, warn the Manchu court that China risked foreign occupation and partition unless the Boxers were checked. Navy Secretary Long was more concerned, and sent the cruiser *Wheeling* to visit the port of Taku on her way to Alaska in April. But Rear Admiral Remey, who now commanded the Asiatic Squadron, told Washington that he needed every ship in his command to deal with the Philippine Insurrection. Remey stationed his second in command, Rear Admiral Louis Kempff, with the cruiser *Newark* at Yokohama and ordered him to monitor events on the mainland, but Kempff could call for support only on the Yangtze Patrol gunboat *Castine* and the old sidewheeler *Monocacy* at Shanghai. On 17 May, when he received a cable from Conger, the American minister, that the situation in Peking was "becoming serious" and asking that a "warship [be sent to] Taku soon," Kempff decided to act. Ten days later the Boxer Army severed the railroad linking Peking and the port of Tientsin.[2]

Kempff arrived off Taku at the mouth of the Peiho River on 29 May, but he discovered that the *Newark* could not cross the bar and so asked Admiral Remey for support. Remey, burdened by the insurrection in the Philippines, believed American interests in China to be "comparatively minor" and refused to reinforce the China station. He was overruled on 6 June by Secretary Long, who ordered him to transfer the cruiser *Nashville,* some smaller shallow-draft vessels, and nearly 150 Marines to Kempff's command. Kempff now feared that the Boxer Army in Peking would storm the Western legation compound, but he too was reluctant to associate the United States with a multinational punitive expedition being arranged in London that month by the Great Powers. However, on 9 June, he organized a landing party of 112 Marines and bluejackets under Captain Bowman McCalla. The following day, McCalla was ordered to entrain with an international force of 2,000 troops under British Admiral Seymour, who was planning to march on Tientsin and then move forward and relieve Peking. Most of the powers had assembled substantial naval forces off the Taku bar by this time, but Lieutenant Victor Blue, who went ashore on 15 June, reported to Kempff that the Chinese had mined the Peiho River and planned to close it off by firing on ships from the nearby Taku forts. The Europeans demanded that the Chinese evacuate those forts; when this ultimatum was rebuffed, they readied an attack. Kempff refused to join the action in the belief that such a move would precipitate a war with China. He asked Washington for guidance but did not receive a reply for a week.

When the bombing of the Taku forts began at 0150 on the morning of 17 June, Commander Frederick W. Wise moved the *Monocacy* upriver so that his ship would be out of the way, but he was angry at Kempff for not allowing him to participate in the action. When a shell from one of the forts hit an American cutter at 0200, however, Kempff changed his mind. The Chinese had been forced to quit the Taku forts, but Kempff now told Wise to join the multinational squadron and advance with it up the Peiho to Tientsin. The same day, Commander E. D. Taussig in the *Yorktown* reached Chefoo and appealed via Remey to Washington for new orders. In an about-face, Remey now backed Taussig's appeal, and Assistant Secretary of the Navy Frank Hackett quickly wired back that the China station was to "act . . . with foreign forces . . . to protect all American interests." Kempff moved with alacrity, ordering Wise to occupy the Tangku railroad station and support Seymour's movement up the Peiho. The Boxers joined imperial troops in blocking this advance, however, and Seymour was forced to retire to Tientsin on 22 June. The following month reinforcements arrived, and in early August the multinational force took the offensive, thrashed several bodies of Chinese troops, and occupied Peking on the 14th. China was prostrate. After protracted negotiations lasting nearly a year, the powers forced Tzu Hsi's court to sign the humiliating Boxer Treaty in 1901, under which China was forced to pay a huge indemnity, disband the Boxers, punish several high-level officials, and allow greater foreign control over the Chinese economy.[3]

The bombing of the Taku forts and the negotiations leading to the relief expedition's offensive awakened Secretary Hay's concern that the powers might try to partition China after they entered the capital. On 3 July 1900 he circularized a second Open Door note, in which he announced that the United States sought a "solution" to the Boxer Rebellion that would "preserve Chinese territorial and administrative entity." European rivalries rather than the Open Door Policy prevented the powers from dismembering China in the Boxer Treaty, but Hay's pronouncement had profound and long-lasting consequences for American policy in the Far East. The negotiation of the Boxer Treaty also forced Washington to reconsider several proposals to establish a base for the Asiatic Squadron on the China coast, a plan advanced strongly by Admiral Dewey after he became chairman of the Navy's General Board in 1900. Hay supported Dewey's plan, and in November opened secret talks with the Chinese about acquiring a lease on Samsah Bay. Ironically, the project was thwarted by the Japanese, who had prior claims to the site and pointed out to Washington that Hay's objective violated his most recent enunciation of the Open Door Policy. Other schemes to establish an American naval base in Chinese waters were put forward over the next several years by Admiral Dewey, who had the wholehearted support of the State Department, but they all ran aground when confronted by the opposition of the other Great Powers or by resistance in Congress to the extension of American responsibility in the Far East.[4]

Hay's Open Door Policy might be construed as committing the United States to defend China's territorial integrity, but there existed no corresponding eagerness to construct a fleet powerful enough to defend American interests in Asian waters. "We have accomplished a great deal in the East," Hay boasted a few years later, "but thus far without the expense of a single commitment or promise." The Samsah Bay project illustrated the new conundrum in American naval policy. Although the Navy was dedicated to building a concentrated battle fleet, American foreign policy obligations were simultaneously becoming more geographically widespread. Overseas deployments thought necessary to uphold marginal interests in Asia, the Pacific, the Caribbean, and Europe persisted well beyond the turn of the century. In 1903, Admiral Robley Evans, commander in chief of the Asiatic Fleet, admitted that overseas naval bases would be vulnerable to an attack by a wartime opponent's fleet, but he nonetheless urged Washington "to obtain a foothold" around the Chinese port of Amoy in the hope of "thwarting the Japanese and perhaps . . . securing the territory for ourselves." With the collapse of this initiative, however, went the last hope for acquiring an overseas base beyond the Philippines.[5]

The rapid accumulation of America's overseas obligations coincided with the swift development of four major technological innovations that greatly increased the fighting power of all large navies and forever revised thinking about how hostile fleets would fight. The first came about when chemists replaced black powder with a propellant made from a compound of nitrogen and cellulose. They discovered that when it was used to fire guns, the resulting muzzle velocity of heavy shells leaving rifled barrels was doubled, thus providing greater striking power and smaller dispersion at far longer ranges. In turn, high-velocity ordnance led to the introduction of longer, heavier gun barrels and stronger gun mountings. During the nineteenth century, naval gunfire had been ineffective beyond about 2,000 yards, but with the introduction of high-velocity ordnance, naval gunners began to expect battles to be fought at 5,000 yards or more.

The second major innovation stemmed directly from the invention of the telescopic sight. Despite significant improvements in naval ordnance during the last three decades of the nineteenth century, the range of gunfire was limited by the gunner's vision— a maximum of about 1,500 yards—until Lieutenant Bradley Fiske introduced the telescopic sight into the fleet. The telescopic sight permitted accurate shooting out to about 7,000 yards. To naval tacticians, these developments meant that a disorganized melee between opposing fleets would be much less likely than in the past.

The greater destructive power of long-range, highly accurate naval gunfire led Navy men to ask how warships might be better protected. Neither armor-clad vessels nor ironclads could fight in rough water because their guns sat too low on the ship, thus necessitating a very low freeboard. The broadside gunports had to be shut in high seas to prevent spray and waves from disrupting the routine of loading and aiming the guns. This equation began to change after the invention in 1890 of Harvey process steel alloy plate—its face hardened by carburizing—which soon replaced compound steel in the manufacture of armor plate. Armor made from Harvey process steel was twice as resistant to gunfire as was common compound steel of equivalent weight, and its use allowed Navy ship designers to design high-freeboard battleships with high-mounted guns that were immune to ocean spray and could fight in rough seas. Lastly, a series of related inventions—including fast-operating breech mechanisms, large cartridge cases, and hydraulic recoil systems—evolved into the quick-firing 4-inch gun battery, a system that for the first time offered the capital ship an effective means of defending itself against opposing torpedo boats.

Paradoxically, vessels and weapons designed to defend the battleship now threatened its primacy. For example, except for a superior formation of capital ships, the greatest threat to a squadron of battleships and cruisers was from hostile torpedo boats. The menace was widely recognized. "We do not think that we shall have, perhaps shall never need, the large fleets of heavy ironclads," Lieutenant Commander W. W. Reisinger wrote in the Naval Institute *Proceedings'* prize essay in 1888, but "a fleet of powerful vessels with the latest and best torpedo outfits, . . . and high-powered guns, will prove the best coast defense, supplemented by the fast sea-going torpedo boats." The basic function of the torpedo boat, however, retarded its evolution into a high-seas combatant. The torpedo boat had to be very small to avoid being detected by an opposing ship and, to avoid being hit by an opponent's main battery, she also had to be very swift. However, the necessary dedication of such a high fraction of its displacement to the engine, the torpedoes, and the torpedo tubes meant that the torpedo boat could not operate very far from a base or, alternatively, from a slow, helpless tender. This limited its tactical utility to the defense of the sea approaches to naval installations, harbor entrances, or coastal shipping lanes.[6]

The Admiralty was worried that foreign torpedo boats might someday threaten the supremacy of Britain's system of battle fleets and far-flung naval bases, so the Royal Navy developed another new small warship, the destroyer, whose original tactical function was to check torpedo attacks against battleships. The Americans followed suit. By the time the Navy's first destroyer, the *Bainbridge*, was laid down in 1899, American naval leaders expected her not only to defend the battleships against enemy motor torpedo boat attacks, but also to launch her own torpedo attacks against an opponent and supplement the cruiser as a tactical scout. The new destroyers soon took over the mission of the torpedo boat, the very threat they had been built to challenge. The torpedo boat could steam for only about 1,000 miles before coaling, but the destroyer, with her greater displacement, greater range, and quick-firing 4-inch guns, made the torpedo boat obsolete. The destroyer also provided a useful type in which to test new materials and systems. Over the next decade high-tensile steel, pressurized main-bearing lubrication, and turbine steam engines were first tried out in American destroyers before they were installed in larger warships. Not only were these technologies applicable to battleships, but they also increased the Navy's ability to deploy powerful, highly flexible station ships to trouble spots in the Western Hemisphere where turmoil threatened Washington's interests. The Navy's General Board recommended building three torpedo boats in 1900, but there was little enthusiasm for this recommendation. Not even the success of Japan's torpedo boats against the Russian fleet in 1904 undermined the conviction that these short-range, low-endurance vessels were of little value to the American fleet.

Spurred on by enthusiasm over the fleet's victories on Manila Bay and off Santiago, Congress authorized the Navy to build three more battleships in the spring of 1899. The battleships *Georgia*, *Nebraska*, and *Virginia* were still considered to be "coastline" vessels, although each ship displaced nearly 15,000 tons and carried eight 8-inch guns and four 12-inch guns. Inflation, promoted in some measure by the war, had pushed their cost up to $6.5 million apiece. In the winter, Congress approved another pair of the same class of battleships, the *New Jersey* and the *Rhode Island*, but a postwar reaction to lavish military spending was mounting, and in 1900 the annual Navy Department appropriation included no funds for capital ship construction.

This brief lapse in the steady growth of the battleship fleet reflected in part a sense that the pace of international events had become too strident, a homegrown American mood that was synchronous with the flowering of a peace movement among the middle classes of Europe. The decade about to close had seen a vast arms race among all the Great Powers, with little corresponding increase of any sense of security. Indeed, the financial burden on the Russians had become so great that on 3 September 1898 they issued invitations for an international conference to promote "national economy and international peace" by putting "an end to the constantly increasing development of armaments." Few of the Great Powers were enthusiastic about this idea, but most Western governments accepted the invitations merely to satisfy loud domestic constituencies.[7]

The First Hague Conference—with twenty-six nations represented, it was the largest diplomatic gathering since the 1815 Congress of Vienna—opened on 18 May 1899. It soon evolved into a tortured exercise that avoided dealing with hard issues. Although the United States was the first to accept Russia's invitation, Hay was "doubtful" that disarmament "would prove effective" given the "temptations to which men and nations may be exposed in time of conflict." Joining a delegation headed by Ambassador Andrew D. White, Captain Alfred Thayer Mahan, already an international figure with a reputation transcending that of any of the other delegates, was chosen to represent the Navy. His views on disarmament were already well known. He wrote that year in *The Interest of America in Sea Power* that military and naval force had "won . . . the greatest triumphs of good in the checkered story of mankind. . . . Man," he trumpeted, "had ascended by the sword," a stance that White believed would "effectively prevent any" lapse into "sentimentality."[8]

Mahan announced that on principle he was against any international regulation of the use of any weapon at sea, but the conference nonetheless adopted a ban on the use of poison gas in naval warfare. Mahan cast the lone vote against it, pointing out that it was "illogical to be tender about a weapon that would asphyxiate men when it is allowable to blow the bottom out of an ironclad at midnight" and drown the crew. After appending a prohibition against the use of expanding "dum-dum" bullets, and a five-year moratorium on the dropping of explosives from balloons, the delegates established an arbitration tribunal in The Hague to adjudicate international disputes. Kaiser Wilhelm II looked upon this with as much skepticism as did Mahan, confiding that he reserved the right in international disputes "to rely on God and my sharp sword."[9]

For the new century, the whole process was instructive. No longer the province of statesmen, generals, and admirals, military and naval policy had come under the scrutiny of a new mass Western politics made possible by telegraphy, widely circulated and cheap newspapers, and the increasing literacy of the lower classes. Despite the evident public support for the peace movements, most of the delegates to the international conference had little use for this cause. Few were blind to Russia's motive in issuing the invitations, and few failed to recognize that there had been no talk of the underlying foreign policy disputes that were stimulating the international arms race. One month after New Year's Day 1900, the Senate approved the First Hague Convention and thanked White and Mahan for their work. The effect of Mahan's contribution to American naval disarmament policy was summed up by the British minister in Washington, Sir Julian C. Pauncefoote, who had told London before the conference even started that the United States "will on no account ever discuss the question of any limitation of naval armaments."[10]

When the Hague Convention was being considered by the Senate, it was warmly supported by William Jennings Bryan, whose loud protests against new battleship construction and the establishment of overseas fleet bases were heard later in the year. Renominated in 1900 by the Democrats, Bryan opposed McKinley's vigorous foreign policy, high protective tariffs, and expansionist naval program. McKinley was a popular chief executive, a crafty politician, and a solid war leader, however, and in the November election he crushed the Democrats, easily winning a second term. William McKinley was at the peak of his powers at his second inaugural. Within the year, however, he was dead from gunshot wounds suffered at the hands of a crazed anarchist, and the country was in mourning. McKinley was a shrewd statesman, but his diplomacy and military and naval strategy were fundamentally that of a counterpuncher who seized the most from each opportunity. He had little curiosity about the great affairs of Europe or the shifting balance of power, and only a limited notion of the perils America faced in her new role as a Great Power.

Chapter Twenty-five

The Big Stick of the Great White Fleet
1901–1908

When Vice President Theodore Roosevelt assumed the presidency following McKinley's assassination, the United States possessed the world's largest economy and greatest untapped military potential. International events seemed to be unfolding at a dizzying pace. TR pushed the nation into the arena of world-power politics, joined the struggle for the mastery of Europe, stabilized a new set of international relationships in the Far East, and strengthened America's hold over its traditional sphere of influence in the Caribbean and Central America. The Navy was the "big stick" of his active foreign policy. Possessing enormous self-confidence in his ability to devise an astute naval policy, Roosevelt believed that any "fairly able man" could manage the shore establishment, but the "systematic development of policy" and the "military efficiency of the fleet" required the president's "attention." One result of this approach was that none of his six secretaries of the Navy was able to put his own print on naval policy. "It is impossible to treat our foreign policy . . . save as conditioned upon the attitude we are willing to take toward our Army, and especially toward our Navy," Roosevelt declared.[1]

TR did not transfigure the Navy, however. He inherited an unbalanced fleet from McKinley—the General Board complained of the "disproportion now existing between various types of war vessels"—and bequeathed an equally unbalanced fleet to William Howard Taft, his successor. He also left the organization of the

Navy Department essentially intact. He intended to expand the fleet, but administering this policy demanded a strong secretary familiar with the Navy, attributes possessed by none of TR's appointees except John D. Long, a holdover from the McKinley era. A member of the Peace Society, Long was an anti-imperialist Republican, uncomfortable with the costs of naval expansion and uneasy with the fact that the United States was becoming a world power. Navy reformers, led by Admirals Mahan and Luce, had for some years advocated the creation of a naval general staff headed by a chief of operations who would direct the squadrons and prepare the fleet for war, but Long stood in their way. He feared that a naval general staff would be a "stimulus to a chief of staff to hereafter seek always direct communication with the president; and a president with aggressive force would easily come to deal with the official who by law is made the working head . . . of the department." Long greatly complicated the issue of reorganization in 1900 by naming Admiral Dewey to preside over the newly created General Board of the Navy, established to collect intelligence and advise the secretary on war plans and shipbuilding.

The creation of the General Board did not satisfy the proponents of a naval general staff, however, for Dewey possessed no command authority over the bureaus or the fleet. In 1904, at the urging of Rear Admiral Henry Clay Taylor, the highly respected chief of the Bureau of Navigation, Navy Secretary William H. Moody asked Congress to create a general staff and to appoint a member of the General Board to serve as chief of operations and the secretary's principal military adviser. Although both TR and Dewey supported the bill, it was opposed by Assistant Secretary Charles Darling, most of the bureau chiefs, and Senator Hale, the powerful chairman of the Naval Affairs Committee, and it died on the Hill. After Dewey's candidate for the chief of operations billet, Rear Admiral Taylor, died the following year, Dewey's support for reform waned, and Congress showed no interest in reviving the issue.[2]

A related issue involved the bureau chiefs. Most of them were line officers who rotated in and out of office every three years. A strong secretary might mold them into an effective management team, but most secretaries had little knowledge of naval affairs or independent sources of technical advice and were often prisoners of the bureau chiefs, who jealously guarded their independence. The problem was sensationalized in a 1908 article by Henry Reuterdahl in *McClure's* magazine following a series of accidents involving the Navy's latest battleships. A minor mishap in one of the *Massachusetts'* gun turrets in 1903 was followed in April 1904 by a real tragedy on board the *Missouri.* Flaming gases from a gun's breech ignited a charge about to be loaded, and the burning powder fell through the hoist into the handling room. The explosions and fires killed thirty men. A temporary solution was found by blowing out the gun barrels with compressed air after each firing. Then a similar explosion in the *Kearsarge* in 1906 killed fifty men, aroused public interest, and led to an inconclusive congressional investigation.[3]

Lieutenant Commander William S. Sims, an inveterate reformer, charged that the battleship turrets were so poorly designed that there was "nothing to prevent a shell or charge . . . from falling to the magazine deck at the bottom of the ship. The danger of explosion . . . as a result of such an accident is obvious." At length the General Board persuaded the Navy's chief constructor, Rear Admiral Washington Lee Capps, to replace the straight hoist with safety hatches, two unconnected hoists, and a separate upper handling room situated between the magazines and the turret. Dewey, Rear Admiral Seaton Schroeder, Captain Bradley Fiske, and other reformers believed that the turret problem was related to the archaic bureau system and the composition of the Board of Construction. The object of much of their criticism, Admiral Capps, defended the battleships' design and argued that filling the Board of Construction with line officers who possessed limited technical expertise made little sense. "The people who built the turrets were not the people who built the guns," Sims grumbled. But most of the reformers like Sims and Fiske were line officers, and Capps pointed out that the design flaws about which his critics complained resulted from majority votes by line officers on the Board of Construction.[4]

The reformers also charged that the bureau system was responsible for the Navy's slowness in adopting advances in naval gunnery following the fleet's poor performance in the Spanish-American War. Dewey's Asiatic Squadron had fired over 5,800 rounds in Manila Bay, but only 2.4 percent hit anything; only 3 percent of the shells fired at Cervera off Santiago found their targets. This stimulated Sims' interest in gunnery, and while serving in the Far East he met another stormy figure, Captain Sir Percy Scott, a British gunnery expert who had devised a system of continuous-aim firing that greatly improved accuracy. When Sims could not arouse interest in this system in the Bureau of Ordnance, he wrote directly to Roosevelt in November 1901. Admitting the "irregularity" of his letter, he claimed that the Navy's "marksmanship is so crushingly inferior" to that "of our possible enemies" that in battle the fleet "would . . . inevitably suffer humiliating defeat." TR replied that Sims was "unduly pessimistic" but encouraged him to keep complaining, and arranged for Sims to be appointed Inspector of Target Practice in the Bureau of Navigation in 1904.

U.S. Navy Department

Admiral of the Navy George Dewey was commander of the Asiatic Squadron, 1897–98; victor at the Battle of Manila Bay; and president of the General Board of the Navy, 1900–15.

Not only did Sims bring Scott's continuous-aim firing system to the fleet, but he was also instrumental in the adoption of Fiske's range-finding fire control system by the Bureau of Ordnance in 1906. Roosevelt tended to agree that the bureau system was responsible for various lapses, but Senator Hale frustrated his every effort to reorganize the Navy, including a last-gasp plan put forth in early 1909 by Moody and Mahan, which Congress ignored.[5]

TR continued McKinley's expansionist naval policy, although he never laid down specific goals for fleet expansion and rejected the one attempt by Admiral Dewey in 1903 to establish a long-term naval shipbuilding program linked closely to the administration's foreign policy goals. Dewey fixed an objective of forty-eight battleships by 1920, assuming that they would be divided between an Atlantic Fleet of thirty-two battleships and a Pacific Fleet of sixteen. This would ensure parity with Germany in the Atlantic and simultaneously assure the defense of the Philippines and a means to uphold the Open Door Policy in China. Every two battleships should be supported by one armored cruiser, seven protected and scout cruisers, three destroyers, and two colliers, and each division of four battleships should be supported by five auxiliaries, supply, repair, and hospital ships, and two transports. Dewey's Naval Scheme required the administration and Congress to agree to build two or three battleships annually and the requisite number of cruisers, destroyers, and auxiliaries.

From $81 million in 1901, Navy appropriations skyrocketed to $118 million four years later, but TR ignored Dewey's plan, improvised naval policy instead, emphasized battleship construction at the expense of a balanced fleet, and seldom gave Congress much guidance about what he wanted. He was mostly interested in building more battleships than Germany or Japan but adjusted his naval policy to satisfy public opinion. He inherited a fleet that contained nine battleships in commission and three 12,500-ton *Maine*-class and five 15,000-ton *Georgia*-class battleships under construction. The trend was toward building faster, heavier battleships, and Roosevelt continued that policy. Often he had to bow to congressional whims on battleship design, however. Between 1902 and 1906, Congress authorized five 16,000-ton, 18-knot *Connecticut*-class battleships, but in 1903 Senator Hale ignored the General Board's protests and forced the Navy to lay down two slower, 13,000-ton, 17-knot *Idaho*-class battleships. Domestic politics molded Roosevelt's naval policy far more than he liked to admit.

Congress was in an economy mood in early 1905, so he trimmed
the General Board's request for three battleships that year and the
next to a replacement level of one battleship annually. As a result,
only the 20,000-ton *Delaware* was authorized in 1906, and the following year her sister ship, the *North Dakota*, was laid down.[6]

The great distance separating America's new Caribbean and
Pacific maritime empires suggested the need for either two independent battle fleets or an isthmian canal to provide a single fleet
with strategy mobility. "The Navy offers the only means of making
our insistence upon the Monroe Doctrine anything but a subject
of derision to whatever nation chooses to disregard it," TR declared. He was mindful that broken canal schemes littered the nation's record since the 1848 Polk-Mallarino Treaty in which New
Grenada, later renamed Colombia, ceded an exclusive right to
construct a waterway through Panama. This was modified by the
1850 Clayton-Bulwer Treaty in which the United States and Britain
agreed to share the right to build and fortify any isthmian canal.
Most nineteenth-century canal schemes, which favored a site
across Nicaragua, were concocted by private firms, but the *Oregon*'s highly publicized 1898 cruise caused McKinley to announce
that "the construction of such a maritime highway is now more
than ever indispensable" and that the government rather than industry would undertake the project.[7]

Continuing this policy, Roosevelt had first to convince Britain
to abandon her canal interests. "If the canal is open to the warships
of an enemy it is a menace for us in time of war," he wrote. "If fortified by us it becomes one of the most potent sources of our possible sea strength. Unless it is fortified it strengthens against us every
nation whose fleet is larger than ours." Inasmuch as Whitehall's concern for the West Indies was ebbing, the British agreed in late 1901
in the second Hay-Pauncefoote Treaty to supersede the 1850 arrangement and release the United States from its earlier obligations. A comic duel now ensued between investors in the rival
Nicaraguan and Panamanian sites. Aware of Central America's
chronic political instability, TR was taking no chances. Before
Congress chose the site for the canal, he ordered Captain Thomas
Perry in the battleship *Iowa* to Panama to survey the approaches to
Panama City and Colón and determine "how to gain quickly the line
of the railroad" in the event of a crisis. He also negotiated with
Colombia to obtain a naval base at Almirante Bay, and Bogatá
agreed, on condition that Congress select Panama as the canal site.[8]

A volcano, which erupted 100 miles from Lake Nicaragua, moved Congress to approve the Panamanian site, and soon after, TR signed the 1903 Hay-Herran Treaty in which Colombia ceded sovereign rights to a canal zone from the Pacific to the Atlantic in return for $10 million. The treaty was popular in Bogotá, but Colombia's president wanted more money and forced his senate to reject the agreement. Refusing to be blackmailed by the "contemptible little creatures in Bogotá," TR confided that he now favored Panamanian independence. Colombia's writ over Panama was never certain, and on ten different occasions in the nineteenth century Panama had been independent. Colombia had repeatedly begged Washington to send gunboats and Marines to secure order in Panama under the 1846 treaty, and Roosevelt himself reluctantly had sent ships to Panama in 1902 to protect the Panama City-Colón railroad.[9]

When the Colombian senate rejected the Hay-Herran Treaty, TR set in motion events that led to Panama's independence. Philippe Bunau-Varilla, a French rogue who represented Pana-

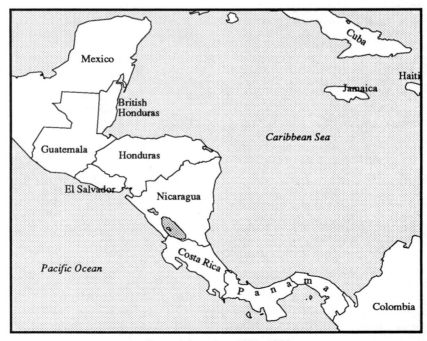

Central America, 1901–1908

manian separatists in Washington, was eager to lead a revolt against Colombia if he could be certain that Roosevelt would recognize his government. On 10 October 1903, TR privately told him that he was "delighted" by the prospect of an independent Panama, but in public the president was unusually restrained. Aware that a revolution was about to erupt, Roosevelt shifted his forces into place. On 19 October, Rear Admiral Glass, the commander of the Pacific Squadron, was directed to send the cruiser *Boston* from San Francisco to San Juan del Sur, Nicaragua. From that station she could support the Panamanians if the uprising succeeded or return to Acapulco if it collapsed. The screw-steamer *Dixie*, carrying a battalion of 400 Marines, stood out of Philadelphia four days later and reached the new naval base on Guantánamo Bay, Cuba, on 29 October. That same day, Commander John Hubbard in the 1,370-ton patrol gunboat *Nashville* reached Kingston, Jamaica, a holding position that put him within thirty hours of Colón.[10]

Roosevelt's supposition that Bogatá would not intervene was upset when Colombia's commanding general in Panama sent troops to the border to prevent an invasion by Nicaragua. A few days later, reinforcements boarded a Colombian Navy gunboat at Cartagena and sailed for Colón. When Bunau-Varilla got word of this movement on 30 October, he warned Washington that Panama's revolt would fail unless these troops could be prevented from reaching the Colón railroad. That afternoon Hubbard received secret orders to "proceed at once to Colón" in the *Nashville* and "prevent any landing of any armed force with hostile intent, either government or insurgent." The *Dixie* was to steam from Kingston to Colón, and the *Boston* was to move from San Juan del Sur to Panama City, there to be joined a few days later by the rest of the Pacific Squadron, now riding at anchor in Acapulco Bay. The *Nashville* stood into Colón at 1730 on 2 November, but when Hubbard went ashore, he found no revolution in progress and everything quiet. In short, Roosevelt had imposed so much secrecy over the operation that his commanders on the scene were unaware of his purposes.[11]

The whole plan was nearly upset by Hubbard's reaction when the transport *Cartagena* carrying 400 Colombian soldiers stood into Colón. "In the absence of any instructions" to prevent them from disembarking before the revolt began, he offered no objection for the moment. The situation was saved by the railroad manager, who sent his rolling stock westward, thereby preventing the Colombian troops from entraining for Panama City. Hubbard changed his mind at dawn the next day when he learned that the rebels had declared Panama's independence. He now put ashore a landing party and warned the Colombian commander that the Americans would not allow the opposing troops to entrain on the grounds that this would "threaten the free and uninterrupted transit of the Isthmus," which the Americans were "pledged to maintain." The Marines in the *Dixie* arrived at Colón on 5 November and the Colombian battalion boarded its transport and returned to Cartagena.[12]

Roosevelt extended diplomatic recognition to Bunau-Varilla's Republic of Panama the next day. With the U.S. Navy now controlling both sides of the isthmus, the Colombians were unable to thwart the revolution. And when rumors reached Washington on 9 November that Bogotá intended to assemble a fleet of steamers and try to land troops in Panama outside the transit zone, the Navy moved a squadron of shallow-draft gunboats to the Caribbean and Roosevelt instructed Admiral Glass to use force to prevent "the landing of men with hostile intent within the limits of the State of Panama." Less than two weeks later, Secretary of State Hay signed the Hay–Bunau-Varilla Treaty with the infant republic. Panama received $10 million for ceding sovereignty to a canal zone across the country and for granting the United States the right to build, operate, and fortify a canal. A bipartisan coalition in the Senate approved the treaty after a short debate, and in 1904 work began on Roosevelt's "big ditch." "I took the Canal Zone and let Congress debate," he later boasted when his naval diplomacy was criticized, "and while the debate goes on, the Canal does also."[13]

The acquisition of the Canal Zone in 1903 planted the pivot of American naval power astride one of the world's most vital sea lines of communications. It also coincided with the emergence of a new German challenge to the American sphere of influence in Latin America. To reorient German naval strategy from coastal defense to a blue water fleet, the young Kaiser Wilhelm II, influenced by Mahan's theory of seapower, had effected a startling change in German naval policy. In 1892, he named to the high command Admiral Alfred von Tirpitz, a leading advocate of replacing Germany's coastal cruisers with battleships. Six years later Tirpitz persuaded the kaiser to approve a naval law authorizing the construction of a fleet of battleships and establishing the concept of "risk" as the basis of German naval strategy. "Germany must have a battle-fleet so strong that, even for the adversary with the greatest sea-power, a war against it would involve such dangers as to imperil his position in the world," he explained. Tirpitz hoped to pose a threat to the Royal Navy of such magnitude that London would not endanger her fleet by siding with the new Franco-Russian Alliance. He also planned to employ the German Fleet to acquire and defend Germany's overseas possessions and to expand her influence in the Far East, Africa, the Pacific, and Latin America.[14]

The Venezuelan affair provided the kaiser with an opportunity to employ his new naval power with British and Italian support. Although TR respected German efficiency, he grew to dislike Wilhelm II, whom he called "restless and tricky," and to distrust Germany's unpredictable meddling outside of Europe in the name of "world politics." His first clash with Germany arose from the kaiser's intervention in Venezuela. Dictator Cipriano Castro, characterized by TR as an "unspeakably villainous monkey," refused to repay debts of $12 million foolishly lent to Venezuela by Germany, Italy, and Britain. In 1901, Lieutenant Commander Nathan Sargant reported that the German gunboat *Viveta* was surveying sites off Venezuela's coast. This was ominous news, and it confirmed Roosevelt's suspicions that the kaiser intended to use the Venezuelan default to increase Germany's influence in Latin America. Nevertheless, in December of that year TR approved punitive action by Germany against Venezuela, but he warned Berlin that he would oppose any territorial acquisitions. During 1902, both Germany and Britain severed diplomatic relations with Venezuela, and the kaiser deployed to the Caribbean a small naval squadron supported by British and Italian ships. They blockaded Venezuelan ports and seized her shipping—an exercise in gunboat diplomacy in the Western Hemisphere that thoroughly alarmed Roosevelt. The threat to Venezuela also attracted Admiral Dewey's attention, and he consistently urged TR to check the growth of German influence in the Caribbean.[15]

Other forces were also at work. Following the Spanish-American War, both Dewey and Mahan urged that the battleship fleet remain concentrated on the East Coast, but Long and just about every other Navy official favored reconstituting the overseas station squadrons. TR even created a permanent European Squadron soon after he entered the White House. However, the acquisition of Puerto Rico and the Guantánamo, Cuba, naval base stimulated interest in expanding the strategic concept of the Monroe Doctrine and applying this new formulation to the Caribbean. If "fortified naval bases could be established in Cuba and Puerto Rico," the General Board reported in 1901, then "our Navy can control the Caribbean." The Naval War College wrote a new tactical plan that summer, which Dewey decided to test in exercises with the North Atlantic Fleet off Culebra, Puerto Rico, during October 1902.

The timing of this battleship concentration was fortuitous inasmuch as Roosevelt soon faced a public uproar over Germany's intervention in Venezuela. Dewey, well known for his anti-German views, took command of the Atlantic Fleet on 8 December, two days before a combined Anglo-German squadron sank two Venezuelan Navy gunboats and bombarded Puerto Cabello. Five days later they landed troops that seized the town of La Guaya. Roosevelt now reasoned that the kaiser's true objective was to acquire a coaling station in the region. "It is the thin end of the wedge and I do not like the move at all," he told Senator Lodge. "A coaling station is what Germany most lacks in our waters and the kaiser could use this commercial station for warships." While Dewey conducted an elaborate exercise to determine whether a German fleet could cross the Atlantic from Europe and establish an advance base in the Caribbean before being obstructed by the Atlantic Fleet, Roosevelt announced that his policy was to "speak softly and carry a big stick." The German ambassador was warned that TR intended to order Dewey, whose fleet included fifty-four warships and colliers from the North Atlantic, European, and South Atlantic Squadrons, to steam for Venezuelan waters unless the kaiser agreed to a plan for international arbitration of his dispute with Cipriano Castro.[16]

Roosevelt, whose position on Germany and the Monroe Doctrine was hardening, also warned Berlin that the United States might intrude in Europe's balance of power politics unless Europe respected American rights in the Western Hemisphere. He had Navy Secretary Moody quietly tell the German ambassador on 2 March 1903 that the North Atlantic Fleet was going to appear soon in European waters as a counterweight to the presence of the German squadron off Venezuela.

Rear Admiral Charles S. Cotton with the European Squadron, composed of the protected cruisers *Chicago*, *Albany*, and *Cincinnati* and the gunboat *Machias*, stood into Marseilles on

30 April to greet President Emile Loubet, who was returning to France from an important state visit to North Africa. The European powers saw the squadron's arrival as a signal of Roosevelt's support for the French position in an ongoing colonial dispute with Germany over Morocco. Loubet was so excited by Cotton's appearance that he invited him to visit Paris, where the Americans were feted during celebrations marking the simultaneous visit of King Edward VII, whose reception in the French capital led to the April 1904 Anglo-French Entente. "The cat is out of the bag," Tirpitz was warned.

The kaiser, unnerved by this shocking turn of events, at once cabled TR and asked him to instruct the European Squadron to visit the German fleet base at Kiel as a neutral gesture. When Roosevelt refused, the German press took up the issue so loudly that Ambassador Charlemagne Tower in Berlin alerted Washington that "this question has assumed a very serious importance." TR reversed himself, and the squadron, augmented by the battleship *Kearsarge*, stood into Kiel in mid-June. Admiral Cotton basked in the friendly welcome. "The naval love feast now going on in Kiel has an air of unreality," commented the *New York Times* on 14 June. "While the host and the guest are exchanging civilities . . . each is preoccupied with the speculations to the figure he would be likely to cut if they met under different conditions." And soon after this, Rear Admiral Albert S. Barker led a division of three new battleships of the North Atlantic Fleet in highly visible maneuvers off the Portuguese Azores. Other pressures were at play. The British, who did not intend to squander American good will, had withdrawn from the Venezuelan affair, thus isolating Germany. As a result, the kaiser agreed that the issue be handled by the International Court at The Hague. To TR's astonishment, however, the court sanctioned German policy.[17]

This decision encouraged Berlin to bring pressure on the Dominican Republic to pay $32 million that it owed to European banks. This in turn moved President Carlos Morales, confronted by economic chaos and a civil war, to beg Washington for protection. Germany wanted "to see how far she could go in testing the Monroe Doctrine," warned Admiral Taylor, and the General Board crafted a new Black War Plan, which had as its "basis an attempt by Germany, in coalition with one or more other European powers, to gain a permanent foothold upon the South American continent north of the Amazon." If war ensued, Dewey believed, the fleet would have to look to the "principle theater of operations being the Caribbean Sea." Thus armed, TR used the opportunity to clarify American foreign policy in the Western Hemisphere.[18]

In December 1904, TR enunciated the Roosevelt Corollary to the Monroe Doctrine. "As a mere matter of self-defense we must exercise a close watch over the approaches to [the Panama] canal, and this means that we must be thoroughly alive to our interests in the Caribbean," he told Congress. "The Monroe Doctrine may force the United States, however reluctantly, in flagrant cases of . . . wrongdoing or impotence, to the exercise of an international police power." Two months later President Morales transferred the Dominican customs house to American oversight, and Roosevelt ordered Captain Albert Dillingham, who commanded the cruiser *Detroit*, to patrol Dominican waters, enforce the customs agreement, and prevent European intervention. Problems elsewhere caused the kaiser to publicly approve of American policy, but he secretly told Tirpitz to prepare plans for a fleet action in the Caribbean should another crisis arise. From this episode Dewey derived the lesson that the Navy's planning "will always be greatly simplified if we bear in mind the clear proposition to prepare for a struggle with this power. Such a struggle is inevitable unless we studiously direct our efforts to prepare for it."[19]

The Caribbean incidents also clarified American naval strategy, and within weeks of the exercises off Culebra, Puerto Rico, in late 1902, Roosevelt decided to concentrate all the modern battleships into a single North Atlantic Fleet. Paradoxically, Mahan opposed this step. "To remove our fleet—battle fleet—from the Pacific would be . . . a confession of weakness," he told Rear Admiral Taylor, the chief of the Bureau of Navigation. "It would mean a revision to a policy narrowly American, and essentially defensive." Roosevelt's decision to consolidate the battle fleet in the Atlantic did not represent, as Mahan feared, a repudiation of the obligation to defend the Philippines, but rather a realistic acknowledgment that protecting American interests in the Caribbean and Europe took precedence over guarding her commonwealth in the Pacific and supporting Open Door diplomacy in the Far East. Although a few older battleships returned to the Pacific Squadron on the West Coast, and the station squadrons were not abolished, the tactical formation of each major command was sorted out into divisions of battleships, cruisers, and destroyers. The Culebra exercises also convinced Dewey that the Navy needed to acquire bases in Cuba, Panama, the Danish West Indies, Costa Rica, Puerto Rico, Peru, and at either Port au Prince or in Samaná Bay in the Dominican Republic, but this policy was so costly that Roosevelt refused to approve it. Instead, Roosevelt was coming around to the view that three strongpoints, combined with the Marine Corps' new mobile advance base force, would be enough to deny a hostile German fleet any basing in the Caribbean littoral. A conservative base policy of developing only the American-owned establishments at Guantánamo, Culebra, and Panama also avoided the tangled question of more overseas territorial acquisitions.[20]

In 1904 Germany confronted a new balance of power in Europe, and the kaiser refused to challenge the Roosevelt Corollary. Following the Boer War, Britain had abandoned her late nineteenth-century policy of "splendid isolation" and signed the 1902 Anglo-Japanese Alliance. With Japan committed to safeguarding Britain's interests in the Far East, the Admiralty turned to deal with the new menace of Tirpitz's Risk Fleet and the kaiser's "world politics." Britain and France secretly agreed to staff talks in 1904 that led to the creation of the Entente understandings, and that same year Admiral Sir John Fisher, the Royal Navy's new First Sea Lord, withdrew Britain's modern battleships from the overseas stations and consolidated them into the Grand Fleet, which he based on the North Sea. He also ignited a new world naval race by building the world's first single-caliber main battery battleship, the *Dreadnought.* The *Dreadnought*'s commissioning made all other battleships obsolete inasmuch as they all were armed with less powerful mixed-caliber main batteries.

The Anglo-Japanese Alliance not only allowed Britain to turn her attention to Germany but also freed Japan to confront Russia without fear of renewed European interference. Japan wanted to annex Korea, but the Russians foolishly refused to agree. The Russo-Japanese War broke out on 6 February 1904, when Japan ended long-stalled negotiations. Two nights later, the Japanese fleet surprised and crushed Russia's Pacific Fleet at Port Arthur, and within days her army had occupied Korea and laid siege to Port Arthur. Not until October did the Russians assemble their larger Baltic Fleet for the voyage to the Far East, and when it sailed into the Straits of Tsushima separating Japan and Korea on 27 May 1905, it was ambushed by Admiral Togo and almost completely destroyed. Three days later the tsar asked Roosevelt to mediate an end to the war, and hard upon this request the president convened a peace conference at Portsmouth, New Hampshire. Aware that both sides were exhausted and needed peace, he tried to salvage Russian honor and a balance of power in the Far East without offending Japan. In the Treaty of Portsmouth, Russia transferred her leaseholds at Darien and Port Arthur to Japan and agreed to Japanese control of southern Manchuria, Korea, and the southern Sakhalin Islands. The agreement brought Roosevelt the Nobel Peace Prize and a new matrix of power both in the Far East and Europe.[21]

The Russo-Japanese War forced Roosevelt to make a new series of major decisions about American strategy and naval policy. When the war broke out, he was uncertain what to do after three years of rapid and very costly shipbuilding. Admiral Dewey's General Board had tried in 1903 to look over the horizon to assess the future of American naval policy. Assuming Germany to be the most probable enemy, Dewey reasoned that the United States required a battleship fleet equal to or greater than Germany's High Seas Fleet so that the Navy might defend the Caribbean against an invasion led by Tirpitz's battleships. Based on this "second power standard," the General Board proposed that the Navy build a fleet consisting of forty-eight battleships over the next two decades. How Dewey arrived at this figure was unclear; the German Naval Law of 1900 authorized a fleet of only thirty-eight battleships by 1920. TR ignored Dewey's Naval Scheme, however, and announced in early 1905 a plan to "maintain" the fleet at the existing level of twenty-eight battleships and twenty armored cruisers. "It does not seem necessary that the Navy should, at least in the immediate future, be increased beyond the present number of units." The outcome of the Russo-Japanese War and the appearance of the *Dreadnought* forced him to reconsider this policy.[22]

In early 1905, Congress authorized the 16,000-ton battleships *South Carolina* and *Michigan*, each of which were to be armed with single-caliber main batteries consisting of eight 12-inch guns on the centerline. Later that year, for the first time, Congress approved a new class of American battleships without placing limits on the tonnage of each vessel. Displacing 20,000 tons and armed with eight guns on the broadside, the battleship *Delaware* was the first American "dreadnought," heralded by Navy Secretary Charles Bonaparte as the "largest and strongest battleship that is known to be afloat." The long-term implication of the introduction of the dreadnought class was not lost on the Americans. "Unless the country—and Congress—are prepared for practically un-limited expenditure, bigger ships mean fewer ships," Mahan had warned Secretary Long several years earlier. On the whole, American battleship designers sought firepower rather than speed or armor defenses. They regarded speed as the most transitory characteristic of a warship, a quality easily degraded by foul bottoms, poor coal, clotted smoke stacks, or damage to the steam engines. Achieving sustained high speed invariably meant sacrificing range, armor, or guns, and Navy men preferred to fight opponents who defended themselves with inferior batteries.[23]

The mix of the caliber of the guns was another issue. Mahan argued that the Japanese had defeated the Russians at Tsushima with their superior quick-firing intermediate batteries, but Admiral Schroeder, Captain Fiske, and Commander Sims held an opposing view. They believed that Russia's inferior big guns, among other factors, had led to Japan's victory. Dewey's General Board had recommended for two years that the Navy's new battleships be armed with single-caliber main batteries and proposed on 28 October 1904 that the battleships *Michigan* and *South Carolina* incorporate this principle. As a result, these ships were armed with eight 12-inch guns and no intermediate batteries, and thus became the precursors to Navy's first *Dreadnought*-type vessels, although their guns were too light to be effective at long range. And, Mahan pointed out, they were poorly prepared to repel torpedo attacks. Whereas mixed-caliber main batteries fired more shells with a greater throwweight than all-big-gun battleships, the mixed battery's guns were brought into action and fired individually, and so did not lend themselves to the newly devised centralized fire control systems.

The issue reached a climax in 1906 when Congress authorized construction of the battleship *Delaware* but set no limit on her tonnage, effectively leaving it for the president to decide. Mahan pressed TR to order that mixed-caliber main batteries be installed on the grounds that the all-big-gun battleships were so expensive that the numbers of battleships in the fleet would be sharply reduced. Sims regarded this as an advantage, however. "For the sum that it would cost to maintain twenty small battleships we could maintain a fleet of ten large ones that would be greatly superior in tactical qualities, in effective hitting capacity, speed protection, and inherent ability to concentrate its gunfire." The launching of the *Dreadnought* in Britain apparently clinched the issue, and on 19 December Roosevelt informed Congress that the *Delaware* would be armed with a single-caliber main battery.[24]

The Bureau of Ordnance announced that it intended "to so arm" American battleships "that they be superior to foreign vessels of equal class in that class." While this was true of the main batteries, American battleships also differed significantly from their European counterparts, differences that reflected the Navy's policy of building in greater range in the American capital ships than other nations' vessels required. The *Dreadnought* was designed to carry 2,700 tons of coal, but her normal load was only 900 tons; American battleships had much larger coal bunkers and usually carried at least two-thirds of their designed load displacement for coal. The uniform-caliber main battery, moreover, paved the way for the introduction five years later of a main-fire control system that coupled several older, dissimilar components: the telescopic central fire director, optical range finders, spotters aloft to report the fall of the shot, and internal electrical communications to link all these elements with one another and with the gun batteries. When the first main fire-control systems were installed in battleships in 1911, the effective range of naval gunfire was extended from about 6,000 yards to nearly 14,000 yards and accuracy was significantly improved.[25]

The debate over the tactical impact of the *Dreadnought*'s innovations coincided with Roosevelt's adoption of a new line in naval policy in late 1905. In March of that year he confided to his friend General Leonard Wood that he had "now reached my mark" for the battle force, a level that "puts us a good second to France and about on a par with Germany." A few months later he announced that he would thenceforth follow a replacement policy that could "be obtained by adding a single battleship to our Navy each year." His indecision over naval policy in late 1905 reflected an uncertainty about the balance of power in Europe following the first Moroccan crisis, an affair in which TR for the first time gingerly committed Washington to the equilibrium of the continent. The kaiser's untimely announcement that he would support Moroccan independence if France tried to annex that country—as she clearly intended to do—created a war scare in Europe and drove Britain into negotiating an unwritten entente with France. Now aware of the results of his rambunctious posturing, the kaiser turned to Roosevelt with a request to mediate the dispute in 1905. TR arranged for the Great Powers to meet at an international conference to settle the matter. Before this meeting convened, however, Roosevelt sent a battleship division to visit the British Mediterranean Fleet at Gibraltar in December 1905, signaling both the sentiments of Americans who favored supporting the new Anglo-French Entente and TR's unwillingness to act solely as a passive broker. He also reversed his earlier stance and asked Congress to authorize building another two *Delaware*-class battleships in 1906 and 1907.[26]

When the envoys of the Great Powers gathered at the sleepy Spanish village of Algeciras in 1906, Germany's demands were opposed by France, Britain, and the United States. The kaiser counted on his partners in the Central Alliance, Austria and Italy, for support, but the Italians were more aggrieved with Austria than with France, and Italy broke ranks with the Central Powers at Algeciras, to the Germans' dismay. France's dominance in Morocco was also backed by the United States. Although the kaiser was appeased, the Germans left the Algeciras Conference with the fear that they had lost one ally and gained two new English-speaking enemies.

France persuaded Russia to repair relations with Britain soon after and they settled four outstanding imperial quarrels in the historic 1908 Persian Convention in which, for the moment, the Russians suspended their nineteenth-century policy of territorial expansion. Roosevelt warmly supported the reinforcement that the Anglo-French Entente brought to the Franco-Russian Alliance. With Italy wavering between the Entente and the Central Powers, he hoped that a new European balance of power would arise, one that would restrain Germany's drive for continental hegemony and the kaiser's impulsive, meddlesome "world politics."

Chapter Twenty-six

The Great White Fleet
1905–1909

European tensions declined following the 1906 Algeciras Conference, and this state of affairs allowed Theodore Roosevelt to shift his attention to the new balance of power in the Far East occasioned by the Russo-Japanese War and the Anglo-Japanese Alliance. Washington's stake in this was governed by the fact that TR inherited not only McKinley's secretary of state, John Hay, but also Hay's Open Door notes. Roosevelt willingly adopted Hay's policy, viewing it as a useful articulation of a long developing American position on China and as a vehicle to maintain a balance of power in the Far East that served to enhance Philippine defense. Although America's relations with Russia in the nineteenth century had been distant but cordial, Roosevelt considered Russia's aggressive policy in Manchuria and Korea following the Boxer Rebellion to be the foremost threat to the Open Door and therefore welcomed the Anglo-Japanese Alliance, as did the Navy's General Board, and he came near to openly siding with Japan in her dispute with Russia the following year. "The mendacity of the Russians is appalling," he told Hay that summer. "The bad feature of the situation from our standpoint is that as yet we can't fight to keep Manchuria open. I hate being in the position of seeming to bluster without backing it up."[1]

Following the Russo-Japanese War there emerged in Washington an overly excited concern for the Open Door Policy and the security of the Philippines, which Roosevelt now labeled Amer-

ica's strategic "heel of Achilles." Rear Admiral Caspar Goodrich of
the Navy's General Board was so alarmed that he told Admiral
Dewey that "the time is ripe for the building of a second fleet." To
prevent a rift with Japan over China, Roosevelt instructed the governor of the Philippines, William Howard Taft, to relay his concern about the islands' security to Prime Minister Taro Katsura
during a visit Taft made to Tokyo in 1905. Katsura assured Taft that
Japan had no interest in the Philippines, and then raised the issue
of Korea. Even before the 1895 Sino-Japanese War, Japan's policy
was to extend its rule over Korea, while Korea looked first to
China, then to the West to maintain her independence. TR took
the line that the United States "cannot possibly interfere for the
Koreans against Japan." Taft was uneasy about his Tokyo assignment, later claiming that he had made no deals there, but he did
comfort Katsura with the news that Washington viewed Japan's position in Korea as a contribution to the peace of Asia.[2]

The euphoria occasioned by the Portsmouth Treaty also revived the peace movement, which called for a second international conference on disarmament. TR announced in December
1905 that he had suggested to Tsar Nicholas II that Saint Petersburg issue the invitations, and the Russians readily agreed to the
American plan. As a result, the delegates of forty-four nations met
for the Second Hague Conference in 1907. To avoid "some Jef-
ferson-Bryan-like piece of idiotic folly," which he reckoned would
put the United States "at a hopeless disadvantage with military
despotism and military barbarians," TR asked Admiral Mahan to
join the American delegation, and he made certain that, unlike
the First Hague Conference, the second one did not have on its
agenda any general proposals for disarmament. Mahan had already persuaded Roosevelt that it would be unwise for the United
States to even raise naval issues—such as the American interpretation of neutral rights or freedom of the seas—given the changing complexion of the global balance of power.[3]

Supporting Roosevelt's prediction that the Second Hague
Conference would do no harm was the fact that the other delegates again traveled to the Netherlands merely to satisfy their domestic public opinions. They agreed to extend the earlier ban on
aerial bombing from balloons and to outlaw laying magnetic
mines at sea and naval bombardments of purely civilian targets
ashore. These measures regulated the conduct of warfare, however, and did nothing to diminish the proliferation or develop-

**Rear Admiral Robley B. "Fig
Bob" Evans and President 7
dore Roosevelt. Evans was
mander in chief of the Atl
Fleet.**

ment of arms or the volume of national arsenals; also, the written
limits were so tempered by qualifications that they were not truly
binding on any of the signatories. In short, the conferees carefully avoided discussing the issues that were cleaving Europe in half
and announced that they would reconvene in 1915. The Senate,
with great fanfare, approved the Second Hague Convention, but
TR felt that "there is more need to get rid of the causes of war than
the implements."[4]

While Roosevelt was busy arranging the international diversion at The Hague, a crisis between Washington and Tokyo was
brewing over immigration, stimulated in part by Japanese confusion over the American system of federal, state, and local government. After 1870, Emperor Meiji, afraid that Japan was overpop-

ulated, encouraged his countrymen to emigrate to Hawaii and California, and over 100,000 Japanese followed his advice. During recessions, they competed for jobs against other Americans on the Pacific coast, and latent animosity and racial bias against the Japanese occasionally percolated into action. In 1906, the San Francisco school board passed a law segregating Japanese children into separate schools. Anti-American mobs rioted in Tokyo to protest, and Japan dispatched a surly complaint to Washington. The Japanese did not believe Roosevelt's assertion that he had no authority to direct a change in local law. Although Roosevelt privately denounced "the infernal fools" in San Francisco, he also warned Japan to clamp down on emigration to prevent further incidents. He considered it "besotted folly" for the West Coast to be "indifferent to building up the Navy while provoking this formidable new power—a power jealous, sensitive, and warlike, and which if irritated could at once take the Philippines and Hawaii from us if she obtained the upper hand on the seas." Washington and Tokyo hurled insults at each other throughout 1907, while TR complained that only the safety of the Philippines "makes the present situation with Japan dangerous."[5]

TR used this nasty episode to move toward some practical foreign policy goals. While the recently constituted Joint Army-Navy Board was drawing up its first plans to defend the Philippines in 1903, TR had become concerned about how quickly the battleships could move from the West Coast to the Far East. At his request, Rear Admiral Robley Evans, then commanding the Asiatic Fleet, was recalled from Yokohama to Honolulu on short notice and then ordered to return to Manila via Guam with his three battleships and a cruiser squadron. Owing to Evans' determined leadership, the entire movement took less than a month. Three years later, on 14 June 1907, Roosevelt asked Dewey to devise a strategy in case war broke out with Japan over the immigration question. Assuming that Japan would invade the Philippines at the outset of the war, the General Board proposed that the Army there withdraw to the Corregidor fortress in Manila Bay and that the Asiatic Fleet's cruisers—no front-line battleships were permanently stationed in the Far East—slowly retire to Hawaii. Because the battleships normally operated with the Atlantic Fleet, the first draft of the Orange War Plan—which outlined strategy and operations in a Pacific war with Japan—provided for a counteroffensive movement from Norfolk around Cape Horn to San Francisco

Bay. After assembling in Hawaii, the fleet would sail into the western Pacific, rescue the Corregidor garrison, and establish an advance base in the Philippines. It would then attack Japan's trade and force a decisive battleship action within the Guam-Luzon-Okinawa triangle. In the final phase of the war, the Navy would establish a second advance base on the China coast or Okinawa, blockade Japan so as to starve her into submission, and await Tokyo's surrender. The entire campaign was expected to take about four months. Because of the lack of a fleet base or coaling stations in the western Pacific, however, the success of the Orange Plan hinged on the U.S. Navy being able to operate its battleships during extended cruises. After the Russian Baltic Fleet's misadventure at Tsushima, this seemed risky. Without a base from which to operate in Philippines waters, many Navy men believed that the fleet could not execute the Orange Plan.

The problem of where to locate the Navy's major Pacific naval base plagued Roosevelt's entire presidency. Soon after Dewey became chairman of the General Board in March 1900, he was ordered to review "possible war situations in the Philippines." He reported after a year of study that Olongapo on Subic Bay was the best site for a fleet base and that such a base was, in turn, necessary to defend the archipelago. Dewey lent his immense prestige to the issue until 1905, but Congress refused to appropriate funds for the project. However, Japan's victory at Tsushima and tensions between Tokyo and Washington moved Congress to allow the Navy to begin constructing the Olongapo facility in 1906. Soon after work began, Major General Leonard Wood, who commanded the Army's Philippine Department, decided that the islands could be defended, as Dewey explained in exasperation, only by "fortifications on the island of Corregidor and a fleet in Manila Bay." And, to Dewey's dismay, Rear Admiral William M. Folger, the commander of the Philippine Squadron, sided with Wood. "The enemy will leave a vessel or two to watch the rat trap at Subic and then take Manila," he warned. Numbed by this hammerlock, the Joint Army-Navy Board tried to compromise in 1908 by agreeing with Dewey that Subic Bay was the best site for a naval base and with Wood that Subic Bay could not be defended on its landward flank. The result was that the Navy was authorized to leave the fleet in Subic until a new base was built near Manila. Roosevelt, furious over this "vacillation," which he felt "justified the most trenchant critics" of the Army and the Navy, now dropped the matter. The naval base question exasperated TR in part because he had already secretly concluded in 1907 that the Philippines were an embarrassing strategic liability. "I don't see where they are of any value to us or where they are likely to be of any value."[6]

Congress was unenthusiastic about building a fleet base in the Philippines in the first place. Besides, the Democrats' opposition to Roosevelt's battleship building program increased after 1905, and peaked in 1907 following the Second Hague Conference. At the same time, negotiations with Japan over immigration policy had reached a brief but tense impasse, which tested Roosevelt's patience with subdued diplomacy. To gain more leverage, on 22 October 1906 he told Maine's Eugene Hale, the chairman of the Senate Naval Affairs Committee, that he wanted to lay down two more battleships to "keep our Navy in such a shape as to make it a risky thing for Japan to go to war with us." The result of this request was that in 1907 Congress authorized the Navy to lay down the battleship *North Dakota* and another *Delaware*-class battleship, and in 1908 funds were approved to build the all-big-gun battleships *Utah* and *Florida*.[7]

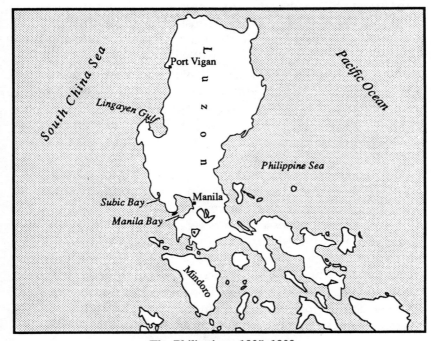

The Philippines, 1905–1909

TR did not believe that an expanded building program would clear the diplomatic trails, so late in 1906 he announced that the Atlantic Fleet would visit the Pacific coast in the coming year. This initial proposal for the voyage of the Great White Fleet was not greeted by unalloyed enthusiasm by Admiral Dewey or other Navy men, who opposed excessive attention to Pacific policy. "At the present time no European nation has a single battleship outside of European waters," Dewey explained, "which fact is a cogent reason that our entire battle fleet should be concentrated on the Atlantic coast." Furthermore, Congress was besieged by protests from New Englanders, who feared that the East Coast would be stripped of its defense. Hale told TR that Congress would not appropriate operating funds for the cruise, but Roosevelt responded sharply that he intended to exercise his constitutional powers as commander in chief and send the fleet to the Pacific coast anyway. Should Congress refuse to bring the ships back, they might stay there.[8]

On the morning of 16 December 1907, Admiral Robley Evans' sixteen white battleships of the Great White Fleet stood out of Hampton Roads, bound for Cape Horn and the uneasy waters of the Pacific Ocean. TR's purpose was avowedly "pacific," although he believed that the movement was "absolutely necessary for us to try in time of peace to see just what we can do in the way of putting a big battle fleet in the Pacific." While the fleet was en route to San Francisco, he ranged Britain's white dominions behind his position and highlighted their unease with the Anglo-Japanese Alliance. Pointing out to Canada her interest in limiting immigration, he also welcomed Australia's support for the "timely demonstration of naval power in the Pacific," and gleefully accepted an invitation for the fleet to visit Melbourne and Sydney as well as Auckland, New Zealand.[9]

Observers on the West Coast were struck not only by the majesty of the battleship fleet but also by its durability during the Latin American leg of the voyage, although it soon became evident that the naval bases and yards at San Diego, Mare Island, and Bremerton would need improving to support fleet operations in the Pacific. The only casualty by the time the fleet reached San Francisco Bay was Roosevelt's favorite admiral, "Fighting Bob" Evans. Old and ill, he was relieved by Rear Admiral Charles Sperry, who hastily prepared for the cruise into the South Pacific. The movement of the Great White Fleet into the Pacific and the announcement that it would visit Australia was coupled with increased diplomatic pressure by Washington on Japan to resolve several outstanding issues, with the result that in February 1908, Tokyo negotiated a "gentlemen's agreement" in which she promised to limit emigration to the United States to a trickle. The Japanese also proposed a joint agreement "to preserve intact" the powers' respective territorial possessions in the Far East while upholding the Open Door Policy. This was followed by an invitation for the Great White Fleet to visit Japan, an offer that TR eagerly accepted.[10]

On 7 July 1908, the American battleships stood out of San Francisco Bay. They arrived in Australian waters in August, and on 18 October reached the port of Yokohama. Sperry and his senior officers were given an audience with the aged Emperor Meiji, who remarked on the "perfect accord" between Japan and the United States, a reference to the forthcoming exchange of notes between Secretary of State Elihu Root and Ambassador Takahira committing both powers to respect the status quo in the Pacific and China's "independence." "The size of the fleet affected the cordiality," boasted the *New York American*. Although TR was satisfied with the Root-Takahira agreement, he had failed to obtain any Japanese pledge to honor China's "territorial integrity" and had tacitly accepted Japan's economic suzerainty over Manchuria. Nonetheless, it was a considerable diplomatic triumph.[11]

When the Great White Fleet stood out of Yokohama, Sperry divided his ships into two squadrons, one of which visited the South China coast while the other stopped off in Manila. They rendezvoused on 1 December, steamed into the Indian Ocean, slipped through the Suez Canal into the Mediterranean, and entered the Atlantic. There they were met by a squadron of four new American battleships, which escorted the Great White Fleet into Hampton Roads on 22 February 1909, ending a fourteen-month-long voyage covering over 45,000 miles. "No other power, not even England, whose drumbeat is heard around the world, ever sent such an enormous fleet around the world," proclaimed one congressman.[12]

Admiral Sperry was more than ever convinced of the need for additional Pacific coast and western Pacific bases. And he had discovered that the movement from the Atlantic coast to the western Pacific, an essential phase of the Orange War Plan strategy, would take at least seventy-five days. Sperry also had difficulty supporting his battleships during the voyage into the western Pacific, and a fiat by Congress that all the coal for the fleet be carried in American vessels had proven to be unworkable. There were too few American colliers to supply the Great White Fleet for the entire voyage, requiring Sperry to take along about twenty foreign colliers and other supply ships. As Senator Hale sourly pointed out, "The greatest fleet of formidable ships the whole world has ever seen" depended "on the indulgence of foreign powers." On the other hand, Sperry marveled that the fleet had been largely self-sustaining and that the battleships were actually in better condition when they arrived home than when they put to sea. Finally, there was little question that the tactical coordination of the fleet had been enormously improved by wireless telegraphy.[13]

Radio communications were about to revolutionize naval operations. In 1888, Lieutenant Bradley Fiske wrapped several turns of insulated wire around two ships, then sent flashes of electrical current through one coil on the cruiser *Atlanta* while listening to the sound in the second ship. Other experiments followed until, in 1896, Guglielmo Marconi set up the first wireless station in England and made the first successful transmission five years later. The Navy purchased its first wireless sets in 1903, and soon Atlantic Fleet ships and naval stations were using twenty German models. Within three years, several shore wireless telegraph stations were broadcasting storm warnings off the Atlantic coast and Washington's Naval Observatory was issuing daily time signals that were transmitted to the Boston Navy Yard and then broadcast to ships at sea. When the Great White Fleet stood out of Hampton Roads in 1907, seventy-five American warships had wireless sets, a number that increased to ninety-three when the fleet returned in 1909.

On other fronts TR kept up his activist naval policy. In 1908, after Congress had appropriated funds to build a pair of *Utah*-class battleships at the height of popular enthusiasm over the voyage of the Great White Fleet, Roosevelt sent up to Capitol Hill another message asking for a total of four new dreadnoughts. The Democrats charged that Roosevelt was stoking the fires of an international naval arms race and, to please their Irish- and German-American constituents, battered TR for siding with the British in several recent international disputes. Rather than attack the popular shipbuilding program directly, however, they moved to restrict the fleet by limiting the displacement of the battleships *Wyoming* and *Arkansas* to 21,000 tons. The Republican majority on the Hill defeated this amendment and enacted the president's program in its entirety. The passage of this expansion act, the success of the Great White Fleet, and the precedent-shattering extension of American influence to Europe and the Far East led Roosevelt to conclude when he left office that the United States was "becoming, owing to our strength and geography, more and more the balance of power of the whole globe."[14]

Chapter Twenty-seven

Dollar Diplomacy
1909–1912

William Howard Taft, whom Theodore Roosevelt selected to be his successor, easily defeated Bryan in his third try for the presidency in 1908. Taft possessed a judicial temper unsuited to making quick decisions, found that he disliked the presidency, and proved to be neither a forceful nor popular chief executive. He was less interested than Roosevelt in Europe's balance of power, but he inherited from TR a host of international troubles. In contrast to Roosevelt's robust nationalism, Taft courted members of the American Peace Society, whose officials annually testified against his own shipbuilding proposals. The influence of the peace lobby was so strong that in June 1910 Congress passed a resolution asking the president to appoint a peace commission that would exploit "existing international agencies for the purpose of limiting armaments . . . by international agreement, and constituting the combined navies of the world" into "an international force for the preservation of universal peace." As one Democrat declared in 1909 during hearings on the annual Navy appropriation, "the prospect of the United States becoming involved in a war is as chimerical and unlikely as a descent on our coasts of an army from the moon." TR, out of office, snorted that the "Navy is an infinitely more potent factor for peace than all the peace societies."[1]

Despite the publication of an expanded battleship building program by the Germans in 1908, Taft was quite willing to abandon Roosevelt's second-power standard and Dewey's Naval

Scheme, and to allow the German fleet to surge ahead of the Americans in numbers of dreadnoughts. Shortly after Taft became president, Germany again intervened in France's sphere of influence in North Africa and thereby provoked the second Moroccan crisis between the Anglo-French Entente and the Central Powers. Taft was personally sympathetic to the Entente's position, but intended to avoid direct involvement in the dispute. He did, however, order the North Atlantic Squadron to visit both France and Britain to demonstrate good will toward the Entente, and pointedly removed from the cruise a proposed visit to the German fleet base at Kiel.

The American battleships arrived off Gravesend in November 1910, and the officers and crews were received in London with extraordinary warmth. Responding to a toast of friendship from the Lord Mayor in the historic Guildhall, Commander William Sims, captain of the battleship *Minnesota*, assured his hosts that "if the time should ever come when the British Empire is menaced by a European coalition, Great Britain can rely on the last ship, the last man, and the last drop of blood from her kindred across the sea." Sims wanted to "shake the old Guildhall" with these sentiments, but Taft, who secretly agreed with Sims's thinking, was swamped by criticism over the remarks. Germany and France appeared to be on the brink of war, and London and Paris had already agreed that the Royal Navy would police the Mediterranean east of Malta and the French fleet at Toulon would cover the seas between Malta and Gibraltar. Unlike Roosevelt, Taft backed away from the issue of French rule in Morocco, publicly reprimanded Sims, and maintained the appearance of being suspicious in his dealings with Britain.[2]

Congressional opposition to military spending during Taft's presidency hurt both services, the Army surely more than the Navy. After the Spanish-American War, the Army had begun to covet its new role as colonial infantry, guarding recently acquired American outposts such as the Panama Canal Zone, Puerto Rico, and the Philippines. But the needs of Caribbean and Gulf defense were modest, whereas the cost of administering the Philippine Islands soared after the insurrection. During the first ten years of American government in the Philippines, $10 million was spent on schools, hospitals, and highways; by 1910, disenchantment in the United States with the cost of Philippine annexation had reached a peak. This political sentiment overcame the War Department's hope that Congress would eventually entrust the defense of the Philippines to a large garrison rather than to a distant but mobile fleet based in the eastern Pacific. Given Taft's background as a former governor of the Philippines, few were surprised that he intended to resolve the naval-base issue, but he told his Navy secretary, George von Gerke Meyer, that he was "not stiff in the matter of having the thing at Manila."[3]

Admiral Dewey and the General Board, of course, still wanted to base the Asiatic Fleet in Subic Bay, but opposition to this scheme was mounting. With the pleasures of the sailors on his mind, Admiral Robley Evans pointed out in 1909 that Olongapo, sixty miles from Manila, was too far from the nighttime attractions of the capital. Even Secretary Meyer recognized that the Army had effectively vetoed the Subic Bay plan once General Wood announced that it could not be defended against a landward attack. When Meyer ordered the Asiatic Fleet to prepare to move to Cavite in Manila Bay, Dewey brought yet another plan before the Joint Army-Navy Board. A large naval base either at Subic or Manila, he now claimed, would be a wasteful luxury considering the forthcoming completion of the Panama Canal, but the establishment of a base at Pearl Harbor in Hawaii would permit the Atlantic Fleet to reach the Philippines before the Japanese could overrun the islands.

Wood countered that, in such a war, the American fleet might arrive in the western Pacific, fight an "indecisive engagement" with the enemy, and then "find itself in Philippine waters with a number of crippled ships," thus being "forced to withdraw to Pearl Harbor, a distance of 5,000 miles for a period of several months." Indeed, Commander Henry S. Knapp of the Naval War College had warned in 1907 that American control of Philippine waters would "not be established the moment our Atlantic Fleet reaches the Philippines" because "it may be months" before Japanese naval forces could be evicted from the area. "Our situation will be well nigh desperate if Olongapo does not succeed in holding out." According to the General Board, the president faced a "question of having a naval station with docking facilities at Olongapo or none at all." Tired of the squabbling, Taft adopted this line of reasoning and decided that it was unnecessary to construct a major fleet base in the Philippines. By this time Dewey had already suggested more than once the alternative of establishing the main American naval facility in the Pacific at Pearl Harbor. Subic and

Cavite, Taft decided, were to be maintained as limited facilities. Congress agreed with this policy, work began on a base at Pearl Harbor in 1909, and the General Board's Orange Plan was revised the following year to account for the fact that Hawaii, not the Philippines, was to anchor the fleet in the Pacific.[3]

General Wood's role in the Philippine naval-base question illustrated his increasing influence over American military policy, a rise that was capped in 1910 when he became the Army's third chief of staff. Leader of the Rough Riders in Cuba and a close friend of Teddy Roosevelt, Wood had Taft's backing in establishing his authority over the Army's bureau chiefs after a bitter contest that stirred reform-minded Navy officers to bring up once again the issue of reorganization of the Navy Department. This time, they believed, they had the support of political progressives, including Secretary Meyer. Instead of backing wholesale reform, however, Meyer settled on a compromise between the radical proposals of Rear Admirals Luce and Mahan, who wanted a naval general staff, and their opponents—the bureau chiefs and their congressional allies on the Senate and House Naval Affairs Committees. Without seeking legislative approval from Congress, Meyer simply divided the tasks of the Navy Department into four functional areas and named an aide to the secretary to coordinate policy for each, the most important being the aide for operations. In effect, the aide for operations assumed some of the responsibility of the chief of the Bureau of Navigation for the deployment and movement of ships and the organization of the squadrons. Later in the Taft administration, this billet was held by Rear Admiral Bradley Fiske, one of the leading reformers. On paper, the aide system seemed to complicate matters; in practice, Meyer found it a useful management tool, and the result was that the issue of a naval general staff lost some of its immediacy.

Secretary Meyer took the matter of "systematizing" naval war plans more seriously than did many line officers, and in 1910 asked Dewey's General Board to consolidate its studies into a Black Plan for war with Germany and an Orange Plan for war with Japan. Germanophobic to the core, Dewey had always stressed the inevitability of an Atlantic conflict, so work on the Orange Plan had languished until Meyer's instruction. The first fully articulated Orange Plan, completed in 1911, was predicated on a war between Japan and the United States erupting over a Japanese violation of the Open Door Policy or aggression against the

Philippines. After Congress declared war, the Atlantic Fleet would sortie around South America, replenish on the West Coast, and steam into the western Pacific. During the three months it would take to do this, Dewey reasoned, the Japanese fleet would probably overrun the Philippines, Hawaii, Guam, Midway, Kiska, and Samoa. From the Pacific coast, the Americans would then take the offensive and the fleet would steam along a "middle route," recapturing Hawaii and Guam, and striking into the Philippine Sea. There they planned to engage and defeat the enemy and liberate the American territories. If, however, Japan still refused to surrender, Dewey now admitted that attacks against her "home territory would likely prove [to be] fruitless." Instead, he advocated a strategy aimed at the "isolation" of Japan, coupled with "the investment and capture of outlying . . . possessions and . . . threats at the repatriation of Korea." As Dewey noted, the major flaw in this strategy was that there was little option to maintaining the battleships in the Atlantic in peacetime. The best the Navy might hope for was some advance warning, "during a period of strained relations," to move them into the Pacific to check a Japanese offensive, from which recovery might be inevitable but also quite costly.[4]

Admiral Dewey reckoned that between the onset of a crisis and an American declaration of war there might not be enough time to send the Atlantic Fleet into the Pacific, even after the Panama Canal was completed. This thinking in part informed his call in his 1903 Naval Scheme for a building policy aimed toward a fleet of forty-eight battleships. In peace, such a fleet could be divided between coasts. In a war with Germany, all the battleships would be reunited in the Atlantic, but in a war against Japan, operations in the Pacific could be undertaken on short notice and a rather formidable force would still remain under the Atlantic command. To reach Dewey's goal, however, the Navy had to lay down four battleships each year—clearly beyond the ability of the Treasury to finance or the willingness of Congress to authorize. As a minimal replacement policy, Taft asked for two battleships in 1909 and two more the next year. He won both fights, but the congressional elections of 1910 reduced Republican control of the Senate and gave the Democrats a majority in the House. Furthermore, a bitter struggle over tariffs and other domestic issues sapped the president's political capital until, by 1911, he was under siege within his own party and his authority over Congress was negligible.

At the same time, the influence of the peace lobby on Capitol Hill had increased substantially. In late 1911, the House Democratic caucus instructed the Naval Affairs Committee to delete any battleships from the authorization bill for the next year. After a stormy session during the summer of 1912, the Republican Senate forced the Democratic House to authorize the 31,400-ton battleship *Arizona*, which was armed with a dozen 14-inch guns. Taft's inability to impose his will on Congress on a issue of naval policy—which normally benefited from bipartisan support—illustrated the self-inflicted debility created by policies of indecision. A moderate caught in the fundamental contradictions of the Progressive era, Taft was trapped between conflicting interests when Secretary Meyer tried to promote greater military efficiency in the Navy Department's eleven shipyards. His plan met with stiff resistance on the Hill. Each of the nine yards on the Atlantic seaboard and the two on the Pacific coast owed their existence to military need, tradition, and political necessity, as did the several additional naval stations that dotted the congressional landscape. Congressmen from these districts invariably inhabited the Naval Affairs Committees and Navy men counted on their support during the annual battles over appropriations. The product of their legislative labors was evidenced by the fact that, during Taft's presidency, naval appropriations steadily increased despite a decline in battleship construction.[5]

It was during Taft's uninspiring presidency that the Navy took on two new technologies that transfigured modern naval warfare—aircraft and submarines. On the eve of the Spanish-American War, Assistant Secretary of the Navy Roosevelt had assembled a panel to examine an experimental flying craft built by Professor Samuel Pierpont Langley, secretary of the Smithsonian Institution. In 1896, his large craft, powered by a small steam engine, had made a successful, uncontrolled, and very brief flight of about 3,000 feet. On 29 April 1898, the Joint Army-Navy Board predicted that, if the aircraft could fly over long distances, they might be used to reconnoiter, communicate between isolated outposts, and bomb enemy camps, forts, and bases. However, the Navy's Board of Construction held that aviation applied "strictly to the land service and not to the Navy."

Langley was at the time sharing his findings with Orville and Wilbur Wright, two inventors who were trying to construct an aircraft for manned flight. Earlier pioneers in this field had developed machines with controls that governed only pitch, the fore-to-aft axis relative to altitude, but they entirely ignored yaw, or lateral movement, and were unaware of the aerodynamic phenomenon of roll. The Wrights discovered that they could control yaw by varying the angle of the wingtips, and that their craft had both lift and lateral balance. The addition of a tail with a rudder increased stability and allowed the pilot to turn the craft during flight. On 17 December 1903, the Wrights made four historic flights in the *Flyer I* along the seashore at Kitty Hawk on North Carolina's desolate Outer Banks. The longest of these flights covered 852 feet and lasted almost one minute. Some Navy representatives witnessed this historic event, but they were discouraged by the fragility and limited flying range of the early Wright biplanes. "This fragile and unreliable invention held no promise for the navy," ruled Victor Metcalf, Roosevelt's secretary of the Navy at the time. The Army felt much the same way, but TR ordered the War Department to buy one of the Wright Brothers' planes.[6]

Within a few years, Admiral Dewey had taken an interest in aviation. He instructed the General Board to investigate the use

The 107-ton Holland submarine *A-2* was launched on 22 July 1901 and commissioned as the (SS-3) in January 1903. Like most of the pre–World War I submarines, she served as a harbo fense and training vessel for the Navy's infant submarine arm. Between 1909 and 1915, large sels towed the *A-2* and five other *A*-class submarines out to the Philippines to improve the de es of Manila Bay.

of aircraft as scouts for the fleet, and persuaded Secretary Meyer to assign Captain Washington Irving Chambers to coordinate naval aviation policy. But the real sparkplug of this early effort was Glenn Curtiss, a flamboyant entrepreneur who hoped that the Navy would become a dependable, long-term customer for his new airframe firm. Chambers had a wooden platform for takeoff laid on the bow of the light cruiser *Birmingham,* which was anchored off Hampton Roads, Virginia, and Curtiss supplied a biplane with a pusher engine and a test pilot, Eugene Ely, who took off on 14 November 1909. After leaving the ship, the plane dipped down into a high wave, but Ely slowly gained altitude and landed safely ashore. Curtiss was a shrewd salesman, and he next offered to train a Navy pilot to fly. Meyer and Chambers agreed, and the Bureau of Navigation ordered Lieutenant Theodore G. Ellyson to report to a barren camp on North Island in San Diego, California, where, with three Army officers and a few civilians, the first American military aviation school opened in 1910.

Curtiss' next objective was to land a plane on the deck of a ship. Chambers selected the armored cruiser *Pennsylvania* for this experiment and arranged for a 120-foot wooden platform to be built on her stern. A means to stop the plane once it had landed perplexed Curtiss until Ellyson suggested stringing twenty ropes athwartships and weighing down the ends of each rope with fifty-pound bags of sand. A simple hook was attached to the tail of the biplane to catch the deck lines. On 18 January 1911, Ely landed a Curtiss biplane on the *Pennsylvania* as she rode at anchor in San Francisco Bay. Mobbed by photographers, he shook hands with Captain Charles Pond, got back in the plane, took off, and flew back to shore. Curtiss had also developed a seaplane that he hoped to sell to the Navy, and, a week later, after trying different shapes for his pontoons, he piloted his seaplane off San Diego Bay in the first takeoff from water. Impressed by this demonstration, Congress appropriated $25,000 for naval aviation on 4 March 1911, and the Navy ordered four A-1 and A-2 Curtiss biplanes. A training camp and airfield were established near Greenbury Point across the Severn River from the Naval Academy in Annapolis. The Wrights sent one of their biplanes in several crates to the Annapolis site. They were assembled by midshipmen, and on 7 September Lieutenant John Rodgers took off from the Academy's Farragut Field and flew for fifteen minutes until he reached Glen Burnie several miles to the north.

The military utility of naval aviation was greatly enhanced by the marriage of manned flight and wireless telegraphy. On 26 July 1912, Ensign Charles Maddox attached a primitive wireless transmitter and an antenna to the A-1 Flying Windmill, and at an altitude of 900 feet Lieutenant Rodgers tapped out a message that was received by the destroyer *Stringham* some three miles away. Despite this achievement, the first policy cleavage in the stormy history of naval aviation was already evident. Chambers, attracted by the safety, economy, and versatility of the seaplane, was funneling the department's small air effort into the development and exploitation of that type at the expense of work on wheeled aircraft and platforms for seaborne launches and landings. By this time, these various experiments had attracted the attention of Rear Admiral Bradley Fiske, the aide for operations, who arranged for Captain Mark Bristol to establish a flying school at the abandoned Navy yard at Pensacola. The Naval Flying School there at first consisted of nine planes and six pilot instructors. With this marginal, inexpensive program, the school prospered. In 1914, the head of the school, Lieutenant Commander Lloyd Mustin, took his small band of naval aviators and four planes down to Vera Cruz, where they flew reconnaissance missions in support of the American occupation.

The small, gasoline-powered internal combustion engine that made manned flight possible also generated renewed American interest in the development of the submarine. In 1875, John P. Holland, an eccentric Irish refugee, had constructed a 16-foot-long tricycle-powered submarine, which he used to practice diving, underwater maneuvering, and surfacing in shallow waters. Within six years he had modified his boat by adding water ballast for natural buoyancy and controls linked to bow-mounted planes for vertical stability. After several false starts, Holland's Torpedo Boat Company obtained a Navy contract to build the *Plunger*, which used a steam engine for surface propulsion and electric batteries to turn the shaft while the vessel was submerged. Meanwhile, Holland's rival, Simon Lake, had rounded up private financing to build the 37-foot *Argonaut,* in which he had installed a gasoline engine and a trailing air hose to the surface to vent the deadly exhaust. Roosevelt accepted Lake's gift of the boat to the Navy during the Spanish-American War, but the improperly vented carbon monoxide fumes were so dangerous that the project was abandoned before she entered the fleet.

Despite repeated setbacks, both Lake and Holland continued to lobby the Navy to buy their submarines, and in June 1900 Congress reluctantly agreed to acquire five boats from Holland. The first, the 64-foot *Holland*, was commissioned on 12 October. Although Holland was ousted from the firm by rivals in 1904, his Electric Boat Company already held a virtual monopoly on building experimental submarines for the Navy, a grip on the market it maintained for most of the next decade.

Simon Lake was equally determined to carve out a niche for his firm, and in 1911 he built the *Seal*, which made 14 knots on the surface and 10 knots underwater. The poorly vented, volatile fumes meant that the early gasoline-engined submarines were impractical for fleet operations, however. The substitution of diesel for gasoline engines changed all this. Rudolf Diesel's 1895 invention of a heavy-oil engine was incorporated by the Admiralty in the British submarine *A-13* in 1908, and soon most European navies replaced their gas engines with diesels. Under license from the Germans, Electric Boat in 1911 laid down the *Skipjack*, the first American diesel submarine; her commanding officer, Lieutenant Chester Nimitz, became one of the Navy's leading authorities on diesel technology. Electric Boat's eventual dominance of the American diesel submarine business meant that the Navy developed little institutional expertise in submarine design and largely had to accept the type of vessels Electric Boat was willing to construct.

The limited range, fragility, and danger of all early submarines suggested that the best mission for the boats was harbor and coastal defense. Admiral Dewey, an early advocate of submarines, told the House Naval Affairs Committee on 23 April 1900 that if the Spanish "had had two of the things in Manila, I would never have been able to hold it with the squadron I had at my disposal." Dewey believed that the submarine was ideally suited for harbor and coastal defense. "With two of these in place in Galveston, all the navies in the world would not be able to blockade the place," he asserted. His support was a powerful stimulant to the development of American submarines. Between 1909 and 1914 the Navy accepted delivery of twenty-five submarines and assigned most of these short-legged vessels to harbor defense patrols. However, in 1913 a squadron of five boats and a tender sailed from Charleston to Colón, Panama, inaugurating a new era in open-ocean operations. Diesel submarines were so new that it was unsurprising that none of the belligerent navies were prepared to deal with submarine warfare in World War I.[7]

Taft's implementation of the Monroe Doctrine in Latin America fell somewhere between Pan American idealism and what critics later labeled Dollar Diplomacy. Secretary of State Elihu Root had assured Latin America in 1906 that Americans sought "no sovereignty except over ourselves," but Taft's Secretary of State, Philander Knox, observed that the real problem was that "the malady of revolutions and financial collapse is most acute precisely in the region where it is most dangerous to us." For this Taft needed a "remedy." He did not find one. The source of most Central American turmoil was President José Zelaya of Nicaragua, who attempted to forge a regional empire out of the five republics by aggression. Zelaya despised American power, baited Washington at every opportunity, refused to repay debts to foreign investors, and sent his army across Nicaragua's frontiers to support friendly factions in Honduras and Guatemala. He was seen as a clear threat to the Canal Zone. Zelaya's adventures ravaged Nicaragua's economy and destroyed its banana trade, the source of most of the country's foreign exchange, and in 1909 the city of Bluefields rose up against his tyranny.

When Zelaya executed two American mercenaries serving with the Bluefields army, Taft ordered the Pacific Fleet to lift a Marine battalion under Major Smedley Butler from Panama to Nicaragua to quell the disorders. With American ships riding at anchor in the port of Corinto in May 1910, Butler landed, occupied Bluefields, and prevented Zelaya's army from crushing the conservative rebels. Zelaya was driven into exile by a new conservative regime headed by Adolfo Díaz, who persuaded Washington in 1911 to take over the customs house in Corinto in return for loans from American banks to pay Nicaragua's national debt. These terms were humiliating, and Zelaya exploited the resulting discontent by launching a new revolt in July 1912, which overthrew the Díaz regime. Díaz's followers regrouped, laid siege to Managua, and cut off rail traffic between Corinto and Leon, a Zelaya stronghold.

Taft now moved to restore order. Rear Admiral H. H. Southerland had just returned with the Pacific Fleet to San Francisco Bay when he was ordered to detach a squadron of eight ships to transport Butler's Marines from Panama back to Corinto. Two weeks later, the Pacific Fleet, led by the battleship *California*, stood into

Corinto, then under siege by the Liberals. Southerland sent Lieutenant William D. Leahy and ten sailors into the town, where they awaited a Liberal attack for forty-eight hours before Butler's Marines came ashore on 14 August. The country was in chaos as a result of the civil war, Southerland reported, and this caused Taft to abandon his earlier neutrality. He dispatched two more Marine battalions from the United States to reinforce Butler at Corinto, and directed Southerland to crush the Liberal uprising. Butler took control of the railroad, seized Leon, and scattered the rebels at Masaya within two months. At the end of the Nicaraguan civil war, Taft withdrew the Marines and the Pacific Fleet, leaving only a legation guard of 100 men and a small ship, while negotiations began in Washington.

Taft supported the Monroe Doctrine with less relish and purpose than had Roosevelt, and he always considered the use of force to be less therapeutic than Dollar Diplomacy, a serum he also applied to the Far East. From McKinley and TR, Taft inherited the Open Door Policy, which required the United States to check Japan's expansion by supporting rival Western interests on the mainland. But once the Great White Fleet returned to Hampton Roads, Virginia, on 22 February 1909, only four armored cruisers remained in the Pacific, and the need to concentrate the Navy's fifteen modern battleships in the Atlantic Fleet severely restricted American freedom of action in the Pacific—until the canal was completed. Furthermore, the small Asiatic Fleet, the most visible symbol of American power in the Far East, was dedicated to defending the Philippines and protecting Americans in China against outrages in the Yangtze River basin and along the south China coast. Taft agreed with the goals of the Open Door Policy, but he pointed out that it "completely disappears as soon as a powerful nation determines to disregard it, and is willing to run the risk of war."[8]

Far Eastern politics grew more complex soon after Taft took office. By 1909, China's ruling Manchu dynasty was helpless, and two years later the imperial government in Peking gave way to a feeble republic. Feuding warlords, many supported by outside powers, effectively split up the country. Japan annexed Korea and increased her influence in Manchuria by grabbing control of the South Manchurian Railroad. To check Japan, Taft sought better relations with Russia, and as a goodwill gesture in 1910 he sent a battleship division commanded by Rear Admiral Charles J. Badger to visit the main Russian naval base at Kronstadt. The tsar welcomed Badger handsomely, but Taft's Russian diplomacy soon came to grief. In 1911, the tsar supported a wave of renewed anti-Jewish pogroms and Taft was criticized for lending support to the Russian regime. He dropped the initiative at once. It was all to no avail as the Russians had already temporarily cast their lot with the Japanese in Manchuria, frustrating Knox's plan to substitute Dollar Diplomacy in the Far East for naval power in the Pacific. How to deal with this new turmoil in Asia was a problem, like many others, that Taft bequeathed to his successors.

Chapter Twenty-eight
Defending the Monroe Doctrine and American Neutrality
1913–1917

In the 1912 presidential race, a split in the Republican majority between Taft and former President Roosevelt led to the election of New Jersey's governor, Democrat Thomas Woodrow Wilson. The Democrats also won control of both the House and the Senate. A strong chief executive, Wilson rewarded William Jennings Bryan for his support in the election by naming him secretary of state, but the president acted largely as his own foreign minister. Soon after taking office, he demonstrated an unusual willingness to use force to impose his will on segments of American society—and other nations—that failed to behave according to his standards. Although Wilson condemned Roosevelt's pugilistic foreign policy, the country found the new president far more willing than his Republican predecessors to employ force as an agent of his moral diplomacy.

To balance his cabinet, Wilson selected as his secretary of the Navy Josephus Daniels, an influential North Carolina newspaper publisher. Narrow-minded and provincial, Daniels knew next to nothing about naval affairs or international politics and held views that reflected an old Jeffersonian distrust of the aristocratic pretensions of the Navy's officer corps. His greatest achievement in office was to improve training programs for sailors at a time when the Navy badly needed a technically skilled enlisted force. He created academic departments at every base and on board every ship for new recruits and directed the Naval Acade-

my to admit sailors from the fleet for the first time. His Jeffersonian philosophy was evident in his support of the Naval Militia
Act in 1914 and in the creation of a permanent militialike naval
reserve a year later.

By any measure, however, Daniels failed the most meager test
of an executive. He was indecisive, refused to lance the boil of
chaos that characterized the department's archaic administrative
structure, and depended almost wholly on his energetic assistant
secretary, Franklin D. Roosevelt, a young New York politician. Co-
incidentally, the influence of Admiral of the Navy George Dewey
had waned, owing to his poor health and advancing age, causing
the General Board to lose much of its old authority over naval policy. Daniels did not support war planning, obstructed joint Army-
Navy collaboration, resisted the creation of the National Defense
Council when the European emergency erupted, and tried in vain
to democratize the Navy, an essentially authoritarian institution.
Enlisted men had been barred from drinking on board ships in
1899, and Daniels extended this prohibition to officers by abolishing the traditional shipboard "wine mess." Apoplectic at this imposition of the new Puritanism of temperance, Rear Admiral
Bradley Fiske, the aide for operations, warned that his fellow officers would now turn to "the use of cocaine and other dangerous
drugs!"[1]

As a result of this lack of leadership, American naval policy
was in a shambles when World War I broke out in Europe. Commander Rufus Zogbaum spoke for many Navy men when he complained that in Washington the "heads of departments had to do
their work surreptitiously in order to get it done." No single professional was responsible for coordinating planning, shipbuilding,
personnel policies, and operations; Daniels was incapable of per-
forming this task. Fiske urged Daniels to adopt a number of preparedness measures in late 1914, but at heart Daniels embraced
pacifism and a narrow view of the impact of international politics
on American interests and security. With Dewey about to retire,
Fiske moved to circumvent the chain of command. In 1914, he
persuaded his allies in Congress to bring forth a bill creating the
office of chief of naval operations, or CNO, to be filled by a senior
admiral who was to exercise command authority over the bureaus
and the fleet. Under Fiske's plan, the CNO was to be responsible
for the "general direction" of the Navy. Daniels opposed the bill
on the specious grounds that a naval general staff on the Prussian

Admiral Bradley Fiske, inventor and
or Operations, 1912–15.

ary of the Navy Josephus Daniels (center seated); Admiral Henry Mayo, commander in chief
Atlantic Fleet (far left seated); and Admiral Robert Coontz (far right seated), c. 1919.

model would undermine or destroy civilian, political control, but many in Congress disliked Daniels and rejected the self-conscious insecurity represented by this argument.[2]

The secretary's attention then turned to diluting the power of the new CNO by having Democrats on the Hill restrict the functions of the Office of Operations and by severely limiting the size of the CNO's staff. The CNO Act passed in 1915, but Daniels got some measure of revenge. He exiled Bradley Fiske to the Naval War College and then selected Captain William S. Benson, the commandant of the Philadelphia Navy Yard, as the first CNO, thus slighting all the other rear admirals. Daniels, who apparently believed Benson to be weak and compliant, expected subservience from the new CNO, but Daniels badly misjudged his man. Benson was an intelligent, crafty bureaucrat who shrewdly manipulated others to his own ends. Rather than quarreling with Daniels, Benson used his technical expertise to make his office invaluable to Daniels and Assistant Secretary Roosevelt. His basic tactic was to stake out a position on an issue akin to that taken by Daniels, then quietly encourage others to lobby him to change his mind. This process usually resulted in a consensus on action within the Navy that not even Daniels could resist. From the aide system Benson inherited the authority to deploy ships and issue operational orders to the fleets, a prerogative that he soon learned to exploit fully to manage strategy. Within a year Daniels could be found on Capital Hill supporting a 1916 act that promoted Benson to the rank of four-star admiral. Nonetheless, Benson was constantly frustrated by his inability to coordinate the work of the material bureaus.

Daniels's narrow-minded, short-sighted moralism reflected many of the attitudes of the president, whose foreign policy was rooted in a Calvinist conception of international morality. Although he denounced TR's *realpolitik*, Wilson found himself upholding the Roosevelt Corollary to the Monroe Doctrine in his dealings with the Caribbean and Central America. None of the Latin American republics was so vital to the security of the United States as Mexico. It had long been in America's interest that Mexico remain politically stable, militarily weak, economically dependent, and unentangled with any of the Great Powers of Europe— conditions that existed after 1876 under Porfirio Díaz's dreary despotism. Díaz was overthrown in 1910 by a liberal coalition led by Francisco Madero, but his frenetic reforms alienated his own supporters and some of them backed a countercoup by General Victoriano Huerta, who shot Madero and seized power. Within weeks, an armed insurgency rose up against Huerta's dictatorship. The United States had theretofore almost always followed the European practice of recognizing the de facto authority of any foreign government in power regardless of its political odor, but Wilson, who believed Huerta's politics to be immoral and his regime illegitimate, announced that he would "not recognize a government of butchers!"[3]

Huerta retaliated by harassing and imprisoning some American nationals in Mexico, and Wilson was soon discussing with his cabinet the need for armed intervention. In October 1913, he ordered Rear Admiral Frank Friday Fletcher to detach a battleship division from the Atlantic Fleet and establish a presence in the Gulf from Vera Cruz to Tampico, where Mexico's important oil industry was concentrated and most American nationals resided. Soon after Fletcher arrived in the flagship *Vermont*, he lamented the "chaotic conditions" ashore but warned Admiral Charles J. Badger, the commander of the Atlantic Fleet, that "it would be unfortunate if we had to land against the consent of the [Mexican] authorities. The temper of the people is such that it would undoubtedly result in war." Wilson was bent on ousting Huerta, however, and in January 1914 the Atlantic Fleet conducted maneuvers in the Caribbean and landed two Marine advance base regiments at Culebra, Puerto Rico. They were reinforced later that month by a Marine battalion from Panama. When the exercise ended, instead of returning to Philadelphia both regiments sailed for American ports on the Gulf coast. Admiral Fiske also strengthened Fletcher's Gulf Squadron by sending the battleships *Florida* and *Utah* to Vera Cruz and the battleships *Connecticut* and *Minnesota* to Rear Admiral Henry Mayo's recently established station off the port of Tampico. Six weeks later, on March 9, as the tension escalated, Fletcher's force off Vera Cruz was strengthened with the arrival of a transport carrying a Marine regiment. This combination of menacing movements and angry pronouncements from Washington was described by Wilson as "watchful waiting" for Huerta to fall.[4]

The Tampico incident led to the occupation of Vera Cruz. Eight members of an American shore party were loading a whaleboat at quayside in Tampico when they were arrested by Mexican troops at gunpoint on 9 April and held for a short time before being released. Mayo flew into a rage. He demanded that the Mexicans punish the responsible officers, formally apologize, and "publicly hoist the American flag in a prominent position and salute it with twenty-one guns." Huerta issued an apology, but he refused to fire the salute. Mayo "will pass by the matter, satisfied with what Huerta has said," Secretary of State Bryan predicted, although he confessed that the admiral "has the whole matter in his hands." Returning to Washington on 13 April, Wilson announced that he was "supporting" Mayo's continued demand for a salute, and that afternoon Fiske cabled Mayo that the president was ordering Admiral Badger to concentrate the Atlantic Fleet in the Gulf of Mexico in a show of force. Yet Huerta did not budge. "The salute will be fired," Wilson now declared.

Wilson was about to ask Congress to approve an expedition against Mexico a week later when Bryan learned that the German steamer *Ypiranga* was en route to Vera Cruz carrying machine guns and ammunition destined for Huerta's army. Mayo was planning to send two Marine regiments ashore to occupy Tampico, but the bar at the mouth of the river prevented him from using his battleships to cover the landing. Moreover, seizing Tampico would not prevent the *Ypiranga* from landing at Vera Cruz. Fletcher had assembled a formidable landing force off Vera Cruz, however, and his battleships could bring their guns to bear on the city, so the General Board urged Wilson to order him to land. Acting quickly, he instructed Mayo not to occupy Tampico but to back out of the Pánuco River and to send ships to reinforce Fletcher at Vera Cruz—a move that left the American community in Tampico without protection. "Several thousand American citizens were left by the Navy at the mercy of Mexican mobs and Huerta's soldiers," recalled Commander Yates Stirling. "These Americans had to be rescued and transported out of the river by foreign warships." Wilson's plan was for Fletcher to land at Vera Cruz, "seize [the] customs house," and "not permit war supplies to be delivered to Huerta or to any other party."[5]

Colonel Wendell Neville's well-armed landing party of Marines and bluejackets stormed ashore on 21 April 1914, entered Vera Cruz, and overwhelmed an aroused but outfought scratch force of Mexican Naval Academy cadets, local militia, and a few federal soldiers. Nine Americans and hundreds of Mexicans died during three days of bitter street fighting. Seaplanes and land-based naval aircraft supported the ships and the assault troops. Riots erupted throughout Mexico, and there were anti-American demonstrations in most Latin American capitals. The "occupation of Vera Cruz placed all foreign and American lives in Mexico in danger," Stirling observed, "and the administration in Washington seemed helpless to devise effective means to protect them." The ABC powers—Argentina, Brazil, and Chile—moved quickly to arrange a truce between Huerta and his principal antagonist, Venustiano Carranza, and to orchestrate an American withdrawal. The Americans pulled out of Vera Cruz on 23 November 1914, but Carranza upset the truce, rejected mediation, drove Huerta from Mexico City, and within days established a new government, which Wilson was quick to recognize. However, Carranza failed to curb Pancho Villa's northern rebels, who raided Columbus, New Mexico, in 1916. Furious over this new ruckus, Wilson ordered Major General John J. Pershing to lead several Army regiments into northern Mexico after Villa. This futile chase was suspended only in early 1917. Mexican resentment of Wilson's intervention in her civil war persisted for many years.[6]

Fear of Germany's policy of "world politics" played a role in Wilson's Mexican embroglio, and it also animated his policy in the Caribbean. The chronically malnourished peasants of Haiti and the Dominican Republic had for decades paid for a politics ruled by elite factions around whom coups and countercoups swirled. For Washington, the central problem was that these governments borrowed heavily from the Germans and French and regularly defaulted on their debts. Under the Roosevelt Corollary, the United States was bound to intervene to collect Europe's debts if it expected restraint by the Great Powers. The new administration hoped to short-circuit this cycle with the Wilson Plan, under which Washington would support elected governments, reorganize their finances, and train a responsible national guard to establish political order. What Wilson failed to realize was that local politicians who accepted American support exposed themselves to attack as pawns of imperial interests.

The Haitian intervention put Wilson's policy to its most severe test. After a fairly free election in 1908, seven presidents held office in Haiti over the next seven years, the *époque des gouvernements éphémères*. In 1913, General Guillaume Sam, a Port au Prince bandit, took power in a bloody coup financed by German banks. Over the next twenty-four months, Marines went ashore to restore order sixteen times, and twice between August 1914 and January

1915 Marine battalions were shipped to Port au Prince to stand by to prevent bloodshed. The situation was so chaotic that Fiske prepared a plan to occupy Cap Haitien or Port au Prince if conditions ashore worsened. His goal was to protect not only the American residents but also European nationals whose presence would otherwise invite the appearance on the scene of naval forces from their homelands. Assistant Secretary of State Robert Lansing opened talks with General Sam about leasing the Mole Saint Nicholas for a naval base, but when Sam rejected the American offer, Lansing reasoned that Haiti intended to sell the site to the German Navy.

While these negotiations were under way, Ronsalvo Bobo, another Haitian thug, raised a peasant army, took Cap Haitien, and laid siege to Port au Prince in July 1915. Sam panicked, massacred all the political prisoners in his jails, and fled to the Dominican Republic's legation. Bobo's army marched into the city, and a mob dragged Sam and his cutthroats from their sanctuaries into the streets and chopped them apart during a torchlight parade. When news of this savagery reached Washington, Wilson announced that he intended to instruct the Haitians that the United States "cannot consent to stand by and permit revolutionary conditions" on the island. Wilson told Lansing, "I suppose there is nothing for it but to take the bull by the horns and restore order." The next day, he ordered Rear Admiral William B. Caperton, who commanded a Caribbean squadron that included the battleship *Washington*, to restore order in Port au Prince.[7]

When Caperton arrived at Port au Prince, he sent a party ashore to disarm Bobo's rioters. A pair of sailors were shot during these sweeps, and Caperton reacted by putting ashore Major Smedley Butler's entire Marine battalion. Butler occupied the city, and Caperton and his chief of staff, Captain Edward Beach, instructed the Haitian Congress to elect a new president who was to sign a treaty that embodied the Wilson Plan and provided for a ten-year American occupation of the country. Bobo's motley army was destroyed by Butler's Marines in a series of ruthless antiguerrilla actions, but simmering disorder among the Haitians continued into the new year. Secretary Daniels then ordered Caperton to abandon the Wilson Plan and establish a national constabulary, the Gendarmerie d'Haiti, commanded by "General" Butler. Haiti was occupied and governed by the Marines for nearly two decades.

After restoring order in Haiti, Caperton shifted his attention to the other side of the island. In the Dominican Republic the regime of Juan Jimenez, an aging tyrant, was burdened by unpaid debts and a revolt led by the minister of war, Desiderio Arias. The basic source of friction was Jimenez's decision to accept the Wilson Plan. In May 1916, Arias's faction impeached Jimenez, and fighting broke out between their partisans in the capital. Furious at the prospect of another Caribbean civil war, Wilson once again ordered Caperton "to restore order" ashore. He shifted the gunboat *Castine* from Haiti to Santo Domingo, and two companies of Marines went ashore to guard the American legation. Caperton soon arrived on the scene and tried to mediate between Arias and Jimenez, but neither would compromise so he decided to support Jimenez by landing more troops and a Marine artillery battery shipped from Haiti. Caperton devised a plan to use the *Castine's* battery to support simultaneous movements by the Marines and Jiminez's army against Arias's stronghold in the Santo Domingo suburbs, but Jimenez refused to shell his own capital and both Dominican armies fled into the interior.

Wilson and Lansing were so frustrated by this turn of events that they told Caperton to take independent action to erect a responsible government. However, the Dominican legislature refused to accept Caperton's proposal for a treaty of occupation embodying the Wilson Plan. Seeing no alternative, he called for more Marines and launched a campaign that decimated the Dominican Republic Army and allowed his successor, Rear Admiral Henry S. Knapp, to establish a military rule over the country. "With the deepest reluctance," Wilson agreed to this expedient on 26 November 1916. Bryan's arbitration treaties and Wilson's insistence that the United States would resort only to peaceful means to pursue its foreign policy were also undermined by Wilson's other interventions elsewhere in the region. Wilson also continued the Marines' occupation of Nicaragua, supported a puppet government in Managua that served Washington's interests, and worked unsuccessfully to get the Americans to build a second canal through the impoverished country.[8]

The moral inconsistencies that characterized Wilson's dabbling in Latin America also expressed themselves in his naval policy. During the 1912 presidential election campaign, Wilson spoke favorably about naval expansion, but the bent of the new administration was obvious early in 1913 when Daniels announced a scheme to nationalize all naval shipbuilding, munitions manufacturing, and oil refining on the grounds that the free market had left the Navy Department at the mercy of monopolists who had charged the government "exorbitant" prices for steel and arms. His plan made only modest headway. To "guard against extravagant and needless expansion" of the fleet, Daniels also proposed that Wilson convene an international conference to limit naval arms, an objective Daniels felt "ought not to be difficult to secure." In an annual report notable for its internal inconsistency, Daniels asked Congress to authorize two more battleships in 1913.[9]

Most Navy leaders wanted a longer-term program and more ships, and Daniels could not keep the dispute under wraps. Rear Admiral Charles Vreeland of the General Board testified before the House Naval Affairs Committee in favor of a report urging Congress to establish the goal of forty-eight battleships—embodied in Dewey's 1903 Naval Scheme—and to lay down four dreadnoughts in 1914. Congressman Richmond P. Hobson, an Alabama Democrat, and Senator Lodge, a Massachusetts Republican, were strong supporters of Vreeland's plan. Hobson backed it on the grounds that the United States had "to have always in the Atlantic a Fleet equal to the German Navy and to have always in the Pacific a fleet equal to the Japanese Navy." Hobson was a retired naval officer and something of a maverick—most Democrats on the Hill opposed fleet expansion. Republican support for the Vreeland's plan was so strong, however, that the Democrats compromised and authorized construction of the 33,400-ton battleships *New Mexico, Idaho,* and *Mississippi.* In spite of this accomplishment, a sharp cleavage was exposed in 1913 over American naval policy, with Daniels and many Democrats on one side and the General Board and most Republicans on the other. This rift grew wider when the United States confronted the problem of the Great War in Europe.[10]

Germany's foreign policy of "world politics" and the reaction of Europe to that menace lay at the root of World War I. None of the Great Powers expected the war to last long. Certainly none supposed that it would end monarchical rule in Russia, Austria, and Germany, weaken Europe's power in Asia and the Middle East, undermine British naval authority, and establish the United States as the arbiter of the balance of power both in the Atlantic and Pacific. The July 1914 assassination of Archduke Franz Ferdinand by a Serbian agent brought Austria to the brink of war with Serbia, leading the Russians, who wanted merely to protect the Serbs by scaring Vienna, to mobilize. Alarmed by the prospect of a Russian invasion of East Prussia and determined to avoid a two-front war, the Germans declared war on Russia's ally, France. On 1 August 1914, the German Army, heading for France, crossed into Belgium, a step that drew in the British, who were obligated to defend Belgian neutrality and could not tolerate German control of the Channel ports. Italy was torn between her treaty with the Central Powers and a chance to recover Trentino and Trieste from Austria; she remained neutral until 1915, when she joined the Allies.

The Royal Navy's control of the English Channel allowed the British to transport four divisions to France within a few weeks. This British Expeditionary Force disrupted the balance of the German offensive at Mons and allowed the French to regroup and obstruct the German drive for Paris. Thereafter, in a succession of flanking battles, the Germans marched up to the Channel, chased by the Allies, until both armies had reached the sea. From the Belgian coast through northern France to the Swiss border, the strategic landscape divided Western Europe in a stalemate that lasted for four years, punctuated periodically by massive ground offensives that seldom gained more than a few square miles of territory at the price of millions of casualties. On the Eastern Front, the Germans easily chased the Russians out of East Prussia in 1914, but their counteroffensive bogged down in Poland's mud by the end of the year. At sea, the contest was less evenly matched. Winston Churchill, the First Lord of the Admiralty, had put Britain's Grand Fleet on alert before London declared war. He stationed this powerful force at Scapa Flow north of Scotland, where Britain's dreadnoughts were poised on distant blockade to prevent the German High Seas Fleet from breaking out of the North Sea into the Atlantic. Although the British Mediterranean Fleet allowed a German battlecruiser and cruiser to escape to the Black Sea, thus making it easier for Turkey to declare war against the Allies, the Royal Navy and other Allied naval forces drove German shipping out of the Atlantic and made it possible for the Allies to overrun most of Germany's colonies and overseas outposts. The German Navy was incapable of defending her far-flung empire, but this had no influence on the outcome of the war.

The European conflict was a "war with which we have nothing to do," declared President Wilson on 4 August, when he issued a neutrality proclamation. This line not only perfectly reflected public opinion but also the unpleasant reality that the United States did not possess the means to join the war at the moment. Wilson's early policy of isolating the United States from the conflict led him to actively discourage American war planning. Upon reading in the *Baltimore Sun* that the Army was writing a plan to use in case Congress declared war on Germany, he threatened to disband the general staff. The interests of the United States as a neutral were transparently biased, however—American trade with Britain and France was much greater than with Germany. Also, the adhesives of American society were the cultural and political freedoms derived from the English heritage. There was considerable anti-British sentiment among Irish- and German-Americans, but pro-German propaganda never could overcome the kaiser's odious image, revelations about German espionage and sabotage in the United States, and, above all else, the brand of aggressor that Germany earned in 1914 by invading neutral Belgium.[11]

Navy men were divided about America's stake in the war. Secretary Daniels supported neutrality without reservations, but Rear Admiral Fiske, the aide for operations, considered this policy "dangerous." A German victory would create "a situation of the greatest possible peril" for the United States, he claimed. Admiral Mahan went further and advocated an immediate alliance with Britain. "The only answer to the sword is the sword," he told Fiske. On the other side was the retired president of the Naval War College, Rear Admiral French Ensor Chadwick, a distinguished historian, who argued that Britain's unwillingness to tolerate Germany as a maritime rival was the cause of the war. "Our interests lie in German success. . . . She can be our only support against Japan," he told Daniels. If Germany were defeated, "the British Empire will turn on us." Apparently most officers disagreed. Mahan, now on his deathbed, had prepared a stout defense of Britain's policy and a detailed argument as to why the United States should oppose the Germans. Daniels wanted to avoid exposing the schism within the Navy between Mahan and Chadwick to public scrutiny, however, so he prohibited active-duty or retired officers from writing about the war. Although Dewey, the chairman of the General Board, had long identified Germany as America's most likely opponent, he privately told Daniels on 1 August

1914 that "if Great Britain is drawn into the war," then "the German fleet will be neutralized as far as any danger from it to our interests in the immediate future is concerned."[12]

At the insistence of Rear Admiral Fiske and Assistant Secretary Franklin D. Roosevelt, the Atlantic Fleet conducted its spring 1915 exercise in accordance with a new version of the Black War Plan. In the exercise the Black Fleet, emulating the Germans, evaded a formation of defending Blue battleships and established a lodgment on the Chesapeake Bay. Although this outcome was inconsistent with Naval War College studies, it emphasized the need to strengthen both coastal and Caribbean defenses. The General Board reviewed the Black Plan and concluded that in the near term neither Germany nor Britain threatened American security. Within a few weeks, however, the General Board revised the Black Plan to take into account the European war. Under the assumption that the United States would remain neutral, Admiral Dewey saw little immediate danger. Should the United States join the Entente, on the other hand, the General Board estimated that the Army could muster an expeditionary force of only 50,000 men, too few to have any military influence in Europe. The board assumed that the German High Seas Fleet would not defeat Britain's Grand Fleet, leaving little for the Atlantic Fleet to do but to guard against an unexpected breakout into the Atlantic by the German battleships. Even this would not, by itself, endanger American or other neutral shipping. However, "at the close of the present war, . . . the defeated belligerents, with the connivance and perhaps the participation of the victors, may seek to recoup their war losses at the expense of . . . the United States," the board warned on 6 August 1915. It did not identify antisubmarine warfare as a peculiar Allied weakness because the Admiralty was closely guarding secret figures about the Allies' early shipping losses to the U-boats. Most American strategists agreed to bend naval policy to the long-term need for a "balanced fleet" to deal with either a German or a British victory in Europe and the nagging conundrum of Philippine defense.[13]

In part because Wilson perceived the European war as a spiritual and a temporal issue, he saw a possible role for himself as a peacemaker and perhaps deluded himself into believing that he could end all war by ending this one. Few Americans were so naive. Wilson's moralism and the course of the fighting moved Washington inexorably from the position of mediator to that of arbitrator. Ironically, the first American dispute with either of the belligerents erupted with London over Britain's blockade policy. When the war broke out, the Royal Navy imposed a naval blockade on the Central Powers as one element of a larger peripheral strategy, at first defining foodstuffs as contraband and later expanding the list of forbidden trade beyond any previous bounds. Holland and the Scandinavian nations were neutrals, and some American ships en route to their ports laden with cargo bound eventually for Germany were seized by the Royal Navy. Dewey condemned British maritime policy as an illegal paper blockade that the Royal Navy could not rigidly enforce. Over transatlantic cable, the State Department and the British Foreign Office debated the finer points of contraband law and the arthritic question of a broken voyage, issues of infinite elasticity given the nature of modern warfare. "The neutral shipper complained bitterly," recalled Captain William V. Pratt, the wartime Assistant CNO, "but he failed to realize that in a war of this character neutral rights in a war zone had to be subordinated to belligerent rights in the same area." The Admiralty solved the problem and deftly smothered American complaints by ordering its prize courts to generously compensate neutral shippers whose cargos had been seized. Within a year, as a result, American trade with the Central Powers was almost shut down.[14]

Germany's strategy of employing submarines to enforce her own blockade of the British Isles created far more transatlantic friction. Admiral Tirpitz had expressed little interest in U-boat development, tactics, or strategy before the war. Thus, when Germany invaded Belgium, the German Navy had in service only eighteen U-boats capable of high-seas operations. Captain Lothair Persius later complained that "Tirpitz had fought all U-boat construction hand and foot," and the size of the U-boat fleet, which operated from bases at the Heligoland Bight, Emden, and Burkum, increased quite slowly as the war progressed. When the war began, the Germans sent out several U-boats to attack British warships. They sank eight enemy vessels and forced the Grand Fleet to evacuate Scapa Flow and retire to a northern anchorage until net and boom defenses were erected at the main base. On the other hand, no frontline battleships were sunk by German submarines during the war, although they did send under nine predreadnoughts, thus illustrating the need for the underwater hull protection incorporated in the dreadnought design. All the

British warships that were sunk had been steaming near a coast-line. The great disparity of speed between a battleship and a sub-marine meant that a U-boat could neither locate an opponent's battle fleet at sea nor, following a chance encounter, maintain con-tact long enough to maneuver into position to launch a torpedo attack. The early losses alarmed the Admiralty, and Churchill tried to check the U-boat offensive by increasing Britain's escort ship-building, organizing the Dover Patrol to protect Allied shipping in the English Channel, and sending a cruiser squadron to Queenstown to defend the western approaches to the Irish Sea. Within a short time, Germany's U-boats ceased to have much in-fluence on the operations of the British battle fleet.[15]

Germany's conquest of Belgium in 1914 left her Navy in pos-session of several bases along the coast of Flanders. Tirpitz want-ed the U-boats to continue to hound the Grand Fleet, but after a terrible row on 4 February 1915, the kaiser overruled him and ap-proved Admiral Hugo von Pohl's plan for a submarine campaign against Allied freighters, transports, and tankers. Although Ger-man diplomats warned that this would provoke neutral protests, the foreign ministry defined a maritime war zone around the British Isles and announced that the blockade would be enforced by U-boats whose captains had been instructed to sink on sight all belligerent ships that entered the restricted area. Within a few days, the Flanders Submarine Flotilla became operational, joining German U-boat squadrons that were already active in the North Sea and the English Channel, and Berlin warned neutral ships to avoid the war zone to prevent "unfortunate mistakes."[16]

The kaiser had already been cautioned that the United States would protest this decision, and Wilson predictably demanded that the Germans obey international laws about commerce raid-ing. In brief, Wilson wanted a U-boat to stop each Allied vessel it intended to attack, search her for contraband, and provide for the safety of the passengers and crew before sinking her. He surely re-alized that this would diminish or negate the strategic value of the submarine blockade as it would prevent the U-boats from attack-ing and escaping quickly—and so reduce the menace of an unex-pected attack. However, Wilson's stance served to protect Ameri-ca's substantial trade with the Entente, whose demand for American foodstuffs, fabricated goods, and munitions was in-creasing daily. He depicted his policy as neutral, intended to hold the Germans to a standard of "strict accountability," and threatened to "take any steps . . . necessary to safeguard American lives and property." These demands were at first ignored by the Germans. Then, on 28 March, the British liner *Falaba*, which was carrying American passengers, was sunk by a German submarine. Torn by divided counsel, Wilson issued another mild protest, announcing that the United States was "too proud to fight."[17]

Over the next three months, Germany's submarine strategy began to bear fruit. British shipping losses soared. Buoyed by this success, Tirpitz deployed U-boats to operate from the Austrian fleet base at Pola, where they attacked Allied commerce in the Adriatic and the Mediterranean. On 7 May 1915, however, another crisis erupted between Germany and the United States. The Cunard liner *Lusitania* was hit by torpedoes fired by a U-boat whose crew believed that the cruise ship was carrying British munitions. The *Lusitania* sank off the Irish coast, and 1,153 passengers and crew, including 114 Americans, died. Americans were indignant over this tragedy. Former President Theodore Roosevelt castigated Wilson for failing to protect the American passengers, Republicans demanded an increased level of military preparedness, and many called for a declaration of war. Pressed by public opinion, Wilson dispatched three notes to Berlin over the next three months in which he defended the right of Americans to travel safely in the war zone and demanded that the U-boats end their campaign of "unrestricted" submarine warfare by taking off all passengers from ships they were about to attack. Finally, on 21 July 1915, he threatened a rupture of diplomatic relations if the Germans sank another liner.

The German reply was restrained. On 19 August, a U-boat sank the liner *Arabic*, and three more Americans were lost. Determined to avoid war with the United States, Prime Minister Bethmann-Hollweg now insisted that the U-boats be instructed to obey traditional prize regulations. From 1 August 1914 to 30 September 1915, German submarines had sunk 792,000 tons of Allied shipping, but the kaiser was not yet ready to risk American belligerency to keep up the commerce raiding strategy, so Berlin issued secret instructions to its U-boat captains not to sink any more Allied liners. On the other hand, the Germans knew that American opinion was not solidly behind Wilson's policy. Secretary of State Bryan strongly objected to the demand for "strict accountability" and resigned over this issue. He was replaced by Robert Lansing, who was more closely aligned with the president's thinking. The lines were drawn on the Hill over a resolution introduced by Senator Thomas P. Gore of Texas and Congressman Jeff McLemore of Oklahoma, which urged the administration to concede the German case on the liner question with the aim of avoiding American involvement in the European war. Some progressive Republicans rallied to support a stiff line against Germany, however, and the Gore-McLemore measure was defeated by both houses in March 1916.

The *Lusitania* incident shook Wilson, and he was moved by Lloyd George's advice that the larger the American military establishment, the more influence the president might exert on the world scene. On 21 July 1915, the same day on which he had threatened to break diplomatic relations with Germany, Wilson told the press that he was reversing his military policy and was directing the War and Navy Departments to draft a major national defense program. He confided to Secretary Daniels that he wanted the American Navy "to stand upon an equality with the most efficient and most practically serviceable" naval force in Europe. Theretofore unbending in his opposition to naval expansion, Daniels within days was calling for more warships. Benson and the General Board proposed "parity" with the Royal Navy as the new standard of American naval policy, a theme soon reflected in the popular slogan of building "a Navy second to none." On a speaking tour to promote his program, Wilson declared his intention to create "incomparably the greatest navy in the world."[18]

The General Board, trying to fathom just what Wilson meant by this, divided the missions of the fleet into four parts. The first was to defend the Monroe Doctrine against German incursions in the Western Hemisphere. The second was to protect the Pacific "strategic triangle" and the Philippines against Japan. The third was to provide Wilson with leverage in his attempt to mediate the war. And, fourth, if Congress declared war, some of the fleet would have to operate in concert with the Allies or as an independent force in the North Atlantic. Reports from the Office of Naval Intelligence profoundly influenced Navy thinking and led the General Board to conclude that the Germans were winning the war. Allied losses on the Western Front were horrendous. The Germans might prevent Anglo-French gains in the west, slowly grind down the Russian Army, and shore up their Austrian allies. Under these circumstances, German naval strategy could decide the war. The High Seas Fleet might triumph in the North Sea in a general action, or German submarines might reduce British shipping to a level below that necessary to sustain ground operations in France. The General Board recognized that if Germany defeated Britain, the cost of victory would be so great it would prevent any immediate pursuit of the kaiser's prewar "world politics." The board estimated, however, that the German fleet might pose a danger to the Monroe Doctrine within a decade after destroying British naval power.

The General Board reasoned that, to repulse a German offensive in the Western Hemisphere or contain the High Seas Fleet in the Atlantic, within six years the American fleet would need to equal the size of the prewar British fleet. The board therefore proposed to increase the size of the fleet to a total of forty-eight battleships by 1922 at a cost of $1.6 billion. This, of course, closely resembled Dewey's 1903 Naval Scheme. Daniels understood Wilson to want "preparedness" as a bargaining tool, but he was deeply repelled by the thought that the United States might actually be drawn into the war. So, in November 1915, he altered the General Board's shipbuilding program by reducing the number of battleships to be built to ten—four 32,600-ton *Maryland*s and six 43,000-ton *South Dakota*s—and by proposing to launch these new vessels within five years. Congress received the measure in January 1916, but its passage was paralyzed by highly charged partisan and regional politics. Republicans, led by Senator Lodge and his son-in-law, Congressman Augustus P. Gardner, demanded more funds for more ships to be completed more quickly than the administration wanted. Many Democrats deserted Wilson, opposed the bill, and attacked not only the naval program but also Wilson's other preparedness measures.

Events across the Atlantic served to unwind this tangle. While the Turks thwarted the Royal Navy's attempt in 1915 to force the Dardanelles Straits and bring Constantinople under the guns of a large Allied fleet, the Germans remained on the defensive in the west. The following year, however, they attacked the key French fortress at Verdun in a costly and unsuccessful bloodletting that momentarily exhausted both armies. Meanwhile, Vice Admiral Reinhard Scheer, the new commander of the High Seas Fleet, was persuading the kaiser to approve offensive operations designed to wrest control of the North Sea from Admiral Sir John Jellicoe's Grand Fleet. Scheer planned a series of ambushes to attrite the British fleet until it was reduced to a strength that he could meet in a battleline engagement, although he was fully aware that attrition was the one result the Germans themselves could least afford. For Britain, the integrity of the Grand Fleet was the linchpin of her war effort. It protected the imports that fed her industry and the British Army on the Western Front. As a result, Jellicoe adopted conservative tactics when he met and checked a German sortie into the North Sea during the great Battle of Jutland on 30 May 1916. Overwhelmed by the fear of losing ships, Jellicoe did not press home his great numerical superiority, but in his defense it was held that he had won a strategic victory inasmuch as Britain still controlled the North Sea and thereafter kept the German High Seas Fleet bottled up in the Baltic.

In the fall of 1916, however, the British had no way of knowing that the kaiser, unhappy with Scheer's conduct off Jutland, soon would turn against another fleet action and decide instead on a second round of unrestricted submarine warfare. The setback at Jutland was minor compared to the Verdun disaster in 1916, a reverse that led to a decision in Berlin to concentrate on the Eastern Front the following year. After this debacle, about the only ray of hope for an eventual German victory lay on the high seas, where the ratio of Allied ships sunk to submarines lost had been about five to one in 1915 but improved to fifteen to one during the next year. The kaiser was subjected to complaints from his admirals that "unrealistic" restrictions on U-boat operations were preventing a victory at sea. And at the end of 1916, Admiral Hennings von Holtzendorf predicted that unrestricted submarine warfare would force Britain to quit the war within six months. Wilhelm II momentarily resisted risking war with the United States, but he soon reasoned that no other solution was in sight.

The Battle of Jutland and Wilson's continuing diplomatic problems with Berlin moved Congress to seek a compromise on the Navy's 1916 shipbuilding program. Senator Tillman of South Carolina, who had earlier opposed the measure, declared on 3 June that Jutland showed the need for more American battleships. Within a few weeks, both houses passed the bill, and on 29 August Wilson signed the 1916 Big Navy Act. This was a three-year plan to lay down 156 new warships with funding for the immediate construction of 56 vessels; 10 battleships and 6 battlecruisers were at the core of this program. The act authorized the construction of four 32,600-ton *Maryland*s armed with eight 16-inch guns, followed by six 43,000-ton *South Dakota*s carrying a dozen 16-inch guns. The six 32,000-ton *Saratoga*-class battlecruisers were to have more armor than similar European types and carry a main battery of ten 14-inch guns. Daniels signed the first contract on 23 October, and Admiral Benson estimated that all the ships would join the fleet before 1922. The United States was plunging "headlong into immediate preparation for war," grumbled Congressman Philip P. Campbell, but the twin objectives of achieving superiority over the German fleet and parity with the Royal Navy drowned out all but a handful of dissidents.[19]

The Democrats had not wanted to desert Wilson's Big Navy Act on the eve of a presidential election that many of them expected him to lose. In 1916, Wilson faced a reunited Republican Party, which nominated Charles Evans Hughes, the governor of New York, but Hughes mistakenly tried to please everyone by stoutly rejecting a firm position on America's interests in the war. While many voters were swayed by the Democrats' simplistic proposition that Wilson had "kept us out of war," the prosperity of the neutral economy and an unwillingness to change leaders in the midst of a great foreign crisis were more important factors in deciding the election. Wilson's diplomacy nicely marched to the tune of public opinion, moving from resolute neutrality to muscular preparedness. By signing the Big Navy Act of 1916, increasing the size of the Army, and hastening munitions production, Wilson snatched from the Republicans their sturdiest issue and in November won a second term in the White House.

One month after the election, Wilson tried for the third time to mediate the war by sending Colonel Edward House, his closest adviser, to Europe with a demand that the Great Powers clearly explain their war aims. London and Paris replied with terms that implied the postwar destruction of German power. The Germans realized that they would alienate Washington should they admit that they wanted to annex Belgium, so they foolishly announced that they would only discuss peace terms at a future date. This third House mission forced Berlin to grapple with the probability of American intervention, however. The new mastermind of German strategy, General Erich von Ludendorff, convinced the kaiser that, even should the United States declare war, Germany could defeat the Allies before a sizable American Army joined the Allies on the Western Front. Ludendorff planned to husband Germany's resources in the west for a massive offensive in 1918, while concentrating in 1917 on the defeat of Russia. His analysis was supported by Admiral Scheer, who estimated that one final U-boat campaign would drive Britain within six months to ask for a compromise peace. Greatly miscalculating the balance of power, the likely outcome of the most effective submarine commerce raiding campaign, and American military potential, the kaiser made the disastrous decision at his headquarters at Pless on 9 January 1917 to resume unrestricted submarine warfare against Allied shipping at the end of the month.

Wilson was stunned by this news. Just before the new German policy took effect, he had announced a newly devised formula consisting of five ingredients for a "peace without victors": an end to the European alliance system, equality of nations, protection of Europe's minorities, postwar disarmament, and the old bromide, "freedom of the seas" for neutrals. After Berlin's announcement, however, he saw no choice but to break diplomatic relations with Germany and order the Navy to arm American merchantmen. Nonetheless, he decided to wait for the Germans to actually conduct unrestricted submarine warfare before taking stiffer measures. At a cabinet meeting on 25 February 1917, Navy Secretary Daniels observed that the fleet "should not [be ordered to] convoy" American merchantmen across the Atlantic as such a move would be "dangerous." Wilson agreed that "the country was not willing that we should take any risks of war."[20]

The Germans were already bracing for an American declaration of war, however, and with this in mind Foreign Secretary Arthur Zimmermann suggested in a cable to his ambassador in Mexico City that a secret alliance among Germany, Mexico, and possibly Japan might be arranged. In return for Mexico's declaration of war against the United States, Germany was prepared to support the recovery of Mexican territory lost in 1848. British intelligence intercepted Zimmermann's telegram containing this preposterous scheme, gave one copy to the White House, and turned others over to the press on 1 March. Germany and Japan had for several years intrigued in Mexico, Mexico's relations with the United States were still strained, and Japan's interest in arranging an anti-American combination with Germany was well known in Washington and greatly feared by the Navy's General Board. The Zimmermann telegram caused a wave of anti-German outrage to sweep over the country, a firestorm for war fed by the news that a U-boat had sunk the unarmed British liner *Laconia* and that three Americans were lost. During the next three weeks,

U-boats also sank an American tanker, three freighters, and an impressive assortment of other Allied merchantmen.

Wilson called on Congress to convene on 2 April. A German counteroffensive in the east had completely undermined Russia in the meantime, forcing Tsar Nicholas II to abdicate, and resulting in the establishment of a provisional government whose foremost figure was Aleksandr Kerensky, a Social Democrat. Wilson could now ask Congress to declare war against Germany without tying himself to the tsar's odious autocracy. "The present German submarine warfare against commerce is a warfare against mankind," he declared. Inasmuch as his policy had failed and "neutrality is no longer feasible," he asked Congress to "lead this great peaceful people into war, into the most terrible and disastrous of all wars, civilization itself seeming to be in the balance. "After a furious debate, a declaration of war was passed by both houses, and on 6 April 1917 the United States entered World War I. The kaiser's overly ambitious, ham-fisted naval policy had finally brought into being the only coalition that could ensure Germany's defeat.[21]

Chapter Twenty-nine

The United States and World War I

1917

The Navy entered World War I with an understandably imperfect knowledge of the course of prior Allied operations. Overwhelming naval power "rested unchallenged in the hands of the
Allies," Rear Admiral William S. Sims, the new president of the
Naval War College, believed. "It appear[ed] impossible that the
Germans could win the war." The reason for this unfounded optimism was that Admiral Sir John Jellicoe, the new First Sea Lord,
had withheld the extent of Britain's merchant tonnage losses not
only from the Americans but also from the British cabinet, on the
grounds that the "facts could not be disclosed without benefitting
the enemy." From information collected by ONI, Admiral
William S. Benson, the CNO, had concluded in 1916 that German
submarines posed a major threat to Britain, but he too believed
that the Royal Navy was succeeding in maintaining control of the
North Atlantic. He told Navy Secretary Daniels in February 1917
that the U.S. Fleet would have "to make war on enemy submarines
within the areas assigned" but also cautioned that American naval
policy should "not only meet present conditions but [also] conditions that may come after the present phase of the world war."[1]

Before Congress declared war, Benson drew up a list of strategic priorities that he implemented once the United States entered
the European conflict. Foremost among these was the deployment
of elements of Admiral Henry Mayo's powerful Atlantic Fleet to
defend "our coasts and our interests" in Latin America. A few

weeks later, during a meeting with Vice Admiral John Browning, who commanded the British Patrol Force in the western Atlantic, he explained that American strategy was "to maintain the fleet intact and to assist in the patrol of the Atlantic and Gulf coasts." To reassure public opinion on the East Coast, he directed Mayo to curtail fleet exercises in the Caribbean in March 1917 and return to the main base at Norfolk. Then, in April, Benson established the Caribbean Patrol Force composed of seventy cruisers, destroyers, and gunboats under the command of a sulphurous old salt, Rear Admiral Henry B. Wilson. Soon after, he negotiated an agreement with the British and French that assigned to the Caribbean Patrol Force the mission of defending Allied shipping, possessions, and interests in the Caribbean and the Gulf of Mexico. Profoundly influenced by the prewar Black War Plan—which presumed a German violation of the Monroe Doctrine— Benson instructed Admiral Wilson to patrol the area for any signs of secret German submarine bases, support the Marines occupying the Dominican Republic, Haiti, and Nicaragua, and establish a highly visible American naval presence in the region. Wilson's Caribbean Force was also to prevent any German U-boats from attacking the large number of American ships steaming to and from the Panama Canal.[2]

In devising a naval strategy to deal with Germany, Benson had to be mindful of the Philippines and the Open Door Policy in China, which had been menaced by Japan during the 1915 crisis over the Twenty-One Demands. Japan would exploit the European war to improve her strategic position in the Far East, Benson assumed, and so he could not afford during the Great War to reduce completely the already weakened Pacific Fleet upon which the defense of the Philippine Islands rested almost totally. Secretary of State Lansing was alert to this problem, however, and during the summer of 1917 he negotiated a compromise with Japan that relaxed tensions for the duration of the Great War. The prospect of this Far Eastern truce, later embodied in the Lansing-Ishii Agreement, permitted Admiral Benson in May to order the commander of the Pacific Fleet, Rear Admiral William B. Caperton, to transfer his four second-line battleships to a new station in the South Atlantic and return a few destroyers to the Atlantic Fleet. The CNO justified this risky step to a skeptical General Board on the grounds that Japan was, for the moment, America's associate in the war against Germany.

Upholding the Monroe Doctrine and defending the Open Door Policy not only complicated the formulation of a naval strategy to defeat Germany but also diminished the resources immediately available to implement it. It was not at all evident at the outbreak of the war whether the greatest danger to the United States lay in the immediate prospect of unrestricted submarine warfare, the continuing threat of a wartime victory by the German High Seas Fleet over the Royal Navy's Grand Fleet, or a victory by the Central Powers over the Allies on the Western Front. Rear Admiral Charles Badger of the General Board pointed out on 5 April 1917 that the Navy had "to keep constantly in view the possibility of the United States being in the not too distant future compelled to conduct a war single handed against some of the present belligerents." Prudence dictated that Benson regard the High Seas Fleet as the Navy's most lethal opponent, at least for the first few months of American belligerency. Accordingly, explained Captain William V. Pratt, the Assistant CNO, the Navy was ready to render "the most hearty cooperation . . . to meet the present submarine situation in European waters or other waters," which was "compatible with an adequate defense of our own home waters" and "the future position of the United States . . . after the successful termination of the present war."[3]

Just before America declared war, President Wilson ordered the Navy to arm merchantmen heading for the War Zone around Britain. Benson at first preferred this to convoying, on the grounds that the U-boats often approached their prey on the surface but were, on the whole, poorly armed. On 12 March 1917, naval gun crews boarded the merchantman *Manchuria* and set up a battery. Over the next twenty months 384 American freighters and tankers were defended by naval armed guard crews, who manned guns, signal platforms, and radios. This policy was surprisingly successful, owing largely to the U-boat's light armament and frail hull and the disinclination of German skippers to surface and exchange gunfire with armed freighters. The American cargo carriers *Navajo* and *Nyanza* both successfully repulsed U-boat attacks, as did the merchantmen *Chincha* and *Paulsboro*. The Navy gun crew defending the stricken cargo ship *Campana* fought for four hours against an attacking U-boat before the vessel had to be abandoned. The defenders of the badly damaged steamer *Norlena* started to leave the vessel after she was hit by a torpedo but changed their minds, returned to their guns, and drove off the op-

Transatlantic AEF convoy en route to France during World War I. Members of the 6th Marine Regiment on board the Navy troopship *Von Steuben* (left) view the troopship *Agamemnon* (right) carrying the Army's 42nd "Rainbow" Division in November 1917.

Admiral William S. Benson, first chief of Naval Operations, 1915–19.

posing submarine, which had mistakenly surfaced. The freighter
J. L. Luckenbach was savagely attacked by a U-boat, but her naval
gun crew kept firing at the submarine for four hours until the badly damaged vessel was rescued by the American destroyer *Nicholson*. And, in the most spectacular success achieved by the armed
merchantmen, the naval gun crew in the *Sea Shell* destroyed a U-
boat on the surface with gunfire when it tried to attack the American tanker in the Mediterranean.

Wilson not only inaugurated the Naval Armed Guard program before America entered the war, but he also instructed Secretary Daniels on 24 March 1917 to "get into immediate communication with the Admiralty . . . and work out a scheme of
cooperation" so as to "save all the time possible." British diplomats
had hoped to negotiate an alliance with the United States for nearly two decades, and the Admiralty now desperately wanted to establish a working relationship with the Navy Department. There
may have been some limited, informal exchange of information
between the two headquarters in 1915 or 1916, but it did nothing
to inform American strategy the following year. Ambassador Walter Hines Page had conveyed from London to Washington a number of requests that a U.S. Navy representative be assigned the Admiralty in 1916, but this idea was ignored until January 1917 when
Assistant Secretary Roosevelt lent his weight to the plan. Still,
nothing happened until 23 March when Page relayed a promise
by the Admiralty to provide a "full and frank" account of "the
whole British naval work since the war began," and Wilson issued
the order to send a high-ranking naval officer to England.[4]

Either Daniels or Benson selected Rear Admiral Sims for this
duty, and he was summoned from Newport to Washington that
weekend. Congress had yet to declare war and Daniels viewed the
establishment of closer relations with the British Admiralty to be
politically ticklish, so he instructed Sims to travel to England under an assumed name and "not even to take any uniforms." Neither Daniels nor Benson knew much about British naval policy, so
they merely told Sims to "keep the Department posted." Benson
also cautioned Sims not to confuse American and British war aims.
"Don't let the British pull the wool over your eyes," Benson
warned, because the Navy did not intend to be "pulling their chest-
nuts out of the fire." Neither Benson nor Daniels detailed
Sims'precise duties or his place in the chain of command, nor did
Sims ask them to spell out the extent of his authority. Even after

Daniels named Sims to command American naval forces in European waters two weeks later, Sims' relationship with the Navy Department, the CNO, and the commander in chief of the Atlantic Fleet remained unclear. Wilson's invitation to Sims a few months later to bypass Daniels and Benson on issues of policy and grand strategy and report instead to the White House as if he were "handling an independent navy" did nothing to relieve this confusion. Furthermore, the initial instructions for Sims, an inveterate Anglophile, were shrouded in Benson's graceless and untimely parting remark that he "would as soon fight the British as the Germans."[5]

On the evening of 31 March, Sims left New York. After an uneventful transatlantic passage, his steamship was struck by a German mine in Liverpool harbor. The passengers safely shifted to an excursion steamer, and the admiral reached London by 10 April. Sims immediately went to the Admiralty, where Jellicoe reviewed the naval war with him and then casually handed him a summary of shipping losses during the first quarter of the year. The total was 1.3 million tons sunk. Losses for April were climbing to nearly 900,000 tons, and the Germans had only fifty-seven U-boats at sea. One of every four ships leaving a British port was being lost to the submarine offensive. Stunned by this appalling revelation, Sims concurred with Jellicoe's overly apocalyptic assessment that Germany would "win unless we can stop these losses—and stop them soon." On the other hand, Jellicoe's dejected conclusion that the Admiralty had "absolutely" no strategic solution to the problem bothered the American's agile mind. Shortly thereafter, Herbert Hoover, the director of American food relief in Europe, warned Sims that British warehouses held only enough grain to last for three weeks. In round numbers, the Allies needed 15 million tons of merchant shipping afloat to sustain both their military operations and their civilian economies. Of the total of nearly 22 million tons afloat on 1 January 1917, the Germans had sunk nearly 10 percent by the time the United States declared war three months later. Based on projected losses of one million tons during each coming month, by October at the earliest the loss of shipping might curtail some British operations on the Western Front.[6]

To defend merchant shipping against the German raiders, Sims proposed that the Allied and American fleets provide naval escorts for convoys of merchantmen transiting the War Zone off the British Isles and at other dangerous chokepoints. Although he may have discussed an escort strategy with Benson in March before leaving Washington, Sims decided after only a few days in

London that this was the only way to counter the German U-boat offensive. When Sims asked Jellicoe "why shipping is not directed to and concentrated to various rendezvous and from there convoyed through the danger zones," the First Sea Lord replied that "the area [of the danger zones] is too large [and] the necessary vessels are not available." Prime Minister David Lloyd George, who discussed naval problems with Sims twice during the admiral's first week in London, found strong support from Sims for his own conviction that Jellicoe should at least organize a trial convoy. "Now that the United States have entered the war," he told the War Cabinet, "it should be possible to find escorts which were formerly impracticable." Following a dramatic visit by Lloyd George to the Admiralty, Sims persuaded the British to accept the proposals of some of their own junior naval planners, release a handful of destroyers from the Grand Fleet to form an ocean escort group, and assign it to defend a convoy of merchantmen routed from Gibraltar to the British Isles. This first convoy, which sailed from Gibraltar on 10 May, lost no ships during its passage to England.[7]

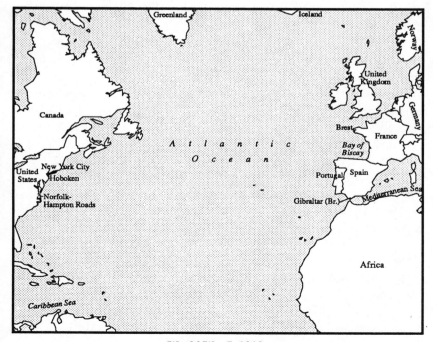

World War I, 1918

Contrary to some accounts, Benson and Sims never tangled over the simple issue of whether merchant ships transiting the danger zones should be organized into convoys and provided with escorts. The questions that divided them were far more vexing and complex. Soon after the successful passage of the first Gibraltar convoy, Sims asked Benson to organize a large transatlantic convoy from Hampton Roads to the British Isles. Concerned about the "probability of the scattering of the convoy" owing to the weather and the "inexperience of personnel and general tension on the merchant vessels" to keep station, Benson responded with an alternative plan that involved a convoy consisting of only four cargo ships escorted by a pair of American destroyers. The second British merchant convoy stood out of Hampton Roads on 29 May, steamed northeast across the great circle route, and reached Liverpool without incident. The success of these trials demonstrated the utility of the convoy strategy to protect British trade and counter the German commerce raiding strategy. They provided only scant evidence as to how to compose a convoy or an escort group, what tactics to adopt, or the relative weight to be given to defending troop or merchant shipping, easily the most difficult question of them all. On 25 June 1917, the Royal Navy formally adopted an escort and convoy strategy for British merchant shipping, withdrew several destroyer divisions from the Grand Fleet to make up a handful of ocean escort groups, and established a convoy section in the Admiralty to coordinate cargo ships' movements. By the end of the month, the shortage of destroyers, cruisers, and other escort vessels among the Allied fleets was clearly acute. Furthermore, the British decision to adopt a convoy strategy did not help the U.S. Navy fix the priority of defending British merchant trade in relation to other strategic demands on American naval forces.[8]

Benson had already been asked by Sims to deploy a destroyer squadron to the Royal Navy's base at Queenstown in Northern Ireland. Unless the American fleet was "thrown into the balance," Sims warned, Britain and France might "be forced to dire straits" and "faced with an unsatisfactory peace." Benson distrusted Sims's assumptions, observing that his "judgment is warped and the weight of what he advocates lessened" by his close identification with the British. Daniels agreed. Benson suspected that the Admiralty had rigged its figures to spread future cargo shipping losses across both merchant navies and put Britain in a relatively more favorable postwar position. Sims was blind to this cruel reality of British maritime policy, Benson believed, because of his genuine affection for the English people. Sims did nothing to allay Benson's suspicions. Indeed, he held the rather naive view that, regardless of future developments, "we can always count upon the support of the British Navy." But Benson's problem in allocating destroyers was more complex than this simple question of British good will. Sims seemed not to comprehend the enormity of the problem Benson faced. The prewar practice of using battleships as the benchmark of naval power had left the American fleet top-heavy and short of escorts in 1917, with the result that Benson had at his disposal that spring only twenty-nine cruisers, forty-two oil-fired destroyers, and twenty-four older coal-burning destroyers. Roughly one-third of the destroyers were being overhauled or repaired, most were undermanned, and many were assigned to training squadrons. Benson had divided up the remainder among the Caribbean Patrol, the Asiatic Fleet, the Pacific Fleet, Admiral Henry Mayo's Atlantic Fleet, an Atlantic Coastal Patrol established by Daniels under pressure from Congress, and Admiral Sims' new Queenstown Force.[9]

Within a few days of Sims' arrival in London, the CNO decided to reduce the Caribbean Patrol by withdrawing a division of six destroyers from that station and deploying them to Queenstown. These ships, led by Commander Joseph K. Taussig, arrived in May at the Irish port. They were greeted by the base commander, Admiral Sir Lewis Bayly, an irascible but experienced martinet who had been charmed into treating the Americans with civility by Sims' considerable diplomatic talents. When, Bayly asked Taussig, would the American destroyers be fit for duty? Taussig later claimed that he replied, "We are ready now, sir," but another witness altered this to "ready when fueled." Because of their hasty formation and hurried deployment, Taussig's ships needed several days before they could join the British on antisubmarine patrols off the Irish coast. These patrols accomplished little, however.[10]

Shortly thereafter, Benson dispatched a second destroyer division to Queenstown and named Rear Admiral Joel Pringle to command all American vessels assigned to the Queenstown Force. The area of operations for which the Queenstown Force was responsible included about 25,000 square miles of War Zone west and south of Ireland, sea lanes that the Admiralty had been unable to patrol before the American destroyers arrived. Even the

British were still not entirely confident with Sims' escort and convoy strategy. Admiral Bayly confided to Sims that he preferred to equip British merchantmen with radios and arm them with naval gun crews, increase the number of destroyers under his command, and institute continual, aggressive sweeps along designated shipping lanes in the western approaches, a patrol strategy that Benson also admired. Then, in May, the Admiralty proposed that Benson send another squadron of destroyers to Halifax to escort an experimental convoy of twenty British merchantmen to Queenstown. This step marked the origin of the transatlantic convoy system, which evolved into the fast HC convoys from Halifax to Londonderry in the spring of 1918. HB convoys sailed from Hampton Roads to the American naval bases at a number of French ports on the Bay of Biscay. Still, a great deal of American shipping, including all shipping to Gibraltar, for instance, was never escorted. Owing to Gibraltar's importance to British trade, however, Benson ordered the Asiatic Fleet to detach five old destroyers for duty in the Mediterranean and directed Rear Admiral Albert P. Niblack to establish an American naval base there alongside the Royal Navy. Benson also positioned an American submarine flotilla at the British base at Berehaven, a defended anchorage about seventy-five miles west of Queenstown, and from there they patrolled the western approaches for U-boats throughout the remainder of the war, again without success.

In June, Benson told Sims, who by now had thirty-two destroyers under his command, that he could release no more escorts from the Atlantic Fleet and that subchasers from the new construction program would not be available until August. Benson's reluctance to deploy more destroyers to the British War Zone provoked another anguished missive from Sims, who complained on 3 July to Pratt, the assistant CNO, about the "tragic . . . spectacle of many dozens of ships, destroyers, yachts, and so forth parading up and down the American coast three thousand miles away from where the vital battle of the war is going on." In response, Benson deployed another six older destroyers to Queenstown later that month.[11]

Woodrow Wilson provided little guidance or support for Benson, and his notions about what to do about the U-boats were often contradictory. Wilson had "always believed in convoying," Daniels wrote in his diary on 6 July, adding that the president "wanted to know why there should not be a single lane for ships to reach Britain, with plenty of patrol boats and hydroplanes so as to make submarine operations there impossible." Benson at one time had studied this proposition, but he now opposed aggressive patrols along a protected shipping lane through the War Zone, arguing that "it is not practicable to thoroughly patrol a single lane by having [a] sufficient number of antisubmarine vessels constantly passing back and forth, thus guarding a constant stream of vessels passing through the lane." Neither Daniels nor Benson ever cleared up this fundamental misunderstanding about the differing escort and convoy strategies. Sims, for instance, was unaware of Wilson's imperfect grasp of the debate over strategy, so when Wilson told him that he could "not see how the necessary military supplies and supplies of food and fuel oil are to be delivered at British ports in any other way than a convoy," Sims totally misunderstood the meaning of the message.[12]

Nevertheless, by the fall of 1917 Anglo-American merchant convoy operations had dramatically reduced Allied losses to the U-boats, although neither the Navy Department nor the Admiralty entirely discounted the gravity of their failure to overcome the German offensive. Whereas 596,629 tons of merchant shipping were lost in May 1917, only 351,748 tons went down in September. Though still high, this second figure demonstrated that the defensive measures adopted by the Allies were saving ships. But success did not come cheaply. Lieutenant Commander David Bagley in the 1,150-ton destroyer *Jacob Jones* arrived at Queenstown with Taussig's squadron on 17 May and spent the next six months patrolling the War Zone off the British Isles, rescuing survivors of sinking ships, and escorting inbound convoys from the United States into English ports and other convoys sailing between Ireland and France. On 6 December, after standing out of Brest, the *Jacob Jones* was steaming for Queenstown when, at 1621, a lookout spotted a torpedo wake 1,000 yards off her starboard bow. Bagley swerved violently to avoid the weapon, but it entered the destroyer's starboard side and exploded, causing so much damage that the depth charges on the deck started to explode and the stern broke off. Bagley ordered his men to abandon ship, but the *Jacob Jones* went under within a few minutes, taking with her sixty-four sailors. Bagley and thirty-five men were saved, however, when Captain Hans Rose, a legendary German submariner, radioed to Queenstown the location of their drifting lifeboats.

Some of the Allied success in reducing the losses to the U-boats was clearly attributable to giving the merchant convoys escorts, but other steps also contributed to the submarines' ultimate defeat. For instance, Lloyd George had not only compelled the Admiralty to adopt Sims' convoy strategy but also completely centralized the supervision of British merchant shipping in May 1917 by sending Sir Eric Geddes to the Admiralty and conferring on him the authority to requisition and manage all privately owned British cargo vessels and transports. Geddes was on the job for only a few days when he discovered that over half of Britain's enormous merchant fleet—mostly liners and larger steamers—were not under government control and were instead sailing under private arrangements, a situation he soon corrected. Geddes' new regime so succeeded in rationalizing the use of shipping that Britain imported more grain in the summer of 1917 than she had one year earlier—despite the apparent success of the U-boat campaign. With the adoption of escorted convoys and tightened shipping controls, a complete plan for Allied transatlantic ocean convoys was ready to be put in place by September 1917.

On the American side, one of Secretary Daniels' most positive contributions to the war effort had been to persuade inventor Thomas Alva Edison to organize the Naval Consulting Board in October 1915. Edison was interested in the work in part because his battery-manufacturing firm had important contracts with the Navy. When the United States entered the war, Edison's group of civilian scientists and inventors and naval officers began to study the problem of antisubmarine warfare, and in the summer of 1917 their reports drew three startling conclusions. First, British merchant shipping between 1914 and 1917 sailed along the same sea lanes that had been used before the war began. Second, over 90 percent of all merchant ship losses to German submarines occurred during the daytime. Although nighttime U-boat attacks were greatly feared by merchantmen, they were largely ineffective. Third, fewer than 5 percent of British merchantmen were fitted with listening devices to locate submarines, and fewer still carried radios with which to broadcast the location of a sighting or an attack. Based on these findings, Edison recommended to the Navy that Allied convoys vary their routes, that merchant ships be equipped with radios and listening devices, that convoys or independently routed merchantmen transit high-risk areas only at night, and that they take refuge in shallow waters or ports in and around the British Isles whenever possible during the daytime. The gradual adoption of these measures helped to turn the tide in the war against the U-boat.[13]

Admiral Benson also acted in July 1917 to diminish the U-boat menace by establishing closer relations between Washington and Paris. He did this not only in response to French pleas for greater diplomatic and military coordination and material assistance but also to prepare the Navy to defend the movement of the American Expeditionary Force to the Western Front. That month the CNO directed Sims to prepare ten Queenstown Force destroyers to operate out of the large French naval base at Brest. The French Navy wanted Benson to establish the major American naval command in Europe at Brest, but both the British Admiralty and Admiral Sims opposed this step and resisted reductions to the Queenstown Force. Moreover, Sims was dead set against any plan to create a rival American naval headquarters in France, confiding bluntly to Benson that he wanted "just one command abroad."[14]

In the meantime, on 4 June, Captain William B. Fletcher with six armed, converted steam yachts left New York bound for Bermuda, coaled at St. George's Bay and again in the Azores, and arrived at Brest on the 4th of July. "In the ancient port . . . but a remnant of the [French] fleet remained," recalled Ensign Joseph Hubbard. "Gone were the seamen that for centuries had given it its glory; gone too were the young men, now fighting and dying on the northern lines of France." Defending transatlantic and coastwise shipping against U-boats operating in the Bay of Biscay quickly became an American responsibility. Once Benson was convinced that the Germans were not conducting U-boat operations in the Caribbean in mid-1917, he further weakened the Caribbean Patrol Force and in October named Vice Admiral Henry B. Wilson to relieve Fletcher in command of the newly independent Brest Force and the first American destroyers that arrived from Queenstown.

Working with French authorities and Vice Admiral Albert Gleaves' Cruiser and Transport Force, Wilson identified Brest and St. Nazaire as the best debarkation ports for the soon-to-arrive AEF. He then devised a plan under which the Brest Force destroyers and armed yachts—later supplemented by newly constructed minesweepers, tugs, and torpedo boats—provided ocean escorts for inbound and outbound troop transports and cargo ships passing through the danger zone and for some French coastal shipping as well. The growing importance of defending the Brest-bound troop transports meant that, within a year, more destroyers operated out of Brest than out of Queenstown. To support Admiral Wilson's operations in France, Benson instructed Sims to organize the American Cross-Channel Naval Service, which escorted Navy colliers from England and Wales to Brest and considerably reduced the losses of those scarce vessels to German submarines. These first steps marked the end of the beginning of the Allies' nearly two-year struggle to overcome the U-boat and to transport the AEF safely to France.[15]

Chapter Thirty
Defeating the U-boat
1918

Defeating Germany in World War I depended on overcoming the U-boat offensive. What prevented the Navy from responding more quickly in the spring of 1917 was not only Admiral Benson's reluctance to shift too many scarce destroyers from the Atlantic Fleet screens and various other stations to Admiral Henry B. Wilson's Brest Force and Admiral Sims' Queenstown Force ocean escort groups but also an overall shortage of escorts large and small. This stemmed from the prewar habit of measuring relative naval power by a battleship standard and from the Navy's peacetime view that destroyers and lesser vessels, aside from those needed to screen the battleships, were mobilization types that should and could be mass produced during the first phase of a major war. Moreover, after the recent passage of the long-awaited 1916 Big Navy Act, Benson was very reluctant to suspend battleship construction, although this policy was advanced by Sims soon after he arrived in London that April. "Our battleships can serve no useful purpose" in the war against Germany, he reported, but for the moment the CNO felt this conclusion to be premature.[1]

Later that month, a British mission led by Foreign Secretary Arthur James Balfour arrived in Washington and urged Daniels and Benson to suspend battleship building and divert those shipyards to the construction of escorts. This was resisted by Rear Admiral Badger, the chairman of the General Board, who preferred to continue building at least half of the ten battleships and six battlecruisers authorized by the Big Navy Act. Otherwise, Badger pointed out, "new alignments of powers after the war," possibly involving Japan, Germany, and even Britain, would find the American fleet "unprepared." By early summer Benson confronted such a grim shortage of oceangoing escorts for both the Cruiser and Transport Force and the Brest Force that he asked the Assistant CNO, Captain William V. Pratt, to investigate the shipbuilding program. Pratt recommended on 6 July that the battleship program be suspended, that shipyards building battlecruisers be turned over to civilian cargo ship construction, and that the Navy build 150 austere, four-stack antisubmarine destroyers and 50 heavy destroyers, in addition to the 66 general-purpose destroyers already laid down. Overriding the General Board's heated objections, Benson moved with amazing speed to implement this policy that very day. Eventually, three classes of four-stack, flush-deck destroyers were built, typified by the 1,100-ton *Caldwell*-class, which made 35 knots and was armed with 4-inch guns and twelve torpedo tubes. This new antisubmarine building program was expected to more than triple the number of destroyers in the fleet, but as a result of an unanticipated shortage of industrial gearcutting capacity, the first of these new ships could not be made ready for sea duty until early 1919.[2]

As an interim solution to the escort shortage, Benson turned to a program to build small oceangoing subchasers that had been sponsored by Assistant Secretary Roosevelt earlier in the year. Roosevelt placed the initial order on 17 March 1917, and the first vessel was delivered in May. The 110-foot, 60-ton wooden-hull subchaser made 17 knots, had a 1,000-mile operating radius, and was armed with 3-inch guns, a pair of machine guns, and, late in the war, a 3-inch nonrecoil 6-pound Davis backblast gun. It also carried the new American Y-gun depth-charge thrower. Prior to the invention of this weapon by the Bureau of Ordnance, ships could attack submerged submarines only by dropping ashcan depth charges off a rack over the stern, a tactic that considerably restricted the escort's lethality. The Y-gun, a set of tubes fixed at an angle like the letter, fired six ashcan depth charges about 100 yards off the attacking vessel's bow, thereby increasing her ability to run down an escaping submarine. Subchasers were also equipped with radios to coordinate operations and report contacts and rudimentary hydrophones to listen for the engine sounds of a nearby submarine. Destroyer hydrophones were use-

World War I emergency subchaser program produced its first escort in July 1917. When the ...m was completed in February 1919, 447 vessels had been built for the U.S. and French fleets. ...10-foot long, 85-ton subchaser (SC-328) carried one 3-inch gun and two machine guns for sur-...ctions and an effective Y-gun depth-charge thrower for use against submerged submarines. ...vessel was equipped with a passive K-tube listening device, but later vessels also operated a ...sophisticated, hull-mounted SC hydrophone tube. The U.S. Navy operated 121 of these ver-...subchasers in European waters during the war, and 100 more were turned over to the French.

...dmiral William Sowden Sims, commander, ...aval Forces Europe, World War I.

less unless the ship's diesel engines were shut down, but the subchaser's small gasoline engine was much quieter and a handful of subchasers, properly coordinated, could search out and locate a submarine at ranges of up to twenty miles under ideal conditions.

The Navy had ordered about 350 subchasers by late April 1917; a total of 441 were delivered during the war, about 50 of which were transferred to the French Navy. Although the versatile subchaser was used not only as a coastal escort but also for harbor defense and minesweeping, her wooden hull did not influence the German contact mine. The subchaser's small fuel tanks also meant that she had to be towed to the European stations. Admiral Joel Pringle discovered that the subchasers' short operating radius, especially in high seas, confined them to waters around the Queenstown base, but by the end of 1917 they were a mainstay of the American escort forces and 235 eventually operated in European waters. An equally ambitious effort by auto magnate Henry Ford to build more than one hundred 500-ton steel-hulled *Eagle*-class escorts in Detroit using mass production methods perfected in automobile manufacturing ran into so many delays that none of these boats was ready to enter the fleet during the war.

The 1917 escort shortage forced Benson to make several other difficult strategic decisions, but then and throughout the war he held to the principle that the Navy's first obligation was to defend American troop transports. Pratt, the Assistant CNO, cautioned Sims that Benson's primary goal was the "safe transportation of American troops to France." Sims believed that defending British merchant convoys was the more urgent mission, but Pratt agreed with Benson's stance that the troop "ships should receive the utmost destroyer protection." Daniels reaffirmed Benson's decision in a stiff directive to Sims on 22 July. "The paramount duty of the destroyers in European waters is principally the proper protection of transports of American troops," he declared. Sims was directed to "be certain to detail an adequate convoy of destroyers and . . . bear always in mind that everything is secondary . . . to ensure protection to American troops."[3]

The need for American troops on the Western Front became evident following the collapse of the French Army's disastrous 1917 Nivelle Offensive. France's new commanding general, Henri Pétain, found that the only way to quell the resulting mutinies was to assure his troops that they would not go on the offensive again until the Americans arrived. The War Department had no plans to meet this need, however, and Secretary of War Newton Baker had confessed to Congress on 7 April that strategic plans "are in the making rather than having been made" and that, furthermore, Wilson had yet to decide to send an army to Europe. Not until 18 May did Congress pass the Selective Service Act and thereby create a draft for the Army, although voluntary enlistments in the Navy and Marine Corps continued until September 1918. The former French commanding general, Field Marshal Joseph Joffre, arrived in Washington soon after and begged the Army chief of staff, General Tasker Bliss, to send at least one American division to France to reassure the Allies that fresh troops were on the way. Bliss agreed to Joffre's plan, and Baker selected General John Pershing to command the AEF in Europe. The Marine Corps commandant, Major General George Barnet, persuaded Bliss to add the hastily assembled 5th Marine Regiment to this newly formed division, but Barnet's success was assured only when Benson agreed to transport the Marines to France on board American warships. Under these same terms, Barnet later got Baker to accept a second Marine regiment, to bring the Corps in France up to a brigade strength of 6,000 men. As a result of his efforts, when the 1st Division assembled in New York in June, the press announced that the Marines would be "the first to fight."[4]

In April 1917, General Bliss estimated that the AEF in France would need about 1 million men, formed into twenty divisions, to hold the Allied line. But when Pershing reached France in July he reported to Washington that he would need at least sixty-six divisions totaling nearly 3 million men "to win the victory" using "numerical superiority." Bliss then developed a new plan to draft and train a much enlarged AEF, which he and his wartime successor, General Peyton March, skillfully implemented. From just over 213,557 men in uniform on 1 April 1917, the Army expanded to over 3.6 million men at the end of 1918. Sixty-two infantry divisions were trained, and when Pershing began offensive operations in 1918, he commanded forty-three divisions totaling nearly 2 million men. Getting these troops to Europe was a vexing issue.[5]

Safely transporting the AEF to France was the Navy's major accomplishment in World War I. To command the naval escorts for the 1st Division, Benson turned to Rear Admiral Albert Gleaves, who had succeeded Sims in command of the renowned Atlantic Destroyer Flotilla in 1916. Benson named Gleaves to command the newly created Cruiser and Transport Force on 29 May

1917 and vested in this organization control of all American troop transport and merchant convoy operations. This force eventually included twenty-four cruisers and a larger number of destroyers drawn from the Atlantic, Pacific, and Reserve fleets and from the Caribbean Patrol. Gleaves established a Newport News Division consisting of two cruiser divisions under Rear Admiral Marbury Johnson and based it at Hampton Roads, the major port of embarkation for the AEF. Also based in Hampton Roads were the twenty-five American and ex-German liners that constituted Rear Admiral Hilary P. Jones' Transport Force.

When Congress declared war, the slow, unseaworthy *Hancock* and the *Henderson,* then still under construction, were the only Navy transports in commission; the Army had in service just four old troop transports and three cargo vessels. Only the twenty-five-year-old Army supply ship *Buford* possessed the speed and fuel capacity for a turnaround transatlantic voyage. The Army acquired and converted fourteen oceangoing steamships, while the Navy turned to the fleet of 104 German merchantmen and passenger liners that had been interned in American ports in 1914 and taken into the Navy three years later. Fourteen of these vessels exceeded 10,000 tons each, and these German liners, after conversion, became the backbone of Admiral Jones's Transport Force. Gleaves identified Hoboken, New Jersey, as a second port of embarkation for the AEF, as the headquarters for his merchant convoy directorate, and as the operating base for the Cruiser Force's New York Division, consisting of three cruiser-destroyer divisions.

Gleaves divided the Transport Force into convoy groups of three to four ships each according to speed and assigned an ocean escort group of five to seven cruisers and destroyers to defend each convoy. The presence of the cruiser in the formation provided the escort group commodore not only with a convenient flagship but also with a means to protect the transports against any lone German surface raider that might break out of the North Sea and enter the North Atlantic. Troop convoys approaching the War Zone off the British Isles were reinforced at prearranged meeting points at sea by destroyers and subchasers from the Queenstown Force, whereas destroyers from the Brest Force rendezvoused with inbound convoys sailing for Brest or St. Nazaire.

The first convoy, carrying 14,000 men of the Army's 1st Division and the 1st Marines, their equipment, and their mules, sailed from Hampton Roads on 14 June 1917 guarded by a powerful escort commanded by Admiral Gleaves in the cruiser *Seattle*. All the escorts, except the destroyers, embarked troops, while the armed Navy transports *Hancock* and *Dekalb* had to double as escorts. Gleaves divided the convoy into four segments according to speed, arranged for all the destroyers to be refueled during the voyage, and asked Sims to have a Queenstown Force destroyer division rendezvous with the convoy and reinforce its ocean escort group during the passage through the War Zone. The worst moment of the voyage came at 2156 on 22 June when the fastest segment, after entering the War Zone, was attacked by a U-boat. Two torpedoes were fired at the *Seattle*; one passed only fifty yards off her bow. However, the entire convoy safely arrived at St. Nazaire between 26 June and 1 July. "We lost nothing but one horse," reported an officer, "and that was a mule!" Owing to an extraordinary effort by his formidable organization, by early 1918 Gleaves could safely transport about 15,000 troops across the Atlantic each month.[6]

Soon after Gleaves organized the Cruiser and Transport Force, Benson decided to integrate the movements of the Transport Force with the established British merchant convoy system and the fledgling American cargo convoy system. On the North American side of the Atlantic, Hampton Roads, New York, and Halifax-Sydney, Nova Scotia, were designated as origination ports for merchant convoys, composed of twenty to twenty-five ships defended by an ocean escort group of one or two destroyers and a few converted minesweepers, subchasers, or lesser vessels. HS convoys sailed from Sydney, HH convoys from Hampton Roads, and HN convoys from New York. In the summer of 1917, Vice Admiral Gleaves arranged for the troop convoys from Hampton Roads to rendezvous in midocean with the fast HX merchant convoys from Halifax for the run across the Atlantic. Eventually, four convoy areas—North Atlantic, Caribbean and Gulf, South Atlantic, and Mediterranean—were identified, and an attempt was made, mostly by the British, to carefully monitor the movement of shipping through this maze. Nonetheless, even at the end of 1918 a large fraction of Allied cargo shipping was untouched by the convoy system and sailed independently.

The primacy of escorting troop shipping never made sense to Sims, and he resisted Benson's essential strategy for the duration of the war. Sims objected to the establishment of the Cruiser and Transport Force on the grounds that it would subtract destroyers from the offensive patrols he had established off Queenstown and complained that there were not enough escorts "to ensure the safety of all vital supplies and prospective movements of our troops and their supplies." In May 1918, he criticized the "excessive demands upon our escort forces for the protection of troops," maintaining that the "safety of vessels carrying merchandise to Europe is hardly less essential . . . than is the safety of troop transports." Strains developed between Benson and Sims as a result. Benson attempted to keep Sims informed of Navy policy, but he often failed to enlist Sims's advice about the other European commands. The outcome was that Benson often had to referee disputes between Sims and Admirals Mayo, Rodman, Henry Wilson, and Niblack. In May 1918, Sims was still complaining that the "lack of more destroyers" lay at the root of continued losses to the U-boats. However, the American naval establishment in Europe grew enormously and by the end of 1918, over 80,000 men and 370 ships had been assigned by Benson to the Navy's commands in Europe, which spread out over forty-five naval bases stretching from Scotland into the Mediterranean. Even this prodigious effort failed to satisfy Sims, who carped in early November 1918 that "our forces have not been thrown into the game."[7]

In the crucial summer of 1917, however, a negotiated relaxation of tensions with Japan brought an end to the Twenty-One Demands crisis and allowed Benson to send more destroyers to Britain, and by 1 August 1917, forty-five of sixty-eight American destroyers were en route to Europe or already operating in the War Zone. There were only twenty-one destroyers left in American waters in September, but Sims was still unsatisfied and accused Daniels and Benson of footdragging. Nominally, Sims served under Admiral Henry T. Mayo, the commander in chief of the Atlantic Fleet, but in practice Sims ignored Mayo and dealt directly with the Navy Department. Mayo deeply resented Sims' anomalous position and repeatedly asked Daniels to shift the Atlantic Fleet's headquarters to London, but Daniels and Benson managed to sidestep the issue for the duration of the war. In London, meanwhile, Sims erected his own general staff in the form of a planning section that had no operational or administrative duties. The British assisted Sims along these lines, provided him with special facilities, and generally tried to stimulate his Anglophilia in the hope that he would influence the Navy Department to adopt a pro-British policy once the war was over.

The organization of troop and cargo shipping also hampered the mobilization of American power. Although Wilson's cabinet decided on 12 July 1917 that "transports during the present war . . . be commissioned in the Navy," confusion reigned in the War Department during the rest of the year over this issue. For example, six months elapsed before Secretary Baker was forced to explain, "in order that there may be no misunderstanding," that only the Navy would man troopships and "other vessels intended for cargo, animals, and munitions." Makeshift arrangements during 1917 prevented many disasters, but at the time this agreement was reached, three separate Navy commands were responsible for troop and cargo shipping, and one of these admirals was afloat. Too often, Benson charged, cargo ships were victims of Navy yard berthing practices, although "more actively engaged in the present war than any other class of vessels in the Navy."[8]

To remedy this, in January 1918 Benson established the Naval Overseas Transportation Service under Captain Charles Belknap, who thereafter provided freighters to the War Department and handled cargo shipping for Navy installations in Europe. By July 1918, the average Navy cargo ship sailed to Britain and back in seventy-two days. Navy operations in Britain, France, and the Mediterranean were solely supported by NOTS, which also shared responsibility with the War Shipping Board for food relief shipments into the Near East. Although shipping shortages continued well into 1918, by the end of the war the Navy Department and the War Shipping Board had built, bought, or confiscated over 3 million tons of cargo and troop shipping to contribute to the war effort. On paper, this was about one-fifth of the Allied shipping pool, but it was so well managed and defended that losses at sea totaled less than 200,000 tons at the end of 1918.

Soon after the United States declared war, Daniels and Benson began to question not only the Royal Navy's inability to defeat the U-boat but also its failure to impose a close blockade on Germany and force the High Seas Fleet into another general action. The source of Britain's conservative approach was Britain's First Sea Lord, Admiral Jellicoe, who had fought the German battle fleet to a tactical checkmate off Jutland, and who was now committed to a purely defensive strategy. He wrote to President Wilson on 1 July 1917 to explain that the primary missions of the Grand Fleet were to protect communications between the British Isles and Britain's armies overseas, enforce the distant blockade of the Central Powers, and guard British maritime trade. Inasmuch as Britain's shipping was not well defended, the Allied navies should "wait for favorable opportunities to engage the elusive enemy fleet." Daniels agreed with Benson that Britain's attitude "represented a failure to prosecute the war" and a regrettable, war-weary lack of "vigor." Even Sims began pressing the Admiralty to take the offensive against the German fleet. Closely aligned with this view was Daniels's conviction that the United States was "playing second fiddle" and that these related problems could be solved only by a "conference to determine upon a joint program." On 16 August Daniels took Admirals Benson and Mayo to the White House, where Wilson explained "the need of an offensive and reiterated his view that we cannot win this war by merely hunting submarines when they have gotten into the great ocean." When Wilson was told by Mayo "not [to] expect too much from offensive antisubmarine operations," he shot back that he at least "expected plans by which America could lead and be the senior partner in a successful naval campaign."[9]

The drive behind an Allied naval strategy conference to clear the air was reinforced by the complaint of Rear Admiral Ralph Earle, the chief of the Bureau of Ordnance, that Sims had proven to be a poor vehicle for transmitting the Navy's views to London because the department still did "not know what the British Admiralty wants us to do." Addressing this problem on 11 August during a secret speech to 300 officers on board the Atlantic Fleet flagship *Pennsylvania,* Wilson urged offensive naval operations against the German fleet and submarine bases. The Allies were "hunting hornets all over the farm and letting the nest alone," he insisted, but "if we crush it, the war is won." This was a peculiar formulation in that few Navy men or senior Allied military officials believed that defeating the U-boat would do more than indirectly contribute to Germany's downfall.[10]

Wilson, Daniels, and Benson did not completely trust Sims' objectivity, so in September 1917 they sent Admiral Mayo to London to review naval strategy with the Allies. After inspecting the Queenstown Force, discussing strategy with Sims and Jellicoe, and visiting Admiral Fletcher's fast growing Brest Force, Mayo reported that the British had no plan to win the war. Naval operations were "carried out from day to day," he wrote, "not according to the effective co-ordination and co-operation of efforts against the enemy." Upon his return to Washington in October, he warned that convoy operations "may, if successful, prevent defeat," but "cannot win the war." Unless "the navies . . . are satisfied to let the armies or political conditions settle the war . . . a more offensive plan is essential." Wilson likewise wondered when the British intended to begin a "real offensive." Mayo had also brought with him a renewed request from Jellicoe to Benson to reinforce the Grand Fleet by sending an Atlantic Fleet battleship division to Scapa Flow to operate under Admiral Sir David Beatty's command. Benson had rejected this proposal once in July on the grounds that the British outnumbered the Germans in modern dreadnoughts by a ratio of two to one and because he wanted to keep the Atlantic Fleet intact. The CNO was mindful of this when he again turned down the scheme in the fall, but in October he was far more concerned with the lack of an overall Allied military strategy and the absence of any recognition by the Allies of the unique American contribution to the war effort.[11]

The Americans believed that these issues were related. As Secretary Baker told the Army War College, Wilson expected the United States to insist on "complete diplomatic and military individuality," since there was no "identity of interest" between the American objectives and those of the Allies—other than defeating Germany. To improve coordination, Wilson directed Colonel House to sail to Europe in November 1917 with a military mission that included both of the service chiefs, Admiral Benson and General Bliss. Their ship stood into Plymouth harbor on the night of 6 November, the nadir of the war for the Allied cause—the day Britain's Passchendaele offensive in Belgium ended in disaster, the Austrians shattered the Italian Army at Caporetto, and the Bolsheviks, who promised to negotiate a separate peace, seized power in Russia. The Allies were "in a terrible mess," reported House's secretary, and "panic" was gripping the high command.[12]

Both Lloyd George and Georges Clemenceau, France's new premier, wanted to exert greater political control over military operations, whereas the Americans sought more interallied coordination and operational independence for their own national forces. The House mission resulted in the establishment of the Allied Supreme War Council, to which Wilson assigned General Bliss, and the Allied Naval Council, to which he named Benson. Although Bliss resigned as Army chief of staff and remained in Europe for the rest of the war, Benson returned to Washington and asked Sims to represent him on the Naval Council in Paris. Relations between the two men continued to worsen, despite this expression of trust. Before Sims had left for London in March 1917, Benson sternly cautioned him about overly identifying himself with British interests. Shortly after Sims arrived in London, Jellicoe invited him to attend the secret daily meetings of the British naval staff, and Sims, beside himself with pride, accepted graciously. That fall Sims was asked to serve as an honorary member of the Admiralty Board, but in November, Benson vetoed this proposal without much sensitivity to Sims' strong personal investment in the honor. Sims even considered redesigning the Navy's uniform so that it would look "practically indistinguishable from the British." It was "absolutely necessary not to view our forces as an entity in themselves but rather as an integral part of the combined Allied naval forces." This view grated on Benson's sense of national pride, his devotion to the U.S. Navy and its unique traditions, his distrust of Britain's motives, and his discouragement with the Admiralty's unwillingness to take offensive measures against the Germans.[13]

During his trip to Europe in November 1917, Benson was disappointed by the unwillingness of the British to devise specific plans for a new Allied naval offensive. The CNO had been less than precise in explaining his own priorities, however. He first urged Jellicoe to increase the strength of the Dover Patrol's sweeps against German surface raiders and even agreed to dispatch Rear Admiral Hugh Rodman's Battleship Division Nine from the Atlantic Fleet to Scapa Flow so that four British battleships might be released for increased patrol operations in the English Channel and the Bay of Biscay. Comprising the coal-burning dreadnought battleships *New York*, *Florida*, *Delaware*, *Wyoming*, *Arkansas*, and *Texas*, Rodman's formation reached the British Isles in early December. They constituted the 6th Battle Squadron of Admiral Beatty's Grand Fleet for the rest of the war. Admiral Rodman's ships did more than simply exercise with the Grand Fleet and await a German sortie. They frequently defended convoys steaming between Britain and Norway against lurking enemy cruisers and often were brought under attack by patrolling U-boats. On 8 February 1918 the *Delaware*, assigned to protect an inbound convoy, was attacked by a U-boat that fired three torpedoes at the fast battleship. The main mission of the U.S. Navy's battleships, however, was to strengthen the already superior British fleet, which contained and immobilized the High Seas Fleet from Jutland until the end of the war.

In the summer of 1918, rumors reached London that the kaiser was about to order the fast German battlecruisers to break out from the North Sea into the Atlantic to attack American troop transport convoys or British shipping. Upon receiving this news, Beatty sent Rodman and three American battleships to the Royal Navy's base at Berehaven as a precaution, but the alarm proved to be false. However, it led Benson to reduce the Atlantic Fleet once again by ordering Rear Admiral Thomas S. Rogers to sail from Hampton Roads for Ireland with his battleship division composed of the coal-burning dreadnoughts *Nevada, Oklahoma,* and *Utah.* Arriving in Bantry Bay on 23 August, Rogers's ships defended inbound troop convoys against a much feared, last minute sortie by Germany's battlecruisers. Indeed, so great was the concern in Allied quarters of a German breakout that Benson at one time even brought up the possibility of basing the entire Atlantic Fleet in European waters, but the Admiralty brushed this aside on the grounds that the British possessed a supply of fuel oil barely sufficient to support their own oil-fired vessels.

On his November 1917 visit to Europe, Benson also raised with the British the issues of tightening the blockade and attacking German naval bases, but Jellicoe did not believe that either step would succeed and Beatty refused to consider offensive operations until the spring of 1918. To escort convoys, the Admiralty in June 1917 had drawn destroyers from his Grand Fleet at the very moment Beatty became convinced that he needed a second screen if he was to check the German High Seas Fleet in another North Sea engagement. Jellicoe and Beatty asked Benson to detach more American destroyers from the Atlantic Fleet to reinforce Sims's Queenstown Force so they might return British destroyers to the Grand Fleet screen, but Benson, locked into his own policy, refused to do this until shortfalls elsewhere could be made up from new American construction.

The CNO also confronted the need to defend American cargo shipping to southern France and Italy, a mission that drew the Navy into the Mediterranean war in 1917. When in June the Admiralty proposed to inaugurate regular convoys between Gibraltar and England, Benson agreed to send a support force composed of two old cruisers, four gunboats, and four Coast Guard cutters to Gibraltar in August. An American naval facility was established at Gibraltar at the same time, thus allowing the British Mediterranean Fleet to strengthen its escort groups, which defended shipping bound for Italy. Occasionally American vessels were assigned to reinforce British ocean escort groups protecting the movement of cargo ships between Gibraltar and Alexandria.

With the near-collapse of the Italians' Alpine Front in 1918, Austrian U-boat operations increased against shipping in the Adriatic. This caused Benson to arrange for American escorts to operate from the Italian naval base at Otranto. When Sims joined the new Allied Naval Council in early 1918 he attempted to improve relations between the Italians and the French and to persuade the Italian Navy to launch an offensive against Pola, Austria's main fleet base. Although he had no more destroyers to spare to back Sims's diplomacy, the CNO did send two subchaser squadrons, thirty-six vessels, to Otranto during the summer to defend Italian shipping and occasionally reinforce convoys between Gibraltar and Alexandria. These Corfu-based subchasers also conducted antisubmarine sweeps in the narrow Otranto Strait to harass Austrian submarines and, late in 1918, joined a combined Anglo-Italian cruiser force that attacked the enemy base at Durazzo. Two Austrian U-boats were trapped and sunk by three intrepid American subchasers during this raid. In addition, Navy aircraft operating from two air stations in Italy conducted antisubmarine patrols over the northern Adriatic. Deep political suspicions between Italy and France undermined Sims's effort to forge a united front, however, and the Italian Navy refused to attack Pola, so the Austrians operated in the northern Adriatic with relative immunity for the rest of the war.

Benson's decision to send naval aircraft to Italy illustrated his recognition of the value of land-based naval aviation to supplement antisubmarine operations. In early 1917, the Navy's entire air establishment consisted of just one air station at Pensacola, about forty officer pilots, and fifty-four fragile biplanes. During the following two years, the Navy purchased more than 2,000 aircraft, 15 small airships, and over 200 observation balloons that, by the end of 1918, were deployed to thirty-five naval air stations stretching from the United States to the Canal Zone to Europe. Soon after the United States declared war, Benson established the first of eight naval air stations eventually opened in the British Isles. Captain Hutch I. Cone, who organized the Navy's air command in France in January 1918, arranged for seaplanes and land-based patrol planes to cover the movement of French convoys across the Bay of Biscay. Because the French had withdrawn most of their aircraft to the Western Front in 1914, Cone's establishment grew quickly, from three stations at Dunkirk and the entrances to the Loire and Gironde rivers to a network of sixteen airfields stretching south to the Spanish border by July 1918. Antisubmarine kite balloon stations were set up at Brest, L'Orient, and La Trinité. Navy aircraft also operated from Gibraltar as well as Italy.

Over 500 planes were assigned to the Europe-based naval air squadrons, the mainstay of which was the Curtiss HS-1L patrol seaplane powered by the rugged Liberty engine and armed with a pair of 180-pound depth charges. Navy air patrols hunted U-boats in the North Sea, over the English Channel, and in the Bay of Biscay. The most prominent of these units was the Northern Bomber Group. This unit was attached to the Dover Patrol, commanded by Admiral Sir Roger Keyes, who used the Americans planes to bomb U-boat bases on the Belgian coast. This campaign was costly and inflicted little damage on the enemy installations. Overall, American naval aircraft made thirty attacks on U-boats in 1918, and although none of the submarines engaged was sunk by aircraft alone, one observer concluded that "in future wars must sea power be assured by air supremacy."

The movement of all these forces to Europe left Benson uneasy about the Navy's ability to defend shipping in American waters. In September 1917, he first raised the issue of how to defend shipping off the East Coast should the Germans deploy U-boats to the western Atlantic, a danger that seemed remote given the more immediate threat to American troop shipping and British merchant convoys in the War Zone. For intelligence on German naval operations, the Navy depended largely on the Admiralty's Room 39 code-breaking organization, and early in 1918 that group told Sims that it had broken the German U-boat cipher and learned that Berlin intended to send a few submarines across the Atlantic to the Western Hemisphere. At first this threat was not wholly appreciated, and Daniels recorded in his diary that spring that "Sims had sent information from the English Admiralty [which] believed [there would be] no danger of submarines on this coast."[14]

Sims' assessment was incorrect—the Germans did intend to send U-boats into American waters. Furthermore, it was not understood by the Navy Department that this German decision was an early confession that the antishipping offensive off the British Isles had failed to knock Britain out of the war. On 1 May, Sims alerted Washington that the long-range cargo-carrying *U-151* had stood out of Kiel and was heading into the Atlantic. "There was a reasonable probability that submarines . . . may arrive off [the] United States coast at any time after May 20 and that they will carry mines," he reported. Five days later off the Delaware Capes the *U-151* sank two coastal schooners, and a week later the 5,000-ton liner *Carolina* and five lesser vessels went under in the same area within the span of a few hours. This single submarine had sunk six ships totaling 15,000 tons by 2 June, and insurance rates for coastal shipping increased overnight by 1,500 percent.

The focus of these alarming losses shifted to the north during the summer as the number of U-boats on station off the Atlantic coast increased to six. On 19 July, the armored cruiser *San Diego* was steaming from Portsmouth down Long Island to New York, where she was scheduled to join a Cruiser Force group assigned to escort a troop convoy to France. She was northeast of Fire Island at 1115 when she collided with a submerged mine whose detonation lifted the stern of the ship out of the water and rattled her fore and aft. Captain H. H. Christy, believing that his ship had been hit by a torpedo, ordered that she be brought up to flank speed and sent the crew to battle stations, but the blast had blown a large hole in the forward end of the engine room and it was flooding. When she listed to port slightly, Christy concluded that she was about to capsize, and ordered his men to abandon ship—although the gun crews continued to fire their batteries at the waves until the sea washed over the mounts. "True to the tradition of the sea," Admiral Gleaves recorded proudly, Captain Christy "was the last man to leave the ship." Twenty minutes after the *San Diego* struck the mine, she disappeared into the ocean. Fortunately, all but six of the crew were saved. One month later, on 10 August, U-boats sank a total of nine coastal schooners about fifty miles off Nantucket. Many of these losses were attributable to the five dozen mines the Germans had planted in a number of places along the mid-Atlantic shipping lanes. The *Minnesota* was cruising about twenty miles off Fenwick Island at the mouth of the Delaware on 29 September when she struck a mine laid by the *U-117*. Although there were no casualties, her starboard side was damaged, but she was saved by good damage control and managed to reach Philadelphia, where she was laid up for extensive repairs.[15]

These losses, which provoked public alarm, outrage on the Hill, and concern within the Navy, seemed to justify Assistant Secretary Roosevelt's scheme to increase the already considerable number of small craft, converted yachts, and Coast Guard cutters that had been commissioned into the coastal patrol forces. The Navy had erected a system of medium radio direction-finding stations along the East Coast to track German submarines operating in the western Atlantic, but this effort seemed not to pay off. Benson now ordered the various naval district commanders to organize local minesweeping forces, which cleared all the principal East Coast harbors and repeatedly swept the major shipping channels, operations that produced some not inconsiderable disruption to normal coastal maritime traffic. Antisubmarine nets were installed at the entrances to every major harbor. Benson also established coastal routing offices in every East Coast port, declared these waters to be danger zones, and ordered all vessels to black out their running lights at night. A handful of destroyer-subchaser hunting groups were formed and sent into the danger zones on patrols, a measure that may have forced the U-boats to move off the coast. Benson asked a planning group headed by Commander Chester W. Nimitz to evaluate the antisubmarine campaign in American waters, and Nimitz predicted in September 1918 that the Germans would reinforce their western Atlantic U-boat flotilla and continue to attack shipping off the East Coast, in the Caribbean, and in the Gulf of Mexico. "Enemy submarines are most likely to operate in southern waters, concentrating on shipping bound to and from the Gulf of Mexico and the Caribbean Sea," he cautioned.[16]

The Caribbean Patrol Force at Key West had been alarmingly weakened in the summer of 1917 when Benson shifted most of the American cruisers and destroyers to the Cruiser and Transport Force and built up the ocean escort groups in European waters. To counter Germany's western Atlantic offensive, Benson ordered the Caribbean Force to institute a makeshift convoy system for individual American oil tankers transiting the Gulf of Mexico in the fall of 1918. Although Caribbean politics had been fairly tranquil since 1916, the prospect of German naval activity in the region revived American concern about renewed disturbances. Cuban waters were thought to be especially vulnerable, and Benson directed Lieutenant Commander H. Kent Hewitt to establish a naval advisory mission in Havana. Eighteen subchasers were transferred to the Cuban Navy, and soon thereafter the Cubans asked Hewitt to take command of their fleet. The war reached a climax in Europe before much more could be done, and merchant shipping in the Caribbean and the Gulf was never organized into convoys. Although the enemy sank about 100,000 tons of shipping in the western Atlantic with an average of only six U-boats on station at any given time during the summer of 1918, the Germans were unable to sustain a high tempo of operations so far from their bases. The voyage across the North Atlantic tested the low endurance of Germany's submarines and allowed them only a limited cruising radius once they arrived on station off the East Coast. Despite the fear that the U-boats would descend on tanker shipping in the Gulf of Mexico, in reality they could not operate south of Cape Hatteras.

The failure of the German Navy's western Atlantic offensive underscored several profound weaknesses in Germany's overall naval strategy. Chaos and inconsistency characterized the German U-boat building program. Instead of accelerating submarine construction in late 1916 when the kaiser decided to resume unrestricted submarine warfare, the German Navy merely implemented a replacement policy, ordering new submarines to be laid down according to the rate of losses at sea. The result was that the U-boat flotillas grew very little during 1917. There were 133 submarines in commission in January 1917, only 144 one year later. During that same period, 87 new boats were built, but 63 were sunk on patrol and 15 more were lost to other causes. The Germans built 373 U-boats during World War I and lost at least 178; each submarine lost cost the Allies about 32 ships, but most of the German losses came after the United States entered the war and improved Allied defensive measures came into play.

One of the most ambitious defensive steps taken by the Allies to defeat the U-boat was the North Sea Mine Barrage, a bold scheme to lay a huge minefield from northern Scotland to Norway, which Admiral Benson first put forth in April 1917. He was ever fearful that the Germans would extend their U-boat operations into the mid-Atlantic, or even to the East Coast or the Caribbean, and he viewed the Mine Barrage as an important means of preventing this. The Admiralty responded on 13 May, however, that it considered the "project of attempting to close exit to North Sea [by mining] . . . to be impracticable. . . . The difficulty will be apprehended when total distance, depth, materials, and patrols required and distance from base of operations are considered." Benson disagreed with this reasoning, and he referred the problem to Admiral Earle of the Navy's Bureau of Ordnance. Earle worked with Ralph C. Browne, an electrical engineer, to devise a way to mass produce the Mark VI mine to which was affixed a 70-foot copper antenna charged with electrical impulses. The mine was designed to explode when a submarine came in contact with a strand of the antenna.[17]

As a result of this work, mining an immense area of the North Sea between Norway and Scotland to bar U-boat movements into the Atlantic became practical for the first time. When Benson told Sims about the project, however, Sims reacted strongly because he did not want Benson to withdraw destroyers, minecraft, or other escorts from the North Atlantic merchant convoys. He argued that the attrition that even a partial barrage might impose on the U-boats was not worth the diversion of escorts from his forces. "Either the barrage is successful or it fails absolutely," he declared, and insisted that an adequate stock of mines was not available to erect an effective minefield system. Sims's true concerns were more parochial. "The convoy is the one sure naval plan," he said, and "no time or material or effort should be diverted from the successful organization or implementation of this plan." Sims invariably followed the Admiralty's lead, and with few exceptions the British were firmly against the North Sea Mine Barrage. The Royal Navy's lack of success in its mining operations was dispiriting. The Harwich Force had earlier planted mines in the Heligoland Bight to prevent U-boats from using that exit, but the Grand Fleet's failure to annihilate the High Seas Fleet at Jutland meant that the British were unable to stop German minesweepers from repeatedly clearing channels through the Heligoland minefields.[18]

Benson revived the issue during his visit to the Admiralty in December 1917 and convinced Eric Geddes, the new First Lord, to overrule Jellicoe's naval staff and approve the strategic concept. After a series of British raids against German bases on the Belgian coast failed early the following year, the Admiralty finally agreed to put Benson's plan into effect. In the summer of 1918, a combined Anglo-American Mining Squadron under Rear Admiral Joseph Strauss laid nearly 75,000 mines in the North Sea along a belt 15 to 35 miles wide stretching 240 miles from the Orkney Islands to Norway's coast near Udsire Light. Captain Henry Wiley recalled that each day, "after the mines were laid, the minelayers dropped the ends of fine piano wire overboard and allowed the wire to run out as they steamed to a marker buoy" at the edge of the minefield. By the end of the year, the Navy had taken delivery of over 100,000 mines, nearly enough to complete the task. Even after the first phase of Strauss's mine-laying operations was finished, however, evaluating the results was difficult. Only four U-boats were lost to the North Sea Mine Barrage, although four more missing German submarines may also have been its victims. The overall effect of the well advertised mining strategy as a deterrent to German operations could not be measured because of the coincident collapse of Germany's naval campaign along with the rest of her war effort.

In March 1918, just as the Allies were about ready to begin sowing the North Sea Mine Barrage, the Germans launched the first of four massive offensives on the Western Front in France and Belgium. These bloodletting drives created another crisis within the Allied military command and led to calls to rush more American troops to France. Admiral Gleaves had assigned nearly all American troops sailing to France to his own Transport Force ships until May, when Pershing demanded that more American divisions be shipped to France to shore up the front. To supplement the Transport Force, Benson arranged with the Admiralty to divert several large, fast British liners from the Canadian troop convoys to Norfolk and Hoboken ports of embarkation. As a result, by July American troops were arriving in France at the remarkable rate of nearly 10,000 men each day. "When Ludendorff . . . launched his great offensive," Gleaves observed, "it was too late. By that time the U-boat had been checked and Allied supremacy of the sea re-established." One of the reasons behind the success of the Cruiser and Transport Force's operations was Gleaves's decision to employ underway refueling for his oil-fired destroyers, using tankers that rendezvoused at predetermined times with each escort group at sea. He had successfully experimented with underway refueling when he commanded the Atlantic Fleet's Destroyer Flotilla in 1916, and found during the war that this technique added considerably to the destroyer support he was able to provide to the Transport Force troop carriers.[19]

Before spring 1918, Germany's U-boat skippers, with few exceptions, confined their operations to the War Zone off the British Isles and the waters to the east of the Azores. On 2 May 1918, however, Captain Edward C. Kalbfus in the westbound troop transport *Pocahontas* unexpectedly encountered an enemy submarine about 1,000 miles west of Brest. After an unsuccessful torpedo attack, the U-boat surfaced and brought the transport under fire with two

rapid-firing guns at a range of 10,000 yards, a distance that was beyond the reach of Kalbfus' small battery. Alarmed at this turn of
events, Kalbfus ordered full speed ahead, adroitly zigzagged
through a frightening hail of shells and fragments, and escaped the
scene by outrunning the enemy. Then, on 31 May, the empty transport *President Lincoln* en route home was torpedoed 500 miles off
the French coast and sank immediately with the loss of twenty-six
officers and men. Captain Raymond Hasbrouck in the *Covington*
had just cleared Brest at 0915 on 1 July 1918 when his transport was
struck on the port bow by a torpedo. She took water and listed badly, so Hasbrouck ordered his crew to abandon ship. The escorting
destroyer *Smith*, accompanied by the destroyer *Warrenton*, soon
reached the scene, took the transport in tow, and headed for Brest,
but the *Covington* sank on the way. Although all but six sailors were
saved, both Wilson and Gleaves later concluded that Hasbrouck
might have saved his ship had he put his damage control plan into
effect immediately after being hit. By contrast, on 15 September
1918 the transport *Mt. Vernon*, steaming at 18 knots in convoy, took
a devastating torpedo hit amidships that killed thirty-six men, but
alert, well-trained damage control parties kept the ship afloat long
enough for her to limp back to Brest at 6 knots.

On the whole, losses to escorted shipping were light. A total
of 388 Tranport Force sailings carried 900,000 AEF troops from
the United States to France during the Great War, while nearly 600
sailings of British, French, and Italian ships transported slightly
over one million more American troops to Europe. The Cruiser
Force escorted all of the American and most of the Allied transport sailings, movements that altogether brought more than 1.7
million men to France before the Armistice. Gleaves realized early on that his battle doctrine would have to emphasize the defensive escort mission rather than offensive, aggressive antisubmarine
operations, although "in so far as was consistent with the accomplishment of this [escort] mission, the doctrine of the Cruiser and
Transport Force was to attack and destroy enemy submarines
whenever circumstances permitted." The results of the occasional attempts to prosecute submarine contacts were disappointing,
but Gleaves claimed that "if in most cases no material damage was
inflicted, these attacking tactics at least had a wholesome effect on
enemy morale." During the war there were twenty-six contacts between Cruiser Force escorts and German U-boats, most resulting
from underwater torpedo attacks.

Sims' Planning Section in London despaired about the lack of aggressive antisubmarine operations, contending as early as 3 April 1918 that "the enemy's submarine campaign cannot be defeated by defensive [escort] measures alone." By November 1918, when about two-thirds of all American destroyers were assigned to escort formations, Gleaves' Transport Force included 123 ocean-going vessels, the largest of these commands. He had put forth his bid to take over the entire North Atlantic convoy system in August of that year, arguing that there was a lack of Anglo-American co-ordination and suggesting that all sailings of British or American merchant shipping that were escorted by American warships "should be placed under one control of our own." Though the British stoutly resisted this move, Benson insisted that the Admiralty agree to transfer responsibility for some of the transatlantic merchant convoys to the Transport Force in September 1918, and the Americans were preparing to make new demands on London before the year was out.[20]

Benson's concern in the fall of 1918 that the Germans would broaden their area of operations was reflected at Sims' headquarters in London where the planners pointed out that the U-boats were now penetrating "farther into the Atlantic and, to a lesser extent, to the North American coast." They warned that "it is physically impossible for us to counter this move by extending the convoy system throughout the Atlantic" since 1,200 ocean escorts "would be required." The Allies never needed to address the problem, however, owing to the success of their armies on the Western Front. The AEF's safe arrival in France that summer allowed Marshal Ferdinand Foch, the director of Allied military strategy, to mount a massive counteroffensive in July and August 1918. The British and French also launched important diversionary offensives in the Balkans against Bulgaria and Austria, and supported the Arab revolt against Turkey. The Turks asked the Allies for an armistice on 30 October, and on 12 November a large Allied fleet sailed into the Sea of Marmora. The fall of Bulgaria opened the gateway to Vienna, and the Austrians sued for peace on 3 November. Already Czechoslovakia, Yugoslavia, and Hungary had declared their independence from the collapsing 400-year-old Austrian Empire.

These blows led Berlin to recall its U-boats from the Atlantic on 10 October in order to put German-American relations on a better footing for the peace talks. According to Daniels, Wilson's cabinet had already "agreed that until German submarines quit sinking passenger ships . . . we could have no armistice and no peace." The kaiser sacked Ludendorff soon after, named a new ministry, and instructed it to seek peace with the Allies by negotiating with Wilson. After exchanging three notes, the Germans realized on 27 October that Wilson was demanding terms that would make it impossible for them to renew the fighting if the peace talks broke down. Moreover, as Daniels recorded, there was to be "no autocratic government in Germany" to negotiate the peace.[21]

Germany's naval command balked at having to suspend all operations and, in a final rash act of defiance, the next day ordered the High Seas Fleet to sortie into the North Sea for a death battle with the combined British and American battleship fleets. Earlier in the war the German Navy's best officers and sailors had been drafted into the submarine service, however, and once the fanatical order became known in the ships, mutiny spread throughout the fleet. The sailors demanded peace and the kaiser's head. Within hours their calls were echoed by a nationwide strike against existing political authority, and by 8 November Germany was swept by revolution. A provisional government assumed power and agreed to Wilson's ceasefire terms, and an armistice went into effect three days later. "On every ship men crowded the decks and cheered madly," wrote Ensign Husband. "The hostilities were ended. It was over, 'Over There.'"[22]

Chapter Thirty-one

The Versailles Treaty
1919

The November 1918 Armistice found President Wilson better prepared to negotiate peace than he had been to wage war twenty months earlier. Soon after the United States had declared war, he announced his intention to create a "steadfast concert of peace" by founding a postwar "partnership of democratic nations" in the form of the League of Nations, one of fourteen points listed as American war aims in January 1918. He sought through "open diplomacy" to achieve "absolute freedom of navigation upon the seas," free trade, immediate German disarmament coupled with a drastic postwar international "reduction in armaments," and territorial adjustments in Europe that would effectively dismember Austria and diminish Germany. The Republicans had successfully attacked Wilson's indifferent record as a war leader, however, and they won control of Congress in November 1918, a stunning repudiation of Wilson's presidency at the climax of a great overseas military victory. This was the basis for ex-president Roosevelt's charge on the eve of the Paris Peace Conference that Wilson's views no longer reflected public opinion. From 12 January to 20 August 1919, the Treaty of Versailles was negotiated by twenty-eight Allied and Associated powers. Scornful of Wilson's lofty idealism and distrustful of his ulterior motives, British Prime Minister Lloyd George and French Premier Clemenceau were determined to reduce the fourteen points in detail.

On one issue the victors agreed. Germany's High Seas Fleet, interned at Scapa Flow, was to be divided up among the Allies or destroyed. As a result, the major Anglo-American maritime controversies at Versailles concerned Wilson's demand for freedom of the seas and the postwar naval balance of power. Because freedom of the seas imperiled classic British blockading strategy, the Admiralty effectively refused to negotiate the issue. As for the balance of power, Admiral Benson was furious about Britain's effort to reestablish her traditional maritime superiority at America's expense; he believed that this would eventually engulf the two Anglo-Saxon powers in a deadly commercial rivalry. Should this transpire, he warned Navy Secretary Daniels, it would be necessary to keep the fleet "in every respect ready for action." Not only did such views conflict with Wilson's stated objective of disarming the victors, they also bore no relationship to international reality. It had for many decades been true that no matter how much British attitudes or foreign policy angered the United States government, armed conflict between the two great English-speaking democracies was simply unthinkable. In a century of international turbulence and discord, of changing alliances and shifting coalitions of power, this was one of the few great international certainties. Navy men who tried to exploit Anglo-American tensions usually found that their arguments fell on deaf ears.[1]

Inasmuch as the German Army had disintegrated and the American and British armies were hastily demobilized during the spring of 1919, only the navies and the French Army were left as objects of disarmament. Therefore, the issue of reducing ground forces was deferred by mutual consent. Most of the minor bartering concerned territorial frontiers in Central Europe that little concerned American security. The war had ripped apart the ancient Austrian Empire, and the conferees at Versailles approved the creation of the independent states of Hungary, Czechoslovakia, Yugoslavia, Albania, and Romania. In a special case, Poland received a swath of East Prussia that tied the Poles to the Germanic city of Danzig, their only seaport, which was to be governed by the League of Nations. Wilson moderated some of France's extreme demands, but he could not prevent them from extracting reparations from Germany, which the French needed to repay war debts to Britain and the United States. To win their points on this and other questions, the Allies threatened not to join Wilson's League unless he appeased them.

Wilson clearly expected the issue of disarmament to divide the victors. The Royal Navy, for reasons of international prestige, wanted to maintain the largest postwar fleet afloat, but in October 1918, shortly before the Armistice, Wilson asked Congress for funds to complete the 1916 Big Navy Act battleship building program. "I want to go into the Peace Conference armed with as many weapons as my pockets will hold so as to compel justice," he told Daniels. Benson ordered work to resume on the two *California*-class battleships, the four *Maryland*s, and the six huge 43,000-ton *South Dakota*s. The British simply could not afford to build ten postwar dreadnoughts—nor, thought Benson, could Japan. Wilson's naval policy threatened to upset the entire postwar maritime balance. Upon hearing this news, Walter Long, the new First Lord of the Admiralty, warned that Britain could not "support the League . . . unless the United States agree to cease the construction of its big naval program." Lloyd George declared that the League would suffer from "complete sterility" if the prewar naval arms race resumed.[2]

Colonel House, Wilson's confidant, "entirely agreed with [Admiral] Benson that it was impossible at this time to promise that the American fleet should always be inferior to the British," but he told the president that "if the League of Nations was to have a chance of life it would not do to start its existence by increasing armaments instead of diminishing them." The Americans were as obdurate about resuming the 1916 program as the British were about avoiding any international commitment to the principle of "freedom of the seas." Benson, arguing that the war had upset the balance of power, cautioned Wilson that "in the past our naval position has derived great strength from the potential hostility of the British and German fleets," which placed the United States in "a position of special strength both in council and decision." The Armistice meant that "all that is now changed," and "we suddenly find the British Navy in a position of unparalleled strength."[3]

In short, Britain threatened to abandon the League unless Wilson compromised on the two powers' relative postwar naval strength. The Admiralty at Versailles, purely for reasons of prestige, sought to maintain the Royal Navy's historic overall superiority. On the other hand, British statesmen believed that possessing the world's largest fleet was somehow related to the strength of their global empire. Ironically, neither the admirals nor the diplomats demanded superiority to provide forces to execute any particular strategic plan or concept. For his part, Admiral Benson insisted that the British agree to Anglo-American naval parity. Wilson and Lloyd George could not bridge this impasse, so they referred it to Colonel House and Lord Robert Cecil, a vocal advocate of the League. Cecil demanded that House agree that the Royal Navy was to have the larger postwar fleet, but House firmly rejected this and proposed an alternative. If Britain joined the League and dropped its demand that the Americans accept perpetual naval inferiority, then Wilson was ready to suspend work on the battleships laid down in late 1916 and withdraw his request to Congress to complete the rest of the Big Navy Act shipbuilding program. Inasmuch as the Americans would go no further, the British had little choice but to accept this arrangement; it was written into the House-Cecil notes of 10 April 1919.

Before the House-Cecil notes were exchanged, Wilson returned briefly to Washington with a draft of the League Covenant. He explained it to Henry Cabot Lodge and other members of the Senate Foreign Relations Committee at the White House on 26 February. The League appeared at first to be a benign instrument that might foster international understanding and somehow prevent another general war. It embodied the principles of collective security, which many considered a better means to keep the peace than the classical balance of power. As a member of the League, the United States was to have one vote in a body to which all nations were eventually to be admitted and treated with equality. International disputes great and small might be submitted to the League. If one party employed force to achieve its ends, then a League peacekeeping force was to be assembled to check and punish the aggressor. It was partly to this end that Wilson wanted Congress to complete the 1916 shipbuilding program, and Admiral Benson had even drafted a plan to establish a permanent international naval police force under the rubric of a League Navy. The foundation of this architecture was Wilson's heartfelt assumption that the powers would view all future threats to the postwar peace and order as unambiguously wrong. One senator left the White House that night sensing that he had been "wandering with Alice in Wonderland and having tea with the Mad Hatter," so naive were Wilson's views about the bitter passions and rancor then gripping the world. The Senators pointed out that the United States was scarcely the political, economic, or military equal of the Latin American or Baltic republics. Moreover, they feared that the Covenant might easily involve American armed forces in League-related conflicts of interest only to others.[4]

Wilson was prepared to make further commitments to preserve the League. Upon returning to Paris, he dissuaded the French from demanding an independent Rhineland by signing an Anglo-American guarantee against future German aggression, the first such military agreement with a European power since the 1778 Alliance. This seemed to be a reasonable step at the time. The Allies in 1919 insisted that Germany limit her postwar army to 100,000 men, maintain no air forces, hand over her battleships and battlecruisers to the British, promise not to construct submarines, and limit her postwar navy to the equivalent of Prussia's old, small mid-nineteenth-century Baltic patrol. Admiral Ludwig von Reuter commanded the High Seas Fleet, which was interned at Scapa Flow, and when he found out that the British planned to take over his ships, he ordered them scuttled on 17 June 1919. Meanwhile, in Berlin, the new German socialist government, threatened at home by a communist revolution, could do no more than make useless gestures against the victors' peace. The German democrats who signed the Versailles Treaty were soon denounced by their countrymen as traitors.

Senator Lodge believed that Wilson's commitment to the League not only violated the Constitution but also created a foolish dependence on foreign interests, so he crafted a set of reservations to the Versailles Treaty that eliminated what he saw as its worst features. Wilson countered, quite correctly, that should the United States amend the treaty, other countries might also demand to revise it. He was unusually rigid on this point, and for reasons that are not altogether clear he steadfastly refused to compromise with Lodge and so ensure that the Senate would approve his handiwork. He rejected any reservations on this basis, and began a speech-making trip around the country to rally the public behind the treaty. Lodge remained behind in Washington and lobbied other senators, who would actually do the voting. On 25 September, Wilson suffered a stroke in Pueblo, Colorado. Only three weeks later the treaty was rejected by the Senate for the first time. Wilson slowly regained his strength, but he still refused to amend the treaty. It was rejected for a second and last time by the Senate in early 1920.

The rejection of the Versailles Treaty did not entirely relieve the United States of its European obligations. The dismemberment of Austria created a number of territorial disputes between Italy and the new south Slav state of Yugoslavia, the major one being rival claims to the territory surrounding the Adriatic port of Trieste. Not wanting to anger either party, Wilson found himself caught up in an intractable squabble and had to dispatch an American squadron to the Adriatic to hold the Trieste area until the League divided the 300-square-mile territory between the contending powers. The Allies were also unable to come to terms with Turkey where the Sultan's old government in Istanbul had collapsed, and Kemal Ataturk's new, revolutionary regime had just moved its capital inland to Ankara. The Chanak War broke out when the Greeks, taking advantage of their historic opponent's prostration, invaded Turkey, only to be thrashed in 1920 by Ataturk's aroused, reconstituted Army. The grisly Chanak War threatened to draw the former Allies into another conflict in the eastern Mediterranean. After the Turks launched a campaign of terror against their own Greek citizens in 1919, Wilson dispatched a squadron built around the 9,500-ton heavy cruiser *St. Louis* to the Turkish coast and ordered Admiral Mark Bristol to protect American lives and interests there. Bristol used his ships to rescue refugees from various Anatolian ports—altogether the Allied squadrons saved over 250,000 Greeks from Turkish vengeance—and to shuttle back and forth across the Black Sea from the Crimea to Istanbul, transporting thousands fleeing from the Russian Civil War to the safety of Asia Minor. Soon after Bristol arrived in the Near East, Wilson persuaded London and Paris to agree that he be named Allied High Commissioner in Turkey. A skillful diplomat, the admiral remained there on his peacekeeping mission until 1929, seven years after the brutal Chanak War was settled following a bloody series of massacres and population transfers that scarred the region for the rest of the century.[5]

From the vantage point of Turkish waters, Admiral Bristol watched the unhappy stream of refugees who fled from the butchery of the Russian Civil War. The Allies were furious with Lenin's Bolshevik regime in Moscow for signing the March 1918 Brest-Litovsk Treaty with Germany, and they worried that munitions they had shipped to Murmansk and Archangel for the use of the Tsarist Army would be handed over to the Germans. A British fleet appeared off Murmansk in May and landed troops who took over the city, and another Allied expedition, which included the old cruiser *Olympia* carrying American troops, took Archangel and the interior cities of Kotlas and Vologda on 2 August. The initial object of these efforts, to safeguard the Allied arms, evaporated after Germany surrendered; but wrangling among London, Paris, and Washington over their relations with Moscow delayed the departure of the American forces from Russia until June 1919. Wilson also agreed to send American troops to Vladivostok in June 1918 to support the rescue of the Czech Legion, then stranded in central Russia, and to prevent the Japanese from establishing themselves in Russia's Maritime Provinces, but he opposed intervening in the Russian Civil War on the grounds that Russians had to "work out their own salvation, even though they wallow in anarchy for a while." An Allied fleet took Vladivostok and a landing force extracted the Czechs, but the powers fell out with one another while the communists gained the upper hand in Russia's bloody Civil War. For the moment, however, Japan's aspirations on the mainland were checked. The Expeditionary Force finally departed Vladivostok after gaining little except the antipathy of Lenin's new government. Thus, the Russian interventions were allowed to drift past usefulness. This was partly a result of Wilson's debility and partly because his attention was centered for twenty-four months on the treaty fight and not much else.[6]

With the upcoming presidential elections, postmortems about the conduct of the Great War quickly assumed a partisan caste. Admiral Sims had not been too careful during the war to conceal his contempt for Secretary Daniels, and trouble between the two seemed bound to boil over after the Armistice. In 1919, Daniels engaged in a campaign of purposeful slights against Sims, who was widely hailed as the premier Navy hero of the war. To relieve Admiral Benson as CNO, Daniels foolishly passed over the senior wartime commanders— Gleaves, Mayo, Sims, and Wilson— and selected Admiral Robert Coontz, who had spent the war supervising the Puget Sound Navy Yard. Sims was again exiled to Newport and the presidency of the Naval War College. In statements, speeches, and congressional testimony, Daniels distorted the character of his prewar and wartime policies and magnified his own role in the Navy's war effort. Sims was enraged. When a list was published of 1,620 awards for wartime service that reflected Daniels' disregard for Sims' recommendations, Sims fired off a long letter to Congress excoriating Daniels and all his works. Captain Pratt, the Assistant CNO, admired Sims, but he recognized that the "real motive behind it was political." A progressive Republican, Sims detested the Democrats and intended to discredit the Wilson administration. Admiral Benson, who was not fond of either man, was now caught in the middle of the Sims-Daniels dispute.[7]

The Republicans, who controlled the Senate Naval Affairs Committee, quickly scheduled hearings on Sims's charges, and they evolved into an inquest into Daniels' administration of the Navy. Sims' aim was not only to expose Daniels on the eve of the elections but also to convince Congress to increase the authority of the CNO over the fleet and the material bureau chiefs at the expense of the secretary. He cast his net too widely, however, and allowed his disdain for Benson to infect his testimony, thus undermining his own case. Benson, who openly agreed with Sims about what the CNO's powers should be, nonetheless vigorously defended wartime naval policy and strategy. Backing Benson were most of the senior officers in Washington, and supporting Sims were some of the Navy's brightest junior captains, but the larger reality was that this internecine bickering screened Daniels from some well deserved criticism. The Senate committee's report was divided along predictably partisan lines. The weariness over naval affairs evoked by the Sims hearings was illustrated when, after the Senate rejected the Versailles Treaty in 1920, the General Board persuaded Daniels to ask Congress to appropriate funds for an interim program of two battleships and one battlecruiser. There was no support for this on the Hill. The Democrats were rudderless and the Republicans awaited a new president who would establish a new postwar foreign policy for the Navy to support. In short, when Wilson left office in 1921, American foreign policy and naval policy were completely adrift.[8]

Chapter Thirty-two

The Era of Naval Disarmament
1921–1925

In 1920, the Democrats faced the tragedy of Woodrow Wilson's stroke, divisions over the Versailles Treaty, and Wilson's insistence that the election was a "referendum" on his treaty. Weariness with international politics, a postwar recession, and a natural Republican majority led in November to the election of a dark-horse candidate, Ohio Senator Warren G. Harding, who brought Republican majorities with him to both sides of Congress. For his secretary of state, Harding chose former New York Governor Charles Evans Hughes, an icy but able figure. Most Republicans opposed reconsidering the treaty, so the issue was dropped. Americans wanted "not experiment but equipoise, not submergence in internationality, but sustainment in triumphant nationality," Harding asserted in his inaugural. He and his Republican successors remained aloof from the European balance of power, and although they contended with Europe's postwar reparations-debts diplomacy against their will, they refused to commit the United States to the Versailles political settlement.[1]

Without explicitly stating it, however, the United States sought a new postwar balance of power in the Far East. Whereas the end of the war saw reduced American interest and influence in Europe, after the Armistice the United States found itself the leading Western power in the Far East and at loggerheads with Japan over a host of issues. After declaring war on Germany in 1915, Japanese forces had overrun the German naval base on China's Kiaochow Peninsula, occupied the German leasehold on the Shantung Peninsula, and took over Germany's central Pacific islands, an empire that included the Carolines, the Marshalls, and most of the Marianas. Then, in 1915, Japan issued her Twenty-One Demands, a vehicle by which she intended to dominate China's government and economy and a direct affront to the Open Door Policy. Wilson, though distracted by events in Europe, was willing nevertheless to take a truly stiff line with Japan, although Admiral Benson and the Navy's General Board cautioned that his approach might bring the two countries to the brink of war. When China appealed to Washington to prevent Japan from occupying the Shantung Peninsula in 1915, however, Assistant Secretary of State Robert Lansing reasoned that "it would be quixotic in the extreme to allow the question of China's territorial integrity to entangle the United States in international difficulties." He followed this general line during important conversations with Ambassador Ishii two years later, which papered over Sino-Japanese problems for the rest of the war. Despite the Lansing-Ishii compromise, Wilson apparently intended to reassert the Open Door Policy at the end of World War I.

Disposing of Germany's Pacific empire was a major source of friction. Britain secretly agreed in 1917 to support Japan's claims to German islands north of the equator in return for Japanese support of the British Empire's acquisition of Germany's much smaller South Pacific holdings. Soon after this agreement was negotiated, the American naval attaché in Tokyo alerted Admiral Benson to "the division of German colonial possessions in the Pacific by Great Britain and Japan." At Versailles two years later, Wilson's devotion to the principles of nationalism and the Open Door Policy was confronted by this sturdy Anglo-Japanese accord. The General Board was emphatic that "continued possession" by Japan of the islands would be a "perpetual menace to Guam, and to any fleet operation undertaken for the relief of the Philippines" under the Orange War Plan. The State Department understood that Japan might gain some minor strategic advantage by holding German Micronesia but assured Wilson that this was of "slight importance." Indeed, Captains Thomas C. Hart and Harry E. Yarnell, who advised Benson during the Versailles Conference, warned that any American move to oust the Japanese from the islands would not be "fair play" and would risk "arousing the enmity of Japan."[2]

The issue was vital to Japan's security. "America has Japan in a strangle grip by her possession of the Aleutian Islands, Hawaii, the Philippines, and Guam," the *Nichi-Bei* newspaper reported on 27 January 1919, "and Japan . . . has broken the cordon by the occupation of German islands." Benson advised Wilson in early 1919 to support Japan's request for a League mandate over Germany's Pacific islands on the condition that the mandate prohibit Japan from erecting fortifications. Wilson linked this issue with China in his diplomacy and negotiated an agreement under which Japan promised to withdraw from the Shantung Peninsula within five years in return for a mandate to govern the Pacific islands as a League trustee. Japanese possession of the mandated islands troubled Navy strategists for the next twenty years. The General Board warned that any of the Marianas might be developed "into submarine bases within supporting distance of Japan" that would create "a perpetual menace to Guam and to any [American] fleet operation undertaken for the relief of the Philippines." For not altogether intelligible reasons, the public's imagination was captured by Japan's occupation of Yap in the Carolines, and a brief war scare gripped both countries in 1920 over this issue. Navy Secretary Daniels told the House Naval Affairs Committee in secret session that year about "the necessity of being prepared if J[apan] should attack us . . . [and Admiral] Coontz gave strategy as to Guam, Philippines, and Hawaii."[3]

As a counterweight to Japan's possession of the Mandates, Harding's secretary of the Navy, Edwin Denby, wanted to continue Wilson's battleship building program, the announced objective of which was to build up to fleet parity with the Royal Navy. Navy men supposed that this would ensure superiority over the Japanese fleet. In March 1921, this program included completion of the battleships and battlecruisers authorized under the 1916 Big Navy Act and the four-stack escort destroyers authorized by the 1917 Destroyer Act. This meant commissioning all four 32,600-ton *Maryland*s, launched in 1920 and 1921, and the six mammoth 43,000-ton *South Dakota*-class battleships. Work had been suspended on these ships during the war, but they were laid down in 1920 and 1921. The program was costly, however, and the most compelling reasons behind it evaporated when the Germans signed the Armistice, the Senate rejected the Versailles Treaty, and the peacekeeping League Navy scheme was abandoned. Nonetheless, the Navy's goal of building up to parity with Britain remained intact. The U.S. Fleet contained sixteen front-line battleships compared to Britain's thirty-three battleships and nine battlecruisers, but the British vessels were much older, needed costly overhauls and improvements following their wartime service, and lacked recent innovations in fire control, communications, and diesel engines. At the moment, the *Maryland*s were the most powerful vessels afloat, and the *South Dakota*s incorporated every known advance in battleship design. The Admiralty had announced plans to lay down four *Hood*-class super-battlecruisers in 1919 and to incorporate in these ships advances shown necessary by the wartime experience. The Japanese followed suit, declaring that they were modernizing their fleet by building eight battleships and eight

nnsylvania soon after she was modernized. The 31,000-ton oil-burning *Pennsylvania*s, a pair
t-dreadnought battleships, were laid down in 1913 and commissioned two years later. Pro-
by 8,000 tons of armor, they carried four triple 14-inch gun turrets. The Navy modernized
*h*ips between 1929 and 1931 by installing new turbines and anti-torpedo blisters on the hull
*t*he waterline and providing two catapults for three scout floatplanes. During the 1930s, the
*l*vania served as the flagship of the U.S. Fleet. Her sister ship, the *Arizona*, was sunk by the
*s*e in Pearl Harbor on 7 December 1941 in the first moments of the attack, but the *Pennsyl*-
*s*caped almost undamaged, saw action in the Aleutians in 1943, and participated, usually as
f a heavy bombardment group, in every major battle of the Pacific campaign, 1944–45, ex-
*v*o Jima. She was one of the victims of the 1946 atomic bomb tests off Bikini Atoll.

battlecruisers by 1927. Japan's naval shipbuilding program appeared to directly threaten British and American interests in the Far East at a time when relations between Tokyo and Washington had already turned sour. However, on the whole, British and Japanese public opinion stood against further naval expansion, as did most Americans.

From the wreckage of Wilson's diplomacy, Idaho's Senator William Borah, a staunch Republican opponent of the Versailles Treaty, extracted the principle of international disarmament and proposed to apply it to stop the looming naval arms race among the Pacific powers. From 1920 to 1936, limiting military forces inevitably meant capping the strength of fleets because no major power except France maintained a large standing army after the Great War. For example, the National Defense Act of 1920 fixed a ceiling on U.S. Army manpower at 125,000, but for nearly two decades neither the White House nor Congress supported even that level of readiness. When Borah turned his attention to naval disarmament in resolutions passed by the Senate in 1920, and again in 1921, he proposed that an international conference set limits on fleet tonnage for each of the Great Powers. British Prime Minister David Lloyd George took up this idea and, in a speech to the House of Commons in June 1921, suggested that an international naval conference be convened. Secretary of State Charles Evans Hughes agreed and decided that he would hold the trumps if the event were staged in Washington. To preempt a British move, within a few days Harding issued invitations to nine nations to attend a conference in the American capital, and they all promptly accepted.

Establishing an American negotiating position prior to the Washington Conference was the source of great anguish within the Navy. The General Board, blind to the temper of the times, stoutly maintained that fleet parity should first be achieved between the United States and Great Britain; only then would negotiations on overall upper limits be prudent. In part this view reflected assumptions of Navy men that the object of diplomacy was to obtain an advantage, not to dispose of it, and they asserted that other powers would do this regardless of American behavior. Fear of the 1916 program was what had caused the British and Japanese to negotiate, they argued, and reducing this program would diminish the incentive for these powers to be conciliatory. "These fifteen [Big Navy Act] capital ships—building—brought Japan to the Conference," the General Board warned. "Scrap them and she will return home free to pursue her aggressive program." The General Board repeated that American policy in the Pacific rested on the defense of the Philippines and the Open Door Policy but resisted understanding that Japan had no interest in the Philippines and that no American statesman favored using force to defend the Open Door. This ignored political reality, Hughes realized, and so he asked Assistant Navy Secretary Theodore Roosevelt, Jr., to find a "more reasonable group" of officers to develop the American negotiating position.[4]

Assistant Secretary Roosevelt, Admiral Coontz, the CNO, and Captain William V. Pratt, representing the General Board, struggled for five months to draft an American naval policy that Hughes would accept, work made difficult by the State Department's refusal to provide specific guidance. The absence of any representatives from the diplomatic service on the Joint Army-Navy Board hindered the development of amalgamated national security planning. Navy Secretary Denby and Admiral Coontz acknowledged that fixing limits was politically attractive, but they insisted that building up to parity with Britain was a more important goal, and the General Board was reflexively opposed to any reductions in fleet strength. When these discussions reached an impasse, Hughes belatedly announced that any treaty had to provide for an immediate end to the construction of all capital ships. Informed by this directive, Coontz devised a formula the key equations of which appeared to satisfy both American strategic demands and the tactical realities of a Pacific war. He assumed that the treaty would measure relative fleet strength by some ratio and decided that the most advantageous and realistic gauge was warship tonnage. Newer ships not only displaced more water, they also sported more and heavier guns, had thicker armor, used heavier oil burners rather than coal-fired boilers, and carried more modern electrical and mechanical systems.[5]

Coontz arrived at acceptable tonnage ratio for capital ships by relying on a contemporary rule of thumb that held that a battleship fleet lost about 10 percent of its overall operational efficiency for every 1,000 miles it steamed away from a major base. Because the Orange War Plan hypothesized an engagement between the Japanese and American fleets in the Philippine Sea, he estimated that the enemy would be over 1,000 miles from his nearest base at Formosa and that the U.S. Fleet would fight at least 5,000 miles from Hawaii. Thus, if the tonnage ratio between the American and Japanese fleets were 10 : 6, then the Americans would have a slight advantage. Inasmuch as Denby demanded Anglo-American parity, Coontz wrote that a tonnage ratio of 10 : 10 : 6, or 5 : 5 : 3, among the American, British, and Japanese fleets had to be the Navy's "last stand." The General Board accepted the 10 : 10 : 6 ratio with reservations but urged the secretary to hold firm to a very large figure for total fleet tonnage. The General Board also agreed to provisions limiting battleship displacement to 35,000 tons and main battery guns to 16 inches. This meant abandoning the six-ship *South Dakota*-class program, a painful concession. Nor did the General Board object to fixing the displacement of cruisers at 10,000 tons or to limiting their main batteries to 8-inch guns. Although Hughes believed that he would have trouble persuading the British and Japanese to accept this plan, he agreed to put it forward.

On 11 November 1921, Admiral Sims and General Pershing celebrated the first Armistice Day by laying wreaths at the new Tomb of the Unknown Soldier. The next day, Hughes addressed the international delegates to the Washington Naval Conference, who sat in the splendor of Constitution Hall only a few blocks from the White House. He electrified his audience when he announced that the Harding administration was proposing a plan to suspend battleship construction for a decade, scrap ships already under construction, and limit the fleets of the great naval powers by tonnage. "Hughes sank in thirty-five minutes more ships than all the admirals of all the world would have sunk in a cycle of centuries," one newsman breathlessly declared. During the following twelve weeks, the conferees debated the details of Hughes' plan. Hughes had the upper hand in the talks for several reasons. He enjoyed strong, immediate support from his staff, as well as from the nearby Navy Department. Also, a "black chamber" of American code breakers had deciphered the Japanese diplomatic code and provided the secretary of state with translations of Tokyo's instructions to its conference delegates. As a result, during the negotiations, Hughes won repeated debating points. Since Japan's naval staff accepted the same rule of thumb that Coontz had used to devise his ratio, when the negotiations started, the Japanese delegates demanded a 10 : 10 : 7 ratio. This would endow Japan with a decided tactical advantage in the western Pacific. The Japanese were also worried that the Americans would someday build a fleet base in the Philippines and thereby upset the ratio system. For his part, Coontz worried that Japan intended to undermine the ratio by building advance bases in the Mandates.[6]

After hard bargaining, they reached a compromise. The British agreed not to fortify their bases to the west of Singapore; the Japanese pledged not to fortify Formosa, Okinawa, or the mandated islands; and the Americans promised not to improve the defenses of the Philippines or Guam. The Japanese secretly promised Hughes that American inspectors could visit the Mandates to ensure compliance with the agreement, but they later ignored this commitment. In return for nonfortification, the Japanese accepted the 5 : 5 : 3 ratio for capital ships. When the Mediterranean powers, Italy and France, agreed on parity, the ratio scheme became 5 : 5 : 3 : 1.75 : 1.75. The delegates also dealt with the issues of definition and duration. They defined a battleship as a warship displacing more than 10,000 tons or carrying a gun greater than 8 inches. They also fixed an upper limit on capital ship tonnage at 35,000 tons and prohibited guns greater than 16 inches. Battleship and battlecruiser construction was to end when ratifications were exchanged, followed by a ten-year "holiday" during which no capital ships were to be laid down. Dealing with lesser types and new technology posed problems. The British desperately wanted to limit the construction and deployment of submarines, but neither the Americans nor the Japanese cared much about this problem. When a disagreement arose as to whether an aircraft carrier was a capital ship, the conference sidestepped the issue, devised a seperate category for this new type of warship, and limited total carrier tonnage according to the 5 : 5 : 3 ratio and individual carriers to no more than 27,000 tons displacement. Other critical systems such as naval aircraft or armaments were too complex to discuss in the brief time remaining, and these matters were not dealt with by the treaty.

The Five Power Treaty was signed by Japan, Britain, France, Italy, and the United States. Under its terms, Britain and America might eventually retain 525,000 tons of battleships and battlecruisers; Japan, only 315,000 tons. This left the U.S. Fleet with eighteen battleships. The earliest American dreadnoughts, the two 20,000-ton *Delawares*, and their predecessors were to be scrapped. The two 22,000-ton *Utahs*, the two *Arkansas*-class, the two *Texas*-class, the two *Nevadas*, and the two 31,400-ton *Pennsylvanias* had been completed before the war. The three 32,000-ton *New*

*Mexico*s were laid down in 1915 and completed just before and just after the Armistice. Work on the two 32,000-ton *California*-class battleships was suspended during the war, but they had entered the fleet in 1920. The Five Power Treaty allowed the Navy to put into commission three 32,600-ton *Maryland*s, the first battleships to carry 16-inch gun main batteries, but the fourth ship of this class, the graceful *Washington*, which was already afloat, could not be commissioned. She was sunk in 1925 by aircraft and naval gunfire.

The treaty also allowed the U.S. Navy and the Royal Navy to build up to 135,000 tons of carriers but limited the Japanese Navy to 81,000 tons of this type. In effect, this allowed the United States and Britain to operate five 27,000-ton *Saratoga*-class carriers, or some equivalent mix of heavy and light carriers, but Japan was limited to only three heavy carriers or an equivalent mix. In Article XIX, which defined nonfortification, the naval powers forswore the right to improve the defenses of their outlying possessions, including Hong Kong, Formosa, Okinawa, the Mandates, the Philip-

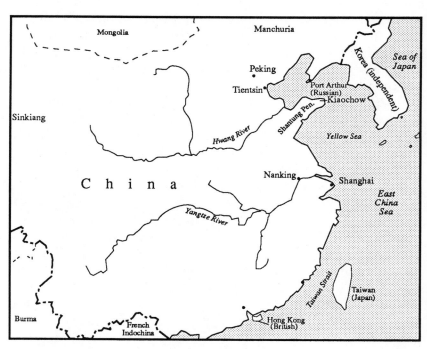

China in the 1920s

pines, and Guam. And each power agreed to a ten-year "battleship-building holiday." The treaty was to remain in effect until 1932, subject to an "escape clause," which allowed any power to abrogate the treaty with two years' notice.

Two other issues dealt with at the Washington Conference directly concerned American naval policy. The Anglo-Japanese Alliance of 1902 was about to come up for renewal at roughly the same time that the conference was scheduled to convene. The Navy increasingly viewed this combination as a menace to American interests—despite repeated British insistence that it simply could not be turned against the United States—and Hughes warned the British not to renew it. Canada and Australia also strongly opposed renewal. The British were horrified at the prospect of offending Japan, however. The negotiators at the Washington Conference found a compromise by persuading Britain and Japan to abandon their alliance and by replacing it with the fig leaf of the Four Power Treaty. Under this agreement, Britain, France, Japan, and the United States promised to maintain the "status quo" in the Pacific. The Japanese, humiliated and indignant at the loss of their valued longtime European partner, signed the Four Power Treaty with great reluctance.

The final issue considered by the Washington Conference was China, torn by civil war since 1911, the victim of a century of abuse by Europe, Japan, and, to a lesser extent, the United States. At the Washington Conference, the bankrupt Peking regime proposed that the Great Powers guarantee the Open Door Policy, which now was thought to mean the maintenance of Chinese territorial and political integrity. At American insistence, this principle served as the cornerstone of the Nine Power Treaty, which enjoined the signatories to respect China's political and territorial independence, but the powers attached so many reservations to the treaty that it had no practical effect. During the conference Hughes did extract two important concessions from Japan on related Far Eastern political issues. He was told by the Japanese in January 1922 that they would withdraw their armies from Russian Siberia and also honor their earlier promise to Wilson to end the occupation of China's Shantung Peninsula. Tokyo, London, Paris, and Washington did not intend to uphold the full spirit of the Nine Power Treaty, however. The unequal treaties, the economic concessions, the treaty port system, and the presence of foreign military and naval forces in China were untouched by the Nine Power Treaty.

Harding viewed the Washington treaties as a measure of his distance from Versailles, the League of Nations, and Wilson's guarantee to France, a point he underscored by boasting that his treaties contained "no entangling alliances." Democrats naturally looked askance at this Republican accomplishment when the treaties came before the Senate for approval. Naval disarmament was popular, but Japan was not, so the Democrats criticized the Four Power Treaty, arguing that Hughes had unwittingly committed the United States to support Japan's new Pacific empire. At the same time, few senators were heedless of the danger of too closely associating the American aims with the defense of China. These concerns caused the Senate to add only one reservation to the treaties. It stated that "no commitment to armed force, no alliance, no obligation to join in any defense" of any foreign territory was implied by the ratification of the three agreements.[7]

Each power ratified the Washington treaties, and Hughes became an international hero. The postconference hyperbole was deafening. "This treaty ends, absolutely ends, the race in competition in naval armament," Hughes declared in *Harper's Weekly*. Harding forecast a coming age when the world would be "more concerned with living to the full fulfillment of God's high intent" than the "agencies of warfare and destruction." Rear Admiral Pratt, who supported the Five Power Treaty, claimed that at the Washington Conference "trust and confidence replaced tension." Admiral Coontz, in a funk, winced at all this "sickly sentimentality."[8]

Navy men over the next two decades condemned the Five Power Treaty for restraining American naval expansion and for lashing the defense of the Philippines to the mainmast of Japanese goodwill. "We must possess bases in the Philippines," Rear Admiral Hilary Jones of the General Board complained in 1924, because they "are vital to our operations in the western Pacific." Nonfortification was "tantamount to abandonment of our ability to protect our interests in the Far East." There was, however, one circle the treaties' opponents found hard to square. The General Board repeatedly bemoaned the insecurity of America's position in the Philippines, but the Navy uniformly resisted the growing movement in Congress to grant independence to the Filipinos. In a polemic published shortly after the Washington Conference adjourned, retired Captain Dudley Knox charged that the United States "no longer possesses the power to defend the Philippines or to support any other American Far Eastern policy." Some Navy

men certainly feared that the absence of an American commitment to defend the archipelago would leave the fleet without
much of a mission, leading perhaps to even greater economies
than the Republicans had already imposed. This was not wholly
self-serving in that both Army and Navy war planners rightly predicted that no degree of Philippine independence could sever
completely the bond of dependence between Washington and
Manila or provide the Filipinos with the means to protect themselves against their powerful Japanese neighbor.[9]

This was not the only flaw Navy men found in the despised
Washington treaties. Scrapping newly constructed ships was particularly painful. The 32,600-ton *Washington*, a most beautiful ship,
was almost ready for service when work was ended, and most of
the six *South Dakota*s were over half complete when they were
scrapped. The Navy's criticism missed the mark, however. Most
Americans favored naval arms limitations for the simple reason
that neither Japan nor the United States had adopted foreign policies so conflicting as to justify fighting a Pacific war. Congress had
long refused to build a fleet base in the Philippines, and the Navy
had occasionally recognized in public that anything less would be
a waste of money. Furthermore, plans to finish the 1916 Big Navy
Act battleship program attracted almost no postwar support outside the Navy and its industrial allies. In sum, Hughes had bar-
gained away chips that he did not possess and negotiated an agreement that restrained the growth of Japan's battleship fleet for at
least a decade. It was unfortunate that few outside the Navy heeded his clear warning that the president and Congress should agree
to "maintain the relative naval strength of the United States" to uphold the status quo.

Chastened by this unhappy experience, the General Board in
June 1922 heralded the Navy's goal of building up to a "treaty
fleet" as the new cornerstone of postwar American naval policy, an
objective that was as unremarkable as the wisp of political support
it attracted. The General Board issued a more practical demand
in April 1923 when it called on Admiral Edward Eberle, the new
CNO, to revise the Orange Plan to take into account the new limits on the fleet. In short, the Navy set about to undo the work of
the architects of the Five Power Treaty. Rather than anchoring the
fleet in the eastern Pacific, for instance, the nonfortification article merely spurred Navy men to devise means to overcome the
lack of an advance base in the western Pacific by developing other

tools to conduct a transpacific campaign. They now feared that the Japanese might overrun the Philippines and Guam long before the U.S. Fleet could be ready to enter the western Pacific. Admiral Hugh Rodman pointed out in 1922 that this underscored the need to improve the primitive fleet base at Pearl Harbor, build another base in San Francisco Bay, and upgrade other Navy facilities on the Pacific coast. There was little support in Congress for this, however. The entire problem "is greatly simplified by the four power agreement," claimed the *Chicago Tribune*, because the treaty had "removed the Philippines from our responsibilities." With this issue "out of the way," the Navy had only to concern itself with an "attack upon our own shores."[10]

Circumventing the limits of the Five Power Treaty became a professional obsession within the Navy during the interwar years, stimulating the development of new systems for the battleships and the growth of naval aviation. New technology was to be the means by which the Navy would reverse the unfavorable balance of power embodied in the Washington treaties. During World War I, Admiral Benson had vigorously supported the development of naval aviation and had stationed the Navy's Northern Bombing Group in France to operate against U-boat bases, patrol shipping lanes, and attack submarines at sea. These operations had little effect on the U-boat war, but they did provide the postwar Navy with a cadre of combat-tested aviators who laid the foundations for interwar naval air policy. The Navy, sharply divided over the relative merits of airships, land-based patrol planes, seaplanes, and carrier-based aircraft, agreed on the need for separate Army and Navy air policies and opposed following the lead of the British, who had amalgamated all air activities into an independent Royal Air Force in 1918. Most Navy men were also against moves to recognize the special character of naval air operations. When Commander Henry C. Mustin, the CNO's wartime air adviser, proposed that avaitors be organized into a "naval flying corps" with an independent administrative status akin to the Marines, the General Board labeled his plan "undesirable" and lashed out at those "extremists" who supported it.

Admiral Sims waved a red flag in front of a bull by proposing in October 1918 that the Navy follow the British lead in naval air policy, and Admiral Benson shunted aside a similar plan put forth in 1919 by Captain N. E. Irwin, who now headed the small Office of Naval Aeronautics. Not even the handful of naval aviators were united on this issue. Irwin's plan was taken up by the General Board which, after lengthy hearings, reported that "to ensure air supremacy . . . fleet aviation must be developed to the fullest extent." It proposed the establishment of a "naval air service" that would be "capable of accompanying and operating with the fleet in all waters of the globe" since in any future fleet engagement the advantage would "lie with the fleet which wins in the air." Indeed, Captain Thomas Hart argued that should aircraft, submarines, and fast light torpedo craft be built to operate with the battle line, then "the Fleet action [such as Jutland] will never occur."[11]

Captain George W. Steele, on the other hand, reminded the General Board that it was "not likely" that "air battles will be fought by a mosquito fleet of the present single-seat fighting landplanes." While Captain Ernest J. King viewed the seaplane as a scout, he pointed out that current radio communications linking seaplanes with the battle fleet commander were unreliable. Given the limited range of these aircraft, King warned that "you aren't even going to get your seaplanes" to the naval battle if the action was too far from land. In addition, the seaplanes "would be played out before their entire usefulness has been developed" against an enemy fleet, and the Americans would "need a reserve that can only come from the aircraft carrier." Agreeing, the General Board proposed to convert the electric-drive fleet collier *Jupiter* into an experimental aircraft carrier by installing a 500-foot-long flight deck on the hull. There was no dearth of opposition to this project. Admiral Hugh Rodman, the commander in chief of the U.S. Fleet, complained that "the conversion of such a valuable collier" was "the poorest possible economy." His attitude changed dramatically, however, after Captain Nathan Twining successfully employed naval aircraft to spot for the fall of shells during a main battery exercise by the battleship *Texas*. In addition to the *Langley*, the old Hog Island merchantmen *Wright* and *Aroostook* were converted in 1922 into seaplane tenders. Owing to the 135,000-ton limit on carrier tonnage fixed by the Five Power Treaty, Coontz decided not to scrap the two battlecruisers laid down in 1920 but instead to convert them into heavy carriers. The *Saratoga* and *Lexington*, redesignated aircraft carriers in July 1922 in accordance with the treaty, were completed in 1927 and entered the fleet two years later.

The Navy's response to these challenges was shaped at least partially by a postwar debate in Congress about the organization of the military departments and American aviation policy.

Brigadier General Billy Mitchell, the wartime commander of the Army's Flying Corps in France, returned to the United States in 1919 espousing a highly publicized plan to create a single cabinet department with overall responsibility for both military and naval aviation. Claiming that the Navy was paying little attention to aviation issues, he complained to the House Military Affairs Committee in 1920 that Secretary Daniels and Admiral Coontz "have distributed these duties among six or seven departments." He made similar charges against the Army. Against Mitchell was arrayed formidable opposition, led by General of the Armies John J. Pershing. "Military and naval air forces should remain as integral parts of the Army and Navy," he testified, stressing the need for battleships and carriers as the "bulwark of the nation's sea defenses." With Congress deadlocked over what to do about Mitchell's proposal for a single military department, Harding intervened on 12 April 1921. He announced a plan to centralize air policy within the Navy by creating a new Bureau of Aeronautics, declaring, "Aviation is inseparable from either the Army or the Navy." At the instigation of Congressman Fred A. Britten, the chairman of the House Naval Affairs Committee, Secretary Denby and Admiral Coontz selected Rear Admiral William Moffett to be the first chief of the new bureau. Then, after a minor struggle over the language of the law, Congress enacted a compromise, stating that the Army was to be responsible for "all aerial operations from land bases" while "Naval Aviation shall have control of all aerial operations attached to a fleet, including fleet shore bases."[12]

Mitchell refused to give up. He tried to prove his point in a dramatic demonstration of the offensive power of level bombing against surface ships by organizing a highly publicized joint exercise in June 1921. He staged an electrifying finale in which the 1st Provisional Air Brigade flew out to sea from Langley Field, Virginia, and in a series of relays at low levels used 2,000-pound bombs to sink the old German battleship *Ostfriesland*, which was riding at anchor off the Virginia Capes. Admiral Moffett immediately complained that Mitchell had violated the prearranged rules for the excercise by allowing his planes to fly too low and drop bombs that were too big, but the photographs and newsreels of the event made a vivid impression on Congress and public opinion as well. Moffett's vigorous advocacy of naval aviation at the expense of the battleship fleet was not always welcomed by the Navy, but his skill in countering Mitchell's campaign for a unified national air department, and a joint Army-Navy aviation policy, was vital during the coming decade in keeping all naval aviation under the wing of the Navy Department.

From the start of his twelve-year tour of duty as its chief, Moffett viewed the Bureau of Aeronautics as more than a material organization like Ordnance or Construction and Repair, and he used his mandate from Harding and Congress to truly "centralize the control of naval activities in Aeronautics." He grasped almost unilateral control of the design and acquisition of naval aircraft; he also erected a substantial shore establishment consisting of air stations and training commands for seaplanes, airships, and carrier aircraft. Still, the number of naval aviators during the decade was small—only 426 officer pilots for 673 aircraft in 1926. This disparity was itself the source of a controversy, and Moffett was forced to create enlisted ranks for pilots. Until 1928 he depended on new ensigns from the Naval Academy to fill out vacancies, but this number was not great enough to meet the demand. Moffett finally persuaded Coolidge's secretary of the Navy, Curtis Wilbur, to allow ensigns with reserve commissions from Naval Reserve Officer Training Course colleges to immediately enter flight training. His greatest accomplishment, however, was converting Navy men into believing that the fleet needed aviation. As Captain Sinclair Gannon told Admiral Coontz, the War Plans Division considered it of "paramount importance" to develop naval air power because in an Orange War "Japanese air can operate in the probable theater of operations from shore bases whereas our aircraft must operate from carriers in the initial stages of the campaign."[13]

The Teapot Dome scandal of 1923 closed out the Harding administration. In the age of the battleship, oil had replaced coal as a strategic concern for the Navy and the nation. After the Civil War, petroleum was discovered in Pennsylvania, the Southwest, and southern California, and by the turn of the century nearly 90 percent of all oil was refined and retailed by John D. Rockefeller's Standard Oil Company. Rockefeller was eventually found guilty of violating the Sherman Antitrust Act and forced by the Supreme Court to divide up Standard Oil into regional firms, but by then the Navy had become a major customer of Rockefeller's ruthless monopoly. When the first oil-fired battleships were laid down, the Wilson administration wisely acquired underground oil deposits at Elk Hills, California, and at Teapot Dome, Wyoming, to provide a strategic reserve for the fleet during national emergencies and as a hedge against increases in the retail price charged by Rockefeller and other refiners.

The low cost of money after World War I meant easy credit, which allowed automobile manufacturer Henry Ford and his competitors to sell millions of cars during the 1920s. Demand for gasoline increased dramatically, but a shortage of refineries boosted the retail price of oil, and this in turn sapped funds from the fleet. Navy fuel allowances were so low that ships' movements were often restricted. Frequent complaints about this from the fleet were passed by Admiral Coontz to Secretary Denby. Interior Secretary Albert B. Fall had a solution to the problem. If the Navy transferred ownership of its reserves to the Interior Department, then he would give the Navy valuable oil certificates, which it could use to buy readily usable fuel stored in above-ground containers. Denby was also told that neighboring drillers were draining off the Navy's underground reserves at Elk Hills and Teapot Dome, so he convinced Harding to approve Fall's scheme. In short order the public learned that Fall had privately sold leases to the Navy Department's oil reserves and pocketed the profits. A sensational Congressional hearing proved Fall's villainy, Harding's lack of guile, and Denby's childlike innocence. Fall went to prison, and the Senate passed a resolution demanding that Denby resign. Soon afterward, Harding unexpectedly fell ill and died.

Chapter Thirty-three

The Failure at the Geneva Conference
1922–1927

Harding was succeeded in late 1923 by his vice president, Calvin Coolidge, the taciturn former governor of Massachusetts, who promised to keep the United States out of the League of Nations and to uphold the Washington Treaty system. Distancing himself from the Teapot Dome scandal, he easily defeated John W. Davis, a feeble Democratic candidate, in a landslide in 1924. Often condemned as isolationist, American foreign policy during Coolidge's presidency merely reflected the favorable balance of power in Europe and the minimal threat to American interests and security in the Far East. The urge to remain aloof from European politics was powerful, however. When Aristide Briand, the French foreign minister, tried to persuade the new secretary of state, Frank B. Kellogg, to renew the American guarantee to defend France against Germany, Kellogg adroitly produced instead a harmless Peace Pact outlawing war, which most nations signed in 1928.

Kellogg favored supplementing his peace pact with another naval disarmament treaty, but he lacked the relentless drive to negotiate such an agreement that had characterized Secretary of State Hughes' diplomacy in 1921 and 1922. Coolidge, an economizer, wanted to expand on naval arms limitation, mostly to reduce federal outlays and lower taxes. The Navy stoutly resisted another treaty, continued to identify Japan as an enemy, and clung to the need to defend the Philippines and uphold the Open Door

**Rear Admiral William Moffett, chief of the
reau of Aeronautics, 1922–33.**

Naval Air Station Pensacola, showing Curtiss Flying Boats and hydroplanes.

Policy. Planning was a byword, and after World War I it was centered almost exclusively on an Orange war with Japan. This was underscored by the disestablishment of the Atlantic Fleet in 1922, the creation of a new U.S. Fleet command in the Pacific, and the movement of the battleships, heavy cruisers, and supporting ships to San Diego and San Pedro, California, that same year. Only a skeletal cruiser-destroyer training squadron was based on the East Coast until 1940.

The Five Power Treaty now forced the Navy to modernize its battleships rather than replace them. "The battleship of the future can be so designed . . . that she will not be subject to fatal damage from the air," asserted Admiral Edward Eberle, who became CNO in 1923. American battleships were clearly vulnerable to air attacks, as evidenced by the sinkings of the old battleships *Virginia* and *New Jersey* in September 1923. Eberle asked Congress the following year to approve a seven-year modernization program, which involved converting the six oldest coal-burning battleships to oil-burners, strengthening the decks of all the frontline battleships to resist air-dropped bombs, improving the gun turrets to allow greater elevation, and adding watertight blister compartments to the hull below the waterline to provide additional anti-torpedo protection. Catapults were installed so that each battleship might operate its own float planes for tactical reconnaissance and spotting. Coolidge delayed Eberle's program for a year, however, on the basis that it might reignite the Pacific naval arms race. "If we are going to have the policy of limitation of armaments," he told the press on 9 January 1925, "we shall never have it by reason of that treaty we have made."[1]

Naval air policy was also in flux. The converted battlecruisers *Saratoga* and *Lexington* would not join the fleet until 1929, but the General Board assumed that, after 1931, when the battleship building "holiday" was scheduled to expire, the Navy's appropriations would be devoured by the need to replace the battle line. Until that time, carriers were the only capital ships that might be built under the Five Power Treaty. After the *Langley* was decommissioned, and after subtracting 27,000 tons apiece for the *Saratogas*, about 69,000 "treaty tons" might still be constructed. How to apportion this tonnage consumed a great deal of thought. Admiral Moffett, the chief of the Bureau of Aeronautics, was the central figure in this debate. The Navy's first carrier, the converted collier *Langley*, operated an air group of about fifteen planes, whereas the *Saratoga*-class carriers operated from seventy-five to ninety aircraft. Assuming that naval air power could be measured by the total number of planes the fleet could deploy, Moffett proposed in 1922 to build three new 23,000-ton carriers, each operating up to seventy-five planes. He pointed out that a heavy carrier provided a more stable deck for air operations in stormy seas. On the other hand, Admiral Sims of the Naval War College insisted that there was a link between control of the airspace over the fleet and the rate at which planes were launched and recovered and that the tempo of flight operations was governed less by the overall aircraft inventory than by the number of flight decks. And Admiral Pratt worried that "in a Pacific war naval control of the air cannot be attained by any arrangement of 135,000 tons, and that in order to secure this, quantity production will have to be resorted to." To give the fleet more than four flight decks by "quantity production" under treaty limits meant building six or seven small 10,000-ton cruiser-carriers or four or five 14,000-ton medium carriers. Moffett gradually came to favor experimenting with a medium carrier.[2]

It was not clear to many Navy men at this time when, or if, the carrier might displace the battleship as the fleet's primary antiship arm. "Aviation is in its infancy and has great possibilities and also limitations," Eberle declared in 1924, but its "present state of development and its achievement do not warrant all the extravagant claims set forth." The "ultimate sea power has remained in the capital ship" owing to "its better armor distribution, its improved underwater protection, its greater accuracy of fire, its increased speed and maneuverability, and . . . its own defending aircraft and other units." Battleship admirals and destroyermen alike sneered at the carrier's poor nighttime and foul-weather defenses against a torpedo attack by fast destroyers or scouting cruisers. The "fundamental duty" of the rest of the fleet, according to Admiral Harris Lanning, the new president of the Naval War College, was "to find the enemy so that the battleships may be brought against him in concentration." If a carrier threatened an opposing battle line, then it would be the first object of an enemy's scout cruisers or fast torpedo attack. "A vessel of the *Saratoga*-type, with its vulnerable flight deck, . . . must seek the protection of the big guns and the anti-aircraft batteries of the battle line after contact with the enemy has been established," wrote Admiral Henry Wiley, the commander in chief of the U.S. Fleet. Moffett and the General Board agreed at least that the carriers needed speed greater than the 20-knot battleships to escape from enemy cruisers, scout for the fleet, and detach from the battle line during a night engagement. Moffett was nonetheless consistent in maintaining that the carrier's air group was the ship's best defense, but by 1926 he had come to agree with the Naval War College that high rates of launch and recovery depended on building a large number of flight decks.[3]

Building a small carrier meant limiting her means of engaging in a gunnery duel. Once Moffett decided to give up armor and Rear Admiral William D. Leahy, the chief of the Bureau of Ordnance, agreed reluctantly to restrict the carrier's gunnery to an antiaircraft battery, the General Board approved a design for the *Ranger*, a 14,500-ton, 29-knot, flush-deck carrier, which could operate about eighty planes. Congress was attracted by the cost—about half the price tag for the *Saratoga*-class conversions—and authorized construction of the ship in 1928. The *Ranger* "would have the immediate result of removing all restrictions upon effective air power at sea," Commander Bruce G. Leighton told the General Board. He was especially concerned about building more carriers for escort and antisubmarine operations, long-range reconnaissance, and attacks on enemy bases. Neither of the two *Saratoga*-class heavy carriers could be risked in such secondary operations, inasmuch as the loss of a single ship would seriously reduce the daylight air defense of the battle line. Leighton proposed instead to build a large number of small carriers for these missions, ships that might operate independently or in small groups. On the other hand, the *Ranger*'s small size meant that she could never operate a full air group of the upcoming second generation of heavy dive and torpedo bombers that were about to enter the fleet.

These heavier planes were the result of the Navy's decision to acquire the radial engine, a design derided in 1919 by Brigadier General Mitchell and the Army Air Service but which was sponsored anyway by Moffett's Bureau of Aeronautics. Early naval aircraft were fragile, unreliable machines, but the durable radial engine solved part of this problem. In 1922, the bureau fixed a minimum standard for water-cooled engines of 50 hours, but the first air-cooled radial engine, the Lawrence J-1, ran smoothly for over 300 hours and so promised to dramatically increase the flying radius and reliability of naval aircraft. Also, the horsepower-to-weight ratio of the radial engine was a major improvement over earlier aircraft engines. The Chance Vought FU biplane fighter had an airspeed of 117 miles per hour, a ceiling of 15,000 feet, and a flying radius of over 200 miles. Greater thrust meant a smaller wingspan, thereby increasing the number of aircraft that might be parked on a carrier deck. Furthermore, metal skins could endure the greater stresses necessary for bombing at steep angles, and naval aviators soon concluded that precision, or dive, bombing was the most effective way to sink opposing ships. Although the Army Air Corps had experimented with dive bombing a few years after the war, Marine aviators were the first to try out the tactic in combat with Augusto César Sandino's Nicaraguan rebels in 1927. That same year Glenn Curtiss delivered to the Navy the first F8C biplane, which was powered by a Pratt and Whitney radial Wasp engine. Armed with 116-pound bombs slung under her wings, the F8C was converted from a fighter into a test dive bomber, and hit targets with twice the accuracy of planes flying level bomb runs.

One of Moffett's major objectives after the establishment of the Bureau of Aeronautics was to create a pool of billets to which naval aviators could aspire; in turn, this would attract younger officers into the specialty. He first convinced Congress to restrict almost all air commands to aviators, then used the lure of these billets to persuade a small number of ambitious junior captains to qualify as naval aviators or observers with the understanding that they would more quickly be rewarded than if they remained in the line. Captains Ernest J. King, William F. Halsey, Frederick Horne, and John Mason Reeves were the most prominent of this group. Reeves took command of the aircraft of the Battle Force in 1923. Alternating between the fleet and duty as assistant chief of the bureau, Reeves was principally interested in the development of tactical air doctrine. The converted carrier *Langley* was used as a school, and in 1925 Reeves employed the principles of labor specialization to increase the size of the air group by six planes.

An effective means of delivering bombs against maneuvering ships was still eluding naval aviators in 1926 when Reeves first became interested in the problem. That March he arranged for trials in which Lieutenant Frank Wagoner's plane, a pair of 100-pound white flour bombs slung under its wings, ascended to 7,000 feet, went into a steep dive, and hit the maneuvering target ship below. Admiral Charles F. Hughes, the commander in chief of the U.S. Fleet, conducted a more elaborate exercise later in the year, during which Reeves sent a squadron of eighteen dive bombers against the fleet flagship *Pennsylvania*. Within thirty seconds, they scored several hits before the antiaircraft gun crews had trained on them. Sustained dive-bombing operations, however, had to await the development of an all-metal monoplane with a radial air-cooled engine, technologies that did not mature for another decade. These early dive-bombing exercises did move Leahy, a battleship admiral, to urge his Bureau of Ordnance to improve defensive antiaircraft gunnery. The future of dive bombing looked bright. "A small high-speed carrier alone can destroy or disable a battleship alone," Admiral Sims told Congress in 1925. In his opinion, the carrier had become "a capital ship of much greater offensive power than any battleship."[4]

The carrier *Lexington* was commissioned in November 1927, and the *Saratoga* before the end of the year. The newly appointed commander in chief, Admiral William V. Pratt, took the U.S. Fleet from San Diego to Hawaii for the annual exercise in early 1928. Before this ritual began, however, the commanding general of the Army's Hawaiian Department proposed to conduct a joint exercise to test Oahu's air defenses, and Pratt agreed. One morning Rear Admiral Reeves stationed his carriers 250 miles off Oahu, just beyond the range of the Army's patrol bombers, and that evening his formation moved to within 100 miles of the island. The next morning Reeves launched a large strike of naval bombers that hit the Hawaiian airfields with loads of flour bombs. Although Hawaii was on alert, the carrier's air group achieved complete tactical surprise. At sea, however, aviation was a wager on the future, and even now only a few Navy men disputed Admiral Lanning's contention that "all types of ships" were "designed and built for the purpose of assisting the battleships in one way or another." In 1927, Admiral Montgomery M. Taylor chaired a board that examined the contribution of naval aviation to fleet tactics and reported in compromising tones that the function of the carriers was to defend the battle fleet and to engage in "scouting and offensive operations at a distance from the battle line."

The first radio telephones were installed in naval aircraft in 1928 for experiments conducted by the *Saratoga*'s air group, tests that raised new questions about air strategy, tactics, and policy, and ultimately led to improved coordination between air and sea operations. Fleet exercises repeatedly underscored the need to quickly launch a large number of aircraft so as to establish an effective defending combat air patrol over the battle line to withstand an opponent's attack. However, despite their aircraft carrying capacity, neither the *Saratoga* nor the *Lexington* could launch many more planes faster than the much smaller *Langley*. This reinforced Moffett's preference for building a large number of small carriers of the *Ranger*-class to enhance the defense of the entire battle line and deploy a powerful offensive arm while still remaining within the tonnage confines of the Five Power Treaty. Moffett went so far as to propose building a 10,000-ton, 650-foot-long "flying deck" cruiser with a 350-foot angled flight deck and a hangar for about twenty-four planes, but he found little support for his plan from the General Board.[5]

How to organize and manage American military aviation were questions of hot dispute while Coolidge was in the White House. Moffett not only championed the cause of shore- and carrier-based naval aviation but also supported an expensive, controversial rigid airship program. "There certainly does not seem to be any very great promise in airplanes for long distance scouting," observed Captain Ernest J. King, the assistant chief of the Bureau of Aeronautics. "It would appear that you would have to go into the dirigibles for that purpose—a very long radius." The Navy's airship was a legatee of the apparent tactical success of German dirigibles in the Great War. Admiral Coontz had directed the government-owned Naval Aircraft Factory to construct the *Shenandoah* in 1919, and she joined the fleet soon after Moffett took over the Bureau of Aeronautics. Coontz had also ordered the airship R-38 from a British firm, but during tests she broke in half, crashed, and killed her entire crew, a harbinger of the string of disasters that was to befall the Navy's Lighter-Than-Air program. To replace the R-38, Moffett signed a contract with the German Zeppelin Company for the ZR-3, an airship commissioned as the *Los Angeles* that operated with the fleet beginning in September 1924.[6]

Navy men looked for the airship to establish communications and surveillance over the Alaska-Hawaii-Panama "strategic triangle," the defense of which was essential to executing the Orange War Plan. Airships were endowed with such great range, lift, and endurance, Moffett argued, that they might eventually replace cruisers as scouts for the Battle Force. He even estimated an airship to be worth three scout-plane cruisers. A natural publicist, Moffett advanced the view that the airship would greatly assist in polar exploration, a benign idea to improve the Navy's public relations at a time when its military functions were held in low repute owing to popular reaction to the carnage of the Great War.

Moffett had tragically underestimated the difficulty of operating dirigibles in bad weather, however, and this problem lay at the root of the dirigible's undoing.

Moffett's airship program provided the basis for a renewed argument by the assistant chief of the Army Air Service, General Mitchell, that the Army and the Navy were ignoring aviation, a problem he said could only be solved by establishing an independent cabinet-level military and civilian air department. Coolidge may have unwittingly encouraged Mitchell to believe that the White House would support his position when the president announced in 1924 that it "would be a little lack of logic in spending a lot of money on battleships and at the same time spending a lot of money on aviation." Mitchell had toured the Far East at his own expense one year earlier, discovered that Japan was interested in military aviation, and discerned indifference to his findings by the Army and Navy commanders in the Philippines and in Washington. Harding had been willing to tolerate Mitchell's iconoclastic rumblings, but Coolidge's policy of retrenchment discouraged such costly new projects. Then, when Mitchell objected to reductions to the Air Service, Army Chief of Staff Pershing exiled him to Fort Sam Houston in Texas.[7]

A few days later, the Navy dirigible *Shenandoah* flew into an electrical storm and crashed near Dayton, Ohio, killing thirteen men out of a crew of forty-two. The accident was caused by a faulty altimeter and poor piloting. "These accidents are the result of the incompetency, the criminal negligence, and the treasonable administration of our national defense by the Navy and War departments," Mitchell told the press. His earlier attacks on the Navy had been supported or tolerated by the Army's general staff, but this impolitic blast indicted not only the admirals but also his superiors in the War Department and Coolidge's policy of retrenchment. It was almost inevitable that Mitchell would be speedily convicted by a court-martial for discrediting the Army and drummed out of the service, which he was.[8]

It was ironic that Mitchell's major quarrel was not with the Navy or the Army but with the policy of dividing aviation between the two military departments—a state of affairs for which the Navy was largely responsible. He also railed against the Republican policy of fiscal retrenchment, the Post Office's air mail flying service, and Coolidge's civil aviation policies, issues of marginal concern to Admiral Moffett. In effect, Mitchell sought to establish air socialism, and he left few in doubt as to who should direct such a national air monopoly. His motives aside, Mitchell's argument against the Navy's airship program was well reasoned, as was his case against building a fleet of aircraft carriers. While agreeing that "aircraft acting from suitable floating aerodromes can destroy any class of surface sea craft on the high seas," he asserted that land-based aircraft would invariably prevail over opposing carrier-based planes. Compared to land-based aircraft, carrier-based planes' fighting characteristics were inherently inferior because of the disproportionately high fraction of their design weight dedicated to absorbing the stresses of carrier landings. And aircraft carriers could not operate enough bombers to inflict significant damage against an enemy's cities or industries, the strategy that Mitchell saw to be the most reasonable and effective for any air force. "Land-based, long-range air power can attack the vital centers of the opposing country directly, completely destroying or paralyzing them," he wrote, a succinct encapsulation of the basic tenet of strategic air power. This new orthodoxy directly conflicted with the Navy's preference of using aircraft for tactical purposes.[9]

Coolidge instinctively opposed Mitchell's proposals. Creating a new air department "runs counter to the general policy of . . . unification, rather than the establishment of new and independent services," he told reporters on 10 February 1925. Mitchell's charges created a public furor, however. To silence his critics, Coolidge named a presidential commission chaired by his political ally, businessman Dwight Morrow, and charged it with studying air policy. Navy Secretary Curtis D. Wilbur arranged for retired Admiral Frank F. Fletcher, a man certain to protect the Navy's interests, to be appointed to the board. Morrow found little support within either the Army or Navy for an independent air force, or for a single, amalgamated national defense department. Moffett was especially effective in influencing the Morrow Board. He countered Mitchell's advocacy of an independent air department by confessing that "such duplication as exists [between the War and Navy Departments] is not only justifiable but . . . decidedly necessary, in order that there may be competition, that there may be rivalry, that there may be initiative; otherwise, there is bound to be stagnation."[10]

Neither Admiral Eberle, the CNO, nor General John L. Hines, the new Army chief of staff, wanted to contend with another competitor for scarce military appropriations. Moreover, infantrymen and artillerymen had their own ideas about how air-craft should be used. Hines testified "that the Air Service, because of the limitations imposed by natural laws on the operation of air-craft as well as the necessity for unity of action, will always be an auxiliary arm or service." Pershing, Hines' predecessor, insisted that the land-based air forces be subordinated to the larger Army. Infantry was "the backbone of the attack, and the role of the other arms is to help it reach the enemy." In short, the Army's orthodoxy was akin to the Navy's. Air power was most effective in a tactical role supporting other arms. Moffett agreed. "Aviation as an inde-pendent force cannot operate across the sea," he claimed. "The thing to do is to put aviation on something . . . and carry it to the enemy, and the only way to carry it is on board something that will float—on board a ship." The Morrow Board was subjected to a great deal of hyperbole. Mitchell's extraordinary forecasts moved Navy Secretary Wilbur to proclaim that he "regard[ed] the state-ment that the next war will be in the air as an absurdity, partaking of the Jules Verne type of literature."[11]

The Morrow Board, acting according to Coolidge's plan, is-sued its report on 30 November 1925, just at the height of public interest in the spectacle of Mitchell's court-martial, a move timed to take the sting out of Mitchell's indictment of the administra-tion. Morrow announced that his panel "did not consider that air power, as an arm of the national defense, has yet demonstrated its value . . . for independent operations of such a character as to jus-tify the organization of a separate department." Coolidge was pleased with this outcome. "The suggestion for a unified depart-ment," he told the press, "is going to prove more or less academ-ic" because it would "not change the practical functioning of the Army and Navy much." The Morrow Board, reflecting the nation's reaction to the ghastly, seemingly pointless slaughter of World War I; also expressed concern that "the belief that new and deadlier weapons will shorten future wars . . . is a dangerous one which, if accepted, might well lead to a readier acceptance of war as the so-lution of international difficulties."[12]

Morrow did urge Coolidge to pay more attention to national air policy and recommended several specific steps, which the pres-ident agreed to take. The Army Air Corps replaced the old, less prestigious Army Air Service, and an assistant secretary of the Navy for aeronautics was named. Although this post was left vacant to save money after 1932, for a few years at least naval aviators had their own political spokesman within the administration and on Capitol Hill. An even more important recommendation of the Morrow Board was that the Navy buy 1,000 aircraft over the next five years to fill out existing patrol squadrons and training units and to increase the number of fighter, scouting, and bomber squadrons for the new heavy carriers *Lexington* and *Saratoga* before they entered the fleet. Under the aegis of the Morrow Board, Moffett also persuaded Congress to reserve the commands of carriers, seaplane tenders, naval air stations, and air squadrons for qualified naval aviators, a step that provided a tremendous incentive for junior officers to enter naval aviation.

Despite the loss of the airship *Shenandoah*, Moffett refused to abandon the Lighter-Than-Air program. He placed orders with the Goodyear Zeppelin Corporation to build the eight-engined superairships *Akron* and *Macon*, each of which was equipped with a hangar and deck and operated four single-seat biplanes to extend the dirigible's range. The *Akron* first flew on 23 September 1931, soon establishing an extraordinary record for endurance, range, and lift. However, she too seemed to be excessively vulnerable to the menace of bad weather.

Attempting to extend the range of fleet operations by employing airships, seaplanes, and fixed-wing aircraft was only one way of using new technology to overcome the disabilities imposed by the Washington Treaties on western Pacific naval operations. The Navy also attempted to persuade Congress and successive Republican administrations to adopt a policy of building up to a "treaty fleet." American diplomats found that the mere prospect of such a shipbuilding policy was just as potent as any reality. Secretary of State Hughes convinced Tokyo in April 1923 that the United States would adopt a treaty fleet policy unless Japan annulled the 1917 Lansing-Ishii Agreement and relaxed her iron grip on Manchuria's economy. However, Rear Admiral Hilary Jones of the General Board viewed such diplomatic victories as trivial when contrasted to the actual balance of Pacific power, and Admiral Eberle felt that the goal of building a "balanced fleet" up to "treaty strength" was more important than winning an occasional Japanese concession.[13]

Prospects for building a treaty fleet brightened momentarily in 1924 when relations between the United States and Japan took a bizarre turn for the worse. A strong earthquake had jolted the metropolitan area of Tokyo and Yokohama one year earlier, killing nearly 100,000 people, destroying the region's new industries, and crippling Japan's economy for nearly a decade. The outpouring of American sympathy and aid was instantaneous. The men of the Asiatic Fleet helped to fight fires and care for the victims in Tokyo, while American warships transported relief supplies from the Pacific coast to Yokohama. The Japanese people were genuinely touched by this humanitarian response, and for a short time euphoria clouded basic differences between the two countries. This spell was broken when Tokyo bitterly accused New York bankers of profiting from Japan's misfortune by charging Japanese lenders a steep premium for reconstruction loans. On the heels of these accusations came congressional passage of the 1924 Immigration Act, which restated the policy of "Oriental exclusion" and effectively shut off immigration from the Far East. Highly sensitive on issues of race and face, the Japanese were furious about "complete exclusion." Ambassador Masanao Hanihara in Washington went so far as to warn of the "grave consequences" attending the bill, a threatening, impolitic diplomatic stance that virtually ensured the measure's enactment.[14]

At about the same time, Japan had announced a major naval program to lay down cruisers, destroyers, and submarines, a move that ran counter to the spirit of the Washington Treaties. The British quickly followed suit. The American response was predictable. "Our lack of cruisers will render it extremely difficult for us to protect our long lines of communication to the western Pacific, protect American commerce, and establish an economic blockade of Japan" in an Orange war, warned Captain Sinclair Gannon of the Navy's War Plans Division. At the height of the controversy over the 1924 Immigration Act, Rear Admiral Hilary Jones of the General Board persuaded Congressman Thomas Butler, the chairman of the House Naval Affairs Committee, to introduce a bill authorizing the construction of eight heavy cruisers. Despite the furor with Japan, Coolidge was opposed to the program, and Butler struggled for two years before he was able to get Congress to appropriate funds to lay down the first five heavy cruisers of the 9,100-ton *Pensacola*-class. This half-hearted effort annoyed Admiral Jones, who proclaimed that "the lack of modern cruisers . . . constitutes the Navy's greatest weakness today. The demand for them . . . [is] urgent." In January 1927, Navy Secretary Wilbur convinced Coolidge to agree to lay down the last three heavy *Salt Lake City*-class cruisers from the 1924 Butler Cruiser Act, and a few days later the Navy asked Congress to authorize the construction of another ten ships of the same type.[15]

The cruiser issue illustrated how closely overall naval policy was linked to the Orange Plan, a strategy that was repeatedly revised during the 1920s. Before World War I, naval strategists had favored a rapid thrust by the U.S. Fleet from the Pacific coast via Hawaii to the Philippines, but their successors were more cautious. Japan's possession of the mandated islands gave her fine advance bases to position her submarines, cruisers, and aircraft athwart the Hawaii-Philippine line of advance. As a result, the 1921 version of the Orange Plan proposed for the first time an island-hopping campaign involving a fleet movement from Hawaii to the Philippines via the Marshalls and Guam. Once an advance base was established in the southern Philippines, Luzon could be recovered. It was obvious that the difficultly of implementing this strategy was directly related to the existing strength of Japan's outposts, and this led to concern among Navy men that Japan intended to violate the Five Power Treaty and fortify the mandated islands. However, these ever-present suspicions were based on such shallow evidence that Assistant Secretary of the Navy Theodore Roosevelt, Jr., was moved to assert in 1923 that Japanese policy was measuring up "not only to the letter but to the spirit of the treaty." And Commander H. R. Hein, the naval attaché in Tokyo, reported that Japanese naval policy was "to do nothing against the provisions of the Washington treaty and to maintain it." Nonetheless, establishing a large, powerful scouting force to advance ahead of the battleships into enemy-held waters assumed unprecedented importance.[16]

It was against this background that negotiating limits on cruisers became the central issue of Great Power naval diplomacy following the Washington Treaties and a burning issue on the public agenda that led eventually to the Geneva Naval Disarmament Conference in 1927. By fixing the displacement of a capital ship at 10,000 tons or more and its guns at greater than 8 inches, the 1922 Five Power Treaty had effectively capped the size and firepower of the cruiser. From the Navy's standpoint, submarine and destroyer construction was less worrisome than was Japan's quick start in laying down fast, modern cruisers. Navy men were especially concerned that the Japanese might overcome with speed what they lacked in firepower. Admiral Eberle concluded that the U.S. Fleet needed about forty 10,000-ton heavy cruisers to campaign in the western Pacific, inasmuch as Japan's heavy cruisers could outgun and outrun all light cruisers and seemed likely to operate with bases nearby. Figuring in his assessment were the facts that Pearl Harbor was still undeveloped as a naval base, and that neither Guam nor the Philippines might be fortified under the Five Power Treaty. For these reasons, he wanted to extend the 5 : 5 : 3 ratio to cruisers, avoid reductions to the limits established at the Washington Conference, and fix the upper limit for cruiser tonnage at 400,000 tons.

By contrast, two strategies informed British naval thinking: dominance in the Atlantic, Mediterranean, and Indian Ocean; and trade defense of the empire's sea lines of communications. To achieve these objectives, the Royal Navy needed cruisers in the Far East, but Japan's decision to build heavy cruisers now threatened Britain's maritime authority from its base at Weihaiwei in China to Singapore and New Zealand. But, because the Royal Navy depended so greatly on her string of imperial bases, she needed few cruisers with long range. For her part, Japan relied exclusively on naval power to defend her regional sphere of influence, she had little interest in light cruisers, and she was strangely indifferent to overall limits. However, the Japanese, ever sensitive to the domestic political implications of accepting an inferior status in international dealings, would demand a revision of the Washington ratio upward to 10 : 10 : 7.

The failure of the 1926 League of Nations Preparatory Commission to lay a basis for an agreement on the cruiser issue augured ill when the naval powers decided to meet on their own the following year in Geneva. The preliminary discussions had run aground when the French proposed to abolish calculating tonnage limits by classes and substitute instead a "global tonnage limit" that accounted for every warship in each fleet but found that none of the other major naval powers liked this idea. The Preparatory Commission's negotiations were "hopeless," Admiral Jones reported to Navy Secretary Curtis Wilbur, and the delegates were "on a circle of talk of infinite radius." When the invitations to the Geneva Conference were finally issued in early 1927, neither the French nor the Italians, locked in their own naval arms race in the Mediterranean, were willing to attend, but Tokyo and London, hoping to be spared a cruiser race with the Americans, accepted with enthusiasm.

The collapse of the preparatory talks presaged the difficulties of the Geneva Naval Conference, which opened on 29 June 1927. The ambassador to Switzerland, Hugh Gibson, and Rear Admiral Jones headed the United States delegation, but Jones was clearly the dominant American presence. One observer remarked that Jones "viewed the world through a porthole," but his problem stemmed less from Navy parochialism than a basic conflict between his instructions and the British position on cruisers. Eberle was "unalterable" in opposing any additional restrictions on improving the Navy's Pacific bases, and the General Board insisted on building just one class of heavy cruiser and an upper total tonnage limit of 400,000 tons. However, the British wanted Jones to accept an Anglo-American limit of fifteen heavy cruisers and fifty-five light cruisers, and a total tonnage limit of over 500,000 tons. Given a preconference agreement to extend the 5 : 5 : 3 ratio to cruisers, this proposal would have had the effect of allowing the Japanese to build up to 325,000 tons at a time when the General Board believed that the U.S. Navy could get no more than 400,000 tons out of Congress. This "gravely endangers the American western Pacific position," Jones recorded. The Navy neither wanted nor needed light cruisers, but Jones included them in a draft treaty, hoping that the British would reciprocate by changing their position and reducing their upper limit. However, Prime Minister Stanley Baldwin instructed his delegates not to budge on the upper-limit issue. Inasmuch as the upper limit proposed by the British was "beyond anything we want to consider," Jones rejected their proposal, and the conference broke up on 4 August.[17]

Coolidge reacted to the adjournment of the Geneva Conference in December 1927 by endorsing the second Butler bill, a measure authorizing the construction of twenty-five modern cruisers, five carriers, nine destroyers, and thirty-two submarines to be built over the next five years. Without a treaty, he told the press, "the size of the Navy . . . will be solely for America to determine." Opposing the bill were various liberals and peace groups who assailed the "war scare" propaganda of the Navy League and other supporters of the legislation. Chairman Butler had "never known such widespread protest to be registered against any measure," and to get it enacted he had to agree to modify the authorization to include only the small 13,500-ton aircraft carrier *Ranger* and fifteen heavy cruisers to be laid down over three years. Vexed by the failure of the Geneva Conference, Coolidge announced on 17 August 1928 that he was "not contemplating at present taking any further steps about the limitation of armaments" until the Five Power Treaty expired in 1932. This declaration and Butler's concessions led Congress to pass the Second Butler Cruiser Act on 5 January 1929, although work proceeded so slowly on the *Ranger* that she did not enter the fleet until 1934. Tokyo and London quickly reacted by accelerating their own cruiser programs. Thus, on the eve of the Great Depression, the efforts of the maritime powers to extend the spirit and concepts of the Five Power Treaty to non-capital ships were grounded on the bar of sharply conflicting national naval needs.[18]

Chapter Thirty-four

The Collapse of the Postwar Order
1929–1932

Coolidge retired in 1928 and the Republicans nominated the prestigious Secretary of Commerce, Herbert Hoover, who easily defeated New York Governor Al Smith, his Democratic challenger. A devout Quaker, Hoover hated the poverty and destruction he had witnessed in Belgium during the Great War. He did not believe in using force as an agent of foreign policy and opposed the creed "that nations even in peace gain in power and add to their prestige and prosperity by dominating armament."[1]

Hoover had no coherent naval policy other than negotiating other disarmament treaties and imposing more restrictions, however; and he could not or did not articulate how such measures alone would lead to greater world order or a long-lasting peace. His crabbed view of the utility of naval power was expressed in a 1931 Navy Day speech in which he declared that he wanted a "navy so efficient and strong that, in conjunction with our army, no enemy may ever invade our country." Inasmuch as defending the continental United States against an invasion by a foreign power had ceased to be a serious concern after the Civil War, Hoover's approach was at least somewhat eccentric. For his part, the new president considered most strategic questions that concerned Navy men to be somewhat unreal—a position based on his view of Japan as a bastion against communism in Asia, his philosophical opposition to a muscular foreign policy, and his quaint conviction that the "great ocean moats" served as an impenetrable defense of

American home territory. He cringed at the cost of the Second Butler Cruiser Act and hoped to postpone the day when the 1922 Five Power Treaty's battleship-building "holiday" expired. Until the Manchurian crisis erupted and wholly discredited the administration's handling of international affairs, Hoover's policy was supported by Secretary of State Henry L. Stimson, a perennial Republican placeholder whose longstanding disdain for the Navy was ill concealed. Within the cabinet, Stimson towered over the distressed figure of Secretary of the Navy Charles Francis Adams, a Boston gentleman who favored naval expansion but who uneasily conformed to Hoover's and Stimson's views.[2]

Hoover's distaste for military policy and naval affairs was given a shot in the arm when in 1929 a fellow pacifist, Labour leader Ramsay MacDonald, became Britain's prime minister for the second time. When MacDonald ordered a slowdown to Britain's cruiser program, Hoover invited him to a summit in the United States to pave the way for another naval disarmament treaty. At the Rapidan Conference in September 1929, MacDonald reduced Britain's minimum demand for cruisers and Hoover agreed that the U.S. Navy would build only twenty-one heavy cruisers and devote its remaining tonnage to light cruisers. They also arranged to convene another international disarmament conference in London within a few months. Because Britain needed to replace all her cruisers by 1940, the Admiralty supported MacDonald's negotiating concept, but most American admirals opposed further concessions on cruisers—with the notable exception of the commander in chief of the U.S. Fleet, Admiral Pratt. The General Board still held that Japan sought "indisputable naval supremacy in the western Pacific" and "absolute dictation" in the affairs of the Far East, but Pratt was an iconoclast who saw less rigidity in Japan's objectives than did Admiral Jones. Pratt reasoned that because the fleet could not conduct an Orange war without more ships and bases and because Hoover and Stimson were bent on signing another treaty, the Navy should offer its civilian masters "guidance," not unbending hostility.[3]

The onset of the worldwide Great Depression in September 1929 completely altered the politics of naval disarmament. Hoover's reaction to the economic collapse was so politically disastrous that he became an object of national scorn and contempt and his authority to conduct foreign policy was impaired. The Republicans lost control of the Congress in 1930, and both parties now tried to outbid each other in calling for retrenchment in federal spending. In 1930, appropriations for the Navy still represented a significant fraction of federal outlays. The country was burdened by "the largest military budget of any nation in the world today," Hoover claimed, "and at a time when there is less real danger of extensive disturbance of peace than at any time in more than half a century." Although international tensions increased during the Depression, no major power's economy had the vigor to support a war against another industrial nation. Thus, foreign policy and the state of the domestic economy eliminated the reasoning behind the earlier calls for naval expansion. Retrenchment made sense, and Admiral Pratt, who became CNO in 1930, admitted openly that cuts were unavoidable. Negotiated, multinational disarmament meant that reducing arms would not jeopardize the essential interests of any of the maritime powers, but it would allow them to trim their naval shipbuilding and operating expenses. As the international depression worsened in the winter of 1930, Tokyo and London were also anxious to reduce naval construction costs.[4]

Secretary Stimson and Admirals Pratt and Jones, who headed the American delegation to the First London Disarmament Conference, which convened on 21 January 1930, were far from united on a negotiating position. Jones agreed with the General Board that the fleet needed twenty-one heavy cruisers. Pratt believed that obtaining Japan's agreement to a treaty was more important. Stimson was unconcerned with the strategic issues and impatient with Jones' seemingly self-serving arguments. Naval officers, he confided to his diary, were "handicapped by a kind of training which tends to make men think of war as the only possible defense against war." For Stimson, no price was too high to reach an accord because no principle was involved. Hoover, who knew that Prime Minister MacDonald also needed a treaty and cared little about the details, supported Stimson, who told MacDonald on 11 February that it "was unlikely that the United States would actually build" any of the 6-inch "treaty cruisers." The president was also especially moved by Japan's call for the abolition of "offensive" vessels such as battleships, aircraft carriers, and heavy cruisers.[5]

At the London Conference, MacDonald accepted a plan to allow Japan to deploy twelve heavy cruisers; Britain, fifteen; and the United States, eighteen. Inasmuch as the Japanese already had eight heavy cruisers in commission and four more laid down, they were likely to accept this arrangement. In October 1929, Japan had announced that she would demand a 10 : 10 : 7 ratio in cruisers, but Stimson nonetheless went to the London Conference assuming that Tokyo needed relief from the arms race and made no preconference preparations to deal with this issue. He agreed with William R. Castle, his ambassador in Tokyo, that the American worry about Japan "is a fantastic fear" and understood that no threat of force lay behind the Open Door Policy. "I cannot imagine Congress declaring war on Japan because of anything Japan might do in China." It was therefore left to Senator David Reed, another American delegate, and Ambassador Tsuneo Matsudaira to solve the problem. Under the Reed-Matsudaira compromise, the United States might build fourteen heavy cruisers between 1930 and 1936, but would delay laying down the last three until 1934, thus giving Japan a practical 10 : 7 ratio in cruisers for several years. Stimson also agreed to parity in submarine tonnage at 52,700 total tons, and a 10 : 10 : 7 ratio in destroyer tonnage, in order to get an agreement covering all types into the treaty. The Navy considered this an important setback to its policy of insisting that Japan be held to a uniform 5 : 5 : 3 ratio for all warships. Destroyers were to be limited to vessels of 1,850 tons or less carrying no greater than 5-inch guns. The 1922 Five Power Treaty had defined a capital ship as any warship over 10,000 tons, and the British now wanted to limit cruisers to 7,000 tons; both the Americans and Japanese stoutly rejected this plan, and as a result only the numbers and armament of cruisers were restricted.[6]

Worldwide reaction to the 1930 London Naval Treaty was generally favorable. The British ratified it promptly. The Japanese Diet followed suit, although fanatical militarists, furious that the treaty embodied naval inferiority, drove the cabinet to resign and assassinated the prime minister that November. Back home, the Navy League, a national lobby, led the opposition to Senate approval, and in the fall of 1931 loudly accused Hoover of "abysmal ignorance" of American naval policy. Admiral Pratt, on the other hand, urged that the agreement be ratified. Neither Britain nor Japan might lay down new heavy cruisers, he pointed out, but the Navy might build fourteen new ships incorporating the latest technology. Even Pratt agreed, however, that the Navy had no need for light cruisers. Navy leaders reasoned that the destroyer restrictions were less important inasmuch as destroyers were thought to be mobilization types that would be constructed in large numbers at the beginning of any major war. Moreover, for several years Congress had refused to authorize a new destroyer building program. At the time the treaty was negotiated, destroyers consumed only slightly more than 15 percent of the fleet's total warship tonnage, the World War I four-stackers were almost obsolete, and within five years only eight modern front-line destroyers would be in service. Indeed, the Navy was badly split between those who wanted to build a few heavy, well-armed destroyers and others who wanted larger numbers of lighter, general-purpose destroyers. As a result of the 1930 London agreements, there was no choice for the Navy but to plan to build large numbers of light, all-purpose destroyers to fight an Orange war. In the end, despite some spirited opposition, the Senate approved the first London Treaty by an overwhelming margin.[7]

The London Treaty provided for parity with the Japanese in submarines at 52,000 tons and set down rules for the conduct of submarine warfare that reflected the outdated but gentlemanly concern for the safety of passengers at risk during commerce-raiding operations. Conceding parity to Japan annoyed the Navy on principle. On the other hand, the Japanese had been building submarines at a heady pace since 1922 and eight years later enjoyed practical equality. In short, this concession reflected an existing ratio. The reason for this was that American submarine policy was in a state of flux. Germany's unrestricted submarine warfare drove Wilson to fury in World War I, but after the Armistice he lost interest in the issue and insisted that it not clutter the Versailles agenda. After the war, many Navy men believed that they should follow Germany's example and develop submarines to conduct commerce-raiding operations. Captain Thomas Hart, a veteran submariner, warned in 1919 that a future war would find "no quicker or more effective method of defeating Japan than cutting off her sea communications." Submarines would be "extremely valuable for . . . operations against Japanese commerce."[8]

Germany's World War I-era U-boats had very short range, as did the wartime and postwar American *R*-class and early *S*-class submarines, and so conducting a successful submarine campaign against Japan's Far East trade seemed somewhat improbable. Hart's experience in 1921 demonstrated the problem. He took a flotilla of ten boats from the New London submarine base on a long cruise into the Pacific, to Hawaii, and then on to Manila. Every one of the vessels broke down, the tender was overtaxed, and the cruise from Hawaii to Manila could not get under way until every submarine was repaired at Pearl Harbor. The newer S-class boats had a limited cruising radius, they were slow, and they had a terrifying record of major accidents. Manual intake values were responsible for several tragedies, and the poorly ventilated Edison electric storage batteries emitted dangerous gasses, which caused small explosions that endangered the submarines and their crews. As a result of an improperly closed valve, the S-5 went down off Cape Hatteras in 1920, although in one of the most heroic incidents of the interwar years, Lieutenant Commander Charles M. Cooke saved his entire crew from a grisly death at the bottom of the Atlantic Ocean.

The General Board was, nonetheless, positive about the future of submarine warfare. By operating independently "off the enemy ports" to "sink merchantmen or men-of-war," American submarines might reduce Japan's naval fleet and cargo shipping and crimp her economy, which was highly dependent on imported raw materials. Before this goal might be realized, however, the Navy had to develop a long-range fleet submarine to conduct transpacific operations, a challenge immensely complicated by the nonfortification article of the Five Power Treaty. The delegates to the 1921–1922 Washington Conference had reacted instinctively to the wartime experience with Germany's U-boats, and when they met, the prospect for further submarine development at first appeared to be poor. The British had proposed to abolish all submarines since these vessels—and aircraft—threatened the Royal Navy's traditional control of chokepoints and lines of communication between its imperial bases. This plan was opposed by the French, who believed that an armada of submarines might be a cheap alternative to an expensive battleship fleet, thus giving France more leverage in Mediterranean affairs. The Navy's General Board characteristically resisted any limitations on submarines or submarine warfare, but announced its satisfaction with a formula requiring submarines to "conform . . . to the rules for surface vessels of war." Senator Elihu Root offered this to the delegates at Washington as a compromise between the French and British positions, and as a way to satisfy American public opinion, which had not forgotten the *Lusitania* tragedy and generally opposed unrestricted submarine warfare against liners or merchantmen.

The issue of nonfortification was linked to submarine strategy through the Navy's assumption that the poorly defended bases in the Philippines and at Guam would be untenable during the early days of an Orange war. Once American submarines fell back to Pearl Harbor, they would face voyages of at least 4,000 miles to return to Philippine waters or to reach stations near Japan. "Nonfortification . . . surrendered in major degree the naval surface control" of the western Pacific, Commander Charles Cooke believed, and this "loss . . . stepped up the importance of long-range submarines in our building program." Inasmuch as the early short-range S-class boats were tied to their tenders, Navy strategists decided to use them as scouts and escorts and have them conform to the movements of the fleet. Interwar submarine doctrine "rigidly locked" American submarines into "direct participation with and support of the fleet, reflected Captain J. C. Wylie, a noted strategist. "They were not envisaged as weapons to be applied primarily to merchant shipping."

In the 1930s Navy submarine doctrine emphasized scouting and attacks against enemy capital ships, and interest in commerce raiding declined, partly because of the belief that it was the strategy of an inferior naval power. The commander of the Blue Fleet in the 1934 annual exercise assigned his submarines to defend Pearl Harbor, report on enemy movements, and "support . . . fleet operations especially against larger enemy warships." Many submariners by this time realized that they would have to develop a more powerful, long-endurance vessel to stake a claim to independent, long-range action. And it was clear that the numbers allowed under the London Naval Treaty would not be adequate for protracted operations. Cooke asked the General Board that year to lay down a 1,150-ton submarine armed with six bow and two stern tubes, which could conduct seventy-five-day war patrols deep into the western Pacific. "Such a vessel approaches the type the construction of which would be inaugurated on a large scale at the declaration of war."[9]

Public interest in naval policy collapsed in 1929 with the onset of the depression and the Senate's approval of the London Treaty. Hoover responded to the economic crisis with a policy of government economy. The General Board proposed the construction of the 7,050-ton Omaha-class as the standard for light cruisers in May 1930, but two years went by before Navy Secretary Adams asked Congress to appropriate funds for a new 10,000-ton "treaty" cruiser carrying 6-inch guns. After the cruiser bill died in Congress, Admiral Pratt admitted privately that Hoover had "not the slightest intention of trying to build up to the treaty limits" before the London Treaty expired in 1936 "because the cost . . . would be too great." The following year Adams nearly resigned when Hoover announced that he was slashing the Navy's 1932 budget and planned to agree to a one-year multilateral moratorium on naval shipbuilding. When Congressman Carl Vinson of the House Naval Affairs Committee countered with a bill to spend $616 million over two years on 120 new ships, the first serious plan to build up to a "treaty fleet," Adams supported the measure, but Hoover kept it from coming to a vote on the Hill. Hoover was uniformly successful in obstructing naval expansion, although Pratt was not overly concerned. The London Treaty "has been one of the most potent factors in eliminating friction between ourselves and Japan," he assured Congress. Instead "of an atmosphere of distrust" that had been a "source of trouble" in the 1920s, the new decade would see "an atmosphere of confidence" among the Pacific powers.[10]

Although American politics turned inward after World War I, politicians and Navy leaders were drawn by the malignant dynamic of Far Eastern politics into the whirlwind of the Chinese civil war. China was "the colony of every nation that has made treaties with her," complained Sun Yat-sen, a Western-educated socialist who organized the Nationalist Party in 1920. He condemned Peking's hapless post-imperial republican regime and established a rival Nationalist government in Canton four years later. Following Sun's death in 1925, Generalissimo Chiang Kai-shek seized control of the Nationalist Party and Army. Carried along by a wave of xenophobia, he launched his successful eastern expedition and extended Nationalist control over much of southern China. Fresh from defeating the warlords of South China later that year, Chiang mounted a northern expedition with the aim of overthrowing four powerful warlords who dominated the discredited Peking regime.

The antiforeign movement, which accompanied this republican phase of China's long revolution, endangered not only the Open Door Policy but also the lives and property of the 14,000 American merchants, missionaries, educators, and their dependents who lived in China. Their special legal rights were first secured in the 1844 Treaty of Wanghia and later in a succession of equally one-sided agreements culminating in the Boxer Treaty of 1901. When revolution broke out, therefore, American policy embraced some profound contradictions. On 10 July 1925, the State Department told London that Coolidge expected "strict adherence" by China to the extrality and tariff treaties, but the president also instructed Secretary of State Kellogg not to use force to interfere in China's internal affairs. On the other hand, the White House could not abandon Americans preaching and trading in China, and Kellogg repeatedly declared his determination to protect their lives and property.[11]

The Navy provided the principal means for achieving these objectives. Admiral Coontz had abolished the Atlantic Fleet and consolidated all the battleships into the U.S. Fleet on the Pacific coast in 1922, but he did not disestablish the Asiatic Fleet. It was charged with defending the Philippines and Guam and with upholding the Open Door Policy in China. Most Americans who preached and traded in China lived in the Yangtze River basin, or in or around one of South China's great treaty ports. For nearly a century their activities had been periodically threatened by pirates, bandits, antiforeign rioters, warlords, and anti-Peking rebels. As a result, in the 1858 Treaty of Tientsin the United States demanded that China give U.S. Navy warships the right to navigate the rivers of China "in pursuit of pirates" and the freedom to "visit all ports." The first patrol on the Yangtze River was conducted in 1854, and over the years these operations increased in frequency as Peking's ability to keep order declined under pressure from the warlords, Japan, and Europe's interventionists. After the Boxer Rebellion was crushed in 1900, American gunboats routinely patrolled the Yangtze and policed the South China coast. The Boxer Treaty also led to the posting of a large Marine legation guard in Peking and an Army regiment at Tientsin forty miles to the east. Nonetheless, the China station was always an isolated outpost. In 1902, the Asiatic Squadron was ungraded to fleet status, but two years later Theodore Roosevelt withdrew all battleships from the Far East.

Over the years the Asiatic Fleet's Yangtze Patrol and South China Patrol remained fairly weak, despite the increasing danger to American interests that came hard on the heels of the Manchu dynasty's collapse in 1911, the subsequent outbreak of the civil war, and Japan's adoption of a policy of muscular expansionism. When a real crisis appeared on the horizon in 1924, the entire Asiatic

Fleet consisted of only one cruiser, twenty four-stack destroyers, twelve submarines, and eleven gunboats. Rear Admiral Charles B. McVay's Yangtze Patrol maintained a supply depot at Hankow, the midpoint of its area of gunboat operations on the river; a smaller three-vessel South China Patrol was stationed at Canton. The Navy's establishment in China was clearly not up to defending American interests in the Far East. The Yangtze Patrol was "small

The 1,207-ton Yangtze Patrol gunboat *Asheville* **(PG-168), c. 1930. The** *Asheville* **was commissioned in 1920 and served on the China station until 1940, with only one brief interruption for duty off Cuba in 1932 and 1933. The Japanese sank her while she was steaming south of Java on 3 March 1942.**

and weak, merely a police force against banditry," admitted Rear Admiral Yates Stirling. McVay reported in 1923 that he had been forced to book commercial passage to Chungking during a crisis there because his gunboats were unable to make the journey up-river during the winter when the water level was low. "Not one of our gunboats on the river is satisfactory for the duty to which it is assigned." American nationals in China were sharply divided over the value of the patrols, many claiming that the gunboats stimu-lated Chinese agitation, others insisting that only the presence of Western naval forces prevented the Chinese from violating the treaties and slaughtering all foreigners. "Our merchant marine on the Yangtze did not appear to be very important," Stirling ob-served, "but there was a principle involved that took no account of expense. It was the maintenance of our right to free navigation of the river, given us by treaty. If China were too weak to protect our trade, than we must take over completely that responsibility."

Although Britain had long ago turned Hong Kong into a crown colony, and the highest-ranking foreign diplomats resided in Peking, the center of Western investments, trade, and mission-ary activity in China was the International Settlement in Shanghai, where a multinational municipal council exercised the powers of local government. To defend Britain's many interests in China, the Royal Navy maintained a large number of cruisers, destroyers, and gunboats in its Far Eastern Fleet, but Britain's traditional dominance in Asia declined after 1904 with the growth of Japanese naval power. As a result, the British tried repeatedly af-ter 1924 to improve their position by involving the Americans in multinational military efforts to defend Shanghai, put down near-by demonstrations, and thwart Chiang's effort to unite the coun-try. Neither Washington nor the Navy's on-scene commanders sympathized with Britain's plight, although protecting American nationals in China necessarily involved the Asiatic Fleet on more than one occasion in tactical cooperation with British forces.

Until 1924, the International Settlement in Shanghai served as a quiet sanctuary for Chinese who sought refuge from the war, but the following year, to draw attention to foreign involvement in China and the need for national unification and revival, the Na-tionalists turned the spotlight on the concession, and the level of antiforeign violence throughout China reached a new mark. Ad-miral Thomas Washington, who now commanded the Asiatic Fleet, landed a small party of Marines at Tsingtao to protect American property in that port during a nearby battle between two warlord armies. The British, who had the most to lose, rightly detected a shrill anti-Western element in Chiang Kai-shek's xenophobic strategy, and in January 1925 they revived an earlier proposal to establish a multinational force under a single command to defend Shanghai's International Settlement. Admiral McVay met with his foreign counterparts in Shanghai on 18 January and reported that the area was safe, and Admiral Washington told the Navy Department a week later that he opposed the British plan. America's diplomats in China mostly agreed. Jacob G. Schurman, the American minister to China, recommended rejecting the British proposal "unless the naval authorities reported that it was imperative . . . for the protection of American and other foreign lives in Shanghai." Secretary of State Kellogg announced that he was turning down the British plan and pointed out that more overt displays of force "would almost certainly aggravate . . . the present widespread antiforeign sentiment among certain classes in China."

The Coolidge administration was bent on avoiding incidents, but the Yangtze Patrol and the South China Patrol still had to defend American lives, and throughout 1925 a series of landings, punitive movements, escort operations, and rescues kept the Asiatic Fleet busy. After a brief lull, on 30 May a Chinese student march in Shanghai turned into a riot in which Sikh police killed at least a dozen demonstrators. A general strike ensued, and antiforeign incidents were reported in other cities. Admiral Washington had already sent three destroyers to Shanghai and now told six more ships to join them. Operational urgency overcame long-term policy. With Kellogg's approval, McVay organized an international landing force of nearly 1,000 men, which went ashore on 2 June and took up key positions in the settlement area. Admiral Washington did not overreact, however, and most of the Asiatic Fleet remained off North China, at Tsingtao, or at the anchorage at Chefoo. The possible repercussions were obvious. Visiting Canton in July, Lieutenant Commander Glenn F. Howell observed that the damage to Sino-American relations "has already been incalculable, and it will take a century's patient work to build it up again to where it was." The last Marines were withdrawn from Shanghai in July, however, and the level of antiforeign violence subsided after Chiang's Nationalist Army entered Canton that month.

In March 1926, Chiang betrayed his sometime communist allies and that summer launched his great northern expedition with the aim of overthrowing the northern warlords and breaking the Peking regime. "There are so many factions that it is difficult to know whether the central government is in possession of much of any authority," Coolidge remarked. Chiang's campaign, accompanied by a fresh round of anti-Western propaganda, disrupted commerce, travel, and communications, and the foreign residents of the treaty ports loudly demanded that the Navy provide them protection. After several American merchant steamers plying the Yangtze were threatened by gunfire from the riverbanks or by commandeering at the hands of local military figures, Admiral Charles S. Williams, the new commander of the Asiatic Fleet, ordered naval armed guards to board these vessels and ensure their safety. Shortly thereafter, Yangtze Patrol gunboats began to escort Standard Oil and Texaco tankers from Hong Kong to Wuchow, and by the end of the year unescorted steamers could not safely navigate the upper Yangtze without naval escorts. "This precaution prevented banditing but made it easier to have an incident with the Chinese military," Stirling recalled. "We found it difficult to differentiate between bandits and national soldiers. They both wear uniforms of sorts."[12]

The Nationalists reached the Yangtze in August 1926 and laid siege to Hankow, then staunchly defended by General Wu P'ei-fu's warlord army. When the battle threatened the international community there, Rear Admiral Henry Hough of the Yangtze Patrol stationed two gunboats in the harbor, ordered the destroyers *Pope* and *Stewart* to join him, and in collaboration with the British and Japanese sent a landing party ashore on 4 September to prevent any more Chinese refugees from the siege from entering the city's international area. Within two days, however, Wu surrendered. Chiang now took a bold step by attempting to establish Nationalist control of navigation on the Yangtze. On 30 August, the Nationalist commander at Wanhsien had seized two British steamers. During an unsuccessful attempt by a British flotilla to recover these vessels, the Royal Navy gunboat *Cockchafer* fired thirty-six shells into the city, causing considerable damage. However, the battle turned against them when the Chinese brought up more artillery and commenced a ferocious counterbattery fire that drove two British gunboats aground and compelled the entire force to withdraw. The Wanhsien incident marked a change in Nationalist policy. Up to that time, Chiang had denounced the treaty system but restrained his troops from challenging it. On 15 September, however, he announced the imposition of a nighttime curfew on the Yangtze, instructed daytime river traffic to register at Nationalist inspection stations near Hankow, and threatened that violators would "be fired upon by [Nationalist] artillery." This clearly violated the treaty regime.

Nationalist troops stationed along the banks of the river had begun to harass Yangtze Patrol gunboats with small-arms fire and, occasionally, field artillery. These clashes climaxed on 14 September when Nationalist artillery brought the American minesweeper *Pigeon* under fire; five days later she was again the victim of Chinese harassment. The *Pigeon* was hit more than 100 times during the two engagements and suffered three casualties, but she suppressed the hostile gunfire after expending over 2,300 rounds. Admiral Hough protested in vain to the local Nationalist general and reinforced his Hankow station by withdrawing two destroyers from Shanghai, now fairly quiet. The situation in Hankow was so dangerous that the British started to evacuate their residents, and Hough prepared to do the same, but at the end of the month an uneasy calm returned to the city. Admiral Williams had already decided to treat Chiang's navigation decrees as an illegal blockade, and Navy Secretary Curtis Wilbur backed his stand. The British and Japanese adopted a parallel line. However, the cumulative effect of Chiang's decrees and the Wanhsien incident moved Hough to suspend American commercial steamer traffic on the upper Yangtze, although his gunboats continued their patrols. Faced with a firm front of foreign resistance, Chiang backed down and the inspection decree was withdrawn on 15 October. He now saw that the Nationalists would soon have to make some concessions to the Western powers.

Just as tension abated on the Yangtze, the Nationalists overran Wanhsien and marched on Shanghai. Although Admiral Williams had decided to return to the Philippines with most of the Asiatic Fleet destroyers, he agreed to reinforce the Shanghai gunboat station, and Admiral Hough discussed plans for the defense of the International Settlement with other naval commanders there in January 1927. American authorities were divided over how to deal with this new threat to the large American population in Shanghai. John V. A. MacMurray, the minister in the city, believed that Hough should be directed to "protect both the integrity of the settlement and foreign life and property." Neither Admiral Williams nor Admiral Hough agreed with this appraisal.

Although Williams changed his plans and hurried back to Shanghai in early January, he preferred to reduce the American presence in China as soon as possible, avoid offending the Nationalists, and be held accountable only for the defense of American lives. In January 1927, State Department Far Eastern expert Stanley Hornbeck explained that the United States should be "considerate of Chinese rights and interests" and "independent of other nations' interests and adverse to any activity which smacks of aggression."

Hornbeck's altruistic formulation offered no solution to the Asiatic Fleet's immediate operational problem. Secretary Kellogg reiterated his support for Hornbeck's line, warning Minister MacMurray that "American sentiment is very strongly opposed to military action in China . . . [or] for the object of maintaining the present status . . . of the International Settlement." On the other hand, Admiral Eberle, the CNO, decided to reinforce the Asiatic Fleet by sending a light cruiser division to Chinese waters in February and by canceling the fleet's normal winter movement to the Philippines. In addition, Eberle shipped more Marines to China from Guam, the Philippines, and Hawaii. The other powers also surged naval forces onto their China stations; by the end of February, the British had deployed an aircraft carrier, five cruisers, nine destroyers, and 8,400 troops to reinforce the Royal Navy's Far Eastern Fleet. Nevertheless, they were hesitant to intervene without American assistance and complained bitterly about Coolidge's decision to act unilaterally. The Japanese, who took a more independent posture, also increased their forces off Shanghai. As a result, by 1 April, there were more than forty British, Japanese, American, French, Spanish, and Italian warships in nearby waters.

Despite various alarms, the city remained calm during February while Chiang attempted to bribe the regional warlord into surrendering. Then, on 20 March, the Nationalists advanced on Shanghai suburbs, a strike erupted in the city, and riots broke out among the Chinese population in the International Settlement. When the municipal council asked for assistance, Admiral Williams reversed his earlier policy and agreed to send a force of 1,700 Marines ashore to patrol the streets and defend the concession's waterworks. Marine Brigadier General Smedley Butler, who arrived to take command of the landing forces five days later, asked Washington to dispatch the 6th Marine Regiment, then in

San Diego, to the Far East. Despite a number of minor gunfights, however, the Nationalist takeover of Shanghai was surprisingly peaceful. The warlord troops tried to break into the International Settlement several times, but the multinational landing force easily held them back. When news of the crisis reached him, Coolidge commented that "the only advantage that could be secured by a larger force would be from sending a very large force," something he was reluctant to do.[13]

Although the spotlight was fixed on Shanghai for several months thereafter, in the days following the crisis of 23 March Admiral Williams had to turn his attention to more menacing developments in Nanking. When the Nationalist Army approached Nanking, it appeared that the defending warlord would retreat without a fight, but Williams feared that the ensuing disorder would imperil American lives. Lieutenant Roy C. Smith, skipper of the destroyer *Noa*, asked for reinforcements in March, but the situation in Shanghai was so volatile that Hough could send only the destroyer *Preston* to that station later in the month. Before she arrived, Smith had begun to evacuate the Americans from Nanking on 22 March, only two days before the Nationalist Army entered the city. Riots broke out, foreign consulates were sacked, and Japanese and British diplomats were attacked.

After a number of American missionaries and educators were shot and killed, the American consul, John K. Davies, and fifty-one other Americans and Englishmen gathered at a house on Socony Hill, which was now defended by a small landing party from the *Noa*. The sailors repulsed one assault on the house by a band of Chinese soldiers, but by early afternoon Davies saw that the position could not be defended much longer and asked Smith for assistance. When the Chinese once again stormed Socony Hill, Smith directed the two American destroyers and the British destroyer *Emerald* to lay down a curtain of fire on the Chinese positions so that the hostages could follow a prearranged plan to escape by rope down a high wall in the back yard leading to the riverbank. When the ships opened fire, the small group raced for the wall, each person climbed down a makeshift rope of bedsheets, and the entire party escaped from the riverbank in three commandeered sampans. "The shellfire had so completely frightened the Cantonese that not a single armed soldier was encountered" during the escape, reported Ensign Woodrow Phelps, who engineered the intrepid plan.[14]

Admiral Hough arrived at Nanking that evening and quickly arranged with the local Nationalist general for the evacuation of another group of Americans. Nonetheless, over 150 Americans remained ashore, and on 25 March Hough asked Williams for reinforcements and alerted him that "it may be necessary to fire upon [the Chinese Army] barracks." Williams refused to detach any ships from the Shanghai force and warned Hough that shelling Nanking "should be a matter for joint determination" by all the foreign naval commanders in the area. For all practical purposes, the American policy of remaining aloof was in shreds. The British promptly joined Hough in a threat to bombard the city, and in response the Chinese soon allowed the remaining foreigners to assemble at the dock, where they were rescued and transported by ship to Shanghai.

Hough met with his European and Japanese counterparts on 26 March. They agreed that "action must be taken without delay whilst the [Nanking] incident is fresh," otherwise "foreigners must evacuate the entire Yangtze Valley and all war vessels must leave the river." Consul Davies told the State Department that "the American policy of conciliation . . . has failed." Admiral Williams equivocated, Secretary Kellogg instructed the Americans not to deliver an ultimatum to the Nationalists, and Navy Secretary Wilbur cautioned Williams that "the policy of this government is not, repeat not, to resort to sending troops." A few days after the Nanking incidents, antiforeign disturbances erupted in cities all along the coast and as far inland as Chungking. The destroyer *Paul Jones* evacuated Americans from Chinkiang, the destroyer *Hubert* saved another group from an aroused Chinese mob at Anking, and the destroyer *Edsall* rescued all Americans from the Foochow district on 1 April.

A few days later more riots broke out in Hankow, and Admiral Williams had to dispatch the cruiser *Cincinnati* and five gunboats to that station to assist in a general evacuation of all foreigners. By this time, he had withdrawn all the American gunboats from the upper rivers and retaliation for the outrages against American lives and property was out of the question. Williams concurred with the assessment of British statesman Winston Churchill, who remarked at the time that "punishing China is like flogging a jellyfish." Minister MacMurray wanted Washington to sign a multinational ultimatum that the British and Japanese were proposing to deliver to Chiang Kai-shek, but President Coolidge stood firmly against more closely associating American policy with Japan and Britain, refused to consider economic sanctions against China, and saw no need for an ultimatum. General Butler agreed with this stance. "We have not sufficient armed men in the United States, let alone here in China, to . . . protect the lives and property of Americans living way off in the bushes," he told General John Lejeune, the Marine Corps commandant.

Late in April, Chiang established his capital in Nanking, moved successfully against his new communist rivals who temporarily held Hankow, and then resumed the northern expedition to topple the regime in Peking and unify the country. To prevent a repetition of the Nanking incident, Admiral Williams reinforced the Marine legation guard in Peking, strengthened the Army regiment at Tientsin, and established a stronger naval presence off the northern port of Tsingtao. In September, he was relieved by Admiral Mark Bristol, a veteran naval diplomat, who was intent on preventing additional friction between the American and Chinese forces. Too often, Bristol confessed after conferring with Chiang, American policy in China had mimicked the British. "The best protection of American interests throughout China . . . will be accomplished by the cultivation of relations with all factions," he declared while disapproving the use of a destroyer as a floating consulate in Nanking. Although Bristol successfully reestablished the Yangtze Patrol and resisted an attempt by the Nationalists to require Chinese pilots on board foreign warships on the river, by early 1928 he had gone on record against the continuation of "gunboat diplomacy" in China. Bristol withdrew the naval armed guards from the commercial steamers on the Yangtze and cautioned Admiral Stirling that, "considering the growing consciousness of the Chinese, it is questionable . . . how much longer foreign men-of-war will be allowed to operate in the interior waters of China."

After Chiang negotiated a settlement of the Nanking incident early in the year, Bristol decided to reduce the level of American forces in North China. However, in April the Nationalist Army invaded Shantung Province and defeated the troops of the Manchurian warlord Chang Tso-lin. To protect their investments and thwart Chiang's campaign, the Japanese landed over 20,000 men, who occupied major strongholds on the peninsula and effectively prevented the Nationalists from occupying the province. Chiang appealed to the Americans to help him evict the Japanese from Shantung, but Admiral Bristol staunchly opposed intervention. "Should the Chinese be permitted to arrive at the conclusion that they could involve the United States in a war which they might start against an aggressor," he warned Washington, "it would encourage them to enter into such a war."

Bristol sympathized with China's plight but was unwilling to range force behind the Open Door Policy. Although American interests in North China were considerably less than in the Yangtze Valley or Shanghai, the fighting on the Shantung Peninsula concerned Bristol so much that he asked Admiral Hughes, the chief of naval operations, to deploy three light cruisers from Hawaii to the Asiatic Fleet to strengthen the American presence off Tsingtao. By the time these ships arrived on station in June, Secretary Kellogg had announced that there would "be no participation by the United States in joint action with the Japanese government" to thwart the advance of the Nationalist Army. Against Butler's advice, in July 1928 Bristol decided to withdraw the Marines from North China in three stages, an evolution that began later that month. Despite a few incidents, this movement proceeded so successfully that by the end of the year only the old legation guard and the 15th Infantry at Tientsin remained in northern China, with a reduced element of 4th Marines at Shanghai. Meanwhile, several newly commissioned gunboats entered the Asiatic Fleet.[15]

Chiang's northern expedition bypassed the Japanese in the summer and fell on the Manchurian Army outside Peking in the fall. In December, Chang Tso-lin, the Manchurian warlord, pledged allegiance to the Nationalist regime, which had already been recognized in July in a tariff agreement by the United States. "We were besought to take very strong military action against China, which I all the time refused to do, thinking that it was much more likely that they would be able to adjust their own differences if we refrained from interfering or doing more than was necessary to protect the lives and interests of our people there," Coolidge told the press on 25 July. At the same time, Washington and Nanking agreed to renegotiate the old unequal commercial and extrality treaties. The Japanese withdrew their forces from the mainland in November 1928, Britain closed the Royal Navy's base at Weihaiwei the following year, and the Western powers abandoned their concessions in five treaty ports in 1930. Chiang's decision to negotiate with the warlords limited the extent of his writ over North China and Manchuria, however, and the Nationalists never completely established order along the coast. Admiral Charles McVay, who relieved Bristol in 1929, announced that his mission was not only the defense of Americans in China but also "the cultivation of friendly relations with the Chinese." However, Admiral Stirling of the Yangtze Patrol cautioned that "it will be some years before conditions along the river will be such as to warrant withdrawal of gunboat protection."[16]

The Nationalists' accord with Manchuria's Chang Tso-lin effectively allowed the "young marshal" to continue to govern his own rich, autonomous province. The Japanese, who had enormous investments in Manchuria and a concession allowing them to operate and defend the vital South Manchurian Railway, grew increasingly concerned about the safety of these privileged interests. When the Nationalists mounted a campaign of anti-Japanese propaganda and a boycott of Japanese products in Manchuria in the summer of 1931, the liberal government in Tokyo downplayed the resulting tensions, a policy that enraged leaders of Japan's Kwantung Army in Korea. "The determination of military circles toward Manchuria is so strong," Emperor Hirohito was warned, "that it is feared that orders given by the central authorities [in Tokyo] may not be carried out." On 18 September 1931, the Kwantung Army staged a fake attack by Chinese impostors on the South Manchurian Railroad north of Mukden, which Japanese generals used to justify a prearranged movement from occupied Korea into Manchuria. Employing Korea as a bridgehead, Japanese troops poured onto the mainland, Mukden and Changchen were occupied the next day, and the Kwantung Army advanced northward to Harbin and Marshal Chang's redoubt at Chinchow. Chiang Kaishek, who had just launched a bandit campaign against Mao Tsetung's small army of communist guerrillas, could not or would not send troops to defend Manchuria. Instead, the Nationalists instituted their nationwide boycott of Japanese goods.

Americans generally sympathized with China's plight, although Admiral Montgomery M. Taylor, who had just taken command of the Asiatic Fleet, distrusted the Chinese and held in contempt the Nationalists' refusal to defend Manchuria. America "has little interest" in the Far East, Rear Admiral William D. Leahy confided to his diary, and "would be wise . . . to keep hands off before it is too late." When the Mukden incident erupted, only the small Asiatic Fleet stood ready to defend American interests in the Far East; its most powerful unit was the flagship cruiser *Houston*, which

Admiral Taylor felt "makes much 'face' for us." Moreover, the fleet commander worried that the Chinese would try to entangle the United States into defending them against Japan. "If the failure of the League and the United States to save Manchuria for China convinces her that she must fight her own battles," he told Pratt, then "the loss will be a good thing." Although Taylor put the Yangtze Patrol and the four destroyers of the South China Patrol on alert, he was not convinced at first that Japan's invasion of Manchuria in any way endangered American interests.[17]

Secretary of State Stimson reckoned that Tokyo was officially defending the invasion for reasons of Japan's domestic politics, and therefore tried to arrange a quick ceasefire in concert with the League of Nations. However, this diplomacy was hamstrung from the start by Japan's recalcitrance, the refusal of Britain and France to take stiff action, and Hoover's unwillingness to support the Open Door Policy by imposing sanctions on Japan. The Nine Power Treaty and the Kellogg-Briand Peace Pact were "solely moral instruments," the president told his cabinet on 19 October, and could be upheld only by "the moral reprobation of the world." It was "contrary to the policy . . . of the United States to build peace on military sanctions," and he specifically refused to apply "sanctions either economic or military, for those are the roads to war." The British and French took much the same line.[18]

The outcome of this multilateral backpeddling was a decision by the League merely to appoint a commission of neutral statesmen to investigate the Mukden incident. Before the Litton Commission arrived in the Far East, however, the liberals in Tokyo resigned, a more militant rival party took power, and the new Japanese government announced its intention to occupy not only Manchuria but also neighboring Jehol Province just north of Peking. With few options left, the secretary of state picked up on a suggestion made by Hoover in November, and on 7 January 1932 enunciated in diplomatic notes to Japan and China what became known as the Stimson Doctrine of Nonrecognition. Under this formula, Washington would not legally recognize any arrangement "which may impair the treaty rights of the United States or its citizens in China . . . or the international policy relative to China." To Stimson's distress, no other major power was willing to follow suit.[19]

Three weeks later, the Shanghai crisis erupted, exposing the asymmetry between the deep American diplomatic involvement in the Far East and the lack of will and available force to defend the

Open Door Policy. Shanghai, the home of a large fraction of the
Western nationals in China, had become the focus of the Nationalists' boycott of Japanese goods. This led to a wave of minor clashes, culminating in a riot on 18 January 1932 during which a Chinese mob attacked five Japanese monks and left one of them dead.
A nearby Nationalist garrison went on alert. The local Japanese
commander, Rear Admiral Koichi Shiozawa, demanded an end to
the boycott. When the Chinese did not respond promptly to his ultimatum, he called for reinforcements from Japan, which arrived
on the 23rd and were deployed to defend the settlement.

Unlike the situation in Manchuria, however, China's forces
around Shanghai were bent on resisting, and the impending battle imperiled the Americans in the International Settlement. At
the time, the Asiatic Fleet, consisting of the *Houston*, nineteen destroyers, a dozen submarines, and nine Yangtze Patrol gunboats,
was dispersed along the China coast and in the Philippines. Admiral Taylor could neither deter the Japanese in Shanghai nor put
up a reasonable bluff. He reminded the Navy Department that his
fleet was far too weak even to pretend a credible defense of the
Philippine Islands. Stimson expected Taylor to stand in the path
of further Japanese moves, however, and on 25 January the secretary of state proposed to London that the British Far Eastern Fleet
join the Asiatic Fleet off Shanghai. "I thought their presence in
Shanghai would tend . . . to convince Japan that we were seriously interested in the threat to our trade and our people" and would
prove that "the powers were interested in China and what happened to her." Taylor, on the other hand, felt that "China is up to
her old tricks trying to get someone, preferably the United States,
to fight her battles for her." For the moment, the British, afraid of
offending Japan, were unwilling to cooperate.[20]

The situation worsened on 29 January. Admiral Shiozawa
ordered the Japanese troops in Shanghai to advance into the
Chinese district of Chapei, a movement that was repulsed by the
Nationalists to the surprise of most observers. The Japanese
brought up their heavy artillery, while Shiozawa ordered his ships
to bombard the Chinese forts, flung air strikes with dive bombers
from his carrier task force against these targets, and landed more
troops. Now fearing a "massacre of foreigners in the International Settlement," the British Admiralty ordered reinforcements
to steam from Singapore to Shanghai, and the Foreign Office reluctantly agreed to Stimson's plan for a joint Anglo-American

naval demonstration. By this time Hoover and Stimson had reached an agreement that Admiral Taylor was to "sail for Shanghai immediately with the *Houston* and such destroyers as are available," and they decided to reinforce the American position at Shanghai by shipping an Army regiment from the Philippines to the embattled Chinese port. Taylor had sympathized with the Japanese in January, but soon after the flagship *Houston* stood into Shanghai on 3 February his assessment of the situation changed completely.

Shiozawa's unprecedented use of aircraft to bomb residential areas of Chapei shocked the West and turned the Americans in Shanghai against the Japanese. And, a few hours after his arrival, Taylor learned that the Japanese fleet had deliberately fired on the American destroyer *Parrott* while she rode at anchor in the vicinity of the Woosung Forts, the key Chinese stronghold in the area. In addition, Marine patrols had had to turn back several Japanese parties that tried to enter the American area of the International Settlement. Stimson failed to anticipate this turn of events, and Taylor was left without any specific instructions as to how to proceed. Inasmuch as he could not bluff Shiozawa and did not want to provoke a war, he decided to "sit tight," protest every Japanese violation of American neutrality and treaty rights, and await the arrival of the British fleet commander, Admiral Kelly, who appeared on the scene two days later in the powerful cruiser *Kent.*

Commanding an imposing force, Kelly was determined not to be cowed by the Japanese. During his first meeting with Shiozawa, he warned that British warships had orders to shoot down any Japanese aircraft that overflew their anchorage. Worried that they were overextended, the Japanese suddenly shifted toward a slightly more conciliatory stance, agreed to ceasefire talks, and sent Vice Admiral Kichisaburo Nomura to relieve the hotheaded Shiozawa on 9 February. The ceasefire talks broke down, however, and Tokyo rejected an Anglo-American effort to mediate the struggle for Shanghai. Nomura reorganized his forces, which now totaled 70,000 troops ashore, and prepared to resume the offensive against the Chinese. On 1 March, Nomura landed troops up the river, outflanking the Nationalists and compelling them to abandon Shanghai. Although Kelly would not tolerate outrages by the Japanese against his ships, he now believed that a Japanese victory in Shanghai was the best insurance of the safety of the international settlement. London agreed.

Stimson was furious, but Hoover once again rejected sanctions. The result was that Stimson's diplomacy was in shambles, and he was left with few choices, especially after he reviewed the strategic balance of naval power in the Pacific with Admiral Pratt. "It was more unequal than I had thought," the secretary of state confided to his diary. On 23 February, he threatened to renounce the Washington and London naval disarmament treaties, a move perhaps stimulated by the fresh conviction that the U.S. Fleet had been disarmed to "the danger point." Stimson shrank from asking Britain or France to invoke the Nine Power Treaty for fear "of the yellow-bellied responses" he would receive from Paris and London. He was thus reduced to reaffirming his Nonrecognition Doctrine and expressing moral outrage against Japanese aggression in an open letter to Senator Borah of the Foreign Relations Committee published on 23 February. Although Japanese diplomat Yosuke Matsuoka had already told the Americans that Tokyo considered the intervention in Shanghai to be a "mess," not until Nomura's forces took the Woosung Forts on 2 March were the Japanese ready to discuss a ceasefire with Chiang's envoys. After long and difficult negotiations, on 5 May 1932 the Japanese and Chinese agreed to terms that called for a mutual pullback. Shortly thereafter, Japanese troops returned to their transports and Nomura's task force stood out of Shanghai that summer.[21]

On 9 March, one week after these talks began, Admiral Taylor started to withdraw the Asiatic Fleet from Shanghai. When the Japanese began to pull out a few weeks later, Navy Secretary Adams told Taylor that "it wouldn't have taken much hard luck or much hasty judgment to have developed a war between Japan and ourselves." Taylor was unappeased. "While international differences between western nations may be settled by agreement and legal argument, in my opinion out here the ability to utilize force is what counts," he complained to Admiral Pratt. The Stimson Nonrecognition Doctrine was a negligible substitute for a strong fleet as a means to uphold the Nine Power Treaty or the Open Door. While the Shanghai crisis flared, Japan's Kwantung Army overran the Manchurian Army's last outpost at Chinchow and occupied Harbin, an area of traditional Russian influence. On 12 March, the Japanese organized a puppet government to rule Manchuria, which they renamed Manchukuo. When the Litton Commission report condemned Japan for this aggression, the Japanese walked out of the League of Nations in a dramatic gesture, effectively closing the door on the era of collective security in the Far East.

During the Manchurian crisis, American public opinion was unified against going to war with Japan to defend the Open Door Policy in China, a practical political reality with which Hoover and Stimson had to reckon. Nevertheless, Admiral Pratt believed that an increased American naval presence in the western Pacific might restrain Japan, although ONI warned him that the Navy was so weakened by economy measures that it could not now conduct an Orange war. After a successful burglary of the Japanese consulate in New York in 1922 by the FBI and ONI that resulted in the theft of Japan's naval code, American codebreakers were able to decipher Japanese diplomatic and naval messages, and during the Manchurian crisis they supplied the CNO with timely reports on Tokyo's moves. He was told that operations in China had brought the Japanese to fully mobilize their fleet, and that it was stronger than the opposing peacetime U.S. Fleet, but Pratt attempted to apply pressure on Tokyo anyway. He had, some months earlier, arranged for the U.S. Fleet to conduct its annual fleet problem involving the Battle Force and a cruiser division in Hawaiian waters during January and February 1932. To pressure Japan, Pratt sent the Scouting Force of cruisers from the Atlantic through the Panama Canal to join the fleet in February, and later reinforced the Battle Force by detaching some ships from the Special Service Squadron in Panama and sending them to Pearl Harbor. Although the Battle Force returned to California that spring, Pratt left a reinforced Scouting Force in Hawaii throughout the year. Nonetheless, the Navy Department decided with regret that the juxtaposition of these movements with Hoover's diplomacy and naval policy demonstrated American weakness rather than strength. As a result, the U.S. Fleet withdrew almost completely to the West Coast and its annual exercise was not conducted in Hawaiian waters for another two years. Funds for such operations, Pratt complained, had been trimmed some time ago by Hoover "to the lowest point consistent with national security." And Stimson, who had ridden roughshod over Admiral Jones' opposition to the London Treaty in 1930, now took to warning Hoover that he was "very much alarmed about the present situation of the Navy."[22]

Related directly to the American position in the Far East and therefore to the Manchurian crisis was an act that Congress passed in 1932 granting eventual independence to the Philippine Islands, whose economy had been savaged by the Great Depression and whose exports entered the American market with a considerable advantage over domestic commodities. Objecting to this competition, the farm bloc on the Hill moved the independence bill through both the House and Senate, despite the impassioned but lonely opposition of Navy Secretary Wilbur. The Filipinos, however, persuaded Hoover to veto the bill. "The Philippines are an ungrateful child whose politicos will continue to agitate [for] independence," complained Captain Adolphus Staton. "The protection they receive from our flag gives them more real independence than they can hope to enjoy, were we to cast them alone." A revised measure, called the Tydings-McDuffie Act, which allowed Philippine exports to enter the American market on more favorable terms, was approved by Congress and signed by President Roosevelt in 1934. It required the Navy to abandon the Cavite naval base on Manila Bay upon independence, although the Navy might hold on to a base on Subic Bay or another site elsewhere in the islands. Independence was not intended to relieve the United States of its obligation to defend the Philippines. As Rear Admiral Harry E. Yarnell pointed out, however, a succession of administrations had "never provided the essentials to a naval defense of the Philippines even when no [disarmament] treaties existed." In short, the American position in the Far East was extremely precarious.[23]

Chapter Thirty-five

Building a Treaty Fleet
1933–1936

The Great Depression swept Hoover out of the White House and brought in Franklin D. Roosevelt and the Democrats' New Deal in March 1933. Roosevelt was a deft politician with aristocratic airs, but his understanding of many issues was suspect and his opinions about the world were ill informed and narrow. Dealing with FDR, complained his second secretary of war, Henry Stimson, was akin to "chasing a vagrant beam of sunshine around a vacant room." Rear Admiral Ben Morrill, the hearty wartime chief of the Bureau of Construction and Repair, recalled that "FDR had obsessions on some things one day and forgot them the next." Roosevelt's short attention span and imperfect grasp of events prevented him from establishing a consistent naval policy and led him to rely on a succession of increasingly powerful uniformed figures in the Navy Department. Stimson, who served five presidents, thought Roosevelt the worst administrator he had known. FDR was a superb orator and a brilliant partisan, and he exploited these skills and a new Democratic coalition to win an unprecedented four terms in the White House. He tried to be not only his own foreign minister but also his own Navy secretary. He appointed to that job Senator Claude Swanson, a shrewd but unimaginative machine politician from Virginia. Swanson was "not much of an administrator," according to Admiral Pratt, the CNO, but he possessed a sure legislative touch. He "let the Navy people run the Navy business" and spent his time "getting funds" for the department on the Hill, observed Lieutenant Commander James Fife.[1]

While in the Senate Swanson had supported a policy of building up to "treaty limits," a line to which he hewed after joining Roosevelt's cabinet. His influence was hampered, however, when he suffered a seizure in early 1934 and was in poor health for the next five years. As a result, the CNO gained more authority over war planning, shipbuilding, and fleet operations. Indeed, Swanson's condition worried Congress so much that in 1936 an act was passed designating the CNO as the acting secretary whenever the incumbent was out of town or ill. Swanson was jealous of the power of his office, however, and when in late 1933 the new CNO, Admiral William Standley, tried to obtain command authority over the bureaus, Swanson cleverly lined up Rear Admiral William D. Leahy, the powerful chief of the Bureau of Navigation, and Rear Admiral Ernest J. King, the new chief of the Bureau of Aeronautics, to oppose any change in the Navy's existing bilineal organization under which the shore establishment generally, including the bureau chiefs, reported to the secretary and the fleet answered to the CNO.

The first step taken by the New Deal in foreign policy was to adopt Hoover's diplomacy of improving relations with Latin America. Roosevelt archly entitled his approach the Good Neighbor Policy, and at the Seventh Inter-American Conference in Uruguay in 1933, Secretary of State Cordell Hull charmed his hosts by agreeing that "no state has the right to intervene in the internal affairs of another." Owing to the Roosevelt-Hoover policy of retrenchment in Latin American affairs, the Navy's Special Service Squadron, based in the Canal Zone, had dwindled to only three vessels, which shuttled between Panama's few ports. In February 1933 Admiral Pratt gave this command to Rear Admiral Charles Freeman, a whimsical irony inasmuch as it had been Freeman's forceful arguments that brought about the establishment of the Special Service Squadron in 1920. Freeman's first act upon taking command was to propose an itinerary of "good will" visits in the Caribbean and Central America to reassert American presence in the region, but Hull abruptly vetoed the scheme.[2]

Roosevelt's Good Neighbor Policy was tested and found wanting when a civil war erupted in Cuba in 1933. Forced to act to protect American citizens and interests, FDR ordered Freeman to concentrate his ships off Cuba, and so many other vessels were summoned to those waters that the Special Service Squadron soon grew to thirty ships. Some visited Cuba's major ports—Havana, Matanzas, Cienfuegos, and Santiago—while others cruised off the Cuban coast, and Freeman initiated a vigorous program of visits to smaller ports. As the crisis ashore worsened, FDR sent a regiment of Marines in transports to stand by in Havana harbor, and the Special Service Squadron's offshore presence convinced Cuba's politicians that Washington intended to reestablish order. At the end of the year, Army Sergeant Fulgencio Batista helped to organize a government with Roosevelt's blessing and imposed on Cuba a supine dictatorship friendly to American interests.[3]

The end of the Cuban crisis altered the operational horizon for the Special Service Squadron. In 1934, at the behest of Congress, Roosevelt ended the occupation of Haiti by withdrawing the Marines, although Admiral Freeman frequently sent ships to visit Port au Prince as a sign of support for that villainous pro-American regime. The end of the anti-American Sandino Revolt also brought the withdrawal of the Marines from Nicaragua in 1933. Two years later, after stability returned to the Caribbean littoral, Admiral Standley persuaded Hull to agree to an active schedule of good will visits in the region to reinforce local perceptions of American interest, power, and authority. Despite this new mandate, the need for the Special Service Squadron was diminishing, a victim of its own success, the Good Neighbor Policy, the unlikelihood of European interference in Caribbean or Central American politics, and accumulating problems in the Far East between the United States and Japan.

Japan's occupation of Manchuria constituted the first forceful revision of the Versailles settlement. The West, demoralized by the Great War and the Depression, backed off from its historic role in the Far East, and its ambivalence encouraged Japanese expansionists to pressure their government to take bolder measures. Roosevelt, who thoroughly disliked the Japanese, saw parallels between American and European interests in the Far East, expected Britain to support the United States in reining in Japan, and tried more than once to establish a Western front to block Japanese expansion. He was wary of Britain, however, and the recent history of the Anglo-Japanese Alliance was never far from his thoughts. If Britain "is even suspected of preferring to play with Japan to playing with us," he said on 9 November 1934, he would "approach" Canada and Australia with the line that their "security is linked with us." FDR was unable by himself to devise a consistent line of policy on the Far East, and he so distrusted the State Department that he refused to allow Secretary Hull to take any initiative on his own. Roosevelt evidenced occasional interest in naval policy and strategy, and even discussed the Orange War Plan at his second cabinet meeting, but until 1939, when the New Deal was thoroughly tarnished, he concerned himself mostly with domestic issues and partisan politics.

One of the ironies of the decade was that Roosevelt, who later fulminated against "isolationists" of both parties, gave a lift to this bipartisan movement in 1934 when a handful of liberal senators proposed to legislate American neutrality in advance of a renewed European war. A Senate subcommittee chaired by two mavericks, Gerald Nye and Bennett C. Clark, investigated the profits of World War I arms manufacturers and insinuated that Wilson had acted under their influence in dealing with Germany and in deciding to enter the Great War. To prevent this history from recurring, the first Neutrality Act was passed by Congress and signed by Roosevelt in August 1935. It prohibited Americans from exporting arms to warring nations or sending ships into war zones, and was amended twice over the next two years to outlaw private loans or public credits to belligerents and to require them to buy American goods only on a "cash and carry" basis.[4]

With the Depression overshadowing foreign affairs, and the 1935 Neutrality Act defining America's view of the balance of power in Europe, naval policy became a prisoner of New Deal politics. Although he would later engage in massive deficit spending, Roosevelt insisted during his first spring in the White House that federal accounts be balanced, despite a raft of new relief programs. One of Hoover's legacies was a proposal, concocted by the Bureau of the Budget in 1932, to divide the fleet into thirds and to rotate each ship into a reserve status every third year. This scheme left Admiral Pratt aghast, but Hoover ordered him to implement it anyway on the grounds of fiscal economy. Pratt was ready with a rotation plan in May 1933 that promised to save about $50 million out of the Navy's annual appropriation of roughly $300 million. He exempted the battleships, carriers, and cruisers from the order, but the rotation plan tied up one-third of the fleet without operating funds over the next year and sharply curtailed the activity of the shore establishment. A congressional outcry forced the administration to modify the plan, but it symbolized the toll that early Depression politics took on the Navy.

Unilateral restraint clearly had failed to influence Japan's international behavior, and it did not fit the activist temper of Roosevelt's New Deal. A few months after his inauguration, FDR abandoned his retrenchment policy and boldly accepted the theories of a British economist, John Maynard Keynes, who claimed that deficit spending would spur economic growth when prices and wages were deflated. The capstone of this phase of the New Deal was the 1933 National Industrial Recovery Act, which allowed the president to set wages, prices, and manufacturing quotas and which provided funds for a massive public works program aimed at increasing employment and consumer demand. It also provided Chairman Vinson of the House Naval Affairs Committee with an opportunity to revive his 1930 "treaty fleet" plan and attach to the NIRA bill a provision giving the Navy $238 million for the "recovery" of naval shipbuilding.

Liberals, radicals, peace groups, and feminists—the intellectual mainstays of the New Deal coalition—attacked Vinson's measure. The powerful Women's Civic League, the YWCA, and the National Council of Jewish Women protested a renewal of the arms race in the Pacific. The Mother's Club of Bridgewater, Virginia, told Navy Secretary Swanson that they were not "raising our sons" to "fight the war the Vinson bill presupposes." Most labor unions, the preferred wards of the New Deal, favored arms reductions and an "isolationist" foreign policy, but the trades split over specifics. Inasmuch as the cost of labor represented about 85 percent of every dollar the Navy spent for shipbuilding, those union members who benefitted from this federal expenditure were eager for the work. The International Brotherhood of Boiler Makers, Iron Ship Builders, Welders, and Helpers was not alone in urging the president to procure more work for the shipyards. The Navy League was praised by Rear Admiral Ernest J. King as a factor in persuading Congress to keep the shipbuilding fund in the act.[5]

Roosevelt wavered. The NIRA was wildly popular and passed easily on 16 June 1933. He signed an executive order allocating $238 million to build thirty-three ships but assured liberals that the funds were being spent for "recovery," not "rearmament." "Japan cannot stand the cost of a naval race," he argued, and the new shipbuilding program would compel Tokyo to agree to a more restrictive naval disarmament system. At the same time, he told Swanson that he favored naval expansion and coyly acted as though he had put something over on other Democrats by claiming that the administration "got away with murder" in burying the shipbuilding monies in the NIRA legislation. Distortions of this sort characterized Roosevelt's entire presidency.[6]

The first task for Admiral William H. Standley as CNO was to shape a building plan around NIRA funding for thirty-three ships. Unfortunately, Standley, tactful and crafty, feuded with the new commander in chief of the U.S. Fleet, Admiral Joseph M. Reeves, with the bureau chiefs, and with the president's cousin, Henry Latrobe Roosevelt, the assistant secretary of the Navy, but somehow Standley always retained FDR's confidence. Standley's plan was to build the 19,900-ton treaty carriers *Yorktown* and *Enterprise*, four 10,000-ton *Omaha*-class cruisers, twenty destroyers, four submarines, and a pair of gunboats for the Yangtze Patrol. The 14,500-ton carrier *Ranger* joined the fleet in January 1934, and it was soon clear that she was too small to sustain the high tempo of air operations that Admiral Reeves expected of the heavy *Saratoga*-class carriers. The General Board had fixed the characteristics of the *Yorktown*-class carriers before the Bureau of Aeronautics was ready to interpret the *Ranger*'s early record, however, and as a result the two new vessels were in many ways legatees of Moffett's small-carrier policy. Because these ships would bring the fleet up to the carrier tonnage limit embodied in the Five Power Treaty, and because the battleship modernization program was nearly complete, after 1934 Admiral Standley replaced destroyers and submarines, increased the Navy's aircraft inventory, and prepared to replace the World War I-era battleships.

In 1933, a great tragedy led to a change of course for the Navy's air policy. On 4 April, three days before the superairship *Macon* was scheduled to make her maiden flight, her sister dirigible, the *Akron*, was struck by an electrical storm during a training flight and crashed near Dayton, Ohio, killing seventy-three men, including Rear Admiral Moffett, who had served for over a decade as chief of the Bureau of Aeronautics. Admiral Leahy, the chief of the Bureau of Navigation, persuaded FDR to name Rear Admiral Ernest J. King, an equally dynamic figure, as Moffett's successor. Thus, it became King's responsibility to establish the major directions for American naval aviation for the next decade. With Roosevelt's blessing, King reduced the Navy's commitment to the

Lighter-Than-Air program, although unfortunately he allowed the *Macon*, the last dirigible in the fleet, to continue to operate. On 12 February 1935, she suffered a structural failure during a storm and sank off Point Sur, California, a final blow that closed the book on the ill-conceived rigid airship endeavor. King accelerated the development of long-range, fixed-wing aircraft instead of dirigibles, encouraged the transition from bulky biplanes to more agile monoplanes for fighter and bomber types, and persuaded Congress to adopt a major expansion program for naval aviators so he could provide aircrews for the small carrier *Ranger* and the treaty-class carriers.

Marginal improvements in aircraft technology continued during the decade. Retractable wheels and enclosed cockpits were proven in the fleet when the FF-1, Grumman's first Navy fighter, began to operate from the *Lexington* in 1933. The first in a long line of successful Grumman fighters, she evolved over the next few years into the firm's first monoplane fighter, the rugged F4F Wildcat, which entered the fleet at the end of the decade. The newly commissioned *Ranger* did not operate torpedo planes because they were very slow, not very maneuverable, and inferior to the recently arrived, agile dive bombers. King did not give up on torpedo planes, however, and awarded Douglas Aircraft a contract to build the first all-metal monoplane to operate with the fleet, the long-range, three-seat TBD-1 Devastator torpedo bomber, which carried a secret Norden bombsight for level bombing operations and a deadly Mark XIII torpedo weighing 2,167 pounds. This aircraft and its ship-killing weapon greatly enhanced the lethality of the carrier air groups.

Admiral King realized that the treaty system had so inhibited the growth of the carrier force that it might be necessary to relieve the existing fleet carriers of secondary functions, such as very long-range scouting, antisubmarine duty, and bombing enemy bases. Thus, the mission of the carrier air group focused increasingly on attacking enemy capital ships and defending the battle line. King advanced the cause of flying boats to provide the fleet with safe, reliable long-range patrol bombers. In 1928, Bureau of Aeronautics engineers asked for bids to build a monoplane with a metal fuselage, which could take off from Alaskan waters and fly to the Canal Zone, or from Hawaii to the Philippines. A furious competition ensued between Martin Aircraft and Consolidated Aircraft, with each winning small contracts for successors to Consolidated's original PY-1, which first flew in 1929. Five years later, in January 1934, a patrol plane squadron flew from San Francisco to Pearl Harbor in a little over twenty-four hours, linking together for the first time the Alaska-Hawaii-Panama strategic triangle. When fitted with bomb racks and a Norden bombsight, the Consolidated PBY Catalina patrol bomber became the workhorse of the U.S. Fleet's Patrol Force.

Because the marginal benefits of new technology were accruing so fast, Admiral King purchased small numbers of each version of most of these aircraft types, with the exception of the PBY Catalina. This policy allowed him to provide the fleet with the most modern planes but denied the Navy the benefits of mass production and low unit costs. Admiral Standley, on the other hand, wanted to reduce the number of different aircraft types in the fleet, to avoid buying surplus planes, and to keep as many pilots as possible deployed with the fleet. The pilot training program was quite expensive, and the overall cost of naval aviation soared during the decade, at the expense of replacement shipbuilding for destroyers and submarines.[7]

Developing the long-legged PBY Catalina was only one element necessary to overcome Japan's geographic advantage in a Pacific war, an edge magnified by the passage of the 1934 Tydings-McDuffie Act granting independence to the Philippines in 1946. These and other developments moved Navy planners to revise the Orange Plan two years later. Again they assumed that Japan would invade Luzon in the Philippines at the outbreak of the war and proposed that the Army retire to Corregidor and the Asiatic Fleet withdraw slowly to Hawaii. The U.S. Fleet would then counterattack in a protracted island-hopping campaign from Hawaii to Luzon. The 1935 plan envisioned an "early movement of the fleet from the Pacific Coast [to Hawaii], . . . [the] ejection of Orange from the Marshalls, . . . a subsequent movement to the Carolines, . . . and a subsequent movement to the Western Pacific," Captain William S. Pye of the War Plans Division reported. He believed that Japan's relative naval power was improving as a result of her first rearmament plan, the U.S. Navy's failure to build up to a treaty fleet, and the likelihood that Japan would soon denounce the Five Power Treaty and fortify the mandated islands.

Overcoming Japanese ships and land-based aircraft in the Mandates and successfully assaulting a succession of well-defended atolls to obtain anchorages for the U.S. Fleet, while moving American land-based aircraft and logistics shipping westward with the battleship-carrier fleet, was all so immeasurably complicating the Orange strategy that Pye's version of the war plan did not even consider operations north of Mindanao. "How rapidly this can be done nobody knows," he lamented. "It may take two years, or it may be done in three months." Captain Robert Downes of the Naval War College predicted that the fleet would have a "hard time" during "an early advance to the westward" since it had "no adequate mining or sweeping material" or "mobile repair facilities," and the fleet marine force was "poorly equipped" and "the fleet train likewise." Without a vastly strengthened amphibious force and an enlarged fleet train, reasoned Captain Harold Train, "It is pretty well established that it could not be done." This, coupled with public evidence that the Japanese were about to initiate a new policy of naval expansion, increased the call on Congress and the White House to build up to a treaty fleet.[8]

Roosevelt, however, intended to renew and extend the 1922 Five Power Treaty at the second London Naval Conference by persuading Japan to accept something less than parity. Attempting to outwardly demonstrate stiffened resolve without paying the price, he belatedly endorsed the 1934 Vinson-Trammel Act, which authorized the construction of 102 ships so as to bring the fleet up to treaty limits by 1942. FDR then turned naval policy on its head, asking for appropriations in 1934 to lay down only one 8-inch gun cruiser and three 6-inch gun cruisers, and sharply questioned Hull when the State Department weighed in and demanded a stronger fleet soon after. Vinson was angry at the White House, but for the moment there was nothing he could do. The liberal vanguard of the New Deal reflexively opposed military spending. "It is wrong," wrote Sara Hubie, a New Deal social worker, "to spend money on armaments that is so much needed for direct relief." FDR's reaction was predictable. Upon signing the Vinson-Trammel Act, he expressed his "hope" that the second London Conference would "extend all existing limitations and agree to further reductions" and thereby allow him to cancel the Navy's shipbuilding program.[9]

Preliminary talks to set the stage for the second London Conference opened in late 1934. "I cannot approve, nor would I be willing to submit to the Senate . . . any new treaty calling for larger navies," FDR instructed Ambassador Norman Davis and Admiral Standley, the heads of the American delegation, at the White House on 3 October. Instead, Davis was "to propose to the British

and Japanese a substantial proportional reduction . . . of 20 percent below existing Treaty tonnage." Davis and Standley thought
that a collaborative Anglo-American approach might force Japan
to back down and agree to new limits, but this assessment reflected a misreading of the trend of Japanese policy. Claiming that the
NIRA program and the Vinson-Trammel Act signaled Washington's intention to renew the Pacific arms race, Japan's Diet enacted its first rearmament program soon afterward. Nor did the
Japanese flinch when Secretary Swanson threatened to fortify the
Philippines and Guam should Tokyo denounce the Five Power and
London Treaties and allow them to lapse. In London a few weeks
later, the Japanese demanded parity in all warship types, including
battleships and aircraft carriers, and at the same time proposed to
abolish all "offensive types." The Americans stiffly rejected both
proposals, as did the British, whose view of Japan had been soured
by the Manchurian affair. It now appeared that the conference was
deadlocked, but FDR instructed Davis and Standley to agree to a
compromise stitched together at the last moment by the British.
The English-speaking powers would acknowledge Japan's "right"
to parity if Japan would reciprocate by agreeing not to put that principle "in practice." Tokyo rejected this formula for appeasement,
however, and the preliminary negotiations ended on 19 December.
Ten days later Japan served formal notice that she would not be
bound by either the Washington or London treaties after 31 December 1936. FDR's naval diplomacy was in shreds.[10]

The breakdown of the preliminary London talks left FDR
with no choice but to ask Congress for an additional Navy appropriation in the 1935 Emergency Relief Act. This measure, enacted on 24 June 1935, provided funds for twenty-four ships, including one aircraft carrier, two light cruisers, fifteen destroyers, and
six submarines. Roosevelt's purpose was again to lever the
Japanese back into the corral of the Washington system when the
second London Naval Disarmament Conference met in December 1935, and he once more instructed his delegates to work toward a 20 percent reduction in overall fleet tonnage. His plans
were soon dashed when American naval intelligence provided the
White House with inaccurate but disturbing reports that Japan
had already violated the limits of the Five Power Treaty. "We had
adopted a policy of retaining the ratios of the defunct Limitation
of Armament treaties" without Japanese participation, Rear Admiral Joseph Taussig, the Assistant CNO, later charged.[11]

Roosevelt, still hoping to get Tokyo to sign a new treaty, was genuinely disturbed when the second London Naval Conference climaxed with Japan's predictable departure from the Washington system. On 7 December 1935, when the conference convened, Japan again formally demanded parity in all types, including capital ships. Ambassador Davis and Anthony Eden, Britain's foreign minister, were in "full agreement" on this issue and rejected Japan's demand on principle. The Japanese walked out on 15 January 1936, and Standley was elated. Now "we don't have to agree on anything," he told Lieutenant Commander F. B. Royal, "in which case after 1 January 1937, the sky will be the limit" on naval expansion. The Washington system, already weakened by the absence or withdrawal of Italy, Germany, and Russia, was now in ruins. This also heralded the end of Europe's reliance on the Versailles settlement in the Far East.

The Europeans took little notice of this, for they were beset by a quarrel of their own. Britain and France had large colonial empires in Africa but protested strongly, though unconvincingly, when Italy, a latecomer to the imperial race, invaded and conquered Ethiopia in 1935. British naval strategists, who saw Benito Mussolini's Italy as a counterweight to Germany, were especially appalled by this turn of events. Locked in a naval race in the Mediterranean, the French and Italians both eschewed fixed ratios for their fleets and showed little further interest in the system by which the major naval powers had institutionalized their own superiority. British and French policy over Ethiopia so antagonized Italy that she moved closer to Germany by signing the 1936 Anti-Comintern Pact.[12]

On 3 January 1936, only a few days before Japan's withdrawal, Roosevelt announced his annual naval program, which he claimed would provide for an "adequate defense" in order "to save ourselves from embroilment and attack." He increased the stakes for Japan by announcing that he intended to initiate a battleship replacement program. As passed by Congress on 3 June, the act authorized the replacement of a pair of battleships if any other signatory of the Five Power Treaty, such as Japan, embarked on its own replacement policy. A few days later, Roosevelt declared that the Navy would lay down twelve submarines, six destroyers, and the two new fast 35,000-ton *North Carolina* and *Washington*, the first battleships built in twenty years. This was intended to screw tight the pressure on Japan, but it only increased Japan's sense of insecurity and isolation and hastened the sense of urgency in Tokyo behind the second rearmament program.[13]

In spite of Japan's departure from the London Conference, Roosevelt, who was standing for reelection in 1936, still believed that he needed a naval disarmament treaty, any treaty, to please the left wing of the Democratic Party. At the London Conference, Ambassador Davis proposed "proportional reductions" among the fleets already afloat, a concept the British predictably rejected. The Americans, in turn, refused to allow Britain to increase her light cruiser tonnage under the formula embodied in the first London Treaty. Riposting, the Europeans asked the Americans to limit battleship displacement to 25,000 tons and to restrict battleships' main batteries to 12-inch guns, but Admiral Standley pointed out that the American fleet intended to fight at "extreme ranges" and needed at least 14-inch guns, which was, nevertheless, a reduction from the 16-inch limit embodied in the 1922 Five Power Treaty.

The final version of the second London Naval Treaty, which contained this qualitative limitation, was signed by the United States, Britain, and France on 25 March 1936. Later that year, however, FDR agreed to a Navy proposal that the new *North Carolina*-class fast battleships be armed not with twelve 14-inch guns but with nine 16-inch guns, since the Japanese refused to agree to arm their new battleships with 14-inch guns. Owing to Japan's decision to abandon the disarmament regime, an escape clause in the second London Treaty was set to be triggered by her refusal to comply with its provisions. "The treaty was so written," according to Captain Royal Ingersoll, one of the drafters, "that we could get out of every clause . . . if we found that Japan was in excess of the quantitative limits." As a result, none of its provisions ever came fully into force.

The treaty "means little as far as the Navy is concerned, except that it does give us a treaty and enables us to keep on talking about the Navy of treaty strength," Standley told Admiral Reeves, but "I have come to the conclusion that we could not have done what we have done towards building up the Navy if it had not been for the Treaty." Many disarmament proponents agreed with California's liberal Senator Hiram Johnson that the treaty was "just like a bed without sheets," but later that year the Senate approved this last interwar attempt to limit naval arms.[14]

Chapter Thirty-six

The Origins of World War II
1937–1939

The Depression completely overshadowed foreign affairs during the 1936 elections, and FDR was returned to the White House for a second term by a historic landslide. Repeated setbacks on domestic policy over the next two years considerably weakened his influence over Congress and his authority in setting foreign policy, however, and criticism of the New Deal's failure to end the Depression was so widespread that he turned his attention to the international scene to revive the Democrats' fortunes in 1940, a shift that coincided with the final collapse of the world power structure embodied in the Versailles and Washington treaties.

Adolf Hitler's Nazi regime had come to power in Germany in 1933, starting a series of events that revised Europe's postwar balance of power. Hitler denounced the Versailles Treaty, demanded that the 1919 settlement be revised, and two years later announced that Germany intended to rearm and would build among other things a dozen U-boats. The British also began to rearm, while attempting at the same time to appease Hitler by bringing Germany into the postwar naval arms limitation system with the Anglo-German Naval Treaty of 18 June 1935, but this failed to curb Germany's appetite for revision. The British had long intended to send a fleet to Singapore if war broke out with Japan, but Hitler's foreign policy and German rearmament now forced them to revise their strategy and to attempt to involve the Americans in the problems of Europe. Britain always "believed that the greatest security against war in any part of the world" lay in "the close collaboration of the British Empire with the United States," Prime Minster Stanley Baldwin told Parliament. But for the moment, American disinterest in Europe made such cooperation a practical impossibility.[1]

The limits on American involvement in European politics were made clear during the Spanish Civil War. This conflict broke out in 1936 when General Francisco Franco's army revolted against an anti-Catholic, socialist government in Madrid. Britain and France embargoed arms shipments to Spain; Russia, Germany, and Italy rushed aid to their respective partisans; and FDR imposed the Neutrality Acts to prevent either Franco's Falangists or the left-wing Loyalists from purchasing arms in the United States. He also used the occasion to announce on 18 September the reestablishment of the European Squadron, which thereafter consisted of an old light cruiser and two four-stack destroyers. These ships evacuated Americans from Spain and remained in European waters until the outbreak of World War II, making port visits and showing the flag. As a demonstration of American power, however, this move was so timid that it failed to reassure either the British or the French or to scare either the Germans or the Italians. Outside aid hardly influenced the outcome of the brutal three-year Spanish war, which ended in 1939 when Franco finally overran Madrid, dealt harshly with his opponents, and established a nonaligned police state. This left France bounded by three fascist powers: Germany, Italy, and Spain.

Joseph Stalin, Russia's dictator, who was during the 1930s bent on establishing a united front with the West against Hitler's Germany, was one of the losers in Spain. FDR consistently pursued a pro-Soviet policy, and he, too, was thinking of erecting a united front, although he intended to construct an anti-Japanese coalition. When Stalin asked for the U.S. Navy's help in rebuilding the small Soviet fleet in 1937, FDR eagerly agreed, but Admiral William D. Leahy, the new CNO, largely ignored White House policy and refused to cooperate with Stalin's New York-based purchasing agent. FDR told Joseph E. Davies, his ambassador to Russia, that he wanted some sort of "liaison" between Washington and Moscow to exchange plans on the "military and naval situations of the United States and the Soviet Union vis à vis Japan," and he ordered Admiral Harry Yarnell, the commander in chief of the Asiatic Fleet, to visit Vladivostok with the cruiser *Augusta* and four destroyers in July 1937. Nothing came of this naval diplomacy, how-ever. Stalin was concerned about Roosevelt's steadfastness and re-fused to be drawn into an anti-Japanese combination while Ger-many menaced his western front.[2]

FDR harbored a lifelong, fanciful hatred of the Japanese, and he was greatly alarmed by Japan's expansionist policy in China. In the span of just five years, Japan had denounced the Washington and London treaties, abandoned the League of Nations, and moved forcefully to increase its holdings on the Asian mainland. After establishing the puppet state of Manchukuo in 1933, the Japanese occupied Jehol Province north of Peking. Chiang Kai-shek's Nationalist regime in Nanking was faced all at once with challenges from the Japanese, Mao Tse-tung's Yunnan-based com-munists, and a cast of regional warlords on whom Chiang de-pended. Although Roosevelt despised the Japanese, he wanted to preserve the Washington treaty system and was reluctant to be-come involved in China. While it should "not be officially and for-mally affirmed," the Open Door Policy "involves no attention or thought . . . of taking [up] arms for the purpose of enforcing our views," wrote Stanley Hornbeck, the State Department's foremost China specialist, in 1934. For many years Navy and Army leaders had accepted the myth that the United States had vital interests in China, but the first months of the Sino-Japanese War exposed this sophistry.

Captain Laurence F. Safford, a legendary figure in modern naval intelligence, later claimed that Navy codebreakers deci-phered Japanese Fleet communications during its 1936 maneu-vers and that this gave Admirals Leahy and Yarnell advance warn-ing that Japan intended to invade China the following year. Nevertheless, the War Plans Division reported in April 1937 that "Japan is not at the moment willing to initiate hostilities with Chi-na." It seems clear that Japan had no intention of going to war with China until the Sian incident that summer, in which Chiang Kai-shek was kidnapped and forced to join the communists in an anti-Japanese coalition. Now Tokyo was forced to act. Japanese troops in Chinese uniforms staged a fake attack on the Japanese-held Marco Polo Bridge south of Peking on 7 July, and the leaders of Japan's Kwantung Army used this as a pretext to justify the occu-pation of Peking and an invasion of southern China. On 15 Au-gust, Vice Admiral Kiyoshi Hasegawa, who commanded the Japanese fleet off Shanghai, launched a drive aimed at overrun-

ning that city, destroying China's air force, and occupying
Chiang's capital of Nanking. Hasegawa landed troops who surrounded Shanghai, and his carrier-based aircraft bombed nearby
Chinese armies. To draw Japan's army away from North China
where he was weak, Chiang counterattacked around Shanghai.
Both sides bombed residential areas, but the Japanese quickly
gained command of the air, created terror in the city, severed the
Nationalists' railroad link between Nanking and Shanghai, and attacked shipping on the Yangtze.

Although Roosevelt condemned Japan's policy, he refused to
do more for the time being. The war was an "opportunity to force
Japan . . . to depart from the mainland of Asia," Leahy observed,
but only if Britain shared "the effort and expense." The American
presence on the scene was largely symbolic, however. Admiral
Yarnell's Asiatic Fleet consisted of his flagship, the cruiser *Augusta*, twelve destroyers, six submarines, and the four large Yangtze
gunboats and six small, shallow-draft gunboats that made up Rear
Admiral David M. LeBreton's Yangtze Patrol. There were 500
Marines in Peking, nearly 800 Army troops at Tientsin, and over
1,000 men of the 4th Marines at Shanghai. Yarnell was in Japan
when the fighting broke out around Peking, but he rapidly moved
the *Augusta* to Shanghai to protect the Americans in the International Settlement. He had the Marines set up barriers to prevent
the opposing troops from entering the American compound and
convinced Leahy to ship the 6th Marines from San Diego to
Shanghai later in the year.[3]

Secretary "Hull wants to do something about it all without
having any definite idea what to do," recorded Interior Secretary
Harold Ickes. Hull rejected several British proposals for an Anglo-
American show of naval force and refused to listen to a plan to impose economic sanctions against Japan. The Yangtze Patrol was "to
provide special protection for American nationals," he told Leahy,
"but [the] protection of property as such is not a primary objective." He hoped that Yarnell would "avoid becoming in any way involved in the conflict between the Chinese and the Japanese or
. . . interfer[ing] with their military operations." The conflicting
demands of Roosevelt's foreign policy meant that this was clearly
too much to expect.[4]

China was desperate. On 2 September the Japanese fleet
tightened its blockade of shipping on the Yangtze. After occupying Shanghai, Admiral Hasegawa's troops advanced up the

The Douglas TBD Devastator was the only U.S. Navy torpedo dive bomber in service in the 1930s and during the first six months of World War II.

President Franklin D. Roosevelt and Admiral William D. Leahy, chief of Naval Operat on board the cruiser *Houston* in the Caribbean in February 1938.

Yangtze Valley toward Nanking, and he ordered all foreign diplomats to leave the city before his carrier-based bombers launched an attack at noon on 21 September. Hull was "in favor of the Americans gradually falling back if the battle line approaches," observed Ickes, but realized that "the trouble is that there is no place for them to move back to." Yarnell raced the gunboats *Guam* and *Luzon* up to Nanking, and on the 20th, Ambassador Nelson Johnson and some of his staff took refuge on board the *Luzon* and watched the next day as the Japanese planes terrorized the undefended city. The Japanese Army then entered the old capital and randomly shot or bayonetted 200,000 Chinese in a bloody rampage known thereafter as the Rape of Nanking. After three months of bloody fighting, Chiang's best officers and 300,000 seasoned troops were dead, so in November he ordered the survivors to withdraw 500 miles up the Yangtze to Hankow, with the Japanese in hot pursuit. The *Luzon* transported Ambassador Johnson up to the new capital of Hankow on 22 November, but the *Guam* and *Panay* stayed behind to evacuate other embassy personnel.[5]

Before acting in any positive way, Roosevelt tested public opinion in a speech on 5 October 1937 by suggesting a "quarantine" of the aggressive powers. That address laid the groundwork for the American position at the Brussels Conference on the Far East, which opened on 3 November. Roosevelt failed utterly as a peacemaker, in part because he sent three envoys to the conference with two sets of instructions. It probably made little difference. Neither Britain nor France was willing to pressure Japan, and neither the Japanese nor the Chinese were willing to compromise, so the conference adjourned without reaching a settlement. So long as the British and the French resisted taking on any Far Eastern commitments, FDR decided, he could not answer Chiang's demand that Washington uphold the Open Door Policy. Treasury Secretary Henry Morgenthau, Jr., did arrange to loan China $25 million, and Roosevelt declined to apply the Neutrality Acts to the Sino-Japanese War, but he consistently refused to use American arms to compel Japan to respect Chinese territorial integrity. His reasoning was often circuitous. For example, he vetoed a proposed deployment of four more cruisers to the Asiatic Fleet to strengthen the American presence in the Far East on the grounds that they would be lost should fighting between Japan and the United States unexpectedly erupt.[6]

During the fighting on the Yangtze, American and British warships, including the *Augusta*, had drawn fire from both sides, moving Yarnell to announce that his ships would return fire "in case of [an] attack" against his forces or American nationals "by planes of any nationality." He reported to the Navy Department that "in giving assistance and protection our naval forces may . . . be exposed to dangers . . . but these risks must be accepted." Someone in ONI leaked Yarnell's strong statement to the press, and Hull complained to the White House that it was provocative. FDR was annoyed but did nothing to assure greater coordination in the future or to lay down a consistent line of policy. Things came to a head in October when, after considerable provocation, Yarnell threatened to have his ships return fire if the Japanese shot at them. Hull was livid, fearing that this would inflame the situation, but when he asked Admiral Leahy to muffle Yarnell, the CNO replied that he would not harry his Asiatic Fleet commander over such a trivial issue. At last, FDR directed Leahy to instruct Yarnell to follow the State Department's "moderate" line. Yarnell was itching to act, but he recognized the futility of the grand advance strategy still embodied in the Orange War Plan. Instead, he took up and fleshed out what he believed to be the strategic concept articulated in the president's recent "quarantine" speech. He proposed a military alliance among the United States, Britain, the Netherlands, and Russia, which would engage Japan in a "naval war of strangulation" against the Japanese economy to bring her to her knees without deploying the U.S. Fleet west of Pearl Harbor. Leahy, aware that Roosevelt liked to toy with blockade, quarantine, and other short-of-war measures that might contain Japan or Germany, urged him to read Yarnell's paper. Yarnell "talks a lot of sense," the president commented, but he did nothing to put the plan into effect.[7]

Yarnell's instant problem was that China was in chaos, and that Hankow was now threatened. Reacting to increased Japanese pressure to shut down the Yangtze Patrol and to recent Japanese attacks on British shipping on the river, on 1 December, Joseph Grew, the American ambassador to Japan, gave the government in Tokyo a schedule of the *Panay*'s upcoming movements. Ten days later, Lieutenant Commander James Hughes welcomed fifteen American refugees on board the *Panay*, which, in company with three self-propelled Standard Oil barges, steamed upriver to avoid Japanese artillery fire. Hughes anchored in the river about twenty-seven miles from Nanking late on the morning of 12 December. The weather was clear when, at 1330, he noticed that twenty-four low-flying Japanese Navy aircraft were approaching his well-marked vessel. Within minutes, they began to bomb and strafe the American formation. Hughes and his crew fought back courageously, but they could neither shoot down nor drive off their attackers with the gunboat's few machine guns. The *Panay* was struck by two bombs and strafing created a shambles topside. Ninety minutes later, Hughes ordered her abandoned, and at 1545 she went down, the first American warship to be sunk by enemy aircraft. Two sailors and one civilian were killed, and forty-three were wounded. The *Bee*, a British ship that went to her aid, was also fired upon. Japanese planes and a nearby patrol boat also shot at the survivors as they boated ashore, but after two frightening nights they were rescued by British and American gunboats and taken to Shanghai.

Reaction to the *Panay* incident was mixed. If the United States waited until Japan defeated China, argued Admiral Meyer, it would "be too late for us to act without serious opposition," thus leading to "war and disaster." A few at home urged action, but many Americans criticized the administration for keeping the Yangtze Patrol on station in the middle of a major war. It was "impossible" for the United States to be neutral any longer, Johnson told Washington, but all Hull would do was to issue a vague threat that the Navy would take "definite and specific steps" to protect American lives and property. Leahy wanted "to get the fleet ready for sea," but he was unwilling to do more without British assistance. Roosevelt agreed to test these waters. Captain Royal E. Ingersoll, the chief of the War Plans Division, was told to go on a secret mission to London to discuss plans for a combined Anglo-American naval demonstration against Japan and to notify the British that the U.S. Navy intended to exceed the tonnage and gunnery limits for battleships fixed by the 1936 London Treaty. In short, one result of the *Panay* affair was to force Roosevelt to abandon any hope that the Washington disarmament system could be reimposed on the Far Eastern balance of power.[8]

Ingersoll left New York at 1000 on 25 December and arrived in Southampton on the last day of 1937. He was aware that, for many years, the Admiralty had planned to send a battle fleet to Singapore if Japan threatened Britain's empire in the Far East. Assuming for the moment that that was still the case, Ingersoll and

Captain Tom Phillips, his British counterpart, drew up a plan for a combined Anglo-American distant blockade of Japanese trade. It called for the Royal Navy to cover the Singapore-Dutch East Indies-Australia line and for the U.S. Fleet to hold the Alaska-Hawaii-Panama strategic triangle. It did not predict how Japan would react, whether she would declare war, or against which blockading fleet she might strike first, nor was any mention made of an Allied offensive into the western Pacific. The plan was impractical, Ingersoll recalled. "It was too great a distance and too few ships to make it effective." Moreover, Prime Minister Neville Chamberlain, whose main worry was the growing crisis in Europe, refused to play. The Ingersoll-Phillips plan might exert a "steadying influence over the world," he thought, but blockading another power was an act of war and "it would be a mistake for us to send ships to the Far East . . . except in the event of a serious aggression by the Japanese." Ingersoll remained in London until 18 January 1938, then returned home and reported to Roosevelt. He "realized how shallow the whole thing was," Ingersoll observed. Furthermore, while Ingersoll was in London, Emperor Hirohito had issued an unprecedented personal apology for the *Panay* incident—timed to coincide with the Christmas season—and this defused American anger over the outrage.

To Admiral Yarnell, the Open Door Policy was now a dead letter, but he was still responsible for the thousands of Americans who remained in China. Japanese aircraft bombed Hankow so thoroughly that Chiang was forced to move his government once again in the summer of 1938, this time 600 miles up the Yangtze to the remote city of Chungking. Yarnell had sent the gunboats *Tutuila* and *Luzon* from Nanking to Hankow, and on 3 August the *Tutuila* transported Ambassador Johnson and his staff on to Chungking. She was stranded there by the blockade until 1941. FDR's only response to the bombing of Hankow was to issue a "moral embargo" on American arms shipments to Japan and Japanese-occupied areas of China.

Because the battle for Hankow was approaching the nearby city of Kinkiang, Admiral LeBreton stationed the gunboat *Monocacy* there to protect sixty American missionaries and businessmen in the area. Japanese operations downriver and Chinese mines upriver made it difficult for her to move, however. A few weeks later, several Chinese mines exploded eighty yards off the vessel and she was showered with fragments. After conferring with Yarnell and

Ambassador Johnson, however, LeBreton ordered the gunboat to remain at Kinkiang. The Japanese entered the city on 27 July, immediately severed contact between the *Monocacy* and the American community ashore, and refused to allow her to steam down to Shanghai for coal. Ambassador Grew asked the Tokyo government to order Japanese authorities in China to lift the blockade, but received a "categorical refusal." The gunboat was now almost out of coal, and Yarnell told Leahy that she had to move, so he set a deadline of 10 September and informed the Japanese. Hull's policy of appeasement was by this point so discredited that he raised no objections to Yarnell's ultimatum. Perhaps moved by Yarnell's stiff position, perhaps by broader considerations, the Japanese backed down, permitted renewed contact between the *Monocacy* and the Americans in Kinkiang, and soon lifted the blockade on her movements.[9]

Hankow fell to the Japanese on 3 October, only days after Canton surrendered, and Tokyo announced that it was establishing a "New Order in Asia" combining Japan, Manchukuo, and occupied China into an economic bloc for Japan's benefit. "The Japs are walking into a swamp," reported veteran China hand Marine Captain James McHugh, the assistant naval attaché in Chungking. "They cannot go ahead and they cannot turn back." McHugh, who had the confidence of Chiang and other Nationalist leaders, wanted the United States to "do something besides defend Chinese principles" by providing China with material support, but when Hull responded to Tokyo on 6 October, his sharply worded note merely cited Japan's violations of various treaties, reiterated the Open Door Policy, and made no mention of sanctions. The Japanese commanders in China were also emboldened by Washington's failure to retaliate after the *Panay* sinking. On 21 December, Admiral Hasegawa ordered that "foreign vessels . . . refrain from navigating the Yangtze" without explicit Japanese permission. Yarnell and his European counterparts agreed to cooperate but not to abrogate their nations' treaty rights in China, although Yarnell realized that Japan's control of the lower river meant that the Yangtze Patrol could no longer perform its mission.[10]

The old *Monocacy* reached Shanghai that winter, but on 10 February 1939 Yarnell had her towed out to deep water and sunk. By this time, Japan occupied all the seaports and the richer parts of China and had established a puppet regime headed by Wang

Ching-wei, an erstwhile Nationalist patriot. Chungking still held out. Japan was trapped in a war it could neither win nor willingly abandon. Nonetheless, Japan adopted an even more adventurous policy in early 1939, opening talks with Italy and Germany about a military alliance and occupying Hainan Island in the Tonkin Gulf. With Europe about to go to war, FDR ratcheted up the stakes by broadening the language of the "moral embargo" on arms sales to Japan and announcing in July that the United States would abrogate the 1911 Treaty of Commerce and Navigation with Tokyo in 1940. The timing of this step could not have been worse.

Only a month later, on 22 August, the world was stunned upon learning of the impending Nazi-Soviet Nonaggression Pact. Japan was outraged. She considered Germany her best friend and Russia the main obstacle to her dominance of East Asia. The Anti-Comintern Pact, long thought to embody a military link between Japan and the European Axis, was a dead letter. The government in Tokyo fell and was replaced by a set of more moderate figures who declared on 4 September, after Germany invaded Poland, that Japan would remain neutral in the European war and would focus instead on consolidating her Greater East Asia Co-prosperity Sphere. Roosevelt was pleased by this momentary détente but was not about to abandon China completely and confided to London that renewed tensions might cause him to impose trade sanctions on Japan and even move the U.S. Fleet from California to Hawaii. All this meant, of course, that the Open Door was firmly shut.

The *Panay* incident forced a painful reappraisal of American strategic planning in the Pacific. Observing that the U.S. Fleet was "woefully weak" without a base in the western Pacific, Rear Admiral Meyer of the 16th Naval District in the Philippines reflected a widely held Navy view that, once Japan had fortified the mandated islands, her fleet could cover all the approaches to the western Pacific. The 1935 revision to the Orange War Plan had altered the Navy's strategy accordingly. Instead of steaming directly from Hawaii into the western Pacific, the fleet was now to acquire bases in the Marshalls and Carolines before progressing into Philippine waters, although this would delay relieving the Philippines and require its garrison to hold out even longer. Meyer was not alone in urging the immediate development of a major naval base in the southern Philippines before the United States was faced by the "disaster" of Chinese capitulation. In late 1937, Admiral Leahy and General Malin Craig, the Army chief of staff, had ordered the Joint Army-Navy Planning Committee to reassess the Orange Plan. One Navy member proposed that the Army ship two divisions to the Philippines before war broke out, or, if that proved impossible, put another two divisions under the command of Admiral Arthur J. Hepburn, the commander in chief of the U.S. Fleet. Hepburn considered using the troops for an amphibious invasion of Truk, a Japanese port in the Caroline group. The Army totaled only 180,000 men, however, and Craig was intent on withdrawing from the Far East, so he rejected both ideas. He and Leahy concurred on the importance of defending the Alaska-Hawaii-Panama triangle, but the Army would no longer agree that it should defend the Philippines while the fleet secured advance bases in the central Pacific before challenging the Japanese fleet at sea. For the moment, joint planning was at an impasse.[11]

Having failed to persuade the Army to accept his revisions of the Orange Plan, Leahy joined with Congressman Vinson and exploited the Sino-Japanese War in convincing Congress to pass the Vinson-Trammel Act in 1938. When Admiral Claude Bloch took command of the U.S. Fleet that year, the total number of American warships stood at 533. This was an increase of about 100 vessels over the past five years, an expansion funded largely by the 1933 NIRA legislation and the much smaller 1935 Emergency Relief of Public Works appropriation. The early "treaty" carriers were completed in 1938, with the commissioning of the 19,000-ton *Enterprise* and *Yorktown* and the 14,700-ton light carrier *Wasp*, and this allowed the Navy to turn to the pressing question of battleship replacement. In October 1937, Roosevelt had agreed to ask Congress to increase the rate of replacement to two battleships each year. After the *Panay* incident, Leahy proposed to double this figure for the coming year and to build two new, fast 35,000-ton *South Dakota* treaty-class battleships. On 21 January 1938, Congress approved the regular annual appropriation, which included funds to construct two battleships, two light cruisers, eight destroyers, and six submarines. One week later, after Captain Ingersoll reported that his mission to London had failed, Roosevelt asked Congress to authorize a 20 percent increase in fleet tonnage and to appropriate funds immediately to build two more *South Dakota*-class battleships, two more 20,000-ton *Hornet* treaty-class carriers, nine light cruisers, twenty-three destroyers, two submarines, and 1,000 naval aircraft. Ingersoll had not returned from England with completely empty hands, as he had persuaded the British to allow the United States to invoke the escape clause in the 1936 London Treaty and thus lay down battleships displacing more than 35,000 tons.

In attempting to persuade Congress to enact the 1938 naval authorization bill, FDR stressed the need to strengthen coastal defense and contended that the fleet at the time was sufficient to defend only one ocean. He also claimed that naval expansion was necessary to maintain the existing treaty ratio with Japan, whose ambitious shipbuilding program was well under way in 1937. The second Vinson bill, Roosevelt insisted, would "keep any potential enemy many hundred miles away from our continental limits." Isolationists, who opposed American involvement in Europe and distrusted British imperialism in the Far East, were concerned by publicity about the Ingersoll mission and angered by hints that the president planned to join with Britain and intervene on behalf of China against Japan. While Hull admitted to Republican Congressman Ludlow that American and British policy followed "parallel lines," Leahy, whose greatest virtue was not truth telling, soothed the Senate with the hairsplitting testimony that "we have no alliances against—or understanding with—any other nation, nor are any contemplated." On its own, he maintained, "the Navy has no foreign commitments," and he asserted that "there has been no talk of giving or receiving assistance" with the Royal Navy. These fabrications calmed the brewing storm on the Hill. Concern was aroused again, however, when on 14 February 1938, three American cruisers stood into Singapore for the opening there of the Royal Navy's new graving dock. Only Hull's honey-coated testimony supporting Leahy's assertions prevented a virtual revolt in the Senate against the administration's foreign policy. Congress was not wholly unsympathetic to the apparent goals of Roosevelt's policy, but his devious methods and unpredictable political tactics were fueling the growing distrust of the administration on the Hill.[12]

Interservice rivalry also complicated naval expansion in 1938. For instance, Major General Henry H. Arnold, the chief of staff of the Army Air Corps, lobbied against the Second Vinson bill on the grounds that the president was shorting land-based air power that, owing to the absence of overseas bases, could provide superior coastal defense and hemispheric security without entangling America in foreign wars. Nevertheless, Leahy understood that the "opposition in Congress . . . does not amount to very much in the way of votes" and Congress easily passed the Second Vinson-Trammel Act in May 1938.

All the powers now were rearming at a furious pace, but Hitler had yet to employ force to overturn the Versailles settlement and resorted instead to a threat-laden diplomacy to gain his objectives. He exploited Chamberlain's policy of appeasement and divisions among Germany's sometime opponents to extort an agreement from Britain, France, and Italy at the Munich Conference in September 1938, which transferred the Sudetenland from Czechoslovakia to Germany. Chamberlain announced that the agreement would lead to "peace in our time," but he nonetheless hurried home and accelerated British rearmament. For the moment, public opinion in Europe and America viewed the Munich settlement as a just way of conciliating Germany and expected it to produce a general relaxation of tensions. Roosevelt was quick to congratulate Chamberlain. "We in the United States rejoice with you and the world at large," he cabled the prime minister. Like other Western statesmen, however, FDR worried that Hitler planned to make even more immoderate territorial demands, so he took the first in a long series of steps aimed at shifting part of the fleet from the Pacific to the Atlantic. He and Leahy agreed to establish an Atlantic Squadron consisting of the old battleships *New York* and *Arkansas*, seven heavy cruisers, and an equal number of destroyers, thus doubling the size of Rear Admiral Alfred Johnson's Atlantic Training Detachment. The president also reaffirmed an earlier directive that the Navy stage its annual 1939 fleet exercise in the Caribbean.[13]

The prewar Navy buildup was accelerated in December 1938 when FDR sent to Congress a report on American naval bases prepared by Admiral Hepburn, the former commander in chief of the U.S. Fleet. The report listed improvements, costing $326 million, needed by twenty-six bases on both the Atlantic and Pacific coasts, in the Pacific, and in the Caribbean. Because the Philippines were to become independent in 1946, Hepburn had turned his attention to Guam. A major base there would not unduly commit the fleet to the western Pacific, but it might support the retirement of the Asiatic Fleet from the Philippines and keep alive the Orange Plan's offensive concept. Hepburn's strategy was ill advised inasmuch as Japanese forces in the surrounding Marianas and Carolines could easily isolate Guam and sever its communications with Hawaii. Even in the unlikely event that this did not happen, a counteroffensive against Japan could not rely on Guam alone. Moreover, although the Five Power Treaty's nonfortification article had lapsed at the end of 1936, the Hepburn Report measure was openly provocative at an inopportune moment. Roosevelt himself trimmed the sum for Guam to only $5 million, and in February 1939 Congress rejected it completely on the advice of the State Department. Most of the other projects Hepburn recommended were approved, however, and the War Department convinced Congress to authorize $500 million to bring the projected strength of the Army Air Corps up to 5,500 planes.

Admiral Leahy, alarmed by the Munich crisis, was now determined to update American strategic planning, and he brought Captain Charles M. Cooke, who had served as the U.S. Fleet's first war plans officer, into the Navy's War Plans Division and instructed him to overhaul the old Orange Plan. For three decades, Navy planners had viewed a Pacific war as pitting the United States against Japan, with neither side aided by allies. This informed Navy positions on such diverse issues as retaining a naval base in the Philippines after independence and the offensive strategy embodied in the Orange Plan. Prior to the 1936 Anti-Comintern Pact, the authors of the various Orange Plans assumed that the California-based U.S. Fleet would operate in the Pacific with little worry about the security of the East Coast or the Monroe Doctrine. The Anti-Comintern Pact, the Rome-Berlin Axis, German rearmament, Hitler's 1938 diplomacy at Munich, and Anglo-French appeasement now caused Cooke to ask how the Navy might approach a war between the Anti-Comintern powers, Japan, Germany, and Italy, and a coalition consisting of Britain, France, Russia, and, possibly, the United States.

Captain Russell Willson, the naval attaché in London, reported in January 1939 that the Admiralty was so alarmed about a European war that it was ready to abandon its longtime plan to reinforce Singapore during a Far Eastern crisis, and Commander T. C. Hampton, a British envoy, reiterated this to Leahy during secret talks in Washington in June. Leahy told Hampton that he had established an Atlantic Squadron earlier that year under Admiral Johnson, and that the small carrier *Ranger*, four heavy cruisers, four destroyers, and two land-based patrol plane wings were being transferred to the Atlantic. "In the event of a war in Europe," he said, "it was the present intention of the president that the U.S.

Fleet should be moved to Hawaii as a deterrent to Japan" so as to allow the Royal Navy to concentrate against Germany and Italy. The CNO was clearly uneasy with this prescription, and this caused him to ask more formally what American strategy should be if the United States became embroiled in a two-ocean war between the slowly emerging coalitions.[14]

The Army, with few divisions to play with, was not eager to address this grand problem, so Cooke suspended meetings of the Joint Board's Planning Committee until his Army counterparts agreed to order the planners to study it. Army planners, applying the Orange Plan to a coalition war, reasoned that the first priority was to defend the Caribbean and the second was to protect the Alaska-Hawaii-Panama strategic triangle. Inasmuch as the Orange Plan assumed that neither Japan nor the United States would be supported by allies, Cooke argued that its venerable strategic prescriptions were no longer valid. Germany's relentless drive to revise Versailles, together with British, French, and Russian weakness, meant that the U.S. Navy might have "to carry out the operations of Atlantic War." Cooke proposed in April 1939 that the Joint Board abandon the Orange Plan and instruct the Joint Planners to prepare five Rainbow Plans, each of which was to assume that either the United States or its opponent was a member of a military alliance. The prospect of becoming involved in a war between global coalitions was truly daunting. "Our present naval strength and building program would probably for the immediate future be sufficient" to conduct an Orange war, noted the Assistant CNO, Rear Admiral Robert Ghormley, but it was "insufficient to undertake an offensive naval war simultaneously in the Atlantic and Pacific." It was not until 30 June 1939, when Rainbow Two was outlined, that the Joint Planners considered how the U.S. Fleet might operate in conjunction with Britain, France, and, possibly, Russia against the Anti-Comintern powers. For the moment the planners decided that the Allies should shoulder the major naval burden in the Atlantic and Mediterranean, while the Americans took the offensive against Japan in the Pacific.[15]

Munich also alarmed Roosevelt, but he reacted slowly. He encouraged Britain and France to resist Hitler's March 1939 demand that Poland cede area surrounding the German-speaking port of Danzig to the Third Reich, and he tried without success to persuade Mussolini to arrange another European peace conference. FDR's own ambivalence and congressional support for the

Neutrality Acts prevented the formulation of a more determined policy. Public opposition to new commitments or intervention did not extend to the issue of preparedness, however. After Munich, many on the Hill proposed vast increases in American military spending. Although Congress resisted plans to fortify Guam or to resume conscription so as to increase the size of the Army, a measure expanding the Army Air Corps was enacted in 1939, as was a major naval shipbuilding program that appropriated funds to build the newly-designed 33-knot, 45,000-ton, post-treaty-class battleships *Iowa* and *New Jersey*, eight destroyers, and eight submarines. Congress also agreed to modernize five aging World War I-era battleships and construct a third set of locks for the Panama Canal wide enough to accommodate the new fast battleships.

The Joint Board's concern about defending the Monroe Doctrine against the Axis was examined in the spring 1939 Fleet Problem XX in the Caribbean, which was intended to test "control of the Atlantic Ocean and South America." The political scenario assumed that an Axis battleship-carrier fleet was escorting a Brazil-bound convoy carrying arms to pro-Axis rebels who threatened Rio's pro-American government. At first, Admiral Edward Kalbfus, a fine battleship tactician, chained the aircraft carriers to the battle line, but later in the exercise he allowed the carrier commander, Vice Admiral Ernest J. King, to form his own task force, which included the *Enterprise* and the *Lexington*, and to operate independently. King decided on an unprecedented division of labor and shifted the *Lexington*'s bombers to the *Enterprise*, replacing them with a squadron of fighters. While the *Lexington*'s air group defended the task force, the *Enterprise*'s bombers successfully raided the opponent's patrol plane bases. Before the battle lines clashed, both sides exposed so many cruisers to aircraft that the function of cruisers as scouts or elements of advance screens for the battleships was left in serious doubt.[16]

Before the battleship formations closed to within 100 miles of one another, Admiral Kalbfus cleared the air of planes, a decision he justified on the grounds that the air forces were exhausted. During the remainder of the Fleet Problem XX, one team's battleships successfully defended the movements of an invasion convoy, leading the commander in chief of the U.S. Fleet, Admiral Bloch, to conclude that the influence of carrier aircraft and submarines on fleet operations was overrated. Kalbfus' decision was entirely in keeping with contemporary naval doctrine. For one thing, to save weight, armored decks had not been installed on American carriers, although the Bureau of Ordnance repeatedly pointed out to the Navy's General Board that wooden flight decks were vulnerable to enemy dive bombers. Several years of operating one or two carriers suggested that a protracted battle would exhaust the air groups and that at some point only the heavily armored new fast battleships would be left to pursue and annihilate the enemy's line. Lastly, neither American nor Japanese carriers could conduct nighttime or foul-weather air operations, but the rugged fast battleships, equipped with improved gunfire directors, radar, and modern radios, could continue, despite poor visibility, to chase, engage, and annihilate a hostile fleet.

New technology was rapidly transforming tactics and strategy, however. Many Navy men understood at the time that the introduction of radar into the fleet was inaugurating a revolution in naval warfare. L. A. Hyland, a scientist at the Naval Research Laboratory, had observed in 1930 that signals from a radio direction finder were deflected by a passing aircraft, and, alert to the military implications of this discovery, other NRL scientists constructed a working radar set for use by ships several years later. The first operational naval radar system was installed in the destroyer *Leary*. Under ideal conditions, it could locate incoming aircraft at a distance of about fifteen miles. Tests of this equipment led Admiral Leahy to approve a crash program that not only aimed at improving the performance of the Navy's radar sets but also at getting them out to the fleet. By late 1941, radar systems had been installed in several destroyers and cruisers and four American battleships, but the tactical function of radar was as yet imperfectly understood.

The Navy also placed great faith in a new torpedo that had been developed by the Newport Torpedo Station. Between the wars, the Bureau of Ordnance supplied submarines in the fleet with two types of torpedoes: an older model that employed a contact exploder to detonate TNT, and the Mark XIV, a newer weapon that was longer, faster, heavier, and more lethal. With features akin to the multispeed destroyer torpedo, the Mark XIV might be set to run at a speed of either 46 knots over 4,500 yards or at 31 knots over 9,000 yards. The major advantages of the Mark XIV were its Torpex charge, a compound that eventually replaced TNT in 1943 and produced about twice the explosive force, and the Mark VI magnetic exploder, a device secretly developed by the Navy after

World War I. The German Navy had used magnetic exploders for some of its mines during the Great War, and shortly after the Armistice, the Bureau of Ordnance experimented with similar mechanisms to produce an influence explosion. This work took on added urgency after battleship building ceased following the Washington Conference in 1922 and most naval powers turned to adding structural protection against torpedoes to their existing battleships. From German theory the Americans devised the Mark VI exploder, which used variations in the direction and intensity of the earth's magnetic field around a ship's hull to trigger a mechanical pistol that set off the explosive charge.

On 8 May 1926, a Mark XIV torpedo fitted with a Mark VI exploder sank an old submarine hulk during secret trials off Newport. Rear Admiral Leahy, who became the chief of the Bureau of Ordnance the following year, was satisfied with this result and decided that the costs of additional tests could not be justified. Not until 1942 was the Mark VI used again at sea against a real hull. And Leahy's successors at the Bureau of Ordnance, especially Rear Admiral William R. Furlong, decided to withhold the Mark VI exploder from the fleet on the grounds of security. Instead, the bureau fitted the torpedoes it supplied to the fleet with dummy warheads, and planned to ship the real warheads out to the fleet in a hurry hard upon a declaration of war. Furlong was particularly resistant to criticism of the Mark XIV. A new bureau chief, Rear Admiral William P. Blandy, reversed this policy in 1941, and a few magnetic exploders were issued to the fleet and training in their use was arranged for a small number of submarine officers at Newport that year. However, the lack of realistic testing and any outside evaluation of either the torpedo or the exploder set in train events that had devastating consequences for American submarine warfare within a few short years.

Interwar submarine building policy was victimized by indifference, disputes over battle doctrine, and a serious split among the Navy's submariners over the necessary displacement and function of the vessel. The gradual resolution of the question of displacement led to the development of the large general purpose fleet submarine. The huge experimental V-class boats of the 1920s could conduct long-distance Pacific patrols, but they were very difficult to maneuver. This in part led to the search for a smaller submarine, one capable of making at least 17 knots and conducting 12,000-mile war patrols. "Such a vessel approaches the type the construction of which would be inaugurated on a large scale at the declaration of war," Commander Cooke told the General Board in 1930. One of the reasons behind the success of this effort was the Navy's decision to craft its own design specifications for new submarines rather than to simply accept the vessels offered by Electric Boat, which had a virtual monopoly of postwar American submarine construction.

In 1933, Congress authorized the Navy to lay down the first of twenty-six *P*-class and *Salmon*-class submarines built over the next six years. They were propelled on the surface by four lightweight Winton diesel-electric engines that turned a generator linked to a new powerful 250-cell Gould battery, which in turn powered the underwater electric-drive propeller shaft. The *P*-class and *Salmon*-class boats were fitted with the first submarine fire-control system, the Mark I Torpedo Data Computer, which took information from the periscope or sonar system on a target's bearing, range, and angle, and computed the proper setting for the torpedo gyroscope to intercept the opposing vessel. The last milestone in interwar submarine construction came in 1940, when Rear Admiral Richard Edwards and Captain Charles Lockwood persuaded the General Board to approve the air-conditioned, 1,500-ton *Tambor*-class fleet submarines, which were armed with six torpedo tubes forward and four aft. After twenty years of trial and error, the Navy had at last developed an attack submarine with the endurance and offensive punch to operate throughout the Pacific.[17]

The decade of the Great Depression witnessed the renewal of American naval power, though at a pace so uneven and unguided that the Navy was clearly not prepared on the eve of World War II to deal with a two-ocean conflict. Under the Butler Cruiser Bill and the two Vinson-Trammel acts, between 4 March 1933 and 1 September 1939, the Navy had constructed four aircraft carriers, seventeen heavy and light cruisers, twenty-seven destroyers, twenty-one submarines, and thirty-seven minor vessels. These figures also illustrated what Roosevelt had not done, owing to his decision to pursue disarmament for several years after the postwar system ceased to impose any restraint on Japanese or German behavior. Although studies initiated by Admiral Standley in 1933 demonstrated that, contrary to long-held opinion, a 30-knot battleship could be built within treaty limits, FDR refused to approve a replacement program until the entire naval disarmament structure was in shambles.

Nor did he take note that the introduction of the fast battleship meant that nearly the entire fleet would have to be replaced, not just the battle line but also the slower cruisers, destroyers, and supporting ships, which were expected to maneuver ahead and around the battleships. Two years after the collapse of the Washington system, eight fast *North Carolina-* and *South Dakota-*class battleships were under construction, but Congress had been asked to authorize only one more carrier, thirty-eight destroyers, twenty submarines, and six light cruisers. In almost every type of warship, the Japanese either deployed more ships than the U.S. Navy or enjoyed parity.

Naval rearmament under the New Deal clearly owed more to Congressman Vinson than to Roosevelt. Unlike FDR, Vinson never vacillated in his dedication to building up to a treaty fleet. And, although even a treaty fleet was certain to be inadequate to execute the Orange Plan, Roosevelt was immune to the restraints of this asymmetry and would soon be eager to increase the burden of American naval obligations.

Chapter Thirty-seven
The Neutrality Patrol
1939–1940

On the morning of 1 August 1939, Admiral Harold R. Stark succeeded Admiral Leahy as chief of naval operations. Tactful, hearty, and cunning, Stark had a rare talent for forging good policy in the absence of clear guidance. Only one month before Stark became CNO, Secretary of the Navy Claude Swanson had died. Frank Knox, the Republican candidate for vice president in 1936, declined the appointment for the time being, so FDR promoted Assistant Secretary Charles Edison to the cabinet. Less interested in policy than inventions and research, Edison knew that he was warming a chair. That same month, Brigadier General George C. Marshall was given four stars and the office of the Army's chief of staff. Roosevelt encouraged Stark and Marshall to work closely together and decided to take a more direct hand in strategic planning by ordering the Joint Army-Navy Board to report directly to the White House on matters of strategy.

This shuffle of American military figures came as Europe braced for war. German troops had occupied Czechoslavkia in March, and soon Hitler demanded that the Poles cede the corridor leading through Poland from East Prussia to the port of Danzig. Poland, already allied with France, refused, and the British issued a guarantee to the Poles at the end of the month. Britain and France then sent a military mission to Moscow in the summer to ask Stalin to defend Poland, but the Poles refused to permit the Red Army to march across Poland and take up positions on the German frontier. The collapse of this diplomatic effort led Stalin to accept Hitler's proposal to partition Poland, an arrangement incorporated into the Nazi-Soviet Nonaggression Pact of 27 August 1939. In short, the two powers ignored at Versailles—Germany and Russia—now joined arms to revise the outcome of World War I.

The German naval training ship *Schleswig-Holstein* stood into Danzig on 1 September 1939, and at 0456 she opened fire on a small Polish garrison on the outskirts of the port, the first shots fired in World War II in Europe. Soon after, the German Army invaded Poland. Both Britain and France declared war on Germany, but they could not prevent the Germans from overrunning Warsaw two weeks later. The French assumed a defensive posture along their Maginot Line, while the British sent a small army to France and the Royal Navy imposed a blockade on Germany and mopped up German shipping. In October after defeating Poland, Hitler, instead of attacking in the west, offered the Allies peace terms, which they rejected. Inasmuch as the Allies were unready to take the offensive and the Germans chose not to do so, many in America ascribed this to a stalemate and Senator Borah called it a "phony war." President Roosevelt declared American neutrality and invoked the Neutrality Act, to which he had an aversion inasmuch as it prohibited private or public credits to any belligerent, the use of American shipping in trade with warring powers, or the export of "arms, ammunition, and implements of war" to either side. American public opinion clearly sympathized with Britain and France. FDR asked Congress to give him discretion in applying the arms embargo. In January 1940 Congress amended the law, over the objections of a small but vocal isolationist minority, to allow "cash and carry" transactions.[1]

When Germany and Britain declared retaliatory blockades and established rival war zones, Roosevelt reacted by announcing on 5 September that the United States was creating a Western Hemisphere Neutrality Zone off the Atlantic and Gulf coasts within which belligerent warships would not be allowed to operate. Following the 1938 Munich crisis, FDR had privately predicted that Hitler, once he dominated Europe, intended to move against the Western Hemisphere, a bizarre assumption that the State Department nonetheless supported. Germany had tried for nearly a decade to forge close ties with Brazil, with only marginal success. The Argentines, who admired Mussolini's Italy, shamelessly took

German military aid but refused to move into Berlin's orbit. A misreading of these events and a renewed dedication to the Monroe Doctrine led Americans to try to prevent the Axis powers from gaining military positions in the New World. Captain Alan G. Kirk, the talented naval attaché in London, was mindful of this concern and cautioned that a German victory in Europe might lead eventually to Italo-German military operations in South America. To check such a move, on 2 October Secretary Hull cajoled most of the Latin American republics into issuing the Declaration of Panama, which contained a prohibition against belligerent operations within 300 miles of North, Central, or South America or the Caribbean islands.

Roosevelt announced that defensive patrolling of this immense Neutrality Zone would be, for the time being, the unilateral responsibility of American naval forces in the region, but Admiral Alfred Johnson's small Atlantic Squadron, established one year earlier, consisted of only the small carrier *Ranger*, a few pre-World War I battleships, and a handful of cruisers and destroyers. At FDR's request, Stark renamed this force the Neutrality Patrol, but the CNO was dismayed at Roosevelt's bemused indifference to the Navy's claim that Johnson did not possess enough ships to conduct such operations. To reinforce the Neutrality Patrol, Stark asked Congress for funds to recommission and modernize forty overage, four-stack World War I-era destroyers, the backbone of the Navy's escort force reserve. In addition, he began to transfer a few lesser ships and supporting vessels from the Pacific Fleet to the Neutrality Patrol. As a result of these measures, Admiral Johnson soon reported that he was able on occasion to extend his North American neutrality patrols beyond the 300-mile limit. What Roosevelt did not tell the public was that the true mission of the Neutrality Patrol was to assist the Royal Navy in locating and sinking German shipping in western hemisphere waters, operations that continued in mid-1940. Not all Navy men were eager to conduct these patrols, and Rear Admiral William Sexton, the chairman of the General Board, pointed out that areas such as the Neutrality Zone "have no justification in international law" and that the United States had "vigorously protested the establishment of such zones" in the past.[2]

Stark, who was mostly concerned about events in Europe, felt that an Allied defeat would create opportunities for Japan to exploit in the Far East, since the U.S. Fleet was "not now fully pre-

pared" for a Pacific war. Soon after the fall of Poland, Chairman
Carl Vinson of the House Naval Affairs Committee urged Stark to
send up to the Hill a new naval program; this bill asked for 400,000
tons of additional naval shipbuilding over the ceiling of 1.5 million tons established in 1938, an increase of about 25 percent. He
also asked for monies to improve the naval base at Guam. Vinson
pushed this through the House, but it then fell into the clutches
of Massachusetts Democrat David Walsh, an eccentric isolationist
who chaired the Senate Naval Affairs Committee. Although Walsh
delayed the bill, it was Roosevelt who, at the critical moment, told
Vinson to slash the measure in the interests of economy. Once
again, FDR's inability to hew to a consistent line of policy put the
brake on American naval rearmament. The funds for Guam were
excised, and the tonnage increase was reduced to 167,000 tons,
about 11 percent of the total fleet authorization. The seeming
stalemate on the Western Front of the "phony war" lessened the
sense of urgency, and Walsh allowed the bill to languish in the Senate until June 1940.[3]

This stalemate bothered Winston Churchill, the new First
Lord of the Admiralty, and in early 1940 he stitched together a
plan to land British and French troops in Norway to cut off
Swedish iron ore shipments to Germany. When Hitler learned that
the Allies were about to land, he ordered the German Army to occupy Denmark on 9 April and his fleet and air force overran Norway from Oslo to Narvik soon after. Chamberlain was persuaded
by Churchill to counterattack at Narvik and at Trondheim to the
south, but the British did not enter Narvik until 28 May. By that
time the front in France had collapsed, and London had already
decided to withdraw from Norway. One German army had crossed
into Holland on the 10th, drawing an Anglo-French force into Belgium, while a second German army slashed through the Ardennes
Forest into northern France, cutting off the Allied forces in Belgium and menacing Paris. The British withdrew to the Channel
coast and were successfully extracted by the Royal Navy and the
Royal Air Force at Dunkirk. Paris was now exposed. On 11 June,
Mussolini declared war, and the French made ready to capitulate
two weeks later. Alsace and Lorraine were ceded to Germany and
the French agreed to pay for German occupation of the northern
third of France until the war ended.

With the Germans holding the Belgian and French coast, the
newly formed British government headed by Churchill now

feared an invasion. To prevent this, they needed to maintain control of the airspace over southern England and the English Channel. The Admiralty knew that the German fleet had been damaged during the Norwegian campaign but worried that the newly reconstituted French collaborationist government of Marshal Henri Pétain, which ruled two-thirds of France and its colonial empire from the resort of Vichy, might hand over the French fleet to the Germans. Roosevelt was also concerned, and he instructed Admiral Leahy, the new ambassador to Vichy France, to warn Pétain not to allow the French fleet to fall into German hands. When France surrendered on 25 June, most of the French fleet had escaped to its North African bases, although a few ships were scattered to other ports in Egypt, the West Indies, and England. French warships at the British fleet base at Alexandria, Egypt, were interned, but the British believed that they needed to neutralize the rest of France's fleet. To this end, Churchill approved a number of operations to capture or disable the overrated French fleet. These attacks met with mixed tactical success and wholly alienated French opinion from the British for a time.

U.S. Navy strategists were profoundly shocked by the fall of France. They had fully realized the implications of the German breakthrough in mid-May. In London, both Ambassador Joseph Kennedy and Captain Kirk reckoned that Britain was on the verge of defeat that summer, and Kirk even predicted that the Germans would invade in August. Kennedy saw this as a reason not to tie American policy too closely to Britain, whereas Kirk viewed it as evidence that military aid was desperately needed. If France's impending surrender led to peace between Germany and Britain, Captain Cooke worried on 22 May, the "loss of the British fleet, or the loss of its effective use, points to the collapse of the British Empire with the consequent complete collapse of the world economic and political structure." Only the United States could prevent this from transpiring, by adopting a Europe-first strategy. As a first step, Cooke urged that a joint Army-Navy mission be sent to Europe to evaluate whether the French and British intended to resist, a proposal that ultimately led in August to Rear Admiral Robert Ghormley's mission to London as special naval observer. For the moment, however, the Navy's most immediate concern was disposition of the French fleet. The War Plans Division proposed on 17 June that the entire U.S. Fleet, less one battleship division, be transferred to the Atlantic. Admiral Stark discussed this with FDR the following day, but the president was more concerned with how Japan would react and tentatively agreed to the move only if France's capital ships fell into German hands.[4]

The German defeat of France galvanized American public opinion behind preparedness. Most Americans still wanted to avoid a war but had the sinking sense that it might not be possible. FDR tried to assemble support for military assistance to Britain. In a speech at the University of Virginia on 10 June, he promised to mobilize the American armed forces and provide military and naval aid to those obstructing the "gods of force" and asked Congress to pass a $1 billion National Defense Act for the War Department. Five days later, Congress hastily passed the Navy's 10,000-Plane Act, which provided for the procurement of that many naval aircraft for the new carriers and forty-eight nonrigid airships for the antisubmarine Neutrality Patrol.[5]

Despite his strong rhetoric, FDR gave no guidance to either the War or Navy departments on how to carry out his new policy of supporting Britain. Captain Cooke, who had heard the president's Charlottesville speech, returned to Washington and urged Stark to take advantage of the opportunity offered by Roosevelt's comments. The CNO jumped at the chance "whole hog." On 14 June, the day before FDR signed the 1940 Naval Authorization Act, Stark and Cooke drafted a formidable shipbuilding program aimed at creating two separate, balanced fleets. Assuming that one command would be conducting major operations in Europe, while another was executing some variant of the Orange Plan in the Pacific, Stark estimated that both fleets would need about eighteen fast aircraft carriers, over 200 small carriers, battleships, cruisers, destroyers, and submarines, and a huge fleet train. At a cost of $4 billion, the program would take eight full years to complete, and would increase the total fleet tonnage by 70 percent. Rear Admiral King spurred the General Board into approving the plan overnight. The White House played only a passive role in the passage of the Two-Ocean Navy Act. FDR's only contribution to this important measure was to give the bill his blessing during a brief telephone conversation with Stark. As presented to Congress by Chairman Vinson, the legislation gave the president the unprecedented authority to shift funds between one class or type and another and to reduce or increase the numbers of ships within a class to be constructed. Amidst the panic of the summer, the Two-Ocean Navy Act sailed through Congress, overcoming minimal opposition.[6]

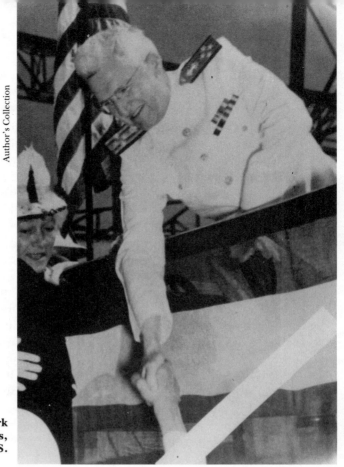

ral Harold R. "Betty" Stark
hief of Naval Operations,
-42 and commander, U.S.
Forces, Europe, 1942–45.

The Two-Ocean Navy Act met one goal of Roosevelt's preparedness policy, but other legislation contained language that reflected congressional unease about aid to Britain. Already, pro-
British writers were urging the Navy Department to transfer
American destroyers to the Royal Navy, whose strength in escorts
was being sapped by the neutrality of the French fleet, Italy's entry into the war, and the escalating German U-boat campaign. Senator Walsh inserted into the National Defense Act of 1940 a provision prohibiting the overseas transfer of any American ships,
munitions, or other war material, unless either the CNO or the
Army chief of staff attested that it was "not essential to the defense
of the United States." The Walsh amendment unintentionally put
the CNO in the awkward position of possessing the legal authority to contravene the policy of his commander in chief.[7]

With a presidential election approaching, FDR needed to
broaden the political base of his cabinet, douse the hot embers of

a personal feud in the War Department between Secretary Harry Woodring and Assistant Secretary Louis Johnson, and create bipartisan support for his legislative program. To do all these things at once, he convinced Henry L. Stimson to replace Woodring at the War Department and Frank Knox to replace Edison as secretary of the Navy. Both Stimson and Knox were liberal Republicans who espoused assistance to Britain, and Knox strongly supported a deal concocted by Roosevelt and Churchill in July to transfer fifty overage, four-stack, World War I-era American destroyers to Britain in return for ninety-nine-year leases on British bases in the West Indies, Bermuda, and Newfoundland.

In June, Stark had agreed to a covert purchase of 50 Navy planes and 750 bombs by Britain, but the "destroyer deal" raised greater issues. For one thing, he had just persuaded Congress to pay for refitting these ships for the Neutrality Patrol. For another, the Walsh Amendment was intended to bar such military aid. To cut this Gordian knot, FDR had his attorney general provide the CNO with an opinion that the bases to be leased were of greater value to American security than the old ships. With Stark's consent, but without any understanding that he was initiating a long-term American policy of overseas military assistance to friendly regimes, Roosevelt on 2 September 1940 consummated the Destroyer Deal.[8]

The peril to Britain seemed to intensify. As this bargain was maturing, on 27 May, Ambassador Joseph Kennedy in London secretly warned Roosevelt to expect the fall of Winston Churchill's newly formed government after France surrendered. With an excess of pessimism, Kennedy believed that "England's only remaining defense is courage . . . not arms." Churchill was supported by Parliament, however, in his rejection of German peace terms in June and in his declaration that Britain would continue alone her war against Germany. Despite these brave steps, Captain Kirk reported from London that the Admiralty expected the Germans to invade the British Isles during August.[9]

The first phase of European war was, in fact, almost at an end. With the conquest of central and western Europe complete, Hitler relaxed, some of the wartime economic measures imposed in Germany were allowed to lapse, and Germans began to enjoy the fruits of victory and their new détente with Russia. Hitler was annoyed by Churchill's rejection of his peace terms, but Germany was not in any way prepared to invade Britain, although Hitler had his military chiefs ready a plan for a landing codenamed Sealion. Admiral Erich Raeder, the commander of the German Navy, knew that his fleet could not wrest control of the English Channel from the Royal Navy, so Hitler turned the problem over to the German Air Force. This provided Reichsmarshal Hermann Göring with the opportunity to boast that bombing Britain would either force London to the peace table, cripple her ability to conduct future military operations, or pave the way for the German Navy to launch the Sealion invasion. Although the German Air Force was not configured to conduct protracted strategic bombing operations, Hitler adopted Göring's strategy anyway, and the air Battle of Britain began in late August 1940.

Churchill would later concoct the fable that the Royal Air Force Fighter Command's victory over the German bombers that fall saved the British Isles from an invasion, but he admitted in private at the time that this was not so. In the contest for air superiority over the Channel and southern England, the British held all the trumps. They were building more aircraft and training more pilots for their fighter squadrons than the Germans and, for the tasks at hand, their aircraft were superior to the German types. The British operated an efficient, radar-based early warning system, and their air marshals devised and followed a rational strategic plan to attrite the enemy and conserve their own fighters. At no time was Fighter Command so battered and in danger of losing so many aircraft that it would be incapable of successfully opposing an invasion. Admiral Raeder knew that the German Navy did not have enough ships, minesweepers, minelayers, troop transports, or specialized landing craft to put the necessary ten divisions ashore on widely scattered, well-defended English beaches, as the Sealion plan called for. Neither did the Germans have enough cargo ships to support ten divisions ashore, even for a few days, or nearly enough antisubmarine escorts to cover the movements of their freighters and tankers back and forth across the English Channel at night.

The German and British air forces dueled over the Channel in daylight, but the Royal Navy owned the night. British ships had swept the Channel and French coasts of barges and small ships in May and mined many of the best Dutch, Belgian, and French anchorages and their own ports in June and July. Nearly 700 fast British patrol boats prevented the Germans from sweeping these minefields or conducting their own countermining operations.

The Germans were not even strong enough in the air to shut down daytime British minelaying operations altogether. Because the German Air Force was preoccupied with Fighter Command in July and August and with bombing London after mid-September, and because the Germans possessed few effective anti-ship weapons and could not operate against darkened, maneuvering warships at night, the Royal Navy operated in its home waters, in the Channel, and off the coast of Europe throughout the air Battle of Britain with near-complete immunity, and in doing so made the danger of an invasion truly negligible. Indeed, nighttime merchant convoys sailed up and down the Channel that summer and fall suffering remarkably few losses. And last, but not least, over 100 destroyers and the Home Fleet's powerful fast battleships and heavy carriers stood poised in the North Sea, ready to descend and engage any approaching German invasion force, although the Home Fleet's commander told the Admiralty in mid-September that the danger of a landing was so slight that he should be allowed to detach some of his destroyers and organize midocean escort groups for inbound merchant convoys.

Churchill, who wanted American aid, now walked a tight-rope—he had to calm his countrymen and alarm Washington. He was remarkably successful. Should Britain fall, the danger to the United States seemed inestimable, and the loss of the British fleet enhanced the threat exponentially. Churchill promised that this would not happen, but by raising the issue he fed Washington's fear that, in a world ulcerated by uncertainty, it just might. To improve Anglo-American coordination, Roosevelt and Stark sent a special naval observer, Rear Admiral Robert Ghormley, to London in mid-August for conversations with the Admiralty. Ghormley eventually discounted the probability of a German invasion, but in his messages to the Navy Department he underlined the bleak military prospects faced by Britain if the war lasted.

When Stark turned his attention from Europe to the Far East, he focused on Japan's willingness to exploit the weakness of the colonial powers in Asia to her advantage. Both Stark and Roosevelt wanted to fill in this new vacuum of power and deter further Japanese expansion. Admiral Leahy's protégé, Admiral James O. Richardson, had taken command of the U.S. Fleet in San Diego in late 1939, and he planned to conduct exercises in Hawaiian waters the following March and steam back to California on 9 May 1940. Roosevelt had agreed as early as 1938 to a Navy plan to send the U.S. Fleet to Hawaii in the event of a crisis in Europe, and when British and German forces clashed in Norway in April, the CNO ordered Richardson to keep the fleet at Pearl Harbor temporarily. Leahy had devised this strategy in early 1938 and explained it to the British in secret conversations that summer. Stark, who apparently agreed with the concept but not with Roosevelt's timing of the move, hoped that it would dissuade Japan from occupying the Dutch East Indies or French Indochina. If Britain also surrendered, however, Stark planned to bring the U.S. Fleet into the Atlantic.[10]

None of this sat well with Richardson, who was wedded to the old Orange Plan strategy of concentrating the fleet on the West Coast. If war with Japan broke out, he intended to raid the Japanese naval base at Truk in the Carolines and follow this up with a grand progression from the Marshalls to the Philippines. In June 1940, Richardson was thrown into a veritable paroxysm by Roosevelt's decision to station his fleet at Pearl Harbor, and he quarreled with Stark's explanation that the move had been taken "because of the deterrent effect which . . . your presence may have on the Japs going to the East Indies." Throughout the summer and fall of 1940, Richardson's protests accumulated in the Navy Department and grew so shrill that Navy Secretary Edison during his last week in office unsuccessfully lobbied the president to replace Richardson with Admiral King.[11]

Richardson repeatedly suggested withdrawing the battleships to San Diego while leaving the submarines in the western Pacific to conduct a campaign of "long-range interdiction of enemy commerce" at the outbreak of war. Then he reversed course and told Admiral Hart that he wanted to send a carrier, four cruisers, and nine destroyers to the Philippines to strengthen the exposed Asiatic Fleet. These wavering opinions alarmed Stark, who finally ordered Richardson to come to Washington to explain his position in person. At the White House on 8 October, FDR explained to Richardson the reasons for leaving the Battle Force at Pearl Harbor, a position that Navy Secretary Knox and Admirals Stark and Leahy supported. Richardson disagreed loudly, arguing that the U.S. Fleet should be readied in peacetime to take the offensive the moment war broke out. Basing the fleet at Pearl Harbor, he insisted, "was undertaken under a completely false premise." No one disputed Richardson's brief that the San Diego-San Pedro complex was a better base than Pearl Harbor, but the Washington command uniformly agreed that the fleet was now obligated to more important tasks. Richardson rejected Stark's concept of splitting the fleet between the Atlantic and Pacific, basing the latter ships in Pearl Harbor to deter Japan and accepting a defensive posture in the Pacific if this failed. Later that day, Leahy apparently suggested to FDR that Richardson be relieved, and Stark moved swiftly to find a replacement.[12]

The CNO had another problem. Rear Admiral Hayne Ellis had recently replaced Admiral Johnson in command of the growing Neutrality Patrol, but Stark was unhappy with Ellis' uninspiring, unimaginative leadership. He had already looked about for a relief for Ellis with the thought of establishing an Atlantic Fleet the following year. FDR agreed to this plan and simply admonished Stark in effect to pick the "meanest SOB's in the Navy" to command the Atlantic and Pacific fleets. Admiral King, now sitting on the General Board, and Rear Admiral Husband Kimmel, who commanded a cruiser force in the Pacific, both fitted this requirement to perfection. Kimmel was already at Pearl Harbor; King, who had just taken command of the Atlantic Neutrality Patrol, was the Navy's only flag officer with command experience in both aviation and submarines. Therefore, Stark told Kimmel to relieve Richardson and ordered King to move up to the Atlantic Fleet command when it was established on 1 February 1941.[13]

In discussing the deployment of the Pacific Fleet with Roosevelt, Stark repeatedly pointed out that now more than ever foreign policy and naval strategy were closely related. If the fleet were split up and a large number of heavy ships were transferred to the Atlantic, for example, then the president might compensate by "maintaining pressure on Japan by the restriction of exports." Stark's voice joined a chorus of other anti-Japanese advisers who had pressured FDR in 1940 to allow the 1911 Treaty of Commerce with Japan to lapse. Exports to Japan of strategic materials and scrap metals were also halted, although no lid was placed on shipments of American oil or most refined oil products. Roosevelt clearly viewed an oil embargo as a major weapon to be wielded only at a moment of the greatest international stress.

The Pacific Fleet's presence in Hawaii reminded Prince Konoye, the Japanese prime minister, about Washington's interests in the Pacific basin, and paradoxically led Japan's naval strategists to consider how to neutralize this threat. Tokyo was less impressed by the World War I-era battleships at Pearl Harbor, however, than by the utter debility in the Far East of her old European rivals and by the strength of the revisionist powers, Germany and Italy, with whom she signed the Tripartite Pact in October 1940. Crafted to ensure American neutrality, this military alliance committed each of the three Axis powers to declare war against the United States if she attacked any of the other signatories. For his part, Hitler saw this as a means of threatening Britain at the reaches of her empire while using "Japan as a club to be held over" the United States. The Tripartite Pact in effect ended the possibility that the U.S. Navy would have the luxury of waging a war on one front.[14]

The European war brought American foreign policy and military strategy to the fore during the 1940 presidential elections and helped to crystallize grand strategy. Roosevelt broke tradition and announced his "availability" for an unprecedented third term. The Democratic platform supported American military and financial aid to Britain and China to resist the Axis, but FDR promised that American "boys are not going to be sent into any foreign war." By nominating Wendell Wilkie, a liberal who agreed with FDR's foreign policy, the Republicans unwittingly denied the country a straightforward choice between noninvolvement and intervention.

Once Roosevelt had been reelected in November, Stark decided to try to bring some coherence to the contradictory policies of rearmament and overseas military assistance in the form of a collaborative Anglo-American strategy. "Not all sure that the British Isles can hold out," he warned that "they do not realize the danger that will exist should they lose in other regions." Stark assumed "that the continued existence of the British Empire . . . combined with building up a strong protection in our home areas, will do most . . . to promote our principle interests." If Germany defeated Britain, then the United States would soon face a hostile world and the probability of going to war with one or more of the remaining Great Powers. "If Britain wins decisively against Germany, we could win everywhere, but . . . if she loses . . . while we might not lose everywhere, we might possibly not win anywhere." But Britain lacked the manpower and industry to reenter German-occupied Europe, thus making American air, land, and ground operations in the Atlantic theater essential. Stark estimated the cost of reentering Europe to be so great that American forces in the Pacific would have to "remain on a strict defensive" until Germany surrendered. Stark's seminal paper, later named Plan Dog, thus called for "an eventual strong offensive in the Atlantic as an ally of Britain and a defensive in the Pacific." Plan Dog was the basic articulation of a "Europe-first" strategy.[15]

Stark reviewed Plan Dog with FDR and he appeared to agree with its prescriptions, and, although he never formally approved it, he sometimes acted as if he had. There were three instant results. First, on 16 December at a meeting of the military chiefs, their civilian secretaries, and Hull, it was agreed that "this emergency could hardly be passed over without this country being drawn into the war eventually." Stark estimated that Britain could tolerate no more than six months of current shipping losses, so the group asked FDR to "consider some method for our Naval cooperation in convoying of shipping to the British Isles." One month later, Roosevelt announced at a White House meeting that the Navy was to stand on the defensive in the Pacific, not reinforce the Asiatic Fleet, and prepare to convoy transatlantic merchant shipping to Britain. Second, expedient aid to Britain was replaced by the Lend Lease program, which Roosevelt sent up to Congress in January 1941. Although Americans sentimentally favored Britain's cause, the Lend Lease bill sailed through Congress mostly because of economic reality. The New Deal, largely dead since 1938, had failed to end the lingering Depression, but in 1940 the economy began to revive as a result of orders for arms and munitions from Britain and from the War and Navy departments. Lend Lease also appeared to be a mechanism to adjust those tensions between American mobilization and overseas military assistance so evident in the haggling over the Destroyer Deal. Alloyed with Lend Lease, of course, was the defense of the transatlantic sealanes, for British losses in 1940 to U-boats and the German air force threatened in some measure to degrade the coin of American assistance.[16]

The third outcome of Plan Dog was the ABC staff conference in Washington in January and February 1941 between representatives of Britain's chiefs of staff and the Joint Army-Navy Board. The British gleefully agreed to Stark's concept of a grand strategy based on the principle of Europe-first, but Britain's specific needs were more difficult for the Americans to meet. The Admiralty badly needed assistance in escorting transatlantic merchant convoys, and Roosevelt on 16 January accepted Stark's case that planning for Atlantic Fleet escort operations had to proceed. This would be the task of King's newly created Atlantic Fleet. On the other hand, the British Empire's security in the Far East was moored to the defense of her naval base at Singapore, but the British fleet was fully occupied in the Atlantic and Mediterranean at the same time that Japan's occupation of northern French Indochina menaced Malaya.

To neutralize this Japanese threat and obstruct a Japanese invasion of Southeast and South Asia, the British wanted Stark to send the Pacific Fleet from Hawaii to Singapore. He refused to do this on the grounds that American national interests required that the fleet defend the Alaska-Hawaii-Panama strategic triangle and support the withdrawal of the Asiatic Fleet from the Philippines. Moreover, he was already planning to transfer a large fraction of the Pacific Fleet to the Atlantic over the coming year, and he optimistically predicted that American operations in the central Pacific at the outbreak of war with Japan would relieve any pressure on Britain in the Indian Ocean. Stark and, to a greater degree, General Marshall, were uneasy about Britain's involvement in the Mediterranean war against Italy, a peripheral strategy that prevented London from dealing decisively with the U-boat offensive in 1944 and from sending a powerful fleet to Singapore to defend their Far Eastern empire. Supplementary conversations exposed a host of differences about procurement issues, and many of these were resolved, but the ABC secret staff talks failed to agree on the "skeleton plan of operations" that Stark had hoped the negotiators would devise. Instead, the talks stimulated the American conviction that the British were overly committed to the Mediterranean and not only wanted to defeat the Axis but also hoped to lever the United States into underwriting the postwar continuance of the British Empire in the Far East.[17]

Chapter Thirty-eight

The Battle of the Atlantic
1940–1941

On 1 February 1941, Admiral Ernest J. King took command of the new Atlantic Fleet with orders to end the neutrality patrols and prepare to escort American transatlantic shipping within two months. All fifty ships of the destroyer deal had been decommissioned in Canada and turned over to the Royal Navy and the Canadians by this time, but British shipping losses were still growing at an alarming rate. The naval war was still "extremely critical," reported Captain Kirk from London on 24 March. The British fleet was being battered everywhere. Britain's 8th Army drove the Italians out of Cyrenaica in January 1941, but Hitler countered by shipping General Erwin Rommel's Afrika Korps to Libya to shore up the Axis defenses. Despite this new threat, Churchill withdrew troops from North Africa to check Germany's successful occupation of Greece and Crete, a move that failed completely and cost the Royal Navy dearly.[1]

The Royal Navy was mauled in the Mediterranean in 1941 and so was unable to staunch the minor German submarine campaign in the North Atlantic against British shipping that year. The German effort was relatively small because Admiral Raeder had persuaded Hitler before the war to rebuild the German fleet around the Z-Plan, a program that aimed to build up a balanced fleet and be ready to challenge the British sometime after 1948. One result of this misguided policy was that Rear Admiral Karl Dönitz' U-boat arm still represented only a small fraction of the prewar German naval effort, and when the war began in 1939, a mere fifty-seven submarines were in commission. Recalling the failure of commerce raiding during the Great War, Hitler assigned submarine construction a low priority and only eighteen U-boats were built in 1939, but with the loss of only nine submarines, the Germans sank 509,000 tons of Anglo-French shipping that year.

Germany's submarine offensive received an invaluable advantage in June 1940 when France surrendered and turned over to the German Navy its bases on the Bay of Biscay. Dönitz transferred most of his operational U-boats there, and Hitler agreed to construct fifty new submarines. In addition, Göring stationed several German Air Force patrol squadrons in Norway, along the English Channel, and around the Bay of Biscay, both to support the U-boat campaign and to conduct independent air attacks on British ports and coastal shipping. Twenty-two U-boats were lost that year, but the Germans sank 2.48 million tons of Allied shipping. This figure declined to 2.33 million tons in 1941 because of Hitler's decision to divert his air forces to Greece and North Africa in the spring, Germany's invasion of Russia in June, and greatly improved British defensive measures. During 1941 the British fleet and the Royal Air Force sank a total of thirty-five U-boats.

A number of factors in addition to ill-conceived grand strategy accounted for Britain's distress in 1941. The Royal Navy's infant Fleet Air Arm had been absorbed by the newly established Royal Air Force during World War I and thereafter was the untended orphan in an organization dedicated to developing its land-based heavy bomber force. Even after the Admiralty recaptured naval aviation in 1937, building carriers and aircraft took second place to a lavish battleship construction program. And, soon after the war broke out in 1939, it was clear to many that the aging First Sea Lord, Admiral of the Fleet Dudley Pound, was unequal to his heavy burdens. He exerted only a negative influence over Prime Minster Churchill, seldom advanced new ideas or new men, and established a highly centralized directorate, which orchestrated several disasters. The Royal Navy, troubled by bad policy and poor leadership at the top, was near the end of its tether. After the passage of the Lend Lease Act in 1941, Pound looked to American industrial production and operational support to rebuild the British fleet and salvage the Admiralty's outrageously ineffective antisubmarine campaign.

Roosevelt's unwavering policy of support for Britain and

World War II, 1940–1941

Stark's Plan Dog strategy led to the large-scale transfer of American ships from the Pacific to the Atlantic during 1941. Captain Kirk pointed out early that year that in spite of the Destroyer Deal, the British badly needed more escorts but would have trouble manning them. Stark saw no alternative but to have the Atlantic Fleet ready itself to prevent a breakout by Germany's heavy ships and begin escorting British convoys later in the year. On 2 April he persuaded Roosevelt to approve moving the carrier *Yorktown*, the battleships *Idaho*, *New Mexico*, and *Mississippi*, four cruisers, and two destroyer divisions from the Pacific to the Atlantic. At the same time, King extended his patrol zones westward in an effort to increase surveillance and hamper U-boat operations.[2]

The following day Stark warned Admiral Husband Kimmel in Hawaii that "the question as to our entry into the war now seems to be 'when' and not 'whether,'" one of a series of messages intended to put Kimmel on notice that the president had subscribed to Stark's strategy of Europe-first. Stark also cautioned Kimmel to expect additional transfers of ships to the new Atlantic Fleet. With a "force utterly inadequate to do it on any efficient scale," Stark told Kimmel that King would soon nonetheless be assigned to escort North Atlantic convoys. It was ironic that part of the redeployment plan was delayed when Japan signed a Nonaggression Treaty with the Soviet Union on 13 April 1941, causing Secretary of State Hull to complain that weakening the Pacific Fleet at the moment would be judged by Japan as "a sign of weakness." FDR agreed, and he ordered Stark to transfer only the *Yorktown* to the Atlantic, a move that was essential, since the *Ranger*—one of only two small Atlantic Fleet carriers—had to be overhauled. The Americans then awaited the Axis' next move.[3]

It came in Europe. Admiral Leahy, the ambassador to France, reported that Vichy was committed to collaboration with Germany, raising anew the fear that the French fleet might fall into German hands, or that Pétain might allow German ground and air forces to operate from French North Africa against Britain's bases at Gibraltar and Malta and against British shipping. Roosevelt's response was twofold. First, on 13 May, he agreed to transfer one battleship division and a carrier to the Atlantic, and Stark ordered Rear Admiral H. Kent Hewitt to take this formation through the Panama Canal in secret to join the Atlantic Fleet in June. This movement completed a larger redeployment that, during the spring of 1941, saw the shift of about one-quarter of the

Pacific Fleet to the Atlantic. Stark assessed this as insufficient, however. If Britain's plight worsened during the summer, he intended to move another third of the Pacific Fleet to the Atlantic in the autumn. Although redeployments were suspended until July owing to the crisis in the Far East, between April and October 1941 King's Atlantic Fleet was nevertheless increased in strength to nearly 200 ships. Roosevelt predicted to Ambassador William Bullitt, then working as an assistant to Navy Secretary Knox, that the result of this strategy would be to bring the United States into the European war through the vehicle of an "incident" that he was "confident that the Germans would give us."[4]

Roosevelt's second response to Vichy's collaborationist policy was to instruct Admiral Stark and General Marshall to prepare to occupy the Portuguese Azores within thirty days. This plan, codenamed Grey, called for King's Atlantic Fleet to land 28,000 troops, about half Army and half Marines, in the Azores, overcome any resistance, and establish American air and naval bases there. Stark was appalled by FDR's orders. Although the landing might be opposed, there were only twenty transports of various pedigrees and the fast liner *America* in the entire theater, the War Department did not have enough equipment or ammunition to support the occupation, and there was no time for a training exercise. King had supervised an amphibious training exercise in the Caribbean in early February—one of the last of the fleet's interwar landing exercises—with Marine Major General Holland Smith's 1st Marine Division, but a great deal more needed to be done before the Atlantic Amphibious Force would be ready for a forced entry. In his report on that event King noted the absence of suitable attack transports and landing craft, misunderstandings about combat loading and unloading, poor ship-to-shore communications, and inadequate naval gunfire support. The material condition of the ten Navy transports was "grotesque," wrote one observer. When queried about the Azores plan, King warned that he had only one small carrier and so could not both defend his ships and prevent opposing aircraft from attacking the beachhead and that, if the Germans stationed air forces at French Dakar, they might attack the invasion force well before it arrived in the Azores. The whole scheme was "a most hazardous undertaking," he told FDR. General Marshall, the Army chief of staff, was prepared to resign over the issue. Roosevelt was apparently immune to the advice. It was ironic that he abandoned the plan only after he mistakenly hinted at it in a nationwide radio address on 27 May, and the Portuguese reacted by announcing that they were reinforcing their Azores garrison and would defend the islands "against attack no matter what side."[5]

Dismayed by this turn of events, and annoyed by Stark's opposition to the Azores invasion, FDR decided to occupy Iceland instead. He had approved the occupation of Greenland by a small American garrison on 9 April 1941, a step taken with the agreement of the Danish government-in-exile in London to prevent Greenland from falling into German hands. Eleven days later he extended the Western Hemisphere Defense Zone, hitherto the Neutrality Zone, across the Atlantic to include the Azores, Greenland, and Iceland. British troops had occupied Iceland, another Danish territory, soon after the war began, but in June 1941 these soldiers were badly needed in Egypt to stop Rommel's drive toward Alexandria and the Suez Canal. Iceland was within range of German airbases in northern Norway, where five German divisions were stationed. However, the Germans were in no position to exploit their apparent advantage, inasmuch as the German Navy could not operate safely in the area. This made Iceland attractive to Roosevelt and King. The CNO, on the other hand, disliked the Iceland stroke, considering it a foolish waste of resources. Nonetheless, the American occupation of Iceland had been agreed on during the ABC staff talks, and the timetable was set for a movement in September 1941.

The Royal Navy's dismal performance against Germany that spring upset this schedule and unnerved the Americans. Britain's Home Fleet was supposed to be blockading Germany's bases, but the German heavy cruiser *Hipper* broke out into the Atlantic in February and sank seven ships of convoy SLS.64 due east of the Azores and then returned safely to Brest. Meanwhile, the pocket battleship *Admiral Scheer* was out hunting in the Indian Ocean, where she sank seventeen British merchant ships. On 15 March, the *Scheer* and the *Hipper* steamed onto the Grand Banks, only 500 miles from Newfoundland, destroyed or captured sixteen ships, and scattered several convoys. Late that month they returned to Norway via the Denmark Strait, the Admiralty being diverted at the moment by the movements of the heavy battlecruisers *Gneisenau* and *Scharnhorst*, which were now operated out of occupied Brest. At the same time, the Royal Navy was feeding aircraft into Malta, but the Axis air forces in Italy destroyed these planes almost as soon as they arrived. In addition, Britain's Mediterranean Fleet was roughly handled by the Germans during the poorly managed battle for Crete. The Germans sank three cruisers and six destroyers and seriously damaged two battleships, one aircraft carrier, and six frontline cruisers. But what thoroughly alarmed the U.S. Navy was the British fleet's error-ridden hunt for the battleship *Bismarck*, a late May misadventure. Although the *Bismarck* was sunk, the action cost the Royal Navy the loss of the battle cruiser *Hood* and damage to the *Prince of Wales*.

American naval leaders were distressed by the Royal Navy's performance against the powerful but unsupported, unescorted German raiders. FDR had told reporters at a White House dinner on 15 March that he intended to assure "the survival of the vital bridge across the ocean—the bridge of ships that carry the army and food for those who are fighting." That same day, he declared

The 1,060-ton destroyer *Chew* (DD-106), a typical World War I-era *Wickes*-class four-stack destroyer, was launched on 26 May 1918 and commissioned on 12 December, just days after the Armistice had been signed. Between the wars she served with the U.S. Fleet in the Pacific, and on 7 December 1941 came under attack by the Japanese at Pearl Harbor. During World War II, she escorted battleships, carriers, troopships, and convoys between Hawaii and the Pacific coast.

a national emergency and ordered all defense forces to repel acts of aggression directed against the Western Hemisphere—which he once again extended far out into the Atlantic. Stark told King, then conducting exercises in the Caribbean, to return to Norfolk, strip his ships for war, apply camouflage paint, and prepare for active duty. About this time, Roosevelt also decided to occupy Iceland so as to position an American battleship-carrier task force in the vicinity of the Denmark Strait in the event of another German breakout. He laid his plan before the British ambassador on 28 May— the day after he had unwittingly sabotaged his own Azores scheme.

A week later, when Washington was finally certain that Hitler was about to invade Russia, Roosevelt directed Stark to land American forces in Iceland in July. This movement took on added urgency on the night of 19 June when the *U-203* began to trail the battleship *Texas* and her accompanying destroyers, which King had stationed between Greenland and Iceland. The chase covered 140 miles, but the poor weather and evasive action of the American ships frustrated the U-boat. When Hitler learned of the incident, he ordered a halt to all attacks on vessels in the North Atlantic until the invasion of Russia, codenamed Barbarossa, was well under way.[6]

FDR was searching for a back door through which to enter the European war, and Iceland seemed an ideal latchkey. The initial concept was to land Marines from the Atlantic Amphibious Force, a two division Army–Marine training command King had established earlier that year, but neither Stark nor King was keen to dismember from the Atlantic Fleet's its only mobile striking force. They were willing, however, for the Atlantic Fleet to use a naval base in Iceland to support future escort operations and reinforce the Denmark Strait. To spare the Amphibious Force, Stark directed General Thomas Holcomb, the commandant of the Marine Corps, to create a new expeditionary brigade by assembling elements of three other Marine regiments. This preserved the Atlantic Amphibious Force and relieved some of King's anxiety about the operation. Stark soon obtained Roosevelt's promise that the Marine brigade in Iceland would be relieved by Army garrison troops at the end of the year.

Rear Admiral David LeBreton, whom King had chosen to conduct the invasion, codenamed Operation Indigo, stood out of Charleston on 22 June with the Iceland Task Force, which consisted of two old battleships, a pair of light cruisers, thirteen destroyers, a transport, and two cargo ships. While LeBreton was heading for Reykjavik, Roosevelt promised to support Iceland's postwar independence from Denmark if the Icelanders would invite the Marines to land on 7 July. They accepted this proposal, and after the Marines had arrived in Iceland, King established a naval air station there with one patrol wing of PBY Catalinas and another patrol wing of PBM Mariners. They were to conduct long-range reconnaissance for German submarines and surface raiders around Iceland and in the Denmark Strait. To provide air cover for the Marines and to put a down payment on Roosevelt's promise to send Army troops to relieve them, General Marshall sent a squadron of Army Air Force P-40 pursuit planes to Iceland in August. King now reorganized the Atlantic Fleet into three major elements. Three task groups, each built around one old battleship, were placed under LeBreton's task force, and King instructed him to establish a Denmark Strait Patrol; rotate his battleships among Iceland, Casco Bay, Maine, and Argentia, Newfoundland; and be ready to take "offensive action against Axis surface raiders." King also told Rear Admiral Arthur L. Bristol, who commanded the Support Force destroyer pool, to deploy one group of destroyers to Casco Bay and another to Argentia and to prepare to provide ocean escort groups once convoy operations had begun. King's initial plan had been to include a heavy ship in each escort group to deal with an attack by enemy raiders, but it now became clear that this could not be done.[7]

To guard the tropics, in April 1941 King had assigned command of the South Atlantic Force to Rear Admiral Jonas Ingram, whose handful of cruisers and destroyers were to patrol an immense area in the South Atlantic bounded by the Cape Verdes, Trinidad, and Brazil. King also asked Ingram to assist the American naval attaché in Brazil, Rear Admiral Toutant Beauregard, whose job it was to persuade the Brazilian dictator General Getulio Dornelles Vargas to support American naval operations in South American waters. The Americans offered Vargas credits, loans, bribes, and protection from a pro-German faction within his own army; but Ingram warned King that Brazil, like many neutrals with no discernible stake in the outcome of the war, "wants to end up on the winning side and is not [now] prepared to gamble." Then, on 21 May 1941, the *U-69* sank the American merchantman *Robin Moor* in the South Atlantic, thus heightening the urgency of extending the Navy's protection to Allied shipping in those waters. After some diplomatic haggling, Vargas agreed to allow the South

Atlantic Force to base several ships at Recife and permit the Navy to establish naval air stations along the northern Brazilian coast. He respected and feared German arms, but Hitler was very far away and the lure of Lend Lease aid was too tempting to ignore.

Admiral Raeder interpreted the establishment of the Recife base and the occupation of Iceland as signals that Washington was about to escalate the naval war, and he nagged Hitler to respond by declaring war on the United States. The German Navy instead received orders to "continue to avoid all incidents" at sea with American naval forces, although Hitler admitted that he would "never call a submarine commander to account if he torpedoes an American ship by mistake." Stretching Hitler's directive to its limit, Dönitz told his U-boat skippers that "darkened warships acting as convoy escorts are to be attacked if the situation makes it necessary." Hitler's restrained policy was the result of Operation Barbarossa, the upcoming invasion of Russia. During the spring, American intelligence had gathered evidence that Hitler intended some time in the near future to invade the Soviet Union, but only after Britain had quit the war. FDR passed this warning on to Stalin, and Churchill relayed more precise alerts, but Stalin believed these alarms were self-serving attempts to provoke him into abandoning the Nazi-Soviet Pact. Neither Western leader understood that the Russians were so committed to the German alliance that they were afraid of provoking Hitler by preparing for war. Thus, when Germany struck on 22 June, the Soviets were caught completely off guard. The German Air Force destroyed the obsolete Red Air Force on the ground, and three German Army groups advanced into Russia along a 2,000-mile front that stretched from Rumania to Finland. They displaced the Red Army everywhere, and by the end of July made camp on the western bank of the Dnieper River, only 200 miles from Moscow.[8]

In the West some reasoned that Germany's invasion of Russia considerably reduced the risk of an Axis threat to Britain, the North Atlantic sealanes, and South America. Most Americans disliked and distrusted the Russian and German regimes in equal measure, and many hoped that a bloodletting between these two totalitarian giants would provide for American security for years to come and eliminate the need to intervene in the European war. Others argued that the geopolitical horizon was more complex, remembering that when the Germans last met the Russians in battle, in 1917, the Germans had thrashed the Russians, the Eastern Front collapsed, Russia fell to the communist revolution, and Russia quit the war, leaving the West to face Germany alone. In 1941 the German Army was an awesome force against which the Red Army was clearly no match. "The best opinion I can get is that it will take anywhere from 6 weeks to 2 months for Hitler to clean up on Russia," Navy Secretary Knox confided to Roosevelt the day after the German invasion. American strategists feared that once Hitler forced Stalin to surrender, he would turn back to the west to deliver a final stroke against Britain. Roosevelt's administration never rigorously and systematically examined how Hitler was to do this, however.[9]

Tragically, Roosevelt did not wait to consider the possibility of an eastern stalemate. With no thought of extracting concessions from Moscow in advance of military assistance, he planned to extend unconditional Lend Lease aid to the Soviet Union soon after the German invasion. Stark, worried that Russia would quickly be defeated and that this would increase the danger to Britain, suggested that Roosevelt also publicly announce that the Atlantic Fleet would begin to escort British transatlantic convoys. Time should not be allowed to pass "without striking hard—the sooner the better," argued Secretary Knox. A presidential proclamation ordering the Navy to escort British shipping would constitute such a flagrant violation of benevolent neutrality, Stark told Roosevelt, that it "would almost certainly involve us in war" with Germany. Congress was less eager to support the Russians, and so it was not until the passage of the second Lend Lease appropriation in late October that a ban on aid to Stalin's barbarous regime was finally lifted.[10]

The uncertainty of the Eastern Front, the revelation of Japanese policy provided by an Army-Navy team of cryptanalysts who read Japan's diplomatic traffic, and the lack of ships in the Atlantic Fleet available to conduct escort operations all fed FDR's natural habit of procrastinating about his next move. On 9 July, he approved the Joint Western Hemisphere Defense Plan prepared by Admirals Stark and King, which assigned to the Atlantic Fleet the mission of protecting the lines of communication from the United States to Iceland. American warships were to defend American or Icelandic shipping, and under this ruse Stark invited the British and Canadians to coordinate their merchant convoy steaming schedules with the arrivals and departures of American escorts and their convoys. Stark told King that his escort commanders need not avoid combat if they encountered Axis submarines, and King promptly instructed his task force and ocean escort groups to destroy any "hostile forces which threaten such shipping." King still did not have enough escorts to defend the British convoys, however, and when Plan No. 4 was brought into effect, the task of escorting foreign flag vessels was suspended for the time being. Furthermore, because the White House was under pressure from Congress to avoid incidents between American naval vessels and German U-boats, Roosevelt refused to make a public announcement of this tidal shift in American maritime strategy. Frustrated, Stark complained that FDR's "policy seems to be something never fixed, always fluid and changing," and he dejectedly offered the president his resignation as CNO. "Only a war psychology," the admiral claimed, could "speed up things the way they should be speeded up." The president refused to accept either Stark's resignation or his case for the urgency of a declaration of war.[11]

Just as Roosevelt was about to order the U.S. Navy to join the Battle of the Atlantic, the picture began to improve. Escorted convoys and coastal air patrols drove the U-boats away from the British Isles in late February 1941, prompting Hitler to announce the extension of the German War Zone to Iceland and Greenland on 25 March. At the same time, German Air Force attacks against British escorts, ports, and shipyards did so much damage that about half of the Royal Navy escort vessels were awaiting repairs in April. Then, in May, armed with Hitler's new directive, Dönitz sent several U-boats to take station south and southeast of Greenland and poised them to pounce on Britain's transatlantic convoys. From only ten U-boats in October 1940, Dönitz's front-line force had grown to thirty submarines by April 1941, and he expected to have a total of fifty operational boats in August. As a result of the expansion of the German area of operations, British merchant shipping losses climbed during the spring, when the Germans took advantage of longer daylight hours and Dönitz began to experiment with wolfpack tactics and night surface attacks against escorted shipping.

During the summer, however, the tide of the Battle of the Atlantic turned against the Germans for the first time. South of Iceland on 9 May, the British destroyer *Bulldog* came upon the *U-110*, which was sinking after having been subjected to a depth charge attack by a British corvette. A British rescue party was put on board, and it recovered an Enigma deciphering machine, along with codebooks and other documents. This coup led directly to the breaking of the German U-boat code, and by July British cryptanalysts at Bletchley Park were deciphering a large volume of radio messages from Dönitz's headquarters to his submarines. By combining this intelligence with other evidence, the Admiralty was able to fix the approximate location of nearly every U-boat in the North Atlantic. In August 1941, the Royal Navy adopted an aggressive strategy of evasive routing, attempting to move every convoy around each U-boat station or beyond the flank of every German wolfpack concentration. In addition, following Hitler's invasion of Russia, the Admiralty strengthened its transatlantic ocean escort groups by reducing the number of destroyers assigned to the Home Fleet and the Channel Patrol. The menace to British ports and merchant shipping from German air operations was lessened when Hitler transferred most of the German Air Force from France to the Russian front. Thus, for the first time in the war, British convoys were defended continuously from Halifax to Liverpool and Londonderry, and between 1 June and 1 September no British ships were lost along the great circle convoy route.

At the same time, the British at last succeeded in persuading the Americans to commit the Atlantic Fleet to escort-of-convoy operations in the northwestern Atlantic. Most of the Atlantic Fleet operated out of Newport, until King shifted some escort groups to a new American naval base established on 15 July at Argentia in Newfoundland. Since February, King had been assembling a powerful Support Force, which totaled nearly thirty destroyers by the end of July and assumed responsibility for escorting all American and Icelandic shipping from the United States to Iceland. Integrating the Support Force into the British and Canadian North Atlantic convoy system proved to be a major hurdle because of the complexity of the communications required to organize and route the convoys, the number of operational and higher headquarters that managed each convoy and its ocean escort groups, and major differences in respective national tactical doctrines. King concluded in July that the Atlantic Fleet still did not have enough ships to form the number of ocean escort groups needed to inaugurate combined convoy operations with the British and Canadians. Churchill was downcast at this news, and, to spur the Americans to provide more support for Britain, he suggested to Roosevelt that they meet for the first time during the war at a summit conference in August.

The resulting Atlantic Conference was needed to establish closer Anglo-American naval, military, and diplomatic coordination following Hitler's invasion of Russia and Japan's occupation of French Indochina. In great secrecy, Admiral King arranged for

Roosevelt to meet Prime Minister Churchill at Newfoundland's Placentia Bay between 9 and 12 August. The most important outcome of this conference was the Atlantic Charter, a confusing statement of principles and war aims that obliged the Allies to work for various political liberties such as self-determination and territorial restoration. To this hastily prepared list Roosevelt attached the traditional American maritime objective of freedom of the seas and the historic Democratic Party goals of free trade and a "permanent system of general security" after the war. He had in mind something akin to the defunct League of Nations. More important to Churchill was Roosevelt's reaffirmation of the secret American commitment to a grand strategy of Europe-first and the president's determined policy of providing virtually unlimited Lend Lease to the British, at the expense of the American armed forces, without demanding strategic concessions in return. Those who objected to this approach were exiled from the White House, according to the Army Air Force chief of staff, Major General Henry Arnold. FDR also lifted Churchill's spirits by promising to hold to a stiff line against further Japanese encroachments in Southeast Asia, but he was still unwilling to make a public pledge to enter the war.[12]

Stark and King met with the British military leaders at Argentia, and they agreed that in September the Royal Navy would withdraw its escorts from the western Atlantic and turn over to the Atlantic Fleet "broad supervision" of Canadian and American escort operations in that strategic area. More particularly, the Atlantic Fleet was to assume responsibility for escorting all fast convoys in the western Atlantic beyond Canadian waters. Stark had already explained King's plan to begin combined Anglo-American convoys in September, convoys that would—to preserve this tissue of American neutrality—include at least one American or Icelandic flag merchantman. Inasmuch as the Canadian Navy's escorts were mostly old or short-legged corvettes, King assigned to them the defense of the slow SC convoys from Halifax to the prearranged meeting point south of Iceland. Even so, the Canadians had to keep a number of British ships in their fleet to fulfill this responsibility. At the same time, the Atlantic Fleet Support Force took on the task of escorting the faster, larger HX and ON transatlantic convoys, and King moved the Fleet Train to Casco Bay, Maine, the American anchorage nearest to the great circle convoy routes. There, he created a destroyer pool to fill out the ocean escort groups, which he attached to the eastbound HX convoys. The westbound ON convoys were met at the midocean meeting point by Support Force units from Argentia, where Bristol's task force headquarters was established to direct these operations.

The menace of another German breakout continued to bother King. The Atlantic Fleet had now grown to include three aircraft carriers, five battleships, and over fifty destroyers. British intelligence had wrongly concluded that the heavy cruiser *Prince Eugen* had sortied from Brest and was headed for the Azores, and the Admiralty asked King for help. He formed a task force composed of the carriers *Wasp* and *Yorktown* and the *Long Island*, a just-commissioned escort carrier built on a merchant marine cargo ship hull, and sent them to Bermuda to rendezvous with the British battleship *Rodney*. Soon after this, it was clear that the Admiralty had issued a false alert. The British also tried to draw the Atlantic Fleet into supporting Churchill's costly strategy of holding on to Britain's imperial position in the Mediterranean by defending Malta, which was besieged by Axis aircraft operating from Italy. Only by having convoys ferry aircraft from Gibraltar to Malta could Malta be defended. On 17 September, the First Sea Lord, Admiral Pound, explained to King that he intended to withdraw three capital ships from the Denmark Strait Patrol to escort Operation Halbred, a supply convoy to Malta. King privately questioned the Malta strategy, but he agreed to reinforce the Argentia Task Force with Admiral LeBreton's three battleships, two carriers, and three heavy cruisers while the British ships were in the Mediterranean. It was now clear that Churchill's strategy of fighting everywhere was severely overtaxing Britain's fleet.

FDR's decision to inaugurate escort-of-convoy operations was intended to create an incident at sea with Germany's U-boats. At 0915 on 4 September 1941, before convoy operations got underway, the recommissioned destroyer *Greer* was about 125 miles southwest of Reykjavik, steaming toward her new assignment in Iceland. A Royal Air Force Hudson medium bomber on patrol passed overhead and signaled the American ship that there was an "enemy U-boat observed submerging about 10 miles northwest." Commander George Johnson, the destroyer division commander, was aboard the *Greer* and decided to trail the German submarine and broadcast its position, although he did not believe that his orders allowed him to attack the U-boat. A few moments later, a sonar contact was acquired, and the *Greer* alerted the British bomber to the location of the *U-652*. At 1032, the Hudson attacked the submarine with four depth charges, but they were far off the mark. While he awaited the arrival of additional British aircraft, Johnson held a position between 200 and 1,000 yards off the stern of the U-boat. The German submarine was unable to escape, so she maneuvered into an attack position, and at 1240 fired one torpedo at the *Greer*. The destroyer's skipper, Lieutenant Commander Laurence H. Frost, swung sharply to present a thin profile to the torpedo, and it passed by 100 yards off his starboard bow. Frost then counterattacked with depth charges, but water turbulence masked the movement of the enemy to his sonar and he was unable to make contact again. The first action in World War II between the American and German fleets ended that evening when the *Greer* was ordered to proceed to Iceland.[13]

Although Rear Admiral Robert Giffen discounted Johnson's report of the attack, King passed on the account to FDR, who exploited the *Greer* incident to justify putting the escort-of-convoy plan into effect, which he hoped would mobilize public opinion behind his war policy. He was unwilling to risk his standing by explaining the entire affair, however. In a nationwide radio broadcast he asserted that he had "sought no shooting war with Hitler," but that "American naval vessels . . . will no longer wait until Axis submarines . . . strike their deadly blow—first." Instead, "our patrolling vessels and planes will protect all merchant ships—not only American ships but ships of any flag—engaged in commerce in our defensive waters." King moved rapidly to implement the new orders. On 16 September, an Atlantic Fleet ocean escort group of destroyers rendezvoused with convoy HX.150 southeast of Newfoundland to begin the first combined Anglo-American escort operation. Eleven days later, most of the Royal Navy's escort groups began to withdraw from the western Atlantic and Admiral Bristol's Argentia-based Support Force assumed responsibility for directing American and Canadian escort operations. This was accepted by Ottawa only because the Canadians expected the U.S. Navy to virtually rebuild Canada's hastily constructed, poorly equipped, ill trained, and greatly overburdened fleet.[14]

German reaction to the entry of the U.S. Navy into the Battle of the Atlantic was measured. Raeder urged Hitler to declare war on the United States, but Hitler rejected this foolish scheme. He was, at this time, concerned that the British might try to divert German troops from the Eastern Front by invading northern Norway, so he instructed Dönitz to station U-boats off the Norwegian coast and to restrict submarine deployments in the western Atlantic. Hard upon this decision he told Dönitz to shift even more U-boats to the waters off Gibraltar and into the Mediterranean to prevent the British from severing the line of communications between Italy and the Axis armies in North Africa. However, on 14 September 1941, Hitler did approve Dönitz's plan to mount a commerce-raiding offensive in Canadian and American waters should hostilities between Germany and the United States break out.

The U-boats' withdrawal to the Mediterranean and Norway in late 1941 was soon known to the British and Americans through Ultra, the codename for a complex, expensive radio intelligence operation that rested on an understanding of the Enigma machine. Enigma was the brand name of a series of cipher machines invented by a German who nearly went bankrupt trying to sell them to businesses and governments in Europe and America after World War I. The German Navy bought a version of the Enigma in 1926 and improved it considerably over the next decade. All the German military services were using Enigma machines by 1939, but each arm had its own set of secret codes and ciphers. Communications security was particularly important to Dönitz, who directed German U-boat operations throughout the war from headquarters on the French coast or, later, from a small Berlin hotel. He adopted a rigid system of control that required frequent location, sighting, and weather reports from the U-boat captains at sea. Thus, the volume of message traffic between his headquarters and the German submarines was relatively high. Dönitz used a special set of naval codes to direct U-boat operations against Allied warships, transports, merchantmen, and convoys, and the Germans generally assumed that these naval codes were particularly secure.

Ironically, even before the war began, the Enigma and some of the German codes were already compromised by the Poles, who built a duplicate of the machine and shipped it to France just before Warsaw fell. It was then sent to London shortly before France surrendered. The product of this effort thereafter was known among a very small group in the British government as Ultra intelligence, a daily batch of partially deciphered messages between various German headquarters and their forces in the field. Seldom, however, were most of these messages completely understood by Allied intelligence agencies during the early years of the war. German naval message traffic, for instance, proved peculiarly difficult for the British to interpret, even during the months when the Enigma cipher was broken. The British began to share Ultra with the U.S. Navy in 1941, and the Americans, while impressed by this British accomplishment, were at the same time sobered by its tactical limitations. Lieutenant Commander Kenneth Knowles, who handled Ultra for the Atlantic theater, recalled that "the geographic position of a U-boat and its operating area were generally unknown unless we possessed the coded chart," a secret document containing the German grid coordinates that identified every square nautical mile of the Atlantic. In addition to the problem of reconstructing the grids, on an almost daily basis during the first half of the war "there were frequent lapses when no 'Ultra' was forthcoming, in some cases of several months' duration."[15]

To supplement Ultra, the Admiralty relied on thirty-five receiving stations extending from Iceland to South Africa in the eastern Atlantic and from Brazil to Halifax in the western Atlantic. This system became increasingly elaborate during 1941 when direct American naval participation in escort operations appeared to be imminent. American naval intelligence analysts "received by facsimile a preliminary fix on three to five bearings within thirty-five minutes of the U-boat's transmission" of operational reports to Dönitz's headquarters. The strategic benefits of this intelligence coup were undeniable, but no Allied naval commander could ever pinpoint the position of all his enemies. Even late in the war, "fixes were designated as to accuracy, the best being . . . 'within fifty miles,'" Knowles remembered, but only "perhaps 15 to 20 percent came within this degree of accuracy."[16]

The Germans were not without resources of their own. Through espionage and hard work, the German deciphering service recreated the Allied convoy code—used to route merchantmen across the North Atlantic—an older, vulnerable U.S. Navy code, which the Navy Department insisted the Admiralty adopt in September 1941. This knowledge allowed Dönitz to establish scouting stations, plant picket lines athwart a convoy's course, and concentrate U-boats into wolfpacks and thereby increase the destructiveness of their attacks. For both sides, a critical factor in operational intelligence was lag time, the minutes or hours or days between the transmission of a message and its interception, deciphering, and translation into useful information by an operational intelligence headquarters. Long lag time plagued the Germans in October 1941, but they reconstructed the Allies' North Atlantic timetable for that month and decided to block three transatlantic convoys: SC.48, a slow eastbound convoy with Canadian escorts, which cleared the Belle Isle Strait on 8 October, and ON.23 and ON.24, a pair of fast westbound convoys guarded by Support Force escort groups. Dönitz, who was devising a plan to intercept these ships, ordered several U-boats to rendezvous at a heading point that intersected with the course adopted by the convoy. Unbeknownst to the Germans, however, Bletchley Park's codebreakers deciphered this initial message and the Admiralty shifted SC.48, ON.23, and ON.24 south of the new U-boat stations. When Dönitz learned of this move, he extended his picket line to the south and so created a dilemma for the Allied headquarters. If SC.48 and ON.23 continued along their assigned routes, they would intersect one another, bunching the targets together in the event of a chance contact. In addition, both convoys were in danger of passing too close to TC.10, a fast troop convoy then steaming to the east. To avoid the U-boat pickets, the Admiralty decided to take this risk. SC.48 and ON.23 were separated and moved to the southeast, while room was made between them for TC.10 to pass safely by.[17]

The Allies stood on the doorstep of a successful evasive routing operation when the Germans counterattacked. Anticipating the possibility that the convoys would shift to the south, Dönitz had previously instructed a few U-boats on patrol in the central Atlantic to head northward to reinforce the southern flank of his picket line. A master in the strategy of convoy attacks, Dönitz took care to balance the need to patrol for targets with the requirement to concentrate the U-boats quickly to achieve a decisive attack once the location of a convoy was fixed. On the evening of 15 October, the U-553 was heading north to join the German picket line when she sighted SC.48 and reported its location to Berlin. With viperlike grace, Dönitz irrigated the area with U-boats from the picket line and dispatched to the scene more submarines that had just arrived in the mid-Atlantic from the German bases in France.

Despair replaced satisfaction in London and Washington when SC.48 began to lose ships. The Admiralty detached four escorts from ON.25 to assist SC.48, and Bristol ordered Captain Hewlett Thebaud with a task unit of five destroyers to break off from ON.24 and head eastward to support SC.48. When Thebaud reached the threatened convoy, he assumed command of a combined ocean escort group of American, British, Canadian, and Free French destroyers and corvettes, each with different routines, doctrines, and training. During this eastward movement, the destroyer *Kearny* was slowed by engine problems, but she caught up with Thebaud's escort group on the night of 14 October and took a station on the port flank of the 7-knot convoy, which had already lost three ships.[18]

In developing escort doctrine during 1941, King was impressed by the limited lethality of most antisubmarine weapons, the defenselessness of poorly escorted merchant convoys, and the inadequate numbers of escorting ships. He disliked the British strategy of evasive routing and hoped to defend the convoys with escort groups so powerful that they could defeat the strongest U-boat concentrations, but he did not have enough ships to do that. Mindful of these problems, he and Bristol crafted a tactical doctrine that stressed the need for a close, tight ring around a convoy's perimeter to prevent enemy submarines from penetrating the formation. The problem was that, owing to the shortage of escorts in 1941, very aggressive patrolling much beyond the perimeter of the convoy and the relentless pursuit of contacts—both highly desirable tactics—were just not possible. Although Thebaud had an unusually large ocean escort group to defend SC.48, he adhered to a conservative battle doctrine. Thus, when the *Kearny* took station, she was about 1,500 yards off the nearest merchantman. He was fully aware that this provided his opponents with the opportunity to stand off the convoy and fire their torpedoes at ranges of 3,000 to 5,000 yards. By the evening of 15 October, Thebaud knew that several U-boats were closing on SC.48. To harass and fend them off, the *Kearny* veered away from the formation and dropped a few desultory depth charges near a reported contact, but to no avail. At 2010, a Norwegian freighter in the center of the convoy suddenly exploded and sank. One hour later, the *U-558* slipped silently into the Allied formation and started firing, and in the space of two minutes, two more merchantmen were torpedoed. Star shells and red flares lit up the area, which was crisscrossed by gunfire and blanketed by smoke from the burning hulks.

By this time, SC.48 was being attacked by half a dozen U-boats, and the tight formation adopted by Thebaud was allowing each enemy submarine to stand off or enter the convoy and fire with relative impunity. The *U-432* drilled a torpedo into a Norwegian tanker at midnight, and the resulting explosion illuminated the entire convoy and outlined the position of every other Allied ship and escort. Lieutenant Commander Anthony L. Danis in the *Kearny* swerved away from the convoy again, dropped a single depth charge, and swung back to rejoin the formation. At the same moment the Canadian corvette *Baddeck* raced ahead of her station to rescue survivors from the tanker. The corvette was heading directly for the *Kearny*. When Danis realized what was happening, he reversed his engines to avoid a collision, thereby bringing his ship to a halt. Still in the water, outlined against the dark sea by the fires of the burning tanker, the *Kearny* was an easy shot for a spread of three torpedoes fired by the *U-568*, one of which struck the destroyer's starboard side below the waterline. Eleven sailors were killed by the explosion and the resulting blaze, but Danis and his experienced, well-trained crew saved their ship that harrowing night, and the next day she was escorted back to Iceland by the *Greer*.

The attack on the *Kearny* was a milestone in the Battle of the Atlantic, for two reasons. First, it pointed to the need to strengthen the escorts and improve their tactics. It underlined the need to allow the destroyers to sweep the wake of the convoys at nightfall for lurking U-boats and to conduct relentless depth-charge counterattacks against attacking U-boats so as to drive them away from the convoy or at least keep them submerged while the convoy steamed away safely. It also moved other escort group commanders to position their escorts about 3,000 yards off the convoy, although this tactic had its own disadvantages. King's doctrine called for aggressive antisubmarine tactics, but this could not now be put into effect until the numbers of escorts increased, their training improved, and their equipment was perfected. Later in the year, Bristol decided that the small corvettes should be positioned closer to the convoy and that the destroyers should be stationed about 5,000 yards off the merchant ship columns. King wanted his ocean escorts to pursue and hunt down attacking U-boats without stint, but he warned Stark that they could not now do so for any length of time "without dangerously reducing the escort strength." Second, the *Kearny* incident had immediate political ramifications. FDR used the action—the main features of which he distorted in a radio broadcast—to justify the claim that "America has been attacked." He was, he said, issuing "orders to the American Navy to shoot on sight" whenever German vessels were encountered. He assumed the public would accept his argument that the *Kearny* was due the right of innocent passage while engaging in clearly non-neutral operations.[19]

Just before the *Greer* incident, FDR had asked Congress to amend the Neutrality Acts to allow the Navy to arm American merchantmen and place naval gun crews on board some cargo ships and permit them to sail into the European War Zones. The ensuing debate in Congress lasted five weeks, punctuated by the *Kearny* incident and another action involving the *Reuben James*. Recommissioned in 1939 and attached to the Neutrality Patrol, the four-stack destroyer *Reuben James* joined the Iceland-based Support Force and operated out of Hvalfjordur after July 1941. She sailed from Argentia on 23 October as one of a five-destroyer ocean escort group defending the eastbound HX.156 convoy. This convoy, consisting of thirty-eight ships, mostly British tankers, was moving to Iceland where Royal Navy escorts were to relieve the Americans and cover the last leg of the voyage. The convoy was attacked several times by U-boats during this passage, but she was soon blanketed by a gale that prevented the Germans from concentrating their forces. A lone boat, the *U-562*, picked up the convoy's trail on the morning of 31 October, however, and reported this to Dönitz, who ordered more submarines to sail to intercepting positions. Unbeknownst to the Germans, the destroyer *Tarbell*'s radio direction finder fixed this transmission close by the convoy, and the *Reuben James* was ordered to run down the contact. At 0535, just after the destroyer turned toward the *U-562*, the Germans fired two torpedoes, which penetrated the *Reuben James*' hull, detonated in her magazine, and created an explosion that ripped the ship apart. Forty-four Americans were rescued, but 115 lost their lives.

The *Reuben James* incident provoked surprisingly little public reaction. When asked if it would lead to war, Roosevelt confessed that he "did not think so." He declared over nationwide radio that the *Reuben James* was the victim of "unprovoked attacks" by German submarines while "on patrol" in the North Atlantic, again suggesting untruthfully that she deserved the neutral right of innocent passage. And when isolationist Senator Burton K. Wheeler disclosed that the Navy was escorting British convoys, Secretary Knox responded that his "statement is not true." During the first week of November, the Senate voted by a fair margin to gut the Neutrality Acts, but the House was more narrowly divided. At the same time, in the South Atlantic, a task group composed of the cruiser *Omaha* and the destroyer *Somers* intercepted the German blockade runner *Odenwald*, seized her as a prize of war, and brought her into San Juan, Puerto Rico, on 11 November on the preposterous charge that she had been engaged in the African slave trade.

Summing up the public mood, Congressman Homer Angell, an Oregon Republican who supported revision, declared, "We should use every means . . . to build up our defenses, to preserve the freedom of the seas, to uphold the Monroe Doctrine, and to protect our Western Hemisphere . . . [but] not send our American troops overseas . . . to engage in this or any foreign war unless we are attacked." Two days later, the House, by an eleven-vote margin, voted to amend the Neutrality Acts. This was "one of the last steps that will plunge this nation into war," reasoned Congressman John M. Coffee, a Democrat from Washington state. Nonetheless, FDR's policy to provoke a war in the Atlantic with Germany was, as December 1941 approached, a complete failure. Perhaps because of this, the most fundamental precept of Plan Dog—that the United States go on the offensive in the Atlantic and at the same time remain on the defensive in the Pacific by not provoking Japan—was about to be violated.[20]

Chapter Thirty-nine
The Passage to Pearl Harbor
1941

On 1 February 1941, Admiral Husband Kimmel took over command of the Pacific Fleet from Admiral Richardson, whom FDR had sacked. A few days earlier, Admiral Stark had sent Captain John McCrea out to Pearl Harbor to explain the Pacific Fleet's new mission to the new commander. McCrea told Kimmel that the CNO had completely abandoned the offensive movement embodied in the traditional Orange Plan strategy and had replaced it with defensive tasks that were subordinate to the grand strategy of Europe-first. Under the old Orange Plan, the Pacific Fleet was to prepare for a strong offensive advance into the central Pacific to relieve the Philippines, but now the Joint Board's new Rainbow Five War Plan obligated the Pacific Fleet only to stage a small raid on the Marshall Islands within six months of the onset of war. Rainbow Five did not require the Pacific Fleet to rush to the aid of Admiral Thomas Hart's Asiatic Fleet in the Philippines. Stark fully expected that in the war's opening phase the Philippines would fall to Japan and the Asiatic Fleet would retire from the western Pacific.

Though Stark informed Kimmel that he would forbid the Pacific Fleet's battleships to operate west of Midway, Kimmel, no less than Richardson, was wedded to an offensive strategy. Indeed, he intended "to start the offensive action by [a] movement against the Marshalls at the earliest possible moment." On 26 November 1941 Kimmel told Stark that, two weeks after the war broke out, he intended to send Vice Admiral William Halsey's three-carrier task force on a four-day, high-speed raid into the Marshalls covered by PBY patrol planes and, at the same time, to position the battleships and cruisers of the Battle Force in the vicinity of Wake Island. Kimmel predicted that Halsey's raids would lure the enemy fleet into the eastern Pacific where his battleships would ambush them and force a classical line-ahead engagement. Stark, determined to impose a defensive cast on American strategy in the Pacific, was altogether unable to discourage Kimmel's excessive optimism. Kimmel found it hard to accept orders that placed the Pacific Fleet on a defensive footing, and Stark utterly failed to insist that he adopt this approach.

Stark's perpetually sunny disposition made it difficult for him to convey his gloom-laden concerns, although his letters to Kimmel in 1941 were filled with foreboding. "That Stark," Treasury Secretary Henry Morgenthau once complained. "His smile doesn't indicate what is going on in his mind." In an attempt to impose a defensive strategy in the Pacific, Stark went so far as to persuade the Joint Board to veto the important American-British-Dutch Agreement, which Admiral Hart had negotiated in April 1941. It called for the Western powers to reinforce Luzon with air forces and submarines that would support the defense of the Philippines and attack the flanks of any Japanese thrust against the Malay Peninsula or the Dutch East Indies. Abandoning the ABD Agreement, however, left Allied planning in the Far East in limbo for the time being.[1]

Neither then nor later did Kimmel grasp the significance of these decisions—that the Atlantic Fleet and Lend Lease enjoyed a far higher priority for new ships, planes, men, and material than did the Pacific or Asiatic fleets. The transfer of carriers, battleships, cruisers, and destroyers from the Pacific to the Atlantic throughout the year was ample evidence that FDR stood behind Stark's strategy, and the CNO repeatedly warned Kimmel not to expect reinforcements at the expense of the Atlantic front. The defense of the fleet itself, and the seaward approaches to Midway, Wake Island, Alaska, Hawaii, and Panama, were—no later than the spring of 1941—without doubt the Pacific Fleet's most important missions.

Relations with Japan, already tense as a result of the Sino-Japanese War, worsened after the outbreak of the European war in 1939. They took a sharp turn in October 1940 when Tokyo signed the Tripartite Pact with Germany and Italy, unwittingly becoming in Western eyes a partner to the Axis alliance. To retaliate, Washington curtailed trade with Japan and by the end of 1940 cut off all exports to Japan except oil. This angered the Japanese, as did Roosevelt's decision in March 1941 to extend Lend Lease assistance to Chiang's Chungking-based Chinese regime. To avoid getting entangled in the European war, Japan's foreign minister, Yosuke Matsuoka, journeyed to Moscow in the hope of reducing Russo-Japanese tensions. The Red Army had clashed briefly with Japanese troops on the Mongolian-Manchurian border in 1939, but Stalin now feared a war on two fronts and he was willing to appease Russia's traditional Far Eastern rival. A five-year Neutrality Pact was signed by Matsuoka and Soviet Foreign Minister V. Molotov on 13 April 1941. Prime Minister Konoye, believing that this would secure Japan's northern flank, now looked to the south where Europe's distress might be turned to Japan's advantage. Tokyo had already, in 1940, compelled Vichy France to allow Japanese troops to occupy northern French Indochina, and soon after Germany invaded Russia in late June 1941, Konoye demanded that the French permit Japan's army to post troops near Saigon and Da Nang and allow a Japanese fleet to operate in the Tonkin Gulf. The French agreed, and on 24 July ships of Japan's Combined Fleet stood into Camranh Bay and Da Nang. The flanks of Southeast Asia and the southwest Pacific were thereafter wholly exposed to Japanese power.

Advance word of this move reached the White House on 8 July 1941, provided by a joint Army-Navy codebreaking team that had, on the basis of a very few messages, built a machine that had deciphered Japan's diplomatic cipher, known as Purple, back in 1940. FDR considered embargoing oil exports to Japan, a strong step since Japan imported 90 percent of the oil she consumed and 80 percent of this total came from the United States. On the other hand, an embargo would merely hasten the arrival of the day when American military demands for oil would be so great that exports would have to be curtailed anyway. However, the Navy "strongly" and "consistently opposed" an embargo since it would confront Japan with the choice between withdrawing from China or going to war with Britain and the United States. Because Admiral Stark did not want to divert attention from his Europe-first strategy, he urged that "no open rupture" with Japan be brought about, "particularly at this time." Yet FDR felt he had no real alternative and on 26 July issued an executive order freezing all Japanese assets and effectively imposing an oil embargo on Japan. The CNO promptly alerted Kimmel that this "policy probably involves war in the near future."[2]

When they learned of the embargo, the Japanese estimated that their oil reserves would last between six and twenty-four months. This dilemma compelled Konoye's cabinet to choose between bowing to American demands that Japan withdraw from Southeast Asia and China, or going to war to conquer the Dutch East Indies, where they hoped to acquire enough oil to fuel Japan's industry and support overseas military operations indefinitely. On 6 September, the war council approved a strategic plan sponsored by the army minister, General Hideki Tojo, the head of a powerful faction of fanatical militarists. Under Tojo's plan, when war was declared the Combined Fleet under Admiral Isoroku Yamamoto was to attack and cripple the American Pacific and Asiatic fleets. Japanese forces would then invade the Philippines, overrun British Malaya, occupy the Dutch East Indies, and renew the campaign against China. Cut off from Allied support, the Chungking government was expected to collapse. In the meantime, Yamamoto would establish a string of fortified air and naval bases along a strong defensive island cordon stretching from the Kuriles in the north to the Marshalls in the central Pacific and the East Indies and the Malay Peninsula in the south. Konoye was fearful of going to war with the United States, however, and had proposed in August to meet Roosevelt at a summit conference in the hope of narrowing their differences; but Secretary of State Hull distrusted FDR's negotiating talents and persuaded him to reject the Japanese offer on 2 October. Humiliated by this unnecessary rebuff, Konoye resigned in favor of Tojo, the foremost sponsor of an unbending policy of expansionism. When Stark apprised Kimmel of this ominous development, Kimmel took the uncharacteristic step of warning his subordinates to concern themselves with the security of Pearl Harbor and even cautioned that a Japanese declaration of war "may be preceded by a surprise attack on Pearl Harbor." He did nothing then or later, however, to assure that new measures were taken to defend the fleet or the base.[3]

Throughout 1941, to keep Japan on edge, Roosevelt tried to get Stark to agree to a number of bizarre movements by elements of the Asiatic and Pacific fleets, which he evidently believed would disconcert Tokyo. Stark resisted each of these gestures on the grounds that it was unwise to provoke the Japanese while the

Atlantic Fleet was being strengthened at the expense of the Pacific. In March, however, FDR overruled the CNO's objections and directed him to send a task force of four cruisers and a division of destroyers to visit American Samoa. Stark did persuade the president to extend the cruise by having the ships visit Australia in March—rather than the Philippines or Singapore, where they could easily be trapped. "I just want to keep them popping up here and there and keep the Japs guessing," FDR explained flippantly. To prevent another such episode, Stark himself now proposed to dispatch a powerful cruiser task force to the waters around Russia's Kamchatka Peninsula on Japan's northern flank. As he expected, this strange scheme forced the State Department to carefully examine the utility of Roosevelt's policy, and on 11 April Secretary Hull successfully argued against the plan at the White House. Roosevelt's vacillation on this issue and others was explained by Rear Admiral Ben Morrill, the chief of the Bureau of Construction, who recorded that "FDR had obsessions on some things one day and forgot them the next." Kimmel complained about the frequent shifts in strategy when he visited Washington in June, and his concern was not allayed by Stark's observation that the balance of power was changing almost daily. Stark apparently was not aware that Kimmel's attitude reflected a degree of inflexibility and unwillingness to adapt that had already infected his command at Pearl Harbor.[4]

The War Department reacted with alacrity in June 1941 to the crisis in the Far East and the new threat to the Philippine Islands. General Marshall recalled to active duty Lieutenant General Douglas MacArthur, who, since 1936, had been in the pay of the Philippine Commonwealth as a field marshal, and put under his command all Army ground and air forces in the Far East. To Marshall's surprise, MacArthur soon threw over decades of strategic planning by deciding to conduct an active defense of the entire Philippine archipelago. Not only did he persuade Marshall to agree to this absurd concept, but the Army's usually astute chief of staff also approved a plan to send several squadrons of new long-range B-17 Flying Fortresses to the Philippines. If their presence failed to deter the Japanese, then MacArthur would have on hand a means to retaliate by attacking Formosa. MacArthur devised no plan to use these planes, however, and Marshall inexplicably failed to insist that he do so. Although this shift of forces to the Far East conflicted with Plan Dog's Europe-first strategy, Admiral Stark encouraged Marshall to reinforce the Philippines; Stark believed this would counterbalance the transfer of ships from the Pacific to the Atlantic Fleet. Sending a handful of bombers to the Philippines would "revolutionize . . . America's strategy in the southwest Pacific, taking her from impotence . . . to a position of great effective power," declared Secretary of War Stimson in a spasm of hyperbole.[5]

Admiral Hart put little faith in MacArthur's prescriptions. After establishing the Asiatic Fleet's headquarters in Manila in October 1940, he began withdrawing the 4th Marines from China, evacuating American dependents from the Far East, and reducing the paralyzed Yangtze Patrol. In the summer of 1941, he ordered his ships not to operate north of the Philippines and crafted a plan to fight a series of delaying actions between Mindanao and the Dutch East Indies. Ordered to shut down the Yangtze Patrol in November, Rear Admiral William A. Glassford found that he had to leave behind the aged gunboats *Wake* and *Tutuila,* but the rest of his vessels were on their way to Manila by the end of the month. Hart expected the Japanese to land on Luzon, and he intended to remain in Manila with his submarines and an understrength patrol wing and harry the invaders while Glassford retired to Surabaya and Balikpapan in the Dutch East Indies with the cruisers, destroyers, and gunboats. By the end of the first week in December, owing to Hart's careful preparations, only the submarine *Sealion* and the old tender *Canopis* were left at Cavite Navy Yard. The rest of the Asiatic Fleet had already put to sea.

Hart implemented his plan in the fall when he learned from deciphered Magic diplomatic intercepts that Tojo was determined to resolve the Pacific crisis. Japan's position was ironic. Because she could not completely defeat China, her leaders were bent on going to war with the United States and Britain. Once at the top, however, Tojo shrank from moving too fast. His cabinet instructed Admiral Yamamoto to organize expeditions to invade Malaya, the Dutch East Indies, and the Philippines and tentatively approved Yamamoto's plan to launch a preemptive attack against the Pacific Fleet at Pearl Harbor. This was the sheerest folly. Yamatomo's strategy aimed not at winning a victory—an end even he understood to be beyond Japan's reach—but at establishing a network of far-flung outposts while hoping the Americans would accept a compromise peace. For his part, Tojo applied his skills to one last attempt to reach a diplomatic settlement with Washington. Japan preferred to avoid war but not if the cost was her absolute hegemony in the Far East. On 20 November, the Japanese delivered a note to Secretary of State Hull proposing that both sides not "make any armed advancement into any of the regions in southeastern Asia and the southern Pacific area excepting the part of French Indochina where the Japanese troops are stationed at present." In return for an American agreement to allow the Dutch East Indies to sell oil to Japan and a promise to "refrain" from supporting Chiang Kai-shek, Tokyo pledged to withdraw its troops from Indochina "upon either the restoration of peace between Japan and China or the establishment of an equitable peace in the Pacific area."[6]

Hull found this to be offensive, but he still hoped to put off a war and so toyed with a "modus vivendi," a three-month diplomatic ceasefire during which more substantive talks could get at basic principles. The terms of Hull's "modus vivendi" required Japan to withdraw her troops from southern Indochina and her fleet from Camranh Bay, in return for which Washington would relax the oil embargo on "a monthly basis for civilian needs." Both Admiral Stark and General Marshall now urged Roosevelt to postpone a showdown with Japan until March 1942, when MacArthur's B-17 bombers would be ready. Stark was attempting to get Roosevelt to hew to the strategy embodied in Plan Dog, whereas Marshall actually believed that a handful of bombers would somehow deter Japan or disrupt an invasion of the Philippines. The "modus vivendi" was one way to suspend the crisis and delay hostilities, although Secretary of War Stimson did not "think that there is any chance of the Japanese accepting it, because it was so drastic." Both Britain and China were eager for the United States to enter the war, and when Roosevelt asked Churchill and Chiang for their comments they each denounced the "modus vivendi" as a form of appeasement. Hull's mind was now changed. Stark and Marshall learned that he was abandoning the "modus vivendi" but not that he had persuaded FDR to reply to Tojo instead with a lengthy denunciation of Japanese foreign policy and a defense of the Open Door, a note that was certain to inflame Tokyo. Its substance was that Japan had to "withdraw all military, naval, air, and police forces from China and from Indochina" before Washington would lift the oil embargo.[7]

At noon on 25 November, FDR conferred with Stark, Marshall, and secretaries Stimson, Knox, and Hull. It was clear that "we were likely to be attacked," and Roosevelt cautioned his circle that "the Japanese are notorious for making an attack without warning."

Stimson confessed that the "question was how we should maneuver them into the position of firing the first shot without allowing too much danger to ourselves." While they hoped to postpone hostilities until the spring of 1942, Stark and Marshall agreed that the United States could not allow Japan to "move against British Malaysia or the Dutch East Indies without attempting to prevent it." FDR had forewarned neither Stark nor Marshall about the substitute for Hull's "modus vivendi," and when the admiral learned of this decision from a deciphered Japanese message, he was stunned. He sent his own urgent message to Admiral Kimmel, which began with the historic statement, "This is a war warning." Stark alerted Kimmel that "negotiations with Japan . . . have ceased and an aggressive move by Japan is expected within the next few days," although the CNO could not be certain where the enemy would first strike. He therefore directed Kimmel to "execute an appropriate defensive deployment preparatory to carrying out the tasks assigned in" the Pacific Fleet's latest war plan. That same day, the major elements of Admiral Chuichi Nagumo's six-carrier Pearl Harbor Striking Force rendezvoused in Tankan Bay in the Kurile Islands and began to steam east into the north Pacific.[8]

Kimmel's reaction to Stark's war warning was somewhat less animated than that of his Army counterpart, Lieutenant General Walter Short, who received not only an alert from General Marshall but also a paraphrased copy of Stark's alarm-laden message. Misled by the confusing wording of the Army message, Short reasoned that Marshall wanted him to defend against sabotage by the large number of Japanese-Americans in Hawaii, so he directed that all Army Air Corps aircraft be parked together in the center of their airstrips, wingtip to wingtip. Short was technically responsible for the defense of Hawaii and the Pearl Harbor base, but Stark had alerted Kimmel in February that "in view of the inadequacy of the Army defenses, the responsibility . . . must rest upon the fleet for its own protection within Pearl Harbor." Kimmel was hardly ignorant of the threat to Pearl Harbor posed by Japan's carriers inasmuch as he had studied a thorough, prophetic March 1941 report on the subject prepared by Rear Admiral Patrick Bellinger and Brigadier General Frederick Martin, the commanders of the land-based air forces in Hawaii. They warned of the possibility of a surprise early-morning attack and outlined the steps that Kimmel had to take to establish a continuous long-range, early-warning reconnaissance patrol. "I decided that I

The battleships *West Virginia* (BB-48) and *Tennessee* (BB-43) in flames soon after the Japanese attack on Pearl Harbor, 7 December 1941.

could not risk having no patrol plane force . . . for the fleet's expected movement into the Marshalls," Kimmel later observed. Because Bellinger did not have enough planes to institute a full-time, 360-degree, long-range patrol, Kimmel not only rejected the Bellinger-Martin plan but also refused to institute a limited, partial patrol regime during periods of extreme diplomatic tension. Using the "patrol planes for searching the Hawaiian Area . . . was of much less value than being prepared to immediately advance those planes to our distant island bases," he asserted.[9]

Nor was Kimmel especially concerned by Stark's urgent war warning. He assumed that Japan was preparing to invade Thailand, the Philippines, or British Malaya, or to attack Russia. Lieutenant Commander Edwin Layton, the fleet intelligence officer, claimed many years later that Kimmel said "that the two messages calling for 'defensive deployment' were non-specific and not set forth in WPL-46," the Pacific Fleet war plan. "If they [CNO] have something definite in mind, why don't they say so? The words 'defensive deployment' cover anything and nothing." In fact, Kimmel wanted to be ready to take the offensive quickly once war erupted, so he began to put into position the forces he would need to lure the enemy fleet into attacking Wake Island. His first step, taken on 28 November, was to order Admiral Halsey in the carrier *Enterprise* to deliver twelve F4F Wildcat fighters to strengthen the Marine garrison on Wake. Before the task force got under way, Kimmel showed Halsey the CNO's war-warning message and indirectly encouraged him to attack any Japanese planes or ships he encountered. This was "as fine an order as a subordinate ever received," Halsey wrote, and when the *Enterprise* stood out of Pearl Harbor, Captain George D. Murray announced that the carrier was "now operating under war conditions."

Although Kimmel put Halsey, his 1904 Naval Academy classmate, on notice, he did not discuss Stark's war warning with his patrol plane commander, Admiral Bellinger, who was unaware of the alert. Nor did Kimmel mention it on 5 December when he instructed Rear Admiral John Newton to take the *Lexington* into the central Pacific and deliver twenty-five scout bombers to Midway's naval air station. Nor was the war warning revealed to Rear Admiral Wilson Brown, whom Kimmel told to take his cruiser-destroyer task force south to conduct landing exercises in the central Pacific at Johnston Island. Kimmel's mind was now focused on arranging his plan to lure the enemy to Wake, not on defending Hawaii. No joint Army-Navy air raid drills were held after 12 November, and Kimmel did not reply to a June message from the Assistant CNO, Rear Admiral Royal Ingersoll, who told Kimmel that the battleships in Pearl Harbor would be vulnerable to an attack by shallow-running torpedoes unless he installed a system of nets and booms. An earlier warning from Washington to this effect had elicited from Admiral Bloch, the naval district commandant, the opinion that "the installation of baffles for the fleet moorings would have to be so extensive that most of the entire channel would be restricted," and Kimmel agreed with this assessment. Neither Kimmel nor Bloch took account of Ingersoll's June alarm, and Kimmel went so far as to claim later that "the Navy Department was convinced that aerial torpedoes would be ineffective in Pearl Harbor and we had discounted that menace."

Just as inexplicable was Kimmel's November decision to discontinue rotating his battleship and carrier divisions in and out of Pearl Harbor. As a result, there were eighty-six ships in Pearl Harbor on the morning of 7 December. "It just happened that the two battleship divisions, one and three, were due to be in [Pearl Harbor] over that weekend, but a couple of inspections. . . . Just the normal schedule had them lined up, jammed up, in the harbor at this time," according to Lieutenant Commander Fitzgerald, then serving on the staff of the battleship-type command. "There was no particular reason. . . . It was just the normal routine, the normal overlap of the [battleship] task forces that occurred over that weekend." Nor did Kimmel seem to take notice of the unusual berthing arrangements. While the Pacific Fleet had not gone to the highest state of alert, other Navy recipients of the "war warning" had. The Asiatic Fleet was ready for war. Over 100 Army aircraft were on full alert in Panama, and the naval district was conducting an aggressive surface and air patrol of the Pacific approaches to the canal, America's most important strategic asset.[10]

By the first week of December, American naval intelligence in Washington had uncovered several clues—mostly from Magic or other radio intelligence—that the Japanese were preparing to attack the Dutch and British Empires and, possibly, the Philippine Islands. FDR and his advisers, confident that they were reading Japan's most closely held secrets, were in the thrall of the Magic intercepts, and this intelligence, if anything, overemphasized Tokyo's interest in the Philippines and the Panama Canal. Every scrap of unambiguous evidence pointed to momentary amphibious invasions of Thailand and Malaya's Kra Peninsula, not to a lightning carrier raid on Hawaii. Indeed, Admiral Hart was so concerned that he agreed to a request from Admiral Tom Phillips, the commander of the newly established British Far Eastern Fleet, to send the destroyers at Balikpapan to Singapore to screen the *Prince of Wales* and *Repulse* in the defense of Malaya. He has no authority whatsoever to do this, and acted wholly on the basis of a rumor from London via Singapore to the effect that Roosevelt had committed the United States to the defense of Britain's empire in southeast Asia.

Stark was not especially fearful of a surprise attack on Pearl Harbor, America's most well-defended outpost, as he believed that Kimmel had instituted long-range air patrols after receiving the Navy's 27 November war warning, and Stark assumed that both the Pacific Fleet and the Army's Hawaiian Department were at the highest state of alert. Neither of these assumptions was correct. Stark had selected Kimmel for the Pacific Fleet because he trusted Kimmel's judgment—an appalling error the CNO partially recognized that fall—and he repeatedly refused to query or badger Kimmel about taking what Stark considered elementary precautions during a time of extraordinary danger. Stark was unaware

that Kimmel did not believe that Japan intended to go to war with
the United States, despite the secret warnings from Washington
and the abundant evidence in the public press to the contrary.
Kimmel, however, was expressing this absurd view as late as 6 December, when he told reporter Joseph C. Harsch that Japan was
about to go on the offensive in north Asia.

Washington now awaited Japan's response to Hull's long note
of late November. On 6 December, the Magic codebreakers deciphered the first thirteen parts of a message from Tokyo to its Washington embassy, the substance of which indicted the Open Door
policy and America's intervention in Far Eastern politics. A copy was
delivered to the White House late that evening. The messenger,
Lieutenant Lester Shultz, claimed in late 1945—when he first told
the story—that he entered the Oval study and handed the thirteen-
part message to the president, who, upon reading it, exclaimed,
"This means war!" Schultz apparently invented this small fiction,
however, as neither of the naval officers on duty at the White House
that memorable night verified his dramatic account.[11]

The first thirteen parts of Japan's last peacetime diplomatic
communication contained neither an ultimatum nor a declaration of war, and the fourteenth and last part, deciphered on Sunday morning, merely announced that Japan was severing diplomatic relations with the United States. Ambassador Nomura was
told to deliver the entire note to Hull at the State Department at
1300 that day. An expert on Japanese intelligence, Captain Arthur
McCollum, discussed the intercept with Stark that morning, pointing out that 1300 in Washington was 0700 in Hawaii and 0200 in
the Philippines, but McCollum did not believe that this was especially significant. Stark thought that the timing meant something,
but he did not know what. If, as he had every right to expect, Admiral Hart and Admiral Kimmel had placed their fleets on alert,
and the forces defending the Panama Canal were ready, the timing of Japan's diplomacy should make no difference. Stark
phoned the White House and talked with FDR, but he rejected an
aide's suggestion that he call Kimmel on his scrambler phone. He
was more worried about the Asiatic Fleet, and neither the latest intercept nor any previous intelligence hinted in any way at an attack on Pearl Harbor. Inasmuch as Stark had nothing to tell Kimmel, he agreed instead to let the Army send another message to
Hawaii, once again telling both Short and Kimmel to "be on the
alert." Given the information available in Washington that Sunday
morning, there was nothing more to do.[12]

List of Abbreviations

AF: Air Force
AR: Annual Report of the Secretary of the Navy
ASC: Armed Services Committee
ASP: American State Papers
CNO: Chief of Naval Operations
FRUS: Foreign Relations of the United States
GenBd: General Board
GPO: U.S. Government Printing Office
HMSO: Her Majesty's Stationery Office
LC: Library of Congress
NA: National Archives
NHC: Operational Archives, Naval Historical Center,
    Washington Navy Yard
OH: Oral History
ONI: Office of Naval Intelligence
PRO: Public Records Office, Kew Gardens, London
RG: Record Group
USNA: Nimitz Library, U.S. Naval Academy, Annapolis,
    Maryland
WPD: War Plans Division

Notes

Introduction

1. Hilary Herbert, "The Lesson of the Naval Review," *North American Review* (June 1893), p. 643.

Chapter One

1. Douglas E. Leach, *Roots of Conflict: British Armed Forces and Colonial Americans, 1677–1763* (Chapel Hill: University of North Carolina Press, 1986); Elsie Engle and Arnold S. Lott, *America's Maritime Heritage* (Annapolis: Naval Institute Press, 1975); Neil R. Stout, *The Royal Navy in America, 1760–1775* (Annapolis: Naval Institute Press, 1973) p. 155; and Arthur Pierce Middleton, *Tobacco Coast: A Maritime History of the Chesapeake Bay in the Colonial Era* (2nd ed.; Baltimore: Johns Hopkins Press, 1984), Ch. 11. For attempts to place Britain's naval power in a wider perspective, see George Modelski and William R. Thompson, *Seapower in Global Politics, 1494–1993* (Seattle: University of Washington Press, 1988), Chs. 3 and 5; and Gerald S. Graham, *Sea Power and British North America* (Cambridge: Harvard University Press, 1941).

2. Stout, *Royal Navy*, p. 161; and Paul M. Kennedy, *The Rise and Fall of British Naval Mastery* (New York: Scribner, 1976), p. 114.

3. William G. Anderson, "John Adams and the Creation of the American Navy," (Unpubl. Ph.D. Diss., State University of New York, Stony Brook, 1975), p. 2; and Frederic H. Hayes, "John Adams and American Sea Power," *American Neptune* (1965), pp. 35–45.

4. James Bradford, "Navies of the American Revolution," in Kenneth J. Hagan, ed., *In Peace and War* (Westport, Conn.: Greenwood Press, 1977), p. 5; and Robert W. Neeser, ed., *The Despatches of Molyneux Shuldham . . . January–July 1776* (New York: Naval History Society, 1913), pp. 38–39.

5. C. Worthington Ford, ed., *Journals of the Continental Congress, 1774–1789* (34 vols.; Washington: LC, 1904–37), Vol. III, p. 274; Bradford, "Navies," p. 7; Anderson, "Adams," p. 4; and Frank C. Mevers III, "Congress and the Navy: The Establishment and Administration of the American Revolutionary Navy by the Continental Congress, 1775–1784" (Unpubl. Ph.D. Diss., Duke University, 1972), Chs. 1–3.

6. William M. Fowler, Jr., *Rebels Under Sail* (New York: Scribner's, 1976), p. 50; Bradford, "Navies," p. 6; and Anderson, "Adams," p. 9.

7. Charles O. Paullin, ed., *Out-Letters of the Continental Marine Committee and Board of Admiralty, August 1776–1780* (New York: Naval History Society, 1914–15), Vol. I, p. 78.

8. William B. Clark and William J. Morgan, eds., *Naval Documents of the American Revolution* (Washington: GPO, 1940–), Vol. III, pp. 636–38; and John J. McCusker, "The American Invasion of Naussau," *American Neptune* (1965), pp. 189–217. Hopkins was addressed as either Admiral or Commodore, but Congress probably did not intend to vest him with overall responsibility for the fleet comparable to Washington's command of the Continental Army. See Frank C. Meev-

ers III, "Congress and the Navy: The Establishment and Administration of the American Revolutionary Navy by the Continental Congress, 1775–1784," (Unpubl. Ph.D. Diss., Duke University, 1972), Ch. 7. Hopkins' views of his many problems can be found in Alverda S. Beck, ed., *The Correspondence of Esek Hopkins, Commander-in-Chief of the U. S. Navy* (Providence: Rhode Island Historical Society, 1933).

9. Neeser, *Shuldham,* p. 38; and Clark and Morgan, *Documents,* Vol. IV, p. 702.

10. Anderson, "Adams," p. 15.

11. Anderson, "Adams," p. 35.

12. Paullin, *Out-Letters,* Vol. II, p. 271, and Vol. I, p. 199.

13. Robert G. Albion and Jennie B. Pope, *Sea Lanes in Wartime: The American Experience, 1775–1945* (2nd ed.; Hamden, Conn.: Archon Books, 1969), p. 37.

14. Albion, *Sea Lanes,* p. 41; Charles O. Paullin, "Birth of a Navy," *Proceedings* (Report.; Jul 1976), p. 21; Eugene S. Ferguson, *Truxtun of the Constellation* (2nd ed.; Annapolis: Naval Institute Press, 1982), p. 102; William J. Morgan, "American Privateering in America's War of Independence," *American Neptune* (Apr 1976), pp. 79–87; and Alan G. Jamieson, "American Privateers in the Leeward Islands, 1776–1778," *American Neptune* (Jan 1983), pp. 20–30.

15. Piers Mackesy, *The War for America, 1775–1783* (Cambridge: Harvard University Press, 1964).

16. Bradford, "Navies," p. 15.

17. William A. Dudley and Michael A. Palmer, "No Mistake About It," *American Neptune* (Fall 1985), p. 256; and Bradford, "Navies," p. 16.

18. Robert W. Nesser, ed., *Letters and Papers Relating to the Cruises of Gustavas Conyngham* (New York: Naval History Society, 1915), pp. 96–97.

19. Armin Rappaport, *A History of American Diplomacy* (New York: Macmillan, 1975), p. 23.

20. Kennedy, *Rise* p. 112.

21. James Bradford, "John Paul Jones," in James Bradford, ed., *Command Under Sail* (Annapolis: Naval Institute Press, 1985), p. 25.

22. Edgar S. Maclay, *A History of the United States Navy* (2nd ed.; New York: Appleton, 1901), Vol. I, pp. 73, 76.

23. Bradford, "Jones," p. 26.

24. Maclay, *Navy,* Vol. I, p. 80.

25. Bradford, "Jones," p. 27; and Maclay, *Navy,* Vol. I, p. 84.

Chapter Two

1. Bradford, "Jones," pp. 28–29.

2. Maclay, *Navy,* Vol. I, p. 123.

3. Maclay, *Navy,* Vol. I, p. 127.

4. John J. McCusker, "The American Invasion of Nassau in the Bahamas," *American Neptune* (Jul 1965), pp. 89–217.

5. Kenneth Scott, "New Hampshire's Part in the Penobscot Expedition," *American Neptune* (Jul 1947), p. 212.

6. Alan G. Jamieson, "The Battle of Grenada and Caribbean Strategy, 1779," in William B. Cogar, ed., *Naval History: The Seventh Symposium of the U. S. Naval Academy* (Annapolis: Naval Institute Press, 1989), pp. 55–62.

7. Kennedy, *Rise,* p. 112.

8. Paullin, *Out-Letters,* Vol. II, pp. 79, 161.

9. Gardner W. Allen, *A Naval History of the American Revolution* (Boston: Houghton Mifflin, 1913), Vol. II, p. 557.

10. John R. Alden, *The American Revolution* (New York: Harper & Row, 1954), p. 241.

11. Rappaport, *Diplomacy,* pp. 26–27.

12. Francis Wharton, ed., *The Revolutionary Diplomatic Correspondence of the United States* (Washington: GPO, 1889), Vol. III, p. 833.

13. John E. Fitzpatrick, ed., *The Writings of George Washington from the Original Manuscript Sources, 1745–1799* (Washington: GPO, 1931–44), Vol. XXII, pp. 499–501.

Chapter Three

1. Harold and Margaret Sprout, *The Rise of American Naval Power, 1776–1918* (Princeton: Princeton University Press, 1939), p. 18.

2. Stephen T. Powers, "The Decline and Extinction of American Naval Power, 1781–87" (Unpubl. Ph.D. Diss., University of Notre Dame, 1965), pp. 173, 237.

3. Powers, "Decline," p. 238; Harry M. Ward, *The Department of War* (Pittsburg: University of Pittsburg Press, 1962); and Thomas Bryson, *Tars, Turks, and Tankers* (Metuchen, New Jersey: Scarecrow Press, 1980), p. 1

4. Sprout, *Rise*, pp. 18–19.

5. Frederick Marks, *Independence on Trial* (2nd ed.; Wilmington, Del.: Scholarly Resources, 1984), pp. 43, 39.

6. Julian P. Boyd et al., eds., *The Papers of Thomas Jefferson* (Princeton: Princton University Press, 1954–), Vol. X, pp. 224–25.

7. Sprout, *Rise*, p. 20.

8. Marks, *Independence*, p. 174; and Sprout, *Rise*, p. 21.

9. Sprout, *Rise*, p. 23; and Marks, *Independence*, p. 181.

10. Fitzpatrick, *Writings . . . Washington*, Vol. XXX, p. 512; and Sprout, *Rise*, p. 26.

11. Rappaport, *Diplomacy*, p. 38.

12. Craig L. Symonds, *Navalists and Antinavalists* (Newark: University of Delaware Press, 1980), pp. 31–32.

13. Dudley W. Knox, ed., *Naval Documents Relating to the United States War with the Barbary Powers* (Washington: GPO, 1939–44), Vol. I, pp. 69–70; Sprout, *Rise*, p. 33; Ray W. Irwin, *The Diplomatic Relations of the United States with the Barbary Powers* (Chapel Hill: University of North Carolina Press, 1931); and Ferguson, *Truxtun*, p. 109.

14. Symonds, *Navalists*, p. 46.

15. James D. Richardson, ed., *A Compilation of the Messages and Papers of the Presidents, 1789–1897* (Washington: GPO, 1896–99), Vol. I, p. 201.

16. Richard Morris, ed., *Great Presidential Decisions* (Philadelphia: Lippincott, 1960), pp. 45–46.

Chapter Four

1. William Stinchcombe, *The XYZ Affair* (Westport, Conn.: Greenwood Press, 1980), pp. 118, 112; Albion, *Sea Lanes*, p. 78; and Alexander deConde, *The Quasi War* (New York: Scribners, 1966).

2. Morris, *Presidential Decisions*, p. 50; and Rappaport, *Diplomacy*, p. 47.

3. Page Smith, *John Adams* (New York: Doubleday, 1962), Vol. II, p. 969; and Charles S. Tansill, "War Powers of the President of the United States," *Political Science Quarterly* (1930), pp. 1–55.

4. Dudley W. Knox, ed., *Naval Documents Relating to the Quasi War with France* (Washington: GPO, 1935–38), Vol. I, pp. 350, 49, 497. On the Pittsburg gunboats, see Leland B. Baldwin, *The Keelboat Age on Western Waters* (Pittsburg: University of Pittsburg Press, 1941), pp. 163–64.

5. William M. Fowler, *Jack Tars and Commodores* (Boston: Houghton Mifflin, 1985), p.42; and Michael A. Palmer, *Stoddert's War: Naval Operations during the*

Quasi War with France, 1798–1801 (Columbia: University of South Carolina Press, 1987).

6. Knox, *Naval Documents . . . Quasi War*, Vol. II, pp. 129–34; and Robert Albion, *The Makers of Naval Policy, 1798–1947* (Annapolis: Naval Institute Press, 1980), p. 182.

7. Symonds, *Navalists*, p. 76.

8. Michael A. Palmer, "The Dismission of Isaac Phillips," *American Neptune* (Spr 1985), pp. 94–103.

9. David F. Long, *Ready to Hazard: A Biography of Commodore William Bainbridge* (Hanover, N.H.: University Press of New England, 1981), p. 22; and Knox, *Naval Documents . . . Quasi War*, Vol. II, p. 327.

10. William J. Morgan, "John Barry," in Bradford, *Command*, p. 64.

11. James D. Phillips, "Salem's Part in the Naval War with France," *New England Quarterly* (Dec 1943), pp. 543–66; and McKee, "Preble," in Bradford, *Command*, p. 76.

12. Fowler, *Jack*, pp. 54–55.

13. Bradford Perkins, *The First Rapprochement: England and the United States* (Philadelphia: University of Pennsylvania Press, 1955); and Harold C. Syrett, ed., *The Papers of Alexander Hamilton* (New York: Columbia University Press, 1961–79), Vol. XXIII, pp. 227–28.

14. Morris, *Presidential Decisions*, p. 55; and *AR* in *ASP: Naval Affairs*, Vol. I, p. 74.

Chapter Five

1. Donald R. Hickey, "Federalist Defense Policy in the Age of Jefferson, 1801–1812," *Military Affairs* (Apr 1981), p. 64; and Anderson, "Adams," p. 102.

2. Charles Goldsborough, *The United States Naval Chronicle* (Washington: J. Willson, 1824), Vol. I, p. 86; and Albion, *Makers*, p. 183.

3. Richardson, *Messages*, Vol. I, pp. 309–12; Thomas A. Bailey, *A Diplomatic History of the American People*, 6th ed. (New York: Appleton-Century-Crofts, 1958), p. 100; and Smith, *Adams*, Vol. II, p. 1051.

4. Albion, *Makers*, p. 184.

5. Glenn Tucker, *Dawn Like Thunder: The Barbary Wars and the Birth of the United States Navy* (Indianapolis: Bobbs-Merrill, 1963), p. 58.

6. Knox, *Naval Documents . . . Barbary*, Vol. I, pp. 378–79.

7. Symonds, *Navalists*, pp. 91–93.

8. Knox, *Naval Documents . . . Barbary*, Vol. III, pp. 171–76; and Albion, *Makers*, p. 184.

9. Charles O. Paullin, *Commodore John Rodgers* (report; Annapolis: Naval Institute Press, 1967), p. 102.

10. Christopher McKee, "Edward Preble," in Bradford, ed., *Command*, pp. 71–96.

11. Spencer C. Tucker, "Mr. Jefferson's Gunboat Navy," *American Neptune* (Apr 1982), pp. 135–41; and Morris, *Presidential Decisions*, p. 67.

12. Fowler, *Jack*, p.104.

13. Fowler, *Jack*, p. 113.

Chapter Six

1. Arthur A. Lipscomb, ed., *The Writings of Thomas Jefferson* (Washington: Thomas Jefferson Memorial Assn., 1903–04), Vol. X, p. 312; and Hickey, "Federalist," p. 66.

2. Lipscomb, *Writings*, Vol. X, p. 312.

3. Bailey, *Diplomatic*, pp. 108–9.

4. Richard Peters, ed., *The Public Statutes at Large of the United States* (report; Washington: Microcard Editions, 1968), Vol. II, p. 330.

5. Hickey, "Federalist," pp. 63–70; Harvey Strum, "The *Leander* Affair," *American Neptune* (Jan 1983), pp. 40–50; and Lipscomb, *Writings*, Vol. X, p. 267.

6. Lipscomb, *Writings*, Vol. XI, pp. 288–89, and Vol. X, p. 267.

7. Anthony Steel, "More Light on the *Chesapeake-Leopard* Affair," *Mariner's Mirror* (Nov 1953), p. 265; Paullin, *Rodgers*, p. 196; and Edwin M. Gaines, "George C. Berkeley and the *Chesapeake-Leopard* Affair of 1807," in John Boiles, ed., *America: the Middle Period* (Charlottesville: University of Virginia Press, 1973), pp. 83–96. On impressment, see Jesse Lemisch, "Jack Tar in the Streets," *William and Mary Quarterly* (Jul 1968), pp. 381–95; and Anthony Steel, "Impressment in the Monroe-Pinckney Negotiation, 1806–07," *American Historical Review* (Jan 1952), pp. 352–69.

8. Sprout, *Rise*, p. 59.

9. Reginald C. Stuart, "James Madison and the Militants," *Diplomatic History* (Spr 1982), p. 148; and Louis M. Sears, *Jefferson and the Embargo* (Durham, N.C.: Duke University Press, 1926), p. 92.

10. Stuart, "Madison," p. 149.

11. Herbert Heaton, "Non-Importation, 1806–1812," *Journal of Economic History* (1944), pp. 194–96.

12. Sprout, *Rise*, p. 63.

13. Sprout, *Rise*, p. 63; and Symonds, *Navalists*, pp. 158–61.

14. Hickey, "Federalist," p. 66; Allan R. Millett and Peter Maslowski, *For the Common Defense* (New York: Free Press, 1984), p. 102; and Morris, *Presidential Decisions*, p. 78.

Chapter Seven

1. Edward K. Eckert, *The Navy Department in the War of 1812* (Gainesville: University of Florida Press, 1973), p. 25; John K. Mahon, *The War of 1812* (Gainesville: University of Florida Press, 1972); Reginald C. Stuart, *United States Expansionism and British North America, 1775–1871* (Chapel Hill: University of North Carolina Press, 1988); James E. Valle, "The Navy's Battle Doctrine in the War of 1812," *American Neptune* (Sum 1984), pp. 171–78; and Clifford L. Egan, "Thomas Jefferson's Greatest Mistake: The Decision for Peace, 1807," *Citadel Conference on War and Diplomacy, 1977* (Charleston, S.C.: Citadel, 1977), p. 96.

2. Hamilton to Decatur, 22 Jun 1812, Letters to Officers, SecNav Letters, USNA.

3. Maclay, *Navy*, Vol. I, p. 384–86.

4. Linda M. Maloney, *The Captain from Connecticut: The Life and Times of Isaac Hull* (Boston: Northeastern University Press, 1986), p. 182.

5. William S. Dudley and Michael J. Crawford, eds., *The Naval War of 1812: A Documentary History* (Washington: Navy Dept., 1985), Vol. I, p. 241.

6. Jones to Rodgers, et al., 22 Feb 1813, Letters to Officers, SecNav Letters, USNA.

7. Eckert, *Navy Department*, p. 25; and Donald G. Shmoette and Fred W. Hopkins, Jr., "The Search for the Chesapeake Flotilla," *American Neptune* (Jan 1983), pp. 5–8.

8. K. Jack Bauer, "Naval Shipbuilding Programs, 1794–1860," *Military Affairs* (Spr 1965), p. 33; and Dean R. Mayhew, "Jefferson's Gunboats in the War of 1812," *American Neptune* (Apr 1982), pp. 101–17.

9. Alfred T. Mahan, *Sea Power in Its Relation to the War of 1812* (Boston: Little, Brown, 1905), Vol. II, p. 151.

10. Maclay, *Navy*, Vol. I, p. 456; Albert Gleaves, *Captain James Lawrence, U. S. Navy* (New York: Putnam, 1904); Carl H. Amme, "Comment," *Naval History* (Fall

1989), p. 8; and Eckert, *Navy Department,* p. 21.

    11. David F. Long, "David Porter," in Bradford, *Command,* pp. 178–85.

    12. Perry to Jones, 10 September 1813, Letters from Captains, SecNav Letters, USNA.

Chapter Eight

    1. John P. Cranwell and William B. Crane, *Men of Marque* (New York: Norton, 1940).

    2. William L. Calderhead, "Naval Innovation in Crisis: War in the Chesapeake, 1813," *American Neptune* (Jul 1976), pp. 206–21.

    3. Julius W. Pratt, "Fur Trade Strategy and the American Left Flank in the War of 1812," *American Historical Review* (1935), pp. 246–73.

    4. Eckert, *Navy Department,* p. 30.

    5. Eckert, *Navy Department,* p. 27.

    6. Millet and Maslowski, *Common,* p. 110.

    7. John H. Schroeder, "Stephen Decatur," in Bradford, ed., *Command,* pp. 208–9.

    8. Robert J. Hanks, "'The Ruinous Folly of a Navy,'" in Clayton R. Barrow, ed., *America Spreads Her Sails* (Annapolis: Naval Institute Press, 1973), p. 9.

    9. James A. Carr, "The Battle of New Orleans and the Treaty of Ghent," *Diplomatic History* (Sum 1979), p. 279.

    10. Mayhew, "Gunboats," pp. 115–17; Eckert, *Navy Department,* p. 33; and Edward Channing, *A History of the United States* (New York: Macmillan, 1905–26), Vol. IV, p. 506.

    11. Eckert, *Navy Department,* p. 34; and Irving Brant, *James Madison* (Indianapolis: Bobbs-Merrill, 1961), Vol. VI, pp. 273–74.

    12. Charles G. Muller, *The Proudest Day: Macdonough on Lake Champlain* (New York: John Day, 1960).

    13. Eckert, *Navy Department,* p. 35.

    14. Fred L. Engelman, *The Peace of Christmas Eve* (New York: Harcourt, Brace, 1962).

    15. Bradford Perkins, *Castlereagh and Adams* (Berkeley: University of California Press, 1964), p. 161; and Irving Brant, "Madison and the War of 1812," *Virginia Magazine of History and Biography,* (1966), pp. 51–67.

Chapter Nine

    1. Long, *Ready,* p. 201.

    2. C. P. Stacey, "The Myth of the Unguarded Frontier, 1815–1871," *American Historical Review* (Fall 1950), p. 10; and Brant, *Madison,* Vol. VI, p. 406.

    3. Frederick Merk, *The Oregon Question* (Cambridge: Harvard University Press, 1976), pp. 17–18.

    4. Edwin M. Hall, "Benjamin W. Crowninshield," in Paolo E. Coletta, ed., *American Secretaries of the Navy* (Annapolis: Naval Institute Press, 1980), Vol. I, pp. 113–28;

    5. Paullin, *Rodgers,* pp. 306–9.

    6. Charles O. Paullin, "Naval Administration under the Navy Commissioners, 1816–1842," *Proceedings* (Jun 1907), pp. 597–642.

    7. Symonds, *Navalists,* p. 197; Sprout, *Rise,* pp. 88–89; and Raymond L. Shoemaker, "Diplomacy on the Quarterdeck," in Robert W. Love, Jr., ed., *Changing Interpretations and New Sources in Naval History* (New York: Garland Press, 1980), p. 173.

    8. Richard Dillon, *We Have Met the Enemy: Oliver Hazard Perry, Wilderness Commodore* (New York: McGraw-Hill, 1978), pp. 214–20.

    9. David F. Long, "The Navy under the Board of Commissioners," in Hagan,

Peace and War, p. 69; and Caspar Goodrich, "Our Navy and the West Indies Pirates," *Proceedings* (Jul and Nov 1916), pp. 1923–37.

10. Goodrich, "Pirates," p. 1936.

11. Samuel F. Bemis, *John Quincy Adams and the Foundations of American Foreign Policy* (New York: Knopf, 1949), pp. 383–85; Harry Ammon, "The Monroe Doctrine: Domestic Politics or National Decision," *Diplomatic History* (Wtr 1981), pp. 60–61; Morris, *Presidential Decisions*, pp. 92, 102; and Dexter Perkins, *A History of the Monroe Doctrine* (Rev. ed.; Boston: Little, Brown, 1955).

12. Morris, *Presidential Decisions*, p. 97; and Samuel E. Morison, *Old Bruin: Commodore Matthew Calbraith Perry* (Boston: Little, Brown, 1967), p. 79.

13. Long, "Porter," p. 191; and *AR: 1823*.

14. Symonds, *Navalists*, p. 231; and Edwin M. Hall, "Samuel Lewis Southard," in Coletta, *Secretaries*, Vol. I, pp. 131–40.

15. Richardson, *Messages*, Vol. II, pp. 361–62; Sprout, *Rise*, pp. 103–4; and Symonds, *Navalist*, p. 233.

16. Richardson, *Messages*, Vol. II, pp. 217–18.

17. *AR: 1823*.

18. Edward Baxter Billingsley, *In Defense of Neutral Rights* (Chapel Hill: University of North Carolina Press, 1967), p. 7.

19. Billingsley, *Defense*, p. 15.

20. Downes to Thompson, 20 Nov 1820, Letters from Captains, SecNav Letters, USNA.

21. T. Ray Shurbutt, "Chile, Peru, and the U. S. Pacific Squadron, 1823–1850," in Craig L. Symonds, ed., *New Aspects of Naval History* (Annapolis: Naval Institute Press, 1981), pp. 201–9; and Maloney, *Hull*, Ch. 13.

22. *AR: 1823*; David H. Finne, *Pioneers East* (Cambridge: Harvard University Press, 1980); Douglas Dakin, *The Greek Struggle for Independence* (Berkeley: University of California Press, 1973); and Paullin, *Rodgers*, Ch. 13.

23. *ASP: Naval Affairs*, Vol. III, p. 177.

24. *AR: 1827*.

25. Judd Scott Harmon, "Marriage of Convenience: The United States Navy in Africa, 1820–1843," *American Neptune* (Oct 1972), p. 265.

26. Harmon, "Marriage," p. 267.

27. Harmon, "Marriage," pp. 268–69; *AR: 1823*; and George Brooke, "The Role of the U. S. Navy in the Suppression of the African Slave Trade," *American Neptune* (Jan 1961), pp. 28–42.

Chapter Ten

1. John H. Schroeder, *Shaping a Maritime Empire* (Westport, Conn.: Greenwood Press, 1985), p. 19.

2. John K. Mahon, *A History of the Second Seminole War, 1835–42* (Gainesville: University of Florida Press, 1967).

3. *Niles National Register* (12 Dec 1829), p. 251; and Sprout, *Rise*, p. 105.

4. W. Patrick Strauss, "John Branch," in Coletta, ed., *Secretaries*, Vol. I, p. 145; and Schroeder, *Shaping*, p. 21.

5. *AR: 1834*.

6. James A. Field, *America and the Mediterranean World, 1776–1882* (Princeton: Princeton University Press, 1969), pp. 141–53.

7. *AR: 1831*; Celia Woodworth, "The USS *Potomac* and the Pepper Pirates," in Barrow, *America*, p. 69; and U.S. House, 22nd Cong., 1st Sess., 27 Jul 1837, House Doc. 485.

8. Arthur M. Schelsinger, Jr., *The Age of Jackson* (Boston: Little, Brown, 1947), p. 65.

9. Woodworth, *"Potomac,"* p. 62.

10. Woodworth, *"Potomac,"* p. 62.

11. Downes to Woodbury, 17 Feb 1832, Letters from Captains, SecNav Letters, USNA.

12. Schroeder, *Shaping,* p. 27–28.

13. *AR:1832;* and J. D. Phillips, *Pepper and Pirates* (Boston: Houghton Mifflin, 1949), pp. 103–6.

14. Curtis T. Henson, Jr., *Commissioners and Commodores: The East India Squadron and America Diplomacy in China* (University: University of Alabama Press, 1982); and Edmund Roberts, *An Embassy to the Eastern Courts* (New York: Harper, 1837).

15. *AR: 1836.*

16. Harold Peterson, *Argentina and the United States, 1810–1960* (New York: University Publ., 1964), p. 96; and Robert W. Love, Jr., "Anglo-American Naval Diplomacy and the Falkland Islands, 1820–1854," (Unpubl. Mss, USNA).

17. William R. Manning, ed., *The Diplomatic Correspondence of the United States Concerning the Independence of the Latin American Nations* (New York: Oxford University, Press, 1925), Vol. I, pp. 3–4.

18. Manning, *Correspondence,* Vol. I, p. 85.

19. Manning, *Correspondence,* Vol. I, p. 85.

20. Duncan to Woodbury, 3 Feb 1832, Letters from Masters Commandant, SecNav Letters; Robert Greenbow, "The Falkland Islands," *Hunt's Merchant's Magazine* (Feb 1842), pp. 14–15; and Parrish to Palmerston, c15 Feb 1831, FO 6–499, PRO.

21. Palmerston to Fox, 22 Mar 1832, FO 6–499, PRO.

22. K. Jack Bauer, "The U. S. Navy and Texas Independence," *Military Affairs* (Apr 1970), p. 45; and *AR: 1836.*

23. Bauer, "Texas Independence," p. 46.

24. Bauer, "Texas Independence," p. 46.

25. Morris, *Presidential Decisions,* p. 316.

26. Bailey, *Diplomatic,* pp. 195–98.

27. Robert C. Thomas, "Andrew Jackson Versus France: American Policy toward France, 1834–36," *Tennessee Historical Quarterly* (Spr 1972), pp. 51–64; John M. Belohlavek, *Let the Eagle Soar: The Foreign Policy of Andrew Jackson* (Lincoln: University of Nebraska Press, 1985), pp. 102–25; and *AR: 1834.*

28. *AR: 1835;* and W. Patrick Strauss, "Mahan Dickerson, in Coletta, *Secretaries,* Vol. I, p. 158.

29. Charles O. Paullin, *Paullin's History of Naval Administration, 1775–1911* (reprint ed.; Annapolis: Naval Institute Press, 1968), p. 197.

30. Sprout, *Rise,* p. 115.

Chapter Eleven

1. Harold D. Langley, *Social Reform in the United States Navy, 1798–1862* (Urbana: University of Illinois Press, 1967), p. 27; *AR: 1833.*

2. *AR: 1841;* and Paolo E. Coletta, *The American Naval Heritage in Brief* (Washington: University Press of America, 1978), p. 102.

3. Paolo E. Coletta, "George E. Badger," in Coletta, *Secretaries,* Vol. I, p. 174.

4. William F. Lynch, *A Naval Life* (New York: Charles Scribner, 1851), p. 150.

5. U.S. Senate, 27th Cong., 1st Sess., Exec. Doc. No 1, 1841, pp. 61–62.

6. Sprout, *Rise,* p. 119.

7. Paullin, *Administration,* p. 189.

8. Geoffrey S. Smith, "An Uncertain Passage: The Bureaus Run the Navy, 1842–1861," in Hagan, *Peace and War,* p. 83.

9. Sprout, *Rise*, p. 119.

10. Bauer, "Shipbuilding," p. 36.

11. U.S. Senate, 37th Cong., 2nd Sess., *CR*, 27 Mar 1862, p. 1394.

12. J. W. McIntire, ed., *The Writings and Speeches of Daniel Webster* (Boston: Little, Brown, 1903), Vol. XII, pp. 21–30; and Kenneth E. Shewmaker, "The War of Words: The Cass-Webster Debate of 1842–1843," *Diplomatic History* (Spr 1981), p. 155.

13. Donald R. Wright, "Matthew Perry and the African Squadron," in Barrow, ed., *America*, p. 84.

14. Wright, "Perry," p. 89.

15. Wright, "Perry", pp. 90–91.

16. C. Ian Jackson, "Exploration as Science: Charles Wilkes and the U. S. Exploring Expedition, 1838–42," *American Scientist* (Sep 1985), pp. 450–61; and William J. Morgan et al., *Autobiography of Rear Admiral Charles Wilkes, USN, 1798–1877* (Washington: GPO, 1979).

17. E. Mobray Tate, "American Contacts with China," *American Neptune* (Jul 1971), p. 182.

18. Tate, "Contacts," p. 182; and Carroll S. Alden, *Lawrence Kearny, Sailor Diplomat* (Princeton: Princeton University Press, 1936).

19. Tate, "Contacts," p. 188; and E. Mobray Tate, "U.S. Gunboats on the Yangtze: History and Political Aspects, 1842–1922," in *Studies on Asia* (Lincoln: University of Nebraska Press, 1966), pp. 21–32.

20. U.S. Senate, 29th Cong., 1st Sess., Doc. No. 139.

21. Frank M. Bennett, *The Steam Navy of the United States* (Pittsburgh: W. T. Nicholson, 1896), p. 67.

Chapter Twelve

1. George M. Brooke, Jr., "The Vest Pocket War of Commodore Jones," *Pacific Historical Review* (Aug 1962), pp. 217–33; and Galbert Workman, "A Forgotten Firebrand: Commodore Thomas C. Jones," *Proceedings* (Sep 1968), pp. 79–87.

2. Kinley J. Brauer, "The United States and British Imperial Expansion, 1815–1860," *Diplomatic History* (Wtr 1988), p. 25; and Norman Graebner, *Empire on the Pacific: A Study in American Continental Expansion* (New York: Ronald Press, 1955).

3. Sprout, *Rise*, p. 130.

4. Jack Sweetman, *The U. S. Naval Academy: An Illustrated History* (Annapolis: Naval Institute Press, 1979).

5. Merrill J. Bartlett, "Commodore James Biddle and the First Naval Mission to Japan, 1845–1846," *American Neptune* (Jan 1981), pp. 25–35.

6. Amos L. Mason, *Memoir and Correspondence of Charles Stedman, Rear Admiral, U. S. Navy* (Cambridge, Mass.: privately printed, 1912), p. 138.

7. Merk, *Oregon*, p. 340.

8. Julius Pratt, "James K. Polk and John Bull," *Canadian Historical Review* (1943), pp. 341–49; Merk, *Oregon*, Ch. 12; and Mark A. DeWolfe Howe, *The Life and Letters of George Bancroft* (New York: Scribners, 1908), p. 282.

9. Rappaport, *Diplomacy*, p. 106.

10. K. Jack Bauer, *Surfboats and Horse Marines: U. S. Naval Operations in the Mexican War, 1846–1848* (Annapolis: Naval Institute Press, 1969), p. 146.

11. John A. Hessey, "Commander John B. Montgomery and the Bear Flag Revolt," *Proceedings* (Jul 1939), pp. 973–80; and George P. Hammond, ed., *The Larkin Papers* (Berkeley: University of California Press, 1951–64), Vol. V, pp. 107–8.

12. Bauer, *Surfboats*, pp. 191–234; and Harold D. Langley, "Robert F. Stockton," in Bradford, *Command*, pp. 286–91.

13. Howe, *Bancroft Letters,* p. 287.

14. Bauer, *Surfboats,* p. 22.

15. Bauer, *Surfboats,* p. 31.

16. Bauer, *Surfboats,* pp. 46–51.

17. Caspar F. Goodrich, "Alvarado Hunter: A Biographical Sketch," *Proceedings* (Mar 1918), pp. 495–514.

18. Milo M. Quaife, ed., *The Diary of James K. Polk* (Chicago: A. C. McClurg, 1910), Vol. II, pp. 465–67.

Chapter Thirteen

1. Bailey, *Diplomatic* p. 273.

2. Brauer, "Imperial Expansion," p. 31; and Bailey, *Diplomatic,* p. 274.

3. Bailey, *Diplomatic,* p. 276.

4. Bauer, "Shipbuilding," p. 38; U.S. Senate, 32nd Cong., 2nd Sess., Doc. 1, p. 320; and Harold D. Langley, "John Pendleton Kennedy," in Coletta, *Secretaries,* Vol. I, p. 272.

5. Albion, *Makers,* p. 310.

6. Albion, *Makers,* p. 311–12; and Morris, *Presidential Decisions,* pp. 194–95.

7. Morison, *Old Bruin,* Chs. 21–28.

8. Vincent Ponko, Jr., *Ships, Seas, and Scientists: U. S. Naval Explorations and Discoveries in the Nineteenth Century* (Annapolis: Naval Institute Press, 1974), pp. 142–157.

9. Bailey, *Diplomatic,* p. 310.

Chapter Fourteen

1. *AR, 1856;* and Richardson, *Messages,* Vol. IV, pp. 2748, 2942.

2. Sprout, *Rise,* p. 142.

3. Richardson, *Messages,* Vol. V, pp. 198–99.

4. Bailey, *Diplomatic,* p. 295; and Sprout, *Rise,* p. 143.

5. U.S. House, 33rd Cong., 2nd Sess., Doc. 93, pp. 129–31.

6. Schroeder, *Shaping,* p. 127.

7. Bailey, *Diplomatic,* p. 277.

8. Richardson, *Messages,* Vol. IV, p. 212.

9. Robert Erwin Johnson, *Far China Station: The U. S. Navy in Asian Waters, 1800–1898* (Annapolis: Naval Institute Press, 1979), p. 74.

10. David F. Long, "A Case for Intervention: Armstrong, Foote, and the Destruction of the Barrier Forts, Canton, China, 1856," in Symonds, *New Aspects,* pp. 220–37.

11. Julius W. Pratt, "Our First 'War' in China: The Diary of William Henry Powell, 1856," *American Historical Review* (Jul 1948), p. 786; and Schroeder, *Shaping,* p. 182.

12. V. F. Boyson, *The Falkland Islands* (Oxford: Clarendon Press, 1924), pp. 123–53.

13. Robert W. Love, Jr., "Anglo-American Naval Diplomacy and the Falkland Islands, 1820–1854," Unpubl. paper delivered at the Society for Historians of American Foreign Affairs, 18 Aug 1983, Washington, D.C.

14. Schroeder, *Maritime,* p. 132.

15. Sprout, *Rise,* p. 146; and Joseph T. Durkin, *Confederate Navy Chief: Stephen R. Mallory* (Columbia: University of South Carolina Press, 1954), p. 99.

16. Schroeder, *Maritime,* p. 132.

17. Schroeder, *Maritime,* p. 131.

18. James M. Merrill, *Du Pont: The Making of an Admiral* (New York: Dodd, Mead, 1986), p. 238.

19. Charles C. Jones, Jr., *Life and Services of Commodore Josiah Tattnall* (Savannah: Morning News Press, 1878), pp. 104–8; and Schroeder, *Shaping*, p. 182.

20. Schroeder, *Maritime*, p. 114.

21. Clare V. McKenna, "The *Water Witch* Incident," *American Neptune* (Jan 1971), p. 10; and John Hoyt Williams, "The Wake of the *Water Witch*," *Proceedings* (Suppl. 1985), pp. 14–19.

22. McKenna, *Water Witch*, p. 13; and Richard C. Froehlich, "The U. S. Navy and Diplomatic Relations with Brazil, 1822–1871," (Unpubl. Ph.D. Diss., Kent State University, 1971), p. 313.

23. McKenna, *Water Witch*, p. 15; and Schroeder, *Maritime*, p. 116.

24. Froehlich, "Brazil," pp. 315–17; and S. R. Franklin, *Memories of a Rear Admiral* (New York: Harper and Bros., 1898), p. 160.

Chapter Fifteen

1. Richard S. West, Jr. *Mr. Lincoln's Navy* (New York: Longmans, Green, 1957), p. 14; and Virgil Carrington Jones, *The Civil War at Sea* (3 vols.; New York: Holt, Rinehart, and Winston, 1960–62).

2. Bailey, *Diplomatic*, p. 446; Howard K. Beale, ed., *Diary of Gideon Welles* (New York: Norton, 1960), Vol. I, Ch. 1; and West, *Navy*, pp. 17–18.

3. John Niven, *The Coming of the Civil War* (Arlington Heights, Ill.: Harland Davidson, 1989), pp. 140–41; and West, *Navy*, pp. 26–27.

4. Kenneth Stampp, *And The War Came* (2nd ed.; Chicago: University of Chicago Press, 1965), pp. 285, 227.

5. David D. Porter, *The Naval History of the Civil War* (Repr.; Secaucus, N.J.: Castle, 1984), p. 360.

6. U.S. Naval War Records Office, *Official Records of the Union and Confederate Navies in the War of the Rebellion* (Washington: GPO, 1894–1927), Series II, Vol. I, pp. 44–45; Bern Anderson, "The Naval Strategy of the Civil War," *Military Affairs* (Spr 1962), pp. 11–21; and Russell F. Weigley, *The American Way of War* (New York: Macmillan, 1973), pp. 93–98.

7. West, *Navy*, p. 103.

8. Stanley Sandler, "A Navy in Decay: Some Strategic Technological Results of Disarmament," *Military Affairs* (Dec 1971), p. 139.

9. E. B. Potter and Chester W. Nimitz, eds., *Sea Power* (Englewood Cliffs, N.J.: Prentice-Hall, 1960), p. 263; William C. Church, *The Life of John Ericsson* (New York: Scribner, 1890), Vol. I, p. 245; and William M. Fowler, Jr., *Under Two Flags: The American Navy in the Civil War* (New York: Norton, 1990), p. 80.

10. Norman B. Ferris, *Desperate Diplomacy* (Knoxville: University of Tennessee Press, 1976), p. 13; Frank J. Merli, *Great Britain and the Confederate Navy, 1861–1865* (Bloomington: Indiana University Press, 1970); and Carlton Savage, *The Policy of the United States toward Maritime Commerce in War* (Washington: GPO, 1934), Vol. I, p. 381.

11. *FRUS: 1861*, pp. 71–80; and D. P. Crook, *The North, the South, and the Powers, 1861–1865* (New York: Hohn Wiley, 1974), p. 78.

12. Crook, *Powers*, p. 64.

13. Marcus W. Price, "Ships That Tested Georgia and East Florida Ports," *American Neptune* (Apr 1955), p. 98.

14. Norman B. Ferris, *The Trent Affair* (Knoxville: University of Tennessee Press, 1977), p. 20.

15. West, *Navy*, p. 96.

16. West, *Navy*, pp. 95, 281.

17. Robert W. Love, Jr., "The End of the Atlantic Slave Trade to Cuba," *Caribbean Quarterly* (Jun 1976), pp. 51–59; Crook, *Powers*, p. 189; and William N. Still, Jr., "Historical Importance of the *Monitor*," in Cogar, *Naval History*, p. 76.

18. Bailey, *Diplomatic,* p. 337; and Crook, *Powers,* p. 226.
19. Crook, *Powers,* p. 181.

Chapter Sixteen
1. Stampp, *War,* p. 291; W. M. Robinson, *The Confederate Privateers* (New Haven: Yale University Press, 1928); and David and Joan Hay, *The Last of the Confederate Privateers* (New York: Crescent Books, 1977).
2. West, *Navy,* p. 271; Raphael Semmes, *Memoirs of Service Afloat During the War Between the States* (New York: Rogers and Isherwood, 1887), p. 757.
3. Nathan L. Ferris, "The Relations of the United States with South America during the American Civil War," *Hispanic American Historical Review* (Feb 1941), pp. 51–78.
4. Albion, *Sea Lanes,* p. 151.
5. Ephraim D. Adams, *Great Britain and the American Civil War* (London: Longmans, Green, 1925), pp. 141–44.
6. NHD, *Civil War Naval Chronology, 1861–1865* (Washington: GPO, 1965), Vol. V, p. 65.
7. Albion, *Sea Lanes,* pp. 148–73; Frank J. Merli, "The Confederate Navy, 1861–65," in Hagan, *Peace and War,* Ch. 7; and William N. Still, Jr., *Confederate Shipbuilding* (Athens: University of Georgia Press, 1969).

Chapter Seventeen
1. *Official Records Navies,* Series II, Vol. II, p. 152.
2. John L. Worden et al., *The Monitor and the Merrimack* (New York: Harper and Bros., 1912), p. 6; and Worden to Welles, 5 Jan 1868, reprinted in *Proceedings* (Feb 1927), pp. 202–3. The definitive account of the engagement is William C. Davis, *Duel Between the First Ironclads* (Baton Rouge: Louisiana State University Press, 1975).
3. Rowena Reed, *Combined Operations in the Civil War* (Annapolis: Naval Institute Press, 1978), p. 139.
4. Reed, *Combined,* p. 127.
5. Reed, *Combined,* p. 162.
6. Robert Erwin Johnson, *Rear Admiral John Rodgers* (Annapolis: Naval Institute Press, 1967), p. 198.
7. Johnson, *Rodgers,* p. 204; Durkin, *Mallory,* p. 214; and Reed, *Combined,* p. 169.
8. Durkin, *Mallory,* p. 220.
9. Durkin, *Mallory,* p. 222.
10. Reed, *Combined,* pp. 179–81.
11. Reed, *Combined,* p. 180.
12. Reed, *Combined,* p. 263.

Chapter Eighteen
1. *Official Records Navies,* Series I, Vol. XXII, p. 336. Also see James M. Hoppin, *The Life of Andrew W. Foote, Rear Admiral, U. S. Navy* (New York: Harper and Bros., 1874.)
2. Porter, *Naval,* p. 143.
3. Johnson, *Rodgers,* p. 167.
4. West, *Navy,* p. 175.
5. Richard S. West, Jr., *The Second Admiral* (New York: Coward-McCann, 1937), p. 149.
6. Lee N. Newcomer, "The Battle of the Rams," *American Neptune* (Apr 1965), pp. 128–39.
7. Porter, *Naval,* p. 256.

8. Carl Sandburg, *Abraham Lincoln: The War Years* (New York: Harcourt Brace, 1939), Vol. II, p. 348.

9. *Official Records Navies*, Series I, Vol. XXV, pp. 103–6.

10. Thomas L. Connelly, "Vicksburg: Strategic Point or Propaganda Device?", *Military Affairs* (Apr 1970), pp. 49–53.

11. Howard C. Westwood, "After Vicksburg, What of Mobile?", *Military Affairs* (Oct 1984), pp. 169–72.

Chapter Nineteen

1. *AR: 1861*; Edward F. Merrifield, "The Seaboard War: A History of the North Atlantic Blockading Squadron, 1861–1865" (Unpubl. Ph.D. Diss., Case Western Reserve University, 1975); and Robert M. Browning, Jr., "From Cape Charles to Cape Fear: The North Atlantic Blockading Squadron During the Civil War" (Unpubl. Ph.D. Diss., University of Alabama, 1988).

2. William N. Still, Jr., "A Naval Sieve? The Union Blockade in the Civil War," *Naval War College Review* (May-June 1983), pp. 43–44.

3. Crook, *Powers*, p. 172.

4. Merrill, *Du Pont*, p. 260.

5. Merrill, *Du Pont*, p. 269.

6. John D. Hayes, ed., *Samuel Francis Du Pont: A Selection from his War Letters* (Ithaca, N.Y.: Cornell University Press, 1969), Vol. II, p. 129; and John Niven, "Gideon Welles and Naval Administration During the Civil War," *American Neptune* (Jan 1975), pp. 59–60.

7. Hayes, *Du Pont*, Vol. II, p. 387.

8. Merrill, *Du Pont*, pp. 293–94.

9. Merrill, *Du Pont*, pp. 295–98.

10. Richard Lester, "Confederate Finance and Purchasing in Great Britain During the American Civil War" (Unpubl. Ph.D. Diss., Manchester, UK, 1962).

11. E. Milby Burton, *The Siege of Charleston* (Columbia: University of South Carolina Press, 1970), p. 248; Price, "Georgia . . . Ports," pp. 97–132; "Ships That Tested the Blockade of Carolina Ports, 1861–1865," *American Neptune* (Jul 1948), pp. 196–214; and "Ships That Tested the Blockade of Gulf Ports," *American Neptune* (Oct 1951), pp. 262–97.

12. William N. Still, Jr., "David Glasgow Farragut," in James C. Bradford, ed., Captains of the Old Steam Navy (Annapolis: Naval Institute Press, 1986), p. 184.

13. Porter, *Naval*, pp. 470–71.

14. Porter, *Naval*, p. 477.

15. Burton, *Siege*, pp. 195–99.

16. Benjamin F. Sands, *From Reefer to Rear Admiral* (New York: Frederick A. Stokes, 1899), p. 256.

17. Porter, *Naval*, p. 692.

18. Mason, *Stedman*, pp. 395–96; and Tamara Moser Melia, "David Dixon Porter," in James Bradford, ed., *Captains of the Old Steam Navy* (Annapolis: Naval Institute Press, 1986), p. 235.

19. Porter, *Naval*, p. 755.

20. Stephen R. Wise, "Lifeline of the Confederacy: Blockade Running During the Civil War" (Unpubl. Ph.D. Diss., University of South Carolina, 1983), pp. 479–84.

21. Price, "Georgia . . . Ports," p. 100; and Burton, *Siege*, p. 249.

22. *Chronology*, Vol. V, pp. 54, 76.

Chapter Twenty

1. Bailey, *Diplomatic*, p. 352. Also see Charles S. Campbell, *The Transformation of American Foreign Relations, 1865–1900* (New York: Harper & Row, 1976).

2. Bailey, *Diplomatic*, p. 354.

3. Kenneth J. Hagan, *American Gunboat Diplomacy and the Old Navy* (Westport, Conn.: Greenwood Press, 1973), p. 150.

4. Rappaport, *Diplomacy*, p. 167.

5. Barry Rigby, "American Expansion in Hawaii," *Diplomatic History* (Fall 1980), p. 358.

6. Sandler, "Decay," pp. 139–40; and William S. Peterson, "Congressional Politics: Building the New Navy, 1876–86," *Armed Forces and Society* (Summer 1988), pp. 489–508.

7. Sprout, *Rise*, p. 166; and Sandler, "Decay," p. 141.

8. Paullin, *Administration*, p. 330.

9. Albion, *Makers*, p. 168.

10. Leonard A. Swann, Jr., *John Roach: Maritime Entrepreneur* (Annapolis: Naval Institute Press, 1965), p. 42.

11. General Order No. 128, 11 June 1869, and General Order No. 131, 18 June 1869, Directives File No. 42, RG 45, NA; Dept. of the Navy, *Regulations, 1870* (Washington: Navy Dept., 1897), pp. 36–37; Sandler, "Decay," pp. 139–40; and Albion, *Makers*, pp. 200–203.

12. Swann, *Roach*, p. 135.

13. Albion, *Makers*, p. 169.

14. Lance C. Buel, "Mariners and Machines: Resistance to Technological Change in the American Navy, 1865–69," *Journal of American History* (Dec 1974), p. 703.

15. Buel, "Mariners," p. 721; and Swann, *Roach*, p. 43.

16. Robert G. Albion, "George M. Robeson," in Coletta, *Secretaries*, Vol. I, pp. 369–80.

17. Lawrence C. Allin, "The First Cubic War—The *Virginius* Affair," *American Neptune* (Jan 1983), pp. 233–48.

18. Richard H. Bradford, *The 'Virginius' Affair* (Boulder: University of Colorado, 1980), pp. 39–54.

19. Allin, "Cubic War," p. 245; and Bradford, *Virginius*, p. 65.

20. Albion, "Robeson," p. 373; and Paullin, *Administration*, p. 336.

21. Paullin, *Administration*, p. 346.

22. Kenneth J. Hagan, "Showing the Flag in the Indian Ocean," in Barrow, ed., *America*, p. 171.

23. Johnson, *Rodgers*, p. 311.

24. Johnson, *Rodgers*, p. 314; and Winfield S. Schley, *Forty-Five Years Under the Flag* (New York: D. Appleton, 1904), pp. 90–95.

25. Paullin, *Administration*, p. 338.

26. Paullin, *Administration*, p. 338.

27. Peterson, "Congressional Politics," pp. 489–508.

28. Robert Seager II, *Alfred Thayer Mahan* (Annapolis: Naval Institute Press, 1975), p. 200

29. Hagan, "Showing," p. 166.

Chapter Twenty-one

1. *AR: 1881*.

2. Johnson, *China Station*, pp. 184–90.

3. Frederick C. Drake, "Robert Wilson Shufeldt," in Bradford, *Captains*, pp. 287–89.

4. Johnson, *China Station*, pp. 184–93.

5. Johnson, *Rodgers*, p. 367; *AR: 1881*; and Donald J. Sexton, "Forging the Sword: Congress and the American Naval Renaissance, 1880–1890," (Unpubl. Ph.D. Diss., University of Tennessee, 1976).

6. Robely D. Evans, *A Sailor's Log* (New York: D. Appleman, 1901), p. 230.

7. B. Franklin Cooling, *Gray Steel and Blue Water Navy* (Hamden, Conn.: Archon Books, 1979), p. 30; and Sprout, *Rise*, pp. 194–95.

8. Sprout, *Rise*, p. 192.

9. *AR: 1883.*

10. Albert Gleaves, *Life and Letters of Rear Admiral Stephen B. Luce, U. S. Navy* (New York: Putnam, 1925), pp. 99–101; and Ronald Spector, *Professors of War* (Washington: GPO, 1977), p. 14.

11. Richard A. West, Jr., *Admirals of the American Empire* (Indianapolis: Bobbs-Merrill, 1948), p. 113.

12. Walter R. Herrick, Jr., *The American Naval Revolution* (Baton Rouge: Louisiana State University Press, 1966), p. 35.

13. William Bainbridge-Hoff, Bureau of Navigation, "Examples, Conclusions, and Maxims of Modern Naval Tactics," (Washington: GPO, 1884), pp. 133, 139–41; and *AR: 1887.*

14. Richardson, *Messages*, Vol. VII, pp. 168–69.

15. Bailey, *Diplomatic*, p. 423.

16. Bailey, *Diplomatic*, p. 424.

17. Herrick, *Naval Revolution*, p. 58.

18. Bailey, *Diplomatic*, p. 425; and Ernest Andrade, "The Great Samoan Hurricane of 1889," *Naval War College Review* (Jan 1981), p. 81.

Chapter Twenty-two

1. Herrick, *Naval Revolution*, p. 91.

2. Herrick, *Naval Revolution*, p. 102.

3. B. Franklin Cooling, *Benjamin Franklin Tracy* (Hamden, Conn.: Archon Books, 1973), p. 116.

4. Francis X. Holbrook and John Nikol, "The Chilean Crisis of 1891–1892," *American Neptune* (Oct 1978), pp. 291–300.

5. Evans, *Log*, p. 259.

6. Herrick, *Naval Revolution*, p. 123.

7. Herrick, *Naval Revolution*, p. 127.

8. Seager, *Mahan*, p. 328.

9. Seager, *Mahan*, pp. 204, 170.

10. Love, *Interpetations*, p. ix.

11. Seager, *Mahan*, pp. 206–7.

12. Seager, *Mahan*, p. 203; and A. T. Mahan, *Naval Administration and Warfare* (Boston: Little, Brown, 1908), p. 167.

13. Merli, "Confederate Navy," in Hagan, *Peace and War*, p. 133.

14. Seager, *Mahan*, p. 209.

15. *AR: 1890.*

16. William T. Sampson, "Outline of a Scheme for the Naval Defense of the Coast," *Proceedings* (Apr 1889), pp. 169–232; and *AR: 1890.*

17. *AR: 1890.*

18. U.S. House, 53rd Cong., 2nd Sess., Exec. Doc. No. 11, p. 37.

19. Hugh B. Hammett, "The Cleveland Administration and Anglo-American Naval Friction in Hawaii, 1893–1894," *Military Affairs* (Feb 1979), pp. 27–32.

20. Cooling, *Gray Steel*, p. 113.

21. Cooling, *Gray Steel*, p. 118.

22. *AR: 1896.*

23. Sprout, *Rise*, p. 221.

24. Bailey, *Diplomatic*, p. 441.

25. Rappaport, *Diplomacy*, p. 188.

26. Rappaport, *Diplomacy*, p. 192.

Chapter Twenty-three

1. Paolo E. Coletta, "John Davis Long," in Coletta, *Secretaries*, Vol. I, pp. 431–32; Herrick, *Naval Revolution*, p. 194; and Lawrence S. Mayo, ed., *America of Yesterday as Reflected in the Journal of John D. Long* (Boston: Atlantic Monthly Press, 1923), p. 157.

2. James A. Field, Jr., *History of United States Naval Operations: Korea* (Washington: GPO, 1962), p. 6.

3. H. P. Willmott, *Empires in the Balance* (Annapolis: Naval Institute Press, 1982), p. 20.

4. Seager, *Mahan*, p. 505.

5. William M. Morgan, "The Anti-Japanese Origins of the Hawaiian Annexation Treaty of 1897," *Diplomatic History* (Wtr 1982), p. 33.

6. Morgan, "Annexation," pp. 37–43; and Spector, *Professors*, p. 96.

7. *AR: 1896*; and Sprout, *Rise*, pp. 228–29.

8. Coletta, *Heritage*, p. 132.

9. Coletta, *Heritage*, p. 153; and Rappaport, *Diplomacy*, p. 193.

10. Coletta, *Heritage*, p. 154; Rappaport, *Diplomacy*, p. 194; John D. Long, *The New American Navy* (New York: Outlook, 1903), Vol. I, p. 145; and Morris, *Presidential Decisions*, pp. 319–22.

11. Ronald Spector, *Admiral of the New Empire* (Baton Rouge: Louisiana State University Press, 1974), pp. 51, 46; and George Dewey, *Autobiography* (New York: Dorrance, 1913).

12. West, *Admirals* ; David F. Trask, *The War with Spain in 1898* (New York: Macmillan, 1981); Spector, *Admiral*, pp. 73–74; Philip Y. Nicholson, "Admiral George Dewey after Manila Bay," *American Neptune* (Jan 1977), pp. 26–39; and Alfred L. Dennis, *Adventures in American Diplomacy* (New York: Dutton, 1928), p. 98.

13. *AR: 1898*, Vol. II, p. 69.

14. Long, *New American Navy*, Vol. I, pp. 148, 206; and Charles E. Clark, *My Fifty Years in the Navy* (Boston: Little, Brown, 1917), pp. 266–71.

15. West, *Admirals*, p. 226; and Maclay, *Navy*, Vol. III, p. 103.

16. Maclay, *Navy*, Vol. III, p. 104; and West, *Admirals*, p. 231.

17. Maclay, *Navy*, Vol. III, 282–88; and Schley, *Forty-Five Years*, p. 382.

18. Edmund Morris, *The Rise of Theodore Roosevelt* (New York: Coward, McCann, 1979), p. 628.

19. George J. Tanham, "Service Relations Sixty Years Ago," *Military Affairs* (Fall 1967), p. 142.

20. Potter and Nimitz, *Sea Power*, p. 184; Tanham, "Relations," p. 144; and Morris, *Roosevelt*, p. 635.

21. Tanham, "Relations," p. 147.

22. Tanham, "Relations," p. 148; and Gardner W. Allen, ed., *The Papers of John Davis Long* (Norwood, Ma.: Massachusetts Historical Society, 1939), p. 210.

23. William J. Hourihan, "The Fleet That Never Was: Commodore John Curt Watson and the Eastern Squadron," *American Neptune* (Apr 1981), p. 93.

24. L. W. Walker, "Guam's Seizure by the United States in 1898," *Pacific Historical Review* (1945), pp. 1–12; and Mayo, *America of Yesterday*, p. 214.

25. Barbara Tomblin, "The United States Navy and the Philippine Insurrection," *American Neptune* (Jul 1975), pp. 183–95; Vernon L. Williams, "The U.S. Navy in the Philippine Insurrection and Subsequent Native Unrest, 1898–1906" (Unpubl. Ph.D. Diss., Texas A & M University, 1985); and Dept. of State, *Correspondence Relating to the War with Spain and Conditions Growing Out of Same, Including the Insurrection in the Philippines and the China Relief Expedition* (Washington: GPO, 1902).

26. Yates Stirling, *Sea Duty: The Memoirs of a Fighting Admiral* (New York: Putnam's, 1939), p. 79.

Chapter Twenty-four

1. William R. Braisted, *The United States Navy in the Pacific, 1897–1909* (Austin: University of Texas Press, 1958), p. 77; Bailey, *Diplomatic*, p. 481.

2. *FRUS: 1900*, p. 110.

3. U.S. House, 57th Cong., 1st Sess., "Bombardment of the Taku Forts in China, 1901," House Doc. No. 645, pp. 12–14. Also see D. W. Wurtzbaugh, "The Seymour Relief Expedition," *Proceedings* (Jun 1902), pp. 207–9; and Joseph W. Taussig, "Experiences During the Boxer Rebellion," *Proceedings* (Apr 1927), pp. 403–10.

4. Bailey, *Diplomatic*, p. 482.

5. Braisted, *Pacific, 1897–1909*, p. 135.

6. W. W. Reisinger, "Torpedoes," *Proceedings* (1888), p. 521.

7. William R. Hawkins, "Captain Mahan, Admiral Fisher, and Arms Control at the Hague, 1899," *Naval War College Review* (Jan 1986), p. 82.

8. Andrew D. White, *Autobiography* (New York: Century, 1904), Vol. II, pp. 250, 346; and Alfred Thayer Mahan, *The Interest of America in Sea Power, Present and Future* (Boston: Little, Brown, 1899), p. 177.

9. Hawkins, "Hague," p. 84–88.

10. G. P. Gooch and Harold W. Temperly, eds., *British Documents on the Origins of the War, 1898–1914* (London: HMSO, 1926–1937), Vol. I, p. 23.

Chapter Twenty-five

1. Morris, *Presidential Decisions*, p. 338; Long, *New American Navy*, Vol. II, pp. 184–85; and Paul T. Heffron, "Paul Morton," in Coletta, *Secretaries*, Vol. I, p. 470.

2. GenBd to SecNav, 12 Oct 1903, File 8557–18, SecNav Records, RG 45, NA; Elting E. Morison, *Admiral Sims and the Modern American Navy* (Boston: Houghton Mifflin, 1942), p. 83; and Paolo E. Coletta, *A Survey of U.S. Naval Affairs, 1865–1917* (Lanham, Md.: University Press of America, 1987), pp. 126–29.

3. U.S. House, 60th Cong., 1st Sess., Committee on Naval Affairs, "Hearings on Estimates Submitted by the Secretary of the Navy, 1908," 1907, pp. 370–74.

4. William S. Sims, "Roosevelt and the Navy," *McClure's* (1922), pp. 56–57.

5. Morison, *Sims*, pp. 80–86, 103; Archer Jones and Andrew J. Keogh, "The Dreadnought Revolution: Another Look," *Military Affairs* (Jul 1985), pp. 124–31; and Robert L. O'Connell, "Dreadnought? The Battleship, the U.S. Navy, and the World Naval Community" (Unpubl. Ph.D. Diss., University of Virginia, 1974).

6. Albert C. Stillson, "Military Policy without Political Guidance: Theodore Roosevelt's Navy," *Military Affairs* (Spr 1962), pp. 18–56.

7. Gordon C. O'Gara, *Theodore Roosevelt and the Rise of the Modern Navy* (Princeton: Princeton University Press, 1943), p. 7; and Rappaport, *Diplomacy*, p. 223.

8. Sprout, *Rise*, pp. 250–51; and Richard W. Turk, "The U.S. Navy and the Taking of Panama, 1901–1903," *Military Affairs* (Sep 1974), p. 92.

9. Bailey, *Diplomatic*, p. 491.

10. Turk, "Panama," p. 93.

11. Turk, "Panama," p. 93; and John Nikol and Francis X. Holbrook, "Naval Operations in the Panama Revolution, 1903," *American Neptune* (Oct 1977), p. 254.

12. Turk, "Panama," p. 94; and Nikol and Holbrook, "Naval Operations," p. 257.

13. Nikol and Holbrook, "Naval Operations," p. 259; John Major, "Who Wrote the Hay-Bunau Varilla Convention?" *Diplomatic History* (Spr 1983), pp. 115–23; and Bailey, *Diplomatic*, p. 497.

14. Gerald Fiennes, *Sea Power and Freedom* (New York: Putnam, 1918), p. 259.

15. Holger H. Herwig, *Politics of Frustration: The United States in German Naval*

Planning, 1889–1941 (Boston: Little, Brown, 1976), pp. 35, 76–92; and Spector, *Admiral*, pp. 145ff and 184ff.

16. Turk, "Panama," p. 92.

17. Herwig, *Frustration*, p. 96; Bailey, *Diplomatic*, p. 499; William J. Hourihan, "The Best Ambassador: Rear Admiral Cotton and the Cruise of the European Squadron, 1903," *Naval War College Review* (Jun 1979), pp. 63–72; William N. Still, Jr., *American Sea Power in the Old World* (Westport, Conn.: Greenwood Press, 1980), p. 149; and Paul Kennedy, *The Rise of Anglo-German Antagonism, 1860–1914* (London: Allen and Unwin, 1980), pp. 257–58.

18. Turk, "Panama," p. 92.

19. Morris, *Presidential Decisions*, p. 341; and Spector, *Admiral*, p. 151.

20. Robert Seager II and Doris McGuire, eds., *Letters and Papers of Alfred Thayer Mahan* (Annapolis: Naval Institute Press, 1975), Vol. III, p. 86.

21. Howard K. Beale, *Theodore Roosevelt and the Rise of America to World Power* (New York: Collier Books, 1968), Ch. 5.

22. Albert Stillson, "The Development and Maintenance of the American Naval Establishment, 1901–1909" (Unpubl. Ph.D. Diss., Columbia University, 1959), Appendix B; and Spector, *Dewey*, pp. 152–53.

23. U.S. House, 59th Cong., 1st Sess., House Report No. 3639; and Mahan to Long, 31 Jan 1900, Mahan Mss, LC.

24. Richard Hough, *Dreadnought* (New York: Macmillan, 1964), p. 36.

25. George T. Davis, *A Navy Second to None* (New York: Harcourt, Brace, 1940), p. 183.

26. O'Gara, *Roosevelt*, p. 10.

Chapter Twenty-six

1. Elting E. Morison, ed., *The Letters of Theodore Roosevelt* (Cambridge: Harvard University Press, 1952), Vol. III, pp. 497–98.

2. Weigley, *Way of War*, pp. 186–88; Goodrich to Dewey, 18 Feb 1905, Dewey Mss, LC; and Field, *Naval Operations . . . Korea*, p. 11.

3. Morison, *Roosevelt Letters*, Vol. V, p. 348.

4. Frederick C. Leiner, "The Unknown Effort: Theodore Roosevelt's Battleship Plan and International Arms Limitation Talks, 1906–1907," *Military Affairs* (Oct 1984), pp. 174–79.

5. Bailey, *Diplomatic*, p. 522; Beale, *Roosevelt and the Rise of America to World Power*, p. 284; and Rappaport, *Diplomacy*, pp. 212–13.

6. Edwin A. Falk, *Fighting Bob Evans* (New York: Cape and Smith, 1931), pp. 390–92; Spector, *Admiral*, p. 163–69; and Morison, *Roosevelt Letters*, Vol. VI, pp. 937–38, and Vol. V, pp. 761–62.

7. O'Gara, *Roosevelt*, p. 11.

8. Richard W. Turk, "Defending the New Empire, 1900–1914," in Hagan, *Peace and War*, p. 197.

9. O'Gara, *Roosevelt*, p. 77; and Braisted, *Pacific, 1897–1909*, p. 227.

10. Braisted, *Pacific, 1897–1909*, p. 234.

11. Bailey, *Diplomatic*, p. 525; and Braisted, *Pacific, 1897–1909*, pp. 231–36.

12. Robert A. Hart, *The Great Fleet* (Boston: Little, Brown, 1965), p. 27.

13. Hart, *Fleet*, p. 55.

14. O'Gara, *Roosevelt*, p. 8.

Chapter Twenty-seven

1. Sprout, *Rise*, p. 287; and Rappaport, *Diplomacy*, pp. 248–49.

2. Edward B. Parsons, "Admiral Sims' Mission in Europe" (Unpubl. Ph.D. Diss.; State University of New York, Buffalo, 1971), p. 48.

3. Spector, *Admiral*, pp. 182–83; William R. Braisted, *The United States Navy in the Pacific, 1909–1922* (Austin: University of Texas Press, 1971), p. 62; and Bradley Fiske, *From Midshipman to Rear Admiral* (New York: Century, 1919), p. 480.

4. Spector, *Admiral*, pp. 184–87.

5. Sprout, *Rise*, pp. 281–98.

6. Robert L. Lawson, *The History of Naval Air Power* (New York: Crown, 1985), p. 10.

7. Clay Blair, Jr., *Silent Victory* (Philadelphia: J. B. Lippincott, 1975), p. 9.

8. Rappaport, *Diplomacy*, pp. 229, 215.

Chapter Twenty-eight

1. Spector, *Admiral*, p. 192.

2. Rufus Zogbaum, *From Sail to Saratoga* (Rome: Privately printed, 1947), pp. 221, 259–60, 309–10; Henry P. Beers, "The Development of the Office of the Chief of Naval Operations," *Military Affairs* (Spr 1946), p. 40; (Fall 1946), p. 10; (Spr 1947), p. 88; (Fall 1947), p. 229; and Robert W. Love, Jr., "Introduction," *The Chiefs of Naval Operations* (Annapolis: Naval Institute Press, 1980), pp. xiii.

3. Jack Sweetman, *The Landing at Veracruz* (Annapolis: Naval Institute Press, 1968), p. 13.

4. Lester D. Langley, *The Banana Wars* (Lexington: University of Kentucky Press, 1983), p. 85; and Whitney T. Perkins, *Constraint of Empire: the United States and Caribbean Interventions* (Westport, Conn.: Greenwood Press, 1981).

5. Sweetman, *Veracruz*, p. 38; Stirling, *Sea Duty*, pp. 147–48; and James H. Alexander, "Roots of Deployment—Vera Cruz in 1914," in Merrill Bartlett, ed., *Assault from the Sea* (Annapolis: Naval Institute Press, 1983), pp. 133–41.

6. Rappaport, *Diplomacy*, pp. 234–38.

7. David Healy, *Gunboats in the Wilson Era* (Madison: University of Wisconsin Press, 1976), p. 129.

8. Richard W. Leopold, *The Growth of American Foreign Policy* (New York: Knopf, 1962), p. 318.

9. *AR: 1913*.

10. Sprout, *Rise*, p. 313.

11. Rappaport, *Diplomacy*, p. 251; and William V. Pratt, "Review of *The Naval History of the World War*," *Proceedings* (Feb 1927), p. 328.

12. Paolo E. Coletta, *Admiral Bradley A. Fiske and the American Navy* (Lawrence: Regents Press of Kansas, 1979), pp. 131–32; Paolo E. Coletta, *French Ensor Chadwick* (Lanham, Md.: University Press of America, 1980), pp. 155–66; Doris D. Maguire, *French Ensor Chadwick: Selected Letters and Papers* (Lanham, Md.: University Press of America, 1981), p. 566; and Herwig, *Frustration*, pp. 152–53.

13. John A. S. Grenville and George B. Young, *Politics, Strategy, and American Diplomacy* (New Haven: Yale University Press, 1966), pp. 326–27; and Herwig, *Frustration*, pp. 155–57.

14. Spector, *Admiral*, p. 200.

15. Philip K. Lundeberg, "The German Naval Critique of the U-Boat Campaign, 1915–1918," *Military Affairs* (1963), p. 105.

16. Bailey, *Diplomatic*, pp. 575–76.

17. Bailey, *Diplomatic*, pp. 577–79.

18. Arthur Link et al., *The Papers of Woodrow Wilson* (Princeton: Princeton University Press, 1966–), Vol. 34, p. 5; and Braisted, *Pacific, 1909–1922*, p. 195.

19. Sprout, *Rise*, p. 342.

20. E. David Cronon, ed., *The Cabinet Diaries of Josephus Daniels* (Lincoln: University of Nebraska Press, 1963), p. 106.

21. Morris, *Presidential Decisions*, pp. 379–87.

Chapter Twenty-nine

1. Mary Klachko with David Trask, *Admiral William Shephard Benson: First Chief of Naval Operations* (Annapolis: Naval Institute Press, 1987), p. 62; David Trask, "William Shephard Benson," in Love, *Chiefs*, pp. 3–22; Thomas G. Frothingham, *The Naval History of the World War* (Cambridge: Harvard University Press, 1926), Vol. III, p. 21; and Trask, *Captains*, p. 48.

2. U.S. Senate, 56th Cong., 2nd Sess., "Naval Investigation Before the Subcommittee on Naval Affairs, 1920," Vol. II, p. 1843; and Tracy D. Kittredge, *Naval Lessons of the Great War* (New York: Doubleday, Page, 1921), p. 196.

3. Trask, *Captains*, p. 58; and Klachko, *Benson*, p. 75.

4. Wilson to Daniels, 24 Mar 1917, Daniels Mss, LC; and Morison, *Sims*, p. 337.

5. Ray Stannard Baker, *Woodrow Wilson: Life and Letters* (New York: Doubleday, Page, 1927–39), Vol. VI, pp. 146–47; "Naval Investigation, 1920," Vol. II, pp. 1181–82; and Trask, "Benson," p. 10.

6. Morison, *Sims*, p. 342.

7. Sims to Daniels, 19 Apr 1917, File 1911–1927 CP, Box 43, RG 45, NA; and Arthur Marder, *From the Dreadnaught to Scapa Flow* (London: Oxford University Press, 1961–70), Vol. IV, pp. 157–58.

8. Eric Grove, "The Reluctant Partner: The United States and the Introduction and Extension of Convoy in 1917–1918" (Unpubl. paper), Author's files.

9. Morison, *Sims*, p. 355; Josephus Daniels, *The Wilson Era* (Chapel Hill: University of North Carolina, 1944–46), Vol. II, p. 86; and *FRUS: 1917*, suppl. 2, Vol. I, pp. 124–26.

10. Morison, *Sims*, p. 377.

11. Trask, *Captains*, p. 90.

12. Cronon, *Daniels' Diary*, p. 173; and Parsons, "Sims," pp. 57–58.

13. Clyde S. McDowell, "American Anti-Submarine World During the World War," (Unpubl. Navy Histories, 1919), USNA.

14. Klachko, *Benson*, p. 68.

15. Joseph Hubbard, *On the Coast of France* (Chicago: A. C. McClurg, 1919), p. 13.

Chapter Thirty

1. Klachko, *Benson*, p. 66.

2. Klackho, *Benson*, p. 73.

3. Klachko, *Benson*, p. 71; and Grove, "Reluctant Partner," p. 19.

4. Russell Weigley, *The History of the United States Army* (New York: Macmillan, 1967), p. 355.

5. Weigley, *Army*, p. 359.

6. Albert Gleaves, *The Admiral: The Memoirs of Albert Gleaves* (repr. ed.; Pasadena: Hope Publ. Co., 1985), p. 146.

7. Klachko, *Benson*, p. 111; and Dean C. Allard, "Admiral William S. Sims and United States Naval Policy in World War I," *American Neptune* (Apr 1975), p. 105.

8. Lewis P. Clephane, *History of the Naval Overseas Transport Service in World War I* (Washington: Naval History Division, 1969), p. 1.

9. Klachko, *Benson*, p. 79; and Cronon, *Daniels Diary*, p. 190.

10. Klachko, *Benson*, pp. 79–81.

11. Klachko, *Benson*, p. 83; and "Naval Investigation," Vol. II, p. 1371.

12. Baker to House, 18 Jul 1917, Box 3, Newton Baker Mss, LC; and Klachko, *Benson*, p. 90.

13. ONI, *The American Naval Planning Section, London* (Washington: GPO, 1923), p. 204; and Sims to Daniels, 17 May 1917, TD File, Subject File, RG 45, NA.

14. Hubbard, *Coast,* p. 111; and Cronon, *Diaries,* p. 309.

15. Albert Gleaves, *A History of the Transport Service* (New York: Doran, 1921), p. 140.

16. Dept. of the Navy, *German Submarine Activities on the Atlantic Coast of the United States and Canada, 1918* (Washington: GPO, 1920), p. 10; T. P. Magruder, "The Navy in the War," *Saturday Evening Post* (16 Feb 1929), pp. 76–89; James M. Merrill, "Submarine Scare, 1918," *Military Affairs* (Wtr 1953), pp. 181–90; and Donald A. Yerxa, "The U. S. Navy in Caribbean Waters During World War I," *Military Affairs* (Oct 1987), p. 186.

17. Frothingham, *Naval History,* Vol, III, p. 79. Also see Edward Breck, *The United States Naval Railway Batteries in France* (reprint; Washington: GPO, 1988).

18. Morison, *Sims,* pp. 413–18.

19. Henry Wiley, *An Admiral from Texas* (New York: Doubleday, Doran, 1932), p. 207; and Gleaves, *Transport,* p. 17.

20. Gleaves, *Transport,* p. 172; and Cronon, *Daniels' Diary,* p. 340.

21. ONI, *Planning,* p. 195; and Grove, "Reluctant Partner," p. 18.

22. Hubbard, *Coast,* pp. 126–27.

Chapter Thirty-one

1. Benson to Daniels, 6 May 1919, Daniels Mss, LC.

2. Cronin, ed., *Daniels' Diaries,* p. 342; and Frederick Moore, *America's Naval Challenge* (Saxton, Penn.: Brandywine Books, 1929), pp. 26–29.

3. Charles Seymour, *The Intimate Papers of Colonel House* (Boston: Houghton Mifflin, 1928), Vol. IV, p. 417; and Ray S. Baker, *Woodrow Wilson and World Settlement* (New York: Doubleday, Page, 1922), Vol. III, p. 210.

4. Rappaport, *Diplomacy,* p. 273.

5. A. C. Davidonis, "The American Naval Mission in the Adriatic, 1918–1921" (Washington: Navy Dept., 1943); and Henry P. Beers, "U. S. Naval Detachment in Turkish Waters, 1919–1924," (Washington: Navy Dept., 1943).

6. Henry P. Beers, "U. S. Naval Forces in Northern Russia, 1918–1919," (Washington: Navy Dept., 1943); and Betty Unterberger, "Wilson and the Bolsheviks," *Diplomatic History,* (Spr 1987), p. 85.

7. Klachko, *Benson,* p. 179.

8. Morison, *Sims,* Ch. 23.

Chapter Thirty-two

1. James D. Richardson, ed., *Messages and Papers of the Presidents* (New York: Bureau of National Literature, 1897–1922); *FRUS: 1944,* Suppl., p. 189; and Ernest Andrade, Jr., "United States Naval Policy in the Disarmament Era, 1921–37" (Unpubl. Ph.D. Diss., Michigan State University, 1966).

2. Earl Pomeroy, *Pacific Outpost: American Strategy in Guam and Micronesia* (Palo Alto, Ca.: Stanford University Press, 1951), p. 69.

3. Pomeroy, *Pacific Outpost,* p. 63; Timothy P. Maga, "Prelude to War: The United States, Japan, and the Yap Crisis, 1918–22," *Diplomatic History* (Sum 1985), pp. 215–31; Gerald E. Wheeler, *Prelude to Pearl Harbor: The United States Navy and the Far East, 1921–1931* (Columbia: University of Missouri Press, 1968), p. 50; Edward S. Miller, "War Plan Orange, 1897–1941: The Blue Thrust through the Pacific," in William Cogar, ed., *Naval History: The Seventh Symposium of the United States Naval Academy* (Wilmington, Del.: Scholarly Resources, 1989), p. 242; and Cronin, ed., *Daniels' Diaries,* p. 505.

4. Wheeler, *Prelude,* p. 56; and Andrade, "Disarmament Era," pp. 35–36.

5. Lawrence H. Douglas, "Robert Edwards Coontz," in Love, *Chiefs,* p. 29; and Roskill, *Naval Policy Between the Wars, 1919–1929* (London: Collins, 1968), pp. 300–30.

6. Thomas H. Buckeley, *The United States and the Washington Conference, 1921–1922* (Knoxville: University of Tennessee Press, 1970), p. 73; and U.S. Senate, 67th Cong., 2nd Sess., "Conference on the Limitation of Armament," Sen. Doc. No. 126, 1922.

7. Andrade, "Disarmament Era," p. 71; and Bailey, *Diplomatic*, p. 646.

8. Douglas, "Coontz," p. 30.

9. Pomeroy, *Pacific Outpost*, pp. 111–12; and Dudley Knox, *The Eclipse of American Sea Power* (New York: Army and Navy Journal, 1922), p. 135.

10. Pomeroy, *Pacific Outpost*, p. 98.

11. Archibald D. Turnbull and Clifford L. Lord, *History of United States Naval Aviation* (New Haven: Yale University Press, 1949), p. 64; and Charles M. Melhorn, *Two-Block Fox: The Rise of the Aircraft Carrier, 1911–29* (Annapolis: Naval Institute Press, 1974), p. 18.

12. Melhorn, *Two-Block Fox*, p. 26–47.

13. Albion, *Makers*, p. 374; Ernest J. King and Walter Muir Whitehill, *Fleet Admiral King: A Naval Record* (New York: Norton, 1952), pp. 208–9; and Gannon to Coontz, 27 Mar 1923, "Budget, 1925, Estimate of the Situation and Base Development Program," WPD Records, OA, NHC.

Chapter Thirty-three

1. "Report of the Special [Eberle Board] on . . . Aviation, Jan 17, 1925," in *Information Concerning the U.S. Navy and Other Navies* (Washington: Navy Dept., 1925), pp. 153–54; and Howard H. Quint and Robert H. Ferrell, ed., *The Talkative President: The Off-the-Record Press Conferences of Calvin Coolidge* (Amherst: University of Massachusetts Press, 1964), p. 157.

2. Melhorn, *Two-Block Fox*, p. 109.

3. Richard W. Turk, "Edward W. Eberle," in Love, *Chiefs*, p. 42; Lanning to GenBd, 23 Oct 1931, Box 54, Harris Lanning Mss, LC; and Wiley, *Admiral from Texas*, p. 308.

4. Clark G. Reynolds, *The Fast Carriers: the Forging of an Air Navy* (New York: McGraw-Hill, 1968), p. 1.

5. Reynolds, *Fast Carriers*, p. 16.

6. Richard Smith, *The Airships Akron and Macon* (Annapolis: Naval Institute Press, 1965), p. xxi.

7. Quint and Ferrell, *Talkative President*, p. 155.

8. Weigley, *Way of War*, pp. 232–33.

9. Weigley, *Way of War*, pp. 233–34.

10. Quint and Ferrell, *Talkative President*, p. 158; and U.S. House, 69th Cong., 1st Sess., Committee on Military Affairs, "Hearings on a Department of Defense and the Unification of the Air Service," 1926, pp. 719–21.

11. *Army-Navy Journal*, 25 Sep 1925, pp. 1–6, 9–15.

12. *Report of the President's Aircraft Board* (Washington: GPO, 1926), pp. 7–21; and Quint and Farrell, *Talkative President*, p. 167.

13. Turk, "Eberle," pp. 39–40, 45.

14. Bailey, *Diplomatic*, p. 693.

15. William Trimble, "Admiral Hilary P. Jones and the 1927 Geneva Naval Conference, " *Military Affairs* (Feb 1979), p. 2; and Gannon, WPD, to CNO, 9 Apr 1923, "Budget, 1925, Estimate of the Situation," OA, NHC.

16. Michael A. West, "Laying the Legislative Foundation: The House Naval Affairs Committee and the Construction of the Treaty Navy, 1926–34" (Unpubl. Ph.D. Diss., Ohio State University, 1980); and U.S. Senate, 70th Cong., 1st Sess., "Records of the Conference for the Limitation of Naval Armament Held at Geneva, Switzerland," Sen. Doc. No. 55, 1928.

17. Trimble, "Jones," p. 2.

18. Andrade, "Disarmament Era," p. 157; and Quint and Farrell, *Talkative President*, p. 171.

Chapter Thirty-four

1. Ray L. Wilbur and Arthur M Hyde, *The Hoover Policies* (New York: Scribner's, 1937), p. 577; and Stephen Roskill, *Naval Policy Between the Wars* (Annapolis: Naval Institute Press, 1976), Vol. II.

2. Charles A. Beard, *The Navy, Defense or Portent?* (New York: Harper, 1932), p. 12; and Herbert Hoover, *The Cabinet and the Presidency, 1920–1933* (New York: Macmillan, 1952), p. 338.

3. Michael K. Doyle, "The U. S. Navy: Strategy, Defense, and Foreign Policy, 1932–1941" (Unpubl. Ph.D. Diss., University of Washington, 1977), p. 142.

4. John R. M. Wilson, "Herbert Hoover's Relations with the Military," *Military Affairs* (Apr 1974), p. 42; and John R. M. Wilson, "Herbert Hoover and the Armed Forces" (Unpubl. Ph.D. Diss., Northwestern University, 1971).

5. Samuel Huntington, *The Soldier and the State* (New York: Columbia University Press, 1962), p. 309; and U. S. Senate, 71st Cong., 2nd Sess., "Abstract of Testimony on . . . the London Naval Treaty," Committee on Naval Affairs, Sen. Doc. No. 197, 1930.

6. Alfred L. Castle, "Ambassador Castle's Role in the Negotiations of the London Naval Conference," *Naval History* (Sum 1989), p. 18.

7. Armin Rappaport, *The Navy League of the United States* (Detroit: Wayne State University Press, 1962), p. 135; and Craig L. Symonds, "William Veazie Pratt," in Love, ed., *Chiefs*, p. 81.

8. J. E. Talbott, "Weapons Development, War Planning, and Policy: The U.S. Navy and the Submarine, 1917–1941," *Naval War College Review* (Spr 1984), pp. 53–71.

9. Cooke to GenBd, 6 Oct 1930, GB420–15, GB Records, OA, NHC.

10. Gerald Wheeler, *Admiral William Veazie Pratt: A Sailor's Life* (Washington: GPO, 1974), p. 341.

11. Bernard D. Coles, *Gunboats and Marines: The U.S. Navy in China, 1925–1928* (Newark: University of Delaware Press, 1983), p. 62; Kemp Tolley, *Yangtze Patrol: The U.S. Navy in China* (Annapolis: Naval Institute Press, 1968); Tate, "Gunboats on the Yangtze," pp. 121–32; Esson M. Gale, "The Yangtze Patrol," *Proceedings* (Mar 1955), pp. 307–315; and F. F. Liu, *A Military History of Modern China, 1924–1949* (Princeton: Princeton University Press, 1956).

12. Stirling, *Sea Duty*, pp. 207–15; and Tate, "Gunboats on the Yangtze," pp. 121–32.

13. Quint and Farrell, *Talkative President*, pp. 263–65.

14. *FRUS: 1927*, Vol. II, pp. 151–63;.

15. Coles, *Gunboats*, pp. 140–71.

16. Quint and Farrell, *Talkative President*, p. 267.

17. Diary entry, William D. Leahy Mss, LC; and Stephen S. Roberts, "The Decline of the Overseas Station Fleets: The United States Asiatic Fleet and the Shanghai Crisis, 1932," *American Neptune* (Jul 1977), p. 188.

18. David MacIsaac, "Commentary," *Cidatel Conference on War and Diplomacy, 1976* (Charleston, S.C.: Citadel, 1977), p. 167; and Leopold, *Foreign Policy*, p. 492.

19. Leopold, *Foreign Policy*, p. 494.

20. Roberts, "Decline," pp. 192–93.

21. Entry, 29 Feb 1932, Henry L. Stimson Diary, Microfilm copy, USNA; Leopold, *Foreign Policy*, p. 496; and Russell D. Buhite, *Nelson T. Johnson and American Policy Toward China* (East Lansing: Michigan State University Press, 1969), p. 74.

22. Roberts, "Decline," p. 201; and Entry, 8 Mar 1932, Stimson Diary.
23. Wheeler, *Prelude*, pp. 21, 183–84.

Chapter Thirty-five
1. Entry, 1 Dec 1941, Stimson Diary; Interview with Morrill in P. L. Greaves to Harry Elmer Barnes, 21 Dec 1962, Kimmel Mss, USNA; and Henry C. Ferrell, Jr., *Claude A. Swanson of Virginia* (Lexington: University Press of Kentucky, 1985), p. 202.
2. Bailey, *Diplomatic*, p. 683.
3. Richard Millett, "The State Department's Navy: A History of the Special Service Squadron, 1920–1940," *American Neptune* (Apr 1975), p. 118ff; and Donald A. Yerxa, "The United States Navy and the Caribbean, 1914–1941" (Unpubl. Ph.D. Diss., University of Maine, 1982).
4. FDR to Norman Davis, 9 Nov 1934, Norman Davis Mss, LC.
5. Stephen E. Pelz, *Race to Pearl Harbor* (Cambridge: Harvard University Press, 1974), p. 79.
6. FDR to Davis, 9 Nov 1934, Davis Mss, LC; and Ferrell, *Swanson*, p. 207.
7. John Walters, "William Harrison Standley," in Love, *Chiefs*, pp. 89–100; Norman Friedman, *U.S. Aircraft Carriers* (Annapolis: Naval Institute Press, 1983), pp. 57–118; and King, *Naval Record*, pp. 247–85. One study pointed out that between 1929 and 1940 the Bureau of Aeronautics faced a peculiar problem that inhibited the development of naval aviation. "The Navy fighter market during the 1930–1935 period accounted for roughly 4 percent of all military aircraft purchased, making it quite unattractive to larger firms requiring large production 'runs' to sustain themselves." At the same time, the Navy's opponents in Congress criticized Admiral King when he was serving as the Chief of the Bureau of Aeronautics for providing airframe firms with "execessive profits" to subsidize production. Great Lakes Aircraft, one of these firms, which built the Navy's dive bombers during the Depression, went bankrupt as a result in 1935. Randolph P. Kucera, "Grumman Aircraft Engineering Corporation and Its 'Familial' Relationship with the U.S. Navy" (Unpubl. Ph.D. Diss., Syracuse University, 1973), pp. 114–15.
8. Pye to Standley, 22 Aug 1935, King Mss, OA, NHC; and Doyle, "Navy . . . 1932–41," pp. 52–57.
9. Pelz, *Race to Pearl Harbor*, p. 79.
10. Meridith W. Borg, "Admiral William H. Standley and the Second London Naval Treaty, 1934–1936," *The Historian* (Feb 1971), pp. 215–36; William H. Standley and Arthur A. Ageton, *Admiral Ambassador to Russia* (Chicago: Regnery, 1955), pp. 32–34; Thomas Bailey, *Presidential Greatness* (New York: Appleton Century, 1966), p. 322; and Nancy Hooker, ed., *The Moffett Papers* (Cambridge: Harvard University Press, 1956), pp. 115–17.
11. Joseph K. Taussig, "The Case for the Big Capital Ship," *Proceedings* (Jul 1940), p. 930.
12. Dept. of State, *The London Naval Conference, 1935; Report of the Delegates . . . and Text of the London Naval Treaty of 1936* (Washington: GPO, 1936), p. 443; Roskill, *Naval Policy*, Vol. II, pp. 315–16; and Standley to F. B. Royal, 12 Feb 1936, Standley Mss, University of Southern California.
13. Davis, *Second to None*, p. 370.
14. Royal Ingersoll OH, USNA; Standley to Reeves, 12 May 1936, Standley Mss.

Chapter Thirty-six
1. Roskill, *Naval Policy*, Vol. II, pp. 306–23; and David Reynolds, *The Creation*

of the Anglo-American Alliance, 1937–41 (Chapel Hill: University of North Carolina Press, 1982), pp. 10–16.

2. Malcolm Muir, Jr., "American Warship Construction for Stalin's Navy Prior to World War II," *Diplomatic History* (Fall 1981), pp. 337–51; and Norman Davis to Hull, 9 June 38, *FRUS: Soviet Union, 1933–39*, p. 391.

3. Laurence F. Safford, "Brief History of Communications Intelligence in the United States," SHR-119, RG 457, NA; WPD, "Annual Estimate of the Situation, FY 1939," 17 Apr 1937, WPD, OA, NHC; Edgar B. Nixon, ed., *Franklin D. Roosevelt and Foreign Affairs* (Cambridge: Harvard University Press, 1969), Vol. II, p. 58; and John Major, "William Daniel Leahy," in Love, ed., *Chiefs*, pp. 103–105.

4. Harold L. Ickes, *The Secret Diary of Harold Ickes* (New York: Simon and Schuster, 1952–54), Vol. II, p. 198; and James H. Herzog, *Closing the Open Door* (Annapolis: Naval Institute Press, 1973), pp. 15–16.

5. Ickes, *Diary*, Vol. II, p. 198.

6. William L. Langer and S. Everett Gleason, *The Challenge to Isolation* (New York: Harper and Bros., 1952), pp. 18–19.

7. Yarnell to Navy Department, 22 Sep 37, File 393, RG 59, NA; and FDR to Leahy, 10 Nov 37, in Donald B. Schewe, ed., *Franklin D. Roosevelt and Foreign Affairs* (New York: Garland, 1979), Vol. III.

8. Buhite, *Johnson*, p. 136; Doyle, "Navy . . . 1932–41," p. 515; Henry H. Adams, *Witness to Power: The Life of Fleet Admiral William D. Leahy* (Annapolis: Naval Institute Press, 1985), p. 101. For the Ingersoll mission, see Royal Ingersoll OH, USNA; and John McVickar Haight, Jr., "FDR's Big Stick," *Proceedings* (Jul 1980), p. 71. On the *Panay* incident, see Tolley, *Yangtze Patrol*; Manny T. Koginos, *The Panay Incident: Prelude to War* (Lafayette, Ind.: Purdue University Press, 1967); Hamilton D. Perry, *The Panay Incident: Prelude to War* (New York: Macmillan, 1969); Masatake Okumiya, "How the *Panay* Was Sunk," *Proceedings* (Jun 1953), pp. 587–96; and Harlan J. Swanson, "The *Panay* Incident: Prelude to Pearl Harbor," *Proceedings* (Dec 1967), pp. 26–37.

9. Herzog, *Closing*, p. 34.

10. William M. Leary, "Portrait of an Intelligence Officer: James McHugh in China, 1937–42," in Cogar, *Naval History*, p. 254; Buhite, *Johnson*, p. 140; and Herzog, *Closing*, p. 24.

11. Doyle, "Navy . . . 1932–41," p. 514.

12. Davis, *Second to None*, pp. 373–75.

13. Frederick Marks, *Wind Over Sand* (Athens: University of Georgia Press, 1988), p. 146.

14. Hampton to DCNS Admiral Danckwerts, 27 June 1939, Adm 116–3922, PRO.

15. Cooke OH, privately held; Major, "Leahy," pp. 112–13; and Ghormley to Leahy, 15 February 1939, WPD, OA, NHC.

16. Patrick Abbazia, *Mr. Roosevelt's Navy* (Annapolis: Naval Institute Press, 1975), pp. 33–50; King, *Naval Record*, pp. 289–90; Franklin G. Percival, "Future Naval War," *Proceedings* (Dec 1940), pp. 1699–1712; and James M. Grimes, "Aviation in Fleet Exercises, 1911–39," History Office, DNCO (Air), Library, NHC.

17. Cooke to GenBd, 6 Oct 1930, GB420–15, GB Records, OA, NHC.

Chapter Thirty-seven

1. Langer and Gleason, *Challenge to Isolation*, pp. 231–35. On Stark, see B. Mitchell Simpson, *Admiral Harold R. Stark* (Columbia: University of South Carolina Press, 1989); and B. Mitchell Simpson, "Harold R. Stark," in Love, *Chiefs*, pp. 119–36.

2. Samuel F. Bemis, "Submarine Warfare in the Strategy of American De-

fense and Diplomacy," (Unpubl. Mss., Navy Dept Library), p. 1. For the Neutrality Patrol and the Atlantic Fleet, see Abbazia, *Roosevelt's Navy*; and Brian Hussey, "The U.S. Navy's Atlantic Fleet and Ocean Escort Operations, September-December 1941" (Draft; Trident Scholar Report, 1991), USNA.

3. Simpson, *Stark*, pp. 16–34.

4. Malcolm H. Murfett, *Foolproof Relations: The Search for Anglo-American Naval Cooperation* (Singapore: Singapore University Press, 1984); Stephen Roskill, *Churchill and His Admirals* (New York: Morrow, 1978), Chs. 8–15; and Cooke to Stark, 22 May 1940 and Crenshaw to Stark, 17 Jun 1940, Strategic Plans Papers, OA, NHC.

5. Langer and Gleason, *Challenge to Isolation*, p. 516.

6. Cooke OH.

7. Langer and Gleason, *Challenge to Isolation*, pp. 521–22.

8. FDR insisted that the World War I-era four-stack destroyers were "on their last legs." Marks, *Wind Over Sand*, p. 162. Roosevelt was fully aware that Stark had gone to considerable trouble to convince Congress to recommission these vessels, however, and that the Navy intended to use them as ocean and coastal escorts. See discussion on this issue in DirWPD to DirFltMaintDiv, 18 Apr 1940, File: "Signed Letters," Box 79, WPD, OA, NHC. Also see "Current Tactical Orders, Destroyers," 1 Oct 1940, U.S. Fleet Publication No. 33, OA, NHC. This document was composed before the author learned that the four-stackers would be transferred to the Royal Navy.

9. *FRUS: 1940*, Vol. I, p. 233; James Leutze, *Bargaining for Supremacy: Anglo-American Naval Collaboration* (Chapel Hill: University of North Carolina Press, 1977), p. 80; and Michael R. Beschloss, *Kennedy and Roosevelt* (New York: Norton, 1980), pp. 205–7.

10. Cooke to Stark, 28 May 40, File A16–3, WPD, OA, NHC; Stark to FDR, 2 June 40, CNO Records, OA, NHC; and Captain Russell Crenshaw to Stark, 17 June 40, File "Signed Letters," Box 79, Series IV, WPD, OA, NHC. Crenshaw was the director of the War Plans Division. For the decision to keep the U.S. Fleet in the Pacific, see Stark to Richardson, 22 June 1940, in U.S. Congress, 79th Cong., 1st Sess., Joint Committee, "Hearings on the Investigation of the Pearl Harbor Attack," 1946, Pt. 1, p. 262.

11. "Hearings . . . Pearl Harbor," Pt. 14, pp. 943–44.

12. George Dyer, *On the Treadmill to Pearl Harbor: The Memoirs of Admiral James O. Richardson* (Washington: GPO, 1973), pp. 307–33, 383–401. Richardson disingenuously claimed that he was surprised by the May 1940 order to hold the U.S. Fleet at Pearl Harbor. He surely knew that Leahy had explained this plan to the British naval attaché, Captain L. A. Curzon-Howe, and an envoy from the Admiralty, Commander T. Hampton, in June 1939, and that the War Plans Division studied this plan for several months thereafter. Hours after Germany invaded Poland, Captain Russell Crenshaw, the director of the War Plans Division, told the CNO that "all of the units in the Pacific should remain in the Pacific, either on the West Coast or in Hawaiian Waters" so as to provide for the "stabilization of the western Pacific." Crenshaw to Stark, 1 Sep 1939, "Steps to be taken in the Event that England and France enter War against Germany," Charles M. Cooke, Jr., Mss. Hoover Inst., Stanford, Conn.

13. Cooke OH; Cooke Mss. King, who was familiar with Richardson's argument, agreed with Stark that Richardson was wrong, but he disagreed with the decision to relieve Richardson over this issue and believed Kimmel to be wholly unsuited for high command. Walter M. Whitehill, "[Admiral King's] Comments on Flag Officers of U.S. Navy," 31 July 1949, Whitehill Mss, Naval War College, Newport, R.I.

14. Simpson, *Stark*, p. 50.

15. Robert E. Sherwood, *Roosevelt and Hopkins* (New York: Harper and Bros., 1948), p. 191; and CNO to SecNav and President, 12 Nov 40; Copy in Cooke Mss.

16. Stetson Conn and Bryon Fairchild, *The Framework of Hemispheric Defense* (Washington: GPO, 1960), p. 94.

17. FDR to Knox, 26 Jan 1941, File: Navy, Box 80, President's Safe File, FDR Mss; Reynolds, *Creation*, pp. 182–85; Leutze, *Bargaining*, Ch. 14; Churchill to Pound, 17 Feb 1941, Adm 116–4877, PRO; "Hearings . . . Pearl Harbor," Pt. 15, pp. 1491–92; and Maurice Matloff and Edwin Snell, *Strategic Planning for Coalition Warfare, 1941–1942* (Washington: GPO, 1953), pp. 30–36.

Chapter Thirty-eight

1. Kirk to OpNav, 24 Mar 41, King Mss, OA, NHC. See also National Defense Research Council, Summary Technical Report of Division 6, Vol. III: "A Summary of Antisubmarine Warfare Operations in World War II," 1946, Library, NHC.

2. Roskill, *Churchill*, pp. 283–99. Waldo Heinrichs claimed that "the navy had to join the battle to save its ships" from the Lend Lease program. See Waldo Heinrichs, *Threshold of War* (New York: Oxford University Press, 1988), pp. 42–44 and p. 144. The Admiralty found it difficult to man the fifty four-stackers, however, and had no trained crews to man additional escort transfers in 1941. ALUSNA London to OpNav, 22 Feb 41, File: "Atlantic Dispatches," Box 122, Series VII, SPD, OA, NHC. Moreover, as Admiral Turner pointed out, there were at the time not enough American destroyers available "for protection of U.S. shipping in Naval Coastal Frontiers." Turner to Stark, 14 Mar 41, "Support Force," File: Signed Letters, Box 81, Series IV, SPD, OA, NHC. In short, the evidence suggests that Roosevelt's decision to transfer the fifty four-stackers to the Royal Navy in 1940 was responsible for the shortage of Atlantic Fleet escorts when the United States entered the war in December 1941, and it was in part this lack of escorts that allowed a handful of German U-boats to operate so successfully against merchant shipping off the East Coast in early 1942.

3. Stark to Kimmel, King, and Hart, 3 Apr 41, King Mss, OA, NHC.

4. Orville H. Bullitt, ed., *For the President: Correspondence Between Franklin D. Roosevelt and William C. Bullitt* (Boston: Houghton Mifflin, 1972), p. 512.

5. William F. Atwater, "The U. S. Army and Navy Development of Joint Landing Operations, 1898–1942" (Unpubl. Ph.D. Diss., Duke University, 1986), p. 136; and Samuel I. Rosenman, ed., *The Public Papers and Addresses of Franklin D. Roosevelt* (New York: Random House, 1938–50), Vol. IX, pp. 185–90.

6. Heinrichs, *Threshold*, p. 31.

7. Abbazia, *Roosevelt's Navy*, p. 215; OpPlan No. 5–41, 14 Jul 41, File: "WPL-51 Navy Western Hemisphere Defense Plan No. 4," Box 147K, Series IX, SPD, OA, NHC; and King, *Naval Record*, p. 345.

8. Abbazia, *Roosevelt's Navy*, pp. 204–5; F. W. Hinsley et al., *British Intelligence in the Second World War* (London: HMSO, 1979–88), Vol. II, p. 174.

9. Knox to FDR, 6 July 41, President's Safe File, FDR Mss.

10. Stark to Cooke, 31 July 41, Cooke Mss. Also see Stark to Cooke, 24 July 41, Cooke Mss.

11. Stark to Cooke, 31 July 41, Cooke Mss.

12. Theodore A. Wilson, *The First Summit: Roosevelt and Churchill at Placentia Bay, 1941* (Boston: Hougton Mifflin, 1969), p. 199.

13. Abbazia, *Roosevelt's Navy*, p. 224.

14. Joseph P. Lash, *Roosevelt and Churchill* (New York: Norton, 1976), pp. 417–18.

15. Kenneth A. Knowles, "Ultra and the Battle of the Atlantic," in Love, *Interpretations*, pp. 446–47.

16. Knowles, "Ultra," p. 447.

17. Abbazia, *Roosevelt's Navy*, pp. 265–68.

18. Jurgen Rohwer, "Ultra and the Battle of the Atlantic: The German View," in Love, *Interpretations*, pp. 428–29.

19. King to Stark, 17 Nov 1941, CNO Records, OA, NHC; and William L. Langer and S. Everett Gleason, *The Undeclared War* (New York: Harper, 1953), p. 757.

20. Com Task Unit 4.1.3 to CNO, 3 Nov 41, "Report of Loss of USS *Reuben James*, File: Task Unit 4.1.3, Serial 23, Box 83, WWII Action Reports, OA, NHC; *New York Times*, 1 Nov 1941; Marks, *Wind Over Sand*, p. 166; Lash, *Roosevelt and Churchill*, p. 428; Reynolds, *Creation*, p. 217; *New York Times*, 20 Nov 1941; and U.S. House, 77th Cong., 1st Sess., *Cong. Record*, 16 Oct 1941, p. 8016 and p. 7986.

Chapter Thirty-nine

1. "Hearings . . . Pearl Harbor," Pt. 17, pp. 2575–98 and Pt. 23, p. 1133; and U.S. Senate, 89th Cong., 1st Sess., Committee on the Judiciary, *The Morgenthau Diary (China)*, 1965, Vol. I, p. 385. On Japanese policy in 1941, see Robert J. C. Butow, *Tojo and the Coming of the War* (Stanford: Stanford University Press, 1961).

2. Simpson, *Stark*, p. 104.

3. "Hearings . . . Pearl Harbor," Pt. 14, p. 1402.

4. Simpson, "Stark," p. 190; and P. L. Greaves to Harry Elmer Barnes, 21 Dec 1962, Kimmel Mss.

5. Waldo Heinrichs, "The Role of the U.S. Navy," in Dorothy Borg and Shumpei Okamato, ed., *Pearl Harbor as History* (New York: Columbia University Press, 1973), pp. 218–23; and Stimson to Roosevelt, 21 Oct 1941, President's Safe File, FDR Library.

6. *FRUS: Japan, 1931–1941*, Vol. II, p. 755.

7. *FRUS: The Far East, 1941*, Vol. IV, pp. 661–64; "Hearings . . . Pearl Harbor," Pt. 11, p. 5433; and *FRUS: Japan, 1931–1941*, Vol. II, pp. 768–70.

8. "Hearings . . . Pearl Harbor," Pt. 9, p. 1403, and Pt. 14, p. 1406.

9. Layton to Love, 28 Mar 1978, Author's files, USNA; Msg, Stark to Kimmel, 10 Feb 1941, Ser. 014412, OA, NHC; Edwin Layton, John Costello, and Roger Pineau, *And I Was There* (New York: Morrow, 1985), p. 226; "Hearings . . . Pearl Harbor," Pt. 23, p. 1133; and Interview with Layton, 26 Apr 1983, Author's files.

10. William F. Halsey and J. Bryan III, *Admiral Halsey's Story* (New York: McGraw-Hill, 1947), pp. 74–75; Bloch to Stark, 20 Mar 1941, OpNav SC Files, OA, NHC; and Interview with Rear Admiral Fitzgerald, 26 Apr 1974, Author's files, USNA.

11. William Heindahl and Geraldine Phillips, "The Navy and Investigating the Pearl Harbor Attack: A Consideration of New Source Material," in Love, *Interpretations*, pp. 400–412; and Samuel E. Morison, *The Two-Ocean War* (Boston: Atlantic, Little, Brown, 1963), p. 53.

12. On 18 May 1945, in a private conversation, McCollum told Kimmel that "the essence of the meeting in Admiral Stark's office was that war would eventuate very shortly and probably commence at 1300 that day. Apparently, nobody had mentioned an attack on Pearl Harbor and he [McCollum] had not considered this probability from the information which had been supplied to him." Memo, Interview with . . . McCollum, 18 May 1945, Kimmel Mss.

Index

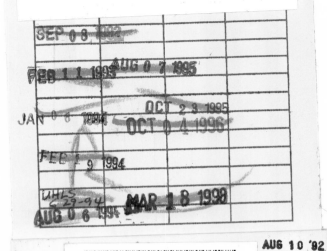